Salafism in Jordan

Since the events of 9/11, Salafism in the Middle East has often been perceived as fixed, rigid and even violent, but this assumption overlooks the quietist ideology that characterises many Salafi movements. Through an exploration of Salafism in Jordan, Joas Wagemakers presents the diversity among quietist Salafis on a range of ideological and political issues, particularly their relationship with the state. He expounds a detailed analysis of Salafism as a whole, whilst also showing how and why quietist Salafism in Jordan – through ideological tendencies, foreign developments, internal conflicts, regime-involvement, theological challenges and regional turmoil – transformed from an independent movement into a politically domesticated one.

Essential for graduate students and academic researchers interested in Middle Eastern politics and Salafism, this major contribution to the study of Salafism debunks stereotypes and offers insight into the development of a trend that still remains a mystery to many.

Joas Wagemakers is an assistant professor of Islamic and Arabic Studies at Utrecht University in the Netherlands. His research focusses mainly on Salafism and particularly Salafi ideology; the Muslim Brotherhood; citizenship, women's rights and rights of the Shi'a in Saudi Arabia; and Hamas. He has published many chapters and articles in this field as well as several books, including: *A Quietist Jihadi: The Ideology and Influence of Abu Muhammad al-Maqdisi* (Cambridge University Press, 2012), *Salafisme* (2014; co-authored with Martijn de Koning and Carmen Becker); and *Islam in verandering: Vroomheid en vertier onder moslims binnen en buiten Nederland* (2015; co-edited with Martijn de Koning).

Salafism in Jordan

Political Islam in a Quietist Community

Joas Wagemakers
Utrecht University

CAMBRIDGE
UNIVERSITY PRESS

CAMBRIDGE
UNIVERSITY PRESS

University Printing House, Cambridge CB2 8BS, United Kingdom

Cambridge University Press is part of the University of Cambridge.

It furthers the University's mission by disseminating knowledge in the pursuit of education, learning and research at the highest international levels of excellence.

www.cambridge.org
Information on this title: www.cambridge.org/9781107163669

First published 2016

A catalogue record for this publication is available from the British Library

Library of Congress Cataloguing-in-Publication data
Wagemakers, Joas, 1979–, author.
Salafism in Jordan : political Islam in a quietist community / Joas Wagemakers.
New York, NY : Cambridge University Press, 2016.
LCCN 2016010372 | ISBN 9781107163669 (hardback)
LCSH: Salafīyah – Jordan. | Islamic fundamentalism – Jordan.
LCC BP195.S18 W34 2016 | DDC 297.8/3–dc23
LC record available at http://lccn.loc.gov/2016010372

ISBN 978-1-107-16366-9 Hardback

Contents

Preface — *page* vii
Acknowledgements — ix
Note on Transliteration, Names and Dates — xii

Introduction — 1
Jordan: A Brief Historical Overview — 2
The Study of Salafism in Jordan — 11
Methodology, Sources and Overview — 19

Part I Ideology — 25

1 Global Salafi Ideology — 27
The Definition, Origins and Spread of Salafism — 28
The Salafi *'Aqīda* — 39
The Salafi *Manhaj* — 51

2 Quietist Salafi Ideology in Jordan — 60
General Quietist Salafi Ideology in Jordan — 60
Quietist Salafi Views on *Īmān* and *Kufr* in Jordan — 74
Quietist Salafism and Politics in Jordan — 82

Part II History — 93

3 The Transnational History of Salafism in Jordan — 95
Salafism in Jordan prior to al-Albani — 96
Al-Albani's Impact on Quietist Salafism in Jordan — 100
The Entrenchment of Quietist Salafi Ideology in Jordan — 109

4 *Fitna*: Quietist Salafi Infighting in Jordan — 118
Prelude to a Conflict: A Loss of Trust — 119
A Crisis of Leadership — 126
The Imam al-Albani Centre — 137

5 Quietist Salafism in Jordan after "9/11" 144
Jordanian Salafis and the State in the Age of Terrorism 145
Salafi Religious Authority in Jordan 157
Salafis in Jordan Today 165

Part III Contestation 177

6 Jihadi-Salafis Join the Fray 179
Jihadi-Salafism in Jordan 179
Contesting Quietist Salafis 188
The Quietists Strike Back 195

7 The Challenge of Political Salafism 201
The Rise of Political Salafism in Jordan 202
The Ideology of the Jam'iyyat al-Kitab wa-l-Sunna 207
The State and Quietist Salafis "Fight" Political Salafism 219

Conclusion 227

Glossary 237
Bibliography 244
Index 289

Preface

During one of my fieldwork trips to Jordan in January 2013, I was reading Andrew Shryock's great book *Nationalism and the Genealogical Imagination*, which deals with the war of words between the Jordanian ʿAbbad and ʿAdwan tribes, the rivalry between two historians from those tribes and their obsession with roots and ideology. During the same period, I was also interviewing Salafis about conflicts between two opposing Salafi camps in Jordan, who are ideologically close but nevertheless on very bad terms with one another. These conflicts concentrated specifically on two men who we will get to know much better in the pages to come and who are both very keen on stressing their ties to their deceased shaykh.

Shryock's book, though about a very different subject than this one focusses on, at one point seemed to intertwine with my interviews since they both dealt with a similar conflict. During the day, I would interview Salafis about their disputes while reading about tribal disputes at night. This was an interesting experience, although it also points to one of the biggest difficulties in my research: untangling the numerous accusations levelled against Jordanian Salafis by other Jordanian Salafis. Though virtually always friendly and hospitable to me, they were often quite hostile towards their "opponents" in these conflicts, which sometimes made me feel rather uncomfortable during interviews.

It would, however, be wrong to characterise Salafism in Jordan solely on the basis of internal conflicts. My interest in the subject was first coined during my research for a previous book on the Jordanian radical scholar Abu Muhammad al-Maqdisi. Through this experience, I got to know Jordan quite well and liked it a lot. Not only was the subject of Salafism in the kingdom wide open from an academic point of view, but the great hospitality of the people, their friendly demeanour and my large number of contacts there made me want to go back. Although Salafis generally do not have a very good reputation, I often found a friendliness and decency among them that were quite striking to me. While Jordan and the Salafi community there certainly have their problems, the nice way I was invited into countless homes and offices is one reason why I hope this book does justice to the Salafism it describes.

Acknowledgements

Writing this book has, in some respects, been a rather arduous exercise since I very often had to wonder whether I had accurately represented everybody's point of view in the sometimes contentious relationships between Salafis in Jordan. How wonderful it is, then, to discard that apprehensiveness altogether and write the acknowledgements to this book, in which I can just thank everybody who helped me in some way during the course of the research for this work or assisted during the writing. The first of these is the Netherlands Organisation for Academic Research (NWO), which awarded me a Veni grant in 2011 and allowed me to start working on this project the following year. I am grateful for the trust they placed in me, and I hope that this book and the many articles and book chapters I have produced since being awarded the grant are proof that it was money well spent.

This book was written while working at the Department of Religious Studies at Radboud University in Nijmegen, the Netherlands. Around the time that I applied for the grant that financed the research project of which this book is a result, the former department of Islam and Arabic was dissolved and integrated into Religious Studies. This was not always easy. Several professors retired without being replaced, and the loss of room in our curriculum for teaching Arabic and other relevant courses, even though these were replaced by other interesting subjects, was a tough blow to the academic study of Islam at Radboud University, not to mention to the morale of particularly some of my older colleagues. Indeed, the loss of so much of our Islam-related teaching time was one of the reasons I eventually left that university for Utrecht University, where I am now employed. Despite all this, however, it was always a joy working there, and that was in no small part because of my wonderful immediate colleagues: Gert Borg, Nicolet Boekhoff-van der Voort, Lieke de Jong, Martijn de Koning, Roel Meijer and Karin van Nieuwkerk. I would like to thank Karin in particular for her great efforts to steer us through these sometimes troubled waters and for trying to secure a good position for me. The fact that I eventually left for a different university was not because of a lack of effort on her part to keep me.

More immediately relevant to this book are those people who helped me by supplying information, websites, articles, books or documents that were somehow related to my research. Through both social media and personal contacts, Assaf David, Tayyeb Mimouni, Reuven Paz, Thomas Pierret and Jillian Schwedler helped me obtain all kinds of information that I would not have had without them. I thank them all for their time and effort on my behalf, and I hope I can return the favours they did me by possibly supplying them with similar information that they are looking for but cannot find.

When doing fieldwork in Jordan, I often visited the home or offices of Hasan Abu Haniyya, Marwan Shahada and Usama Shahada, who not only provided me with many names and phone numbers of interesting people but were also willing to discuss my research with me from their various points of view. I thank them for their hospitality, their kindness and their knowledge on the subject of this book. While in Jordan, I always stayed at research institutes, including the Institut français du Proche-Orient (IFPO), the American Center of Oriental Research (ACOR) and the British Institute in Amman (BIA). I would like to thank the staff at all of these institutes for taking such good care for me. Special thanks are due to Barbara Porter, the director of ACOR, for bringing me into contact with other researchers who shared my interests and saving those wonderful long articles on American politics from her copies of *The New Yorker* for me.

Most important of all for the research done for this book are the people I interviewed all over Jordan. Although I was sometimes refused an interview or, at other times, had to overcome a bit of scepticism, I was generally warmly welcomed by the many Salafis and others I spoke to. Their hospitality, the time they spent talking to me and their willingness to share their knowledge was often truly amazing. This is particularly the case since, in order to cross-check my findings, I often confronted them with uneasy questions that related to episodes of their lives that they would much rather forget. I thank them for their willingness to talk about these issues to a researcher who was not only a stranger and a complete outsider, but was also planning to write a book about these very things. It goes without saying that this book would not have seen the light of day if they had not been open to the idea of discussing Salafism in Jordan with me.

While writing the proposal for this book and the manuscript itself, I was fortunate enough to be aided by the expert help from Cambridge University Press' staff, including the former African, Middle Eastern and Islamic Studies editor Will Hammell and his successor Maria Marsh, as well as Cassi Roberts and Ramya Ranganathan. I thank them for their advice, their excellent work and particularly Maria's great enthusiasm for the entire project. I would also like to thank the anonymous peer reviewers for taking the time to read the manuscript and for offering valuable advice. The same applies to Jonathan Brown, Emad Hamdeh, Bernard Haykel, Martijn de Koning, Henri Lauzière, Harald Motzki and Jacob Olidort, who were kind enough to read parts of the manuscript and send me their comments. I am particularly grateful to Roel Meijer, who read the entire manuscript and shared with me his insights on how it could be improved. Although these scholars' comments were always useful and have helped make the book a better one, any mistakes left in the end result are, of course, mine alone.

Most of the work on this book that I could do behind my desk was done while listening to AccuJazz.com and many other sources of wonderful jazz. As such, this book was written to Joe Henderson's solid swing, John Coltrane's sheets of sound and Kurt Elling's velvety vocalese, which made working on this project – as great as it was in and of itself – even better. Come to think of it, I hope the musical inspiration I got from these and many other great musicians is not too obvious from the text since I can imagine that a book reflecting such wild improvisations is perhaps not very pleasant to read.

Last but not least, I would like to thank my family. Not only was this project a burden on them because I went to Jordan for several month-long periods throughout the past few years, but during the four and a half months that it took me to write this book, I was often up working till late at night rather than spending time with my wife. Although this was difficult for all of us, at least I have a book to show for it, while their reward is less clear. I therefore dedicate this book to them, hoping that my wife will see that its contents made it worth the effort and that my children will one day understand why their father was off to far-away Jordan so often.

Note on Transliteration, Names and Dates

The system of transliteration used in this book is the one used by the *International Journal of Middle East Studies* (IJMES). I have, however, also decided to make a distinction in transliteration that IJMES does not make: the Arabic *alif maqṣūra* is transliterated as "-á" to distinguish it from a *tāʾ marbūṭa* ("-a") and an *alif ṭawīla* ("-ā"). Furthermore, I have transliterated common words (like Qurʾan/Qurʾān), names and titles of books in the footnotes but not in the text itself. Finally, some words, such as *ḥadīth*, have not been given their accurate Arabic plural forms (*aḥādīth*) but a simplified English one (*ḥadīth*s).

Jordanians have a tendency to drop certain parts of names for reasons of convenience. A prominent Jordanian Salafi shaykh called Muhammad b. Musa Al Nasr, for example, is generally known as Muhammad Musa Nasr. When referring to him and others in footnotes and the bibliography, I will use their full names, but the more popular use of names is adopted in the actual text of this book. Salafi shaykhs also tend to be known under different names, depending on how many of their forefathers they choose to include, for example, which may also differ from occasion to occasion. The full name of prominent Jordanian Salafi shaykh ʿAli al-Halabi, for instance, is Abu l-Harith ʿAli b. Hasan b. ʿAli b. ʿAbd al-Hamid al-Halabi al-Athari, parts of which he drops or adds in articles or on covers of books. I have decided to give these names as mentioned in the article or book in the footnotes, sometimes with a few added elements to make them more consistent with other uses of the same name, but to blend them all into one name in the bibliography.

Finally, although Jordanians commonly use the Christian calendar, many Salafi publications mentioned in the footnotes use only the Islamic date of publication (i.e., by referring to Islamic months and years *anno hegirae*). I have decided not only to mention these for easier reference to the original, but also to include the corresponding Christian dates in square brackets for reasons of clarity. These dates were converted using a website linked to the Institute of Oriental Studies at Zurich University in Switzerland.[1]

[1] This website can be found at www.oriold.uzh.ch/static/hegira.html (accessed 8 April 2015).

Introduction

In August 2008, when I was in Jordan for fieldwork, I took a cab from downtown Amman to Beirut for several interviews. The ride took us through several seemingly never-ending customs procedures in Syria and again in Lebanon. In the car with me were three Lebanese people who not only applauded when I gave my best rendition of *Bhibbak Ya Lubnan* ("I love you, oh Lebanon") by the country's famous singer Fairouz, but also quizzed me extensively about my research. After I had explained that I was focussing on Salafism, one of the Lebanese people in the car told me: "You know, you can talk about Salafism here in Jordan, but you must be careful not to do that in Lebanon. That country is not like Jordan." Although I was not quite sure what to make of this warning, it has always struck me that Jordan, despite being a country in which you can supposedly "talk about Salafism", is a place whose Salafi community is rarely talked about by Western academics. To a much lesser extent, one could, in fact, say the same about the country of Jordan itself.

One of the best books on the history of the modern Middle East is William L. Cleveland and Martin Bunton's aptly named *A History of the Modern Middle East.*[1] A quick look at the bibliography of that volume suggests, however, that Jordan – the country on which this book focusses – has played little more than a supporting role in the region's history, getting a mere ten lines of suggestions for further reading.[2] By comparison, Turkey and Syria get more than half a page each, while Egypt gets about three-and-a-half pages of suggested publications.[3] Although numerous studies on Jordan have appeared throughout the years, their number perhaps pales in comparison to the works on regional powerhouses such as Egypt and Iraq or violently unstable states like Lebanon.

1 William L. Cleveland and Martin Bunton, *A History of the Modern Middle East* (Boulder, CO: Westview Press, 2013 [1994]).
2 *Ibid.*, 558–59. 3 *Ibid.*, 552–56.

As mentioned, this relative lack of studies on Jordan, in general, is also indicative of the number of academic titles that deal with the subject of this book: Salafism in Jordan. Comparatively little attention has been paid to Jordan's Salafi community, despite the fact that it has hosted some of the biggest names in Salafism, which I define as the type of Islam whose adherents claim to follow an idealised group of early Muslims known as "the pious predecessors" (*al-salaf al-ṣāliḥ*, hence the name "Salafism") as closely and in as many spheres of life as possible. Merely a decade ago, the Jordanian leader of the Iraqi branch of al-Qaʿida and precursor to the Islamic State (IS), Abu Musʿab al-Zarqawi (1966–2006), was second only to Osama bin Laden (1957–2011) in being the most-wanted terrorist in the world. Similarly, perhaps the two most important radical Islamist scholars (*ʿulamāʾ*, sing. *ʿālim*) alive today, Abu Qatada al-Filastini (b. 1960) and Abu Muhammad al-Maqdisi (b. 1959), are both Jordanian citizens. In fact, Jordan was home to perhaps the greatest and most influential twentieth-century scholar of the traditions of the Prophet Muhammad (*ḥadīth*s), Muhammad Nasir al-Din al-Albani (1914–1999), for the last two decades of his life. Apart from their ties to Jordan, what these men have in common is that they are all Salafis, though of different branches, as we will see later on.

Thus, one can safely say that Salafism in Jordan matters. This book is meant to give that subject the attention it deserves by focussing entirely on the ideology, history and contestation of Salafism in Jordan. As will be explained in more detail later in this introduction, this study concentrates on what Salafism in Jordan is, how its relationship with the state changed and why this happened. Before delving into this subject, however, I will first give a brief historical overview of Jordan (with special emphasis on the role of Islam) in order to provide context to the Salafi community in that country. This introduction will then give a critical overview of the current literature on Salafism in Jordan and indicate what this book contributes to the existing publications on this subject. It continues with an explanation of the method and sources used for this study and concludes with an overview of what will be dealt with in the chapters to come.

Jordan: A Brief Historical Overview

The area covered by Jordan nowadays has a long and interesting history dating back to centuries before Christ and was once the backdrop to significant dynasties and cities – such as the Nabatean kingdom of Petra, the remains of which can still be seen in the similarly named southern Jordanian city today. From the seventh century AD onwards, the area was conquered by the troops of the new Muslim religion that came out of the Arabian Peninsula, thereby slowly Islamising and Arabising a land whose inhabitants had adhered to various religious traditions and had spoken several languages before the Muslim conquest.[4] The different empires that ruled the area now known as Jordan divided the land into several military or administrative areas that were sometimes part of Greater Syria (al-Sham) and sometimes belonged to different empires altogether.[5] This practice was continued by the Ottomans, the last of the Muslim empires to rule the area, who conquered the land in 1516 and divided it into various districts.[6]

According to Rogan, the area now known as Jordan – despite not constituting a clear administrative unit – did have a common culture during late nineteenth-century Ottoman rule. The comparatively homogeneous religious make-up of the country (virtually all its Muslims were Sunnis, peacefully co-existing with a sizeable Greek Orthodox Christian minority) and a culture of hospitality common among both Muslims and Christians ensured a relatively tolerant atmosphere.[7] The latter aspect of this culture – hospitality – points to an important factor in Jordan's social and political life: tribalism.[8] As Alon has shown, the different tribes of Jordan have played an important role in the making of the country[9] and, indeed, tribal issues – ranging from honour-related matters to questions of genealogy – can still cause conflicts and division in modern-day Jordan.[10] It was in this context – an area ruled by the Ottoman Empire and populated by tribes – that the history of modern-day Jordan began.

[4] Kamal Salibi, *The Modern History of Jordan* (London and New York: I.B. Tauris, 2006 [1993]), 8–17.

[5] *Ibid.*, 17–26.

[6] Eugene L. Rogan, "Bringing the State Back: The Limits of Ottoman Rule in Jordan, 1840–1910," in *Village, Steppe and State: The Social Origins of Modern Jordan*, ed. Eugene L. Rogan and Tariq Tell (London and New York: British Academic Press, 1994), 34–45; *id.*, *Frontiers of the State in the Late Ottoman Empire* (Cambridge: Cambridge University Press, 1999), 23–36.

[7] *Id.*, *Frontiers*, 36–41.

[8] For an overview of the different Jordanian and Palestinian tribes and their descent, see ʿAwnī Jaddūʿ al-ʿUbaydī, *Sukkān al-Urdunn wa-Filasṭīn: Al-Manābit wa-l-Uṣūl* (Amman: no publisher, 2014).

[9] Yoav Alon, *The Making of Jordan: Tribes, Colonialism and the Modern State* (London and New York: I.B. Tauris, 2009 [2007]).

[10] Andrew Shryock, *Nationalism and the Genealogical Imagination: Oral History and Textual Authority in Tribal Jordan* (Berkeley, Los Angeles and London: University of California Press, 1997).

Independence and Beyond

Although Arab nationalism goes back further than the beginning of the twentieth century, the push for Arab independence from the Ottoman Empire began in earnest during the First World War (1914–1918), when the emir of Mecca, Husayn b. ʿAli (c. 1853–1931), decided to collaborate with the European colonial forces that increasingly came to dominate the Middle East and to launch the Arab Revolt (1916). Husayn hailed from a Hashimite dynasty, descending from the same Hashim clan that the Prophet Muhammad himself is said to have belonged to, thus giving him some religious prestige. In return for fighting the Ottoman Empire, the British promised Husayn and his sons independence in the Middle East.[11] In the case of the land eventually known as Jordan, this resulted in Husayn's son ʿAbdallah being installed by the British colonial powers as "emir of Transjordan" in 1921.[12] While limited in his power by Britain, which was ultimately and formally in charge of the new state, ʿAbdallah nevertheless managed to unite the tribes in the area under his control in such a way as to forge a more or less unified whole.[13] The country was formally made independent in 1946, when ʿAbdallah received the title of "king".[14]

At the same time, ʿAbdallah was also actively engaged in establishing and cultivating relations with the growing Zionist movement in neighbouring Palestine.[15] Although this did not lead to any lasting peace between them, it did sow the seeds of an enduring relationship between Israel and the Jordanian regime that has continued – with its ups and downs – until this very day. ʿAbdallah's actions were frowned upon by some Palestinian nationalists, however, who saw his relations with the Zionists as attempts to sell out what they saw as their homeland. As a result of such feelings of resentment, King ʿAbdallah was eventually assassinated by a Palestinian nationalist in 1951, when the former visited the al-Aqsa Mosque in Jerusalem.[16]

King ʿAbdallah was briefly succeeded by his son, Talal (1909–1972), who proved to be mentally unstable and therefore unfit for the job of

[11] The classic account of the colonial machinations surrounding the Arab Revolt against the Ottoman Empire is George Antonius, *The Arab Awakening* (New York: Capricorn Books, 1965 [1946]).

[12] Philip Robins, *A History of Jordan* (Cambridge: Cambridge University Press, 2004), 17–19; Mary C. Wilson, *King Abdullah, Britain and the Making of Jordan* (Cambridge: Cambridge University Press, 1987), 39–53.

[13] Alon, *Making*, 65–71. [14] Robins, *History*, 56–8.

[15] For an extensive treatment of these relations, see Avi Shlaim, *The Politics of Partition: King Abdullah, the Zionists, and Palestine 1921–1951* (Oxford: Oxford University Press, 1998 [1988]).

[16] *Ibid.*, 415–21.

king.[17] Talal's reign was a politically eventful one, however, since demands for liberal constitutional reform and more democratisation rose to a frenzy during this period. This was the situation inherited by Talal's son Husayn (1935–1999), who was inaugurated as king in 1953 and almost immediately reversed the liberalising measures adopted during his father's reign.[18] Yet attempts to limit the power of the monarch constituted only one of the challenges facing the young King Husayn. Another threat to his regime was presented by the Egyptian President Gamal ʿAbd al-Nasir (Nasser; r. 1954–1970), whose republican, socialist policies constituted a direct challenge to the monarchical, conservative leadership of Jordan and other kingdoms in the region. Moreover, Nasser enjoyed support within the country itself and it was only through a royal clamp-down on Jordanian Nasserists that a coup was averted in 1957.[19]

A further challenge to the Jordanian regime was presented by the Arab-Israeli conflict. Apart from direct hostilities with Israel, the war in 1948 had also led to a huge influx of Palestinian refugees and the incorporation of the West Bank into Transjordanian territory, which was then renamed "Jordan". The war in 1967 further increased the number of Palestinians fleeing to Jordan but also led to the loss of the West Bank to Israel. The presence of Palestinian refugees often led to tensions between "East Bank Jordanians" and "Palestinian Jordanians" in politics, society and with regard to the Palestinian–Israeli conflict. These came to a head in September 1970, when some Palestinian militant factions hijacked several planes and staged a coup against King Husayn. This episode in Jordan's history, which became known as Black September, led to the violent removal of Palestinian militant groups from Jordanian soil, at a cost of thousands of (mostly Palestinian) lives.[20]

Since the 1970s, the threat of Nasserism has dissipated and the Palestinian question has become much more of a problem between Palestinians and Israelis, rather than between Palestinians and

[17] Robins, *History*, 75–82.

[18] Naseer H. Aruri, *Jordan: A Study in Political Development (1921–1965)* (The Hague: Martinus Nijhoff, 1972), 89–115.

[19] *Ibid.*, 134–50. For a comprehensive treatment of the Nasserist challenge to Jordan, see Uriel Dann, *King Hussein and the Challenge of Arab Radicalism: Jordan, 1955–1967* (New York and Oxford: Oxford University Press, 1989).

[20] Nigel Ashton, *King Hussein of Jordan: A Political Life* (New Haven and London: Yale University Press, 2008), 136–57; Avi Shlaim, *Lion of Jordan: The Life of King Hussein in War and Peace* (New York: Albert A. Knopf, 2008), 315–45. For broader discussions on relations between "East Bank" and "Palestinian" Jordanians, see Adnan Abu-Odeh, *Jordanians, Palestinians & the Hashemite Kingdom in the Middle East Peace Process* (Washington, DC: United States Institute of Peace, 1999); Marc Lynch, *State Interests and Public Spheres: The International Politics of Jordan's Identity* (New York: Columbia University Press, 1999), 74–139.

Jordanians. In fact, the Jordanian regime supported the Palestinian–Israeli peace process that started in the early 1990s and even made peace with Israel itself in 1994. Although the relationship between the two countries has been rocky sometimes, the situation that King Husayn's death in 1999 left behind for his son ʿAbdallah II when the latter succeeded his father was far more stable than what he had ever enjoyed himself. To be sure, King ʿAbdallah II was confronted with new challenges of his own – particularly the rise of radical Islamism and its repercussions, which will be discussed later – but on the whole, these threats were not existential.[21] This has led to a situation in which the Jordanian regime – consisting of the Royal Court (*al-dīwān al-malikī*) and the army and affiliated security services[22] and supported by individual members of a political elite of loyalists in government and parliament – is in a relatively secure position today.

Islam in Jordan

In their study on Islamists and the state in Jordan, Abu Rumman and Abu Haniyya refer to the Jordanian system of governance as one of "conservative secularism" (*al-ʿalmāniyya al-muḥāfaẓa*). The authors use this term to indicate that Jordan has never been a religious or theocratic state in the sense of applying Islamic law (*sharīʿa*) as its sole source of legislation, but instead has a civil constitution giving rights to all its citizens. At the same time, however, it has always projected a conservative image in politics, with its anti-revolutionary monarchy, its strong reliance on tribes, its Hashimite heritage and its support for loyal Islamic organisations.[23] The latter two factors are more explicitly relevant with regard to the topic of Islam in Jordan and deserve some closer attention.

The Hashimite heritage of the Jordanian royal family played an important role in the various kings' efforts to establish their credentials over their kingdom, although their descent from the Prophet Muhammad may not necessarily have been a huge factor in ʿAbdallah's success of uniting the tribes of Transjordan.[24] The kings of Jordan have nevertheless

[21] For more on the transition from King Ḥusayn to King ʿAbdallāh II, see Curtis R. Ryan, *Jordan in Transition: From Hussein to Abdullah* (Boulder, CO: Lynne Rienner Publishers, 2002).

[22] Beverley Milton-Edwards and Peter Hinchcliffe, *Jordan: A Hashemite Legacy* (London & New York: Routledge, 2009), 36–7, 97–8.

[23] Muḥammad Abū Rummān and Ḥasan Abū Haniyya, *Al-Ḥall al-Islāmī: Al-Islāmiyyūn wa-l-Dawla wa-Rihānāt al-Dīmuqrāṭiyya wa-l-Amn* (Amman: Friedrich Ebert Stiftung, 2012), 23–30.

[24] Gudrun Krämer, "Good Counsel to the King: The Islamist Opposition in Saudi Arabia, Jordan, and Morocco," in *Middle East Monarchies: The Challenge of Modernity*, ed. Joseph Kostiner (Boulder, CO: Lynne Rienner Publishers, 2000), 269; Asher Susser,

seemed proud of their prophetic heritage and have used it to shore up their legitimacy in their discourse. Jolen, in her study of King Husayn's speeches, has shown that Islam, Islamic history and the royal family's Hashimite descent were important factors in the king's efforts to legitimise the regime's policies.[25] Similarly, King ʿAbdallah II regularly and proudly refers to his Hashimite heritage and prophetic descent in his autobiographical work *Our Last Best Chance*.[26]

Although, as mentioned, Jordan is not a religious state (*dawla dīniyya*) the way Saudi Arabia or Iran is, the prophetic heritage and genealogical credentials of the country's kings, as well as the generally religious make-up of Jordan's population, have translated into several official Islamic institutes. The first of these is the office of supreme judge (*qāḍī al-quḍāt*) of Islamic legal (*sharʿī*) courts. These courts function alongside regular Jordanian courts and pass verdicts on the basis of the *sharīʿa* in personal status issues of Muslims and several other matters on which the parties involved agree.[27] The second institute is the Ministry of Religious Endowments (*awqāf*, sing. *waqf*). This ministry deals with the upkeeping and control of, for example, mosques, religious schools, sites of Islamic heritage and Qurʾan memorisation centres.[28] The third major official Islamic institute is the Fatwa Department (Daʾirat al-Iftaʾ), which was established in Jordan in 1921 and is the central authority for giving out fatwas to the Jordanian population. It has had changing relations with the Ministry of Religious Endowments – sometimes being part of it, enjoying independence at other times – and has been influenced by two different schools of Sunni Islamic law: the Hanafi school and the Shafiʿi school.[29]

Islamic institutes and organisations in Jordan are not all controlled by the regime, of course, and many forms of Islamic civil society have

"The Jordanian Monarchy: The Hashemite Success Story," in *Middle East Monarchies: The Challenge of Modernity*, ed. Joseph Kostiner (Boulder, CO: Lynne Rienner Publishers, 2000), 87.

[25] Judith Jolen, "The Quest for Legitimacy: The Role of Islam in the State's Political Discourse in Egypt and Jordan (1979–1996)" (PhD diss., Catholic University Nijmegen, 2003), 155–64. This was especially the case with regard to the Hashimite claim to Jerusalem. See Kimberly Katz, *Jordanian Jerusalem: Holy Place and National Spaces* (Gainesville, FL: University Press of Florida, 2005).

[26] King Abdullah II of Jordan, *Our Last Best Chance: The Pursuit of Peace in a Time of Peril* (New York: Viking, 2011), xx, 3–4, 20, to mention just a few references.

[27] Abū Rummān and Abū Haniyya, *Al-Ḥall*, 39–43. [28] *Ibid.*, 43–9.

[29] *Ibid.*, 49–53; Michael Robbins and Lawrence Rubin, "The Rise of Official Islam in Jordan," *Politics, Religion & Ideology* 14, no. 1 (2013): 63–4. I would like to thank Assaf David for bringing this article to my attention. The other two schools of law in Sunni Islam are the Mālikī and Ḥanbalī schools. For more on this subject, see Wael B. Hallaq, *Sharīʿa: Theory, Practice, Transformations* (Cambridge: Cambridge University Press, 2009), 60–71.

developed over the past few decades, including hospitals, charitable societies and political parties.[30] At the same time, Jordanian civil society is heavily controlled bureaucratically by the regime because the latter wants to make sure that organisations, institutes and societies do not pose any security or political threat to the state's hegemony.[31] The need for Islamic and other organisations and institutes to register their existence, goals and leaders with the relevant ministry is therefore of the utmost importance for the Jordanian regime to maintain control.[32] In the context of this book, the registration of these organisations is somewhat less important, but their ideological persuasion is all the more so, because it helps explain how a doctrinally strict movement such as Salafism asserts itself in this Islamic landscape in Jordan.

The first major religious stream among Jordanian Muslims can be found in Sufism, a spiritual trend within Islam – almost as old as the religion itself – that is found all over the world. Although Sufism has taken various forms throughout the history of Islam, ranging from relatively orthodox, text-based approaches to more mystical and ascetic practices, Sufis generally have in common that they seek to "strive for a personal engagement with the Divine Reality".[33] They are often organised in "orders" (*ṭuruq*, sing. *ṭarīqa*) led by a shaykh, who may have considerable influence over his followers. In the case of Jordan, Sufism has long existed in the country as a popular and – importantly – moderate and decidedly apolitical form of Islam focussing on the spiritual aspects of religion through its various orders, rather than party-politics and everything that entails.[34]

A second and similarly apolitical trend within Jordanian Islam can be found in the Jamaʿat al-Tabligh. This movement, which originally dates back to nineteenth-century India and the teachings of Mawlana Muhammad Ilyas (1885–1944), focusses on personal piety, Qurʾan

30 Janine A. Clark, *Islam, Charity, and Activism: Middle-Class Networks and Social Welfare in Egypt, Jordan, and Yemen* (Bloomington and Indianapolis, IN: Indiana University Press, 2004), 82–114; Egbert Harmsen, *Islam, Civil Society and Social Work: Muslim Voluntary Welfare Associations in Jordan between Patronage and Empowerment* (Amsterdam: Amsterdam University Press, 2008).

31 Quintan Wiktorowicz, "Civil Society as Social Control: State Power in Jordan," *Comparative Politics* 33, no. 1 (October 2000): 43–61.

32 For an overview of Islamic organisations of various kinds in Jordan and some basic information about them, see Hamed Dabbas, "Islamic Centers, Associations, Societies, Organizations, and Committees in Jordan," in *Islamic Movements in Jordan* (translation George A. Musleh), ed. Jillian Schwedler (Amman: Al-Urdun al-Jadid Research Center/ Sindbad Publishing House, 1997), 193–259.

33 William C. Chittick, "Ṣūfi Thought and Practice," in *The Oxford Encyclopedia of the Islamic World*, vol. V, ed. John L. Esposito (Oxford: Oxford University Press, 2009), 207.

34 Ḥasan Abū Haniyya, *Al-Ṭuruq al-Ṣūfiyya: Durūb Allāh al-Rūḥiyya; Al-Takayyuf wa-l-Tajdīd fī Siyāq al-Taḥdīth* (Amman: Friedrich Ebert Stiftung, 2011), 9–12, 145–8.

memorisation and – crucially – the transmission (*tablīgh*, hence the name of the movement) of its message. The group made a habit of engaging in *gasht*, a Persian word denoting the practice of "making rounds" in the vicinity of mosques in order to call people to prayer and the study of the Qur'an. The movement began its activities in the early twentieth century with a message of personal piety and Islamic observance, education and propagation.[35] It also established a distinct programme and method for adherents to the movement to follow, which – among other things – dictates that followers should spend three days a month working on behalf of the group.[36] Perhaps unsurprisingly for such a strongly missionary movement, the Jama'at al-Tabligh spread to various regions in India and, eventually, also to other countries and continents, reaching the Arab world – including Jordan – in the early 1950s.[37]

It is not clear how many followers the Jama'at al-Tabligh movement currently has in Jordan. This is even less clear for a much more radical and overtly political organisation that is the third important ideological Islamic trend in Jordan: the Islamic Liberation Party (Hizb al-Tahrir al-Islami). Founded in 1952 by the Palestinian shaykh Taqi al-Din al-Nabhani (1910–1974), the Islamic Liberation Party was, in a sense, the opposite of the Jama'at al-Tabligh as it did not so much focus on social, missionary and charitable activities but concentrated instead on the founding of an Islamic state or caliphate in the Muslim world.[38] Given this clearly political and potentially even revolutionary goal – the regimes of the Muslim world could, after all, easily be seen as obstacles towards this objective – the Islamic Liberation Party is a controversial group in many countries, including in the West. In Jordan, the movement was nevertheless represented in parliament in the 1950s, albeit only briefly and marginally.[39] It is an interesting group because of its single-minded striving for the re-establishment of the caliphate in a way that goes back much further than that of, for example, the Islamic State in Iraq and Syria, but it was never a mass movement in Jordan and only seems to enjoy very little support in Jordanian society today.

35 Muhammad Khalid Masud, "The Growth and Development of the Tablīghī Jamā'at in India," in *Travellers in Faith: Studies of the Tablīghī Jamā'at as a Transnational Islamic Movement for Faith Renewal*, ed. Muhammad Khalid Masud (Leiden: Brill, 2000), 3–11.

36 *Ibid.*, 21–8.

37 Marc Gaborieau, "The Transformation of Tablīghī Jamā'at into a Transnational Movement," in *Travellers in Faith: Studies of the Tablīghī Jamā'at as a Transnational Islamic Movement for Faith Renewal*, ed. Muhammad Khalid Masud (Leiden: Brill, 2000), 126–30.

38 Abū Rummān and Abū Haniyya, *Al-Ḥall*, 397–408. For more on the Islamic Liberation Party, see Suha Taji-Farouki, *Fundamental Quest: Hizb al-Tahrir and the Search for the Islamic Caliphate* (London: Grey Seal Books, 1996).

39 Aruri, *Jordan*, 112.

A fourth and final ideological trend within Islam in Jordan and one that straddles the social and missionary activities of the Jamaʿat al-Tabligh on the one hand and the political zeal of the Islamic Liberation Party on the other is the Muslim Brotherhood. Founded in Egypt in 1928 by Hasan al-Banna (1906–1949), the movement was more or less meant to preach a general message of Islam for the masses and rather quickly spread to other parts of the world, including Jordan, where a local branch was founded by ʿAbd al-Latif Abu Qura (1906–1967) in Amman in 1945. The activities of the group were limited to social, educational and charitable work in the first few decades of its existence, all in the service of Islam.[40] Given the Hashimite credentials of King ʿAbdallah, it is perhaps not surprising that he allowed an Islamic group like the Muslim Brotherhood to "function as a purely religious organization",[41] maybe to allow them to act as a conservative and apolitical antidote to the rising tide of pan-Arab nationalism. The king may thus have had opportunistic reasons to allow the Muslim Brotherhood, which explicitly sought his blessing, and he subsequently looked upon the group with some suspicion, perhaps aware of its political potential and certainly realising that the Brotherhood's strongly anti-Zionist ideas were at odds with his own, more conciliatory tendencies towards the Jews in Palestine. Generally speaking, however, relations between the king and the Muslim Brotherhood were good.[42]

Under King Husayn, the ties between the regime and the Brotherhood remained strong in general, although the relationship did become more strained over the years. This was partly due to the removal of the Nasserist threat from Jordan, which both parties considered a common enemy, but also because of the increased politicisation of the Brotherhood under the guidance of its leader Muhammad ʿAbd al-Rahman Khalifa (1919–2006), who took over from the less political Abu Qura in 1952. The group began to speak up more explicitly about the Palestinian question and the need to apply the *sharīʿa* at the state level and actively participated in parliamentary elections until these were suspended after the attempted Nasserist coup in 1957.[43] The period following the suspension of parliamentary elections – during which the Brotherhood crucially supported the regime in its crackdown on

[40] Ali Abdul Kazem, "The Muslim Brotherhood: The Historic Background and the Ideological Origins," in *Islamic Movements in Jordan* (translation George A. Musleh), ed. Jillian Schwedler (Amman: Al-Urdun al-Jadid Research Center/Sindbad Publishing House, 1997), 13–18; Ibrāhīm Gharāyiba, *Jamāʿat al-Ikhwān al-Muslimīn fī l-Urdunn, 1946–1996* (Amman: Markaz al-Urdunn al-Jadīd/Dār Sindbād li-l-Nashr, 1997), 45–53.

[41] Marion Boulby, *The Muslim Brotherhood and the Kings of Jordan, 1945–1993* (Atlanta, GA: Scholars Press, 1999), 46.

[42] *Ibid.*, 46–7. [43] *Ibid.*, 50–72.

Palestinian militants in 1970 – allowed the group to expand its social activities. When elections were held again in 1989, the group participated and was quite successful and in 1992 it founded a political party, the Islamic Action Front (IAF).[44] Through this party, the Brotherhood has since become even more politicised and thus more willing to discard its traditional reflexive loyalty in favour of a critical attitude and seeking influence. The regime has responded to this by taking electoral measures to limit the group's parliamentary weight.[45] Mostly as a result of this, the Brotherhood – which has become the biggest and most visible Islamist movement in Jordan – has often boycotted parliamentary elections over the last two decades, leaving the relationship during the later years of King Husayn and those of his son, King ʿAbdallah II, quite tense at times.[46]

The Study of Salafism in Jordan

Jordan is thus a country with an overwhelmingly Sunni Muslim population, a royal family with a strong religious pedigree and various Islamic institutes and organisations, both at the level of the regime and within society and politics in general. It is this context to which Salafis in Jordan seek to make their own ideological contribution. The study of Salafism as a global phenomenon has greatly increased over the past decade and books on this trend as a whole have appeared in various languages.[47] The same applies to general studies on Salafism in Gulf countries such as Kuwait[48] and especially Saudi

[44] Jillian Schwedler, *Faith in Moderation: Islamist Parties in Jordan and Yemen* (Cambridge: Cambridge University Press, 2006), 65–9.

[45] Abla M. Amawi, "The 1993 Elections in Jordan," *Arab Studies Quarterly* 16, no. 3 (1994): 15–17; Frédéric Charillon and Alain Mouftard, "Jordanie: Les elections du 8 novembre 1993 et le processus de paix," *Monde Arabe Maghreb Machrek*, no. 144 (1994): 45–6; Jillian Schwedler, "A Paradox of Democracy? Islamist Participation in Elections," *Middle East Report*, no. 209 (1998): 28.

[46] Abū Rummān and Abū Haniyya, *Al-Ḥall*, 74–81, 126–36.

[47] Martijn de Koning, Joas Wagemakers and Carmen Becker, *Salafisme: Utopische idealen in een weerbarstige praktijk* (Almere: Parthenon, 2014); Roel Meijer, ed., *Global Salafism: Islam's New Religious Movement* (London: Hurst & Co., 2009); Bernard Rougier, ed., *Qu'est-ce que le salafisme?* (Paris: Presses Universitaires de France, 2008); Behnam T. Said and Hazim Fouad, ed., *Salafismus: Auf der Suche nach dem wahren Islam* (Freiburg: Herder, 2014).

[48] Carine Lahoud-Tatar, *Islam et politique au Koweït* (Paris: Presses Universitaire de France, 2011), esp. 81–107, 189–220; *id.*, "Koweït: Salafismes et rapports au pouvoir," in *Qu'est-ce que le salafisme?* ed. Bernard Rougier (Paris: Presses Universitaires de France, 2008), 123–35; Falah Abdullah al-Mdaires, *Islamic Extremism in Kuwait: From the Muslim Brotherhood to al-Qaeda and other Islamist Political Groups* (London and New York: Routledge, 2010); Zoltan Pall, *Kuwaiti Salafism and its Growing Influence in the Levant* (Washington, DC: Carnegie Endowment for International Peace, 2014).

Arabia,[49] which have – for various reasons, as we will see later on – been instrumental in the spread of Salafism (including in Jordan). Other countries in the Arab world that have lengthy general studies dedicated to their Salafi communities include Egypt,[50] Lebanon[51] and Yemen.[52] To a much lesser extent, this is also the case for

[49] Muhammad Al Atawneh, *Wahhābī Islam Facing the Challenges of Modernity: Dār al-Iftā in the Modern Saudi State* (Leiden: Brill, 2010); Mohammed Ayoob and Hasan Kosebalaban, ed., *Religion and Politics in Saudi Arabia: Wahhabism and the State* (Boulder, CO: Lynne Rienner Publishers, 2009); David Commins, "Le salafisme en Arabie Saoudite," in *Qu'est-ce que le salafisme?* ed. Bernard Rougier (Paris: Presses Universitaires de France, 2008), 25–44; *id.*, *The Wahhabi Mission and Saudi Arabia* (London and New York: I.B. Tauris, 2006); Michael Cook, "On the Origins of Wahhabism," *Journal of the Royal Asiatic Society* 2, no. 2 (1992): 191–202; Natana J. DeLong-Bas, *Wahhabi Islam: From Revival and Reform to Global Jihad* (Oxford: Oxford University Press, 2004); Abdulaziz H. al-Fahad, "From Exclusivism to Accommodation: Doctrinal and Legal Evolution of Wahhabism," *New York University Law Review* 79, no. 2 (2004): 485–519; Nabile Mouline, *Les clercs de l'islam: Autorité religieuse et pouvoir politique en Arabie Saoudite, XVIIIe-XXIe siècle* (Paris: Presses Universitaires de France, 2011); Madawi Al-Rasheed, *Contesting the Saudi State: Islamic Voices from a New Generation* (Cambridge: Cambridge University Press, 2007); *id.*, "The Local and the Global in Saudi Salafi Discourse," in *Global Salafism: Islam's New Religious Movement*, ed. Roel Meijer (London: Hurst & Co., 2009), 301–20; *id.*, "The Minaret and the Palace: Obedience at Home and Rebellion Abroad," in *Kingdom without Borders: Saudi Arabia's Political, Religious and Media Frontiers*, ed. Madawi Al-Rasheed (London: Hurst & Co., 2008), 199–219; Reinhard Schulze, *Islamischer Internationalismus im 20. Jahrhundert: Untersuchungen zur Geschichte der islamischen Weltliga* (Leiden: Brill, 1990); Saeed Shehabi, "The Role of Religious Ideology in the Expansionist Policies of Saudi Arabia," in *Kingdom without Borders: Saudi Arabia's Political, Religious and Media Frontiers*, ed. Madawi Al-Rasheed (London: Hurst & Co., 2008), 183–97; Elizabeth Sirriyeh, "Wahhabis, Unbelievers and the Problems of Exclusivism," *BRISMES Bulletin* 16, no. 2 (1989): 123–32; Guido Steinberg, *Religion und Staat in Saudi-Arabien: Die wahhabitische Gelehrten, 1902–1953* (Würzburg: Ergon Verlag, 2002); *id.*, "Saudi-Arabien: Der Salafismus in seinem Mutterland," in *Salafismus: Auf der Suche nach dem wahren Islam*, ed. Behnam T. Said and Hazim Fouad (Freiburg, etc.: Herder, 2014), 265–96; *id.*, "The Wahhabi Ulama and the Saudi State: 1745 to the Present," in *Saudi Arabia in the Balance: Political Economy, Society, Foreign Affairs*, ed. Paul Aarts and Gerd Nonneman (London: Hurst & Co., 2005), 11–34; Joas Wagemakers, "The Enduring Legacy of the Second Saudi State: Quietist and Radical Wahhabi Contestations of *al-Walā' wa-l-Barā'*," *International Journal of Middle East Studies* 44, no. 1 (2012): 93–110.

[50] Richard Gauvain, *Salafi Ritual Purity: In the Presence of God* (London and New York: Routledge, 2013).

[51] Zoltan Pall, *Lebanese Salafis between the Gulf and Europe: Development, Fractionalization and Transnational Networks of Salafism in Lebanon* (Amsterdam: Amsterdam University Press, 2013); *id.*, "Salafism in Lebanon: Local and Transnational Resources" (PhD diss., Utrecht University, 2014); Robert G. Rabil, *Salafism in Lebanon: From Apoliticism to Transnational Jihadism* (Washington, DC: Georgetown University Press, 2014).

[52] Laurent Bonnefoy, "How Transnational is Salafism in Yemen?" in *Global Salafism: Islam's New Religious Movement*, ed. Roel Meijer (London: Hurst & Co., 2009), 321–41; *id.*, "L'illusion apolitique: Adaptations, évolutions et instrumentalisations du salafisme Yéménite," in *Qu'est-ce que le salafisme?* ed. Bernard Rougier (Paris: Presses Universitaires de France, 2008), 137–59; *id.*, "Salafism in Yemen: A 'Saudisation'?" in

other Arab countries such as the Palestinian territories,[53] Sudan[54] and Syria[55] as well as non-Arab Muslim countries such as Indonesia,[56] Pakistan[57] and Turkey.[58] In recent years, several studies have also been published on Salafism in general in non-Muslim parts of the world, including Europe as a whole,[59] and also individual European countries such as Great Britain,[60] Germany,[61]

Kingdom without Borders: Saudi Arabia's Political, Religious and Media Frontiers, ed. Madawi Al-Rasheed (London: Hurst & Co., 2008), 245–62; *id.*, *Salafism in Yemen: Transnationalism and Religious Identity* (London: Hurst & Co., 2011); *id.*, "Violence in Contemporary Yemen: State, Society and Salafis," *The Muslim World* 101 (2011): 324–46; François Burgat and Muhammad Sbitli, "Les salafis au Yémen ou ... la modernisation malgré tout," *Chroniques yéménites* 10 (2002); Bernard Haykel, *Revival and Reform in Islam: The Legacy of Muhammad al-Shawkani* (Cambridge: Cambridge University Press, 2003); *id.*, "The Salafis in Yemen at a Crossroads: An Obituary of Shaykh Muqbil al-Wadi'i of Dammaj (d. 1422/2001)," *Jemen Report* 2 (2002): 28–37.

53 Khaled Hroub, "Salafi Formations in Palestine: The Limits of a De-Palestinised Milieu," in *Global Salafism: Islam's New Religious Movement*, ed. Roel Meijer (London: Hurst & Co., 2009), 221–43.

54 Noah Salomon, "The Salafi Critique of Islamism: Doctrine, Difference and the Problem of Islamic Political Action in Contemporary Sudan," in *Global Salafism: Islam's New Religious Movement*, ed. Roel Meijer (London: Hurst & Co., 2009), 143–68.

55 Arnaud Lenfant, "L'évolution du salafisme en Syrië au XXe siècle," in *Qu'est-ce que le salafisme?* ed. Bernard Rougier (Paris: Presses Universitaires de France, 2008), 161–78.

56 Noorhaidi Hasan, "Ambivalent Doctrines and Conflicts in the Salafi Movement in Indonesia," in *Global Salafism: Islam's New Religious Movement*, ed. Roel Meijer (London: Hurst & Co., 2009), 169–88; *id.*, *Laskar Jihad: Islam, Militancy, and the Quest for Identity in Post-New Order Indonesia* (Ithaca, New York: Cornell Southeast Asia Program Publications, 2006); *id.*, "Saudi Expansion, the Salafi Campaign and Arabised Islam in Indonesia," in *Kingdom without Borders: Saudi Arabia's Political, Religious and Media Frontiers*, ed. Madawi Al-Rasheed (London: Hurst & Co., 2008), 263–81; Din Wahid, "Nurturing the Salafi *Manhaj*: A Study of Salafi *Pesantren*s in Contemporary Indonesia" (PhD diss., Utrecht University, 2014).

57 Mariam Abou Zahab, "Salafism in Pakistan: The Ahl-e Hadith Movement," in *Global Salafism: Islam's New Religious Movement*, ed. Roel Meijer (London: Hurst & Co., 2009), 126–42.

58 Samet Yilmaz, "Der Salafismus in der Türkei," in *Salafismus: Auf der Suche nach dem wahren Islam*, ed. Behnam T. Said and Hazim Fouad (Freiburg: Herder, 2014), 350–78.

59 Samir Amghar, *Le salafisme d'aujourd'hui: Mouvements sectaries en Occident* (Paris: Michalon Éditions, 2011); *id.*, "Quietisten, Politiker und Revolutionäre: Die Entstehung und Entwicklung des salafistischen Universums in Europa," in *Salafismus: Auf der Suche nach dem wahren Islam*, ed. Behnam T. Said and Hazim Fouad (Freiburg: Herder, 2014), 381–410.

60 Sadek Hamid, "The Attraction of 'Authentic' Islam: Salafism and British Muslim Youth," in *Global Salafism: Islam's New Religious Movement*, ed. Roel Meijer (London: Hurst & Co., 2009), 384–403.

61 Claudia Dantschke, "'Da habe ich etwas gesehen, was mir einen Sinn gibt.' – Was macht Salafismus attraktiv und wie kann man diesem entgegenwirken?" in *Salafismus: Auf der Suche nach dem wahren Islam*, ed. Behnam T. Said and Hazim Fouad (Freiburg: Herder, 2014), 474–502; Nina Wiedl, "Geschichte des Salafismus in Deutschland," in *Salafismus: Auf der Suche nach dem wahren Islam*, ed. Behnam T. Said and Hazim Fouad (Freiburg: Herder, 2014), 411–41.

France[62] and the Netherlands.[63] Finally, quite some attention has also been paid to Salafism in its various forms on the internet.[64]

Compared to the number of general studies on Salafism in other countries, relatively little attention has been paid to the phenomenon as a whole in Jordan. The existing literature on Salafism in Jordan focusses heavily on only one branch of this trend, namely the radical (and sometimes violent) movement in the country known as Jihadi-Salafism.[65] Certain aspects of this sub-trend have received special attention, such as

[62] Mohamed-Ali Adraoui, "Être salafiste en France," in *Qu'est-ce que le salafisme?* ed. Bernard Rougier (Paris: Presses Universitaires de France, 2008), 231–41; *id.*, *Du Golfe aux banlieues: Le salafisme mondialisé* (Paris: Presses Universitaires de France, 2013); *id.*, "Salafism in France: Ideology, Practices and Contradictions," in *Global Salafism: Islam's New Religious Movement*, ed. Roel Meijer (London: Hurst & Co., 2009), 364–83; Romain Caillet, "Trajectoires de salafis français en Égypte," in *Qu'est-ce que le salafisme?* ed. Bernard Rougier (Paris: Presses Universitaires de France, 2008), 257–71.

[63] Martijn de Koning, "Changing Worldviews and Friendship: An Exploration of the Life Stories of Two Female Salafis in the Netherlands," in *Global Salafism: Islam's New Religious Movement*, ed. Roel Meijer (London: Hurst & Co., 2009), 404–23; De Koning, Wagemakers and Becker, *Salafisme*, 140–74; Ineke Roex, "Leven als de profeet in Nederland: Over de salafi-beweging en democratie" (PhD diss., University of Amsterdam, 2013).

[64] Carmen Becker, "Following the Salafi Manhaj in Computer-Mediated Environments: Linking Everyday Life to the Qurʾān and the Sunna," in *The Transmission and Dynamics of the Textual Sources of Islam: Essays in Honour of Harald Motzki*, ed. Nicolet Boekhoff-van der Voort, Kees Versteegh and Joas Wagemakers (Leiden: Brill, 2011), 421–41; *id.*, "Muslims on the Path of the Salaf al-Salih: Ritual Dynamics in Chat Rooms and Discussion Forums," *Information, Communication & Society* 14, no. 8 (2011): 1181–203; *id.*, "Learning to be Authentic: Religious Practices of German and Dutch Muslims Following the Salafiyya in Forums and Chat Rooms" (PhD diss., Radboud University, Nijmegen, 2013); Mamoun Fandy, "CyberResistance: Saudi Opposition Between Globalization and Localization," *Comparative Studies in Society and History* 41, no. 1 (1999): 124–47; Joshua Teitelbaum, "Duelling for Daʿwa: State vs. Society on the Saudi Internet," *Middle East Journal* 56, no. 2 (2002): 222–39; Dominique Thomas, "Le role d'Internet dans la diffusion de la doctrine salafiste," in *Qu'est-ce que le salafisme?* ed. Bernard Rougier (Paris: Presses Universitaires de France, 2008), 87–102.

[65] Abū Rummān and Abū Haniyya, *Al-Ḥall*, 283–368; *id.*, *Al-Salafiyya al-Jihādiyya fī l-Urdunn baʿda Maqtal al-Zarqāwī: Muqārabat al-Huwiyya, Azmat al-Qiyāda wa-Ḍabābiyyat al-Ruʾya* (Amman: Friedrich Ebert Stiftung, 2009); Anouar Boukhars, "The Challenge of Terrorism and Religious Extremism in Jordan," *Strategic Insights* 5, no. 4 (2006); International Crisis Group (ICG), *Jordan's 9/11: Dealing with Jihadi Islamism*, ICG Middle East Report no. 47 (Amman and Brussels, 2005); Brian Katulis, Hardin Lang and Mokhtar Awad, *Jordan in the Eye of the Storm: Continued U.S. Support Necessary as Regional Turmoil Continues* (Washington, DC: Center for American Progress, 2014), esp. 14–19; Yair Minzili, "The Jordanian Regime Fights the War of Ideas," in *Current Trends in Islamist Ideology*, vol. V, ed. Hillel Fradkin, Hussain Haqqani and Eric Brown (Washington, DC: Hudson Institute, 2007), 55–69; Murad Batal al-Shishani, "Jordan's New Generation of Salafi-Jihadists Take to the Streets to Demand Rule by Shariʿa," *Terrorism Monitor* 9, no. 18 (2011): 7–9; Joas Wagemakers, "Contesting Religious Authority in Jordanian Salafi Networks," in *Perseverance of Terrorism: Focus on Leaders*, ed. Marko Milosevic and Kacper Rekawek (Amsterdam, etc.: IOS Press, 2014), 118–22.

the rise of the movement in the early 1990s[66] and the Palestinian background of some Jordanian radical Salafis.[67] Two major personalities within Jordan's Jihadi-Salafi movement have also been the subject of in-depth studies, namely the late leader of al-Qaʿida in Iraq, Abu Musʿab al-Zarqawi,[68] and his former mentor, Abu Muhammad al-Maqdisi.[69] The latter's criticism of the violent and allegedly extreme tactics in Iraq of the former have also been treated in a detailed way,[70] as have the conflicts between supporters of both men.[71] Other aspects of Jordanian Jihadi-Salafism that have been dealt with in the literature are al-Maqdisi's ideology[72] and the accusation that his criticism of al-Zarqawi represents

66 Beverley Milton-Edwards, "Climate of Change in Jordan's Islamist Movement," in *Islamic Fundamentalism*, ed. Abdel Salam Sidahmed and Anoushiravan Ehteshami (Boulder, CO: Westview Press, 1996), 125–34; Joas Wagemakers, "A Terrorist Organization that Never Was: The Jordanian 'Bayʿat al-Imam' Group," *Middle East Journal* 68, no. 1 (2014): 59–75.

67 Ḥazim al-Amīn, *Al-Salafī al-Yatīm: Al-Wajh al-Filasṭīnī li-"l-Jihād al-ʿĀlamī" wa-"l-Qāʿida"* (Beirut and London: Dār al-Sāqī, 2011), esp. 61–85, 133–47; Petter Nesser, "Abū Qatāda and Palestine," *Die Welt des Islams* 53, nos. 3–4 (2013): 416–48; Joas Wagemakers, "In Search of 'Lions and Hawks': Abū Muḥammad al-Maqdisī's Palestinian Identity," *Die Welt des Islams* 53, nos. 3–4 (2013): 388–415.

68 Jean-Charles Brisard (with Damien Martinez), *Zarqawi: The New Face of Al-Qaeda* (New York: Other Press, 2005); Fuʾād Ḥusayn, *Al-Zarqāwī: Al-Jīl al-Thānī li-l-Qāʿida* (Beirut: Dār al-Khayyāl, 2005); Nibras Kazimi, "Zarqawi's Anti-Shiʿa Legacy: Original or Borrowed?" *Current Trends in Islamist Ideology*, vol. IV, ed. Hillel Fradkin, Hussain Haqqani and Eric Brown (Washington, DC: Hudson Institute, 2006), 53–72; Loretta Napoleoni, *Insurgent Iraq: Al Zarqawi and the New Generation* (New York: Seven Stories Press, 2005).

69 James Brandon, "Jordan's Jihad Scholar al-Maqdisi is Freed from Prison," *Terrorism Monitor* 6, no. 7 (2008): 3–6; Romain Caillet, *Le proces d'Abū Muḥammad al-Maqdisī et le delit d'opinion dans un état autoritaire* (http://ifpo.hypotheses.org/2556 (accessed 24 March 2015), 2011); Joas Wagemakers, *A Quietist Jihadi: The Ideology and Influence of Abu Muhammad al-Maqdisi* (Cambridge: Cambridge University Press, 2012), 29–50.

70 Eli Alshech, "The Doctrinal Crisis within the Salafi-Jihadi Ranks and the Emergence of Neo-Takfirism," *Islamic Law and Society* 21, no. 4 (2014): 422–33; Steven Brooke, "The Preacher and the Jihadi," in *Current Trends in Islamist Ideology*, vol. III, ed. Hillel Fradkin, Husain Haqqani and Eric Brown (Washington, DC: Hudson Institute, 2006), 52–66; Nibras Kazimi, "A Virulent Ideology in Mutation: Zarqawi Upstages Maqdisi," in *Current Trends in Islamist Ideology*, vol. II, ed. Hillel Fradkin, Husain Haqqani and Eric Brown (Washington, DC: Hudson Institute, 2005), 59–73.

71 Alshech, "Doctrinal," 433–6; Murad Batal al-Shishani, "The Dangerous Ideas of the Neo-Zarqawist Movement," *CTC Sentinel* 2, no. 9 (2009): 18–20; *id.*, "Jihad Ideologue Abu Muhammad al-Maqdisi Challenges Jordan's Neo-Zarqawists," *Terrorism Monitor* 7, no. 20 (2009): 3–4; *id.*, "The Neo-Zarqawists: Divisions Emerge between Jordan's Salafist Militants," *Terrorism Focus* 5, no. 39 (2008); Joas Wagemakers, "Invoking Zarqawi: Abu Muhammad al-Maqdisi's Jihad Deficit," *CTC Sentinel* 2, no. 6 (2009): 14–7.

72 Dirk Baehr, *Kontinuität und Wandel in der Ideologie des* Jihadi-Salafismus (Bonn: Bouvier Verlag, 2009), 117–36; Orhan Elmaz, "Jihadi-Salafist Creed: Abu Muhammad al-Maqdisi's Imperatives of Faith," in *New Approaches to the Analysis of Jihadism: Online and Offline*, ed. Rüdiger Lohlker (Göttingen: Vienna University Press, 2012), 15–36; Daurius Figueira, *Salafi Jihadi Discourse of Sunni Islam in the 21st Century: The Discourse of*

or is part of a revision of his ideas.[73] Since the conflict in Syria, in which various Islamist groups rebelled against the regime of Syrian President Bashar al-Asad, the role of the Jordanian Jihadi-Salafi community in this civil war has also become the subject of some publications.[74]

The radical trend within Salafism in Jordan has thus been analysed in quite a number of publications. This should probably in part be seen in the context of the increased interest in Salafism from a security perspective, particularly after the terrorist attacks of 11 September 2001 ("9/11"). Given the importance of al-Zarqawi, al-Maqdisi and Abu Qatada al-Filastini to groups such as al-Qaʿida, it is perhaps not surprising that a lot has been written about them, although at least some of these publications were motivated by a clear interest in ideology, not terrorism.[75] In any case, the more widespread, more popular and more peaceful trends within Salafism in Jordan have received nowhere near this amount of attention. Pioneering work has been done on the subject by Wiktorowicz.[76] Yet although his publications should be credited as seminal at a time when much of the world had never even heard of Salafism,

Abu Muhammad al-Maqdisi and Anwar al-Awlaki (Bloomington, IN: iUniverse, Inc., 2011), 1–76; Aḥmad Ḥusnī, "Qirāʾa fī Kitāb *Imtāʿ al-Naẓar fī Kashf Shubhāt Murjiʾat al-ʿAṣr*," *Al-Misbār*, no. 5 (2007): 167–73; International Institute for Counter-Terrorism, *The Jihadi Forums: An Open Forum with Abu Muhammad al-Maqdisi* (www.ict.org.il/Article.aspx?id=155 (accessed 24 March 2015), 2010); Ṭāhir al-Sharqāwī, "Abū Muḥammad al-Maqdisī … Thunāʾiyyat al-Muqaddas wa-l-ʿUnf," *al-Misbār*, no. 5 (2007): 131–43; Joas Wagemakers, "Defining the Enemy: Abū Muḥammad al-Maqdisī's Radical Reading of Sūrat al-Mumtaḥana," *Die Welt des Islams* 48, nos. 3–4 (2008): 348–71; *id.*, "De 'godfather' van de jihad: Abu Mohammed al-Maqdisi," *ZemZem: Tijdschrift over het Midden-Oosten, Noord-Afrika en islam* 3, no. 3 (2007): 79–85; *id.*, "A Purist Jihadi-Salafi: The Ideology of Abu Muhammad al-Maqdisi," *British Journal of Middle Eastern Studies* 36, no. 2 (2009): 281–97; *id.*, *Quietist*, 51–249; *id.*, "The Transformation of a Radical Concept: *Al-Walaʾ wa-l-Baraʾ* in the Ideology of Abu Muhammad al-Maqdisi," in *Global Salafism: Islam's New Religious Movement*, ed. Roel Meijer (London: Hurst & Co., 2009), 81–106.

73 Nelly Lahoud, "In Search of Philosopher-Jihadis: Abu Muhammad al-Maqdisi's Jihadi Philosophy," *Totalitarian Movements and Political Religions* 10, no. 2 (2009): 205–20; Joas Wagemakers, "Abu Muhammad al-Maqdisi: A Counter-Terrorism Asset?" *CTC Sentinel* 1, no. 6 (2008): 7–9; *id.*, "Reclaiming Scholarly Authority: Abu Muhammad al-Maqdisi's Critique of Jihadi Practices," *Studies in Conflict & Terrorism* 34, no. 7 (2011): 523–39.

74 Kirk Sowell, *Jordanian Salafism and the Jihad in Syria* (www.hudson.org/research/11131-jordanian-salafism-and-the-jihad-in-syria (accessed 24 March 2015), 2015); Joas Wagemakers, "Jihadi-Salafism in Jordan and the Syrian Conflict," in *Religious Extremism in Insurgency & Counterinsurgency in Syria: A New Launching Pad for Global Terrorism*, ed. Nico Prucha (London and New York: Routledge, forthcoming).

75 Wagemakers, *Quietist*, vii–viii.

76 Quintan Wiktorowicz, *The Management of Islamic Activism: Salafis, the Muslim Brotherhood, and State Power in Jordan* (Albany, NY: State University of New York Press, 2001), 111–46; *id.*, "The Salafi Movement in Jordan," *International Journal of Middle East Studies* 32, no. 2 (2000): 219–40. See also Quintan Wiktorowicz, "Anatomy of the Salafi Movement," *Studies in Conflict & Terrorism* 29, no. 3 (2006): 207–39; *id.*,

they are sometimes slightly ill-informed – Wiktorowicz refers to al-Albani as "al-Bani",[77] for example, which suggests he does not realise the shaykh's Albanian origins – somewhat shallow according to today's standards and quite dated. This last point is particularly the case as so much has happened to the Salafi community in Jordan since the late 1990s, when Wiktorowicz did his research, as we will see later on.

Since Wiktorowicz's work, only a few publications have appeared dealing (sometimes marginally) with the mainstream, non-radical Salafi movement in Jordan in European languages[78] and specific claims made in some of these will, in fact, be challenged in this book. The only subject within mainstream Salafism in Jordan that has really received substantial attention is the person of Muhammad Nasir al-Din al-Albani. Many hagiographical works have been dedicated to him by Salafis themselves,[79] but academics have also written about him, yet mostly in the context of Saudi Arabia[80] or from the perspective of his study of *ḥadīth*s.[81] By contrast, almost no attention is paid to al-Albani in the Jordanian context.[82] This is somewhat different in Arabic publications

"The Salafi Movement: Violence and Fragmentation of a Community," in *Muslim Networks from Hajj to Hiphop*, ed. Miriam Cooke and Bruce B. Lawrence (Chapel Hill and London: University of North Carolina Press, 2005), 208–34. The latter two studies were partly based on Wiktorowicz's fieldwork in Jordan, although they do not explicitly or extensively deal with Salafism in that country.

77 See, for example, Wiktorowicz, *Management*, 121.

78 Romain Caillet, "Note sur l'espace public salafi en Jordanie," in *Villes, pratiques urbaines et construction nationale en Jordanie*, ed. Myriam Ababsa and Rami Daher (Beirut: Presses de l'ifpo, 2011), 307–27; Bacem Dziri, "'Das Gebet des Propheten, als ob Du es sehen würdest': Der Salafismus als 'Rechtsschule' des Propheten?," in *Salafismus: Auf der Suche nach dem wahren Islam*, ed. Behnam T. Said and Hazim Fouad (Freiburg: Herder, 2014), 150–7; Juan José Escobar Stemmann, "Islamic Activism in Jordan," *Athena Intelligence Journal* 3, no. 3 (2008): 14–8; Daniel Lav, *Radical Islam and the Revival of Medieval Theology* (Cambridge: Cambridge University Press, 2012), 107–19, 122–66; Jacob Olidort, *The Politics of "Quietist" Salafism* (Washington, DC: The Brookings Institution, 2015), 20–2; Wagemakers, "Contesting," 113–18.

79 The number of works on al-Albānī is too numerous to mention. A sample of these works can be found on al-Albānī's website, www.alalbany.net/ (accessed 24 March 2015).

80 Stéphane Lacroix, "L'apport de Muhammad Nasir al-Din al-Albani au salafisme contemporain," in *Qu'est-ce que le salafisme?* ed. Bernard Rougier (Paris: Presses Universitaires de France, 2008), 45–64; *id.*, "Between Revolution and Apoliticism: Nasir al-Din al-Albani and his Impact on the Shaping of Contemporary Salafism," in *Global Salafism: Islam's New Religious Movement*, ed. Roel Meijer (London: Hurst & Co., 2009), 58–80.

81 Kamaruddin Amin, "Nasiruddin al-Albani on Muslim's Sahih: A Critical Study of his Method," *Islamic Law and Society* 11, no. 2 (2004): 149–76; Jonathan Brown, *The Canonization of al-Bukhārī and Muslim: The Formation and Function of the Sunnī Ḥadīth Canon* (Leiden: Brill, 2007), 321–34; Emad Hamdeh, "The Emergence of an Iconoclast: Muḥammad Nāṣir al-Dīn al-Albānī and His Critics" (PhD diss., University of Exeter, 2014).

82 An exception is Olidort, *Politics*, 15–19, who does spend a few pages on al-Albānī's time in Jordan.

on Salafism in Jordan. A booklet published by the Dubai-based Al-Misbar research centre dedicated entirely to al-Albani appeared in 2010,[83] and Abu Rumman and Abu Haniyya have published two non-academic books (partly) dealing with the subject of mainstream, non-radical Salafism in Jordan as a whole.[84] While their books are good sources of information, they are sometimes not very analytical, occasionally quite repetitive and rather unevenly structured. Moreover, they virtually leave out crucial episodes in the development of Salafism, including those in which Abu Haniyya himself was heavily involved.

As has become abundantly clear from the above, mainstream Salafism in Jordan is an under-researched subject and the literature on this topic – including works in Arabic – is not only very limited and often quite short, but also of a mixed quality. Briefly put: no academic book on Salafism in Jordan exists at the moment. This is the case despite the fact that Jordan is a very interesting case study of Salafism: as described above, it has a very wide array of Islamic activists who can employ their activities relatively freely, ranging from uncontroversial groups such as the Jamaʿat al-Tabligh to organisations that are under fire or even prohibited in other Arab countries, such as the Islamic Liberation Party and the Muslim Brotherhood. Moreover, considering the country's strong ties to Western states as well as its geographical position in between some of the biggest conflicts in the region (the Palestinian–Israeli conflict, the 2003 war in Iraq and the war between the Syrian regime and various militias since 2011), Jordan is a theatre where not just domestic but also regional and even international trends play out. This has also strongly affected the country's transnational Salafi movement, as we will see later on. Furthermore, given the fact that Jordan has had a relatively open political culture towards Islamists for years, it is interesting to see how Jordanian Salafis deal with this and how they (and the state) have been affected by the revolts in the Arab world since 2010 (the "Arab Spring"). Finally, the relatively open atmosphere that can be found in Jordan allows us to take a very close look at what factors have contributed to the dynamics within the Salafi community and to see how religious arguments, transnational trends, personal ambitions, state influence and

[83] *Rimāḥ al-Ṣaḥāʾif: Al-Salafiyya al-Albāniyya wa-Khuṣūmuhā* (Dubai: Markaz al-Misbār li-l-Dirāsāt wa-l-Buḥūth, 2010).

[84] Abū Rummān and Abū Haniyya, *Al-Ḥall*, 219–79; *id.*, *Al-Salafiyya al-Muḥāfaẓa: Istrātījiyyat "Aslamat al-Mujtamaʿ" wa-Suʾāl al-ʿAlāqa "al-Muntasiba" maʿa l-Dawla* (Amman: Friedrich Ebert Stiftung, 2010). Abū Rummān recently also published a book on Jordanian Salafī personalities of various types. See Muḥammad Abū Rummān, *Anā Salafī: Baḥth fī l-Huwiyya al-Wāqiʿiyya wa-l-Mutakhayyala ladá l-Salafiyyīn* (Amman: Friedrich Ebert Stiftung, 2014).

regional/international developments have helped shape the movement, rather than focussing on only one or a few of these.

There is thus not just a dearth of publications on Salafism in Jordan, but the latter country is also a hugely interesting case study for this topic in and of itself. This book therefore seeks to address both points by dealing with the non-radical and apolitical sub-trend within Salafism in Jordan – which I refer to as "quietist Salafism", as we will see in Chapter 1 – from its beginnings in the 1950s until the present day. More specifically, I focus on the relationship between these quietist Salafis and the Jordanian state, arguing that a process of "domestication" has taken place, transforming an apolitical and subservient yet independent community into one that is explicitly loyal to the regime. Unlike the reputation of some quietist Salafi scholars as slavish lackeys to their regimes suggests, however, I argue that this domestication process of Salafism in Jordan has actually been a much more nuanced and complex development that cannot be ascribed to a single factor.

Methodology, Sources and Overview

As briefly alluded to earlier, the main question this book focusses on is threefold: (1) what is (quietist) Salafism in Jordan; (2) how did its relationship with the state change into one of loyalty; and (3) why did this domestication take place? Because of my background in Islamic studies as well as my personal interest, this book will focus more on Salafis' text-based ideology – broadly defined here as a more or less coherent set of ideas – than on their daily practices in Jordan, although the latter are definitely also dealt with. A focus on the textual side of Salafism is, in a sense, also inherent to the subject, however, since Salafis – more than any other trend within Islam – concentrate on what they see as the emulation of the first three generations of Muslims. Salafis claim to know and understand the reality of these "pious predecessors" through texts and texts alone. Therefore, academics studying Salafism, "like the Salafi, simply cannot afford to ignore the precise details of the textual tradition", as Gauvain states.[85] Salafis' study of the Qurʾan and the *ḥadīth*s enables them, in their view, to recreate exactly what the *salaf* once did and to describe it in such a detailed way "as if you see it", as part of the subtitle of a Salafi book puts it.[86]

[85] Gauvain, *Salafi*, 23–4.

[86] Muḥammad Nāṣir al-Dīn al-Albānī, *Ṣifat Ṣalāt al-Nabī – Ṣallá llāh ʿalayhi wa-l-Sallam – min al-Takbīr ilá l-Taslīm ka-annaka Tarāhā* (Beirut and Damascus: Al-Maktab al-Islāmī, 1987).

Methodology

Despite the importance of texts and the ideological theory found therein, this book certainly has relevance for the fields of political and social science too, particularly with regard to the study of Islamism. One framework used by academics who work in these disciplines and focus on Islamist groups is Social Movement Theory (SMT).[87] Concentrating on actors' ability to mobilise their resources, survive and thrive amidst differing political opportunities and constraints and frame their contentious message to appeal to potential followers, scholars using SMT for the analysis of Islamists often deal with ideology and ideas as mere instruments or resources to mobilise people, rather than sources of inspiration that are important in and of themselves.[88] Another question dealt with by political scientists is whether "moderate" Islamist organisations serve as a means to express contention legally and thereby act as a "firewall" against radicalisation or, on the contrary, serve as a "conveyor belt" towards radicalisation.[89] A third theoretical framework sometimes used in the study of Islamists is the inclusion-moderation thesis, which holds that including actors in the political system of a country causes them to moderate their ideology. Although inclusion does indeed appear to have led to moderation of Islamists in some cases,[90] Schwedler has shown that this thesis does not always hold up[91] and Hamid even argues that it is sometimes suppression, not inclusion, which leads Islamists to moderate their views.[92]

[87] Books on SMT include Donatella Della Porta and Mario Diani, *Social Movements: An Introduction* (Malden, MA: Blackwell Publishing, 2006 [1999]); Doug McAdam, *Political Process and the Development of Black Insurgency, 1930–1970* (Chicago: University of Chicago Press, 1999 [1982]); Sidney Tarrow, *Power in Movement: Social Movements, Collective Action and Politics* (Cambridge: Cambridge University Press, 2011 [1994]).

[88] See Mohammed M. Hafez, *Why Muslims Rebel: Repression and Resistance in the Islamic World* (Boulder, CO: Lynne Rienner, 2003), 19–20. See also Ann Swidler, "Culture in Action: Symbols and Strategies," *American Sociological Review* 51 (1986): 273–86, in which the author famously describes "culture" (in a very broad sense) as a "'tool kit' of symbols, stories, rituals, and world-views" that people use to solve problems and call others to action. The best-known work on SMT applied to Islamism is probably Quintan Wiktorowicz, ed., *Islamic Activism: A Social Movement Theory Approach* (Bloomington and Indianapolis, IN: Indiana University Press, 2005).

[89] See, for example, Marc Lynch, "Islam Divided Between *Salafi-jihad* and the *Ikhwan*," *Studies in Conflict & Terrorism* 33, no. 6 (2010): 467–87, especially 480–2.

[90] Dalacoura makes this case, for example, with regard to the Muslim Brotherhood in Jordan. See Katerina Dalacoura, *Islamist Terrorism and Democracy in the Middle East* (Cambridge: Cambridge University Press, 2011), 127–30.

[91] Schwedler, *Faith.*

[92] Shadi Hamid, *Temptations of Power: Islamists and Illiberal Democracy in a New Middle East* (Oxford: Oxford University Press, 2014).

While this book does not tackle these theories head on, it does touch upon and contribute to them from the perspective of Islamic studies by delving into Salafi ideology as a relevant source of inspiration in and of itself, not just as an instrument used to mobilise others. This is not to suggest that ideology is never used for this purpose; on the contrary, it clearly is. Yet I also hold that believers – including Salafis in Jordan – view their ideology as important simply because they see it as the truth. Although Salafi ideas are shaped and developed in the context their adherents live in, I do believe these views as such should be taken seriously, even if only because Salafis themselves do this too. This book also shows that at least some Salafis in Jordan view themselves as a bulwark or "firewall" against radicalisation and as best suited to help prevent ideological "extremism", although the challenges to their discourse from radical Salafis as well as from their own midst show that the situation is more nuanced than it seems. Indeed, a shared set of basic ideas may mean that, at least for some, quietist Salafism is a "conveyor belt" towards a more radical form of Salafism, although this appears to be exceptional. Finally, this book contributes to the debate on the inclusion-moderation thesis by showing that it was not simply state pressure or, conversely, the lack thereof that caused the leadership of quietist Salafis in Jordan to become more domesticated (or more "moderate"), but that this was a much more complex process in which Salafis' own agency should certainly not be discounted. As such, my focus on ideology and texts is not just based on my academic background and personal interest, but also on my ability to use this approach to contribute to debates in the political and social sciences from a perspective that is often ignored by scholars working in those fields.

In trying to find out what texts were decisive in my study on quietist Salafism in Jordan, I combined historical and empirical methodologies by not only building on previous research (including my own on Jihadi-Salafism and al-Maqdisi) but starting out with fieldwork during which I talked to or interviewed virtually all of the major (and many of the minor) players involved in Salafism in Jordan today. Based on their advice and my own efforts to collect books, articles and fatwas on (especially) Salafis' relations with the Jordanian state and related topics, I gradually got to know the relevant texts about the subject. After reading and analysing these, I was frequently left with questions that I tried to get answered during subsequent fieldwork trips, about which I would often receive, photocopy and buy new books, which – in turn – would yield new questions. I repeated this process until I felt I had a firm command of the subject.

At the same time, my research methods also showed me some clear limits to what I could do. Most importantly, and besides obvious limitations in time and money, I was not able to interview female Salafis because of the general Salafi prohibition of contact between unrelated men and women. Although I did have a chance to speak briefly with some Salafi women in Jordan, these meetings were far too short and insignificant to attach any value to in terms of research. To a certain extent, this does not matter too much since the leadership, the ideological production and the organisation of Salafism in Jordan is extremely male-dominated. At the same time, however, women probably constitute about half of Salafis in Jordan and also have important roles as wives, mothers and preachers for other women and, as such, form a very significant part of the phenomenon of Salafism in Jordan today. The role of women and their rights within Salafism are therefore certainly dealt with in this book, but virtually only from the perspective of their male counterparts, simply because that was the best I could do as a man. It therefore goes without saying that the study of Salafi women in Jordan is still uncharted territory and thus wide open for a female researcher to engage in.

Sources

The sources of this book, apart from a thorough reading of the secondary literature on Salafism in general and in Jordan in particular, firstly consist of the primary ideological and historical writings of Jordanian Salafis themselves. These were bought at bookshops in Amman, but also elsewhere in Jordan, given to me by the authors (or their followers), photocopied or downloaded from the internet. They include books, newspaper articles (partly collected at the newspaper archive in the main library of the University of Jordan in Amman), fatwas, YouTube clips and audio tapes. I also made extensive use of two Jordanian Salafi magazines, *Al-Asala* and *Al-Qibla*, as far as they were available to me.[93] Most of these sources are not available outside Jordan and have never been used before in academic publications, certainly not systematically.

A second source of my research consists of the interviews I held in Jordan. Building on my fieldwork in that country in 2008 and 2009,

[93] The issues of *Al-Aṣāla* (no longer published) that were available to me were nos. 1–31 and 35–54, which corresponds with the period of 15 Rabīʿ al-Thānī 1413 (13 October 1992) to 15 Muḥarram 1422 (9 January 2001) and 15 Shaʿbān 1422 (15 November 2001) to 15 Dhū l-Ḥijja 1427 (5 January 2007). Apparently, parallel issues of *Al-Aṣāla* were published around the year 2000 with similar dates or they were simply incorrectly dated. With regard to *Al-Qibla*, I have been able to obtain issues no. 2 (Spring 2002) to 4/5 (2003), nos. 10/11 (November 2005), nos. 16 (January 2008) to 18 (January 2009) and nos. 20 (April 2010) to 24 (June 2013).

I went on five additional month-long research visits throughout the period 2012–2014. All in all, this amounted to six months of fieldwork, during which I conducted 70 semi-structured interviews (some on condition of anonymity) with academics, journalists and – overwhelmingly – Salafis (from young adults to elderly men, of varying levels of education, with various occupations) from all over the country and had informal conversations with many more. Some refused to be interviewed because I am not a Muslim, because of suspicions about my motives or because my research topic reminded them of a life they once lived but had long left behind. Generally speaking, however, I was welcomed by almost everyone I contacted.

A third source used for the research on this book consists of the Salafi lessons I attended during my fieldwork at the Haj Hasan Mosque and the Khalayila Mosque in Amman, the Al-Rahma Mosque in Marj al-Hammam, the Imam al-Albani Centre in Amman and the al-Jasir Mosque in Irbid. The lessons were taught by both major quietist Salafi scholars in Jordan, as well as by slightly younger, upcoming shaykhs from the kingdom, all focussing mostly on doctrine and gaining knowledge. Before, after and in between these lessons, which amounted to between 55 and 60 hours in total, I also had the opportunity to speak with many young Salafi students from all over the country.

Overview

This book is divided into three parts: ideology, history and contestation. Part I, on idealogy, is divided into two chapters. Chapter 1 focusses on the ideological origins of and divisions and diversity within Salafism, the general concepts and ideas that dominate the Salafi worldview and how Salafis apply these in practice. It is based mostly on secondary sources and constitutes a framework on which the rest of the book builds. Chapter 2 concentrates on the ideological contribution that Jordanian quietist Salafis have made throughout the years by showing how they interpret and apply the more general concepts introduced in Chapter 1, how they deal with the contentious issue of faith (*īmān*) and how they frame their views on politics in general and in Jordan in particular. This chapter shows that quietist Salafis have long had a deeply apolitical ideology.

Part II of the book focusses on the history of Salafism in Jordan and is divided into three chapters. The first of these – Chapter 3 – deals with the historical origins of Salafism in Jordan and shows how al-Albani came to dominate the trend in the 1980s and 1990s. It also shows that events in Saudi Arabia and Kuwait in the early 1990s hardened and entrenched the already apolitical attitude of quietist Salafis in Jordan. Chapter 4 deals with the various conflicts that erupted or became apparent after the death of al-Albani in 1999 and profoundly affected the Salafi community in Jordan we know today. It shows that the loss of such a major scholar, who had acted as a bulwark of independence from the regime, opened the door towards more loyalty to the state. Chapter 5 deals with how the Jordanian state and quietist Salafi scholars have tacitly cooperated since 2001, how quietist Salafi scholars maintain their religious authority, particularly in light of the conflicts after al-Albani's death, and what it means to live as a Salafi in Jordan today.

Part III of this book, which is divided into two chapters, deals with the contestation of Salafism in its quietist form by other Salafis in Jordan. Chapter 6 deals with the rise of Jihadi-Salafism in Jordan in the 1990s, how this sub-trend has challenged quietists since then and how the latter have tried to counter this contestation with ideological arguments of their own. Chapter 7, finally, deals with the rise of a more politicised form of Salafism in Jordan, particularly after the so-called Arab Spring, and how the state and quietist Salafis have dealt with that. This chapter shows that quietist Salafis, because of all the preceding factors furthering their loyalty to the state, could be counted upon by the regime to denounce the rise of Islamism and revolution in the Arab world after 2010 in ways that suited the state's own agenda. This, as the conclusion to this book notes, completed a process of complex, long-term and multi-faceted domestication of the quietist Salafi community in Jordan.

Part I

Ideology

1 Global Salafi Ideology

Salafism has a bad reputation. I cannot count the number of times that I was told by Salafis in Jordan that "the West" has a wrong and very generalised view of Salafism. Although the irony of that statement, being rather generalising itself, was often lost on them, it does make some sense. The trend as a whole is often associated with violence and terrorism, particularly in popular discourse, even though most Salafis never engage in either of these.[1] Such stereotypes are not limited to Western countries, however. Pall, for instance, recalls how a Lebanese person, who was probably used to associating Salafism with violence and militancy as well, once referred to some Salafi youngsters as "very good guys" but was shocked to hear them described as "Salafis", as if these two do not go together.[2]

However, a less drastic "accusation" against Salafis in general – that they are very strict and have views about, for example, non-Muslims that are at odds with what most people adhere to – hits closer to home. The general ideology espoused by Salafis is one that is quite different from what even most Sunni Muslims believe in, although this is not always apparent. This chapter delves into the ideology of global Salafism in three parts: firstly, I deal with the definition, origins and spread of Salafism; secondly, I describe and analyse the most important concepts in modern-day Salafi ideology that will be used throughout this book; and thirdly, the divisions within Salafism with regard to applying this ideology in practice are described. This chapter, as such, not only forms a general yet comprehensive treatment of global Salafi ideology in and of itself, but also acts as the basis on which the next chapter, which looks specifically at Jordanian ideological contributions, builds.

[1] Christian Caryl, "The Salafi Moment," in *The New Salafi Politics* (Washington, DC: Project on Middle East Political Science, 2012), 8–10.
[2] Pall, *Salafism*, 18.

The Definition, Origins and Spread of Salafism

In their article on the Ghost Dance movement in the United States, the Rastafari movement of Jamaica and the Maya movement of Guatemala, Price, Nonini and Fox Tree refer to these trends as "grounded utopian movements". By this term, they mean "thoroughly modern movements" that may "have emerged, persisted, disappeared, and re-emerged across decades, even centuries" and that make "use of cultural resources such as religious beliefs, the creation of new cultural formations and meanings, and the manifestation of culturally-embedded movement practices." Such movements are "utopian" because "they point to a[n] 'ideal place' (utopia) [...] and[,] by implication, to a better time and more satisfying social relationships and identifications". Rather than concentrating on "instrumental action with respect to states and capitalism", they focus on "group integrity and identity". These movements are also "grounded" in the sense that their "identities, values, and imaginative dimensions of utopia are culturally focussed on real places, embodied by living people, informed by past lifeways, and constructed and maintained through quotidian interactions and valued practices that connect the members of a community".[3] Salafism, as has been pointed out elsewhere,[4] can also be seen as such a grounded utopian movement, focussing on the "ideal place" or "utopia" of the first generations of Islam, while simultaneously being grounded in the very real places Salafis live in and the actual people they meet.

The Definition of Salafism

It is precisely the focus on the utopia of *al-salaf al-ṣāliḥ* that leads me to refer to Salafis – i.e., those who claim to follow the *salaf* as closely and in as many spheres of life as possible – as such. According to several *ḥadīth*s ascribed to the Prophet Muhammad, "the best of my (i.e., Muhammad's) community" (*khayr ummatī*) or "the best people" (*khayr al-nās*) are "my generation (*qarnī*) and then the ones who follow them (*thumma lladhīna yalūnahum*) and then the ones who follow them (*thumma lladhīna yalūnahum*)".[5] This suggests that the first three

[3] Charles Price, Donald Nonini and Erich Fox Tree, "Grounded Utopian Movements: Subjects of Neglect," *Anthropological Quarterly* 81, no. 1 (2008): 128–9.

[4] Martijn de Koning, "'Moge Hij onze ogen openen': De radicale utopie van het 'salafisme'," *Tijdschrift voor Religie, Recht en Beleid* 2, no. 2 (2011): 49–51; De Koning, Wagemakers and Becker, *Salafisme*, esp. 20–1.

[5] These traditions exist in slightly different forms. See *Ṣaḥīḥ al-Bukhārī*, book 57 ("Kitāb Faḍā'il Aṣḥāb al-Nabī"), chapter 1 ("Faḍā'il Aṣḥāb al-Nabī"), nos. 2–3; *Ṣaḥīḥ Muslim*, book 44 ("Kitāb Faḍā'il al-Ṣaḥāba"), chapter 52 ("Faḍl al-Ṣaḥāba, thumma lladhīna Yalūnahum, thumma lladhīna Yalūnahum"), nos. 2533–6.

generations of Islam are the best that ever lived, and it is also these three that are usually equated with *al-salaf al-ṣāliḥ*.

As straightforward as this may seem, the *ḥadīth*s mentioned above are actually rather unclear. Even if we assume that these traditions are reliable sources of what really happened,[6] it is not entirely obvious what "my generation" means. As has been pointed out by several scholars, it is unclear whether this refers to an actual generation (and exactly how many years that would entail) or to a century of Muslims. The latter explanation would, for example, allow certain scholars revered by Salafis, such as Ahmad b. Hanbal (780–855), to be included among the *salaf*.[7] Despite this lack of clarity, Salafis manage to distil a fairly homogeneous body of doctrines from this utopian period that they try to emulate, although not one that they can all agree on, as we will see later.

In naming and labelling a group of people, it is not uncommon to look at what the object of study calls itself. However, in the case of Salafis, that is slightly problematic. Some Salafis refer to themselves simply as "Muslims", "the people of the Prophetic practice and the community" (*ahl al-Sunna wa-l-jamāʿa*)[8] or "followers of *al-salaf al-ṣāliḥ*". The first is analytically impractical since "Muslims" suggests far too wide a group. The second label is somewhat subjective and more or less a synonym for "Sunni Muslims", which is more narrow than "Muslims" but still too broad to be useful. The third label, finally, may mean the same as "Salafis", making it slightly redundant, or may loosely refer to a more

[6] For more on the academic debate on the authenticity of the sources of Muḥammad's life, see Andreas Görke, "Prospects and Limits in the Study of the Historical Muḥammad," in *The Transmission and Dynamics of the Textual Sources of Islam: Essays in Honour of Harald Motzki*, ed. Nicolet Boekhoff-van der Voort, Kees Versteegh and Joas Wagemakers (Leiden: Brill, 2011), 137–51. One could argue that academic questions about the sources' authenticity do not really matter in this respect since the important thing here is whether Muslims believe them to be authentic. This is correct, yet Muslims themselves, not least the *ḥadīth*-scholar al-Albānī, are sceptical of the authenticity of some traditions of Muḥammad's life as well, though not these particular ones. For more on al-Albānī's methods in this respect, see Amin, "Nasiruddin."

[7] Bernard Haykel, "On the Nature of Salafi Thought and Action," in *Global Salafism: Islam's New Religious Movement*, ed. Roel Meijer (London: Hurst & Co., 2009), 38–9; Christina Hellmich, "Creating the Ideology of Al Qaeda: From Hypocrites to Salafi-Jihadists," *Studies in Conflict & Terrorism* 31 (2008): 117; Justyna Nedza, "'Salafismus': Überlegungen zur Schärfung einer Analysekategorie," in *Salafismus: Auf der Suche nach dem wahren Islam*, ed. Behnam T. Said and Hazim Fouad (Freiburg: Herder, 2014), 96–100.

[8] For more on the origins of the term *ahl al-Sunna wa-l-jamāʿa* from a Salafi perspective, see Muḥammad ʿAbd al-Hādī al-Miṣrī, *Maʿālim Manhaj Ahl al-Sunna wa-l-Jamāʿa* (Amman: Jamʿiyyat al-Kitāb wa-l-Sunna – Lajnat al-Kalima al-Ṭayyiba, 2011), 69–74. Interestingly, this author is typical of many Salafis in the sense that he claims the term *ahl al-Sunna wa-l-jamāʿa* for Salafis by describing its beliefs and characteristics as those of Salafism, as if "ordinary" Sunni Muslims do not really fit into this category. See *ibid.*, 49–130.

general way of following the *salaf* that is not limited to the Salafis discussed in this book but can also be found among other Sunni Muslims. In principle, the terms "Salafi" and "Salafism" used in this study are therefore labels that *I* use to denote the people dealt with in this book, based on their common characteristic of claiming to emulate the utopia of the *salaf* very closely and as much as possible, rather than a term derived from what Salafis call themselves. In practice, however, major Salafi scholars also refer to themselves as such, and labelling oneself a "Salafi" is a common practice among Jordanians whom I too describe as Salafis, meaning that their own label and mine converge.[9]

The Origins of Salafism

The trend we call "Salafism" today – the defining feature of which is the strict emulation of the utopia of the "pious predecessors" in every sphere of life – is often described by its adherents as nothing more than simply Islam in its pure and unadulterated form. The Salafi movement analysed in this book is, however, of far more recent origin and has its roots in the twentieth century. Still, a general desire to emulate the *salaf* in some way – though less detailed, less broadly applied and less focussed upon than by modern-day Salafis – is much older and goes back into history almost as far as Islam itself, to the eighth century. Until that period (but after Muhammad's death in 632), Muslims had mostly relied on the Qurʾan, the different *sunan* (practices; pl. of Sunna) of an authoritative group of early believers, the latter's considered opinion (*raʾy*) and scholarly consensus (*ijmāʿ*) when they wanted to have answers to their questions on religion. On the basis of these sources, the early schools of Islamic law (*madhāhib*, sing. *madhhab*) developed. In opposition, however, to this "lived tradition", as espoused by the *ahl al-raʾy* (the people of considered opinion), a different trend developed. Followers of the latter – known as the *ahl al-ḥadīth* (the people of the Prophetic tradition or traditionists) – claimed that the increasing number of *ḥadīth* texts that were found and ascribed to Muhammad as his authentic sayings were of greater value than the "lived tradition" of the *ahl al-raʾy* and should therefore be focussed on instead.[10]

[9] This is perhaps a result of al-Albānī's statement that Salafis should always refer to themselves as such as shorthand for "Muslims following the Book and the Sunna according to the method of the pious predecessors". See www.youtube.com/watch?v=8uyWHf5FJ_M (accessed 25 March 2015). See also the statement on this issue by major Salafi shaykh Muḥammad b. Ṣāliḥ al-ʿUthaymīn, who arrives at the same conclusion as al-Albānī, at www.youtube.com/watch?v=Fe_8UmoELZk (accessed 25 March 2015).

[10] N.J. Coulson, *A History of Islamic Law* (Edinburgh: Edinburgh University Press, 1999 [1964]), 39–52; Joseph Schacht, *An Introduction to Islamic Law* (Oxford: Oxford University Press, 1982 [1964]), 29–34.

Although the *ahl al-ḥadīth* faced stiff opposition from the *ahl al-ra'y* in the eighth and early ninth centuries, it was clear that the growing body of texts about Muhammad was a religious source that could not be ignored. The *ahl al-ḥadīth* argued that their reliance on Prophetic *ḥadīth*s was more consistent and more authentic than the *ahl al-ra'y*'s "lived tradition" because the former was based on concrete texts that could directly be ascribed to the Prophet himself. Why, after all, rely on people's considered opinion when one can – through the use of *ḥadīth*s – supposedly have direct access to the views of the Prophet himself? Thus, it was not surprising that, while the *ahl al-ḥadīth*'s position did not become mainstream, the focus on the Prophetic traditions that they argued for was incorporated into Islamic law as one of the major sources of the *sharī'a* by Muhammad b. Idris al-Shafi'i (767–820). This middle ground, as it were, between the two approaches of the *ahl al-ḥadīth* and the *ahl al-ra'y* went on to form the legal basis of what became known as Sunni Islam from the ninth century onwards and was generally adopted by most Muslims.[11]

The general desire to base one's beliefs and practices directly on the Qur'an and the prophetic Sunna – as early traditionists such as Ibn Hanbal advocated and as Salafis also want today – thus goes back to the formative period of Islamic legal schools. This is not to suggest that twenty-first-century Salafis are modern-day equivalents of the *ahl al-ḥadīth* – although at least some Salafis seem to view themselves that way[12] – but simply that they share a core tenet in their approach to Islamic tradition.[13] Importantly, this is also the key legal difference between Salafis and "ordinary" Sunni Muslims, who also view the first generations of Islam as the purest form of the religion.[14] The latter see the Prophet and his companions as exemplary and as people whose model should be followed by adhering to a school of Islamic law, which in itself takes into account things like the interests of the Muslim community and considered scholarly opinions. Salafis, by contrast, try to interpret and apply the sources of Islam through the prism of

[11] Coulson, *History*, 52–61; Hallaq, *Sharī'a*, 55–9; Schacht, *Introduction*, 35–48.

[12] See, for example, Aḥmad b. Muḥammad al-Dahlawī al-Madanī, *Tārīkh Ahl al-Ḥadīth: Ta'yīn al-Firqa al-Nājiya wa-annahā Ṭā'ifat Ahl al-Ḥadīth* (Medina: Maktabat al-Ghurabā' al-Athariyya, 1417 AH [1996/1997]), in which the author applies terms such as "the saved sect" (*al-firqa al-nājiya*), which is often used for Salafis, to the *ahl al-ḥadīth*. Interestingly, the *ḥadīth*s used in the book were verified and commented upon by 'Alī al-Ḥalabī, probably the most prominent Jordanian quietist Salafi scholar today.

[13] See also Adis Duderija, "Neo-Traditional Salafi Qur'an-Sunna Hermeneutics and Its Interpretational Implications," *Religion Compass* 5, no. 7 (2011): 314–25.

[14] Haykel, "Nature," 34.

the first Muslim generations only, mostly without recourse to schools of law or extra-textual sources.[15]

Although those advocating a "Salafi" approach to the sources – i.e., bypassing the *madhāhib* and taking the Qur'an and the Sunna of the *salaf* as their only guide – have always been a minority, this trend did not die with Ibn Hanbal. It was picked up again by the Syrian Hanbali scholars Ibn Taymiyya (1263–1328) and his student Ibn Qayyim al-Jawziyya (1292–1350), who argued that blind emulation (*taqlīd*) of any school of law should be discarded. The alternative was direct and independent interpretation of the Qur'an and the Sunna (*ijtihād*)[16] for scholars and – according to some – simply "following" (*ittibā'*) these sources for "ordinary" believers.[17] A similar desire was expressed by Yemeni scholars such as Muhammad b. Ibrahim b. al-Wazir (d. 1436) and Muhammad b. Isma'il al-San'ani (1688–1768), who both rejected *taqlīd* when there were authentic *ḥadīth*s contradicting received Islamic legal opinions.[18] These and others, in turn, were a great influence on the nineteenth-century Yemeni scholar Muhammad b. 'Ali al-Shawkani (d. 1834), who shared his predecessors' dismissal of *taqlīd* and advocated finding direct evidence in the original texts.[19]

The tendency to rely only on the Qur'an and the Sunna, at the expense of extra-textual sources or the blind following of a *madhhab*, could also be found outside the Arab world. On the Indian subcontinent, the

[15] Jonathan A.C. Brown, "Is Islam Easy to Understand or Not? Salafis, the Democratization of Interpretation and the Need for the Ulema," *Journal of Islamic Studies* 26, no. 2 (2015): 117–44. This difference is perfectly summed up in the title of a book written by a staunch Syrian Sunni critic of Salafism, Muḥammad Sa'īd Ramaḍān al-Būṭī: "Salafism is a blessed temporal period, not an Islamic legal school." See Muḥammad Sa'īd Ramaḍān al-Būṭī, *Al-Salafiyya Marḥala Zamaniyya Mubāraka Lā Madhhab Islāmī* (Beirut/Damascus: Dār al-Fikr al-Mu'āṣir/Dār al-Fikr, 2010 [1988]).

[16] The exact history of *ijtihād* and when this tool ceased to be employed by scholars – if at all – is somewhat controversial. For more on this, see Mohammed Fadel, "The Social Logic of *Taqlīd* and the Rise of the *Mukhtaṣar*," *Islamic Law and Society* 3, no. 2 (1996): 193–233; Wael B. Hallaq, "On the Origins of the Controversy about the Existence of *Mujtahid*s and the Gate of *Ijtihād*," *Studia Islamica* 63 (1986): 129–41; *id.*, "Was the Gate of Ijtihad Closed?" *International Journal of Middle East Studies* 16, no. 1 (1984): 3–41; Haykel, *Revival*, 76–108; Sherman Jackson, "*Taqlīd*, Legal Scaffolding and the Scope of Legal Injunctions in Post-Formative Theory," *Islamic Law and Society* 3, no. 2 (1996): 165–92; Rudolph Peters, "Idjtihād and Taqlīd in 18th and 19th Century Islam," *Die Welt des Islams* 20, nos. 3–4 (1980): 131–45; Muhammad Qasim Zaman, *The Ulama in Contemporary Islam: Custodians of Change* (Princeton and Oxford: Princeton University Press, 2002), 17–19.

[17] Haykel, "Nature," 43–4. The difference between *taqlīd* (blind emulation of a *madhhab*) and *ittibā'* (following a Qur'ānic verse or *ḥadīth* itself directly) is further explained in al-Madanī, *Tārīkh*, 116–17.

[18] Brown, *Canonization*, 314–18.

[19] *Ibid.*, 315; Haykel, *Revival*, 10. For more on al-Shawkānī's specific position on *taqlīd* and *ijtihād*, see Haykel, *Revival*, 89–108.

eighteenth-century scholar Shah Wali Allah (1703–1762) thought along similar lines. Although he was very concerned with communal cohesion and therefore quite tolerant of popular religious practices that modern-day Salafis would frown upon, Shah Wali Allah believed that excessive recourse to *madhāhib* had led Muslims away from Islam's original message and that this should therefore be discarded. At the same time, however, he did recognise the value of the schools of law *as such* for their role in bringing order to a Muslim community (*umma*) under fire in his home country.[20] The teachings of Shah Wali Allah and others inspired the *ahl-e ḥadīth* movement on the Indian subcontinent in the nineteenth century,[21] which – like the original *ahl al-ḥadīth* movement discussed earlier – advocated a supposedly purer and more authentic form of Islam through direct recourse to the Qurʾan and Sunna by scholars. The *ahl-e ḥadīth* movement has, in fact, been active in India and Pakistan till this very day.[22]

Also active until today and related to the *ahl-e ḥadīth* movement in India is the so-called Wahhabi movement, named after the eighteenth-century reformer Muhammad b. ʿAbd al-Wahhab (1703–1792). Hailing from the central Arabian region of Najd, Ibn ʿAbd al-Wahhab tried to "cleanse" Islam as he saw it from the popular and syncretistic religious rituals and customs it had acquired throughout time, using the utopia of the *salaf* as his guide. In doing so, he explicitly built on the work of earlier scholars such as Ibn Taymiyya and tried to revert directly to the Qurʾan and the Sunna.[23] Although he initially encountered hostility against his views among his own people and even his own family,[24] he eventually allied himself with the tribal leader Muhammad b. Saʿud (d. 1765) and together they conquered large parts of the Arabian Peninsula. This way, Wahhabism became the dominant Islamic trend in Saudi

[20] Brown, *Canonization*, 318–21.

[21] For more on the origins of this movement, see Barbara Daly Metcalf, *Islamic Revival in British India: Deoband, 1860–1900* (Oxford: Oxford University Press, 2002 [1982]), esp. 268–96.

[22] Abou Zahab, "Salafism," 126–42.

[23] Interestingly, a student of mine once told me he had read one of Ibn ʿAbd al-Wahhāb's books, the famous *Kitāb al-Tawḥīd*, and noticed that there was "really nothing new in the book, just Qurʾān and Sunna". Although a lack of originality is not something authors generally like being accused of, I told my student that Ibn ʿAbd al-Wahhāb would most probably have been proud to hear that.

[24] Hamadi Redissi, "The Refutation of Wahhabism in Arabic Sources," in *Kingdom without Borders: Saudi Arabia's Political, Religious and Media Frontiers*, ed. Madawi Al-Rasheed (London: Hurst & Co., 2008), 157–81; Samer Traboulsi, "An Early Refutation of Muḥammad ibn ʿAbd al-Wahhāb's Reformist Views," *Die Welt des Islams* 42, no. 3 (2002): 373–415.

Arabia and it has remained this way ever since.[25] The ideological kinship between Wahhabism and the *ahl-e ḥadīth* movement was clear from, among other things,[26] the fact that several Arabian scholars went to study in India, including the prominent shaykh Saʿd b. ʿAtiq (1862/3–1930), who studied there for nine years at the behest of his father, Hamd b. ʿAtiq (d. 1883).[27]

The interest in generally wanting to revert to the Qurʾan and the Sunna is the key element that all groups and scholars mentioned in this section had in common, which they share with modern-day Salafis. This does not mean, however, that all of them were Salafis themselves, nor that they were all exactly alike. Wahhabi scholars, for example, were more likely to follow the Hanbali school of Islamic law, rather than discard this practice in favour of *ijtihād*, and focussed mostly on cleansing the creed (*ʿaqīda*) of Islam. Some other reformers dealt with above were much more negative about *taqlīd* and concentrated on the study of Islamic law (*fiqh*), rather than on creedal issues.[28] It is also worth noting that the equation that is often made between Wahhabism on the one hand and Salafism on the other is not entirely accurate. Given its strong ideological similarities with Salafism, Wahhabism – a term rejected by adherents to this trend – can certainly be seen as Salafi, but the opposite is not always true. Apart from the difference in approach towards *ijtihād* and *taqlīd*, Salafism represents the international trend whose adherents claim to emulate the *salaf* as strictly and in as many spheres of life as possible, while Wahhabism is its Najdi version, being (at least initially) more local than Salafism and also perhaps somewhat less tolerant.[29]

[25] Studies describing the rise of early Wahhabism in Saudi Arabia in greater detail include Commins, *Wahhabi*, 10–30; Madawi Al-Rasheed, *A History of Saudi Arabia* (Cambridge: Cambridge University Press, 2002), 15–23; George S. Rentz, *The Birth of the Islamic Reform Movement in Saudi Arabia: Muḥammad b. ʿAbd al-Wahhāb (1703/4–1792) and the Beginnings of Unitarian Empire in Arabia* (London: Arabian Publishing Ltd., 2004); Alexei Vassiliev, *The History of Saudi Arabia* (London: Saqi Books, 2000 [1998]), 64–139.

[26] A very accessible – though somewhat spectacularly titled – work on the relations between Wahhābī scholars and the like-minded shaykhs in India is Charles Allen, *God's Terrorists: The Wahhabi Cult and the Hidden Roots of Modern Jihad* (Cambridge, MA: Da Capo Press, 2006).

[27] Dziri, "Gebet," 145–8; Lacroix, "Between," 62; Steinberg, *Religion*, 249.

[28] Dziri, "Gebet," 141–4; Haykel, "Nature," 42–3; Lacroix, "L'apport," 46–7; *id.*, "Between," 61–2, 65–6. This is not to say that Saudi scholars never make use of *ijtihād*, however, as several scholars have pointed out. See Gauvain, *Salafi*, 140, 162; Qasim Zaman, *Ulama*, 152.

[29] Allen, *God's*, 50; Hala Fattah, "'Wahhabi' Influences, Salafi Responses: Shaikh Mahmud Shukri and the Iraqi Salafi Movement, 1745–1930," *Journal of Islamic Studies* 14, no. 2 (2003): 145–6; Haykel, *Revival*, 14, 127–30.

Another point of confusion about Salafism can be found in the trend of, as Haykel puts it, "enlightened Salafism" (*al-Salafiyya al-tanwīriyya*).[30] This term is often associated with modernist reformers such as Jamal al-Din al-Afghani (1838/9–1897) and Muhammad ʿAbduh (1849–1905),[31] but – as Lauzière has shown – this is likely more because of a mix-up in labels than because of the actual beliefs of these two men. Moreover, it is unlikely that either of these two men claimed to be Salafis or saw themselves as part of a Salafi trend.[32] This does not mean that "enlightened" or "modernist" Salafis did not exist, however. Several nineteenth- and twentieth-century thinkers and scholars in Iraq[33] and particularly Syria,[34] such as Mahmud Shukri al-Alusi (1856–1924) and Jamal al-Din al-Qasimi (1866–1914), could also be labelled "Salafi" in the sense that they, too, fully geared their beliefs towards returning to the *salaf*. They did so, however, with partly different objectives. While the Salafis dealt with in this book reach back to the utopia of the *salaf* in order to "purify" Islam and try do so on the basis of the Qurʾan and Sunna alone, "enlightened" Salafis were mostly concerned with modernising the religion and, among other methods, applied rationalism to achieve this. They wanted to remove "backward" elements such as *taqlīd* from Islam in order to rebuild the religion from the bottom up, as it were, and to make it compatible with the challenges of the modern age.[35] It is this latter aspect, about which the Salafis dealt with in this book –

30 Haykel, "Nature," 45.

31 For more on the ideas and beliefs of these two men, see Albert Hourani, *Arabic Thought in the Liberal Age, 1798–1939* (Cambridge: Cambridge University Press, 1983 [1962]), 103–60.

32 Henri Lauzière, "The Construction of *Salafiyya*: Reconsidering Salafism from the Perspective of Conceptual History," *International Journal of Middle East Studies* 42, no. 3 (2010): 373–6. See also, however, Frank Griffel, "What Do We Mean by 'Salafī'? Connecting Muḥammad ʿAbduh with Egypt's Nūr Party in Islam's Contemporary Intellectual History," *Die Welt des Islams* 55, no. 2 (2015): 186–220, esp. 200–13.

33 Fattah, "Wahhabi"; Itzchak Weismann, "Genealogies of Fundamentalism: Salafi Discourse in Nineteenth-Century Baghdad," *British Journal of Middle Eastern Studies* 36, no. 2 (2009): 267–80.

34 David Dean Commins, *Islamic Reform: Politics and Social Change in Late Ottoman Syria* (New York and Oxford: Oxford University Press, 1990); Munʿim Sirry, "Jamāl al-Dīn al-Qāsimī and the Salafi Approach to Sufism," *Die Welt des Islams* 51, no. 1 (2011): 75–108; Itzchak Weismann, "Between Ṣūfī Reformism and Modernist Rationalism: A Reappraisal of the Origins of the Salafiyya from the Damascene Angle," *Die Welt des Islams* 41, no. 2 (2001): 206–37; *id.*, *Taste of Modernity: Sufism, Salafiyya, and Arabism in Late Ottoman Damascus* (Leiden: Brill, 2001), 263–304.

35 Haykel, "Nature," 45–7; Wagemakers, *Quietist*, 6–7.

frankly – do not really care, that constitutes the most important difference between "enlightened" and "purifying" Salafis.[36]

The Spread of Salafism

The general attempt to emulate the utopia of the *salaf* is thus an old and widespread phenomenon in the history of Islam. This, again, does not mean that the scholars and groups mentioned above were all Salafis *avant la lettre*, but they were indeed precursors to the current Salafi movement in the sense that they all tried to go directly to the earliest textual sources (the Qurʾan and the Sunna). Moreover, this general claim of wanting to return to the beginning of Islam, although it is not as specific and pervasive as modern-day Salafis express it, may nevertheless help explain the spread of Salafism today. A focus on the Qurʾan and the Sunna provides Muslims with a great source of authenticity, giving the impression that they are merely doing what the sources are saying. Given that Salafis are the ultimate advocates of such a method, this approach – although contested by other Muslims, as we will see below – allows Salafis to adopt an attitude of supposed religious purity and authority, which may well be an attractive feature to many Muslim youngsters searching for answers in life.[37] Furthermore, some of the scholars and movements mentioned earlier, although often not Salafis themselves, may well have contributed to a renewed appreciation of the study of particularly *ḥadīth*s. This may, indirectly, also have aided the rise of the Salafi trend dealt with in this book, which – as mentioned – has its roots in the twentieth century. The trend that stimulated and facilitated the spread of Salafism in that period more than any other was Wahhabism.

Before explaining the Saudi-Wahhabi role in the spread of Salafism in the twentieth century, it should be clear that this factor must not be exaggerated.[38] Apart from the influence of other Salafi movements already in existence, independent of Wahhabism, it is important to remember that the *salaf*, the Qurʾan and the Sunna are of great importance to *all* Sunni Muslims. As such, the general tendency to be influenced by early Islam is not beholden to Salafis alone, but finds a much wider audience. Although Salafis and "ordinary" Sunnis have different

[36] The more modernist Salafis in particularly Syria have nevertheless been of great importance to Salafism in Jordan and continue to inspire the more politically minded Salafis in the kingdom. That issue requires a separate publication, however.

[37] See, for example, Martijn de Koning, *Zoeken naar een "zuivere" islam: Geloofsbeleving en identiteitsvorming van jonge Marokkaans-Nederlandse moslims* (Amsterdam: Bert Bakker, 2008).

[38] See also Bonnefoy, *Salafism*, 5–13, who points this out as well in the context of his work on Yemen.

ways of approaching the *salaf* – as an authoritative example that should be followed directly and meticulously or as a model best emulated through the prism of the *madhāhib*, respectively – one could say that a certain tendency to reach back to early Islam is, in a sense, inherent in Sunni tradition. This is not to suggest that Sunni Muslims are all potential Salafis, but simply to point out that they may have a certain susceptibility for Salafis' tendency to focus on the early period of Islam. In fact, if one glosses over the ideological differences between Salafis and "ordinary" Sunnis, it is easy to see the former as nothing more than just very pious Sunnis, and this is indeed how some – both outsiders as well as Muslims – think of Salafis.[39]

These caveats notwithstanding, it is clear that Saudi Arabia and Wahhabism did have a great impact on the rise of Salafism. This can be ascribed to three main factors: the rise of the oil industry in the Gulf in general and Saudi Arabia in particular; the anti-revolutionary propaganda emanating from the Saudi kingdom since the 1960s; and the desire for an alternative to Nasserism after the Arab military defeat against Israel in 1967. Firstly, the discovery of Saudi oil in the 1930s[40] yielded enormous profits for the kingdom when it was fully exploited after the Second World War and – partly for lack of Saudi personnel capable of running the oil industry – attracted many Arabs and Muslims from outside. These men not only made a living in Saudi Arabia, but were simultaneously influenced by Wahhabi Islam and often returned home with much more conservative views than when they first came. Fandy has shown, for example, how such oil workers from Egypt, upon their return home, used the money they earned to set up a religious infrastructure that later formed the basis of the Salafi Jamaʿa Islamiyya group.[41]

Secondly, Saudi Arabia also actively supported the spread of Wahhabism, financed by its oil profits. The military coup led by Nasser in Egypt in 1952 had brought to power a republican, socialist and secularist regime that actively sought to find like-minded allies in the region, in opposition to the "conservative" monarchies of countries such as Saudi Arabia and – as we saw in the Introduction – Jordan. At the same time, Nasser's regime quickly started repressing the Muslim Brotherhood in

[39] Hamid, "Attraction," 387–90; Thomas Hegghammer, "Jihadi-Salafis or Revolutionaries? On Religion and Politics in the Study of Militant Islamism," in *Global Salafism: Islam's New Religious Movement*, ed. Roel Meijer (London: Hurst & Co., 2009), 249. This does not mean, of course, that non-Salafis are not pious.

[40] David Holden and Richard Johns, *The House of Saud: The Rise and Rule of the Most Powerful Dynasty in the Arab World* (New York: Holt, Rinehart and Winston, 1981), 110–20.

[41] Mamoun Fandy, "Egypt's Islamic Group: Regional Revenge," *Middle East Journal* 48, no. 4 (1994): 617–19.

Egypt, a phenomenon that could also be seen under other military regimes in the region, such as Syria. Many of these Brothers fled persecution at home and ended up in Saudi Arabia, where their activism and higher education helped them obtain jobs in the Saudi education system that was being set up. This, in turn, allowed them to assist the kingdom in its efforts to spread a conservative and pro-monarchical Wahhabi message through organisations such as the Muslim World League[42] as a counterweight to the revolutionary rhetoric that Cairo was spreading.[43] These efforts were increased after the Islamic Revolution in Saudi Arabia's neighbour Iran in 1979, when the kingdom also felt threatened by the Shiʿi revolutionary zeal coming from Teheran. This way, Wahhabism was spread to large parts of the Muslim world.[44]

Thirdly, the defeat of the Arab armies in the war against Israel in 1967 dealt a blow to the pan-Arab, socialist policies that Nasser had advocated. His assertive and confrontational leadership had inspired like-minded groups in countries such as Algeria, Libya and Syria and had given Arabs across the region hope of a better future and victory over Israel. When the latter dream fell apart in 1967, many were devastated and started looking for an alternative ideology to which they could adhere. In this context, the Arab world provided fertile ground for the Wahhabi message spread from Saudi Arabia.[45] It is important to note, however, that the growing religiosity in Egypt was also stimulated by Nasser's successor, President Anwar al-Sadat (r. 1970–1981), who sought a clear identity for his own rule that was distinct from his predecessor's socialism. As such, he allowed Islamic movements more freedom and space than Nasser had ever given them, thereby facilitating the influence of Wahhabism.[46]

Saudi Arabia, through its spreading of Wahhabism, has thus had a major influence on the blossoming of Salafism in the Muslim world. Apart from the factors already mentioned, however, it should be clear that Saudi influence in the spreading of Salafism cannot simply be equated with Saudi control over this trend. It is important to point this out, since

[42] For more on this organisation, see Schulze, *Islamischer*.
[43] Gilles Kepel, *The War for Muslim Minds: Islam and the West* (translation Pascale Ghazaleh) (Cambridge, MA, and London: Belknap/Harvard University Press, 2004), 170–3. See also Al-Rasheed, *Contesting*, 73–4, where the author states that the importance of foreign Muslim Brothers in this process, rather than Saudis themselves, should not be overstated.
[44] For a detailed study of Saudi Arabia's efforts to spread Wahhabism and its role in the country's foreign policy, see Shehabi, "Role."
[45] Gilles Kepel, *Jihad: The Trail of Political Islam* (translation Anthony F. Roberts) (Cambridge, MA, and London: Belknap/Harvard University Press, 2002), 62–5.
[46] *Ibid.*, 65.

Saudi Arabia is sometimes accused of supporting all kinds of terrorist movements and the ideologies underpinning them through its missionary efforts.[47] The fact that the kingdom has long been involved in disseminating the conservative and strict message of Wahhabism does not mean that such an ideology, in the hands of radicals, cannot start taking on a life of its own. Indeed, this is also what al-Sadat found out in Egypt when some of the Salafi trends he had allowed to become more prominent radicalised in a way that neither he nor Saudi Arabia had intended, turned against him and ultimately assassinated him in 1981.[48] Such radicals may, therefore, have been inspired by the Wahhabi message coming from Riyadh, but apparently did not feel bound by its conservative and non-revolutionary elements. This suggests that Salafism encompasses different ideological trends, which is indeed the case.

The Salafi *ʿAqīda*

The great value Salafis attach to the utopia of the *salaf* is, to a certain extent, shared by some other groups and scholars throughout Islamic history, as we have seen above. What sets modern-day Salafis apart from many of these historical precursors to their movement is the meticulousness and the comprehensive nature with which they approach the *salaf*. This pertains to the way they define themselves, to how they approach Islamic tradition and to the legal consequences this often has (i.e., following a *madhhab* or not). Yet the most important dimension of Salafis' focus on the "pious predecessors" concerns their theological views, which result in a typically Salafi *ʿaqīda*. This means that the supposed "purity" that Salafis strive for in their emulation of *al-salaf al-ṣāliḥ* is also translated into creedal issues that, again, set them apart from other Muslims, including "ordinary" Sunnis, but now not from a legal but from a theological perspective.

Salafis link this "purity" to a collection of slightly differing *ḥadīth*s in which the Prophet is said to have stated that Jews and Christians have split up into 71 or 72 sects (*firqa*), while his *umma* would split up into 73 sects, "all of which are in hell, except for one. That is the group (*jamāʿa*)". This

47 Examples of studies making this point include Dore Gold, *Hatred's Kingdom: How Saudi Arabia Supports the New Global Terrorism* (Washington, DC: Regnery Publishing, Inc., 2003); Stephen Schwartz, *The Two Faces of Islam: Saudi Fundamentalism and Its Role in Terrorism* (New York: Anchor Books, 2003).

48 For more on the radical groups responsible for the assassination of al-Sādāt, see Johannes J.G. Jansen, *The Neglected Duty: The Creed of Sadat's Assassins and Islamic Resurgence in the Middle East* (New York: MacMillan, 1986); Gilles Kepel, *Muslim Extremism in Egypt: The Prophet and the Pharaoh* (translation Jon Rothschild) (Berkeley and Los Angeles: University of California Press, 2003 [1986]).

"group" is also referred to as "*al-firqa al-nājiya*" (the sect saved [from hellfire]) or "*al-ṭāʾifa al-manṣūra*" (the victorious group). The latter term is taken from a *ḥadīth* stating that "a group (*ṭāʾifa*) from my *umma* will remain committed to the truth (*ʿalá l-ḥaqq*)".[49] Salafis believe that these labels refer to them, since they claim to be the group that remains steadfast in its search for "true" Islam and will thus ultimately be victorious and be saved from going to hell. Given the obvious importance of belonging to this group, it is not surprising that Salafis base their creed entirely on the utopia of the *salaf*, believing that this *ʿaqīda* is "the truth" to which they should remain committed.[50]

The Centrality of *Tawḥīd*

The most important concept in the Salafi *ʿaqīda* – and one that, again, reaches back to the very beginning of Islam – is the unity of God (*tawḥīd*). The Islamic confession of faith (*shahāda*) states: "There is no god but God (*lā ilāha illā llāh*) and Muhammad is the messenger of God." The first half of this statement points to the centrality of strict monotheism in Islam which, given the clear break with the polytheism (*shirk*) in Mecca that the Prophet is said to have intended his new religion to be, is perhaps not surprising. To Salafis, however, *tawḥīd* means more than just monotheism. They divide it into three different aspects of unity, each of which is important: *tawḥīd al-rubūbiyya* (the unity of Lordship), *tawḥīd al-ulūhiyya* (the unity of divinity, also known as *tawḥīd al-ilāhiyya* or *tawḥīd al-ʿibāda* [the unity of worship]) and *tawḥīd al-asmāʾ wa-l-ṣifāt* (the unity of [God's] names and attributes).

Firstly, *tawḥīd al-rubūbiyya* denotes the idea that God is the sole Lord and Creator. This is the most basic aspect of *tawḥīd* and the one that most approaches the English term "monotheism".[51] This branch of *tawḥīd*, however, did not so much distinguish Muslims from Arabian polytheists, since they are also said to have believed in a single Creator, meaning that Muslims – according to some scholars – needed more to affirm their new identity as true monotheists. The second aspect of the unity of God,

49 See, for example, *Ṣaḥīḥ al-Bukhārī*, book 56 ("Kitāb al-Manāqib"), chapter 27 ("Bāb"), nos. 834 and 835; book 92 ("Kitāb al-Iʿtiṣām bi-l-Kitāb wa-l-Sunna"), chapter 10 ("Qawl al-Nabī Ṣallá llāh ʿalayhi wa-Sallam: Lā Tazālu Ṭāʾifatun min Ummatī Ẓāhirīna ʿalá l-Ḥaqq wa-Hum Ahl al-ʿIlm"), no. 414.

50 Haykel, "Nature," 34; Wiktorowicz, *Management*, 120. For an overview of the various *ḥadīth*s used by Salafis with regard to this issue, see al-Miṣrī, *Maʿālim*, 36–47; Abū ʿAbd al-Raḥmān Muḥammad b. Surūr Shaʿbān, *Al-Shaykh al-Albānī wa-Manhajuhu fī Taqrīr Masāʾil al-Iʿtiqād* (Riyadh: Dār al-Kiyān, 2007), 656–66. It may be assumed that not just Salafis believe they belong to this group and that other Muslims make similar claims.

51 According to the *Concise Oxford Dictionary*, monotheism is "the doctrine that there is only one God".

tawḥīd al-ulūhiyya, provided them with this since it refers to the necessity of worshipping God alone.[52] Finally, *tawḥīd al-asmāʾ wa-l-ṣifāt* refers to the absolute uniqueness of God in all his names and attributes and to the idea that God is incomparable to anything or anyone else.[53]

The latter aspect of *tawḥīd* is an important one in distinguishing Salafis from many other Muslims, including many "ordinary" Sunnis, from a theological perspective and requires some explanation. The Qurʾan mentions several attributes of God that are doctrinally controversial, such as body parts that include a face (*wajh*; see Q. 55: 27), eyes (*aʿyun*; see, for example, Q. 54: 14) and hands (*yad*; see Q. 38: 75; 67: 1). At the same time, Q. 42: 11 states that "like Him there is naught" (*laysa ka-mithlihi shayʾun*),[54] raising questions as to the exact form of God's hands, for example. The Qurʾanic text says that God has hands, but if these are "like naught" (i.e., unlike anything else), what do they look like? Different trends within Islam came up with different ways to solve this problem when debates first took place on these issues centuries ago. Some scholars took verses describing God's attributes literally, leading to accusations that they were anthropomorphists ignoring Q. 42: 11. Others, including the mediaeval rationalist Muʿtazila movement, interpreted such verses metaphorically, while Hanbalis simply accepted the literal texts as they are, without speculating about how they should be explained. A middle way was found by the Ashʿariyya and Maturidiyya streams within Islamic theology, which would later become what could be described as "orthodox" Sunni Islam, by adhering mostly to the Hanbali line of accepting the texts "without [asking] how" (*bi-lā kayfa*), but allowing somewhat more speculation as to their true nature.[55] The Salafi position is virtually the same as the Hanbali one and is described by Gharaibeh as "transcendental anthropomorphism", meaning that Salafis do believe God has a certain form based on the relevant verses, but they do so without descriptive designation (*bi-lā takyīf*). Instead, they accept that God must be different from the human form that we are familiar with.[56]

[52] Mohammad Gharaibeh, "Zur Glaubenslehre des Salafismus," in *Salafismus: Auf der Suche nach dem wahren Islam*, ed. Behnam T. Said and Hazim Fouad (Freiburg: Herder, 2014), 110.

[53] Haykel, "Nature," 38–9; Wiktorowicz, *Management*, 113–15.

[54] This verse from the Qurʾān and all others used in this book were taken from A.J. Arberry, *The Koran Interpreted* (New York: Touchstone, 1955). The verse numbering used is not that of Arberry, however, but the more standard form of numbering used by Egyptian editions of the Qurʾān.

[55] Nader el-Bizri, "God: Essence and Attributes," in *The Cambridge Companion to Classical Islamic Theology*, ed. Tim Winter (Cambridge: Cambridge University Press, 2008), 122–31.

[56] Gharaibeh, "Glaubenslehre," 112–24.

Such debates on *tawḥīd al-asmāʾ wa-l-ṣifāt* have a much greater importance than they seem to suggest since they show what status the alleged revelation (*waḥy*) of the Qurʾanic text has and to what extent it may be complemented by such extra-textual sources as rationalism (*ʿaql*) in deciding theological issues. For Hanbalis, the revelation as expressed in the texts was of supreme importance, even if – as we saw above – this meant that its exact meaning was not entirely clear. For the Muʿtazila, on the other hand, rationalism played a major role in their speculative theology (*kalām*). Salafis, perhaps unsurprisingly, strongly resemble or are even exactly the same as Hanbalis in this respect, taking the texts at face value and rejecting rationalism and speculation, thereby distancing themselves not only from the Muʿtazila but also, to a lesser extent, from "orthodox" Sunni Islam as embodied by the Ashʿari and Maturidi approaches to Islamic theology. Thus, Salafis' views on *tawḥīd al-asmāʾ wa-l-ṣifāt* and, more broadly, on the status of scripture, further underline the difference between their own way of thinking and that of "ordinary" Sunnis.

Maintaining Purity

The different positions Salafis take with regard to *tawḥīd* and scripture, even in relation to fellow Sunnis, suggest that they adhere to a branch of Islam that is distinctive and perhaps even somewhat exclusive. This is, indeed, the case. The idea of not belonging to the majority of Sunnis who have supposedly deviated from "the straight path" (*al-ṣirāṭ al-mustaqīm*) is succinctly expressed in the term *ghurabāʾ* (strangers). This term is a reference to several *ḥadīth*s stating that "Islam began as a stranger (*inna l-Islām badaʾa gharīban*) and it will return as it began (*wa-sayaʿūdu kamā badaʾa*), as a stranger".[57] That this term is meant in a positive way becomes clear from one of the *ḥadīth*s, which adds the words "so good tidings (*ṭūbá*) to the strangers (*al-ghurabāʾ*)".[58] This positive connotation is confirmed by another *ḥadīth*, which states: "Be in the world (*kun fī l-dunyā*) as if you are a stranger or a traveller (*ʿābir al-sabīl*)."[59] Given Salafis' exclusivity in their ideology, the term *ghurabāʾ*, just like other concepts such as *al-firqa al-nājiya* and *al-ṭāʾifa al-manṣūra*, is interpreted as a positive confirmation of the correctness of what they believe in. Seen in such a way, being ostracised by society (including by other

[57] *Ṣaḥīḥ Muslim*, book 1 ("Kitāb al-Īmān"), chapter 65 ("Bāb Bayān anna l-Islām Badaʾa Gharīban wa-innahu Yaʾziru bayna l-Masjidayn"), nos. 145–6. No 146 has a slightly different text, stating that "it will return as a stranger, as it began".

[58] *Ibid.*, no. 145.

[59] See *Ṣaḥīḥ al-Bukhārī*, book 76 ("Kitāb al-Riqāʾiq"), chapter 3 ("Bāb Qawl al-Nabī Ṣallá llāh ʿalayhi wa-Sallam: Kun fī l-Dunyā ka-annaka Gharībun"), no. 425.

Muslims) is something to be proud of, as it appears to underline that Salafis are "the strangers" referred to in these *ḥadīths*, striving for their utopia without ever finding a home.[60]

Maintaining the "purity" of Islam among Salafis is not just found in their desire to remain distinct from other Muslims. It also involves "cleansing" Islam of the "religious innovations" (*bidaʿ*, sing. *bidʿa*) that Salafis believe have crept into the religion as a result of the centuries-long use of extra-textual means in the formation of Islamic law,[61] and especially Sunni doctrine, like the aforementioned tools of considered opinion and speculative theology. This desire to "cleanse" Islam can focus on matters of law and doctrine, but often also extends to other things that cannot be traced directly to the *salaf*, such as certain words and concepts, clothing and – in rare cases – even technology.[62] The reason *bidaʿ* are considered so wrong by Salafis is that they constitute practices apparently not used by the Prophet and his companions themselves and were condemned by the former in an oft-cited *ḥadīth*, which states that "every novelty (*muḥdatha*) is an innovation (*bidʿa*) and every innovation is an error (*ḍalāla*) and every error is in hell (*fī l-nār*)".[63] This is not to say that Salafis are against renewal (*tajdīd*). Indeed, Wahhabism has been discussed in the context of eighteenth-century *tajdīd*[64] and the Salafi shaykh Muhammad Nasir al-Din al-Albani has been referred to as a "renewer" (*mujaddid*) by his followers,[65] thus indicating that Salafis view this term positively. The key difference between *bidʿa* and *tajdīd* is that the former is an addition to the words and practices of the *salaf*, which Salafis consider illegitimate, while the latter is seen as the revival of Islam, believed to be sent by God himself in the form of a *mujaddid* who comes "at the turn of every century".[66]

60 De Koning, Wagemakers and Becker, *Salafisme*, 128–9; Benno Köpfer, "*Ghuraba'* – das Konzept der Fremden in salafistischen Strömungen: Von Namen eines Terrorcamps zum subkulturellen Lifestyle," in *Salafismus: Auf der Suche nach dem wahren Islam*, ed. Behnam T. Said and Hazim Fouad (Freiburg: Herder, 2014), 442–73, esp. 449, 451–60.

61 For more on this process, see Hallaq, *Sharīʿa*, 48–51; Schacht, *Introduction*, 60–2.

62 Wiktorowicz, *Management*, 116–17.

63 This is the first *ḥadīth* mentioned by the Jordanian Salafī scholar ʿAlī al-Ḥalabī, for example, in his book dedicated to the subject of *bidʿa*. See ʿAlī b. Ḥasan b. ʿAlī b. ʿAbd al-Ḥamīd al-Ḥalabī al-Atharī, *ʿIlm Uṣūl al-Bidaʿ: Dirāsa Takmīliyya Muhimma fī ʿIlm Uṣūl al-Fiqh* (Riyadh and Jeddah: Dār al-Rāya li-l-Nashr wa-l-Tawzīʿ, 1992), 6.

64 John O. Voll, "Renewal and Reform in Islamic History: *Tajdid* and *Islah*," in *Voices of Resurgent Islam*, ed. John L. Esposito (Oxford: Oxford University Press, 1983), 37–42.

65 See, for example, Muḥammad Nāṣir al-Dīn al-Albānī, *Al-Salafiyya: Haqīqatuhā, Uṣūluhā, Mawqifuhā min al-Madhāhib, Shubha ḥawlahā li-Faḍīlat al-Shaykh al-Mujaddid Muḥammad Nāṣir al-Dīn al-Albānī*, ed. ʿAmr ʿAbd al-Munʿim Salīm (n.p.: Dār al-Ḍiyāʾ, 2006).

66 Ella Landau-Tasseron, "The 'Cyclical Reform': A Study of the *Mujaddid* Tradition," *Studia Islamica* 70 (1989): 79–117. The words quoted are on 79.

The primary concept used by Salafis to remain committed to their own beliefs and practices on the one hand and to stay away from everything else on the other is *al-walāʾ wa-l-barāʾ* (loyalty and disavowal). It refers to the absolute loyalty and dedication that Salafis should display towards God, Islam and fellow Muslims and the disavowal and rejection they must simultaneously show towards all things that cause Muslims to deviate from these. The concept is typically Salafi in the sense that it almost epitomises Salafism's tendency to remain closely attached to religious "purity" and, as such, can be used to ward off everything Salafis see as a threat to Islam.[67] This way, *al-walāʾ wa-l-barāʾ* could be seen as a concept that keeps Salafis from having close relationships with others and hampers their integration into broader society, particularly in non-Muslim countries.[68] Despite this very Salafi character of the concept, it actually has a long history and is rooted in terms dating back to the pre-Islamic period.[69]

Al-walāʾ wa-l-barāʾ as used by Salafis nowadays finds expression on a personal, political and legislative level. The first pertains to all kinds of personal issues such as greeting people, clothing, the celebration of holidays and, generally put, the ability to show one's own religion (*iẓhār al-dīn*). In practice, this means that Salafis should greet Muslims in one way and non-Muslims in another, not imitate adherents to other faiths or wear clothing that is considered un-Islamic (such as ties, jackets and trousers) and only celebrate *ʿīd al-aḍḥá* (the feast of the sacrifice) and *ʿīd al-fiṭr* (the feast of breaking the fast) at the expense of supposedly "un-Islamic" holidays like Christmas or even the birthday of the Prophet. Several Salafi scholars, going back to at least Ibn Taymiyya, have stated that such practices could cause believers to deviate from the "purity" of

[67] Joas Wagemakers, "Framing the 'Threat to Islam': *Al-Wala' wa-l-Bara'* in Salafi Discourse," *Arab Studies Quarterly* 30, no. 4 (2008): 1–22.

[68] For more on these dimensions in a Western context, see Uriya Shavit, "Can Muslims Befriend Non-Muslims? Debating *al-walāʾ wa-l-barāʾ* (Loyalty and Disavowal) in Theory and Practice," *Islam and Christian-Muslim Relations* 25, no. 1 (2014): 67–88; *id.*, "The Wasaṭī and Salafī Approaches to the Religious Law of Muslim Minorities," *Islamic Law and Society* 19 (2012): 416–57.

[69] Wagemakers, "Transformation," 82–91. See also Mouline, *Clercs*, 107, where the author offers the interesting theory that "[l]oyalty and disavowal, which certain Islamic trends adopted at one moment or another in their historical trajectory, was without any doubt inspired by the Jewish principle of *amixia* (exclusivism or misanthropy)". The author only offers secondary sources showing that such a concept may have existed in Judaism, however, and does not show any evidence regarding how, when or why this concept was supposedly adopted from Jews by Muslims. His reasoning also ignores much contrary evidence that suggests that *al-walāʾ wa-l-barāʾ* has pre-Islamic roots, was adopted by early Muslims in a different and Islamised form and, as such, became part of the Islamic scriptural tradition, from where it was used by various groups and trends.

Islam and should therefore be left alone.[70] If Salafis are entirely unable to show their religion, they are even encouraged to express disavowal of their surroundings by striving for emigration (*hijra*) to a Muslim country in which this is possible.[71] It is also partly for this reason that Salafis have a negative view of adherents to other branches of Islam, such as Sufis or Shiʿas, whose theology, rituals and practices they consider deviant.[72]

The political interpretation of *al-walāʾ wa-l-barāʾ* is tied to relations between states and dictates that Muslim countries should display solidarity among each other and not side with non-Muslim states in military conflicts, particularly if the victim of such an alliance is another Muslim country. Concretely, many Salafis contend that believers should refrain from asking non-Muslims for help (*al-istiʿāna bi-l-kuffār*) or actively aid these non-Muslims themselves (*iʿānat al-kuffār*) in case of a conflict. Heavily rooted in Saudi history, where the situation of asking non-Muslims for help against other Muslims occurred several times,[73] this is a form of *al-walāʾ wa-l-barāʾ* that is more controversial among Salafis, unlike the first one, on which all of them basically agree. The different viewpoints on this type of *al-walāʾ wa-l-barāʾ* stem from doctrinal motives, with some Salafis distinguishing between different forms of help asked from or given to non-Muslims (some being admissible while others are not), as well as from more political ones, with some Salafis being willing to criticise their regimes while others decide to remain subservient.[74]

The third and final form of *al-walāʾ wa-l-barāʾ* is even more controversial and refers to legislation applied in Muslim countries. The idea behind this is that the complete loyalty that Salafis should display towards God must also be seen in a country's legislation, meaning that it must be based entirely on the *sharīʿa* and not on so-called "man-made laws" (*qawānīn*

[70] Wagemakers, "Framing," 5–7; *id.*, *Quietist*, 149–51; *id.*, "Salafistische Strömungen und ihre Sicht auf *al-walaʾ wa-l-baraʾ* (Loyalität und Lossagung)," in *Salafismus: Auf der Suche nach dem wahren Islam*, ed. Behnam T. Said and Hazim Fouad (Freiburg: Herder, 2014), 70–2; *id.*, "Transformation," 85–90.

[71] *Id.*, *Quietist*, 150. For more on the supposed duty to emigrate to Muslim countries, see Alan Verskin, *Oppressed in the Land? Fatwās on Muslims Living under Non-Muslim Rule from the Middle Ages to the Present* (Princeton: Markus Wiener Publishers, 2013).

[72] Haykel, "Nature," 41. For more on Salafī views of Shiʿas, including other factors that play a role, see *id.*, "Jihadis and the Shiʿa," in *Self-Inflicted Wounds: Debates and Divisions within al-Qaʿida and Its Periphery*, ed. Assaf Moghadam and Brian Fishman (West Point, NY: Combating Terrorism Center, 2010), 208–23; Guido Steinberg, "Jihadi-Salafism and the Shiʿis: Remarks about the Intellectual Roots of anti-Shiʿism," in *Global Salafism: Islam's New Religious Movement*, ed. Roel Meijer (London: Hurst & Co., 2009), 107–25; Joas Wagemakers, "Soennitische islamisten en de erfenis van de Islamitische Revolutie," *ZemZem: Tijdschrift over het Midden-Oosten, Noord-Afrika en islam* 4, no. 4 (2008): 55–9.

[73] Wagemakers, "Enduring."

[74] *Id.*, "Framing," 7–9; *id.*, *Quietist*, 151–60, 179–83; *id.*, "Salafistische," 72–3.

waḍʿiyya). If the legislative systems in Muslim countries are nevertheless based on such "un-Islamic" laws – and particularly Jihadi-Salafis believe that they are – this form of *al-walāʾ wa-l-barāʾ* dictates that these should be disavowed and resisted. This should preferably be done through jihad, since that is the clearest way of expressing disavowal of Muslim regimes and their "man-made laws". This form of *al-walāʾ wa-l-barāʾ* is clearly distinct from the previous two and seems to have been conceived and adopted only by the Jordanian Jihadi-Salafi scholar Abu Muhammad al-Maqdisi and has therefore been less influential.[75]

The Divisiveness of *Īmān*

The concept of *al-walāʾ wa-l-barāʾ* was the first one we saw on which Salafis have different points of view – although this is also the case with *tawḥīd*, as we will see later on. An even more divisive doctrinal issue among Salafis is, however, the question of what constitutes faith and when one can be accused of engaging in its opposite: unbelief (*kufr*). Both terms may initially not have had the exact meaning ascribed to them here,[76] but they are treated as such by Salafis, which is what is important now. Discussions on the opposition between *īmān* and *kufr* go back to the formative period of Islamic theology and have found their way into treatises on the correct Muslim *ʿaqīda*.[77]

The first issue debated in discussions on faith relevant to this book is the question of what constitutes *īmān*. Some scholars and trends, including the eponymous "founder" of the Hanafi school of Islamic law, Abu Hanifa al-Nuʿman b. Thabit (d. 767), and the Hanafi scholar Abu Jaʿfar Ahmad b. Muhammad al-Tahawi (d. 933),[78] believed that faith existed in the heart and through speech, but not in acts.[79] A similar position was taken by the early Islamic Murjiʾa ("postponers") trend,[80] which is said to

[75] *Id.*, *Quietist*, 166–79; *id.*, "Salafistische," 74; *id.*, "Transformation," 91–5.

[76] For an in-depth discussion of the terms *kufr* and *īmān* in pre- and early *Islamic* periods, see Toshihiko Izutsu, *Ethico-Religious Concepts in the Qurʾān* (Montreal: McGill University Press, 2002), 119–77, 184–202.

[77] See, for example, A.J. Wensinck, *The Muslim Creed: Its Genesis and Historical Development* (London: Frank Cass & Co. Ltd., 1965).

[78] One of the best-known works by al-Ṭaḥāwī, *Al-ʿAqīda al-Ṭaḥāwiyya*, has been of great importance to Muslim scholars, including al-Albānī, who has commented on this text and its *ḥadīth*s. See Muḥammad Nāṣir al-Dīn al-Albānī, *Al-ʿAqīda al-Ṭaḥāwiyya: Sharḥ wa-Taʿlīq* (Beirut: Al-Maktab al-Islāmī, 1993); *Sharḥ al-ʿAqīda al-Ṭaḥāwiyya li-l-ʿAllāma Ibn Abī l-ʿIzz al-Ḥanafī* (Beirut/Cairo: Al-Maktab al-Islāmī/Dār al-Salām, 2011);

[79] William Montgomery Watt, *The Formative Period of Islamic Thought* (Oxford, One World, 1998 [1973]), 132–3; Wensinck, *Muslim*, 103, 125–6.

[80] Wilferd Madelung, "Early Sunni Doctrine Concerning Faith as Reflected in the *Kitāb al-Īmān* of Abū ʿUbayd al-Qāsim b. Sallām (d. 224/839)," *Studia Islamica* 32 (1970): 233; *id.*, *Religious Trends in Early Islamic Iran* (New York: State University of New York Press, 1988), 15; J. Meric Pessagno, "The Murjiʾa, Īmān and Abū ʿUbayd," *Journal of the*

have applied "postponement" (*irjāʾ*) to the judgement over Muslims' faith, leaving this decision to God instead.[81] The Murjiʾa refrained from labelling sinful acts as *kufr*, as long as Muslims did not verbally confirm their sinful intention behind such acts,[82] and they even seem to have applied this reasoning to allegedly clear acts of polytheism, such as idol-worshipping.[83]

A different position in the debate on what constitutes faith was taken by the aforementioned rationalist Muʿtazila movement, the Hanbalis,[84] the eponymous "founder" of the Ashʿariyya school of Islamic theology, Abu l-Hasan al-Ashʿari (874–936) – though not his followers – and the early Islamic Khawarij[85] trend. They believed that acts were part of *īmān* and that, subsequently, faith could not be deprived of them.[86] This position eventually resulted in the idea that faith is found in belief (*iʿtiqād*) or assent (*taṣdīq*) in the heart (*bi-l-qalb*), speech (*qawl*) or verbal confirmation (*iqrār*) showing this faith

American Oriental Society 95, no. 3 (1975): 383, 386–7; Joseph Schacht, "An Early Murciʾite Treatise," *Oriens* 17 (1964): 106–7.

[81] Wilferd Madelung, *Der Imam al-Qasim ibn Ibrahim und die Glaubenslehre der Zaiditen* (Berlin: Walter de Gruyter & Co., 1965), 229–30; William Montgomery Watt, *Islamic Philosophy and Theology* (Edinburgh: Edinburgh University Press, 1962), 32–3.

[82] Schacht, "Early," 109, 113.

[83] Khalid Blankinship, "The Early Creed," in *The Cambridge Companion to Classical Islamic Theology*, ed. Tim Winter (Cambridge: Cambridge University Press, 2008), 46; G. van Vloten, "Irdjā," *Zeitschrift der Deutschen Morgenländischen Gesellschaft* 45, no. 2 (1891): 163; Watt, *Formative*, 124. Given the strong similarities between particularly Abu Hanifa's views and those of the Murjiʾa in this respect, the former is often seen as one of the latter. See Blankinship, "Early," 44; Josef van Ess, *Theologie und Gesellschaft im 2. und 3. Jahrhundert Hidschra*, vol. II (Berlin and New York: Walter de Gruyter, 1992), 534–44; Wilferd Madelung, "The Early Murjiʾa in Khurāsān and Transoxania and the Spread of Ḥanafism," *Islam* 59 (1982): 36.

[84] For an overview of different creeds ascribed to Ibn Ḥanbal, see Saud al-Sarhan, "The Creeds of Aḥmad Ibn Ḥanbal," in *Books and Bibliophiles: Studies in Honour of Paul Auchterlonie on the Bio-Bibliography of the Muslim World*, ed. Robert Gleave (n.p.: Gibb Memorial Trust, 2014), 29–44.

[85] For more on the Khawārij, who left (Ar.: *kharaja*, hence the name Khawārij) the Muslim community after a dispute, see K.H. Pampus, *Über die Rolle der Ḫāriǧīya im frühen Islam* (Wiesbaden: Verlag Otto Harrassowitz, 1980); Elie Adib Salem, *Political Theory and Institutions of the Khawarij* (Baltimore, MD: Johns Hopkins University Press, 1956); Hussam S. Timani, *Modern Intellectual Readings of the Kharijites* (New York: Peter Lang Publishing, 2008). For more on the modern relevance of the Khawārij, see also Jeffrey T. Kenney, *Muslim Rebels: Kharijites and the Politics of Extremism in Egypt* (Oxford: Oxford University Press, 2006); Nelly Lahoud, *The Jihadis' Path to Self-Destruction* (New York: Columbia University Press, 2010); Joas Wagemakers, "'Seceders' and 'Postponers'? An Analysis of the 'Khawarij' and 'Murjiʾa' Labels in Polemical Debates between Quietist and Jihadi-Salafis," in *Contextualising Jihadi Thought*, ed. Jeevan Deol and Zaheer Kazmi (London: Hurst & Co., 2012), 147–50, 153–7.

[86] Watt, *Formative*, 134–6.

with the tongue (*bi-l-lisān*) and corresponding acts with the limbs (*al-a'māl bi-l-jawāriḥ*).[87]

A second issue related to *īmān* that was debated in early Islamic discussions was the question of whether faith could increase and decrease (*yazīdu wa-yanquṣu*) or should be seen as one indivisible entity that was either present or not. The majority position among early Islamic scholars seems to have been that good deeds increased faith and bad ones decreased it, implying that faith was flexible.[88] The minority position, held by adherents to the Hanafi school of law, the Khawarij and the Murji'a, stated that *īmān* was inflexible, could not increase or decrease and was thus left intact or taken away entirely by a single sin,[89] although the Murji'a later modified this view somewhat.[90]

These debates on faith, though old and seemingly obscure, are of great importance to Salafis. Not only do they want their views on this issue to be "correct" from the point of view of the sources,[91] but their insistence on keeping their creed "pure" also dictates that they realise exactly what is part of *īmān* and – perhaps just as important – what to reject as *kufr*. Like the Mu'tazila, Hanbalis, al-Ash'ari and the Khawarij, Salafis generally believe that faith is expressed through belief in the heart, speech with the tongue and acts with the limbs. Moreover, like the majority of scholars – but unlike the Khawarij and the Murji'a – they believe faith can increase and decrease.[92]

In deciding what should be seen as unbelief, Salafis distinguish three levels of faith on which sins can take place. The first and most basic of these, *ṣiḥḥat al-dīn* (the soundness of the religion), refers to tenets of Islam that form its foundation (*aṣl*) – like the belief in the existence of God and his role as the Creator – and, as such, any disbelief in them can be seen as *kufr*. The second level of faith, *wājib al-dīn* (the compulsory of the religion), pertains to aspects of Islam whose violation is considered a major sin (*kabīra*, pl. *kabā'ir*)[93] or disobedience (*ma'ṣiya*), like eating pork or

87 Madelung, "Early Sunnī," 233. 88 *Ibid.*, 244; Watt, *Formative*, 135–6.

89 L. Gardet, "Īmān," in *Encyclopaedia of Islam New Edition*, vol. III, ed. B. Lewis, V.L. Ménage, Ch. Pellat and J. Schacht (Leiden: Brill, 1986), 1173; Meric Pessagno, "Murji'a," 386, 393–4; Wensinck, *Muslim*, 45.

90 Blankinship, "Early," 45, 47.

91 The proof texts taken from the Qur'ān and the Sunna to underpin the doctrinal position of Salafis on this issue are too numerous to list here, but an overview of them is given in 'Abdallāh al-Jarbū', "Al-Īmān al-Shar'ī wa-l-Dalālat al-Nuṣūṣ 'alayhi," *Al-Aṣāla* 6, no. 36 (15 Shawwāl 1422 [31 December 2001]): 30–4.

92 Wagemakers, "Seceders," 160–3.

93 Major sins should be distinguished from minor sins (*ṣaghā'ir*, sing. *ṣaghīra*), which are rarely discussed in this regard, probably because they are never equated with *kufr*. For more on minor sins and the difference with major sins from a Salafī perspective, see Abū 'Ubayda Mashhūr b. Ḥasan Āl Salmān, "Al-Farq bayna l-Ṣaghīra wa-l-Kabīra," *Al-Aṣāla*

drinking wine, but not unbelief in and of itself. The third level, *kamāl al-dīn* (the perfection of the religion), includes aspects of Islam that are commendable (*mustaḥabb*) and which, if violated, do not constitute a sin. For a discussion of the Salafi views on *kufr*, this level of faith is less important.[94]

Salafis generally argue that any sin at the level of *ṣiḥḥat al-dīn* is *kufr* and justifies calling the culprit an unbeliever (*kāfir*, pl. *kuffār*).[95] Such an application of *takfīr* (excommunication; calling a Muslim an unbeliever) is only justified at the level of *wājib al-dīn* as well if the person guilty of a major sin indicates that he or she (1) acted out of conviction (*iʿtiqād*), despite knowing Islam prohibits this expression or act; (2) gave himself or herself permission to do something (*istiḥlāl*) by making something that is forbidden (*ḥarām*) allowed (*ḥalāl*); or (3) expressed negation (*jaḥd* or *juḥūd*) of the message of Islam. If a sinner is "guilty" of any of these three conditions, he or she is not just a sinner (*fāsiq*), but also a *kāfir*. If, on the other hand, major sins are committed out of ignorance (*jahl*), under compulsion (*ikrāh*), by mistake (*khaṭaʾ*) or because of another legitimate excuse, they are simply seen as *kabāʾir*, not *kufr*. On the basis of these different categories, Salafis distinguish major unbelief (*kufr akbar*), which includes sins at the level of *ṣiḥḥat al-dīn* and those major sins that are supported by *iʿtiqād, istiḥlāl* or *jaḥd*, from minor unbelief (*kufr aṣghar*), which includes *kabāʾir* not supported by any conditions of conscious intent. While major unbelief is reason to pronounce *takfīr* over a Muslim, minor unbelief is not.[96]

The discussion on how *īmān* is expressed, what constitutes *kufr* and when *takfīr* is allowed becomes much more practical when applied to one of the most contentious issues within Salafism today: the excommunication of the rulers (*takfīr al-ḥukkām*) of Muslim countries for not applying

7, no. 40 (15 Dhū l-Ḥijja 1423 [17 February 2003]): 19–26; *id.*, "Al-Farq bayna l-Ṣaghīra wa-l-Kabīra – 2," *Al-Aṣāla* 8, no. 41 (15 Ṣafar 1424 [18 April 2003]): 54–60; *id.*, "Al-Farq bayna l-Ṣaghīra wa-l-Kabīra – 3," *Al-Aṣāla* 8, no. 42 (15 Rabīʿ al-Thānī 1424 [16 June 2003]): 43–53; *id.*, "Al-Farq bayna l-Ṣaghīra wa-l-Kabīra – 4," *Al-Aṣāla* 8, no. 43 (15 Jumādá l-Ākhira 1424 [14 August 2003]: 51–8; *id.*, "Al-Farq bayna l-Ṣaghīra wa-l-Kabīra – 5," *Al-Aṣāla* 8, no. 44 (15 Shawwāl 1424 [10 December 2003]): 45–9.

[94] Wagemakers, "Transformation," 97–8.

[95] There are ways in which a person "guilty" of *kufr* can be excused, such as if he or she was forcibly compelled to act or speak this way or if he or she was ignorant of the sinful nature of a particular deed or expression. Salafī scholars do not always agree as to when such excuses apply, however. For a partial discussion of this phenomenon, see *id.*, "An Inquiry into Ignorance: A Jihādī-Salafī Debate on *Jahl* as an Obstacle to *Takfīr*," in *The Transmission and Dynamics of the Textual Sources of Islam: Essays in Honour of Harald Motzki*, ed. Nicolet Boekhoff-van der Voort, Kees Versteegh and Joas Wagemakers (Leiden: Brill, 2011), 301–27.

[96] *Id.*, "Transformation," 98–9.

Islamic law (entirely). Salafis believe that not adhering to the *sharīʿa* in ruling a country is a form of *kufr* on the basis of Q. 5: 44: "Whoso judges not (*wa-man lam yaḥkum*) according to what God has sent down – they are the unbelievers (*al-kāfirūn*)." Based on Q. 9: 11 ("They [Jews and Christians] have taken their rabbis and their monks as lords (*arbāban*) apart from God [. . .]"), Salafis believe that following people or laws other than God's is like taking and worshipping these "as lords apart from God" and thus as a violation of the *tawḥīd al-ulūhiyya* mentioned above. How to judge such an act of not ruling "according to what God has sent down" – which is seen as referring to the *sharīʿa* – is something Salafis do not agree on, particularly since the Qurʾan labels people guilty of this not just "unbelievers" but also "evildoers" (*ẓālimūn*) and "the ungodly" (*fāsiqūn*) in verses 45 and 47 of the same *sūra*. Although these terms are clearly negative as well, they may be less drastic than "unbelievers".[97]

Based on the different distinctions given above, roughly four positions on the application of *takfīr* to political leaders can be distinguished. The first may be called a Murjiʾa position, which means that acts are not part of faith. Since not applying the *sharīʿa* is a supposedly sinful *act*, it does not diminish a leader's *īmān* at all and therefore no *takfīr* is applied. The second position holds that not applying (parts of) the *sharīʿa* is an act of *kufr aṣghar* and only becomes *kufr akbar* – and thus a reason for *takfīr* – if the leader in question expresses *iʿtiqād, istiḥlāl* or *jaḥd*. Scholars supporting a third position agree with the second one, but state that some leaders systematically apply a secular or "un-Islamic" system of laws through an exchange (*tabdīl*) of the *sharīʿa*. If that is the case, scholars holding the third position say that *iʿtiqād, istiḥlāl* or *jaḥd* is no longer necessary to justify *takfīr* since the systematic nature of leaders' "un-Islamic" rule is proof enough of their unbelief. While Salafis hold either the second or third positions in this debate, a fourth position might be seen as that of the Khawarij. It entails that even if not applying the *sharīʿa* is merely a major sin, this is nevertheless reason to apply excommunication, since the Khawarij believed that any *kabīra* was a justification for *takfīr*.[98] Although the first and fourth positions are perhaps somewhat theoretical given the fact that they are based on positions held by historic movements, they are nevertheless quite relevant to current intra-Salafi discussion on faith, as several publications have pointed out[99] and as we will see in later chapters.

[97] *Ibid.*, 96–7, 99–101. [98] *Id.*, *Quietist*, 64–6.
[99] Kenney, *Muslim*; Lav, *Radical*, 86–191; Wagemakers, "'Seceders'."

The Salafi *Manhaj*

The differences in Salafi views we saw above with regard to *tawḥīd, al-walāʾ wa-l-barāʾ* and *īmān/kufr* are real and meaningful to the people involved, but they are all found at the level of the Salafi *ʿaqīda* and thus merely theoretical. Salafis also translate many of these views into an applied method (*manhaj*), however, and thereby create fault lines between different categories of Salafis that give a clearer and more practical picture of how they are divided among themselves. The term *manhaj* is explained by the Saudi Salafi scholar Salih b. Fawzan al-Fawzan (b. 1935) as referring to the method of (1) reading the Qurʾan and the Sunna literally and without recourse to rationalism or speculation; (2) refraining from religious innovations in the area of worship (*ʿibāda*); and (3) engaging with society and current affairs.[100] In categorising Salafis on the basis of their *manhaj*, they are alike in the first two respects, as we saw above, but differ greatly with regard to the third, which is also why this is generally taken as the measure by which Salafis are divided.

The most common way to categorise Salafis on the basis of *manhaj* is found in a very influential article by the American political scientist Quintan Wiktorowicz, who divides Salafis into "purists", "politicos" and "jihadis".[101] Although this division has been criticised,[102] Wiktorowicz's categorisation of Salafis has been adopted – sometimes independently and sometimes in a slightly modified form – by a great number of scholars writing on Salafism.[103] Other scholars have tried to move the categorisation away from Salafism and towards various types of Islamism, since Salafism is too ideological a term that does not in itself tell us much about Salafis' involvement in politics or violence,[104] or have come up with an alternative classification altogether.[105] As I have pointed out in detail elsewhere, the former is true but not very relevant in a book dealing with Salafism, while the latter creates more problems than it tries to

[100] Ṣāliḥ b. Fawzān al-Fawzān, *Why Manhaj?* (http://turntoislam.com/community/threads/why-manhaj-methodology-by-shaykh-saalih-bin-fawzaan-al-fawzaan.25431/ (accessed 1 April 2015), n.d.).

[101] Wiktorowicz, "Anatomy," 208.

[102] Lav, *Radical*, 122; Wagemakers, "Purist," 283–5, 296; *id., Quietist*, 9–10.

[103] See Amghar, *Salafisme*, 35–70; *id.*, "Quietisten," 384–408; Bonnefoy, *Salafism*, 44; Burgat and Sbitli, "Salafis," section V; Gauvain, *Salafi*, 37–47; Haykel, "Nature," 48–9; De Koning, Wagemakers and Becker, *Salafisme*, 50–6; Peter Mandaville, *Global Political Islam* (London and New York: Routledge, 2007), 248–9; Rabil, *Salafism*, 3, 8–12, 34–50; Bernard Rougier, "Introduction," in *Qu'est-ce que le salafisme?* ed. Bernard Rougier (Paris: Presses Universitaires de France, 2008), 15–18; Wagemakers, "Purist,"; *id., Quietist*.

[104] Hegghammer, "Jihadi-Salafis," 248–57.

[105] Pall, *Lebanese*, 22–8; *id.*, "Salafism," 34–43.

solve.[106] The following categorisation of Salafis therefore not only builds on but also corrects and provides more detail to Wiktorowicz's division of Salafis.[107]

Quietist Salafis

Probably the biggest branch within Salafism consists of the people I call quietist Salafis. I refer to them as such because their *manhaj* with regard to society is characterised by political quietism. They stay away from politics and instead focus on studying Islam, educating others in it through the prism of Salafism and propagating this message to others (*da'wa*) as their *manhaj* of contributing to society. This group includes the most prominent Salafi *'ulamā'* of the twentieth century, including the late Grand Mufti of Saudi Arabia Muhammad b. Ibrahim Al al-Shaykh (d. 1969), his successor in this position shaykh 'Abd al-'Aziz b. Baz (d. 1999), the Saudi scholar Muhammad b. Salih al-'Uthaymin (d. 2001), the Yemeni shaykh Muqbil b. Hadi al-Wadi'i (d. 2001) and the aforementioned late Syrian-Jordanian *'ālim* Muhammad Nasir al-Din al-Albani. Among major scholars of the twenty-first century, Saudi shaykhs such as the aforementioned Salih b. Fawzan al-Fawzan and Rabi' b. Hadi al-Madkhali (b. 1931) are perhaps the most prominent.[108]

The idea that quietist Salafis are "apolitical" is the defining feature in my definition of them and therefore merits some extra attention. Given the close ties with the rulers that such quietists may have, particularly in Saudi Arabia, and the discreet advice (*naṣīḥa*) that they sometimes give to the *walī al-amr* (ruler), one could argue – as Meijer has done – that they are playing politics in a covert yet powerful way. This suggests that they are political after all.[109] Moreover, one could argue that avoiding party politics, parliament and elections is also inherently political since it implicitly supports the political status quo. Furthermore, Mandaville argues that politics encompasses much more than just elections and

[106] Joas Wagemakers, "Revisiting Wiktorowicz: Categorising and Defining the Branches of Salafism," in *Salafism after the Arab Awakening: Contending with People's Power*, ed. Francesco Cavatorta and Fabio Merone (London: Hurst & Co., 2016).

[107] See *ibid.* for a comprehensive and much more detailed critique of Wiktorowicz's categorisation and the alternatives that have been proposed. See also *id.*, "Salafistische," 55–79.

[108] For more information on the Saudi scholars mentioned, see Mouline, *Clercs*; Al-Rasheed, *Contesting*. For more on Muqbil b. Hadi al-Wadi'i, see Haykel, "Salafis." More information on al-Albānī can be found in Olidort, "Politics," 15–19 and will also be given in Chapter 3.

[109] Roel Meijer, "Introduction," in *Global Salafism: Islam's New Religious Movement*, ed. Roel Meijer (London: Hurst & Co., 2009), 17–24, esp. 17.

parliaments and also includes claims of identity and ethics.[110] Finally, Olidort – in a critique of my description of quietists as not engaged in politics – points out that quietist Salafis actually do engage in politics in their books and articles by writing about contentious political subjects such as the Palestinian–Israeli conflict and the civil war in Syria.[111]

All of these points make sense. For the purpose of this book, however, my delineation of politics is more restricted than Meijer's and more practical than Mandaville's. As such, I define quietist Salafis as those Salafis who focus on the study, education and propagation of their views and stay away from politics in the sense that they do not engage in contentious political action through demonstrations, party politics, parliamentary opposition, political mobilisation or policy discussions. In that sense, quietist Salafis are apolitical. Olidort's contention that I suggest quietists avoid political discussion, finally, is based on a misunderstanding of my work. I never stated or suggested that quietists avoid political subjects in their writings. Rather, I meant that they avoid political *action* and only write about political issues such as the Palestinian question and the war in Syria as *religious* issues pertaining to things like piety and doctrine, not political interests and the like.[112]

The political quietism of quietist Salafis does not mean that they believe political action is wrong in principle, but simply that the rule of a country should be left to the rulers for now and that society should first be prepared for the establishment of an Islamic state through education and *daʿwa* because it is not ready for that yet. This reasoning could be seen as a pragmatic way of legitimising one's own lack of involvement in politics, particularly because one can basically use it to defer political action indefinitely, arguing that truly Islamic politics requires a truly Islamic society that has not materialised yet. Still, as the next chapter makes clear, there is a real ideological conviction behind quietists' a-political views, at least in Jordan, and they frequently label political groups such as the Muslim Brotherhood "*ḥizbī*" (partisan) for their organisational allegiance. A similar reasoning applies to quietists' views on jihad. The fact that they are not Jihadi-Salafis does not mean that they are against jihad. In fact, quietist Salafis see jihad – in the sense of a military struggle bound by the rules of Islam and waged against non-Muslim invaders of the abode of Islam (*dār al-Islām*) – as an integral part

110 Peter Mandaville, *Transnational Muslim Politics: Reimagining the Umma* (London and New York: Routledge, 2004 [2001]), 8–14.
111 Olidort, "Politics," 4–5.
112 Olidort himself seems to realise this as well, in fact. See *ibid.*, 16–17, 21–2, 23 (footnote 71).

of their religion and distinguish it clearly from the terrorism they associate with groups such as al-Qaʿida, which they reject.[113]

Quietist Salafism, however, is not a homogeneous trend, but can be split up into various sub-trends with respect to their exact positions towards the rulers of their countries. As I have pointed out in greater detail elsewhere,[114] I firstly distinguish "aloofists", a sub-trend of quietist Salafism whose adherents want to remain aloof of political action altogether because they believe society is not ready for it yet, because it necessarily entails compromises that sully the "purity" of their religion or because politics is fickle, while Islam is steady and eternal.[115] As a result, they not only remain aloof of political action altogether, but also maintain a certain independence of and distance from the rulers. This trend of aloofists is primarily associated with the Syrian-Jordanian scholar Muhammad Nasir al-Din al-Albani.

A second sub-trend within quietist Salafism is that of the "loyalists", by which I mean those quietists who share the aloofists' rejection of political action, but can – and often are – called upon to show their loyalty to their regime by justifying the latter's policies through fatwas. As such, they are much closer to their rulers than aloofists and also support them more explicitly. In Saudi Arabia, many loyalists are simply state employees working in one of the country's many religious organisations. This sub-trend includes major *ʿulamāʾ* like ʿAbd al-ʿAziz b. Baz and Muhammad b. Salih al-ʿUthaymin.

A third sub-trend that is related to the second one may be called "propagandists". Like the loyalists, they are on good terms with their regimes – particularly Saudi Arabia – but take this loyalty a step further by actively propagating the legitimacy of the Saudi state and – more importantly – fiercely denouncing the more politicised (Salafi) critics of the regime. These quietist Salafis are sometimes referred to as "Jamis" or, especially, "Madkhalis"[116] because of their ties to Saudi shaykhs Muhammad b. Aman al-Jami (d. 1996) and particularly the aforementioned Rabiʿ b. Hadi al-Madkhali.[117]

113 Bonnefoy, *Salafism*, 91–101; Gauvain, *Salafi*, 12; Rabil, *Salafism*, 243–4; Behnam T. Said, "Salafismus und politische Gewalt under deutscher Perspektive," in *Salafismus: Auf der Suche nach dem wahren Islam*, ed. Behnam T. Said and Hazim Fouad (Freiburg: Herder, 2014), 207–21.

114 Wagemakers, "Revisiting"; *id.*, "Salafistische," 57–60.

115 See also *id.*, *Quietist*, 76.

116 A website actively refuting these propagandists ("the Madkhalis") is http://madkhalis.com/ (accessed 3 April 2015), not to be confused with a website defending the same group, which can be found at www.themadkhalis.com/md/ (accessed 3 April 2015).

117 For more on the strongly polemical and propagandist nature of al-Madkhalī's discourse, see Roel Meijer, "Politicising *al-Jarḥ wa-l-Taʿdīl*: Rabīʿ b. Hādī al-Madkhalī and the Transnational Battle for Religious Authority," in *The Transmission and Dynamics of the*

Apart from Saudi Arabia, important quietist Salafi groups belonging to any of these three sub-trends can be found in the form of the Ansar al-Sunna al-Muhammadiyya (Followers of the Muhammadan Sunna) in Egypt,[118] the Jam'iyyat Ihya' al-Turath al-Islami (Revival of the Islamic Heritage Association; from the second half of the 1990s) in Kuwait[119] and the Jam'iyyat Waqf al-Turath al-Islami (Endowment of Islamic Heritage Association) in Lebanon,[120] to name just a few examples. In Jordan, quietist Salafism is traditionally informally organised, by contrast, but was heavily influenced by the aloofist quietism of al-Albani. In this book, I argue that the domestication of the quietist Salafi community in Jordan entailed – among other things and for various reasons – a distinct shift from al-Albani's aloofism to a much more loyalist approach.

Political Salafis

Contrary to quietist Salafis, political Salafis – as I label them – do engage in political debate, various types of activism (demonstrations, political parties, petitions, etc.) and frequently run for parliament in elections. They share their basic ideology with other Salafis, but adhere to a *manhaj* of dealing with society that is characterised by a much stronger political commitment than that of quietists. This trend within Salafism has roots in different places. Perhaps the most prominent one is related to a phenomenon we saw earlier in this chapter, namely the flight of various prominent Muslim Brothers to Saudi Arabia from repression in Egypt and Syria in the 1960s. These Muslim Brothers did not only work in the Saudi educational system and help spread Wahhabism, but their more sophisticated political outlook also influenced a generation of students at Saudi universities, including prominent scholars such as Safar al-Hawali and Salman al-'Awda,[121] leading to a trend of politicised Salafism known as the *ṣaḥwa* (awakening). This trend gained adherents in the 1970s and 1980s, but did not burst out into the open until the Iraqi invasion of Kuwait in 1990, which culminated in the Gulf War of that year. When

Textual Sources of Islam: Essays in Honour of Harald Motzki, ed. Nicolet Boekhoff-van der Voort, Kees Versteegh and Joas Wagemakers (Leiden: Brill, 2011), 375–99, esp. 383–92.

118 Hazim Fouad, "Postrevolutionärer Pluralismus: Das salafistische Spektrum in Ägypten," in *Salafismus: Auf der Suche nach dem wahren Islam*, ed. Behnam T. Said and Hazim Fouad (Freiburg: Herder, 2014), 230–5.

119 Pall, *Kuwaiti*, 8–10; *id.*, "Salafism," 68–79.

120 *Id., Kuwaiti*, 14–15; *id., Lebanese*, 59–62; *id.*, "Salafism," 123–31. See also Rabil, *Salafism*, 93–107.

121 For more on these two men, see Mamoun Fandy, *Saudi Arabia and the Politics of Dissent* (New York: Palgrave, 1999), 61–113.

Saudi Arabia, afraid that Iraq might also invade its territory, allowed 500,000 American troops to be stationed in the kingdom to protect it, political Salafis were among the most prominent Saudis leading the protests against this decision with demonstrations, petitions and calls for political – but Islam-based – reform. This way, a clear trend of Brotherhood-influenced political Salafism emerged in Saudi Arabia that was, however, also repressed again after the Gulf War.[122]

A second source of political Salafism was the aforementioned Jamʿiyyat Ihyaʾ al-Turath al-Islami from Kuwait. Founded in 1981, it quickly became an umbrella organisation for all kinds of Salafi activities, including political action like running for parliament. The more politically active character of the Jamʿiyyat Ihyaʾ al-Turath al-Islami was mostly due to the ideology and writings of their main religious authority, the originally Egyptian Salafi scholar Abu ʿAbdallah ʿAbd al-Rahman b. ʿAbd al-Khaliq (b. 1939), who believed Islam was an all-encompassing system that should also include politics. This type of thinking became controversial after the Gulf War, however, during which both Saudi adherents to the *ṣaḥwa* and followers of Ibn ʿAbd al-Khaliq criticised the Saudi decision to allow the American soldiers into the kingdom. This resulted in Ibn ʿAbd al-Khaliq's being ousted from the Jamʿiyyat Ihyaʾ al-Turath al-Islami and the association as a whole was subsequently turned into a quietist group, which it has remained since.[123] In both its earlier, political form as well as its later, quietist form, it has been quite influential, for example in Lebanon.[124]

Based on these two political Salafi movements, as well as indigenous sources of influence, two different types of political (or, as they say in Jordan, "reformist") Salafi trends have emerged. One of these is quite politically savvy, but does not engage in party politics or running for parliament, either because it does not want to or because it is not allowed to. The Saudi *ṣaḥwa* movement is an example of this trend and so is the Jamʿiyyat al-Kitab wa-l-Sunna (the Book and Sunna Association) in Jordan, as we will see in Chapter 7. The second trend within political Salafism does engage in parliamentary work, is interested in all aspects of politics and tries to influence the rule of the country as political parties

[122] This phenomenon has been analysed in detail in *ibid.*; Stéphane Lacroix, *Les islamistes saoudiens: Une insurrection manquée* (Paris: Presses Universitaires de France, 2010); Al-Rasheed, *Contesting*; Joshua Teitelbaum, *Holier than Thou: Saudi Arabia's Islamic Opposition* (Washington, DC: Washington Institute for Near East Policy, 2000).

[123] Lahoud, *Islam*, 190–7; *id.*, "Koweït," 126–34; Pall, *Kuwaiti*, 6–8, 10–12; *id.*, *Lebanese Salafis*, 87–97; *id.*, "Salafism," 66–72.

[124] Pall, *Kuwaiti*, 12–17.

usually do.[125] As mentioned, this trend has not only existed for a long time in Kuwait, but has also come to the fore in Morocco[126] and, particularly after the "Arab Spring",[127] in Egypt.[128]

Jihadi-Salafis

The third and final branch of Salafism distinguished here is that of Jihadi-Salafism. Although the name suggests otherwise, Jihadi-Salafis are not just Salafis who believe in the legitimacy of jihad because, as mentioned, all Salafis see jihad as integral to Islam. Rather, I define Jihadi-Salafism as the branch of Salafism whose adherents believe that jihad should not just be waged against non-Muslim invaders of the *dār al-Islām* ("classical jihad"), but who believe that jihad may also be launched within the Muslim world against so-called "apostate" leaders for their alleged unwillingness to apply the *sharīʿa* in full. This revolutionary jihad was influenced by the radical Egyptian Muslim Brotherhood ideologue Sayyid Qutb (1906–1966)[129] but also has its roots in radical readings of the Salafi tradition itself.[130] As Gerges has pointed out, the idea of fighting Muslim regimes ("the near enemy") was later changed by some into a strategy of first attacking the United States and other Western countries ("the far enemy") so as to make them withdraw support from Muslim regimes, which – in turn – would then be more vulnerable to Jihadi-Salafi revolutionary jihad.[131] This third type of jihad – global jihad – was controversial within Jihadi-Salafi circles, but nevertheless became widely

[125] It should be mentioned that there are also Salafis who run for parliament but do so because they believe parliament is a new platform for their *daʿwa*. As such, they are not engaged in politics to talk about, for example, the economy, taxes and the country's defence budget, but purely see politics as a new arena in which they can spread their religious message. Such Salafis are therefore better described as quietists in a political guise. See also Pall, *Lebanese*, 26.

[126] Mohammed Masbah, "In Richtung politischer Partizipation: Die Mäßigung der marokkanischen Salafisten seit Beginn des 'Arabische Frühlungs'," in *Salafismus: Auf der Suche nach dem wahren Islam*, ed. Behnam T. Said and Hazim Fouad (Freiburg: Herder, 2014), 297–319.

[127] For a more general analysis of the rise of political Salafism after the "Arab Spring", see *The New Salafi Politics* (Washington, DC: Project on Middle East Political Science, 2012).

[128] Fouad, "Postrevolutionärer," 235–8; Jacob Høigilt and Frida Nome, "Egyptian Salafism in Revolution," *Journal of Islamic Studies* 25, no. 1 (2014): 33–54; Stéphane Lacroix, *Sheikhs and Politicians: Inside the New Egyptian Salafism* (Doha: Brookings Institution, 2012), esp. 1–6.

[129] The number of publications on Quṭb is too great to mention here. One publication dealing with his ideological influence on Egyptian radical Islam is Kepel, *Muslim*, 36–67.

[130] Wagemakers, *Quietist*, 165–74.

[131] Fawaz A. Gerges, *The Far Enemy: Why Jihad Went Global* (Cambridge: Cambridge University Press, 2005).

known through attacks such as "9/11" in the United States and the July 2005 bombings in London.

A crucial stage in the formation of such ideas was the war in Afghanistan from 1979 to 1989. When the Soviet Union invaded this Muslim state in 1979 as part of its Cold War efforts to buttress communist regimes in various countries, many Muslims from across the Arab world saw this as an opportunity to wage jihad against the "godless" Soviets. Although the Soviet invasion was in many ways a "classical jihad" and thus attracted all kinds of Muslims, not just Jihadi-Salafis, it nevertheless proved an excellent training ground for militants and a school of radical ideology where a cross-fertilisation took place between various Islamists, Salafis and other Muslims, thus aiding the emergence of Jihadi-Salafism.[132] The organisation that eventually sprang from this group of "Afghan Arabs" was al-Qaʿida,[133] initially led by the Saudi businessman Osama bin Laden and currently headed by the Egyptian physician Ayman al-Zawahiri (b. 1951).[134]

Jihadi-Salafism was not limited to the al-Qaʿida network based in Afghanistan/Pakistan, however, and local branches of the organisation emerged after 2001, with the best-known being the ones in Saudi Arabia[135] (and later Yemen[136]), North Africa,[137] Iraq[138] and – more

[132] Anwar ul-Haq Ahady, "Saudi Arabia, Iran and the Conflict in Afghanistan," in *Fundamentalism Reborn? Afghanistan and the Taliban*, ed. William Malley (New York: New York University Press), 117–19; Kepel, *Jihad*, 136–44; Bernard Rougier, "Le jihad en Afghanistan et l'emergence du salafisme-jihadisme," in *Qu'est-ce que le salafisme?* ed. Bernard Rougier (Paris: Presses Universitaires de France, 2008), 65–86; Barnett Rubin, "Arab Islamists in Afghanistan," in *Political Islam: Revolution, Radicalism, or Reform?* ed. John L. Esposito (Boulder, CO, and London: Lynne Rienner, 1997), 184–9.

[133] Jason Burke, *Al-Qaeda: The True Story of Radical Islam* (London and New York: I.B. Tauris, 2004 [2003]), 72–5; Rougier, "Jihad," 67–8.

[134] General books on the history and development of the global jihad movement that al-Qāʿida represents are Jarret M. Brachman, *Global Jihad: Theory and Practice* (London and New York: Routledge, 2009); Burke, *Al-Qaeda*; Devin R. Springer, James L. Regens and David N. Edger, *Islamic Radicalism and Global Jihad* (Washington, DC: Georgetown University Press, 2009).

[135] Thomas Hegghammer, *Jihad in Saudi Arabia: Violence and Pan-Islamism since 1979* (Cambridge: Cambridge University Press, 2010), 161–226.

[136] Gregory D. Johnsen, *The Last Refuge: Yemen, al-Qaeda, and America's War in Arabia* (New York and London: W.W. Norton & Co., 2013); Bryce Loidolt, "Managing the Global and Local: The Dual Agendas of Al Qaeda in the Arabian Peninsula," *Studies in Conflict & Terrorism* 34, no. 2 (2011): 102–23; Michael Page, Lara Challita and Alistair Harris, "Al Qaeda in the Arabian Peninsula: Framing Narratives and Prescriptions," *Terrorism and Political Violence* 23, no. 2 (2011): 150–72.

[137] Jean-Pierre Filiu, "The Local and Global Jihad of al-Qaʿida in the Islamic Maghrib," *Middle East Journal* 63, no. 2 (2009): 213–26.

[138] Mohammed M. Hafez, *Suicide Bombers in Iraq: The Strategy and Ideology of Martyrdom* (Washington, DC: United States Institute of Peace, 2007).

recently, in the form of Jabhat al-Nusra – in Syria.[139] This is not to suggest that all forms of Jihadi-Salafism are necessarily connected to al-Qaʿida. In Lebanon, for example, Jihadi-Salafism is rooted in the specific Lebanese context of sectarianism and Palestinian refugee camps.[140] More recently, the break-away from al-Qaʿida by the Islamic State in Iraq and al-Sham (ISIS), known as "the Islamic State" since it announced the founding of a caliphate on 29 June 2014, seems to represent the latest interpretation to Jihadi-Salafism that is not only more violent but also more state-focussed.[141]

All of the branches of Salafism mentioned above are present in some way in Jordan too, meaning that quietist Salafis in that country have also had to deal with them. In the following chapters, we will see how this initially aloofist quietist community of Salafis in Jordan gradually became much more loyalist and was domesticated through a very apolitical ideology (Chapter 2), its response to the influence of political Salafism from the Gulf (Chapter 3), the death of al-Albani (Chapter 4), implicit cooperation between the state and quietists (Chapter 5) and the confrontation with Jihadi-Salafis (Chapter 6) and political ones (Chapter 7). Thus, the first new topic we must turn to is the local interpretation and application of the general Salafi ideology in Jordan by the kingdom's quietist community.

[139] International Crisis Group (ICG), *Tentative Jihad: Syria's Fundamentalist Opposition*, Middle East Report no. 131 (Damascus and Brussels, 2012), 10–14. For more on other Jihādī-Salafī groups operating in Syria, see Aron Lund, *Syria's Salafi Insurgents: The Rise of the Syrian Islamic Front*, UI Occasional Papers no. 17 (www.ui.se/eng/upl/files/86861.pdf, March 2013 (accessed 28 October 2014)); Jeffrey White, Andrew J. Stabler and Aaron Y. Zelin, *Syria's Military Opposition: How Effective, United or Extremist?*, WINEP Policy Focus 128 (www.washingtoninstitute.org/policy-analysis/view/syrias-military-opposition-how-effective-united-or-extremist, September 2013 (accessed 31 October 2014)).

[140] Simon Haddad, "Fath al-Islam in Lebanon: Anatomy of a Terrorist Organization," *Studies in Conflict & Terrorism* 33, no. 6 (2010): 548–69; Rabil, *Salafism*, 132–52; Bernard Rougier, *Everyday Jihad: The Rise of Militant Islamism among Palestinians in Lebanon* (translation Pascale Ghazaleh) (Cambridge, MA, and London: Harvard University Press, 2007 [2004]); *id.*, "Fatah al-Islam: Un réseau jihadiste au coeur des contradictions libanaises," *Qu'est-ce que le salafisme?* ed. Bernard Rougier (Paris: Presses Universitaires de France, 2008), 179–210; Bilal Y. Saab and Magnus Ranstorp, "Securing Lebanon from the Threat of Salafist Jihadism," *Studies in Conflict & Terrorism* 30, no. 10 (2007): 825–55.

[141] Aymenn Jawad al-Tamimi, "The Dawn of the Islamic State of Iraq and ash-Sham," in *Current Trends in Islamist Ideology*, vol. XVI, ed. Hillel Fradkin, Hussain Haqqani, Eric Brown and Hassan Mneimeh (Washington, DC: Hudson Institute, 2014), 5–8; *id.*, "The Islamic State of Iraq and al-Sham," *Middle East Review of International Affairs* 17, no. 3 (2013): 19–23; Aaron Y. Zelin, *The War between ISIS and al-Qaeda for Supremacy of the Global Jihadist Movement*, WINEP Research Notes no. 20 (www.washingtoninstitute.org/policy-analysis/view/the-war-between-isis-and-al-qaeda-for-supremacy-of-the-global-jihadist, June 2014 (accessed 11 July 2014)), 2–6.

2 Quietist Salafi Ideology in Jordan

In the first chapter, we saw that global Salafi ideology consists of a coherent yet controversial and – even among Salafis – contested set of ideas. This is particularly the case with regard to the creedal issue of *īmān* and *kufr* and the questions about *takfīr* that this leads to, as well as the methodological issue of how to deal with society and politics. Such contestations of the Salafi *ʿaqīda* and *manhaj* sometimes run parallel to the categories of quietist, political and Jihadi-Salafis that I distinguished earlier, but not always. This chapter delves into the details of quietist ideology adhered to by Salafis in Jordan and shows that some creedal issues are heavily contested among this local community too.

In what follows, I will first deal with Jordanian Salafi views of the central concepts encompassed by the Salafi ideology we saw in Chapter 1, as well as broader ideas based on their *ʿaqīda*. Then I will move on to the highly controversial issue of faith, unbelief and excommunication among Jordanian Salafis, which has long been the most contested creedal issue within the community. Finally, I will deal with the quietists' *manhaj* by analysing their views on politics. This chapter shows that the way Jordanian quietists strive for their utopia of the *salaf* is a decidedly apolitical one, thus providing an ideological basis for the domestication of their community.

General Quietist Salafi Ideology in Jordan

The quietist Salafi community in Jordan is part of a global Salafi trend that strives to emulate the utopia of the *salaf*. Since this utopia is embodied in texts whose literal words do not differ from country to country, one might expect Salafism to be the same everywhere. In many respects, this is indeed the case. In some, however, it is not. Although this chapter is not meant to compare Salafism in Jordan with similar trends elsewhere, it is nevertheless important to look at precisely what Salafis in Jordan believe, rather than assuming that they are just the local Jordanian branch of a global trend.

To Be or Not to Be a Salafi

It should not come as a surprise that a movement that claims to have distilled such a coherent set of doctrines from a certain period of time – the first three generations of Islam – holds the people who embodied this era in very high esteem indeed. The quietist Salafi movement in Jordan is no different in this respect,[1] although it does add an interesting dimension to the concept of *al-salaf al-ṣāliḥ*. According to Salafis in Jordan, the companions of the Prophet were "the best people" referred to in the *ḥadīth* mentioned in the previous chapter and "one cannot imagine an idea, understanding or method that is sounder (*aṣaḥḥ*) and more correct (*aqwam*) than the understanding of the pious predecessors and their method".[2] They are, in fact, "the embellishment of this community (*zīnat hadhihi l-umma*) with regard to understanding, knowledge and work"[3] and, as one Jordanian Salafi claims, plenty of evidence for this can be found in the sources of Islam.[4] According to al-Albani, the reason for divisions within Islam lies in "not returning to the understandings, ideas and views of our pious predecessors"[5] and it is therefore that one should refer to oneself as "Salafi", since understandings of Islam not directly derived from the *salaf* are inevitably flawed.[6] Interestingly, two leading Jordanian quietist scholars – Muhammad Musa Nasr and Basim b. Faysal al-Jawabira – have stated that, although they distinguish between the first three "best generations" (*qurūn al-khayr*) of Islam and later scholars who followed them, even the latter may be seen as part of the *salaf*. Muhammad Musa Nasr even went so far as to say that if he lived meticulously according to the example of the first three generations, he could become part of the *salaf* himself, thereby acting as an example worthy of emulation to others.[7]

1 Abū Rummān and Abū Haniyya, *Al-Salafiyya al-Muḥāfaẓa*, 18–20.
2 Salīm al-Hilālī, "Limādha l-Manhaj al-Salafī," *Al-Aṣāla* 1, no. 1 (15 Rabīʿ al-Thānī 1413 [13 October 1992]): 17–18.
3 *Ibid.*, 23.
4 Yūsuf b. Aḥmad Āl ʿAlāwī, *Al-Ṣaḥāba Jīl al-Qudwa* (n.p.: no publisher, 2013), 14–25.
5 Al-Albānī, *Al-Salafiyya*, 35.
6 *Id.*, "Masāʾil wa-Ajwibatuhā: Al-Masāʾil al-Lubnāniyya (2)," *Al-Aṣāla* 2, no. 9 (15 Shaʿbān 1414 [28 January 1994]): 86–9.
7 Interviews with Muḥammad b. Mūsá Āl Naṣr, Amman, 20 June 2012; Bāsim b. Fayṣal al-Jawābira, Amman, 26 June 2012. In an informal conversation with a Salafī in the northern Jordanian town of al-Ṭayba on 23 June 2014, I was also told that Salafīs, provided they live meticulously according to the example of the *salaf*, can become *salaf* themselves, even with reference to Q. 9: 100. This verse states that "And the Outstrippers, the first of the Emigrants and the Helpers (*wa-sābiqūn al-awwalūn min al-muhājirīn wa-l-anṣār*), and those who followed them in good-doing (*wa-lladhīna ittabaʿūhum bi-iḥsān*) – God will be well-pleased with them [...]".

This stretching of the term "*salaf*" to include scholars clearly not part of the first three generations of Islam does not mean that Jordanian Salafis have views about the term "Salafism" that differ from what we saw earlier. In the words of one Salafi shaykh, "Salafism" is simply Islam "on the basis of the Book and the Sunna according to the understanding of the pious predecessors".[8] More specifically, Salafism entails "the *manhaj* of the *salaf*, which is the method of the group (*al-jamāʿa*) that is rightly-guided (*al-rāshida*) in its faith" and includes "the unity of God", "commanding right and forbidding wrong (*al-amr bi-l-maʿrūf wa-l-nahy ʿan al-munkar*)",[9] the "application of the texts of Islam" and "knowledge" (*ʿilm*).[10] According to an article in the Jordanian quietist Salafi journal *Al-Asala*, "following the way of the believers – the companions [of the Prophet], may God be pleased with them – is an Islamic legal duty (*wājib sharʿī*)" and anyone who adheres to this rule but refuses to call himself a Salafi "has turned himself into fool (*fa-qad safiha nafsuhu*)".[11]

The categorisation of Salafism I have given above – quietist, political and Jihadi-Salafis – is not one that Jordanian quietists agree with, however. In fact, the different branches of Salafism in Jordan all claim that they represent "true" Salafism and the quietists are no exception in this respect. Under the title "Salafism is One", an article in *Al-Asala* states that

> some scum (*baʿḍa l-raʿāʿ*) from among the people of ignorance (*al-jahl*) and innovation (*al-ibtidāʿ*) [claim that] Salafism has [different] types!! They have said: traditional Salafism (*al-Salafiyya al-taqlīdiyya*),[12] Jihadi-Salafism, renewing Salafism (*al-Salafiyya al-tajdīdiyya*), official Salafism (*al-Salafiyya al-rasmiyya*), legitimate Salafism (*al-Salafiyya al-sharʿiyya*) and reformist Salafism (*al-Salafiyya al-iṣlāḥiyya*). [...] In this, they – all of them – are beside the truth.[13]

8 Interview with Aḥmad Muṣliḥ, Amman, 29 January 2013.

9 For more on this specific duty in the history of Islam, see Michael Cook, *Commanding Right and Forbidding Wrong* (Cambridge: Cambridge University Press, 2001). Jordanian quietist Salafī publications on this topic include ʿAlī b. Ḥasan b. ʿAlī b. ʿAbd al-Ḥamīd al-Ḥalabī al-Atharī, ed., *Ḍawābiṭ al-Amr bi-l-Maʿrūf wa-l-Nahy ʿan al-Munkar ʿinda Shaykh al-Islām Ibn Taymiyya* (n.p.: Al-Aṣāla, 1994); Muḥammad Ibrāhīm Shaqra, "Ḍawābiṭ al-Amr bi-l-Maʿrūf wa-l-Nahy ʿan al-Munkar Tadhkīran li-l-Khāṣṣa wa-Bayānan li-l-ʿĀmma," *Al-Aṣāla* 3, nos. 15–16 (15 Dhū l-Qaʿda 1415 [15 April 1995]): 36–44; ʿUthmān Muʿallim al-Ṣūmālī, "Baʿḍ al-Ḍawābiṭ fī Fiqh al-Amr bi-l-Maʿrūf wa-l-Nahy ʿan al-Munkar," *Al-Aṣāla* 4, no. 22 (15 Jumādá l-Ākhira 1420 [26 September 1999]): 60–6.

10 Aḥmad Salām, "Hal Naḥnu Qawm Salafiyyūn (1)?" *Al-Aṣāla* 3, nos. 13–14 (15 Rajab 1415 [18 December 1994]): 117–20.

11 "Al-Salafiyya Ẓāhira – bi-Idhn Allāh," *Al-Aṣāla* 7, no. 38 (15 Rabīʿ al-Awwal 1423 [27 May 2002]): 5–6.

12 This is the Arabic term often applied in Jordan to the phenomenon I refer to as "quietist Salafism".

13 "Al-Salafiyya. Wāḥida," *Al-Aṣāla* 6, no. 31 (15 Muḥarram 1422 [9 April 2001]): 5.

As an alternative, quietist Salafis dismiss the different labels applied to Salafism as "media terms" or "names not found among the scholars". They reject other types of Salafism as "not true Salafism" or as political movements in a Salafi guise. Jordanian quietists claim that they – and not other types of supposed Salafis – really adhere to the *manhaj* of the pious predecessors through their focus on knowledge and insistence on *da'wa*.[14]

Quietist criticism of the term "Jihadi-Salafism" is often followed by the assertion that quietists are not against jihad as such. They do, however, believe that it should conform to the rules of Islam,[15] including being ordered by the *walī al-amr*,[16] and cannot be equated with violence or terrorism.[17] This attitude of being in favour of jihad in principle, but limiting its application to what quietists see as its "proper" use as embodied by the *salaf*, is illustrated by quietist publications in Jordan. Although some stress that jihad is "not limited to fighting with weapons because calling to God (*al-da'wa ilá llāh*)" is "the greatest and most beneficial

[14] *Liqā' Ṣaḥafī ma'a Mawqi' (… Awar Jū …) ma'a Shaykhinā 'Alī b. Ḥasan al-Ḥalabī – Ḥafiẓahu llāh* (www.alhalaby.com/play.php?catsmktba=3181, 5 July 2012 (accessed 1 April 2013)); *Liqā' al-Shaykh 'Alī al-Ḥalabī fī Ṣaḥīfat al-Sūsina* (www.alhalaby.com/play.php?catsmktba=3172, 3 July 2012 (accessed 1 April 2013)); interviews with Salīm al-Hilālī, Amman, 28 January 2013; 'Abd al-Mālik Besfort Maxhuni, al-Zarqā', 18 January 2014. Some Salafis, however, reject this claiming of the mantle of Salafism altogether. Interview with Amīn al-Tubāsī, al-Ḥuṣn, 22 January 2014.

[15] Books describing the rules of jihad include Muhammad Hamidullah, *The Muslim Conduct of State* (Lahore: Sh. Muhammad Ashraf, 1996); Majid Khadduri, *The Islamic Law of Nations: Shaybānī's Siyar* (Baltimore: The Johns Hopkins Press, 1966); *id.*, *War and Peace in the Law of Islam* (Baltimore: The Johns Hopkins Press, 1955); Rudolph Peters, *Jihad in Classical and Modern Islam* (Princeton: Markus Wiener Publishers, 1996); Isam Kamel Salem, *Islam und Völkerrecht: Das Völkerrecht in der islamischen Weltanschauung* (Berlin: EXpress Edition, 1984). For more on the history and development of jihad, see Michael Bonner, *Jihad in Islamic History* (Princeton and Oxford: Princeton University Press, 2006); Richard Bonney, *Jihād: From Qur'ān to bin Laden* (New York: Palgrave, 2004); David Cook, *Understanding Jihad* (Berkeley and Los Angeles: University of California Press, 2005); Reuven Firestone, *Jihad: The Origin of Holy War in Islam* (Oxford: Oxford University Press, 1999); Alfred Morabia, *Le Gihad dans l'Islam medieval: Le "combat sacré" des origins au XIIe siècle* (Paris: Albin Michel, 1993).

[16] Other conditions include having the capacity to wage jihad. This may seem obvious, but one of the points quietists criticise radical Muslims for is their alleged willingness to engage in fights that they are not capable of waging in the first place. For more on these conditions, see 'Uthmān b. Mu'allim al-Ṣūmālī, "Shurūṭ al-Jihād fī Sabīl Allāh," *Al-Aṣāla* 6, no. 31 (15 Muḥarram 1422 [9 April 2001]): 62–8.

[17] *Liqā' Ṣaḥafī*. More detailed treatments by quietist Salafis of the legitimacy of jihad that adheres to the *sharī'a* – as opposed to terrorism – see Abū 'Abdallāh 'Umar b. 'Abd al-Ḥamīd al-Buṭūsh, *Kashf al-Astār 'ammā fī Tanẓīm al-Qā'ida min Afkār wa-Akhṭār* (Amman: Al-Dār al-Athariyya, 2009); 'Alī b. Ḥasan b. 'Alī b. 'Abd al-Ḥamīd al-Ḥalabī al-Atharī, *Ijābat al-Sā'il 'an Ḥukm Asliḥat al-Dammār al-Shāmil* (Amman: Al-Dār al-Athariyya, 2009), esp. 5–12; Yūsuf Sulaymān, "Kalima ḥawla l-Jihād," *Al-Aṣāla* 3, no. 17 (15 Dhū l-Ḥijja 1416 [4 April 1996]): 96–8.

form of jihad at this time",[18] jihad as such – for example in the life of the Prophet[19] – is praised and a "martyr" killed while waging jihad in Bosnia in the 1990s is even eulogised.[20] On the other hand, quietist Salafis publishing in Jordan make abundantly clear that revolts against Muslim rulers should not be seen as jihad[21] – as Jihadi-Salafis claim – and that suicide bombings as used by groups like al-Qaʿida are not legitimate.[22]

Thus, quietist Salafis in Jordan may have more specific ideas on how to define and categorise the *salaf* and Salafis, but they do not really differ from the global Salafi ideology we saw in Chapter 1. The same applies to Salafism's other basic characteristics. The general Salafi emphasis placed on *ḥadīth*s was certainly shared by al-Albani,[23] as was the rejection of *madhāhib*[24] and scepticism of extra-textual sources of Islamic law.[25] It must be said, however, that al-Albani went further in these than Salafis like Muhammad b. ʿAbd al-Wahhab, who al-Albani considered a great reformer and scholar,

[18] Abū l-Ḥasan al-Maʾribī, "Rafʿ al-Ḥijāb ʿan al-Farq bayna Daʿwat Ahl al-Sunna wa-Daʿwat Ahl al-Bidaʿ wa-l-Aḥzāb," *Al-Aṣāla* 5, no. 27 (15 Rabīʿ al-Ākhir 1421 [18 July 2000]): 58.

[19] Muḥammad Khalīl Hirās, "Jihād al-Rasūl – Ṣallá llāh ʿalayhi wa-Sallam – fī Sabīl al-Tawḥīd," *Al-Aṣāla* 10, no. 50 (15 Ramaḍān 1426 [18 October 2005]): 15–18.

[20] Umm Muḥammad al-Fātiḥ, "Ilá Mawākib al-Ṣādiqīn 1," *Al-Aṣāla* 2, no. 7 (15 Rabīʿ al-Thānī 1414 [2 October 1993]): 40–8; *id.*, "Ilá Mawākib al-Ṣādiqīn 2," *Al-Aṣāla* 2, no. 8 (15 Jumādá l-Ākhira 1414 [30 November 1993]): 63–9.

[21] ʿUthmān Muʿallim Maḥmūd al-Ṣūmālī, "Al-Farq bayna l-Jihād fī Sabīl Allāh wa-l-Khurūj ʿalá l-Ḥukkām," *Al-Aṣāla* 4, no. 21 (15 Rabīʿ al-Ākhir 1420 [29 July 1999]): 43–50.

[22] Abū ʿUbayda Mashhūr b. Ḥasan Āl Salmān, "Al-ʿAmaliyyāt al-Fidāʾiyya: A-Hiya Intiḥāriyya?! Am Istishhādiyya?! Al-Ḥalqa al-Ūlá," *Al-Aṣāla* 6, no. 36 (15 Shawwāl 1422 [31 December 2001]): 35–45; *id.*, "Al-ʿAmaliyyāt al-Fidāʾiyya: A-Hiya Intiḥāriyya?! Am Istishhādiyya?! Al-Ḥalqa al-Thāniya," *Al-Aṣāla* 7, no. 37 (15 Ṣafar 1423 [28 April 2002]): 41–7; *id.*, "Al-ʿAmaliyyāt al-Fidāʾiyya: A-Hiya Intiḥāriyya?! Am Istishhādiyya?! Al-Ḥalqa al-Thālitha," *Al-Aṣāla* 7, no. 38 (15 Rabīʿ al-Awwal 1423 [27 May 2002]): 44–57; *id.*, "Al-ʿAmaliyyāt al-Fidāʾiyya: A-Hiya Intiḥāriyya?! Am Istishhādiyya?! Al-Ḥalqa al-Rābiʿa," *Al-Aṣāla* 7, no. 39 (15 Jumādá l-Ākhira 1423 [24 August 2002]): 28–41; *id.*, *Al-Salafiyyūn wa-Qaḍiyyat Filasṭīn fī Wāqiʿinā l-Muʿāṣir* (Nicosia: Markaz Bayt al-Maqdis li-l-Dirāsāt al-Tawthīqiyya, 2006 [2002]), 37–79. These works were primarily written to answer the question of whether suicide bombings are suicide. Shaykh Mashhūr states – citing al-Albānī – that they are not, but can only be done on the orders of "the leader of the army" (*qāʾid al-jaysh*), not individually. See *ibid.*, 63.

[23] Iyād Muḥammad al-Shāmī, *Ārāʾ al-Imām al-Albānī al-Tarbawiyya* (Amman: Al-Dār al-Athariyya, 2009), 53–6; Muḥammad Nāṣir al-Dīn al-Albānī, *Manzalat al-Sunna fī l-Islām wa-Bayān annahu Lā Yustaghná ʿanhā bi-l-Qurʾān* (Al-Ṣafāt: Al-Dār al-Salafiyya, 1984). For an analysis of the role *ḥadīth*s played in al-Albānī's Salafism, see Brown, *Canonization*, 325–31; Hamdeh, "Emergence," 171–226.

[24] Al-Albānī, *Al-Salafiyya*, 14–16, 93–107; Hamdeh, "Emergence," 95–170.

[25] Shaʿbān, *Al-Shaykh*, 125–31.

but who he did not see as having completely detached himself from the Hanbali *madhhab*.[26]

Given the critical attitude that Salafism has towards other trends within (Sunni) Islam, particularly through its rejection of parts of the orthodox Islamic legal and theological tradition, it is not surprising that other Muslims object to some of the tenets of Salafism. Of particular importance in this respect is the largely Syrian-led effort to delegitimise Salafism on legal and doctrinal grounds, especially in the work of the Syrian scholar Muhammad Saʿid Ramadan al-Buti (1929–2013).[27] Pierret even speaks of an "anti-Salafi international" consisting of a network of like-minded orthodox Muslim scholars in the Middle East, South Asia and the West.[28] Al-Buti and other such *ʿulamāʾ* have engaged in fierce debates with al-Albani, particularly about the latter's rejection of the *madhāhib*[29] and the works of Salafism's critics – including especially al-Buti's – have also been refuted in Jordanian quietist publications.[30]

However, criticism of Salafism in Jordan has not just been a foreign issue. Not only are there ties between the "anti-Salafi international" and the Jordanian Royal Aal al-Bayt Institute for Islamic Thought,[31] at which al-Buti was a Senior Fellow,[32] but scholars within Jordan itself have also criticised al-Albani for his dismissal of Islamic legal schools and his allegedly faulty authentification process of *ḥadīths*.[33] One Jordanian critic of Salafism, Ibrahim al-ʿAsʿas, particularly deserves to be mentioned

[26] Hamdeh, "Emergence," 45–6; Aḥmad Ṣāliḥ Ḥusayn al-Jabbūrī, *Juhūd al-Imām al-Albānī Nāṣir al-Sunna wa-l-Dīn fī Bayān ʿAqīdat al-Salaf al-Ṣāliḥīn fī l-Īmān bi-llāh Rabb al-ʿĀlamīn* (Amman: Al-Dār al-Athariyya, 2008), 12–17; Shaʿbān, *Al-Shaykh*, 717–23.

[27] See, for example, al-Būṭī, *Al-Salafiyya*.

[28] Thomas Pierret, *Religion and State in Syria: The Sunni Ulama from Coup to Revolution* (Cambridge: Cambridge University Press, 2013), 126.

[29] Hamdeh, "Emergence," 95–170, esp. 97–127.

[30] ʿAlī b. Ḥasan [al-Ḥalabī], "Hadhihi l-Daʿwa.. Man la-hā?!" *Al-Aṣāla* 2, no. 11 (15 Dhū l-Ḥijja 1414 [26 May 1994]): 32–4; Muḥammad Farīz Manfikhī, "Waqfāt maʿa Kitāb Al-Salafiyya Marḥala Zamaniyya Mubāraka Lā Madhhab Islāmī (li-Muḥammad Saʿīd al-Būṭī) (Al-Ḥalqa al-Ūlá)," *Al-Aṣāla* 3, nos. 13–14 (15 Rajab 1415 [18 December 1994]): 73–86; *id.*, "Waqfāt maʿa Kitāb Al-Salafiyya Marḥala Zamaniyya Mubāraka Lā Madhhab Islāmī li-Muḥammad Saʿīd al-Būṭī, Al-Ḥalqa al-Thāniya," *Al-Aṣāla* 3, nos. 15–16 (15 Dhu l-Qaʿda 1415 [15 April 1995]): 62–74; Abū ʿAbdallāh al-Shāmī, "Al-Duktūr al-Būṭī min Khilāl Kutubihi!!!" *Al-Aṣāla* 2, no. 11 (15 Dhū l-Ḥijja 1414 [26 May 1994]): 59–66; *id.*, "Al-Duktūr al-Būṭī min Khilāl Kutubihi!! (2)," *Al-Aṣāla* 2, no. 12 (15 Ṣafar 1415 [24 July 1994]): 64–70. For detailed Jordanian quietist publications critical of Ashʿarī/Māturīdī theology, see Shākir b. Tawfīq al-ʿĀrūrī, *Al-Ashʿariyya fī Mīzān al-Ashāʿira – Al-Juzʾ al-Awwal* (n.p.: no publisher, 2011); ʿAbd al-Raḥīm [b.] Ṣamāyil al-Sulmī, "Maṣādir al-Talaqqī ʿinda Ahl al-Bidaʿ," *Al-Aṣāla* 2, no. 7 (15 Rabīʿ al-Thānī 1414 [2 October 1993]): 28–35.

[31] Pierret, *Religion*, 126–7.

[32] See http://aalalbayt.org/en/news.html (accessed 9 April 2015).

[33] Brown, *Canonization*, 325.

since he used to be involved with Salafi groups himself.[34] Al-ʿAsʿas, a researcher and writer from Amman, sees Salafism as polemical and divisive and objects to the term "Salafism" – even going so far as to call its use a *bidʿa*[35] – since the alleged purity and authority that has come to be associated with it by its followers "has become a reason in the splitting of the ranks of the Muslims".[36] This criticism, which portrays Salafism as divisive and as driving Muslims apart rather than uniting Sunnis around a group of early predecessors they all hold dear, is not limited to al-ʿAsʿas but is actually heard more often in Jordan.[37]

The Salafi *ʿAqīda*

The basic elements of Salafism in Jordan are thus not really different than elsewhere, but how about the all-important Salafi creed? The core tenets of the Salafi *ʿaqīda* are, again, shared by Jordanian adherents to quietist Salafism.[38] Thus, they similarly state that one should try to be part of *al-ṭāʾifa al-manṣūra* or *al-firqa al-nājiya* and believe that Salafism represents this group.[39] Moreover, numerous Jordanian quietist publications emphasise the concept of *tawḥīd* and its various aspects[40] – as well as

[34] He refuses to refer to himself as "Salafī" and states that he never was a Salafī according to the meaning it has now. Interview with Ibrāhīm al-ʿAsʿas, Amman, 14 January 2013.

[35] Yūsuf al-Daynī, "Rimāḥ al-Ṣaḥāʾif: Al-Iḥtirāb ʿalá Tamthīl al-Salafiyya bayna l-Albāniyya wa-Khuṣūmihā," in *Rimāḥ al-Ṣaḥāʾif: Al-Salafiyya al-Albāniyya wa-Khuṣūmuhā* (Dubai: Markaz al-Misbār li-l-Dirāsāt wa-l-Buḥūth, 2010), 23–4; Marwān b. Aḥmad Shaḥāda, "Al-Salafiyya al-Albāniyya: Qirāʾa Naqdiyya," in *Rimāḥ al-Ṣaḥāʾif: Al-Salafiyya al-Albāniyya wa-Khuṣūmuhā* (Dubai: Markaz al-Misbār li-l-Dirāsāt wa-l-Buḥūth, 2010), 129.

[36] Ibrāhīm al-ʿAsʿas, *Al-Salaf wa-l-Salafiyyūn: Ruʾya min al-Dākhil* (Beirut: Dār al-Bayāriq, 1994), 30.

[37] See, for instance, Muḥammad Abū Ṣaʿīlīk, "Al-Salafiyya allatī Nurīdu," *Al-Sabīl* June 28, 2005: 11.

[38] For basic Jordanian treatments of the Salafī *ʿaqīda*, see al-Shāmī, *Ārāʾ*, 52–3; Salīm al-Hilālī, "Marāḥil Tadwīn al-ʿAqīda," *Al-Aṣāla* 1, no. 1 (15 Rabīʿ al-Thānī 1413 [13 October 1992]): 11–14.

[39] Al-Albānī, *Al-Salafiyya*, 18–19; Abū Usāma Salīm b. ʿĪd al-Hilālī, *Limādhā Ikhtartu l-Manhaj al-Salafī?* (Cairo: Dār al-Imām Aḥmad, 2008), 43–75; *id.*, "Man Hiya l-Ṭāʾifa al-Manṣūra?" *Al-Aṣāla* 1, no. 2 (15 Jumādá l-Ākhira 1413 [11 December 1992]): 30–9.

[40] Muḥammad Nāṣir al-Dīn al-Albānī, *Al-Masāʾil al-ʿIlmiyya wa-l-Fatāwá al-Sharʿiyya: Fatāwá l-Shaykh al-ʿAllāma Muḥammad Nāṣir al-Dīn al-Albānī fī l-Madīna wa-l-Imārāt*, ed. ʿAmr ʿAbd al-Munʿim Salīm (Ṭanṭā: Dār al-Ḍiyāʾ, 2006), 7–20; *id.*, *Al-Salafiyya*, 61–4, 156–70; *id.*, *Al-Tawḥīd Awwalan Yā Duʿāt al-Islām!!* (n.p.: Dār al-Hudá al-Nabawī, 1999); Ḥusayn al-ʿAwāyisha, *Limādhā l-Islām wa-l-Tawḥīd?* (http://alawaysheh.com/print.php?id=248, 16 February 2011 (accessed 2 April 2013)); ʿAlī b. Ḥasan [al-Ḥalabī], "Aqsām al-Tawḥīd," *Al-Aṣāla* 1, no. 4 (15 Shawwāl 1413 [8 April 1993]): 23–6; Muḥammad b. Ṣāliḥ al-ʿUthaymīn, "Kalimat al-Tawḥīd: Faḍluhā wa-Maʿnāhā," *Al-Aṣāla* 3, nos. 15–16 (15 Dhū l-Qaʿda 1415 [15 April 1995]): 13–16; ʿAbdallāh b. Muḥammad al-Jawnam, "Shurūṭ Lā Ilāha illā llāh," *Al-Aṣāla* 4, no. 24 (15 Shawwāl 1420 [22 January 2000]): 21–5; Muḥammad b. ʿAbd al-Raḥmān al-Khamīs, "Al-Tawḥīd

the rejection of its opposite, *shirk*[41] – as being of paramount importance and they are equally adamant that *bida'* should be fought at all levels of Islamic tradition.[42]

The seriousness with which Salafis in Jordan approach the "purity" of their *'aqīda* and the far-reaching emphasis they place on not engaging in religious innovations is not just apparent from the number of publications dedicated to these subjects, however, but is also exhibited in the lengths to which Salafis go to "cleanse" their creed. The example of combining two prayers on rainy days so that people do not have to go to mosque in such weather more than is necessary illustrates this perfectly. Apparently somewhere around the early 2000s, a dispute seems to have arisen among Jordanian quietists about whether this practice was allowed, with some Salafis who were against this accusing others favouring it of committing a major sin. As a result, Muhammad Musa Nasr wrote a booklet about this issue, stating that numerous *ḥadīth*s prove that

'inda Ahl al-Sunna wa-Aqsāmuhu," *Al-Aṣāla* 6, no. 31 (15 Muḥarram 1422 [9 April 2001]): 25–31; Muḥammad Badr Mansī, "Ahammiyyat al-Tawḥīd fī Wāqi' al-Muslimīn Jamā'āt wa-Afrādan 1," *Al-Aṣāla* 1, no. 5 (15 Dhū l-Ḥijja 1413 [6 June 1993]): 13–17; *id.*, "Ahammiyyat al-Tawḥīd fī Wāqi' al-Muslimīn Jamā'āt wa-Afrādan 2," *Al-Aṣāla* 1, no. 6 (15 Ṣafar 1414 [6 June 1993]): 17–20; 'Abd al-Mu'man Muḥammad al-Nu'mān, "Maqām al-Tawḥīd . . .," *Al-Aṣāla* 2, no. 12 (15 Ṣafar 1415 [24 July 1994]): 13–14.

41 Shākir b. Tawfīq al-'Ārūrī, "A'ẓam al-Dhunūb: al-Shirk," *Al-Aṣāla* 2, no. 7 (15 Rabī' al-Thānī 1414 [2 October 1993]): 12–15; 'Abd al-'Aẓīm b. Badawī, "Maẓāhir Shirkiyya 1," *Al-Aṣāla* 2, no. 8 (15 Jumādá l-Ākhira 1414 [30 November 1993]): 14–17; *id.*, "Maẓāhir Shirkiyya 2," *Al-Aṣāla* 2, no. 9 (15 Sha'bān 1414 [28 January 1994]): 14–16; *id.*, "Al-Taḥdhīr min al-Shirk wa-l-Ḥathth 'alá l-Tawḥīd," *Al-Aṣāla* 2, no. 11 (15 Dhū l-Ḥijja 1414 [26 May 1994]): 17–24; 'Alī b. Ḥasan [al-Ḥalabī], "Al-Shirk . . . bayna l-Qubūr . . . wa-l-Quṣūr!!" *Al-Aṣāla* 1, no. 3 (15 Sha'bān 1413 [8 February 1993]): 18–20; Muḥammad [b.] Mūsá [Āl] Naṣr, "Wa-Man Yushriku bi-llāh fa-ka'annamā Kharra min al-Samā'," *Al-Aṣāla* 1, no. 1 (15 Rabī' al-Thānī 1413 [13 October 1992]): 5–8; *id.*, "Taḥdhīr al-Birriyya min 'Ibādat al-Aṣnām al-Bashariyya," *Al-Aṣāla* 1, no. 2 (15 Jumādá l-Ākhira 1413 [11 December 1992]): 25–9.

42 Muḥammad Nāṣir al-Dīn al-Albānī, "Kull Bid'a Ḍalāla," *Al-Aṣāla* 4, no. 21 (15 Rabī' al-Ākhir 1420 [29 July 1999]): 73–7; *id.*, *Ṣalāt al-'Īdayn fī l-Muṣallá Hiya l-Sunna* (Beirut and Damascus: Al-Maktab al-Islāmī, 1986); *id.*, *Taḥdhīr al-Sājid min Ittikhādh al-Qubūr Masājid* (Beirut and Damascus: Al-Maktab al-Islāmī, 1398 [1377; 1978 [1957/1958]]); *id.*, *Al-Tawassul: Anwā'uhu wa-Aḥkāmuhu* (Beirut and Damascus: no publisher, 1397 [1395; 1977 [1975]]); Ḥusayn al-'Awāyisha, *Kalima fī l-Da'wa wa-l-Taḥdhīr min al-Bid'a* (http://alawaysheh.com/print.php?id=445, 4 October 2012 (accessed 2 April 2013)); al-Ḥalabī, *'Ilm*; Salīm al-Hilālī, "Min Bida' al-Ṣiyām wa-l-Qiyām fī Ramaḍān," *Al-Aṣāla* 1, no. 3 (15 Sha'bān 1413 [8 February 1993]): 73–4; *id.*, *Maṭla' al-Fajr fī Fiqh al-Zajr bi-l-Hajr wa-ma'ahu Bayān Manhaj al-Salaf al-Ṣāliḥ fī Mu'āmalat Ahl al-Bida' wa-l-Ahwā'* (Cairo: Dār al-Imām Aḥmad, 2005), 53–151; Abū 'Abd al-Raḥmān Hishām al-'Ārif al-Maqdisī, "Madá Khaṭūrat Ahl al-Ahwā' wa-l-Bida'," *Al-Aṣāla* 7, no. 37 (15 Ṣafar 1423 [28 April 2002]): 19–26; al-Ma'ribī, "Raf'," 55–9; Muḥammad [b.] Mūsá [Āl] Naṣr, "'Āqibat Ahl al-Bida'," *Al-Aṣāla* 5, no. 27 (15 Rabī' al-Ākhir 1421 [18 July 2000]): 17–18; *id.*, *Jarīmat al-Ghishsh: Aḥkāmuhā wa-Ṣuwarihā wa-Āthārihā l-Mudammira* (Dubai: Maktabat al-Furqān, 2008).

combining two prayers in a mosque because of rain is actually allowed.[43] The fact that a booklet was written about this issue and that a dispute arose over it in a country in which it rains very little and mosques are ubiquitous shows that this issue was mostly one of doctrinal "purity", not one of great practical relevance. To Salafis, however, the need to search for "the truth" – even if it is mostly of theoretical value – is of paramount importance.

This emphasis on religious "purity" among Jordanian Salafis can also be found in their views on *al-walāʾ wa-l-barāʾ*. As we saw in Chapter 1, this concept has roughly three different forms among Salafis today of which only two are commonly adhered to among Salafis and it is also as such that it can be found among Jordanian quietists. Sometimes, the concept is discussed in a general way,[44] but it is clear that Salafi publications from Jordan deal with the two most prominent forms of *al-walāʾ wa-l-barāʾ* distinguished earlier. With regard to "loyalty and disavowal" in the personal sphere, al-Albani emphasises that Muslims must not resemble (*yushbihu*) non-Muslims "in their worship (*fī ʿibādātihim*), their feasts or in their clothing (*al-azyāʾ*) that is specific to them", a duty that "many Muslims – regrettably – have left today".[45] Muhammad Musa Nasr sees *al-walāʾ wa-l-barāʾ* as a tool against "Westernisation" (*al-taghrīb*). The latter, he states, has led to nominal Muslims who "do not know [anything] about [their] Islam and [their] religion, except for the name". They "live the life of Westerners and unbelievers" and become "part of the West".[46]

Statements such as these are based on deeply held Salafi views on *al-walāʾ wa-l-barāʾ*, but are also rooted in the much more widely held belief that Islam in general is threatened by Western cultural influences.[47]

43 Muḥammad b. Mūsá Āl Naṣr, *Iʿmāl al-Naẓar fī l-Radd ʿalá Man Ankara l-Jamʿ fī l-Ḥaḍar bi-ʿUdhr al-Maṭar* (Amman: Al-Dār al-Athariyya, 2003). A reference to the dispute can be found in *ibid.*, 4–5.

44 ʿAlī [b.] Ḥasan [al-Ḥalabī], "'... Lā Tattakhidhū ʿAduwwī wa-ʿAduwwakum Awliyāʾ...'," *Al-Aṣāla* 1, no. 6 (15 Ṣafar 1414 [4 August 1993]): 8–9; Abū ʿUzayr ʿAbd al-Ilāh Yūsuf al-Yūbī al-Ḥasanī al-Jazāʾirī, *Masʾalat al-Īmān fī Kaffatay al-Mīzān* (Amman: Dār al-Maʾmūn, 2006), 199–203; Muḥammad ʿAbd al-Raḥmān al-Khumayyis, "Mafāhīm Khāṭiʾa ḥawla l-Awliyāʾ," *Al-Aṣāla* 2, no. 9 (15 Shaʿbān 1414 [28 January 1994]): 71–5.

45 Muhammad Nasir al-Din al-Albani, *Jilbāb al-Marʾa al-Muslima fī l-Kitāb wa-l-Sunna* (Hebron and Amman: Maktabat Dandīs, 2002), 161.

46 Abu Anas Muḥammad b. Mūsá Āl Naṣr, "Makhāṭir Taghrīb al-Mujtamaʿāt al-Muslima," *Al-Aṣāla* 10, no. 49 (15 Jumādá l-Ākhira 1426 [22 July 2005]): 29.

47 See, for instance, Quintan Wiktorowicz and Suha Taji-Farouki, "Islamic NGOs and Muslim Politics: A Case from Jordan," *Third World Quarterly* 21, no. 4 (2000): 685–6, 693, 695. The belief that Islam is "under attack" is by no means limited to Jordan. Gallup, for example, found that the idea that Islamic values are declining because of various types of Western cultural influence was widely held in the Muslim world in 2002.

The Jordanian Salafi shaykh Marwan al-Qaysi, for example, speaks of "the cultural invasion" (*al-ghazw al-thaqāfī*) that, he states, has continually been launched by Western forces on the Muslim world.[48] Similarly, Jordanian quietists regularly write about "unbelievers" or even "Crusaders" waging war on Islam[49] and portray the Palestinian–Israeli conflict as part of a much longer struggle with Jews.[50] This probably also partly explains the stress some Jordanian Salafis place on loyalty and solidarity to Muslims in various trouble spots[51] or their emphasis on the need to be loyal and committed to God at all times.[52]

Such forms of *walāʾ* touch upon the second, political form of "loyalty and disavowal". Interestingly, while many political Salafis in Saudi Arabia saw the Saudi decision to invite 500,000 American troops into the kingdom to protect it from a possible Iraqi invasion as a case of "asking unbelievers for help" and thus as a sinful form of *walāʾ* to non-Muslims, Jordanian quietist publications try to downplay the gravity of states' requests for such help. They distinguish asking non-Muslims for help to serve one's own interests but without love for the unbelievers' religion (*muwālāt*) from total loyalty to non-Muslims (*tawallī*) and state that only the latter is a form of *kufr*.[53]

See Gallup, *Poll of the Islamic World: Perceptions of Western Culture* (www.gallup.com/poll/5458/poll-islamic-world-perceptions-western-culture.aspx, 12 March 2002 (accessed 10 April 2015)).

48 Marwān al-Qaysī, "Al-Thaqāfa . . . wa-l-Ghazw al-Thaqāfī 1," *Al-Aṣāla* 2, no. 7 (15 Rabīʿ al-Thānī 1414 [2 October 1993]): 63–6; *id.*, "Al-Thaqāfa . . . wa-l-Ghazw al-Thaqāfī 2," *Al-Aṣāla* 2, no. 8 (15 Jumādá l-Ākhira 1414 [30 November 1993]): 57–62.

49 "Aḥwāl al-ʿĀlam al-Islāmī," *Al-Aṣāla* 1, no. 2 (15 Jumādá l-Ākhira 1413 [11 December 1992]): 78; "Aḥwāl al-ʿĀlam al-Islāmī," *Al-Aṣāla* 1, no. 5 (15 Dhū l-Ḥijja 1413 [6 June 1993]): 78; "Aḥwāl al-ʿĀlam al-Islāmī," *Al-Aṣāla* 3, nos. 15–16 (15 Dhū l-Qaʿda 1415 [15 April 1995]): 133; Muḥammad b. Mūsá Āl Naṣr, *Ḥarb Ṣalībiyya Jadīda Yaʿuddu la-hā Bābā l-Fātīkān* (www.almahajjah.net/Pages/3_ReportS_Pages/Arciv_Report_HrbFtekan.htm, n.d. (accessed 2 April 2013)).

50 "Lā Salām illā bi-l-Islām," *Al-Aṣāla* 2, no. 8 (15 Jumādá l-Ākhira 1414 [30 November 1993]): 5–7; "Ṣirāʿunā maʿa l-Yahūd Ṣirāʿ Wujūd Lā Ṣirāʿ Ḥudūd," *Al-Aṣāla* 5, no. 30 (15 Shawwāl 1421 [11 January 2001]): 5–6.

51 Muḥammad [b.] Mūsá [Āl] Naṣr, "Wujūb Taʿāwun al-Muslimīn ʿalá l-Birr wa-l-Taqwá," *Al-Aṣāla* 1, no. 2 (15 Jumādá l-Ākhira 1413 [11 December 1992]): 7–11; *id.*, *Wujūb Taʿāwun al-Muslimūn* [sic!] *ʿalá l-Birr wa-l-Taqwá* (http://almahajjah.net/print.php?action=printf&&id=155, 16 May 2010 (accessed 2 April 2013)).

52 "Al-Ḥubb fī llāh.. wa-.. l-walāʾ," *Al-Aṣāla* 1, no. 2 (15 Jumādá l-Ākhira 1413 [11 December 1992]): 81–2.

53 Ḥusayn al-ʿAwāyisha, *Masʾalat al-Muwālāt* (http://alawaysheh.com/print.php?id=504, 16 February 2013 (accessed 2 April 2013)); al-Buṭūsh, *Kashf*, 118–28; ʿAbd al-Muḥsin b. Nāṣir Āl ʿUbaykān, "Ḥukm Muwālāt wa-Muẓāharat al-Kuffār?" *Al-Aṣāla* 8, no. 44 (15 Shawwāl 1424 [10 December 2003]): 13–17; See also Muḥammad Nāṣir al-Dīn al-Albānī et al., "Masāʾil ʿAṣriyya fī l-Siyāsa al-Sharʿiyya," *Al-Aṣāla* 1, no. 2 (15 Jumādá l-Ākhira 1413 [11 December 1992]): 19–22; Abū l-Ḥārith ʿAlī b. Ḥasan al-Ḥalabī al-Athari, "Al-Walāʾ wa-l-Barāʾ.. wa-l-Balāʾ!" *Al-Aṣāla* 11, no. 54 (15 Dhū l-Ḥijja 1427 [6 December 2006]): 18–20; Saʿd al-Ḥaṣīn, "Fī l-Walāʾ wa-l-Barāʾ al-Sharʿī wa-l-Ḥarakī," *Al-Aṣāla* 4,

The concept of *al-walāʾ wa-l-barāʾ* is interesting with regard to Jordanian quietists because it not only shows how they differ from political Salafis, but it also allows us to see some of al-Albani's independence and aloofist quietism. As Hamdeh has shown, al-Albani did not hesitate to hold controversial ideological positions if he could find a *ḥadīth* to back it up and would often insist on his position being the only correct one.[54] This was also the case with respect to the personal dimension of *al-walāʾ wa-l-barāʾ*. In an infamous fatwa, al-Albani once stated that Palestinians who could not properly practise their religion under Israeli occupation should make the *hijra* to a Muslim society.[55] In a country – and a Salafi community – that is largely made up of Jordanians of Palestinian descent who often have very strong feelings against Israel, such a fatwa is unlikely to go down well and it was indeed criticised for its lack of political sensitivity.[56] To al-Albani, however, this was probably purely a religious matter related to *barāʾ*: disavowing unbelievers by keeping one's distance from non-Muslims. It was also as such that he was defended by others, who pointed to relevant Prophetic examples and similar rulings by earlier scholars.[57]

Al-Albani's independence of and aloofness with respect to political interests and sensibilities was also on display in a statement that was directly related to the political dimension of *al-walāʾ wa-l-barāʾ*. With regard to the Saudi decision to allow 500,000 "unbelieving" American soldiers into the country during the Gulf War, al-Albani stated that this was a case of *al-istiʿāna bi-l-kuffār*, thereby making it illegitimate. In fact, he even stated that it was a duty to wage jihad against American troops in Iraq.[58] Despite the fact that the Saudi regime had received explicit approval for its decision from the Wahhabi religious establishment – including its leader ʿAbd al-ʿAziz b. Baz,[59] who is revered by Salafis in Jordan as one of the greatest scholars of the twentieth century – al-Albani would not budge. According to his secretary, ʿIsam Hadi, Saudi scholars even came to Jordan to convince al-Albani to change his mind,

no. 20 (15 Muḥarram 1420 [1 May 1999]): 22–5, in which other distinctions between (verdicts based on) *al-walāʾ wa-l-barāʾ* are made.

[54] Hamdeh, "Emergence," 194–226. For an early example of this polemical attitude, see Muḥammad Nāṣir al-Dīn al-Albānī, *Kashf al-Niqāb ʿammā fī Kalimāt Abī Ghurra min al-Abāṭīl wa-l-Iftirāʾāt* (n.p.: no publisher, 1978 [1975]).

[55] Verskin, *Oppressed*, 151–3. [56] Wiktorowicz, *Management*, 169, note 76.

[57] Muḥammad Ibrāhīm Shaqra, "Kalimat Ḥaqq fī Futyā l-ʿAllāma Muḥammad Nāṣir al-Dīn al-Albānī ḥawla Hijrat al-Muḍṭahadīn min al-Muslimīn," *Al-Aṣāla* 2, no. 7 (15 Rabīʿ al-Thānī 1414 [2 October 1993]): 49–62; *id.*, *Mādhā Yanqimūna min al-Shaykh?!* (n.p.: no publisher, n.d.).

[58] Abū Rummān and Abū Haniyya, *Al-Salafiyya al-Muḥāfaẓa*, 47.

[59] Mordechai Abir, *Saudi Arabia: Government, Society and the Gulf Crisis* (London and New York: Routledge, 1993), 178.

but the latter refused and insisted that the Iraqi army – despite Saddam Husayn's bad intentions and secular outlook – consisted of Muslims, while the American military was made up of Jews and Christians.[60]

Minorities and Women

Given Jordanian Salafis' emphasis on the "purity" of their creed and the necessity to remain loyal to Muslims and disavow others, it is not surprising that they often treat religious minorities and particularly their beliefs with what one might summarise as non-violent scepticism. This applies, first of all, to other religions. The idea of, for example, inter-religious dialogue is often seen as a potential source of sullying the "purity" of Islam and it is therefore vehemently rejected by various Jordanian quietist Salafis and their publications.[61] One scholar states that people who call for "the unity of religions (*waḥdat al-adyān*), religious tolerance (*al-tasāmuḥ al-dīnī*) and human brotherhood (*al-ikhwa al-insāniyya*)" "want that to uproot the root of Islam (*ijtithāth aṣl al-Islām*) and to obliterate the truth of God's religion (*maḥw ḥaqīqat dīn Allāh*) from [Muslims'] souls".[62] Serious enquiries by Jordanian Salafis into actual other religions, such as Judaism or Christianity, show the same attitude. They are either looked at through the prism of Islam[63] or dealt with in a polemical way, for example by focussing on controversial issues such as the role of *tawḥīd* in Christianity (as opposed to the allegedly polytheistic idea of a holy trinity)[64] or the supposed role of the Prophet Muhammad in the Bible.[65]

Although other religions such as Judaism and Christianity are presumably further removed from Salafism than different branches within Islam

[60] Interview with ʿIṣām Hādī, Amman, 19 January 2013.

[61] ʿAlī b. Ḥasan al-Ḥalabī al-Atharī, *Al-Iʿlān bi-Barāʾat Ahl al-Sunna wa-l-Īmān min Daʿwá "Waḥdat al-Adyān"* (www.alhalaby.com/play.php?catsmktba=2242, 2 August 2010 (accessed 2 April 2013)); Saʿd al-Ḥaṣīn, "Al-Taqrīb bayna Ahl al-Firaq wa-l-Adyān am Radduhum Jamīʿan ilá l-Waḥyayn?" *Al-Aṣāla* 9, no. 47 (15 Dhū l-Qaʿda 1425 [27 December 2004]): 50–4; Al-Lajna al-Dāʾima li-l-Buḥūth wa-l-Iftāʾ, "Waḥdat al-Adyān aw al-Taqrīb baynahā," *Al-Aṣāla* 4, no. 18 (15 Muḥarram 1418 [23 May 1997]): 22–8; Salmān al-ʿUmarī, *Ḥiwār Jarīdat* Al-Jazīra *maʿa l-Shaykh Yūsuf al-Barqāwī* (www.al-sunna.net/articles/file.php?id=3213, 23 Dhū l-Ḥijja [10 April 1999] (accessed 21 February 2013)).

[62] ʿAlī b. Ḥasan al-Ḥalabī, *Kalāmī fī Takfīr al-Qawl bi-"Waḥdat al-Adyān" – wa-Mā ilayhā – qabla Iḥdá wa-ʿIshrīn Sana* (www.alhalaby.com/play.php?catsmktba=2331, 26 August 2010 (accessed 2 April 2013)).

[63] Hishām al-ʿĀrif al-Maqdisī, "Al-Yahūd wa-l-Naṣārá fī Ḍawʾ al-Qurʾān wa-l-Sunna," *Al-Aṣāla* 6, no. 31 (15 Muḥarram 1422 [9 April 2001]): 7–12.

[64] Shākir Tawfīq al-ʿĀrūrī, *Daʿwat Nabī llāh ʿĪsá – ʿalayhi l-Salām – ilá l-Tawḥīd Wafqa l-Tawrāt wa-l-Injīl* (n.p.: no publisher, 2009).

[65] Aḥmad Daydāt, *Mādhā Taqūlu l-Tawrāt wa-l-Injīl ʿan Muḥammad – Ṣallá llāh ʿalayhi wa-Sallam?* (Al-Dammām: Dār Ibn al-Jawzī, 1990).

itself, Jordanian Salafis are probably more critical of Sufism and Shi'ism. The practices of the former as perceived by Salafis – including the belief in the omnipresence of God (*waḥdat al-wujūd*), knowledge of the supernatural (*'ilm al-ghayb*), the ritual involving the repeated mentioning of one of God's names (*dhikr*) and invocations of the deceased (*du'ā' al-amwāt*) – are rejected by al-Albani as an "error" or even "polytheism".[66] This is even more the case with Shi'as, who are accused of adhering to a religion that started as a Jewish attempt to strike Islam from within, one of whose followers helped the Mongol invaders to conquer Baghdad in the thirteenth century and who are currently assisting Iran in its supposedly evil plots.[67] This mixture of historical and conspiratorial claims is typical of Salafi discourse on Shi'ism, although there are also clearly religious arguments, such as the allegedly polytheistic Shi'i veneration of 'Ali and Husayn, respectively the son-in-law and grandson of Muhammad.[68] Jordanian quietist scholars point out that calls to engage in dialogue with Shi'as or to see them as equals to Sunnis are wrong.[69] Shi'as, quietist publications state, supposedly curse the companions of the Prophet Muhammad, but also engage in secret plans with Iran, Syria, the Lebanese Shi'i Hizbullah organisation and others to dominate the region.[70]

[66] Sha'bān, *Al-Shaykh*, 724–36. See also Abū Usāma Salīm b. 'Īd al-Hilālī, *Manzalat al-'Ilm wa-l-'Ulamā' 'inda l-Ḥarakāt al-Islāmiyya al-Mu'āṣira* (Cairo: Dār al-Imām Aḥmad, 2008), 33–50, where the author criticises them for their supposed lack of and wrong kind of knowledge. For a comprehensive Jordanian quietist Salafi critique of Ṣūfism, see *id.*, *Al-Jamā'āt al-Islāmiyya fī Ḍaw' al-Kitāb wa-l-Sunna bi-Fahm Salaf al-Umma* (Amman: Al-Dār al-Athariyya, 2004), 106–93.

[67] Muḥammad b. Mūsá Āl Naṣr, *Al-Rāfiḍa wa-Dawruhum fī l-Manṭiqa* (www.almahajjah.net/Pages/3_ReportS_Pages/Arciv_Report_Rafedah.htm, n.d. (accessed 2 April 2013)); "Al-Rawāfiḍ al-Shī'a wa-Mawāqifuhum al-Shanī'a min Ahl al-Sunna wa-l-Sharī'a!!" *Al-Aṣāla* 11, no. 54 (15 Dhū l-Ḥijja 1427 [6 December 2006]): 5–6.

[68] This is certainly a point of severe criticism Salafis have against Shi'as since it clashes with the strict ideas Salafis have on *tawḥīd*, but it was clearly less present in contemporary Jordanian quietist writings on Shi'ism. An example, however, can be found in Abū Ṭalḥa 'Umar b. Ibrāhīm Āl 'Abd al-Raḥmān, *Ḥukm al-Sharī'a fī l-Zawāj min al-Shī'a* (Cairo: Dār al-Minhāj, 2004), in which the author argues against marrying Shi'i wives.

[69] 'Alī b. Ḥasan al-Ḥalabī al-Atharī, *Al-Shī'a Fitnat al-'Aṣr Yā Sa'ādat Muftī Miṣr!* (www.alhalaby.com/play.php?catsmktba=969, 12 December 2009 (accessed 2 April 2013)); Sa'd b. Muḥammad b. 'Abd al-Laṭīf, "Qirā'a fī l-Mu'tamar al-Khāmis li-l-Taqrīb bayna Ahl al-Sunna wa-l-Shī'a!!" *Al-Aṣāla* 1, no. 5 (15 Dhū l-Ḥijja 1413 [6 June 1993]): 41–5.

[70] Abū Muḥammad al-Atharī, "Nashāṭ al-Rāfiḍa fī Turkiyā," *Al-Aṣāla* 2, no. 9 (15 Sha'bān 1414 [28 January 1994]): 64–70; 'Alī b. Ḥasan al-Ḥalabī al-Atharī, *Risāla ilá Kull Man Wallāhu llāh Umūr al-Muslimīn fī l-Muḥādharat min Tasallul al-Shī'a 'ibra l-Mutaṣawwifīn* (www.alhalaby.com/play.php?catsmktba=3470, 5 May 2013 (accessed 2 July 2013)); *id.*, *Al-Shī'a Taghzū "Miṣr"! bi-Amwālihā wa Shubhātihā wa-Shahwātihā; fa-ntabihū wa-Tayqaẓū wa-ḥdhanū!* (www.alhalaby.com/play.php?catsmktba=3438, 7 April 2013 (accessed 11 April 2013)).

A less conspiratorial but all the more conservative idea found among Jordanian quietist Salafis is contained in their views on women.[71] Writings published by quietist Jordanians show that Salafis generally call on women to be pious and obedient,[72] most specifically towards their husbands, whom they should serve, respect, listen to, love and ask permission from.[73] Apart from more general characteristics, like faith, it is such qualities, a female quietist Salafi writes, that make one a good Muslim woman.[74] Men are also encouraged to help their wives in housekeeping, to be good to their spouses, to cooperate with them, to spend time with them and to correct them in a friendly way. They are also called upon not to meddle in their wives' daily affairs and to be careful with punishing them.[75] Together, men and (particularly) women are supposed to raise their children in this spirit and to guard them from influences that can lead them away from Islam.[76]

Outside of the family, women are forbidden to have certain jobs[77] and, in fact, are strongly encouraged to stay indoors as much as possible[78] and not to travel without a male family member accompanying them (*maḥram*),[79] although they are allowed to pray at a mosque.[80] Many of the prohibitions towards women among quietist Salafis in Jordan are related to the concepts of *ikhtilāṭ* (gender-mixing) and *khalwa* (seclusion), which Salafis reject if unrelated people of opposite sexes are involved. Situations in which unrelated men and women share a cab or

71 For more on this issue, see Ḥasan Abū Haniyya, *Al-Mar'a wa-l-Siyāsa min Manẓūr al-Ḥarakāt al-Islāmiyya fī l-Urdunn* (Amman: Friedrich Ebert Stiftung, 2008), 25–33. Some quietist Salafis in Jordan, however, do see Western influence in the Muslim world and women's rights organisations as a conspiracy against Muslim women. See Abū Rummān and Abū Haniyya, *Al-Ḥall*, 255–7.

72 'Abd al-Ṣamad b. Muḥammad al-Kātib, "... ilayka Ayyatuhā l-Mar'a al-Muslima," *Al-Aṣāla* 2, no. 9 (15 Sha'bān 1414 [28 January 1994]): 59–61.

73 Marwān al-Qaysī, "Al-Usra wa-Qawā'id al-Sulūk al-'Ā'ilī 2," *Al-Aṣāla* 1, no. 3 (15 Sha'bān 1413 [8 February 1993]): 44–6.

74 Umm 'Abdallāh Najlā' al-Ṣāliḥ, "Ukhtāhu Kūnī Khayr Mutā'," *Al-Aṣāla* 11, no. 53 (15 Rajab 1427 [10 August 2006]): 77–81.

75 Marwān al-Qaysī, "Al-Usra wa-Qawā'id al-Sulūk al-'Ā'ilī 1," *Al-Aṣāla* 1, no. 2 (15 Jumādá l-Ākhira 1413 [11 December 1992]): 67–70.

76 Muḥammad b. Muḥammad b. Aḥmad al-Mahdī, "Ḥuqūq al-Ṭifl al-Tarbawiyya fī l-Islām," *Al-Aṣāla* 2, no. 10 (15 Shawwāl 1414 [28 March 1994]): 44–8.

77 Muḥammad Nāṣir al-Dīn al-Albānī, "Masā'il ... wa-Ajwibatuhā," *Al-Aṣāla* 3, no. 17 (15 Dhū l-Ḥijja 1416 [4 April 1996]): 70.

78 *Id.*, "Al-Fatāwá," *Al-Aṣāla* 4, no. 19 (15 Dhū l-Qa'da 1419 [3 March 1999]): 74–5; *id.*, *Al-Fatāwá Kuwaytiyya wa-l-Fatāwá al-Ustrāliyya* (Cairo: Dār al-Ḍiyā', 2007), 79.

79 Lajnat al-Fatwá fī Markaz al-Imām al-Albānī, "Rukn al-Fatāwá," *Al-Aṣāla* 10, no. 50 (15 Ramaḍān 1426 [18 October 2005]): 73.

80 Al-Albānī, *Al-Fatāwá*, 80; Khayr al-Dīn al-Wānilī, "Al-Aḥkām allatī Tamyīz bi-hā l-Mar'a 'an al-Rajul 2," *Al-Aṣāla* 6, no. 35 (15 Sha'bān 1422 [2 November 2001]): 63; *id.*, "Al-Aḥkām allatī Tamyīz bi-hā l-Mar'a 'an al-Rajul 3," *Al-Aṣāla* 6, no. 36 (15 Shawwāl 1422 [31 December 2001]): 65.

are in a mosque together, for example, should be avoided or a clear separation should be used between them so as to avoid temptation and strife (*fitna*).[81] It should be mentioned that the overwhelming majority of these articles were, in fact, written by men, although I have also found some written by a female quietist Salafi.[82]

While al-Albani was just as strict in his views on women's rights as other Jordanian quietist Salafis, this issue was again one in which he displayed his independence, just as we saw before with regard to *al-walāʾ wa-l-barāʾ*. Many Salafis believe, probably based on Hanbali rulings, that women should not just cover their hair but also their shoulders and faces in public. Al-Albani, however, states in a ruling that the parts of the body a woman is supposed to cover (*ʿawra*) do not include the face and the shoulders and he uses *ḥadīth*s to make his case for this position.[83] Unsurprisingly, given the importance of Hanbali jurisprudence to Salafis, particularly among Wahhabis in Saudi Arabia, al-Albani's ruling on this issue was quite controversial.[84] Within Jordan itself, however, it was not so much al-Albani's views on the Muslim veil, but his stance on faith that was heavily contested.

Quietist Salafi Views on *Īmān* and *Kufr* in Jordan

The issue of faith – and particularly its opposite, unbelief, and the related question of excommunication – is a very divisive one among Muslims in general, as we saw in Chapter 1. Precisely because this is the case, it is an excellent means for Salafis to show how they differ from other Muslims. Since Salafis often define themselves by pointing out who they are not and what they disagree with,[85] the characteristics and limits of faith are not just important for doctrinal reasons and for the political implications that they have, but also for reasons of self-definition. As we saw previously, however, the Salafi utopia is a divided one in this respect, with Salafi

81 Muḥammad Nāṣir al-Dīn al-Albānī, "Masāʾil wa-Ajwibatuhā," *Al-Aṣāla* 2, no. 10 (15 Shawwāl 1414 [28 March 1994]): 39–40; al-Wānilī, "Al-Aḥkām [...] 2," 62; *id.*, "Al-Aḥkām allatī Tamyīz bi-hā l-Marʾa ʿan al-Rajul 4," *Al-Aṣāla* 7, no. 37 (15 Ṣafar 1423 [28 April 2002]): 58.

82 Umm ʿAbdallāh Najlāʾ al-Ṣāliḥ, "ʿAwāmil Bināʾ Shakhṣiyyat al-Marʾa al-Muslima," *Al-Aṣāla* 8, no. 44 (15 Shawwāl 1424 [10 December 2003]): 77–82; *id.*, "Dawr al-Marʾa al-Muslima fī Tamkīn al-Waḥda al-Islāmiyya," *Al-Aṣāla* 10, no. 48 (15 Rabīʿ al-Awwal 1426 [24 April 2005]): 73–82.

83 Al-Albānī, *Jilbāb*, esp. 3–23, 96–117. For a more comprehensive treatment of al-Albānī's views of women's rights, see *id.*, *Al-Masāʾil*, 232–68.

84 Lacroix, "Between," 66.

85 This can be seen on many Salafī websites, ranging from the quietist www.salafipublications.com to the Jihādī-Salafī www.tawhed.ws, where special sections can be found on issues such as "deviant sects".

scholars choosing two different positions in the debate on *takfīr* of the rulers. Quietist Salafis in Jordan are equally divided on this issue and on the underlying ideas about what constitutes faith and unbelief. Therefore, and given its continuing importance to Jordanian quietists after the death of one of the central figures in the debates on this question (al-Albani),[86] this subject must be dealt with in some detail here.

Al-Albani on *Īmān, Kufr* and *Takfīr*

The discussion on faith and related issues among Salafis in Jordan starts with al-Albani's controversial thoughts on this topic. Al-Albani – as both his followers and his critics acknowledge – believes that *īmān* consists of belief in the heart, speech with the tongue and acts with the limbs,[87] explicitly criticises the Hanafi scholar al-Tahawi's views on faith (which exclude acts)[88] and states that *īmān* can both increase and decrease.[89] As such, his thoughts on this issue seem to correspond with the Salafi position we saw in Chapter 1. Al-Albani was nevertheless criticised by several scholars as having ideas on faith akin to those of the Murji'a, who excluded acts from faith and believed it neither increased nor decreased. The most prominent critique of such "Murji'ī" ideas was published by the Saudi political Salafi scholar Safar al-Hawali, who mentioned al-Albani several times with regard to this issue in his PhD thesis, *Zahirat al-Irja' fi l-Fikr al-Islami* (The Phenomenon of Postponement in Islamic

[86] "Bayān min Hay'at Kibār al-'Ulamā' ḥawla Mas'alat al-Takfīr," *Al-Aṣāla* 5, no. 28 (15 Jumādá l-Ākhira 1420 [26 September 1999]): 90–3; "Fatāwá l-Lajna al-Dā'ima fī Mas'alat al-Ḥukm bi-Ghayr Mā Anzala llāh," *Al-Aṣāla* 5, no. 29 (15 Sha'bān 1421 [13 November 2000]): 77–8; "Ḥiwār ma'a Faḍīlat al-Shaykh Faqīh al-Zamān Muḥammad b. Ṣāliḥ al-'Uthaymīn Ḥafaẓahu llāh," *Al-Aṣāla* 5, no. 28 (15 Jumādá l-Ākhira 1420 [26 September 1999]): 71–8; 'Alī b. Ḥasan b. 'Alī b. 'Abd al-Ḥamīd al-Ḥalabī al-Atharī, *Masā'il 'Ilmiyya fī l-Da'wa wa-l-Siyāsa al-Shar'iyya* (Amman: Al-Dār al-Athariyya, 2010), 19–31; Fatḥī Sulṭān, "Ḍawābiṭ al-Kalām fī Anwā' al-Kufr wa-Taqsīmātihā," *Al-Aṣāla* 5, no. 29 (15 Sha'bān 1421 [13 November 2000]): 66–76.

[87] Sha'bān, *Al-Shaykh*, 427–9.

[88] Muḥammad Abū Ruḥayyim, *Ḥaqīqat al-Īmān 'inda l-Shaykh al-Albānī* (www.tawhed.ws/dl?i=d7pgztyu, 2001 (accessed 27 March 2013)), 22; 'Alī b. Ḥasan b. 'Alī b. 'Abd al-Ḥamīd al-Ḥalabī al-Atharī, *Al-Ta'rīf wa-l-Tanbi'a bi-Ta'ṣīlāt al-'Allāma al-Shaykh al-Imām Asad al-Sunna al-Humām Muḥammad Nāṣir al-Dīn al-Albānī – Raḥimahu llāh – fī Masā'il al-Īmān wa-l-Radd 'alá l-Murji'a* (www.alhalaby.com/play.php?catsmktba=3430, 2009 (accessed 19 April 2013)), 51.

[89] 'Alī b. Ḥasan b. 'Alī al-Ḥalabī al-Atharī al-Salafī, *Al-Radd al-Burhānī fī l-Intiṣār li-l-'Allāma al-Muḥaddith al-Imām al-Shaykh Muḥammad Nāṣir al-Dīn al-Albānī* ('Ajman: Maktabat al-Furqān, 2002), 30–5, 168–9; Al-Jabbūrī, *Juhūd*, 90–4; Sha'bān, *Al-Shaykh*, 427–9; 'Abd al-Mun'im Muṣṭafá Ḥalīma "Abū Baṣīr" [al-Ṭarṭūsī], *Al-Intiṣār li-Ahl al-Tawḥīd wa-l-Radd 'alá Man Jādala 'an al-Ṭawāghīt: Mulāḥaẓāt wa-Rudūd 'alá Sharīṭ "Al-Kufr Kufrān" li-l-Shaykh Muḥammad Nāṣir al-Dīn al-Albānī* (Beirut: Dār al-Bayāriq, 1996), 212.

Thought).[90] This book has been dealt with extensively in the secondary literature[91] and needs no further attention here, but the Jordanian criticism of al-Albani does.

According to Muhammad Abu Ruhayyim, a quietist Salafi shaykh from al-Zarqaʾ, al-Albani's words about *īmān* sometimes – though not always[92] – include acts in faith, but do so in a very specific way that is related to the three different levels of faith we saw in Chapter 1. While al-Albani considers both belief in the heart and speech with the tongue as a pillar (*rukn*) of faith, meaning that it has relevance on any level of faith (the soundness, the compulsory or the perfection of the religion), Abu Ruhayyim states that al-Albani saw acts as only a condition (*sharṭ*) at the level of *kamāl al-dīn*. In other words, Abu Ruhayyim claims that to al-Albani, any sinful belief in the heart or speech with the tongue can in itself undo a Muslim's faith (if it takes place at the level of *ṣiḥḥat al-dīn*) or decrease a believer's *īmān* (if it takes place at the level of *wājib al-dīn*). With regard to sinful *acts*, however, Abu Ruhayyim contends that al-Albani only saw them as possibly "perfecting" one's faith, but not as able to decrease a Muslim's *īmān*, let alone remove his faith altogether. In practice, this means that al-Albani believed acts could harm a person's faith if they were supported by sinful beliefs or speech, but not in and of themselves, Abu Ruhayyim states.[93] That position, in turn, is very similar to excluding acts from *īmān* altogether, as the Murjiʾa did.[94]

Without wanting to take a position in this debate myself, it must be said that there is actually quite a lot of evidence to support Abu Ruhayyim's analysis of al-Albani's views on faith.[95] Some of his followers even implicitly acknowledge that this is the case.[96] The *de facto* leader of the quietist Salafi community in Jordan, ʿAli al-Halabi, does not accept this, however, and staunchly defends his late teacher. He claims that al-Albani does contend that acts are a pillar of faith and that people who commit sinful acts can be labelled *kuffār*, but adds explanatory footnotes in which the examples of such "acts" are actually forms of

[90] Ṣafar b. ʿAbd al-Raḥmān al-Ḥawālī, *Ẓāhirat al-Irjāʾ fī l-Fikr al-Islāmī*, vol. II (www.tawhed.ws/dl?i=xc88bqeg, 1985/6 (accessed 15 April 2015)), 152, 186–7, 193.

[91] Kepel, *War*, 182–4; Lav, *Radical*, 86–119, esp. 107–19; Wiktorowicz, "Anatomy," 231–2. Al-Albānī is said to have considered al-Ḥawālī's book one of "deviance" (*al-inḥirāf*). See ʿIṣām Mūsá Hādī, *Muḥaddith al-ʿAṣr al-Imām Muḥammad Nāṣir al-Dīn al-Albānī kamā ʿAraftuhu* (Al-Jubayl: Dār al-Ṣadīq, 2003), 72. Al-Albānī's Jordanian student ʿAlī al-Ḥalabī has written a book refuting al-Ḥawālī. See his *Gleaming Pearls in Destroying the False Claim that Imaam al-Albanee Agrees with the Murjiʾah!* (https://sunnahtube.files.wordpress.com/2013/05/salafimanhaj_gleamingpearls.pdf, 2006–2008 (accessed 15 April 2015)). The book was originally published in 2002.

[92] Abū Ruḥayyim, *Ḥaqīqat al-Īmān*, 18–21. [93] *Ibid.*, 28. [94] Lav, *Radical*, 161–2.

[95] See also *ibid.*, 111–14. [96] Al-Jabbūrī, *Al-Juhūd*, 226; Shaʿbān, *Al-Shaykh*, 491.

speech (not pronouncing the Islamic confession of faith and insulting God or the Prophet).[97] In other words, al-Halabi seems to suggest that the only acts that can be labelled *kufr* in and of themselves are, in fact, not acts at all but forms of speech. It thus seems as if al-Halabi is quite aware of the common Salafi position on this issue and, possibly out of loyalty to his shaykh, wants to ascribe these views to al-Albani, but is honest enough to indicate – albeit through a flurry of terms and concepts and thus only very implicitly – that al-Albani really did not see acts as a pillar of faith equal to belief and speech.

At least part of the confusion surrounding al-Albani's views on unbelief and on what levels of faith it takes place has to do with the distinction he makes between *kufr ʿamalī* and *kufr iʿtiqādī*, two terms that are difficult to translate literally and which I will refer to here as "*kufr* of action" and "*kufr* of belief", respectively. The former refers to sinful acts that constitute *kufr* but do not as such expel the culprit from Islam, while the latter term refers to actual unbelief in a person's heart, which does place the person guilty of this outside the religion.[98] The terms are slightly misleading because they both incorporate the word "*kufr*", suggesting that both are full-blown forms of unbelief, while in fact only the latter is, but in a different way than *kufr aṣghar* and *kufr akbar*, two terms we saw in the previous chapter. This is probably also the reason why there is sometimes confusion about this issue, even among Jordanian Salafis themselves.[99] In any case, al-Albani adopts these terms from the mediaeval scholar Ibn Qayyim al-Jawziyya and uses them to label as mere *kufr ʿamalī* sinful acts referred to as "*kufr*". This way, he essentially defangs the accusation of *kufr* against acts by stating that the form of *kufr* referred to in texts is actually only a form of unbelief that does not expel the culprit from Islam. Following this line of thinking, al-Albani even goes so far as to state that altogether leaving prayer (*tark al-ṣalāt*) is not, in and of itself, an act of *kufr* that places a Muslim outside his or her religion.[100]

Whether acts are or can be *kufr* as such, so without verbal affirmation of the culprit's unbelief, is a question that becomes more political when

[97] Al-Ḥalabī, *Al-Radd*, 30, 32. See footnote 1 on both pages.

[98] Abū Ruḥayyim, Ḥaqīqat al-Īmān, 66–72; Mūsá b. ʿAbdallāh Āl ʿAbd al-ʿAzīz, ed., *Al-Maqālāt al-Manhajiyya fī "Ḥizb al-Taḥrīr" wa-l-Jamāʿāt al-Takfīriyya min "Al-Majalla al-Salafiyya" li-l-Imāmayn Ibn Bāz wa-l-Albānī* (Riyadh: Dār al-Buḥūth wa-l-Dirāsāt al-Muʿāṣira wa-l-Tarājum, 2006), 25; al-Ḥalabī, Al-Radd, 197–206. See also Lav, Radical, 112, 141.

[99] Al-Ṭarṭūsī, *Al-Intiṣār*, 79–94, 114–153.

[100] Muḥammad Nāṣir al-Dīn al-Albānī, *Ḥukm Tārik al-Ṣalāt* (Riyadh: Dār al-Jalālayn, 1992), 38–45; *id.*, *Al-Masāʾil*, 21–5. See also Khālid b. Muḥammad b. ʿAlī al-ʿAnbarī, *Al-Ḥukm bi-Ghayr Mā Anzala llāh wa-Uṣūl al-Takfīr* (Cairo: Dār al-Minhāj, 2003), 241, however, as well as Lav, *Radical*, 111–14.

applied to the aforementioned Q. 5: 44. As we saw in Chapter 1, Salafis believe that this verse indicates the unbelief of "[w]hoso judges not according to what God has sent down", which, as many see it, also includes rulers who do not govern according to the *sharīʿa*. According to al-Albani, this verse refers to *kufr* of action and he cites the early Muslim scholar ʿAbdallah b. ʿAbbas (c. 619–687) as stating that this was "unbelief less than unbelief (*kufr dūna kufr*)".[101] Since he claims, however, that this verse was originally revealed with regard to Jews, who adhered to a different religion than Islam altogether and whose *kufr* was thus automatically one of belief, not just of action, these Jews were "guilty" of *kufr* of belief.[102] This is also the reason, al-Albani states, that the Jews of this verse cannot be compared to the rulers of Muslim countries. While the former adhered to a different religion, the latter are at least nominally Muslims.[103]

For al-Albani, this naturally leads to a position on *takfīr* of the rulers of the Muslim world that is highly restricted. He states that explicit proof of a sinner's sinful intentions through *iʿtiqād, istiḥlāl* or *jaḥd* is necessary for *takfīr* to be allowed.[104] Since modern-day Muslim rulers are often careful to pay at least lip service to Islam rather than to indicate that they have consciously or intentionally rejected Islam in favour of another legal system, this makes *takfīr* of the rulers a largely theoretical issue for al-Albani. This apparently also applies to *tabdīl*. Even in cases where a ruler completely exchanges the *sharīʿa* for another system of laws, al-Albani claims that proof of the ruler's sinful intentions is necessary to label him or her a *kāfir*.[105] Such a position places al-Albani in the second category that I distinguished in the previous chapter with regard to *takfīr* of Muslim rulers, which many of his students in Jordan seem to have followed.

[101] Al-Albānī, *Tārik*, 40. For Jordanian treatments of these words by Ibn ʿAbbās in the context of Q. 5: 44, see ʿAlī [b.] Ḥasan [b.] ʿAlī [b.] ʿAbd al-Ḥamīd al-Ḥalabī al-Atharī, *Al-Qawl al-Maʾmūn fī Takhrīj Mā Warada ʿan Ibn ʿAbbās fī Tafsīr wa-Man Lam Yaḥkum bi-mā Anzala llāh fa-Ulāʾika Hum al-Kāfinūn* (Al-Dammām: Dār al-Hijra, 1989), esp. 7–10, 18–26; Muḥammad Ibrāhīm Shaqra, *Tanwīr al-Afhām ilá baʿḍ Mafāhīm al-Islām* (www.saaid.net/book/open.php?cat=1&book=43, 2000 [1985] (accessed 5 October 2013)), 98–104. See also al-ʿAnbarī, *Al-Ḥukm*, 150–7, 203–5, 239–40.

[102] Shaʿbān, *Al-Shaykh*, 461–5. See also Wagemakers, "Transformation," 99–101.

[103] Al-Ṭarṭūsī, *Al-Intiṣār*, 84–108. For an extensive treatment of Q. 5: 44 in this context, see Lav, *Radical*, 151–8.

[104] Āl ʿAbd al-ʿAzīz, *Al-Maqālāt*, 27–8; al-Jazāʾirī, *Masʾalat*, 184–6.

[105] Al-Jazāʾirī, *Masʾalat*, 209–15. Al-Albānī was not alone in holding this position, however. Ibn Bāz thought along similar lines. See Wagemakers, *Quietist*, 65.

Wavering between al-Albani and Others

Although quietist Salafi scholars in Jordan dutifully state that faith consists of belief, speech and acts and that it can increase and decrease,[106] the awkward situation of apparently wanting to defend al-Albani while trying to square his different views on faith with the more standard ones generally espoused by Salafis was not limited to ʿAli al-Halabi. This ambiguity was clearest in his writings, however. In some cases, al-Halabi states that acts themselves, such as prostrating before an idol (*al-sujūd li-l-ṣanam*), can lead to *kufr*, although he does not explicitly state what type of *kufr*, leaving open the option that he only refers to the less serious *kufr ʿamalī*.[107] At other times, he is vaguer about faith, suggesting that he believes acts of unbelief do not just take place on the level of *kamāl al-dīn*, but also on the more serious level of *wājib al-dīn*.[108]

The positions of other quietist Jordanian scholars on this issue are sometimes characterised by the same ambiguity. In a document written to clarify the scholars' views on this issue, senior quietist Jordanian *ʿulamāʾ* Husayn al-ʿAwayisha, Muhammad Musa Nasr, Salim al-Hilali, ʿAli al-Halabi and Mashhur b. Hasan state that acts are part of faith but only – except for prayer – on the level of *wājib al-dīn* or *kamāl al-dīn*, suggesting that no act in and of itself can make one a *kāfir*.[109] On the very next page, however, they argue that

> among *kufr* of action – or speech – there is also that which expels from the religion in and of itself (*bi-dhātihi*) and does not require *istiḥlāl* in the heart. This is what is contrary to faith from every viewpoint, for example: insulting God (*sabb Allāh*) – the most high – vilifying the Messenger (*shatam al-rasūl*)[,] may God pray over him and give him peace[,] prostrating before an idol (*al-sujūd li-l-ṣanam*) and throwing the Qurʾan (*al-muṣḥaf*) in the garbage (*fī l-qādhūrāt*).[110]

Such a point of view is, in fact, different from al-Albani's, although the latter could perhaps argue that such acts betray unbelief in the heart and therefore are not in and of themselves forms of *kufr*, but only because they necessarily require intentions of unbelief. These ambiguities contrast with

[106] This is ubiquitous in quietist Salafī writings in Jordan. See, for example, ʿAlī b. Ḥasan b. ʿAli b. ʿAbd al-Ḥamīd al-Ḥalabī al-Atharī, *Al-Tabṣīr bi-Qawāʿid al-Takfīr* (Cairo: Dār al-Minhāj, 2004), 12–17.

[107] *Ibid.*, 45–6. [108] *Id.*, *Al-Taʿrīf*, 26.

[109] Ḥusayn b. ʿAwda al-ʿAwāyisha, Muḥammad b. Mūsá Āl Naṣr, Salīm b. ʿĪd al-Hilālī, ʿAlī b. Ḥasan al-Ḥalabī al-Atharī and Mashhūr b. Ḥasan Āl Salmān, *Mujmal Masāʾil al-Īmān al-ʿIlmiyya fī Uṣūl al-ʿAqīda al-Salafiyya* (www.mediafire.com/view/?ehqmw6g0mr599bn, 29 August 2000 (accessed 5 April 2013)), 4. See also "Hal al-ʿAmal Sharṭ Ṣiḥḥa fī l-Īmān am Sharṭ Kamāl?" *Al-Aṣāla* 5, nos. 25–6 (15 Muḥarram 1421 [20 April 2000] – 15 Rabīʿ al-Awwal 1421 [18 June 2000]): 135.

[110] Al-ʿAwāyisha et al., *Mujmal*, 5.

the much clearer statements by Abu Ruhayyim, who says that acts should not be distinguished from belief and speech since all could take place on all levels of faith.[111] Similarly clear statements are given by Muhammad Ibrahim Shaqra, a Jordanian quietist scholar who used to side with al-Albani in this matter[112] but later changed his mind and openly supported Abu Ruhayyim's views on faith.[113]

The same ambiguity can be found on the question of whether leaving prayer as such – so without proof of sinful intention – makes one an unbeliever. The supposedly clarifying document by Jordanian quietist scholars mentioned above only makes clear that there is a difference of opinion on this matter among the *ʿulamāʾ* and that even major scholars like Ibn Baz and al-Albani disagree with one another on this.[114] This latter remark is confusing, however, since it clashes with a later remark by al-Halabi that Ibn Baz and al-Albani *do* agree on this issue.[115] Al-Halabi's own position on someone who abandons prayer is no clearer. In his introduction to al-Albani's book on this matter, he acknowledges that the scholars differ on this question, but concludes that carefulness in this matter is called for and that leaving prayer should therefore not be seen as *kufr* that expels from Islam if it is not accompanied by sinful intentions.[116] In a later publication, however, al-Halabi seems to conclude that leaving prayer in itself *is kufr.*[117] It would be easy to view these differing statements by al-Halabi as proof that he is misleading his readers. I believe, however, that such contradictions may be explained by pointing to the often painstaking efforts al-Halabi makes to defend al-Albani's position on this matter and to square the circle of the latter's slightly distinct views on faith.

The question of *īmān* is drawn into politics again when it touches upon Q. 5: 44. Like al-Albani, quietist Salafi publications in Jordan describe that verse as referring to Jews. They similarly claim that the unbelief of not ruling "according to what God has sent down" is, in fact, a form of *kufr* that does not expel from Islam (described as either *kufr ʿamalī* or *kufr aṣghar*) since it is – in the words of Ibn ʿAbbas we also saw above – "unbelief less than unbelief". This only changes, they state, if the person ruling on the basis of something other than "what God has sent down"

[111] Abū Ruḥayyim, *Ḥaqīqat al-Īmān*, esp. 42; *id.*, *Ḥaqīqat al-Khilāf bayna l-Salafiyya al-Sharʿiyya wa-Adʿiyāʾihā* (www.tawhed.ws/dl?i=ynh8cqba, 1998 (accessed 16 April 2015)), 11–68.

[112] See al-Ṭarṭūsī, *Al-Intiṣār*.

[113] Muḥammad Ibrāhīm Shaqra, introduction to *Ḥaqīqat al-Īmān ʿinda l-Shaykh al-Albānī* by Muḥammad Abū Ruḥayyim (www.tawhed.ws/dl?i=d7pgztyu, 2001 (accessed 27 March 2013)), 5–8.

[114] Al-ʿAwāyisha et al., *Mujmal*, 6.

[115] Al-Ḥalabī, *Al-Taʿrīf*, 113–14.

[116] Al-Albānī, *Ḥukm*, 5–21.

[117] Al-Ḥalabī, *Al-Taʿrīf*, 113–15.

does so with sinful intentions.[118] On the question of *tabdīl* of the *sharīʿa*, al-Halabi remains ambiguous, citing statements that automatically assume sinful intention in cases of a total exchange of Islamic law for something else and therefore consider it *kufr akbar*, but also ones that still require *istiḥlāl*, *iʿtiqād* or *juḥūd* in such instances.[119] Al-Halabi also explicitly notes that this difference of opinion exists among Salafi scholars.[120] Given al-Halabi's carefulness in expressing *takfīr*[121] and his unwillingness to take a clear stand on this issue, Abu Ruhayyim criticises him for his views and claims that *tabdīl* of the *sharīʿa* is unbelief, with or without signs of sinful intentions.[122]

Considering the fact that many quietist Salafi scholars often take a position on faith that is close to al-Albani's or, in any case, refuse to adopt a clearly distinctive stance, they should also be placed in the second category with regard to *takfīr* of the rulers that we saw in Chapter 1. Because of the similarities between their views and al-Albani's, they are equally open to the charge of being Murjiʾa, and Shaqra implicitly labels them as such. Although his book on this subject does not mention either al-Albani or any of the other Jordanian quietist scholars by name, he does speak of "the neo-Murjiʾa (*al-Murjiʾa al-judud*)" and, given his disagreements with them on the question of faith, it seems obvious who he means by this.[123] That is, in fact, also how the quietist scholars editing the journal *Al-Asala* interpret Shaqra's publications, which is why they dedicated a special double issue to refuting his ideas on faith, including his assertion that they are Murjiʾa.[124] Shaqra's implicit claim, spurious though it may be, does point to an important aspect about quietist Jordanian scholars' views on faith, namely that they are so careful in their treatment of *kufr* and *takfīr*, that they essentially leave impious but nominally Muslim rulers off the hook, even if they do not rule "according to what God has sent down". This ideologically motivated quietism is also found in their concrete views on politics in Jordan.

118 Khālid b. ʿAlī b. Muḥammad al-ʿAnbarī, "Faṣl al-Khiṭāb fī Man Lam Yaḥkum bi-l-Sunna wa-l-Kitāb," *Al-Aṣāla* 1, no. 6 (15 Ṣafar 1414 [4 August 1993]): 12–16; *id.*, "Al-Ṭarīq ilá l-Ḥukm bi-Mā Anzala llāh," *Al-Aṣāla* 2, no. 10 (15 Shawwāl 1414 [28 March 1994]): 17–19. See also ʿAlī b. Ḥasan b. ʿAlī b. ʿAbd al-Ḥamīd al-Ḥalabī, introduction to *Al-Taḥdhīr min Fitnat al-Ghulūw fī l-Takfīr* by Muḥammad Nāṣir al-Dīn al-Albānī (Bīr Nabālā: Sharikat Nūr, 2002 [1996]), 19–22, 28–32, 42.

119 Al-Ḥalabī, introduction to *Al-Taḥdhīr min Fitnat al-Ghulūw*, by al-Albānī, 22–6.

120 *Ibid.*, 34–5. 121 *Id.*, *Al-Tabṣīr*, 23–35.

122 Abū Ruḥayyim, *Ḥaqīqat al-Khilāf*, 69–90.

123 Muḥammad Ibrāhīm Shaqra, *Ayna Taqaʿu "Lā ilāha illā llāh" fī Dīn al-Murjiʾa al-Judud?* (www.saaid.net/book/open.php?cat=88&book=1312, n.d. (accessed 25 September 2013)).

124 "Masʾalat al-Irjāʾ," *Al-Aṣāla* 5, nos. 25–6 (15 Muḥarram 1421 [20 April 2000] – 15 Rabīʿ al-Awwal 1421 [18 June 2000]): 115–32.

Quietist Salafism and Politics in Jordan

The practical question of how to deal with Jordanian politics and society is not so much one of *ʿaqīda*, but one of *manhaj*. As we saw in Chapter 1, however, the *manhaj* that Salafis apply to strive for their utopia of the "pious predecessors" revolves around more than just politics and society. An article in the Jordanian quietist journal *Al-Asala* acknowledges this, stating that their method of dealing with the texts (relying on the Qurʾan and the Sunna, understanding them through the prism of the *salaf*, rejecting the application of speculative theology to them, etcetera), for example, is also part of the Salafi *manhaj*.[125] With regard to politics and society, Jordanian quietists – like their brethren elsewhere – believe in peacefully spreading and propagating their beliefs.[126] This focus on *daʿwa* is necessary since, as one Jordanian quietist says, people live in darkness and need "the light of God (*nūr Allāh*)" to shine into their hearts and the way to make this happen is *daʿwa*.[127] Although quietists in Jordan acknowledge that there are different means to spread the message of Islam at different times,[128] they do point out that *daʿwa* – in any situation – needs to be based on the Qurʾan and the Sunna according to the understanding of the *salaf*[129] and the propagators of this message need to be fully committed to God and the Prophet.[130]

General Jordanian Quietist Beliefs on Politics

In Jordan, the quietist *manhaj* of dealing with society through *daʿwa* is often referred to as *al-taṣfiya wa-l-tarbiya* (cleansing and education), a term ascribed to al-Albani[131] that has been adopted by the larger quietist Salafi community in the kingdom.[132] The term *taṣfiya*, according to al-Albani, refers to the process of (1) removing from the Islamic creed those aspects considered alien to it, like "divine attributes and their

[125] ʿAbdallāh b. Ṣāliḥ al-ʿUbaylān, "Durūs fī Manhaj al-Salaf," *Al-Aṣāla* 4, no. 22 (15 Jumādá l-Ākhira 1420 [26 September 1999]): 35–7.

[126] *Ibid.*, 38.

[127] Salīm al-Hilālī, "Al-Daʿwa.. wa-l-Nūr..," *Al-Aṣāla* 1, no. 1 (15 Rabīʿ al-Thānī 1413 [13 October 1992]): 37–8..

[128] Muḥammad Nāṣir al-Dīn al-Albānī, "Masāʾil wa-Ajwibatuhā," *Al-Aṣāla* 4, no. 18 (15 Muḥarram 1418 [23 May 1997]): 72–3.

[129] *Id.*, "Al-Daʿwa al-Salafiyya: Uṣūluhā ... Maqāṣiduhā ... Asbāb al-Nuhūf [sic!] bi-hā," *Al-Aṣāla* 5, no. 27 (15 Rabīʿ al-Ākhir 1421 [18 July 2000]): 7.

[130] Muḥammad b. Mūsá Āl Naṣr, *Awluwiyyāt al-Daʿwa ilá llāh* (www.almahajjah.net/Pages/3_ReportS_Pages/Arciv_Report_aulauiat.htm, n.d. (accessed 2 April 2013)).

[131] Muḥammad Abū Rummān, "Al-Māḍī fī l-Ḥāḍir ... al-Taṣfiya wa-l-Tarbiya ʿinda l-Albānī," in *Rimāḥ al-Ṣaḥāʾif: Al-Salafiyya al-Albāniyya wa-Khuṣūmuhā* (Dubai: Markaz al-Misbār li-l-Dirāsāt wa-l-Buḥūth, 2010), 65–88, esp. 71–88.

[132] Abū Rummān and Abū Haniyya, *Al-Salafiyya al-Muḥāfaẓa*, esp. 57–65.

metaphorical interpretation (*al-ṣifāt al-ilāhiyya wa-ta'wīlihā*)"; (2) the purifying of Islamic jurisprudence "from faulty independent interpretations (*al-ijtihādāt al-khāṭi'a*) that differ with the Book and the Sunna"; and (3) purging books of Qur'anic exegesis (*tafsīr*) and other areas of Islamic knowledge from "weak *ḥadīth*s" (i.e., ones that cannot be attributed to the Prophet with certainty).[133] *Tarbiya*, in turn, refers to the raising of a generation of Muslims on "this cleansed Islam (*hādha l-Islām al-muṣaffá*)" without "any influence of infidel Western education".[134]

The concept of *al-taṣfiya wa-l-tarbiya* not only represents the long-term plan that al-Albani had for the Muslim community but also exemplifies his quietist attitude towards politics and society, choosing to focus on an intellectual project of cleansing and teaching Islam, rather than translating his views into some sort of political action.[135] This was very clearly expressed in his statement that

> we think that the *umma* is not in need of revolutions, assassinations and strife (*thawrāt wa-ghtiyālāt wa-fitan*), but is in need of faith education (*al-tarbiya al-īmāniyya*) and intellectual cleansing (*al-taṣfiya al-fikriyya*). This is among the most successful means of returning the *umma* to its might and glory (*'izzihā wa-majdihā*).[136]

As an agenda for the future, as a means to deal with society and as – in the words of one Jordanian quietist publication – "the preparation of the Muslim individual (*al-fard al-Muslim*) for [this] world and the hereafter",[137] *al-taṣfiya wa-l-tarbiya* remains the guiding *manhaj* for quietist Salafis in Jordan today.[138]

The fact that al-Albani and other quietist Salafis in Jordan have focussed on *al-taṣfiya wa-l-tarbiya* does not mean that they reject politics altogether or believe that politics is not part of Islam. Al-Albani realised that in the situation the Muslim world was in in the 1960s and 1970s, truly Islamic politics was impossible because of dictatorship, divisions

133 Al-Jabbūrī, *Juhūd*, 38–9; Sha'bān, *Al-Shaykh*, 93–4; al-Shāmī, *Ārā'*, 89–90.

134 Al-Jabbūrī, *Juhūd*, 39; Sha'bān, *Al-Shaykh*, 94.

135 Abū Rummān and Abū Haniyya, *Al-Salafiyya al-Muḥāfaẓa*, 69–70.

136 Al-Albānī et al., "Masā'il 'Aṣriyya," 23. See also Sha'bān, *Al-Shaykh*, 95. For a comprehensive treatment of the subject of *al-taṣfiya wa-tarbiya* by al-Albānī himself, see Muḥammad Nāṣir al-Dīn al-Albānī, *Al-Taṣfiya wa-l-Tarbiya wa-Ḥājat al-Muslimīn ilayhimā* (Amman: Al-Maktaba al-Islāmiyya, 1421 [2000/2001]). For a detailed study of the importance of this subject to al-Albānī, see Shāmī, *Ārā'*, 81–297.

137 Khālid Muḥammad 'Alī al-Ḥāj, "Al-Islām wa-l-Tarbiya," *Al-Aṣāla* 3, nos. 15–16 (15 Dhū l-Qa'da 1415 [15 April 1995]): 49.

138 See, for example, 'Alī al-Ḥalabī, *Al-Taṣfiya wa-l-Tarbiya: Muḥāḍara li-l-Shaykh al-Ḥalabī* (www.alhalaby.com/play.php?catsmktba=1078, 14 December 2009 (accessed 1 April 2013)); al-Hilālī, *Al-Jamā'āt*, 546–58.

among Muslims and their supposed ignorance about their religion. His secretary, ʿIsam Hadi, describes al-Albani's views on politics as if it were a pyramid:

> We want to go to the top of the pyramid, the caliphate, but the pyramid has a base and you have to build the base before you can reach the top. That is why shaykh Nasir (i.e., al-Albani) used to believe that the best thing to do for us as Salafis is not to work in politics, not just because there are rulers who oppress us and watch us, but because the Muslim group (*al-jamāʿa al-Muslima*) is not prepared for political action because they have not been raised or educated well about the correct Islam.[139]

It was precisely in response to al-Albani's realisation that "in the present circumstances, the good policy is to stay away from politics (*min al-siyāsa tark al-siyāsa*)" that he developed his agenda of *al-taṣfiya wa-l-tarbiya.*[140] Al-Albani did believe, however, that politics was part of Islam, but simply wanted to "*thaqqif, thumma kattil*" (educate [first], conglomerate next)[141] in order to prepare it for an Islamic state in the long run.[142]

Jordanian quietist Salafis see the concept of *al-taṣfiya wa-l-tarbiya* in the context of what they call "the jurisprudence of reality" (*fiqh al-wāqiʿ*), which al-Albani defines as

> the inquiry into what is of interest to Muslims from among that which is related to their affairs or the deceit of their enemies; to warn them and encourage them: reality-wise (*wāqiʿiyyan*), not through theoretical words (*kalāman naẓariyyan*), or keeping oneself busy with the affairs of the unbelievers and their news [. . .].[143]

The idea that Muslims should take an interest in what goes on around them and the issues related to themselves and to those threatening their interests can be used as a stepping stone towards political activism, of course. To Jordanian quietists, however, it is directly related to *al-taṣfiya wa-l-tarbiya* since knowledge of reality can facilitate the effectiveness of *daʿwa*. As such, al-Halabi, in a book about the subject, complains that many propagators of

139 Interview with ʿIṣām Hādī, Amman, 19 January 2013.
140 Lacroix, "Between," 69–70.
141 Interviews with ʿIṣām Hādī, Amman, 19 January 2013; Usāma Shaḥāda, Amman, 7 June 2012.
142 Abū Rummān and Abū Haniyya, *Al-Salafiyya al-Muḥāfaẓa*, 72; Muḥammad Zāhid Kāmil Gūl, "Al-Khiṭāb al-Siyāsī li-l-Salafiyya al-Albāniyya," in *Rimāḥ al-Ṣaḥāʾif: Al-Salafiyya al-Albāniyya wa-Khuṣūmuhā* (Dubai: Markaz al-Misbār li-l-Dirāsāt wa-l-Buḥūth, 2010), 97–101. See also Abū ʿUbayda Mashhūr b. Ḥasan Āl Salmān, *Al-Siyāsa allatī Yurīduhā l-Salafiyyūn* (Amman: Al-Dār al-Athariyya, 2005), 19.
143 Muḥammad Nāṣir al-Dīn al-Albānī, *Suʾāl wa-Jawāb ḥawla Fiqh al-Wāqiʿ* (Amman: Al-Maktaba al-Islāmiyya, 1422 [2000/2001]), 29–30.

Islam (*duʿāt*) do not understand what goes on around them and do not study it.[144]

Fiqh al-wāqiʿ is thus clearly meant by Jordanian quietists as an intellectual engagement with politics and society in order to use it as a means to further their own *manhaj* of preaching Islam, not for politics as an end in itself. Al-Halabi points to various Qurʾanic verses about remaining loyal to Islam and Muslims and keeping one's distance from non-Muslims that should serve as "invariables" (*thawābit*) on how to engage with reality.[145] "Politics in the *fiqh al-wāqiʿ*", al-Halabi writes, "is the application of [these] invariables of the Book and the Sunna to the novelties of the era (*mustajiddāt al-ʿaṣr*)".[146] This deeply quietist position naturally results in an attitude that rejects political means such as demonstrations, strikes or revolts to change reality[147] and focusses instead on religious ways like *daʿwa, al-taṣfiya wa-l-tarbiya* and "returning the *umma* to the Book and the Sunna according to the understanding of the *salaf*".[148]

This attitude can clearly be discerned in Jordanian quietists' views of international affairs, particularly those concerning Muslims. There is a strong tendency in quietist publications from Jordan to see conflicts in which Muslims are involved as resulting from their lack of understanding of or their deviation from the Qurʾan and the Sunna.[149] Muslims' alleged ignorance, ideological deviance but also disunity and less than total commitment to God and the *sharīʿa* are mentioned as the reasons for the "weakness" of the Muslim world.[150] This conviction that religious

144 ʿAlī b. Ḥasan b. ʿAlī b. ʿAbd al-Ḥamīd al-Ḥalabī al-Atharī, *Fiqh al-Wāqiʿ bayna l-Naẓariyya wa-l-Taṭbīq* (Ramallah: Sharakat al-Nūr, 1420 [1999/2000] [1412 [1991/1992]]), 11.

145 *Ibid.*, 29–32.

146 *Ibid.*, 40. Mashhūr b. Ḥasan actually gives an example of what the second caliph ʿUmar b. al-Khaṭṭāb would have done if he had been confronted with the Gulf Crisis in 1990, pointing out that he would have applied the basic principles of Salafī politics, namely to base his solution on the Qurʾān and the Sunna and the *ijtihād* of a consultation council, he would reject the most injust solution and apply what the scholars decide. See Āl Salmān, *Al-Siyāsa*, 24–6.

147 ʿAlī b. Ḥasan Abū Lūz, "Ẓāhirat al-Iʿtiṣāmāt wa-l-Muẓāharāt wa-l-Thawrāt al-Shaʿbiyya wa-l-Iḍrāb fī Fatāwá l-Aʾimma wa-l-ʿUlamāʾ," *Al-Aṣāla* 5, no. 30 (15 Shawwāl 1421 [11 January 2001]): 59–61; Salīm al-Hilālī, "Al-Salafiyyūn wa-l-Siyāsa," *Al-Aṣāla* 4, no. 18 (15 Muḥarram 1419 [23 May 1997]): 32.

148 Al-Hilālī, "Al-Salafiyyūn," 30–1. The words quoted are on 30. See also Mashhūr b. Ḥasan b. [Āl] Salmān, "Al-Fitan wa-ʿAwāmil al-Taghyīr," *Al-Aṣāla* 2, no. 8 (15 Jumādá l-Ākhira 1414 [30 November 2013]): 11–13; Abū l-Ḥārith ʿAlī b. Ḥasan al-Ḥalabī, "Madārik al-Naẓar fī l-Siyāsa bayna l-Taṭbīqāt al-Sharʿiyya wa-l-Infiʿālāt al-Ḥamāsiyya," *Al-Aṣāla* 5, no. 28 (15 Jumādá l-Ākhira 1420 [26 September 1999]): 48–9.

149 Abū Rummān and Abū Haniyya, *Al-Ḥall*, 257–8.

150 "Wāqiʿunā l-Alīm wa-Mustaqbalunā l-Wāʿid," *Al-Aṣāla* 6, no. 35 (15. Shaʿbān 1422 [2 November 2001]): 10–11; ʿAbd al-ʿAzīz b. Bāz, "Asbāb Ḍaʿf al-Muslimīn Amām ʿAduwwihim wa-Wasāʾil al-ʿIlāj li-Dhālika 1," *Al-Aṣāla* 8, no. 42 (15 Rabīʿ al-Thānī 1424 [16 June 2003]): 54–7; *id.*, "Asbāb Ḍaʿf al-Muslimīn Amām ʿAduwwihim

factors are to blame for political conflicts is strongly connected with Jordanian quietists' views that, deep down, conflicts involving Muslims are religious in nature and are rooted in the idea that "never will the Jews be satisfied with thee, neither the Christians, not till thou followest their religion" (Q. 2: 120).[151] The conflict in Bosnia in the 1990s, for instance, is framed as a battle "between the unity of God and polytheism".[152] The solution to international problems such as Palestinian suffering in the Gaza Strip is therefore obvious to the Jordanian quietist scholar al-Halabi: "The return to the religion, the true religion, the religion based on the Book and the Sunna".[153] Another quietist scholar from Jordan calls on Gazans to "flee to God".[154] The idea that such major international conflicts can really be countered by studying and preaching Islam[155] may sound naïve and Jordanian quietists certainly understand that, in the short term, *da'wa* is not going to stop Israeli military actions against the Palestinians. Yet Salafis in Jordan are not thinking in short-term solutions, but are in it for the long run and believe, as one Jordanian scholar puts it, that "the future is Islam's".[156]

Quiestist Political Views Applied to Jordan

Jordanian quietists' strong focus on *al-taṣfiya wa-l-tarbiya* as a long-term solution to the Muslim world's ills is complemented by another aspect of quietism: a subservient attitude towards the rulers. Al-Albani, for example, not only rejected military coups against Muslim rulers,[157] but also believed that obedience (*ṭā'a*) to the *walī al-amr* was necessary for the proper rule of the *umma*.[158] For the aloofist al-Albani, that was as far as the relationship with rulers went: he remained subservient to them, but did not seek to influence them and maintained his independence to focus

wa-Wasā'il al-'Ilāj li-Dhālika 2," *Al-Aṣāla* 8, no. 43 (15 Jumādá l-Ākhira 1424 [14 August 2003]): 34–7; *id.*, "Asbāb Ḍa'f al-Muslimīn Amām 'Aduwwihim wa-Was ā'il al-'Ilāj li-Dhālika 3," *Al-Aṣāla* 9, no. 45 (15 Ṣafar 1425 [6 April 2004]): 40.

151 "Ḥaqīqat al-'Udwān," *Al-Aṣāla* 7, no. 40 (Dhū l-Ḥijja 1423 [17 February 2003]): 4.

152 "Aḥwāl al-'Ālam al-Islāmī," *Al-Aṣāla* 1, no. 1 (15 Rabī' al-Thānī 1413 [13 October 1992]): 75.

153 'Alī b. Ḥasan b. 'Alī b. 'Abd al-Ḥamīd al-Ḥalabī al-Atharī, *Al-'Udwān al-Ghāshim 'alá Ghazzat Hāshim* (Amman: Al-Dār al-Athariyya, 2009), 43.

154 Muḥammad b. Mūsá Āl Naṣr, *La-Kum Allāh Yā Ahlunā fī Ghazza al-Abiyya* (www .almahajjah.net/Pages/7_Others_Files/GAZA_File.htm, n.d. (accessed 2 April 2013)).

155 "Iṭfā' al-Fitna," *Al-Aṣāla* 9, no. 45 (15 Ṣafar 1425 [6 April 2004]): 5–6; Salīm al-Hilālī, "Al-Mujtama' al-Islāmī al-Mu'āṣir wa-l-Taḥaddī al-Ḥaḍārī 1," *Al-Aṣāla* 9, no. 45 (15 Ṣafar 1425 [6 April 2004]): 30.

156 Salīm al-Hilālī, *Al-Mustaqbal li-l-Islām bi-Manhaj al-Salaf al-Kirām* (Cairo: Dār al-Imām Aḥmad, 2007).

157 Al-Albānī, "Masā'il wa-Ajwibatuhā," *Al-Aṣāla* 2, no. 10, 43.

158 Sha'bān, *Al-Shaykh*, 643–8.

on *al-taṣfiya wa-l-tarbiya* instead.[159] His Jordanian students, however, have gone somewhat further in their relationship with the rulers. Nowadays, Jordanian quietists similarly reject *takfīr* of and revolts against Muslim or non-Muslim rulers because they generally abhor the *fitna* they believe this will result in[160] and see King ʿAbdallah II of Jordan as their *walī al-amr* because he maintains peace and security.[161] Yet they also distinguish between *ṭāʿa*, which implies merely that one obeys and does not revolt against any ruler, and *bayʿa* (oath of fealty), which is a more active pledge of allegiance not just given to anyone.[162] Although *bayʿa* in Islam was first pledged to the caliph only,[163] quietist Salafis in Jordan today also express the willingness to extend this pledge to King ʿAbdallah II,[164] who they see as a truly Sunni ruler worthy of their allegiance,[165] and – in a further sign that they are closer to loyalist quietist Salafism than the aloofist al-Albani ever was – are willing to serve him with advice too.[166]

Neither aloofist independence and subservience nor loyalist allegiance and advice means, however, that Salafis are not interested in who is elected to parliament. Although they discourage people from running for public office since they do not see elections as the proper way to work towards the establishment of an Islamic state, they do acknowledge

159 Interview with Aḥmad Muṣliḥ, Amman, 29 January 2013.

160 Al-Ḥalabī, *Ḍawābiṭ*, 7, 39; interviews with Muḥammad b. Mūsá Āl Naṣr, Amman, 20 June 2012; Iṣḥāq b. Yaḥyá, Amman, 11 June 2012; ʿAlī al-Ḥalabī, Amman, 27 June 2012; Bāsim b. Fayṣal al-Jawābira, Amman, 26 June 2012.

161 *Liqāʾ Ṣaḥafī*; interviews with Ziyād al-ʿAbbādī, Amman, 26 June 2012; Muḥammad b. Mūsá Āl Naṣr, Amman, 20 June 2012; Mashhūr b. Ḥasan Āl Salmān, Amman, 27 June 2012; Bāsim b. Fayṣal al-Jawābira, Amman, 26 June 2012; Akram Ziyāda, Amman, 28 June 2012; lesson by Bāsim b. Fayṣal al-Jawābira, Imām al-Albānī Centre, Amman, 14 June 2014.

162 Interview with Bāsim b. Fayṣal al-Jawābira, Amman, 26 June 2012.

163 Saʿūd b. Mulūḥ b. Sulṭān al-ʿAnzī, "Al-Bayʿa bayna l-Ḍawābiṭ al-Sharʿiyya wa-l-Tanẓīmāt al-Ḥizbiyya," *Al-Aṣāla* 8, no. 41 (15 Ṣafar 1424 [18 April 2003]): 34–5; ʿAlī [b.] Ḥasan [b.] ʿAlī [b.] ʿAbd al-Ḥamīd [al-Ḥalabī], *Al-Bayʿa bayna l-Sunna wa-l-Bidʿa ʿinda l-Jamāʿāt al-Islāmiyya* (Amman: Al-Maktaba al-Islāmiyya, 1985), 18.

164 The idea of pledging allegiance to a king in the form of a *bayʿa* is not limited to Salafis or Jordan, however. See Elie Podeh, "The *Bayʿa*: Modern Political Uses of Islamic Ritual in the Arab World," *Die Welt des Islams* 50, no. 1 (2010): 117–52, esp. 141–4, which deal with Jordan.

165 Interviews with Muḥammad b. Mūsá Āl Naṣr, Amman, 20 June 2012; Bāsim b. Fayṣal al-Jawābira, Amman, 26 June 2012. In a book from the 1980s, ʿAlī al-Ḥalabī gives the impression that *bayʿa* is a duty upon Muslims, but only towards the caliph, although it is not always clear if he also sees modern-day rulers as "imams". See al-Ḥalabī, *Al-Bayʿa*, 20–3.

166 "Al-Salafiyya Ẓāhira," 7; Akram Ziyāda, *"Fasād" al-Salafī, Lā "al-Fasād" al-Salafī* (www.majles.alwkah.net/t9059/, 30 October 2007 (accessed 22 November 2013)); interviews with ʿAlī al-Ḥalabī, Amman, 27 June 2012; Mashhūr b. Ḥasan Āl Salmān, Amman, 27 June 2012. See also ʿAbd al-ʿAzīz b. Bāz, "Min Fatāwá l-Shaykh ʿAbd al-ʿAzīz b. Bāz," *Al-Aṣāla* 4, no. 21 (15 Rabīʿ al-Ākhir 1420 [29 July 1999]): 79.

that parliament exists and that this is a reality they have to deal with. As such, al-Albani supported voting for the Front Islamique du Salut (FIS), an Islamist party that ran for parliament in Algeria in the 1990s.[167] His support for this was rooted in the concept of *al-maṣāliḥ wa-l-mafāsid*, which can roughly be translated as "advantages and disadvantages". Al-Albani argues that voting was "the smallest disadvantage" (*al-mafsada al-ṣughrá*) in this matter, since it entailed using a non-Islamic means (elections) that can nevertheless be employed to ward off "the greatest disadvantage" (*al-mafsada al-kubrá*) of a secular (and possibly anti-Islamic) parliament.[168] This emphasis on the "interest" (*maṣlaḥa*) of the Muslim community has also caused today's Jordanian quietist scholars to look upon elections and parliament as less than ideal, but with which they are nevertheless willing to engage by voting for "the least bad" candidates from an Islamic point of view.[169]

Quietist Salafis' position on voting and elections is, of course, not exactly a ringing endorsement of democracy. In fact, although Jordanian quietists support the application of mutual consultation or counsel (*shūrá*),[170] a concept Islamists often liken to or even equate with parliaments and democracy,[171] they clearly reject the latter. Democracy, quietist Jordanian *ʿulamāʾ* argue, is based on the people – rather than on God – as the source of legislative authority and, as such, results in laws that clash with the *sharīʿa*.[172] Moreover, quietist Salafi scholars in Jordan object to the idea that the majority gets to decide what happens, rather than just following the supposedly obvious truth, as expressed in the Qurʾan and the Sunna.[173] These reasons for rejecting

[167] "Ajwibat al-ʿAllāma al-Albānī ʿalá Asʾilat Jabhat al-Inqādh – al-Jazāʾir," *Al-Aṣāla* 1, no. 4 (15 Shawwāl 1413 [8 April 1993]): 15–22, esp. 19–20.

[168] *Ibid.*, 20.

[169] *Liqāʾ al-Shaykh*; interviews with Bāsim b. Fayṣal al-Jawābira, Amman, 26 June 2012; Fatḥī al-Mawṣilī, Amman, 23 January 2013; ʿAlī al-Ḥalabī, Amman, 27 June 2012; Salīm al-Hilālī, Amman, 28 January 2013; Akram Ziyāda, Amman 28 June 2012. This attitude towards voting may suddenly sound very pragmatic. Particularly given the Jordanian regime's emphasis on voting and the legitimacy it supposedly derives from that, quietists' acceptance of voting in elections could perhaps be explained as a way of helping the regime maintain its credibility. Maybe this is partly correct, but the fact that the staunchly independent al-Albānī also supported this (and in an Algerian context, from which the Jordanian regime could not benefit directly) suggests that this position is at least somewhat ideologically inspired rather than just based on support for the regime.

[170] Ṣāliḥ b. Ghānim al-Sadlān, "Wāqiʿ al-Umma al-Islāmiyya al-Dāʾ wa-l-Dawāʾ," *Al-Aṣāla* 1, no. 4 (15 Shawwāl 1413 [8 April 1993]): 46; Shaʿbān, *Al-Shaykh*, 636–41.

[171] Uriya Shavit, "Is *Shura* a Muslim Form of Democracy? Roots and Systemization of a Polemic," *Middle Eastern Studies* 46 (2010): 349–74.

[172] Al-Albānī et al., "Masāʾil ʿAṣriyya," 17; interview with Muḥammad b. Mūsá Āl Naṣr, Amman, 20 June 2012.

[173] *Liqāʾ al-Shaykh*; interviews with Ziyād al-ʿAbbādī, Amman, 26 June 2012; Akram Ziyāda, Amman, 28 June 2012.

democracy also explain the main difference quietist Salafis discern between democracy, on the one hand, and *shūrá*, on the other: whereas the former is allegedly alien to Islam and can therefore result in "un-Islamic" rulings, the latter is part of Islamic tradition[174] and its results must therefore always remain within the limits of Islam.[175]

It almost speaks for itself that quietist Salafis in Jordan, given their ideologically inspired subservience to the regime as well as their rejection of political activism and democracy, are also against groups that do engage in contentious political action. Generally speaking, al-Albani was not against establishing groups (*jamāʿāt*) as such, as long as they adhered to the Qurʾan and the Sunna[176] and did not demand their members to pledge fealty to their leaders since that would be a *bidʿa*.[177] Political parties, on the other hand, only engage in sinful politics and cause division within Islam, al-Albani states.[178] Similar arguments are used against "partisanship" (*ḥizbiyya*)[179] by today's scholars of quietist Salafism in Jordan and the writings they spread. Political parties, they say, create a sense of loyalty and allegiance towards the party and its leadership, rather than to Islam, God and Muslims alone. This naturally leads to disunity and division, which in turn causes at least some Muslims to go astray.[180]

Fellow Muslims who, according to quietist Salafi scholars, have gone astray by founding groups in Jordan are sometimes accused of

[174] See Q. 42: 38, for example, which states "[...] their affair being counsel between them (*wa-amruhum shūrá baynahum*) [...]". This entire *sūra* is named "Shūrá," in fact. Consultation is also said to have been used for political purposes in early Islam. See, for example, M. J. Kister, "Notes on an Account of the Shura Appointed by ʿUmar b. al-Khattab," *Journal of Semitic Studies* 9 (1964): 320–6.

[175] *Liqāʾ al-Shaykh.* [176] Shaʿbān, *Al-Shaykh*, 685–91.

[177] *Ibid.*, 681–8; Ḥasan Sulaymān, "Mawqif al-Salafiyya al-Albāniyya min al-Jamāʿāt al-Islāmiyya," in *Rimāḥ al-Ṣaḥāʾif: Al-Salafiyya al-Albāniyya wa-Khuṣūmuhā* (Dubai: Markaz al-Misbār li-l-Dirāsāt wa-l-Buḥūth, 2010), 147–8.

[178] Al-Albānī, "Ajwibat al-ʿAllāma," 19–20; al-Albānī et al., "Masāʾil ʿAṣriyya," 19.

[179] ʿAlī b. Ḥasan [al-Ḥalabī], "Al-Salafiyya ... wa- ... l-Ḥizbiyya ...," *Al-Aṣāla* 1, no. 2 (15 Jumādá l-Ākhira 1413 [11 December 1992]): 51–3.

[180] *Id.*, *Al-Hudá wa-l-Nūr fī Hatk Sutūr al-Ḥizbiyya Dhāt al-Shunūr wa-Bayān annahā min Ḍalālāt al-Bidaʿ wa-Muḥaddathāt al-Umūr* (n.p.: Mānshūrāt Muntadayāt Kull al-Salafiyyīn, 2012), 10–13, 18–19, 27–32; *id.*, "Naṣāʾiḥ wa-Tawjīhāt Faḍīlat al-Shaykh ʿAlī b. Ḥasan ʿAlī al-Ḥalabī," in *Naṣāʾiḥ wa-Tawjīhāt al-Mufakkirīn wa-ʿUlamāʾ al-Islām li-l-Jamāʿāt wa-l-Aḥzāb al-Islāmiyya*, ed. Niẓām Salāma Sakkijhā; (Amman: Al-Maktaba al-Islāmiyya, 1999), 307–8; Abū l-ʿAbbās ʿImād Ṭāriq b. ʿAbd al-ʿAzīz al-Mukhtār, *Taḥdhīr al-Nāṣiḥīn min al-Taḥazzub li-l-ʿUlamāʾ wa-l-Murabbīn* (Amman: Al-Dār al-Athariyya, 2008), 37–65; Muḥammad Ibrāhīm Shaqra, "Al-Dīmuqrāṭiyya wa-l-Taʿaddudiyya al-Ḥizbiyya," *Al-Aṣāla* 1, no. 1 (15 Rabīʿ al-Thānī 1413 [13 October 1992]): 26–8; interviews with Muḥammad b. Mūsá Āl Naṣr, Amman, 20 June 2012; ʿAlī al-Ḥalabī, Amman 27 June 2012; Bāsim b. Fayṣal al-Jawābira, Amman, 26 June 2012.

"extremism" (*al-taṭarruf, al-ghulūw*) by them.[181] Apart from Jihadi-Salafis, who are often accused of this but who we will deal with in Chapter 6, it is probably mostly Hizb al-Tahrir that forms the target of the charge of "extremism", most likely because of their radical and highly politicised call for a caliphate and their supposedly deviant beliefs.[182] Not radical, but – according to quietists in Jordan – all the more deviant and, importantly, ignorant is the Jamaʿat al-Tabligh. Although Jordanian quietists acknowledge the group's piety and commitment to Islam, they do not approve of its non-Salafi ideas, its supposed *bidaʿ* and its lack of attention to studying.[183]

As we saw in the introduction, the Muslim Brotherhood combines some of the social activities that the Jamaʿat al-Tabligh is known for with the politicised character of Hizb al-Tahrir. From a Jordanian quietist point of view, this is doubly bad, especially as the Jordanian Brotherhood has, throughout the past decades, become less and less of a *daʿwa* organisation and has increasingly focussed on politics[184] and, through its oppositional character, contrasts sharply with the subservience found among quietist Salafis. Doctrinally, too, the Muslim Brotherhood is found lacking among Jordanian Salafis, even though some of the more hawkish members of the Brotherhood hold views on, for example, democracy that are quite similar to those espoused by Salafis.[185] In my conversations with Salafis, the Muslim Brotherhood – including its hawkish members – was often dismissed as unscholarly and shallow in its beliefs. This became painfully clear when a Salafi journalist interviewed the then leader of the Jordanian branch of the Muslim Brotherhood, ʿAbd al-Majid al-Dhunaybat, in 2002. The former was keen to ask al-Dhunaybat about doctrinal details that Salafis focus on so much, in order to define the Brotherhood ideologically, but got very general replies, quite possibly because the interviewee simply did not know the answer.

181 Muḥammad Ibrāhīm Shaqra, "Al-Taṭarruf al-Dīnī ... Maʿná!!" *Al-Aṣāla* 1, no. 2 (15 Jumādá l-Ākhira 1413 [11 December 1992]): 46–50.

182 Abū Rummān and Abū Haniyya, *Al-Ḥall*, 268–9; *id.*, *Al-Salafiyya al-Muḥāfaẓa*, 97–8; al-Hilālī, *Al-Jamāʿāt*, 369–470; Sulaymān, "Mawqif," 150–1.

183 Abū Rummān and Abū Haniyya, *Al-Ḥall*, 268; *id.*, *Al-Salafiyya al-Muḥāfaẓa*, 97; Abū ʿUbayda Mashhūr b. Ḥasan Āl Salmān, *Al-Imām al-Albānī wa-Jamāʿat al-Tablīgh: ʿAwāṣim wa-Qawāṣim, Sawābiq wa-Bawāʾiq* (Amman: Al-Dār al-Athariyya, 2010), esp. 278–339; al-Hilālī, *Al-Jamāʿāt*, 471–531; *id.*, *Manzalat*, 61–72; Shaʿbān, *Al-Shaykh*, 698–702; Sulaymān, "Mawqif," 149–50.

184 Interview with Shadi Hamid, Amman, 11 August 2008.

185 See, for example, Muḥammad ʿAbd al-Qādir Abū Fāris, *Al-Mushāraka fī l-Wizāra fī l-Anẓima al-Jāhiliyya* (n.p.: no publisher, 1991). Abū Fāris is a well-known hawkish scholar (i.e., opposed to engaging with the Jordanian regime) affiliated with the Jordanian Muslim Brotherhood and a prolific writer. Hawkish members of the Muslim Brotherhood often – though not always – also hold more conservative views on various issues.

When the journalist finally asked al-Dhunaybat whether he believed Ibn Hanbal had "erred in his position with regard to the inquisition of the creation of the Qur'an" – a classic theological controversy that Salafis are very interested in but that the Brotherhood really does not care about – an increasingly exasperated al-Dhunaybat simply answered: "We are with the Sunnis."[186]

The Jordanian Muslim Brotherhood thus represents more or less everything in an Islamic movement that quietist Salafis do not want. The latter object to the group's partisanship, its supposed lack of understanding of Islam and its members' allegiance to their leaders through a pledge of fealty.[187] In fact, the Brotherhood has become such a lightning rod for criticism of everything that is allegedly wrong with Islamism, that one Jordanian quietist scholar even accuses the group of "deviance in creed, distancing from the Sunna, falling into polytheism, reviving *bida*ʿ, the glorification of innovators [...], as well as partisanship, armament and following the method of the Khawarij in *takfīr*, shedding blood and causing revolutions". The Muslim Brotherhood, he states, is "the most dangerous [movement] to Islam and Muslims".[188] Hyperbolic perhaps, but it does show the vehemence with which quietist Salafis in Jordan defend their striving for a utopia through *al-taṣfiya wa-l-tarbiya* and criticise those who differ with them. It also underlines once more that quietist Salafism in Jordan has always been underpinned by a strongly apolitical ideology – even if the aloofist al-Albani sometimes took positions differing from those some of his more loyalist students later held – which facilitated the movement's domestication process. Yet how this process took place has also been shaped by the historical context in which Salafism in Jordan has existed throughout the years, which is what we must now turn to.

186 "Fī Ḥiwār Maftūḥ maʿa l-Murāqib al-ʿĀmm li-Jamāʿat al-Ikhwān al-Muslimīn fī l-Urdunn," *Al-Qibla* 1, no. 3 (Summer 2002): 98.

187 Abū Rummān and Abū Haniyya, *Al-Ḥall*, 266–7; *id.*, *Al-Salafiyya al-Muḥāfaẓa*, 94–6; al-Hilālī, *Al-Jamāʿāt*, 195–367; *Liqāʾ al-Shaykh*; Shaʿbān, *Al-Shaykh*, 692–7; Sulaymān, "Mawqif," 146–9.

188 Muḥammad Māhir ʿAbd al-Karīm al-Khaṭīb, *Ḥarakat al-Ikhwān al-Muslimīn: ʿAraḍ wa-Naqd* (Amman: Al-Baynūnī, 2012), 5.

Part II

History

3 The Transnational History of Salafism in Jordan

"The Salafi movement in Jordan began in the 1970s as the result of individuals exposed to Salafi thought while studying abroad in Lebanon, Syria and Egypt."[1] Thus Wiktorowicz begins a very brief section on Salafi history in Jordan. Although this statement is partly incorrect – the Salafi movement in Jordan has roots that go back further than the 1970s, as we will see in this chapter – it rightly points to the transnational ties among Jordanian Salafis and their influence on the movement's historical development. These ties, particularly with Syria, Egypt, Saudi Arabia and Kuwait, have shaped how Jordan's quietist Salafi community functions today, although indigenous Jordanian developments have also been of great importance, of course.

In this chapter, we first look at the history of Salafism in Jordan prior to the settlement of Muhammad Nasir al-Din al-Albani in the kingdom in the early 1980s, which has been all but ignored in the secondary literature, both in Western languages and in Arabic.[2] It was in this period that influences from Syria and Egypt on Jordanian Salafis were strongest. We then move on to the person of al-Albani and the impact this Syrian had on the historical development of the quietist Salafi trend in Jordan. Finally, we turn to events in Saudi Arabia and Kuwait and the imprint they left on the quietist Salafi community in Jordan until al-Albani's death in 1999. As we will see, all of these factors have influenced the way in which Jordanian Salafis strive to realise their desired utopia of the *salaf*. In turn, this has affected, underlined and entrenched their apolitical ideology, leading to their further domestication as a movement that is implicitly loyal to the regime.

[1] Wiktorowicz, *Management*, 120.

[2] Abū Rummān and Abū Haniyya (*Al-Ḥall*, 235–6; *Al-Salafiyya al-Muḥāfaẓa*, 42–3) and Wiktorowicz (*Management*, 120; "Salafi," 222, 229–30) incorrectly give the impression that Salafism in Jordan started with al-Albānī.

Salafism in Jordan Prior to al-Albani

To Salafis in Jordan, he is always *the* shaykh. When Jordanian quietist Salafis nowadays talk about anyone this way, it is al-Albani they are referring to. Indeed, in the little attention that is paid to the history of Salafism in Jordan in the secondary literature, al-Albani features prominently.[3] This is indeed correct, since al-Albani certainly did play a major role in the development and growth of Salafism in Jordan, yet it goes too far to label him "the founding father of [quietist] Salafism" in the kingdom, as some do.[4] This does not do justice to the people – both Jordanians and others – who introduced and preached a Salafi message in the kingdom long before al-Albani arrived in Jordan.

The Roots of Salafism in Jordan

As we saw in the introduction, Jordan is an overwhelmingly Sunni Muslim country, with the only minority of any numerical significance being the Christian community. Some authors state that the type of Sunni Islam adhered to in Jordan at the beginning of its foundation as an emirate in 1921 was mostly of a "popular (*shaʿbī*) and Sufi" nature, suggesting it was far removed from the strictly text-based character of Salafism.[5] The most prominent scholar of the quietist Salafi community in Jordan today, ʿAli al-Halabi, does not fundamentally dispute this, but he does claim that there are strong indications of a Salafi presence in the emirate even at that time. This was partly the case, he states, because of local Muslims who went to Mecca for the Islamic pilgrimage (*ḥajj*) in the 1920s and picked up Salafi teachings there, which they subsequently brought back with them upon their return.[6]

Al-Halabi also claims that the emirate was founded in an intellectual climate in which Syrian Salafi reformers such as Muhammad Rashid Rida (1865–1935)[7] and Muhibb al-Din al-Khatib (1886–1969)[8] played

[3] Abū Rummān and Abū Haniyya, *Al-Salafiyya al-Muḥāfaẓa*, 29–36; Wiktorowicz, *Management*, 120–1; *id.*, "Salafi," 222, 229–30.

[4] Abū Rummān and Abū Haniyya, *Al-Salafiyya al-Muḥāfaẓa*, 29. [5] *Id.*, *Al-Ḥall*, 234.

[6] ʿAlī b. Ḥasan b. ʿAlī b. ʿAbd al-Ḥamīd al-Ḥalabī al-Atharī, *Mujmal Tārīkh al-Daʿwa al-Salafiyya fī l-Diyār al-Urdunniyya* (Amman: Al-Dār al-Athariyya, 2009), 14.

[7] For more on Muḥammad Rashīd Riḍā's life and beliefs, see Hourani, Arabic, 222–44; Umar Ryad, *Islamic Reformism and Christianity: A Critical Reading of the Works of Muḥammad Rashīd Riḍā and His Associates (1898–1935)* (Leiden: Brill, 2009); Simon A. Wood, *Christian Cricitisms, Islamic Proofs: Rashīd Riḍā's Modernist Defense of Islam* (Oxford: Oneworld, 2008).

[8] For more on Muḥibb al-Dīn al-Khaṭīb, see Sayyid Muhammad Rizvi, "Muhibb al-Din al-Khatib: A Portrait of a Salafi-Arabist (1886–1969)" (MA thesis, Simon Fraser University, 1991).

a prominent role through their writings, their journals and their personal ties with the emir of Mecca, Husayn b. ʿAli, and his son, the later King ʿAbdallah of Jordan.[9] More specifically, al-Halabi discerns Salafi leanings among several official Jordanian Muslim scholars in the days of the emirate and early decades of the kingdom. These scholars included shaykh ʿAbdallah al-Qalqili (1899–1969), a former mufti of Jordan, and the former supreme judge of the kingdom, Ibrahim al-Qattan (1916–1984), both of whom expressed strong reservations against the tenets of Sufism.[10] While anti-Sufi views do not make one a Salafi, al-Halabi implicitly describes these scholars as such. This is even more the case with the first supreme judge in the emirate of Jordan, Muhammad al-Khadir al-Shinqiti (1868–1935), who was not only critical of Sufism but is also said to have been a Salafi in creedal issues and with regard to the attributes of God, which – as we saw in Chapter 1 – is a theological matter on which Salafis have fairly distinct views.[11]

Whether or not the people mentioned above can really be described as full-blown Salafis is difficult to judge. This question is, however, perhaps less important than the observation that, in any case, these men were probably isolated examples of what could be described as Salafi tendencies – even if they held important official religious positions – with little connection to the Islam professed by their contemporaries in Jordan. This is not to deny that they had an impact on the Jordanian population, which they probably did, but simply to state that their presence does not seem to have constituted what one might call a Salafi "trend" in any way. This changed, however, in the 1950s.

The Beginnings of a Trend

It may seem as if Salafism in Jordan, at least with regard to its roots, was entirely a foreign-inspired affair. Although we will see later on that Jordanian Salafis themselves had a great impact on the country's Salafi movement as well in more recent decades, this was indeed the case. The reason for this was that until the 1970s, there was little possibility for students of Islam to get a solid religious education at Jordanian institutes, forcing them to go abroad if they wanted to become Muslim scholars.[12] If they ended up in Saudi Arabia, this often influenced them in such a way that they would take the Salafi knowledge acquired there back

[9] Al-Ḥalabī, *Mujmal*, 17–30.
[10] *Ibid.*, 35–40; interview with Mashhūr b. Ḥasan Āl Salmān, Amman, 27 June 2012.
[11] Al-Ḥalabī, *Mujmal*, 31–2; interview with Usāma Shaḥāda, Amman, 7 June 2012.
[12] Murād Shukrī Suwaydān, "Thalāthūn ʿĀmman min Tārīkh al-Daʿwa al-Salafiyya fī l-Mamlaka al-Urdunniyya (1980–2010)" (unpublished manuscript in possession of the author, n.d.), 3; Wiktorowicz, *Management*, 120.

home with them. Some, however, went to Al-Azhar University, the venerable orthodox centre of Islamic learning in Egypt. Two of these, Ahmad al-Salik (1928–2010) and Muhammad Ibrahim Shaqra (b. 1933), ended up as Salafis when they came back home in the 1950s and thereby laid the basis of the Salafi trend in Jordan.

The story of Ahmad al-Salik began in Turkey, where he was born and partly raised but which he left when he was six. His father, Muhammad al-Salik, was apparently convinced that sending his son to a Turkish secular school would not be beneficial to his religious beliefs and thus emigrated with his family for religious reasons. After travelling to several countries, the al-Salik family ended up in Jordan, where Muhammad became a prominent preacher at the al-Husayni Mosque in Amman, the biggest and most important mosque in Jordan at that time.[13] Muhammad al-Salik was not a Salafi, however, but a Sufi and a mosque was founded in his name – the Al-Salik Mosque – in the al-Hashimi al-Shimali neighbourhood in Amman. Ahmad, like his father Muhammad, was also a Sufi and went to study at Al-Azhar University in Cairo in 1952. During his studies there, he is said to have been greatly influenced by Salafi books that he apparently read outside the orthodox Azhar curriculum, including the writings of Ibn ʿAbd al-Wahhab, and by the time he returned to Jordan in 1956, he had more or less become a Salafi and began preaching in the Al-Salik Mosque in al-Hashimi al-Shimali.[14] As such, he became an important source of influence among the budding Salafi community, which was still in its infancy at the time.[15]

Ahmad al-Salik's companion in much of his early career was Muhammad Ibrahim Shaqra, a Palestinian who had fled to Jordan with his family when he was still a teenager in 1948.[16] Like al-Salik, he went to study at al-Azhar in Egypt in 1952 and by the time he returned a few years later, he had similarly become convinced that Salafism was the way forward.[17] He went to the same al-Hashimi al-Shimali neighbourhood in Amman and started preaching there at the Al-Takruri Mosque, which was only a few hundred metres away from the Al-Salik Mosque.[18] His

[13] ʿIṣām Mūsá Hādī, "Ḥayāt Aḥmad al-Sālik" (unpublished manuscript in possession of the author, n.d.), 14–15.

[14] Interview with ʿIṣām Hādī, Amman, 19 January 2013.

[15] Interviews with Ziyād al-ʿAbbādī, Amman, 26 June 2012; Muḥammad Abū Ruḥayyim, Amman, 16 January 2013.

[16] Interview with Muḥammad Ibrāhīm Shaqra, Amman, 27 June 2012.

[17] ʿĀṣim Muḥammad Ibrāhīm Shaqra, *Al-Rudūd al-ʿIlmiyya al-Sunniyya Yaruddu fī-hi l-Kitāb ʿalá Mā Jāʾa min Hujūm ʿalá l-Shaykh Muḥammad Ibrāhīm Shaqra fī ʿadaday* al-Aṣāla 25 wa-26 (n.p.: no publisher, 2000), bāʾ-jīm; interview with ʿIṣām Hādī, Amman, 19 January 2013.

[18] Interview with ʿIṣām Hādī, Amman, 19 January 2013.

closeness with al-Salik was consolidated even further when he married the latter's sister.[19] In the early 1960s, Shaqra went to Saudi Arabia to take up the position of professor of Arabic at the newly founded Islamic University of Medina, where he met important Salafi shaykhs, such as ʿAbd al-ʿAziz b. Baz, and deepened his Salafi tendencies.[20] Upon his return to Jordan a few years later, he and Ahmad al-Salik gained an increased following because of their sustained Salafi preaching, emphasising *tawḥīd*, rejecting *bidaʿ* and alternating their preaching in each other's mosques. Because of this and due to his and al-Salik's high stature as Azhar-educated *ʿulamāʾ* – even though they deviated from that institute's orthodox teachings – Shaqra became perhaps the most important scholar of Jordan's Salafi trend in the 1960s and 1970s.[21]

The early Salafi trend in Jordan was supported even further by several other scholars who joined the movement slightly later. These included the originally Palestinian ʿAbd al-Rahim Saʿid, the father of the current leader of the Muslim Brotherhood in Jordan, Hammam Saʿid (b. 1944),[22] and Yusuf al-Barqawi (d. 2009), a mufti and teacher at various mosques in al-Zarqaʾ.[23] Although the latter was said to have been influenced by Hanbali thought later in life and eventually got involved in a dispute with al-Albani over the validity of *madhāhib* because of this, which pitted al-Albani's students against him as well,[24] he was nevertheless eulogised on the main Jordanian Salafi internet forum, *Kull al-Salafiyyin*, when he died in 2009.[25]

Perhaps the most important scholar who joined the Salafi movement in Jordan slightly later but prior to al-Albani was Muhammad Nasib al-Rifaʿi (1915–1992). Born in Aleppo in a religious Sufi family, he later turned to Salafism.[26] He is said to have met his fellow Syrian al-Albani in 1945[27] and actually got in trouble for his Salafi beliefs since a crackdown on supposed "Wahhabi agents" acting on behalf of Saudi Arabia meant

[19] Shaqra, *Al-Rudūd, jīm*.
[20] *Ibid.*, *jīm-ḥāʾ*; interview with Muḥammad Ibrāhīm Shaqra, Amman, 27 June 2012.
[21] Shaqra, *Al-Rudūd, dāl*; interviews with Ziyād al-ʿAbbādī, Amman, 26 June 2012; Muḥammad Abū Ruḥayyim, Amman, 16 January 2013; ʿIṣām Hādī, Amman, 19 January 2013.
[22] Abū Rummān and Abū Haniyya, *Al-Ḥall*, 235.
[23] For more on al-Barqāwī's views, see al-ʿUmarī, *Ḥiwār*.
[24] Interview with ʿIṣām Hādī, Amman, 19 January 2013.
[25] ʿAlī b. Ḥasan al-Ḥalabī, *Wafāt Faḍīlat al-Shaykh Yūsuf al-Barqāwī – ʿAlam min Aʿlām Madīnat al-Zarqāʾ* (www.kulalsalafiyeen.com/vb/printthread.php?t=11556, 21 October 2009 (accessed 21 February 2013)). See also the many responses to al-Ḥalabī's original post on this forum.
[26] ʿIṣām Mūsá Hādī, "Ṣafaḥāt min Ḥayāt al-ʿAllāma Muḥammad Nasīb al-Rifāʿī" (unpublished manuscript in possession of the author, n.d.), 5–6.
[27] *Ibid.*, 11–12.

al-Rifaʿi was targeted by the Syrian regime and arrested. Once released, he moved to Lebanon in the 1970s, but left because of the civil war in that country and ended up in Jordan, where he settled in the aforementioned Amman neighbourhood of al-Hashimi al-Shimali in 1976. Given the strong Salafi presence in that area of the capital, with Shaqra and al-Salik preaching in the Al-Takruri Mosque and Al-Salik Mosque, he quickly joined them in their *daʿwa* and, as such, is said to have helped expand the Salafi trend in Jordan.[28] Like al-Barqawi, al-Rifaʿi was extensively eulogised by Jordanian quietists when he died in December 1992.[29]

Al-Albani's Impact on Quietist Salafism in Jordan

All of the early Salafi scholars mentioned so far were foreign-born (Palestinian, Turkish, Syrian) and often studied abroad as well. The same applies to the man whose influence turned Salafism in Jordan from a budding trend into a substantial movement with international recognition: Muhammad Nasir al-Din al-Albani. Born in Shkodër in Albania in 1914, the young al-Albani grew up in a poor but religious family. From the early 1920s on, Albania was ruled by the secularist prime minister and later president and even king Ahmet Zogu (1895–1961), who wanted to modernise Albania in a way similar to what Mustafa Kemal Atatürk (1881–1938), the first president of Turkey, had done in the early Turkish Republic. Like Ahmad al-Salik, whose father did not want to send him to a secular Turkish school for fear of what it would do to his son's religious beliefs, al-Albani was taken away from the Albanian school system by his father, Nuh Najati l-Albani, because of its secularism. The young al-Albani's family therefore emigrated to Damascus in French-occupied Syria.[30] It was here that his search for the utopia of the *salaf* began.

Al-Albani Prior to Coming to Jordan

The family al-Albani grew up in were strict followers of the Hanafi school of Islamic law and the young Muhammad started his religious

[28] *Ibid.*, 13–17.

[29] Muḥammad Ibrāhīm Shaqra, "Al-Shaykh Muḥammad Nasīb al-Rifāʿī: Ṣafḥa Daʿwiyya Ṭuwiyat?!" *Al-Aṣāla* 1, no. 3 (15 Shaʿbān 1413 [8 February 1993]): 21–9; Murād Shukrī, "Al-Shaykh Muḥammad Nasīb al-Rifāʿī – Raḥimahu llāh," *Al-Aṣāla* 1, no. 3 (15 Shaʿbān 1413 [8 February 1993]): 30.

[30] Hamdeh, "Emergence," 39; Al-Jabbūrī, *Juhūd*, 49–50; Shaʿbān, *Al-Shaykh*, 49–51; Usāma Shaḥāda, *Al-Daʿwa al-Salafiyya: Maqālāt fī Mafhūmihā, Tārīkhihā wa-Tab āyunihā ʿan Jamāʿāt al-ʿUnf wa-l-Taṭarruf* (n.p.: no publisher, n.d.), 121; al-Shāmī, *Ārāʾ*, 47; Muḥammad b. Ibrāhīm al-Shaybānī, *Mukhtaṣar Kitāb al-Albānī: Jihāduhu wa-Ḥayātuhu l-ʿIlmiyya* (Kuwait: Markaz Makhṭūṭāt wa-l-Turāth wa-l-Wathāʾiq, 1998), 7.

education by being taught Hanafi *fiqh* by his father (who also trained him as a watch repairman), as well as local teachers.[31] From an early age, however, al-Albani is said to have had a suspicion of Sufism and he gradually moved away from the Hanafi *madhhab* and the blind following of Islamic schools of law in general. This attitude was stimulated by his reading of the leading Muslim reformist journal of the day, *Al-Manar*, which was published by the aforementioned Muhammad Rashid Rida[32] and which encouraged al-Albani to individually take up the study of *ḥadīths* as a path towards reform and away from *madhāhib*.[33]

However, the influence Rida had on al-Albani was not an isolated phenomenon. It seems that al-Albani was thoroughly influenced by a milieu that was heavily impacted by modernist Syrian Salafis, including Muhammad Bahjat al-Bitar (1894–1976), a student of the aforementioned Jamal al-Din al-Qasimi.[34] In fact, Syrian Salafis set up several organisations in the 1930s, including *Al-Tamaddun al-Islami* (Islamic civilisation),[35] which published a journal by the same name[36] to which al-Albani regularly contributed.[37] Indeed, in the 1980s – when he had already moved to Jordan – al-Albani even published new versions of books by modernist Salafis like Rida and al-Qasimi upon which he commented in the footnotes or whose *ḥadīths* he checked for authenticity.[38] Apart from a shared desire to emulate the *salaf* by emphasising *tawḥīd* and rejecting *bidaʿ*, modernist Salafis seem to have had in common with al-Albani that they were sceptical of Sufism and – especially – rejected *taqlīd*

31 Hamdeh, "Emergence," 39; al-Shāmī, *Ārāʾ*, 48–9.
32 Abū Rummān and Abū Haniyya, *Al-Salafiyya al-Muḥāfaẓa*, 31; al-Albānī, "Masāʾil wa-Ajwibatuhā," *Al-Aṣāla* 2, no. 10, 41; Brown, *Canonization*, 321; Hamdeh, "Emergence," 86–8, 261; al-Jabbūrī, *Juhūd*, 52; ʿAbd al-ʿAzīz b. Muḥammad b. ʿAbdallāh al-Sadḥān, *Al-Imām al-Albānī Durūs wa-Mawāqif wa-ʿIbar* (Riyadh: Dār al-Tawḥīd, 2008), 31–9; Shaʿbān, *Al-Shaykh*, 52; al-Shāmī, *Ārāʾ*, 49.
33 Abū Rummān and Abū Haniyya, *Al-Salafiyya al-Muḥāfaẓa*, 32; Brown, *Canonization*, 321–3; Hamdeh, "Emergence," 39–40; Shaḥāda, *Al-Daʿwa*, 121–3, 127–8; al-Shāmī, *Ārāʾ*, 49; Samīr b. Amīn al-Zuhayrī, *Muḥaddith al-ʿAṣr Muḥammad Nāṣir al-Dīn al-Albānī* (Riyadh: Dār al-Mughnī, 1421 [2000 [1999]]), 14–15. However, for differences between al-Albānī and Riḍā, see Hamdeh, "Emergence," 87.
34 Lacroix, "L'apport," 48–9; *id.*, "Between," 63–5; interview with Fatḥi al-Mawṣilī, Amman, 23 January 2013.
35 For more on this organisation from the point of view of one of its recent leaders, see Ahmad Mouaz al-Khatib, "Al-Tamaddun al-Islami: Passé et present d'une association réformiste Damascène," *Maghreb-Machrek*, no. 198 (2008–9): 79–89. I would like to thank Thomas Pierret for providing me with this article.
36 Pierret, *Religion*, 104.
37 These and other articles by al-Albānī were collected and published in Nūr al-Dīn Ṭālib, ed., *Maqālāt al-Albānī* (Riyadh: Dār al-Aṭlas, 2000).
38 Muḥammad Jamāl al-Dīn al-Qāsimī, *Iṣlāḥ al-Masājid min al-Bidaʿ wa-l-ʿAwābid* (Beirut and Damascus: Al-Maktab al-Islāmī, 1983); Muḥammad Rashīd Riḍā, *Ḥuqūq al-Nisāʾ fī l-Islām* (Beirut and Damascus: Al-Maktab al-Islāmī, 1984).

of the schools of Islamic law.[39] In the latter sense, at least, al-Albani may well have had more in common with modernist Salafis from Syria than with Wahhabi scholars from Saudi Arabia during his lifetime, who were more likely to rely on the Hanbali *madhhab*.[40]

Despite being influenced by Syrian Salafism and thus presumably having ideological allies among them, it appears that al-Albani did not have many like-minded fellow scholars in Syria. One of the few people who seems to have shared his views, although in a more moderate fashion (he is said to have had good ties with certain Sufi scholars, for example), was ʿAbd al-Qadir al-Arnaʾut (1924–2004). Like al-Albani, he was originally Albanian but lived in Damascus now, had little formal education but was considered a major and largely self-taught scholar and also made his living as a watch repairman.[41] Doctrinally, al-Arnaʾut similarly focussed on the study of *ḥadīth*s, was part of the same Syrian Salafi milieu that al-Albani also belonged to and did not follow a particular *madhhab*.[42]

Interestingly, al-Albani also found kindred spirits in the Syrian branch of the Muslim Brotherhood, which had been founded in 1939. This may sound odd, given quietist Jordanian Salafis' rejection of the Brotherhood's goals and methods, which we saw in Chapter 2. There are three reasons why this was not as strange as it seems, however. Firstly, although al-Albani was in close contact with members of the Syrian Muslim Brotherhood and even gave lessons to them,[43] he never actually became a member of the organisation, probably indicating a desire to keep his distance from the group. Secondly, the Syrian Muslim Brotherhood was divided into a Damascene wing, which was strongly Salafi in its beliefs and was led by men such as Mustafa al-Sibaʿi (1915–1964), ʿIsam al-ʿAttar (b. 1927) and Zuhayr al-Shawish (1925–2013), and a more Sufi, Ashʿari wing from Aleppo, which was led by people like ʿAbd al-Fattah Abu Ghudda (1917–1997) and Saʿid Hawwa (1935–1989). Not surprisingly, it was the Salafi wing from Damascus with which al-Albani was most closely associated.[44]

[39] Shaḥāda, *Al-Daʿwa*, 123, 134; interview with Wāʾil al-Batīrī, Amman, 11 January 2014.

[40] This dimension should not be exaggerated, however, since many Saudi scholars – certainly nowadays – also use *ijtihād* instead of *taqlīd* of the Ḥanbalī *madhhab*. Interview with ʿAbd al-Malik Besfort Maxhuni, al-Zarqāʾ, 18 January 2014. As mentioned in Chapter 1, the exact relations between al-Albānī and the Jordanian Salafī trend on the one hand and the Syrian Salafī reform movement on the other really deserve a separate publication, however, and will not be dealt with in more detail here.

[41] Pierret, *Religion*, 105–6.

[42] "Tarjamat Faḍīlat al-Shaykh al-Muḥaddith ʿAbd al-Qādir al-Arnāʾūṭ (Raḥimahu llāh)," *Al-Qibla* 4, nos. 10–11 (November 2005): 39–43.

[43] Abū Rummān and Abū Haniyya, *Al-Salafiyya al-Muḥāfaẓa*, 94; Sulaymān, "Mawqif," 145.

[44] Abū Rummān and Abū Haniyya, *Al-Salafiyya al-Muḥāfaẓa*, 33; Gūl, "Al-Khiṭāb," 94–5.

Thirdly, quietist Salafis' opposition to *ḥizbiyya* and political activism does not mean that they are totally against establishing Islamic groups in general. In fact, al-Albani may not have been entirely against this, as long as such groups remained true to the Qur'an and the Sunna as he saw it, although it appears al-Albani remained sceptical of Islamist political parties throughout his life.[45]

The reason al-Albani never got more involved with the Muslim Brotherhood in Syria than he actually did seems to have had a lot to do with his aloofist quietism. As we saw before, al-Albani was a scholar who stuck to his beliefs if he thought he had a Qur'anic verse or a supposedly authentic *ḥadīth* to back them up, irrespective of politics or rulers' interests. The same aloofness from political considerations, expressed in a strong ideological independence, seems to have guided both his willingness to engage with the Salafi wing of the Syrian Muslim Brotherhood and his unwillingness to join them officially and become a member.[46]

Such an aloofist attitude, with its ideological stubbornness and principled apoliticism, is also likely to create enemies and, indeed, al-Albani had plenty of them in Syria. Apart from the aforementioned shaykh al-Buti, other Syrian scholars – particularly those of a Sufi persuasion and/or the more orthodox followers of a *madhhab* – criticised al-Albani as an "erroneous Wahhabi" (*Wahhābī ḍāll*).[47] One Salafi author states that al-Albani "patiently put up [with this criticism] and bore the grievances [that he felt as a result]".[48] Perhaps, yet this is not the impression one gets when reading about these debates, particularly with the Syrian Brotherhood-leader ʿAbd al-Fattah Abu Ghudda of the group's Sufi wing, in which al-Albani was sometimes joined by prominent Brotherhood-member Zuhayr al-Shawish,[49] of the group's Damascene Salafi wing.[50] Accusations of arrogance, calling each other names and rising tempers seem to have been frequent elements of the discussions and disputes in which al-Albani was involved.[51]

Part of the discussions between al-Albani and his opponents dealt with the former's scholarly credentials. Having been largely self-taught, al-Albani was open to the charge that he never enjoyed a proper religious education and was "merely" a watch repairman. Interestingly, al-Albani

[45] Abū Rummān and Abū Haniyya, *Al-Salafiyya al-Muḥāfaẓa*, 92–3; Pierret, *Religion*, 107; Sulaymān, "Mawqif," 142–6.
[46] Interview with Ibrāhīm al-ʿAsʿas, Amman, 14 January 2013. See also Olidort, *Politics*, 13.
[47] Al-Jabbūrī, *Juhūd*, 56–7; Shaḥāda, *Al-Daʿwa*, 123; al-Shāmī, *Ārāʾ*, 51.
[48] Al-Shāmī, *Ārāʾ*, 51.
[49] Although initially on very good terms with Shāwīsh, al-Albānī's relationship with him would later sour. For more on this, see Hamdeh, "Emergence," 43, footnote 51, 266–7.
[50] Pierret, *Religion*, 107. [51] Hamdeh, "Emergence," 202–5.

himself was proud of the latter factor and stressed that his daytime job allowed him to be financially and politically independent of any employer or regime.[52] Although al-Albani was fiercely defended against his critics, particularly in later years, by his supporters and students,[53] the opposition against him in Syria became more powerful and local religious authorities saw him as a Salafi rabble-rouser and apparently frequently frustrated his travels in the country by calling the police.[54]

In such a climate of increased pressure, it was perhaps not surprising that al-Albani accepted the offer to take up a teaching position at the newly founded Islamic University of Medina in Saudi Arabia in 1961. He was invited there by his friend and fellow scholar Ibn Baz, who shared his interest in the study of *ḥadīth*s. He is said to have been extremely popular among students in Medina.[55] One Salafi writing about this period even states: "When [al-Albani] used to enter the university in the morning, you almost could not see [his] car among the many students who were circling around it, greeting the shaykh, asking him questions and calling for fatwas from him."[56] Hyperbole perhaps, but al-Albani does seem to have enjoyed a genuine popularity among students and his presence in Medina gave a tremendous boost to the study of *ḥadīth*s, causing some students to question their professors' use of these and demanding authentication of the traditions of the Prophet according to al-Albani's standards.[57]

Al-Albani's popularity among students at the Islamic University of Medina was not always shared by his colleagues there. It has been suggested that they were simply jealous of his success among students, but there was most probably (also) something else going on, namely al-Albani's insistence on *ijtihād* and rejection of the *madhāhib*, which contrasted sharply with the Hanbali *fiqh* that many Wahhabi scholars in Saudi Arabia followed at the time. Al-Albani's approach not only differed with that of particularly the Saudi mufti, Muhammad b. Ibrahim Al al-Shaykh, but also resulted in specific rulings that clashed with the prevailing Saudi

52 *Ibid.*, 67–8.

53 See, for example, Aḥmad b. Ibrāhīm Abū l-ʿAynayn, *Al-Intiṣār li-l-Ḥaqq wa-Ahl al-ʿIlm al-Kibār wa-l-Radd ʿalá Man Ramá l-Shaykh Muḥammad Nāṣir al-Dīn al-Albānī Raḥimahu llāh bi-l-Tasāhul* (Kuwait: Maktabat al-Imam al-Zuhbī, 2004); ʿAmr ʿAbd al-Munʿim Salīm, *Barāʾat al-Dhimma bi-Nuṣrat al-Sunna: Al-Difāʿ al-Sunnī ʿan al-Albānī wa-l-Jawāb ʿan Shubah Ṣāḥib "Al-Taʿrīf"* (Ṭanṭā: Dār al-Ḍiyāʾ, n.d.).

54 Pierret, *Religion*, 107. For more on al-Albānī's stay in prison, see al-Sadḥān, *Al-Imām*, 48–53.

55 Interestingly, however, Shaqra worked at the same university at the same time but claims he was unaware of al-Albānī's presence there. A possible explanation of this is that they may have been employed at different departments or faculties. Interview with Muḥammad Ibrāhīm Shaqra, Amman, 27 June 2012.

56 Al-Jabbūrī, *Juhūd*, 59.

57 Lacroix, "L'apport," 51–3; *id.*, "Between," 65–7.

Hanbali ways.[58] These included the aforementioned belief that it is not compulsory for women to cover their faces in public, differing ideas on how to hold the hands during prayer, al-Albani's view that wearing shoes in a mosque was allowed and his statement that a niche in a mosque (*miḥrāb*) indicating the direction of prayer (*qibla*), though very common, was actually a *bidʿa*.[59]

As a result of al-Albani's popularity and/or such ideological controversies, his contract was not renewed in 1963, forcing him to leave the Islamic University of Medina.[60] This eventually led al-Albani back to Syria, which had not become much more welcoming to his unabashedly Salafi views in the meantime. In fact, his continuing criticism of others even got him arrested and imprisoned for a short period on the charge of defaming Sufi shaykhs in 1967.[61] He was apparently arrested and put in gaol again a few years later.[62] All of this probably stimulated al-Albani to look for a chance to leave Syria altogether. That chance would come from Jordan.

Al-Albani in Jordan

Al-Albani's first visit to Jordan is said to have occurred through shaykh Muhammad Ibrahim Shaqra, who travelled to Damascus and met with some Salafis there, including al-Albani, in 1966. Shaqra was apparently so impressed by al-Albani's knowledge that he asked the latter to visit Jordan.[63] A year later, the same request came from Ahmad al-Salik, who had been told about al-Albani by Shaqra and met him in Damascus too. Shortly thereafter, al-Albani went to Jordan for a period of three days while staying with al-Salik and giving some lessons in the al-Hashimi al-Shimali neighbourhood in Amman.[64] This attracted so much attention from Salafis that al-Albani started going to Jordan every month for lessons and *daʿwa*, with people coming from the nearby cities of al-Zarqaʾ and al-Salt to hear him speak in people's homes. This increased even more when al-Albani's daughter ʿUnaysa married a Jordanian Salafi, Nizam Sakkijha, and went to live in the kingdom, giving her father a good reason to stay in Jordan for longer periods of time.[65] This development was abetted by the growing tensions between Islamists and the regime in Syria in the late 1970s, which is likely to have spilled over into state repression of Salafi

58 *Id.*, "L'apport," 51–2; *id.*, "Between," 65–6.
59 Hamdeh, "Emergence," 48.
60 Lacroix, "L'apport," 52; *id.*, "Between," 66.
61 Pierret, *Religion*, 107.
62 Hamdeh, "Emergence," 42–3.
63 Shaqra, *Al-Rudūd, dāl*; interview with Muḥammad Ibrāhīm Shaqra, Amman, 27 June 2012.
64 Interview with ʿIṣām Hādī, Amman, 19 January 2013.
65 Al-Ḥalabī, *Mujmal*, 107–8; interview with Usāma Shaḥāda, Amman, 7 June 2012.

scholars like al-Albani too, creating an even greater desire to stay in the relatively stable Kingdom of Jordan.[66]

Interestingly, al-Albani's popularity also extended to the Muslim Brotherhood in Jordan, many of whose members came to benefit from his knowledge and listen to his lessons by visiting him at his home and inviting him to theirs in the 1970s. In fact, the Brotherhood's interest in al-Albani is said to have gone so far that the organisation even allowed him to use their own centres to speak to audiences. Yet al-Albani, being the independent and principled scholar that he was, stuck to his beliefs and did not shy away from criticising major leaders from the Brotherhood's past, such as founder Hasan al-Banna and ideologue Sayyid Qutb. This, together with the growing number of Brotherhood members who felt attracted to al-Albani's message – including Mashhur b. Hasan, who is now one of the most prominent Salafis in Jordan – caused the organisation to boycott al-Albani and to prohibit members from attending his lessons.[67]

Al-Albani's ability to convince others to follow his beliefs was on display even more clearly with regard to the Tali'at al-Ba'th al-Islami (Vanguard of the Islamic Renaissance), a small radical group that split from the Muslim Brotherhood in Jordan in late 1973. The reason the group left the Brotherhood is said to have been related to the October War between Israel on the one hand and Egypt and Syria on the other earlier that year. More specifically, a debate ensued within the Brotherhood over the question of whether it is allowed to fight Israel under the banner of supposedly apostate regimes such as those in Egypt and Syria.[68] Led by a man called Muhammad al-Ra'fat, a former prominent member of the Muslim Brotherhood in Jordan, the Tali'at al-Ba'th al-Islami apparently felt that this was not allowed and they are said to have begun excommunicating religious scholars and even society as a whole.[69] The Brotherhood, unhappy about this development, asked al-Albani to intervene and the latter – after three days of long discussions that went on well into the night – managed to convince them that their views were wrong. Subsequently, all members of the group – including Basim al-Jawabira, who became al-Albani's student and is now one of the most prominent quietist Salafi scholars in Jordan – abandoned their radical beliefs.[70]

66 Interview with 'Iṣām Hādī, Amman, 19 January 2013.
67 Al-Ḥalabī, *Mujmal*, 108–10; interview with Muḥammad Abū Ruḥayyim, Amman, 16 January 2013.
68 Interview with Salīm al-Hilālī, Amman, 28 January 2013.
69 Interview with Usāma Shaḥāda, Amman, 7 June 2012.
70 Abū Rummān and Abū Haniyya, *Al-Salafiyya al-Muḥāfaẓa*, 43–4; al-Ḥalabī, *Mujmal*, 110–11; interviews with Salīm al-Hilālī, Amman, 28 January 2013; Bāsim b. Fayṣal al-Jawābira, Amman, 26 June 2012.

Such occurrences not only raised al-Albani's stature in the eyes of Jordanian Salafis but also ensured that more and more people started following him and his beliefs. Indeed, major Salafi scholars from various countries have praised al-Albani's knowledge, particularly of *ḥadīth*s,[71] and the list of Saudi and Syrian students who learned from him at one point or another is a veritable *Who's Who* of Salafi shaykhs in those two countries today.[72] In Jordan, too, the most prominent Salafi scholars today – ʿAli al-Halabi, Mashhur b. Hasan, Muhammad Musa Nasr, Husayn al-ʿAwayisha and others – are all students of al-Albani's.[73] Part of his popularity was not only due to his knowledge and ability to convince others but also because of his steadfast personality. Mashhur b. Hasan writes:

> The venerable scholar al-Albani is not like the rest of the *ʿulamāʾ* – despite their erudition and their standing (*ʿalá faḍlihim wa-makānatihim*) – because he is among those for whom God has gathered strength in [pursuing] the truth, showing it and calling to what he believes in (*al-daʿwa ilá mā yaʿtaqidu*) through clear expressions (*bi-ʿibārāt ṣarīḥa*), not covertly (*min ghayr khafāʾ*) and without confusion (*lā labs*). No reluctance and no hesitation (*lā taraddud wa-lā takalluʾ*)![74]

Al-Albani's student Muhammad Musa Nasr similarly describes him as remaining true to his methodology of *daʿwa* and steadfast in pursuit of the truth. In fact, he says al-Albani "did not know any deceit and did not waver in his position" and would not move from his point of view "if the proof was clear to him".[75]

These statements are perhaps somewhat hagiographical. Yet views about al-Albani being single-minded are ubiquitous, including among his opponents, and are backed up by ideological positions that showed his aloofist quietism, as we saw in the previous chapter. Remaining principled and steadfast, however, can possibly lead to becoming

[71] Al-Jabbūrī, *Juhūd*, 17–25.
[72] *Ibid.*, 55–6; Shaḥāda, *Al-Daʿwa*, 143–8; al-Shāmī, *Ārāʾ*, 69–72.
[73] Al-Jabbūrī, *Juhūd*, 56; Shaḥāda, *Al-Daʿwa*, 148–51; al-Shāmī, *Ārāʾ*, 72. This connection with al-Albānī is something his Jordanian student like to stress. One of the ways in which some scholars in Jordan are attacked is to state that they were never really al-Albānī's students and particularly ʿAlī al-Ḥalabī has had to defend himself against this "accusation". See, for example, ʿAlī al-Ḥalabī, *Hal Aqarra? Am Nafá? ʿAlī al-Ḥalabī bi-annahu Tilmīdh al-Albānī* (www.alhalaby.com/play.php?catsmktba=1193, 22 December 2009 (accessed 1 April 2013)); *id.*, *Kayfa Naruddu ʿalá Man Yatamassaku bi-Kalām al-Shaykh: Annaka Lasta min Talāmīdhihi?* (www.alhalaby.com/play.php?catsmktba=229, 14 November 2009 (accessed 1 April 2013)).
[74] Mashhūr b. Ḥasan Āl Salmān, introduction to *Juhūd al-Imām al-Albānī Nāṣir al-Sunna wa-l-Dīn fī Bayān ʿAqīdat al-Salaf al-Ṣāliḥīn fī l-Īmān bi-llāh Rabb al-ʿĀlamīn*, by Aḥmad Ṣāliḥ Ḥusayn al-Jabbūrī (Amman: Al-Dār al-Athariyya, 2008), 6.
[75] Interview with Muḥammad b. Mūsá Āl Naṣr, Amman, 20 June 2012.

stubborn and ill-mannered, which al-Albani himself admitted to being,[76] as did his students.[77] Such an attitude, though perhaps admirable to one's followers, is likely to be seen as annoying and pig-headed by one's opponents. Indeed, it is said that members of the Jordanian Muslim Brotherhood tried to have al-Albani, who had more or less come to live in Jordan by the late 1970s, exiled for stimulating the growth of a Salafi movement that was increasingly critical of the Brotherhood.[78]

Although the Jordanian Muslim Brotherhood's attempt to have al-Albani banned from the kingdom failed, the success of his Salafi movement also attracted negative attention from the Jordanian regime itself.[79] Not exactly sure who this foreign shaykh was and what this "Salafism" he preached entailed and possibly afraid that his growing movement could prove to be a source of political opposition, the regime decided to confront al-Albani and to exile him in the late 1970s or early 1980s. He was therefore forced to leave and spent time in Syria, Lebanon and the United Arab Emirates.[80] In the meantime, however, the war between Iran and Iraq (1980–1988) had broken out, pitting a Sunni Arab country – and staunch Jordanian ally at the time[81] – against a Shiʿi Persian state. Groups such as the Muslim Brotherhood, while sceptical of Shiʿi Islam, initially tended to look favourably upon the Islamic Revolution in Iran in 1979 and the Islamic Republic that resulted from this.[82] Salafis, on the other hand, were deeply suspicious and highly critical of Shiʿas and Iran and Muhammad Ibrahim Shaqra was openly involved in warning people against the supposed dangers of Shiʿi "unbelievers".[83]

Shaqra's anti-Shiʿi preaching apparently came to the attention of King Husayn and the latter invited him to hear more about Shiʿi Islam. Shaqra is said to have told him about the alleged danger that Shiʿas represented and bluntly stated that the government had made a mistake in demonising the leader of the Islamic Revolution in Iran, ayatollah Ruhollah Khomeini (1902–1989), without resorting to Muslim scholars about this issue. The king is not only said to have been convinced by what Shaqra told

[76] Hamdeh, "Emergence," 85–6. [77] Brown, *Canonization*, 325.
[78] Hamdeh, "Emergence," 54.
[79] Wiktorowicz, *Management*, 121; interview with Bāsim b. Fayṣal al-Jawābira, Amman, 26 June 2012.
[80] Interview with ʿIṣām Hādī, Amman, 19 January 2013.
[81] Nigel Ashton, *King Hussein of Jordan: A Political Life* (New Haven and London: Yale University Press, 2008), 210–83; Randa Habib, *Hussein and Abdullah: Inside the Jordanian Royal Family* (translation Miranda Tell) (London: Saqi, 2010), 83–8.
[82] Rudi Matthee, "Egyptian Oppostion on the Iranian Revolution," in *Shiʿism and Social Protest*, ed. Juan R. I. Cole and Nikki R. Keddie (New Haven and London: Yale University Press, 1986), 251–65.
[83] Interview with ʿIṣām Hādī, Amman, 19 January 2013.

him, but he was also impressed enough with what he had just heard to offer Shaqra something in return. Apparently, Shaqra took this opportunity to ask the king if he could facilitate al-Albani's return to Jordan and convinced him that al-Albani was equally sceptical of Shiʿi Islam and did not form a danger to the security of the kingdom at all. King Husayn subsequently got al-Albani to return to Jordan in 1983, which is when he finally settled there.[84]

The Entrenchment of Quietist Salafi Ideology in Jordan

Salafism in Jordan was thus a transnational affair from the beginning, with Salafis studying in Saudi Arabia and Egypt and others coming from Syria, most importantly al-Albani, of course. The latter's aloofist quietism greatly contributed to a deeply apolitical Salafi ideology, although the first signs of how the Jordanian regime could possibly use this trend could already be seen in King Husayn's handling of al-Albani's temporary exile. Yet transnational connections also influenced Salafism in Jordan in a different way, namely through the rise of political Salafism in Saudi Arabia and Kuwait, which represented a way of striving for the utopia of the *salaf* that quietists in Jordan were very much against. This, in turn, caused them to double down on the apoliticism of their own ideology, thereby becoming more susceptible to domestication by the regime in the future.

Impact of Foreign Events on Quietist Salafism in Jordan

As we saw in Chapter 1, the 1980s saw the rise of political Salafism in Saudi Arabia through the *ṣaḥwa*, represented most prominently by the scholars Salman al-ʿAwda and Safar al-Hawali, and in Kuwait through the Jamʿiyyat Ihyaʾ al-Turath al-Islami, headed by shaykh ʿAbd al-Rahman b. ʿAbd al-Khaliq. Both of these burst into the open after the Gulf War in 1990, when they criticised the Saudi regime's decision to allow 500,000 American soldiers on its soil and were subsequently repressed after hostilities had ended. This repression was not just a policy undertaken by the regime, however, but also involved quietist Salafis in both countries, who became (more) aware of the "danger" of other types of Salafism and sometimes started taking increasingly fervent positions against them. As mentioned, Salafis more loyal to the regime took over the Jamʿiyyat Ihyaʾ al-Turath al-Islami in Kuwait and shaykhs

[84] Shaqra, *Al-Rudūd, hāʾ*; interviews with ʿIṣām Hādī, Amman, 19 January 2013; Muḥammad Ibrāhīm Shaqra, Amman, 27 June 2012.

such as the propagandist quietist Rabiʿ b. Hadi al-Madkhali vehemently criticised political Salafis for their opposition to the Saudi regime.

Although these events took place outside Jordan, they had a profound effect on the Salafi community in the kingdom, too. With regard to Saudi Arabia, it was clear that Jordanian Salafi ties with Wahhabi scholars were strong because al-Albani and Shaqra had worked and many others had studied at the Islamic University of Medina, but also for reasons of ideological kinship and because Saudi Arabia was (and is) seen as a source of inspiration to quietists everywhere.[85] An added factor in Jordan was the financial assistance Saudi Arabia gave to quietist Salafis, allowing them to publish their writings, work as full-time scholars and enjoy a financial leverage that other Salafi groups more critical of the Saudi regime clearly lacked. As Wiktorowicz points out, however, this does not mean that Jordanian quietist Salafis simply preached an apolitical message because that was what Saudi Arabia paid them for – their deep-rooted ideological quietism alone shows that this is what they believed in anyway – but such financial aid did, perhaps, encourage scholars even more to adhere to this trend.[86]

Given the challenge that the *ṣaḥwa* presented to the Saudi regime, it was not surprising that some of the increased emphasis placed on apoliticism and loyalty to the Saudi state influenced Salafis in Jordan as well. The latter were, after all, not oblivious to what was happening in their neighbouring country and were equally sceptical of the partly Muslim Brotherhood-inspired *ṣaḥwa*. This was particularly clear in the relations between the Saudi al-Madkhali and the Jordanian al-Halabi. The latter is said to have strengthened his ties with the former and to have asked al-Albani – as others did, too – to condemn Salman al-ʿAwda and Safar al-Hawali for things they had supposedly said, which al-Albani refused because he did not want to judge anyone simply on the basis of a few words. This changed, however, when al-Albani obtained a copy of al-Hawali's aforementioned PhD thesis *Zahirat al-Irjaʾ*, in which the author criticised what he saw as the Murjiʾa of this day and age, including al-Albani. The latter read the book and strongly condemned it. When al-Halabi heard about this, he is said to have immediately phoned al-Madkhali, informing him of the fact that they had finally got to the point where al-Albani condemned al-Hawali.[87]

The PhD thesis written by al-Hawali had been supervised by Muhammad Qutb (1919–2014), the younger brother of Sayyid Qutb

[85] Abū Rummān and Abū Haniyya, *Al-Ḥall*, 221, 273–4.
[86] Wiktorowicz, *Management*, 125–6.
[87] Hādī, *Muḥaddith*, 72; interview with ʿIṣām Hādī, Amman, 19 January 2013.

and one of the Egyptian Muslim Brothers in Saudi Arabia who had helped shape the *ṣaḥwa*. Similarly, Salman al-ʿAwda had been strongly influenced by the Syrian scholar Muhammad Surur (b. 1938), who had also fled to Saudi Arabia as a member of the repressed Muslim Brotherhood but who later adopted a more Salafi creed while staying true to the Brotherhood's political activism.[88] The *ṣaḥwa* was thus intimately connected, both ideologically and personally, with the Muslim Brotherhood[89] and the hardening apoliticism among Jordanian quietists therefore did not just express itself in fiercer rhetoric against al-Hawali,[90] but – perhaps also for lack of a political Salafi movement in Jordan itself at the time – against the Muslim Brotherhood as well.[91] Indeed, while the Salafi criticism of the Brotherhood mentioned in Chapter 2 is partly rooted in their long-held and ideologically motivated scepticism of that organisation, it is simultaneously part of the anti-Brotherhood Salafi backlash that could be found among quietist Salafis in various countries in the region after the Gulf War.[92]

Increased criticism of the Muslim Brotherhood among Jordanian quietist Salafis was probably clearest in their changing views on Sayyid Qutb. Although al-Albani had long been critical of Qutb for not being a religious scholar and for his supposedly deviant views and remained so throughout his life, he refused to apply *takfīr* to him and pointed out that Qutb's execution by Nasser's regime in Egypt was unjust since it only took place because he had called people to Islam.[93] Al-Albani also stated that Qutb, though not a Salafi, did show "a strong tendency towards the Salafi *manhaj* at the end of his life".[94] While al-Albani's Jordanian followers were perhaps less nuanced in their views of Qutb from the start, even they were initially not entirely negative about him. In a book published in 1985, for example, al-Halabi cites approvingly from Qutb's Qurʾanic exegesis *Fi Zilal al-Qurʾan* (In the Shade of the Qurʾan)[95] and adds the words "may God have mercy on him" (*raḥimahu llāh*) to his name, a common way to honour the deceased of whom one has a favourable view.[96]

After the Gulf War, when the supposed danger of anything tied to the Muslim Brotherhood (and especially Sayyid Qutb) had become clear through the opposition in Saudi Arabia and Kuwait, there was less

88 Kepel, *War*, 174–8.
89 For more on the influence of Sayyid Quṭb on al-Ḥawālī's work, see Lav, *Radical*, 88–91.
90 See, for instance, al-Ḥalabī, *Gleaming*.
91 The Muslim Brotherhood was also one of al-Madkhalī's most important targets of criticism. See Meijer, "Politicising," 384–6.
92 Interview with Muʿādh al-ʿUtaybī, Irbid, 19 January 2014.
93 Hamdeh, "Emergence," 53–4. 94 Al-Albānī, *Al-Fatāwá*, 27.
95 Sayyid Quṭb, *Fī Ẓilāl al-Qurʾān* (Cairo: Dār al-Shurūq, 1980/1).
96 Al-Ḥalabī, *Al-Bayʿa*, 7.

room for such nuanced and relatively positive views, both politically and ideologically. Thus, in the 1990s, al-Halabi published another book in which he warned against "some who deviate in *manhaj*" and mentioned "the literary writer (*al-kātib al-adīb*) Sayyid Qutb" as "the most prominent" among them. Moreover, he no longer added the words "*raḥimahu llāh*" to Qutb's name, but used "*ghafara llāh la-hu*" (may God forgive him), a subtle way of indicating disagreement with someone no longer alive.[97]

As Meijer has shown, Qutb was also "the main ideological enemy" targeted by al-Madkhali's attacks.[98] One Jordanian analyst even states that "if you look at all the books by Rabiʿ al-Madkhali and his followers, you will find that they are only interested in attacking Sayyid Qutb [...], Safar al-Hawali [...] and Hasan al-Banna [...]".[99] These words may be an exaggeration, but propagandist quietist Salafis in the Netherlands, for example, did engage in literally blacklisting the people they referred to as "Qutbis", partly as a result of the differing Salafi responses to the invitation of American troops to Saudi Arabia.[100] Interestingly, when making the negative statement about Qutb mentioned above, al-Halabi refers directly to al-Madkhali, stating that "the venerable professor, shaykh Rabiʿ b. Hadi [al-Madkhali] – may God make use of him – has already refuted [Qutb] in several independent books".[101]

In later writings, al-Halabi approvingly cites the words of Saudi Chief Mufti shaykh ʿAbd al-ʿAziz b. ʿAbdallah Al al-Shaykh (b. 1943), who is best described as a loyalist quietist Salafi, when he refers to Qutb's words as containing "deviance, extremism and inconsistencies".[102] In a later fatwa, al-Halabi even goes so far as to say that merely quoting Qutb – which, as we saw above, he himself was also "guilty" of – though not serious enough to make one stop being a Salafi, is a mistake in and of itself.[103] Such views are not limited to al-Halabi, moreover, but can be found among other quietist Salafi scholars in Jordan too, who are equally critical of Qutb.[104]

[97] Al-Ḥalabī, *Fiqh*, 5–6.
[98] Meijer, "Politicising," 386–7. The words cited are on 386. See also Lav, *Radical*, 127–8.
[99] Shaḥāda, "Al-Salafiyya," 127.
[100] De Koning, Wagemakers and Becker, *Salafisme*, 150–3.
[101] Al-Ḥalabī, *Fiqh*, 6, footnote 1.
[102] ʿAlī al-Ḥalabī, *Taʾyīd, lā Taqlīd maʿa Kalimat Faḍīlat al-Shaykh al-Muftī fī Sayyid Quṭb* (www.alhalaby.com/play.php?catsmktba=1133, 16 December 2009 (accessed 2 April 2013)).
[103] Cited in Saʿd b. Fatḥī b. Saʿīd al-Zaʿtarī, *Tanbīh al-Faṭīn li-Tafāhut Taʾṣīlāt "ʿAlī al-Ḥalabī" l-Miskīn wa-llatī Khālafa bi-hā Nahj al-Salaf al-Awwalīn* (Cairo/Fez: Dār ʿIlm al-Salaf/Dār al-Tawḥīd, 2009), 62.
[104] Sulaymān, "Mawqif," 148. See also Abū Rummān and Abū Haniyya, *Al-Ḥall*, 232.

While the rise of the *ṣaḥwa* in Saudi Arabia had ideological repercussions in Jordan, there was no comparable Jordanian political Salafi movement. This began to change with another development related to the Gulf War, namely the exodus of some 400,000 Palestinians from Kuwait, who had moved there from the late 1940s to the early 1960s as refugees or as migrant labourers.[105] Their leaving came about after the Palestine Liberation Organisation (PLO) had tilted towards favouring Iraq after its invasion of Kuwait in 1990, causing the latter to expel virtually its entire Palestinian community.[106] Because some 350,000 of them had originally come from either Jordan or the West Bank, which was Jordanian territory between 1948 and 1967, they were officially Jordanian citizens and several hundred thousand Palestinians therefore went to Jordan after their expulsion.[107]

Apart from the economic, social and political repercussions that the influx of hundreds of thousands of Palestinians had on Jordan,[108] their settling in the kingdom also influenced Salafism there because quite a number of them were Salafis. Considering the major impact that ʿAbd al-Rahman b. ʿAbd al-Khaliq and his Jamʿiyyat Ihyaʾ al-Turath al-Islami, which was then still a political Salafi group, had on Salafism in Kuwait, it is not surprising that a significant number of the Salafis who came to Jordan in the early 1990s were politicos as well.[109] These included Usama Shahada and Ihsan al-ʿUtaybi, both of whom are currently prominent political Salafis in, respectively, Amman and the northern city of Irbid, as we will see in Chapter 7.

Kuwaiti political Salafis presented a challenge to the quietist Salafism prevalent in Jordan, not just because of its different views on politics, but also because of its alternative way of organising. While quietist Salafis in Jordan focussed on *al-taṣfiya wa-l-tarbiya* and were therefore mostly a trend seeking doctrinal reform, the political Salafis from Kuwait brought with them a much more organised, activist and outgoing type of Salafism. Its adherents viewed Salafism as entailing more than just

[105] Shafeeq Ghabra, "Palestinians in Kuwait: The Family and the Politics of Survival," *Journal of Palestine Studies* 17, no. 2 (1988): 63; Ann M. Lesch, "Palestinians in Kuwait," *Journal of Palestine Studies* 20, no. 4 (1991): 42–3.

[106] Palestinians themselves, however, were deeply divided over this issue and often supported Kuwait. See Lesch, "Palestinians," 45–7; Yann le Troquer and Rozenn Hommery al-Oudat, "From Kuwait to Jordan: the Palestinians' Third Exodus," *Journal of Palestine Studies* 28, no. 3 (1999): 37–8.

[107] Lamia Radi, "Les Palestiniens du Koweit en Jordanie," *Monde arabe Maghreb Machrek*, no. 144 (1994): 55; Le Troquer and al-Oudat, "Kuwait," 38.

[108] For a detailed analysis of the Palestinian-Jordanian community from Kuwait, see Le Troquer and al-Oudat, "Kuwait," 39–49.

[109] Interviews with Ḥasan Abū Haniyya, Amman, 9 June 2012; Usāma Shaḥāda, Amman, 7 June 2012; Iḥsān al-ʿUtaybī, Irbid, 28 January 2014.

studying and preaching and believed it also included parliamentary participation, collective action for good causes and things as simple as making collective trips through the country.[110] Although it took several years for this trend to grow into something substantial in Jordan and there was no backlash against political Salafis in the kingdom comparable to the one directed against the *ṣaḥwa* and the Muslim Brotherhood, the influx of Kuwaiti Salafis can only have underlined the quietist fears emanating from events in Saudi Arabia. This way, the Palestinian exodus from Kuwait is likely to have abetted the entrenchment of quietist Salafi ideology in Jordan.

Quietist Salafism Prior to al-Albani's Death

One of the reasons Kuwaiti political Salafism differed so much from quietist Salafism in Jordan is that the latter was very informally organised, working through grass-roots networks and meetings in people's homes, rather than through official organisations and sermons in mosques. There are three reasons for this. Firstly, when King Husayn allowed al-Albani back into Jordan, the security services explicitly stated that they did not want any disturbances or mass meetings, partly out of fear of what Salafism might stand for.[111] This way, the regime prevented mosques from becoming Salafi centres of learning and kept Salafism from becoming an organised trend. Secondly, al-Albani's experiences with state repression of certain organised Islamic activities in Syria led him to believe that the formal organisation of Salafism was unwise and he published a fatwa in which he stated it was forbidden. Although he later softened his views on this issue because of the more welcoming climate in Jordan and even issued a second fatwa allowing formally organised Salafi activities, many Salafis nevertheless stuck to his earlier ruling.[112] Thirdly, as pointed out in the introduction, Jordan subjects formal organisations, parties and groups to a strict regime of rules and regulations, thereby controlling them bureaucratically. Informal networks therefore provide Salafis with more freedom of movement since formal organisations are more easily subjected to state control and interference.[113]

All of this meant that during the 1980s and the 1990s, al-Albani's lessons were very informally organised. In fact, it would even be better

[110] Interview with Iḥsān al-ʿUtaybī, Irbid, 28 January 2014.
[111] Interviews with ʿIṣām Hādī, Amman, 19 January 2013; ʿAlī al-Ḥalabī, Amman, 27 June 2012; Bāsim b. Fayṣal al-Jawābira, Amman, 26 June 2012.
[112] Wiktorowicz, *Management*, 131–2; *id.*, "Salafi," 226.
[113] *Id.*, *Management*, 113, 129–31, 132; *id.*, "Salafi," 221–2, 227; interview with Akram Ziyāda, Amman, 28 June 2012. For more on the structure of these Salafi networks in the 1990s, see Wiktorowicz, *Management*, 133–46; *id.*, "Salafi," 229–37.

to state that al-Albani did not give lessons at all. He would just visit Salafis at their houses or have them visit him at his house, at which they would eat, drink and talk to one another, with plenty of room for questions. Although some sources mention a "weekly programme" (*barnāmij usbūʿī*) that al-Albani apparently followed, including the occasional use of certain books,[114] it seems his *taṣfiya* was expressed in studying and writing while his *tarbiya* was mostly limited to these informal meetings, in which there was actually little formal teaching involved.[115] To outsmart the security services, they would plan such meetings simply as visits from friends during which they just talked about religious issues.[116] Other ways in which al-Albani taught others was by speaking to them on the phone, an activity for which he is said to have reserved about two hours every day, and by having his meetings with Salafis recorded on audio tapes by one of his students, Abu Layla, who accompanied al-Albani on his visits to record his sessions and spread them around.[117]

Al-Albani's distinct way of "teaching" others means that whenever I call someone a "student" of al-Albani's, this should be seen in the context of the above. Nevertheless, today's leading quietist Salafi scholars in Jordan – ʿAli al-Halabi, Mashhur b. Hasan, Muhammad Musa Nasr, Husayn al-ʿAwayisha, Basim b. Faysal al-Jawabira and Akram Ziyada – all benefited greatly from their meetings with al-Albani. These men were born in the 1950s and 1960s, and through their numerous publications, their closeness to al-Albani, their publishing of the quietist Salafi journal *Al-Asala* and their relative seniority in knowledge, experience and age, they gradually rose to the fore as the new generation of quietist scholars in Jordan. These men were all of Palestinian descent, as were most early Salafis. The reason for this was simple: the al-Hashimi al-Shimali area in Amman where al-Albani and other Salafi shaykhs lived and taught was mostly inhabited by Palestinian-Jordanians and the same applied to nearby areas such as al-Rusayfa and al-Zarqaʾ. Interested Salafis would come from such cities or refugee camps and visit al-Albani in Amman, from where they would take their knowledge home and often teach it to others.[118] Simultaneously, Abu Layla's increasing collection of audio tapes was spread throughout the country and al-Albani would also visit

114 Al-Jabbūrī, *Juhūd*, 57–8; Shaʿbān, *Al-Shaykh*, 55–6.
115 Shaḥāda, *Al-Daʿwa*, 131–2; interviews with Ziyād al-ʿAbbādī, Amman, 26 June 2012; Muḥammad b. Mūsá Āl Naṣr, Amman, 20 June 2012; Aḥmad Muṣliḥ, Amman, 29 January 2013; Murād Shukrī, Amman, 17 January 2013.
116 Interview with ʿIṣām Hādī, Amman, 19 January 2013.
117 Interview with Muḥammad Aḥmad Abū Laylá l-Atharī, al-Ruṣayfa, 26 January 2013.
118 Interviews with Shākir al-ʿĀrūrī, Amman, 23 January 2013; ʿAbd al-Malik Besfort Maxhuni, al-Zarqāʾ, 18 January 2014; Ṣāliḥ al-Laḥḥām, Amman, 21 January 2013; Walīd ʿUthmān Tāsh, al-Zarqāʾ, 26 January 2014.

Salafis in cities elsewhere in the kingdom.[119] This way, Salafism reached every city in Jordan, including those inhabited by East Jordanians, such as al-Karak and Maʿan in the south and Irbid in the north. Still, because the major quietist shaykhs either lived in or eventually moved to Amman, quietist Salafism in Jordan became more and more centred in the capital of the country.[120]

The quietist Salafi community that resulted from these developments was mostly, though certainly not entirely, of Palestinian descent in the 1990s. Economically speaking, they were often from the poorer classes of society at that time, although exceptions to this rule could also be found, of course.[121] With regard to education, many Salafis did not go to or did not finish university in the 1980s and 1990s, which is even true for some of Jordan's most prominent quietist scholars, such as ʿAli al-Halabi. Others, like Muhammad Musa Nasr, Husayn al-ʿAwayisha and Basim al-Jawabira, have PhDs, however.[122] Interestingly, although many quietist Salafis I spoke with were not raised in the tradition of Salafism, they virtually always had religious backgrounds, having lived pious lifestyles from an early age with groups such as the Muslim Brotherhood or the Jamaʿat al-Tabligh.[123]

Jordanian quietist Salafis, despite their more entrenched apolitical ideology as a result of events in Saudi Arabia and Kuwait in the 1990s, could still have continued focussing on *al-taṣfiya wa-l-tarbiya* for years to come without becoming more loyal to the Jordanian regime. The utopia they strove for, in other words, could have been an apolitical and subservient yet simultaneously independent and aloofist one, if the movement had continued in the spirit of al-Albani. Towards the second half of

[119] Interviews with Abū l-Ḥajjāj Yūsuf b. Aḥmad Al ʿAlāwī, Māḥiṣ, 21 January 2014; ʿAbd al-Malik Besfort Maxhuni, al-Zarqāʾ, 18 January 2014; ʿĀyish Labābinā, Irbid, 14 January 2014.

[120] Interviews with ʿĀyish Labābinā, Irbid, 14 January 2014; Ṣāliḥ al-Laḥḥām, Amman, 21 January 2013.

[121] Abū Rummān and Abū Haniyya, *Al-Ḥall*, 238; *id.*, *Al-Salafiyya al-Muḥāfaẓa*, 106; interview with Ḥasan Abū Haniyya, Amman, 9 June 2012.

[122] Abū Rummān and Abū Haniyya, *Al-Ḥall*, 273; *id.*, *Al-Salafiyya al-Muḥāfaẓa*, 107; interviews with Ḥasan Abū Haniyya, Amman, 9 June 2012; Muḥammad Abū Ruḥayyim, Amman, 16 January 2013; Muḥammad b. Mūsá Āl Naṣr, Amman, 20 June 2012; Mashhūr b. Ḥasan Āl Salmān, Amman, 27 June 2012; Shākir al-ʿĀrūrī, Amman, 23 January 2013; Muḥammad b. Aḥmad Abū Laylá l-Atharī, al-Ruṣayfa, 26 January 2013; Ṣāliḥ al-Laḥḥām, Amman, 21 January 2013.

[123] Interviews with Ziyād al-ʿAbbādī, Amman, 26 June 2012; Shākir al-ʿĀrūrī, Amman, 23 January 2013; Salīm al-Hilālī, Amman, 28 January 2013; Aḥmad Muṣliḥ, Amman, 29 January 2013; Akram Ziyāda, Amman, 28 June 2012. One could argue that statements about pious lifestyles are attempts to portray their youth as more religious than it really was. Perhaps this is the case, but from a Salafi point of view, saying that one was once a member of the Brotherhood or a Tablīghī is not a sign of showing off one's Islamic credentials.

the 1990s, however, disputes began to appear among quietist Salafis in Jordan, which were not caused but exacerbated by the death of the only man who had the stature and authority to hold the community together: Muhammad Nasir al-Din al-Albani. His passing on 2 October 1999 after having been ill for almost two years[124] left the quietist Salafi community in Jordan in disarray and created a gap that nobody was really able to fill. How this had an impact on the further domestication of Jordanian quietists is what we will see in the next chapter.

[124] Al-Shāmī, *Ārā'*, 76.

4 *Fitna*: Quietist Salafi Infighting in Jordan

After al-Albani died in 1999, the Jordanian quietist Salafi journal *Al-Asala* dedicated an entire issue to the passing of the scholar who had meant so much to their community. The major quietist shaykhs cooperated in lamenting the loss of the man who had played a hugely important role in turning their budding trend into a movement. Muhammad Ibrahim Shaqra and Akram Ziyada eulogised al-Albani;[1] Muhammad Musa Nasr referred to his death as "the catastrophe (*nakba*) of the era",[2] using a term normally applied to the Palestinians' dispersal and loss of their homeland; Salim al-Hilali praised al-Albani's qualities as an expert on *ḥadīth*s,[3] while Mashhur b. Hasan, ʿAli al-Halabi and Husayn al-ʿAwayisha did the same with regard to their shaykh's knowledge on *fiqh*,[4] *ʿaqīda*[5] and the "cleansing" of Islamic tradition,[6] respectively. A poem published in this issue of *Al-Asala* even went so far as to refer to al-Albani as "the Ibn Taymiyya of the twentieth century".[7] From a Salafi point of view, a greater compliment than that is hardly imaginable.

The grief and the sense of loss over al-Albani's death among Jordanian quietist scholars were no doubt genuine. Yet their unified praise for their late shaykh also hid the deep fissures that had developed among them. In fact, only a few years after these *ʿulamāʾ* lamented in unison the passing

[1] Muḥammad Ibrāhīm Shaqra, "Jaffat al-Ṣuḥuf wa-Rufiʿat al-Aqlām," *Al-Aṣāla* 4, no. 23 (15 Shaʿbān 1420 [24 November 1999]): 15–20; Akram b. Ziyāda, "Ṭūbá li-Man Lam Yanqaṭiʿ ʿAmalahu ʿanhu," *Al-Aṣāla* 4, no. 23 (15 Shaʿbān 1420 [24 November 1999]): 50–2.

[2] Muḥammad [b.] Mūsá [Āl] Naṣr, "Nakbat al-ʿAṣr.. bi-Mawt Imām al-ʿAṣr," *Al-Aṣāla* 4, no. 23 (15 Shaʿbān 1420 [24 November 1999]): 21–7.

[3] Salīm al-Hilālī, "Shaykhunā al-Albānī.. Muḥaddithan," *Al-Aṣāla* 4, no. 23 (15 Shaʿbān 1420 [24 November 1999]): 28–32.

[4] Mashhūr b. Ḥasan Āl Salmān, "Maʿālim fī Fiqh al-Shaykh al-Albānī," *Al-Aṣāla* 4, no. 23 (15 Shaʿbān 1420 [24 November 1999]): 33–6.

[5] ʿAlī al-Ḥalabī, "Al-ʿAllāma al-Albānī wa-Juhūduhu fī l-ʿAqīda," *Al-Aṣāla* 4, no. 23 (15 Shaʿbān 1420 [24 November 1999]): 37–9.

[6] Ḥusayn al-ʿAwayisha, "Manhaj al-Shaykh al-Albānī fī l-Tazkiya," *Al-Aṣāla* 4, no. 23 (15 Shaʿbān 1420 [24 November 1999]): 44–5.

[7] Khayr al-Dīn [al-]Wānilī, "Ibn Taymiyyat al-Qarn al-ʿIshrīn," *Al-Aṣāla* 4, no. 23 (15 Shaʿbān 1420 [24 November 1999]): 63–4.

of their teacher, they were not on speaking terms with each other anymore. As Mashhur b. Hasan put it: "After his death – may God the Exalted have mercy on him – the *fitna* appeared",[8] although he acknowledges that this strife between the scholars was rooted in the final years of al-Albani's life.[9] Given the great impact that the intra-Salafi conflicts after al-Albani's death had on the quietist community in Jordan, it is rather surprising that the existing literature on Salafism in Jordan pays very little attention to them and does not really make an effort to explain what happened.[10] Only Lav partially deals with these intra-Salafi conflicts in detail, but sees them as rooted in theological differences.[11] As I have pointed out elsewhere, the conflicts between quietist Salafi scholars in Jordan after al-Albani's death were essentially *not* about ideology but about the leadership of the community.[12] Even this leadership struggle, however, was only part of a wider set of problems confronting the quietist Salafi community after 1999.

In this chapter, we will deal with the intra-Salafi conflicts that occurred shortly before and after al-Albani's death. In what follows, I will first deal with the accusations of plagiarism levelled against some Salafi scholars, particularly ʿAli al-Halabi, and the ties of the latter to the publication of a controversial book by Jordanian quietist Murad Shukri. I will then deal with the charges of theological deviance against al-Halabi and his covert leadership struggle with Muhammad Ibrahim Shaqra. Finally, this chapter analyses the founding of the Imam al-Albani Centre by the victorious party in this power struggle – al-Halabi and his allies – and the accusations of fraud and theft against the director of this centre, Salim al-Hilali. A thorough analysis of these conflicts shows not only that the utopia of the *salaf* was perhaps further away than ever for Jordanian Salafis in this period but also that the victory of al-Halabi's loyalist quietist inclinations over the more critical and independent tendencies represented by Shaqra ensured that by the early 2000s the quietist Salafi community in Jordan was ready to be fully domesticated by the regime.

Prelude to a Conflict: A Loss of Trust

The man central to several of the conflicts that erupted prior to and after al-Albani's death in 1999 was ʿAli al-Halabi. Born in al-Zarqaʾ in 1960 to a family of Palestinian refugees originally from Jaffa, al-Halabi met al-Albani in 1978 and was heavily influenced by him. In fact, he became one

[8] Mashhūr b. Ḥasan, introduction to *Juhūd*, by al-Jabbūrī, 5. [9] *Ibid.*, 6.

[10] Abū Rummān and Abū Haniyya, *Al-Ḥall*, 234, 241–3; *id.*, *Al-Salafiyya al-Muḥāfaẓa*, 36, 39, 49–53; Shaḥāda, "Al-Salafiyya," 120, 126–7.

[11] Lav, *Radical*, 140–66. [12] Wagemakers, "Contesting," 113–18.

of al-Albani's most prominent students and became actively involved in the Salafi movement's *da'wa* activities.[13] Despite having no formal education as a religious scholar,[14] al-Halabi became a prolific author, writing and editing well over two hundred books and booklets[15] and countless articles,[16] which is impressive even when compared to the large number of publications by his fellow scholars in Jordan.[17] Being a full-time scholar who can live off the financial assistance he gets from Saudi and other international Salafi organisations, his work as a preacher and the proceeds from his books, he has more or less become the *de facto* leader of and official spokesman for quietist Salafism in Jordan today, although he refuses to talk about himself that way.[18]

Accusations of Plagiarism

Al-Halabi's prominent position among quietist Salafis in Jordan today perhaps suggests that his stature was similar to that of al-Albani in the sense that Salafis in general looked up to him. This, however, was not the case. Even during al-Albani's lifetime, rumours started to appear that al-Halabi was not entirely honest and had ascribed (parts of) other people's books to himself. More specifically, al-Halabi was accused of plagiarising a book by the Kuwaiti shaykh 'Abd al-Rahman b. 'Abd al-Khaliq and publishing a revised version under his own name as *Kalimat ila l-Ukht al-Muslima* (Words to the Muslim Sister).[19] When the news about this reached the original author, he apparently contacted al-Albani, who confronted al-Halabi with what he had done. The latter is said to have apologised profusely, to have claimed that he only wanted to engage in *da'wa* and that it was never his intention to do anything wrong. Given al-

[13] 'Alī b. Muḥammad Abū Haniyya, *Tuḥfat al-Ṭālib al-Abī bi-Tarjamat al-Shaykh al-Muḥaddith 'Alī b. Ḥasan al-Ḥalabī* (n.p.: Manshūrāt Muntadayāt Kull al-Salafiyyīn, 2011), 9–14; interviews with 'Alī al-Ḥalabī, Amman, 19 January 2009, 27 June 2012.

[14] His knowledge was built up by studying on his own, spending a lot of time with al-Albānī and attending individual lectures and classes given by Salafī scholars in Saudi Arabia and elsewhere. See Abū Haniyya, *Tuḥfat*, 20–1.

[15] An overview of these can be found in Abū Haniyya, *Tuḥfat*, 95–118.

[16] Virtually all of al-Ḥalabī's writings can be found on his website: http://alhalaby.com/ (accessed 7 May 2015).

[17] For an overview of the publications of other quietist Salafī scholars in Jordan, see their websites: www.mashhoor.net/ (Mashhūr b. Ḥasan); http://alawaysheh.com/index.php (Ḥusayn al-'Awayisha); and http://almahajjah.net/ and http://almahajjah.net/Pages/2_Dr_Pages/2_1_DR.htm (Muḥammad b. Mūsá Āl Naṣr). All of these websites were still available on 7 May 2015.

[18] Interview with 'Alī al-Ḥalabī, Amman, 19 January 2009.

[19] Interviews with 'Iṣām Hādī, Amman, 19 January 2013; Ṣāliḥ al-Laḥḥām, Amman, 21 January 2013. Although it is quite common for Salafīs to use the same sources and arguments as other scholars, al-Ḥalabī's actions apparently went further than this, meaning he may have copied Ibn 'Abd al-Khāliq's actual choice of words.

Halabi's lack of an academic education and relative youth at the time, this explanation is perhaps less implausible than it sounds.[20]

When I asked al-Halabi about this accusation, he admitted that it was true, but downplayed its importance and stressed that it happened decades ago.[21] Al-Albani is said to have blamed this type of behaviour on a lack of education, yet made it quite clear that he objected to it.[22] He only did so privately, however, not publicly.[23] Al-Albani's refusal to disavow his students' behaviour in public may have contributed to a climate in which scepticism of al-Halabi in general could flourish. One author claims al-Halabi is ignorant,[24] regularly makes mistakes[25] and sometimes cites sources that are actually deviant.[26] Other sources claim al-Halabi committed plagiarism with more than just one book[27] or did not always get his references to other books right.[28]

What to make of all this? Although the rumours about al-Halabi's alleged plagiarism after he falsely ascribed Ibn ʿAbd al-Khaliq's book to himself are widespread,[29] almost none of the people who personally told me they believed al-Halabi was guilty of this wanted to be quoted as such because they did not have any evidence.[30] Moreover, one staunch and outspoken critic of al-Halabi's told me that he believed al-Halabi had not engaged in plagiarism for years.[31] Furthermore, al-Albani's secretary ʿIsam Hadi states that "the enemies of al-Halabi still take [his plagiarism of Ibn ʿAbd al-Khaliq's book] as typical of him or his faults. They still remind him of the sin he committed when he was young."[32] Given the

[20] Interview with ʿIṣām Hādī, Amman, 19 January 2013.

[21] Interview with ʿAlī al-Ḥalabī, via e-mail, 17 June 2013.

[22] Wāʾil al-Batīrī, *Luṣūṣ al-Nuṣūṣ* (www.tawhed.ws/r?i=0504091k, n.d. (accessed 12 November 2012)), 2; Hādī, *Muḥaddith*, 74–5.

[23] Interview with ʿIṣām Hādī, Amman, 19 January 2013.

[24] Ibn Ḥamd al-Atharī, *Mudhakkira fī l-Rudūd ʿalá Jahālāt al-Ḥalabī wa-Sariqāt al-ʿIlmiyya* (http://alathary.net/vb2/attachment.p ... ntid=695&stc=1, n.d. (accessed 8 November 2012)), 4–6.

[25] *Ibid.*, 28–32. [26] *Ibid.*, 16–24.

[27] ʿAbd al-ʿAzīz b. Fayṣal al-Rājiḥī, *Al-Fāriq bayna l-Muḥaqqiq wa-l-Sāriq* (www.saaid.net /Doat/rajhi/1.htm, published at various dates in 2000 and 2002 (accessed 8 November 2012)).

[28] Khālid al-Ḥāyik, *Hakadhā Badaʾa "Musalsil al-Sariqāt" ʿinda Man Yantasibūna li-l-Salaf Zūran!* (www.tawhed.ws/r?i=0504096s, 18 Jumādá l-Ūlá [25 May 2008] (accessed 12 November 2012)). See also ʿAbdallāh b. Muḥammad al-Shamrānī, *Mazāliq fī l-Taḥqīq* (www.tawhed.ws/r?i=72ffkf2o, n.d. (accessed 28 March 2013)).

[29] There is, in fact, an entire website dedicated to refuting al-Ḥalabī: http://alhalaby.net/ main/Default.aspx (accessed 7 May 2015).

[30] An exception was my interview with Muḥammad Abū Ruḥayyim, Amman, 16 January 2013.

[31] Private conversation with a former Salafī who preferred to remain anonymous, Amman, January 2014.

[32] Interview with ʿIṣām Hādī, Amman, 19 January 2013.

fact that I have not been able to obtain the relevant texts in order to check claims of al-Halabi's plagiarism myself and that some of the accusations – particularly those of sloppy footnotes and references to "deviant" books – do not always justify the serious charge of plagiarism, it is perhaps fair to say that we can only be absolutely sure that al-Halabi was guilty of this once, namely with regard to Ibn ʿAbd al-Khaliq's book.

Al-Halabi was not the only quietist Jordanian scholar accused of plagiarism. His colleague Mashhur b. Hasan is also said to have used other people's work without proper reference, as claimed by an author who wrote an (unpublished) book about this topic.[33] One Jordanian Islamist analyst mentions that the phenomenon of plagiarism among quietist shaykhs is widespread. Although he does not tell his readers explicitly who he means, he uses a play on the accused scholars' first names, saying that "the highest of them (*aʿlāhum*)" is involved, as well as another who has "famous (*mashhūra*) books" and one who "boasts through perfect (*salīm*) speech". Particularly because he accentuates these words, it is clear that he is referring to ʿAli al-Halabi, Mashhur b. Hasan and Salim al-Hilali, respectively.[34]

Al-Hilali is targeted in particular by critics for his alleged plagiarism. Several authors claim that he actually stole most or even all of what he wrote from other scholars.[35] This is most likely an exaggeration, but several accusers have come up with highly detailed writings indicating what publications al-Hilali has supposedly used under his own name.[36] One Jordanian critic also accuses al-Hilali of using such long citations that readers simply forget that these are not his own words.[37] Jordanian Islamist analyst Waʾil al-Batiri specifically accuses al-Hilali of plagiarising

[33] Abū Ṣuhayb al-Ḥāyik, *Liqāʾ maʿa l-Shaykh Rāʾid Ṣabrī ḥawla Sariqāt Mashhūr Ḥasan Āl Salmān li-Kutubihi wa-Kitābihi "Kashf al-Mastūr ʿan Sariqāt Mashhūr"* (www.addyaiya.com/uin/arb/Viewdataitems.aspx?ProductId=309, 27 Muḥarram 1430 [24 January 2009] (accessed 8 November 2012)).

[34] Wāʾil al-Batīrī, *ʿIṣābat al-Surrāq al-Muttaḥida!* (www.tawhed.ws/r?i=1502094c, n.d. (accessed 12 November 2012)), 1–2.

[35] Abū ʿAbdallāh ʿAbd al-Raḥīm b. al-ʿArabī al-Atharī, *Difāʿan ʿan Mashāyikh al-Urdunn* (www.kulalsalafiyeen.com/vb/showthread.php?t=15620, 24 March 2010 [originally published Shawwāl 1428 [October–November 2007]] (accessed 7 February 2013)), 18; Wāʾil al-Batīrī, *Sariqa ʿIlmiyya* (www.tawhed.ws/r?i=0606091d, n.d. (accessed 12 November 2012)), 2.

[36] Abū Ṣuhayb Khālid al-Ḥāyik, *Fa-ltaqamahu l-Ḥūt* (www.tawhed.ws/r?i=1502092n, 11 Jumādá l-Ūlá 1429 [17 May 2008] (accessed 29 November 2013)), esp. 27–38; Aḥmad al-Kuwaytī, *Al-Kashf al-Mathālī ʿan Sariqāt Salīm al-Hilālī* (http://alhalaby.net/main/articles.aspx?article_no=412, n.d. (accessed 7 May 2015)), 30–9, 43–91. With regard to the latter publication: I have made use of a pdf version of this book that is no longer available online. I will refer to that version in later footnotes since the version mentioned here is an html document, which cannot be referred to precisely.

[37] Al-Kuwaytī, *Al-Kashf*, 21–2.

the work of Sayyid Qutb and has written an entire book in which he lists al-Hilali's supposed attempts to adopt the almost literal words by Qutb into his work. Although the use of editions by al-Batiri that are no longer available made checking his claims impossible for me, the charges against al-Hilali are so detailed and sustained throughout the works criticising him, that they seem quite believable.

Al-Halabi's Role in Murad Shukri's Book

The question of whether or not the accusations of plagiarism against al-Halabi, Mashhur b. Hasan and al-Hilali are entirely true is perhaps one that a police investigator, rather than an academic researcher, should answer. Moreover, for this book the most important aspect about this topic is that there is a widespread perception among some Jordanian Salafis that several of their scholars are guilty of plagiarism, which has led to a loss of trust in them. In al-Halabi's case, this perception was confirmed not only by his actual plagiarism of Ibn ʿAbd al-Khaliq's book but also by the dubious role he played in a book by a fellow Jordanian Salafi called Murad Shukri.

In 1994, the Jordanian quietist Salafi Murad Shukri published a book entitled *Ihkam al-Taqrir li-Ahkam Masʾalat al-Takfir* (The Precision of the Decision for Rulings on the Question of Excommunication). Possibly because of the fact that Shukri was not a scholar, but more what Salafis usually refer to as "a knowledge seeker" (*ṭālib ʿilm*),[38] it was perhaps deemed appropriate to put a more established name on the cover of the book as well, to indicate that its contents had been properly checked and vetted. This is quite common with Salafi books and in this case ʿAli al-Halabi's name was included on the cover as having "read [the book] and watched over its character (*qāma ʿalá ṭabʿihi*)". The inside cover further stated that al-Halabi had "verified" the book (*rājaʿahu*).[39]

When it was published, the book did not go down very well with some Salafis. The problem was that Shukri's book deals with the important subjects of *īmān, kufr* and *takfīr* and – controversially – seems to suggest that acts of unbelief should almost always be accompanied by a verbal

[38] The term "*ṭālib ʿilm*" is certainly a positive one to Salafis, since it indicates that a person seeks Islamically correct knowledge (*ʿilm sharʿī*) and is not someone with activist, political or academic motives. At the same time, the term "*ṭālib ʿilm*" is clearly lower in rank than "*ʿālim*", which is only applied to scholars. In my conversations with Jordanian Salafis on these terms, it became clear to me that they make no formal distinction between them and that (the perception of) greater knowledge, age and experience distinguishes an *ʿālim* from a *ṭālib ʿilm*.

[39] Murād Shukrī, *Iḥkām al-Taqrīr li-Aḥkām Masʾalat al-Takfīr* (Riyadh: Dār al-Ṣamīʿī, 1994).

affirmation of *kufr* (showing *iʿtiqād, istiḥlāl* or *jaḥd*) in order to qualify as such.[40] Moreover, he also claims that certain questions with regard to *kufr* (such as whether or not someone who abandons prayer is a *kāfir*), rather than being straightforward and clear cut, are actually matters of *ijtihād*. In this case, this means that they are issues on which Muslims can legitimately disagree and which should be left to major scholars.[41] Furthermore, Shukri also approvingly cites the mediaeval scholar Ibn Hajar al-ʿAsqalani (1372–1449) as stating that acts are part of faith, but only on the level of *kamāl al-dīn*, meaning that acts can perfect *īmān*, but cannot damage it or take it away entirely. This, Shukri maintains, is different from what the Murjiʾa believed, since they rejected acts as a part of faith altogether.[42]

These ideas bear a strong resemblance to the ones espoused by al-Albani and, in defence of his teacher, by al-Halabi, as we saw in Chapter 2. That same chapter also made clear, however, that some Jordanian Salafis, including Muhammad Abu Ruhayyim, strongly disagreed with them. In the case of Shukri's book, Abu Ruhayyim believed that it showed clear traces of the thinking of the Murjiʾa and decided to write a refutation of it named *Haqiqat al-Khilaf bayna l-Salafiyya al-Sharʿiyya wa-Adʿiyaʾiha fi Masaʾil al-Iman* (The Truth of the Disagreement between Legitimate Salafism and Its Impostors on Questions of Faith). This book was read by a fellow Salafi,[43] who was subsequently inspired by it to send Shukri's book to the Saudi Permanent Council for Knowledge Studies and Fatwas (Al-Lajna al-Daʾima li-l-Buhuth al-ʿIlmiyya wa-l-Iftaʾ) to ask for the scholars' opinion about it.[44] The Saudi scholars responded through a fatwa in which they state that the book contains traces of "the *madhhab* of the Murjiʾa", "who say that a sin does not hurt faith and for whom *īmān* is confirmation in the heart and unbelief only [exists through] negation (*takdhīb*)". They therefore call upon Shukri and the book's publisher to repent and ask God for forgiveness.[45]

[40] *Ibid.*, 31–5. [41] *Ibid.*, 35–45. [42] *Ibid.*, 61–5.

[43] This person is identified as Ibrāhīm al-Ḥamadānī in the full text of the fatwa he asked for. See Abū Ruḥayyim, *Ḥaqīqat al-Khilāf*, 135.

[44] Interview with Muḥammad Abū Ruḥayyim, Amman, 16 January 2013.

[45] Al-Lajna al-Dāʾima li-l-Buḥūth wa-l-Iftāʾ, "Fatwa no. 20212" (www.alifta.net/Search/ResultDetails.aspx?languagename=ar&lang=ar&view=result&fatwaNum=&FatwaNumID=&ID=10899&searchScope=3&SearchScopeLevels1=&SearchScopeLevels2=&highLight=1&SearchType=exact&SearchMoesar=false&bookID=&LeftVal=0&RightVal=0&simple=&SearchCriteria=allwords&PagePath=&siteSection=1&searchkeyword=217133216177216167216175032216180217131216177217138#firstKeyWordFound, n.d. (accessed 8 May 2015)). The complete text of the fatwa, including its date (3 June 1998), is also produced in Abū Ruḥayyim, *Ḥaqīqat al-Khilāf*, 135–7.

While this matter seemed to be entirely about doctrine, with Abu Ruhayyim apparently only concerned with the alleged theological mishaps in Shukri's book, there was clearly more going on. Firstly, by the time Shukri's book was published, al-Halabi had already gained a reputation as a serial plagiariser among some Jordanian Salafis, including Abu Ruhayyim, even if this was not (entirely) justified. Secondly, it had also become clear that even at that time Abu Ruhayyim did not agree with al-Halabi's own views on faith, quite apart from anything Shukri wrote, as we will see later. Thirdly, Abu Ruhayyim clearly looked at al-Halabi with disdain as someone who was "inferior" to him not only in age (Abu Ruhayyim was born in 1949) but – more importantly – also in education. While al-Halabi, as mentioned, did not receive any formal religious training, Abu Ruhayyim studied at the Faculty of Shariʿa of the University of Jordan and the Umm al-Qura University in Saudi Arabia, specialising in *ʿaqīda*, about which he also wrote his PhD thesis.[46] Given this context, it becomes clear that the core issue at stake here is not so much doctrine but religious scholarly authority[47] and it is not surprising that when Abu Ruhayyim saw al-Halabi's name on the cover of Shukri's book, he decided to criticise it at least partly for that reason. Indeed, when I interviewed Abu Ruhayyim, he was far less concerned with the actual author of the book (Shukri) than with the role played by al-Halabi, who he clearly considers a stealing Salafi charlatan whose name he did not even want to utter out loud.[48] His disgust for al-Halabi was further underlined by his references to him as "Halabi" in his writings, so without the use of the Arabic definite article "al-", which can be considered – and was surely meant by Abu Ruhayyim as – an insult.[49]

It did not end there, however. When Shukri's book was published, the author discovered only then that al-Halabi's name was also on the cover, even though the latter had not played any role in the book whatsoever.[50] According to al-Halabi himself, he had been asked by the publisher to add his name to the book for marketing reasons.[51] Considering that Salafis

[46] *Liqāʾ Shabakat Anā l-Muslim maʿa l-Shaykh al-Duktūr Muḥammad Abū Ruḥayyim* (www.saaid.net/leqa/1.htm, n.d. (accessed 21 February 2013)).

[47] Wagemakers, "Contesting," 115–16. For more on the definition of religious authority, see Chapter 5.

[48] Interview with Muḥammad Abū Ruḥayyim, Amman, 16 January 2013.

[49] See, for example, Muḥammad Abū Ruḥayyim, introduction to *Masʾalat al-Īmān fī Kaffatay al-Mīzān* by Abū ʿUzayr ʿAbd al-Ilāh Yūsuf al-Yūbī al-Ḥasanī al-Jazāʾirī (Amman: Dār al-Maʾmūn, 2006), 5–18. In Arabic, this dropping of the definite article in a person's name may – but does not have to – indicate a dismissive attitude towards someone. In the case of "al-Ḥalabī" ("the man from Aleppo"), Abū Ruḥayyim's leaving out the definite article is perhaps best translated as "just someone from Aleppo".

[50] Interview with Murād Shukrī, Amman, 17 January 2013.

[51] Abū Ruḥayyim, *Ḥaqīqat al-Khilāf*, 5, footnote 3.

often add the names of the scholars who checked and revised their work to their own names on the covers of their publications to lend some extra scholarly credentials to them, it is not unlikely that al-Halabi is speaking the truth. Yet when the Saudi Permanent Council issued its fatwa condemning Shukri's book, al-Halabi, rather than admitting that he had made a mistake by allowing his name to be used on the cover of a book he had nothing to do with, wrote a letter to the Permanent Council downplaying their criticism.[52] Moreover, he also distanced himself from the book and its contents.[53]

Thus, while al-Halabi was probably only guilty of wrongly lending his name to a book with which he had no connection – possibly even with the objective of doing Shukri a favour – and mishandling the aftermath of this string of events, all the parties involved became very angry with him for reasons of their own. Firstly, Shukri felt he had been betrayed by al-Halabi, first by adding his own name to the book and later for disavowing the publication's contents.[54] Indeed, when I spoke to him some 15 years after all this happened, Shukri was still quite angry over this issue.[55] Secondly, other Jordanian Salafis undoubtedly felt confirmed in their suspicions of al-Halabi as an unrepenting plagiariser because – in their perception – he had once again lent his name to a book that was not his. Finally, to Abu Ruhayyim, the idea that al-Halabi was involved with this book – even though he was not – underlined his views of him as a Murjiʾi in Salafi clothing, which was particularly bad given his reputation as a plagiariser. This perception also encouraged Abu Ruhayyim to set his sights on al-Halabi's own publications.

A Crisis of Leadership

Al-Halabi was thus being criticised from different sides for things he probably was not guilty of. Doctrinally, however, there clearly was a difference between him and Abu Ruhayyim with regard to matters of faith and unbelief, like there was with Muhammad Ibrahim Shaqra, as we saw in Chapter 2. Lav's account of the conflict between the different quietist Salafi scholars in this period focusses entirely on ideological differences between the main protagonists and states: "It is certainly true that bitter and ugly rivalries developed among the Jordanian salafis in al-Albānī's last years and following his death. We cannot ignore however that

[52] *Ibid.*, 138–41.
[53] *Id.*, introduction to *Masʾalat* by al-Jazāʾirī, 6; interview with Usāma Shaḥāda, Amman, 10 January 2013.
[54] Interview with Usāma Shaḥāda, Amman, 10 January 2013.
[55] Interview with Murād Shukrī, Amman, 17 January 2013.

the acrimony centered on one main issue[: the question of faith]."[56] Although Lav has generally done a very good job of what he set out to do, namely to describe and analyse the ideological debates between the different actors in these conflicts, he is mistaken to see the question of faith – though important from a doctrinal point of view – as the main issue in the disputes between Jordanian quietist Salafis in this period. Three reasons can be given for this.

Firstly, the saga described earlier, with its accusations of plagiarism and al-Halabi's role in the publication of Shukri's book, is entirely missing from Lav's account of the conflict. This is crucial because it shows that Abu Ruhayyim and al-Halabi did not enter the conflict with Shaqra, which this section partly focusses on, as blank slates but actually had a history of animosity towards each other that is not only important in and of itself, but also influenced their discussions on faith. Moreover, the account given earlier also shows that this animosity was based on more than just ideology, but was actually mostly an attempt by Abu Ruhayyim to "get" al-Halabi in a contest over religious scholarly authority. Secondly, because Lav's intention was not to deal with every publication related to this question,[57] he ignores some writings that show that the conflicts were about more than just theology. Thirdly, Lav did not do any fieldwork, meaning that he never talked to any of the protagonists in these conflicts. This is essential, since – as I have pointed out elsewhere – these disputes were written about in theological terms partly to hide very personal ambitions regarding the leadership of the quietist Salafi community in Jordan after al-Albani's death.[58] Mostly limiting oneself to written sources about these conflicts therefore gives the impression that the main issue is, indeed, more about theology than it really is, as this section will show.

Abu Ruhayyim Takes on al-Halabi

While the accusations of plagiarism against various quietist scholars were made and the problems surrounding Shukri's book occurred, al-Halabi continued publishing books. One of these was called *Al-Tahdhir min Fitnat al-Takfir* (The Warning against the Strife of Excommunication), originally published in 1996.[59] The book was actually based on a transliterated version of a tape by al-Albani called *Fitnat al-Takfir*

[56] Lav, *Radical*, 163. [57] *Ibid.*, 140. [58] Wagemakers, "Contesting," 118.

[59] ʿAlī b. Ḥasan b. ʿAlī b. ʿAbd al-Ḥamīd al-Ḥalabī al-Atharī, ed., *Al-Taḥdhīr min Fitnat al-Takfīr* (n.p.: no publisher, 1996). I would like to thank Tayyeb Mimouni for providing me with a photocopy of this book.

(The Strife of Excommunication),[60] which seems to have been a more structured and succinct version of a discussion between al-Albani, Shaqra and a then unknown Jordanian Salafi called Sami al-ʿUraydi[61] that took place earlier.[62] (Although al-Albani's *Fitnat al-Takfir* was also published in edited form by someone else in two editions,[63] that version did not attract much attention.) In the book, al-Halabi presents what he believes are the correct ideas about faith, unbelief and excommunication, particularly with regard to rulers. Since these have been dealt with in Chapter 2, there is no need to go into them again.[64]

Just like with the refutation of Shukri's book, when Abu Ruhayyim was more interested in al-Halabi's (non-existent) contribution than in the book's author, he now also apparently chose to ignore the fact that *Al-Tahdhir min Fitnat al-Takfir* was actually based on a fatwa by al-Albani, with whom he disagreed but who he at least saw as a scholar. Instead, he seemed bent on "exposing" al-Halabi, who he considered an uneducated fraud.[65] As with Shukri's book, Abu Ruhayyim claimed al-Halabi's publication contained ideas akin to those of the Murjiʾa but, more importantly in this case, also misrepresented and twisted the ideas of some major Salafi scholars. Given his views on al-Halabi's own scholarly credentials, particularly when compared to those of Abu Ruhayyim himself, the latter was simply not going to accept this book.[66]

The exact order of things is not entirely clear since my sources contradict each other somewhat at this point, but Abu Ruhayyim's initial response to the book appears to have been that he went to al-Albani and confronted him with al-Halabi's alleged misrepresentation of major Salafi scholars. Moreover, he claims to have asked al-Albani to take firm action against al-Halabi, ensuring this would not happen again, yet al-Albani was unwilling to do so.[67] Al-Halabi apparently heard about Abu Ruhayyim's accusations against him, however, and asked him if they

[60] Muḥammad Nāṣir al-Dīn al-Albānī, *Fitnat al-Takfīr* (www.saaid.net/book/open.php?cat=1&book=174, n.d. (accessed 8 May 2015)).

[61] Lav, *Radical*, 141. Al-ʿUraydī would later play an important role in Jabhat al-Nuṣra, the Syrian wing of al-Qāʿida.

[62] This conversation was recorded on a series of tapes called *Al-Kufr Kufrānī* (There are Two Kinds of Unbelief) and can be found in transliterated form in al-Ṭarṭūsī, *Intiṣār*. Lav mistakenly conflates these *Al-Kufr Kufrānī* tapes with the *Fitnat al-Takfīr* tape, which al-Ḥalabī used as the basis for his book. See Lav, *Radical*, 140–1.

[63] Abū Anas ʿAlī b. Ḥusayn Abū Lūz, *Fitnat al-Takfīr* (Riyadh: Dār al-Waṭan, 1417 [1996–7]); *id., Fitnat al-Takfīr* (Riyadh: Dār Ibn Khuzayma, 1997).

[64] For a brief overview of al-Ḥalabī's views in this specific book of his, see Lav, *Radical*, 141–2.

[65] Interview with Muḥammad Abū Ruḥayyim, Amman, 16 January 2013. [66] *Ibid.*

[67] Abū Ruḥayyim, introduction to *Masʾalat* by al-Jazāʾirī, 7; interview with Muḥammad Abū Ruḥayyim, Amman, 16 January 2013.

could have a debate about the topic of faith and unbelief that was to be moderated by Shaqra. Abu Ruhayyim agreed to the debate, but only reluctantly, as he later made quite clear to me:

> The one called ʿAli Hasan [al-Halabi] asked for a debate with me. I, of course, asked "Who is this ʿAli Hasan?" He did not even finish secondary school. Secondary school! Who is he, saying that he wants to debate me? [...] He does not have any knowledge, absolutely none at all![68]

The debate, which was quite heated at times,[69] took place in 1997, but did not convince either party that they were wrong. It did convince Abu Ruhayyim, however, that al-Halabi was unrepentant of his "deviance".[70] This belief was confirmed when, shortly after the debate in 1997, al-Halabi wrote another book himself – *Sahyat Nadhir bi-Khatar al-Takfir* (A Warning Cry on the Dangers of Excommunication) – that argued about the perils of "extremism in *takfīr*" along similar lines as his earlier book.[71] Enraged about this, Abu Ruhayyim therefore decided to write a refutation of this book himself called *Tahdhir al-Umma min Taʿliqat al-Halabi ʿala Aqwal al-Aʾimma* (The Warning of the Muslim Community against the Comments of al-Halabi against the Sayings of the Imams).[72]

Abu Ruhayyim did not leave it at this, however. Having already inspired someone else to ask the Saudi Permanent Council for Knowledge Studies and Fatwas for a ruling on Shukri's book, Abu Ruhayyim now decided to ask the council for a fatwa himself, but this time about al-Halabi's two controversial works.[73] The fatwa was published in July 2000[74] and it criticised al-Halabi precisely on the two points that Abu Ruhayyim had asked about: the supposed Murjiʾa-type of ideas about faith and the misrepresentation of major scholars. The fatwa states that *kufr* does not just occur if it is accompanied by unbelief in the heart, as al-Halabi is said to have suggested, but can also be found in, for example, acts. Moreover, the Saudi scholars also claim that al-Halabi

68 Interview with Muḥammad Abū Ruḥayyim, Amman, 16 January 2013.
69 Audio recordings of the entire debate can be found at *Munāẓarat Muḥammad Abū Ruḥayyim li-ʿAlī al-Ḥalabī*, parts 1–4 (www.tawhed.ws/c?i=296, n.d. (accessed 11 May 2015)).
70 Abū Ruḥayyim, introduction to *Masʾalat* by al-Jazāʾirī, 6.
71 ʿAlī b. Ḥasan b. ʿAlī b. ʿAbd al-Ḥamīd al-Ḥalabī al-Atharī, *Ṣayḥat Nadhīr bi-Khaṭar al-Takfīr* (www.alhalaby.com/play.php?catsmktba=2925, 1997 (accessed 22 April 2013)).
72 Abū Ruḥayyim, introduction to *Masʾalat* by al-Jazāʾirī, 6. This refutation of al-Ḥalabī's book, together with Abū Ruḥayyim's work criticising Shukrī's publication, was later combined into one book, the aforementioned *Ḥaqīqat al-Khilāf bayna l-Salafiyya al-Sharʿiyya wa-Adʿiyāʾihā*. See Abū Ruḥayyim, *Ḥaqīqat al-Khilāf*, 8.
73 Abū Ruḥayyim, introduction to *Masʾalat* by al-Jazāʾirī, 11–12; interview with Muḥammad Abū Ruḥayyim, Amman, 16 January 2013.
74 Al-Jazāʾirī, *Masʾalat*, 403–5.

has twisted or misrepresented the words of several major *'ulamā'*, including the mediaeval shaykh Ibn Taymiyya and the late Saudi mufti Muhammad b. Ibrahim Al al-Shaykh, and they therefore state that it is not allowed to print, publish or circulate these books.[75]

Al-Halabi's fellow quietist scholars in Jordan speak highly of him and some of them state that even if the Permanent Council was right and he did make mistakes, they are clearly outweighed by the good things al-Halabi has written in his publications. Moreover, they claim that al-Halabi has benefited from the fatwa written against his books.[76] This suggests, perhaps, that al-Halabi humbly accepted the criticism against his publications and corrected his alleged mistakes. This was not the case, however. Al-Halabi first wrote a document that constituted a reply to the fatwa by the Permanent Council and in which he presented his case again.[77] Al-Halabi's point is not so much that the Permanent Council is entirely wrong, as he describes it in a new introduction to his first controversial book, but that he published his books against "extremists in *takfīr*" and that this is a good cause. Moreover, he claims that if mistakes were made (and he acknowledges that he did make mistakes), these also affect the value of the rest of the book.[78]

What al-Halabi seems to be saying is that he may have made mistakes, but that the scholars of the Permanent Council should perhaps have ignored these in light of the greater good that the book would do. In fact, he may even have wanted to suggest that their fatwa undermined the value of his book to such an extent that its use in the refutation of "extremists in *takfīr*" would now be far smaller. In any case, several Saudi scholars did not take too kindly to al-Halabi's critique of their fatwa and contributed to a new book by the Saudi scholar Muhammad b. Salim al-Dawsari, in which the latter once again explained why al-Halabi was wrong.[79] One of the contributing shaykhs writes in his introduction that

[75] Al-Lajna al-Dā'ima li-l-Buḥūth wa-l-Iftā', "Fatwa no. 21517" (www.alifta.net/Search/ResultDetails.aspx?languagename=ar&lang=ar&view=result&fatwaNum=&FatwaNumID=&ID=10901&searchScope=3&SearchScopeLevels1=&SearchScopeLevels2=&highLight=1&SearchType=exact&SearchMoesar=false&bookID=&LeftVal=0&RightVal=0&simple=&SearchCriteria=allwords&PagePath=&siteSection=1&searchkeyword=216185217132217138032216173216179217134032216167217132216173217132216168217138#firstKeyWordFound, n.d. (accessed 11 May 2015)). See also Lav, *Radical*, 165–6.

[76] Interviews with Muḥammad b. Mūsá Āl Naṣr, Amman, 20 June 2012; Mashhūr b. Ḥasan Āl Salmān, Amman, 27 June 2012.

[77] 'Alī b. Ḥasan b. 'Alī al-Ḥalabī al-Atharī, *Al-Ajwiba al-Mutalā'ima 'alá Fatwá l-Lajna al-Dā'ima ḥawla Kitābay* al-Taḥdhīr *wa-*Ṣayḥat Nadhīr *fī l-Radd 'alá Du'āt al-Takfīr* (www.4salaf.com/vb/showthread.php?t=5986, n.d. (accessed 21 February 2013)).

[78] *Id.*, introduction to *Al-Taḥdhīr min Fitnat al-Ghulūw* by al-Albānī, 5–10.

[79] Muḥammad b. Sālim al-Dawsarī, *Raf' al-Lā'ima 'an Fatwá l-Lajna al-Dā'ima* (www.tawhed.ws/dl?i=ev70m465, n.d. (accessed 3 September 2009)).

the scholars whose fatwa criticised al-Halabi are "more knowledgeable than [al-Halabi], greater in age than he and more advanced in knowledge of the creed". Rather than being grateful and thanking these scholars and revising his work, he states, al-Halabi wrote a "refutation of the [Permanent] Council".[80] Al-Halabi, in turn, countered this critique of his critique of the fatwa with yet another book criticising al-Dawsari.[81]

To Abu Ruhayyim, whose main gripe against al-Halabi was his lack of scholarly credentials, this only added insult to injury. He blames him for holding the Permanent Council in contempt by refuting them, instead of humbly admitting he was wrong, and by only "adding other lies" to his supposedly already existing ones.[82] Of course, the fact that al-Halabi, in the early 2000s, also wrote a book directly refuting Abu Ruhhayim's criticism of al-Albani's views on faith did not help either.[83] Still, the conflict between al-Halabi and Abu Ruhayyim, fierce and transnational though it was, remained within the scholarly sphere and did not have any further ramifications. This changed, however, when Muhammad Ibrahim Shaqra got involved.

The Leadership of the Quietist Salafi Community

As we saw in Chapter 2, Shaqra – though initially siding with al-Albani on the question of faith – eventually drifted towards Abu Ruhayyim's point of view and implicitly started referring to al-Halabi and other quietist Salafi scholars in Jordan as "neo-Murjiʾa". This suggests that Shaqra was very much like Abu Ruhayyim, yet this was not the case. Abu Ruhayyim, as we saw above, was against al-Halabi from the start, seeing him as weak, untrustworthy and deviant with regard to religious authority.[84] The relationship between Shaqra and al-Halabi seems to have been a good one, however. Shaqra apparently had a favourable view of al-Halabi and even singled him out to accompany him on visits to other people.[85] Conversely, even after the debate with Abu Ruhayyim in

[80] Saʿd b. ʿAbdallāh b. ʿAbd al-ʿAzīz Āl Ḥumayyid, introduction to *Rafʿ al-Lāʾima ʿan Fatwá l-Lajna al-Dāʾima*, by Muḥammad b. Sālim al-Dawsarī (www.tawhed.ws/dl?i=ev70m465, n.d. (accessed 3 September 2009)), 11.

[81] ʿAlī b. Ḥasan b. ʿAlī b. ʿAbd al-Ḥamīd al-Ḥalabī al-Atharī, *Al-Tanbīhāt al-Mutawāʾima fī Nuṣrat Ḥaqq al-Ajwiba al-Mutalāʾima ʿalá Fatwá l-Lajna al-Dāʾima wa-l-Naqḍ ʿalá Aghālīṭ wa-Mughālaṭāt* Rafʿ al-Lāʾima*!!!* (United Arab Emirates: Maktabat Dār al-Ḥadīth, 2003).

[82] *Liqāʾ Shabakat Anā l-Muslim* (this source contains the words quoted); interview with Muḥammad Abū Ruḥayyim, Amman, 16 January 2013. See also al-Jazāʾirī, *Masʾalat*, 38.

[83] Al-Ḥalabī, *Al-Radd*.

[84] The concept of religious scholarly authority will be dealt with in greater detail in Chapter 5.

[85] Interview with ʿIṣām Hādī, Amman, 19 January 2013.

1997,[86] which Shaqra – as moderator – apparently decided in favour of the former,[87] al-Halabi still spoke highly of Shaqra, referring to him in words such as "my teacher Ab[u] Malik [Shaqra] – may God aid him" and "my father teacher (*ustādhī l-wālid*) Abu Malik – may God be beneficial to him".[88]

Thus, a mere two years before al-Albani's death, Shaqra and al-Halabi seem to have got along fine but only a year after their shaykh's passing, they were in open conflict with one another, disputing each other's views on faith. The reason for this cannot only have been that they had different ideas on *īmān*, since this had been apparent for some time and, moreover, had not caused a conflict with al-Albani – who differed with Shaqra on this point as well – either. This suggests that Shaqra, like Abu Ruhayyim, may have been willing to put up with al-Albani's supposedly deviant views on faith since the latter was at least a scholar, but that he was not going to accept this from a younger and less scholarly person like al-Halabi. This explanation would be incorrect as well, although the factor of religious scholarly authority does play a role here, but in a different way than with the dispute between al-Halabi and Abu Ruhayyim.

After al-Albani died in 1999, the question of who should lead the quietist Salafi community in Jordan arose. Although al-Albani had never actually been the official "leader", everyone seems to have understood that he was "the shaykh". According to al-Halabi, al-Albani's foremost students wanted to transfer that label onto Shaqra, but the latter wanted to have the explicit leadership over the community, which they refused.[89] If this is true, their rejection may have been caused by their traditional refusal to become a formally organised group or, as some quietist Salafis suggest, because both men had leadership ambitions.[90]

In any case, it was clear that Shaqra and al-Halabi were both qualified for the leadership of the Jordanian quietist Salafi community, though in different ways. As mentioned, Shaqra was an Azhar-educated man who had been of great importance to the early Salafi trend in Jordan and who had been instrumental in getting al-Albani to come to Jordan and later,

[86] Al-Ḥalabī, *Ṣayḥat*, 4, footnote 2.

[87] Interview with ʿIṣām Hādī, Amman, 19 January 2013. Shaqra's siding with Abū Ruḥayyim does not appear to have been a polemical move, however. Shaqra can be heard repeatedly trying to calm al-Ḥalabī down in a friendly way during the debate and it seems that Shaqra simply felt that Abū Ruḥayyim had better arguments.

[88] Al-Ḥalabī, *Ṣayḥat*, 4, 6 (see also footnote *alif* on this page), 14. The words cited can be found on 4.

[89] Interview with ʿAlī al-Ḥalabī, Amman, 27 June 2012.

[90] Interviews with Bāsim b. Fayṣal al-Jawābira, Amman, 26 June 2012; Bassām Nāṣir, Amman, 16 June 2013; Usāma Shaḥāda, Amman, 10 January 2013; Murād Shukrī, Amman, 17 January 2013.

after the latter had been expelled, to return to the kingdom. Al-Halabi, by contrast, was almost 30 years younger and lacked Shaqra's education. The latter, however, was a senior civil servant who regularly met and had befriended King Husayn and several Jordanian princes. While this brought him professional benefits, it led to the neglect of his scholarly studies and his close relationship with al-Albani and the Salafi community. By contrast, al-Halabi was a full-time scholar who could dedicate almost all of his time to studying, writing and preaching, thereby surpassing Shaqra in knowledge and publishing far more books. Moreover, as a relatively young Palestinian refugee, al-Halabi was naturally closer to many of the similarly young quietist Salafis in Jordan than the older and slightly elitist Shaqra and frequently mingled among them.[91] As a result, it was al-Halabi – not Shaqra – who became the *de facto* leader of the quietist Salafi community in Jordan.

The fact that Shaqra was overtaken in his religious authority by al-Halabi and the realisation that he was not accepted as "leader" of the quietist Salafi community on his own terms must have hurt, particularly since Shaqra seems to have felt entitled to the position. In my interview with him, he claimed to have been the first Salafi in Jordan and repeatedly stressed his own contributions to Salafism in the kingdom and his links to al-Albani:

> I was the one who spoke with King Husayn and put in a good word for [al-Albani] with [the king]. I directed [the king] so that he would have [al-Albani] return to Jordan another time. Indeed, he returned to Jordan though my putting in a good word for him with King Husayn. The bond between me and the shaykh was firm. People met with shaykh Nasir [al-Albani] and I was the reason. [The Salafi *da'wa*] was spread among the cities and the villages in Jordan through my influence. I brought this Salafi *da'wa* with shaykh Nasir – may God have mercy on him. I brought this Salafi *da'wa* to the mosques of the kingdom, its schools and its universities. [This way,] people were greatly influenced by the knowledge of shaykh Nasir. You could say that I was the one who found a ready market for shaykh Nasir, helped [his *da'wa*] and spread the Salafi *da'wa* in Jordan among youngsters and among the major scholars. With shaykh Nasir al-Din al-Albani, I was the first who brought the Salafi *da'wa* [to Jordan], helped shaykh Nasir contact the people and called the people to this blessed *da'wa*.[92]

Given such explicit words by Shaqra about his own contribution to the history of Salafism in Jordan, it is not surprising that virtually all quietist

[91] Interviews with ʿAbd al-Fattāḥ ʿUmar Abū l-Ḥārith, Amman, 14 January 2013; ʿIṣām Hādī, Amman, 19 January 2013; ʿAlī al-Ḥalabī, Amman, 27 June 2012; Usāma Shaḥāda, Amman, 7 June 2012.

[92] Interview with Muḥammad Ibrāhīm Shaqra, Amman, 27 June 2012.

Salafis in Amman[93] with whom I discussed this matter either implicitly or explicitly stated that the core of the conflict between Shaqra and al-Halabi was really about leadership ambition, not theology.[94]

Although the main reason for the conflict between Shaqra and al-Halabi was not ideological, their rhetoric suggested otherwise. In fact, the differences of opinion about faith between Shaqra and others prior to al-Albani's death were exactly that: differences of opinion. They existed and they were real, but they were not allowed to turn into a conflict until after al-Albani died. Quickly after it became apparent that Shaqra would not succeed al-Albani as leader of the quietist Salafi community, he revised several of his earlier writings from the 1980s and 1990s to bring them in line with his new ideas on faith.[95] The fact that he only revised these books after he was rejected as leader of the Salafi community could be a coincidence, of course, but it suggests that he doubled down on his theological difference with other Jordanian quietists out of frustration at being rejected as leader.[96]

The response to Shaqra's revisionism came swiftly: an aforementioned special double issue of the quietist Salafi journal *Al-Asala* was dedicated to refuting one of the books Shaqra had revised, concentrating particularly on the book's linguistic analysis,[97] its treatment of a person who leaves prayer,[98] the focus on Ibn ʿAbbas' words "*kufr dūna kufr*",[99] its analysis of the question of *irjāʾ*[100] and, finally, the role of acts in faith.[101]

93 These conflicts took place in Amman among shaykhs who lived or spent much of their time in that city. Salafis outside of Amman, probably because they did not witness these disputes personally, are often much less aware of the aspects of religious authority and leadership ambition involved in these conflicts, which is why they tend to see them in theological terms, as we will see later on.

94 Abū Rummān and Abū Haniyya, *Al-Salafiyya al-Muḥāfaẓa*, 107; interviews with Muḥammad b. Mūsá Āl Naṣr, Amman, 20 June 2012; Ibrāhīm al-ʿAsʿas, Amman, 14 January 2013; ʿAlī al-Ḥalabī, Amman, 27 June 2012; Bāsim b. Fayṣal al-Jawābira, Amman, 26 June 2012; Bassām Nāṣir, Amman, 16 June 2013; Marwān Shaḥāda, Amman, 11 January 2013; Usāma Shaḥāda, Amman, 10 January 2013; Muḥammad Ibrāhīm Shaqra, Amman, 27 June 2012; Murād Shukrī, Amman, 17 January 2013.

95 Muḥammad Ibrāhīm Shaqra, *Irshād al-Sārī ilá ʿIbādat al-Bārī* (I have not been able to locate this book); *id.*, *Hiya l-Salafiyya Nisbatan wa-ʿAqīdatan wa-Manhajan* (www.saaid.net/book/open.php?cat=1&Book=44, 2000 [1992] (accessed 5 October 2013)); *id.*, *Tanwīr*, 33–114, esp. 33–59.

96 He also critically refers to other Jordanian Salafis in his new introduction to the book. See *id.*, *Hiya*, 9.

97 "Bayna Lughat al-ʿArab wa-Fahm al-Salaf," *Al-Aṣāla* 5, nos. 25–6 (15 Muḥarram 1421 [20 April 2000] – 15 Rabīʿ al-Awwal 1421 [18 June 2000]): 17–24.

98 "Takfīr Tārik al-Ṣalāt," *Al-Aṣāla* 5, nos. 25–6 (15 Muḥarram 1421 [20 April 2000] – 15 Rabīʿ al-Awwal 1421 [18 June 2000]): 25–77.

99 "Taḥrīr Qawl Ibn ʿAbbās – Raḍiya llāh ʿanhu: 'Kufr Dūna Kufr'," *Al-Aṣāla* 5, nos. 25–6 (15 Muḥarram 1421 [20 April 2000] – 15 Rabīʿ al-Awwal 1421 [18 June 2000]): 79–114.

100 "Masʾalat al-Irjāʾ . . . !" 115–32.

101 "Hal al-ʿAmal," 132–49.

Although the special issue concentrated on refuting Shaqra with regard to most of the controversial themes related to *īmān*, it did so in a very non-polemical and even polite way. In fact, it did not even mention Shaqra's name, nor the title of the book it was refuting and every article was published anonymously, all presumably in order not to embarrass Shaqra.[102]

Shaqra apparently did not appreciate this, however, since ʿAsim Muhammad Ibrahim Shaqra, one of Shaqra's sons, wrote a spirited defence of his father in response to the double issue of *Al-Asala*. Interestingly, although he uses most of the book to defend his father's views on faith, he echoes Muhammad Shaqra's own words cited earlier by starting this discussion with a polemical introduction in which he emphasises his father's precedence in Salafism, his contribution to *daʿwa* in Jordan, his ties to al-Albani and his help to the latter when he was in need.[103] He mockingly refers to the anonymous authors of the articles in *Al-Asala* by nicknames[104] and pointedly writes about the Saudi Permanent Council's fatwa against al-Halabi.[105] In a further indication that he sees his father as possessing greater religious authority than his competitors, ʿAsim Shaqra writes that the authors of the special double issue of *Al-Asala* "were [still] wrapped in the cloths of their mothers while 'the shaykh'[106] (i.e., Muhammad Ibrahim Shaqra) was working hard to found the [Salafi] *daʿwa* and spreading it".[107]

ʿAsim Shaqra's book in defence of his father appears to have been the beginning of this discussion turning into something rather nasty. It seems that it was only at this point – around and after 2001 – that Muhammad Ibrahim Shaqra openly started using the label "neo-Murjiʾa" to describe his opponents[108] and that he started siding with Abu Ruhayyim in the latter's criticism of al-Albani's views on faith.[109] This, to al-Halabi and his

[102] The title only became clear in ʿĀṣim Shaqra's defence of his father, written in response to the special issue of *Al-Aṣāla*, where the author wrote that the book in question was his father's work *Irshād al-Sārī ilá ʿIbādat al-Bārī*. See Shaqra, *Al-Rudūd, alif*.

[103] *Ibid., dāl-yāʾ*. [104] *Ibid., alif*. [105] *Ibid., kāf*.

[106] This is a sarcastic reference to the way the special issue of *Al-Aṣāla* refers to Shaqra in order to avoid his name.

[107] Shaqra, *Al-Rudūd, hāʾ*.

[108] Shaqra, *Ayna; id., Al-Dufūʿāt al-Ghawānī wa-l-Istinbāṭāt al-Rawānī li-Iẓhār Wajh al-Ḥaqq fī Masʾalat ʿIṣmat Azwāj al-Nabī – Ṣallá llah ʿalayhi wa-Sallam – allatī Ikhtalafa ʿalayhā Nasīb al-Rifāʿī wa-Nāṣir al-Dīn al-Albānī* (n.p.: no publisher, 2003), 3–4.

[109] *Id.*, introduction to *Ḥaqīqat al-Īmān* by Abū Ruḥayyim, 5–8, esp. 6. See also *id., Al-Dufūʿāt*, 9–16. In 2010, Shaqra even wrote the introduction to a book that openly accused al-Ḥalabī of being a Jahmī, referring to a shadowy sect within early Islam that is said to have equated faith only with conviction in the heart. See Muḥammad Ibrāhīm Shaqra, introduction to *Al-Kāshif fī Tarājuʿ ʿAlī al-Ḥalabī al-Jahmī al-Zāʾif*, by Abū ʿUzayr ʿAbd al-Ilah Yūsuf al-Yūbī al-Ḥasanī al-Jazāʾirī (www.tawhed.ws/dl?i=17051001, 2010 (accessed 4 October 2013)), 5–12, as well as the book itself.

supporters, was the final straw. Al-Halabi describes how he and other quietist Salafi shaykhs from Jordan and elsewhere visited Shaqra and confronted him with his accusations against al-Albani.[110] Although the meeting seemed to have ended with reconciliation and Shaqra taking back his words about al-Albani, al-Halabi claims he quickly found out that Shaqra had apparently not changed his mind at all and was giving false accounts of the meeting, causing him to repeat his arguments against Shaqra's theological reasoning all over again.[111]

In later years, al-Halabi sometimes reminded Shaqra of his criticism of al-Albani[112] and in 2013, a reconciliation meeting was even held at which al-Halabi and several other prominent Jordanian quietist shaykhs were present. During this meeting, at which Shaqra was apparently absent for health reasons, al-Halabi and the others once again stated that they felt it was their duty to stand up for al-Albani's views on faith – even after his death – and that this was the most important aspect of the conflict for them.[113] Although Shaqra is now in his eighties and the conflict seems to have lain dormant for the last few years, al-Halabi may have spoken the truth: it could indeed be the case that he and his fellow students of al-Albani first and foremost did not want to see their teacher slandered and were never in this conflict for reasons of religious authority, leadership or power. Shaqra, on the other hand, would most probably never have used the label of "neo-Murjiʾa" were it not for his frustration over being rejected as a leader of the quietist community in Jordan, particularly given his record of service to al-Albani and Salafism in the kingdom.

The conflict between al-Halabi on the one hand and Abu Ruhayyim and Shaqra on the other did not just create a lot of bad blood between the leading Salafi shaykhs in Jordan, but it also shook up power relations in Jordanian Salafism. This is particularly relevant with regard to Salafi relations with the state since the latter ended up with a more regime-friendly Salafi leadership than under al-Albani's guidance or under the possible direction of Shaqra. After all, like al-Albani, al-Halabi and his like-minded fellow scholars, as winners of this battle over the leadership of quietist Salafism in Jordan, were less likely to hold the rulers of Jordan to account than Abu Ruhayyim and Shaqra because they only treated acts as part of *kamāl al-dīn*, making *takfīr* of the king or politicians highly

[110] ʿAlī b. Ḥasan b. ʿAlī b. ʿAbd al-Ḥamīd al-Ḥalabī al-Atharī, *"Qālū lā Ḍayr . . . ": "Wa-l-Ṣulḥ Khayr . . . " Awrāq . . . fī Kāʾinat "al-Ṣulḥ wa-l-Ittifāq" maʿa l-Shaykh Muḥammad Shaqra . . . Faqra Faqra!* (Amman: Al-Dār al-Athariyya, 2004), 8–18.

[111] *Ibid.*, 19–74.

[112] *Id.*, *Al-Shaykh Muḥammad Ibrāhīm Shaqra.. Shukran Jazīlan la-ka* (www.alhalaby.com/play.php?catsmktba=3169, 28 June 2012 (accessed 1 April 2013)).

[113] *Id.*, *Kalimatī fī Majlis al-Ṣulḥ maʿa Faḍīlat al-Shaykh Muḥammad Shaqra – Wafaqahu llāh* (www.alhalaby.com/play.php?catsmktba=3461, 25 April 2013 (accessed 7 May 2013)).

improbable, as we saw in Chapter 2. At the same time, they were more loyalist than the aloofist al-Albani. The Jordanian regime thus ended up with a Salafi leadership that was both doctrinally and politically more favourably disposed to the state than the possible alternatives. This, in turn, made the Jordanian Salafi community more susceptible to domestication by the regime, a process that was reinforced by the founding of the Imam al-Albani Centre.

The Imam al-Albani Centre

The conflicts between Murad Shukri, Muhammad Abu Ruhayyim, Muhammad Ibrahim Shaqra and ʿAli al-Halabi created a group of disgruntled and increasingly marginalised quietist Salafis that included the former three and their supporters. At the same time, the disputes left the leadership of the quietist Salafi community in Jordan in the hands of al-Halabi and his allies, who included Mashhur b. Hasan, Muhammad Musa Nasr, Husayn al-ʿAwayisha, Basim b. Faysal al-Jawabira, Akram Ziyada and Salim al-Hilali. In an informally organised movement like quietist Salafism in Jordan until the early 2000s, such power relations were sometimes expressed through influential positions such as being on the editorial board of the *Al-Asala* journal, in which particularly Muhammad Musa Nasr played a major role and, to a lesser extent, also al-Halabi, Mashhur b. Hasan and Salim al-Hilali. Yet precisely because the Salafi trend in Jordan was so informally organised, such relations were not tied to official positions or government patronage and were therefore not set in stone. This was particularly the case considering the fact that an unknown number of quietist Salafis in Jordan had witnessed the ugly disputes between their scholars and may not have automatically sided with the victorious party. The dynamics of intra-Salafi power relations changed, however, when the Jordanian regime entered the fold, which definitively decided the leadership contest in favour of one of the parties, but did not end the drama.

The Founding of the Imam al-Albani Centre

In 2001, the Imam al-Albani Centre for Knowledge and Methodological Studies (Markaz Imam al-Albani li-l-Dirasat al-ʿIlmiyya wa-l-Manhajiyya) was founded,[114] located in a specially designated building on the outskirts of Amman. Unlike the situation under al-Albani's leadership, when Salafis

[114] Abū Rummān and Abū Haniyya, *Al-Ḥall*, 240; Shaḥāda, "Al-Salafiyya," 120; interview with Salīm al-Hilālī, Amman, 28 January 2013. See also the centre's website: http://al albany.org/pageother.php?catsmktba=6753 (accessed 9 June 2015).

met in each other's homes and spread their message through talks and audio tapes, quietist Salafism in Jordan now had a building, a fixed phone number and a fax machine. Using these means, the Imam al-Albani Centre became the focal point for quietist Salafi lessons, *daʿwa* activities, fatwas and publications (including *Al-Asala*). As will be recalled from Chapter 2, however, founding centres and organisations was not something that many Jordanian Salafis were in favour of, including al-Albani himself when he was in Syria, although he later changed his mind about this when he saw that circumstances in Jordan were more suitable for organised Salafism. This explains why, more than a decade after the foundation of the Imam al-Albani Centre, al-Halabi was still defending its very existence against critics who were against such organised Salafi activities altogether. According to al-Halabi, as long as Salafi organisations were ideologically sound and did not create divisions, there was nothing wrong with them, which also seems to have been al-Albani's point of view.[115]

The reason for the founding of the Imam al-Albani Centre was not, however, because some Salafis in Jordan suddenly, after al-Albani's death, came round to the view that organisations were not so bad after all, but because the regime got involved.[116] As we saw in the Introduction, the Jordanian state strives to control civil society organisations and groups through rules and regulations, thus using bureaucracy to ensure that none of them pose a political or security threat. The informally organised Salafi movement in Jordan, which was still relatively unknown but certainly growing in the kingdom at the time, operated almost entirely outside of the regime's gaze. With the loss of al-Albani, the regime may well have believed that this was the right moment to strive for more control over this trend, either because it felt the movement would be more malleable now or because it saw Salafis as possibly going into all kinds of undesirable directions without their shaykh.

Whatever the case may be, the regime must have realised the desirability of bringing Salafism in Jordan under bureaucratic control and is said to have discussed this idea with the direct students of al-Albani, calling them to ask whether they felt Shaqra or al-Halabi should be the leader of this endeavour. Although not everybody was enthusiastic about this idea, it quickly became clear that the regime was going to go ahead with the plan of founding an official Salafi centre anyway, so those closest to al-Albani expressed their preference for either Shaqra or al-Halabi.[117]

[115] ʿAlī al-Ḥalabī, *Radd Qawl Man Qāla bi-Taḥrīm al-Jamʿiyyāt Muṭlaqan* (www.alhalaby.com/play.php?catsmktba=3179, 4 July 2012 (accessed 1 April 2013)).

[116] Shukrī refers to the regime as "the father" and the Imām al-Albānī Centre as "the son". Interview with Murād Shukrī, Amman, 17 January 2013.

[117] Interview with ʿIṣām Hādī, Amman, 19 January 2013.

The regime ended up founding the Imam al-Albani Centre with Salim al-Hilali as its director, Muhammad Musa Nasr as his deputy and al-Halabi, Mashhur b. Hasan and Husayn al-ʿAwayisha acting as leading members. Other quietist Salafis allied to these five were also made members of the centre.[118]

The founding of the Imam al-Albani Centre thus drew quietist Salafism into the regime's sphere of influence and brought it under its bureaucratic control. This is not even denied by al-Halabi, who states that the centre was founded "to coordinate [al-Albani's students'] efforts with regard to *daʿwa* and knowledge in a manner of knowledge-based brotherhood (*bi-ṣūra akhawiyya ʿilmiyya*), on the one hand, and in an official and orderly way (*bi-ṭarīqa niẓāmiyya rasmiyya*), on the other".[119] Al-Halabi also says that the Imam al-Albani Centre, precisely because it is under regime control, provides quietist Salafism with official cover from any accusations of being Salafi "extremists".[120]

Given the different and more radical trends within Salafism that also exist and are often under fire in Jordan, as we will see later on, the Imam al-Albani Centre thus gave useful protection to al-Halabi and his allies from being lumped together into the same category with such trends. Moreover, by making the Imam al-Albani Centre the officially approved representative of Salafism in the kingdom, the regime also consolidated the leadership position of al-Halabi and his allies *vis-à-vis* Shaqra and his supporters. Because of both factors, quietist Salafism in Jordan lost even more of the independent and aloofist character it had had under al-Albani's leadership and increasingly became a loyalist movement that was close to the regime. Although this process was only completed later on, when the regime's agenda became increasingly intertwined with that of official quietist Salafism, the founding of the Imam al-Albani Centre was nevertheless an important step in the further domestication of the quietist Salafi movement in Jordan.

Accusations of Theft against Salim al-Hilali

The founding of the Imam al-Albani Centre as the representative of quietist Salafism in Jordan also brought with it the possibility of greater funding, both from inside Jordan and internationally, since the movement no longer just consisted of individual adherents but actually had official status now. One of the groups from abroad supporting the Imam

118 Abū Rummān and Abū Haniyya, *Al-Ḥall*, 240–1; *id.*, *Al-Salafiyya al-Muḥāfaẓa*, 107; Shaḥāda, "Al-Salafiyya," 120; interview with Salīm al-Hilālī, Amman, 28 January 2013.

119 Al-Ḥalabī, *Mujmal*, 113.

120 Interview with ʿAlī al-Ḥalabī, Amman, 27 June 2012.

al-Albani Centre was the Kuwaiti Jamʿiyyat Ihyaʾ al-Turath al-Islami, which – as we saw in Chapter 1 – had become a thoroughly quietist Salafi group after the Gulf War. Somewhere around 2006 or 2007 – the exact year is unclear – the director of the Imam al-Albani Centre, Salim al-Hilali, was accused of embezzling money donated to the centre, which eventually led to his giving up his role as one of the prominent shaykhs of the quietist Salafi community and almost resulted in the end of the centre's activities.

The discovery of the alleged theft by al-Hilali is said to have happened when Muhammad Musa Nasr went to Kuwait to attend activities organised by the Jamʿiyyat Ihyaʾ al-Turath al-Islami. Representatives of the latter reportedly asked him how the money they had sent to the Imam al-Albani Centre had been spent. Muhammad Musa Nasr, given the fact that he was deputy director of the centre, should have known about this but apparently did not, leading to suspicions. Apparently the money, which was meant for *daʿwa* activities, sacrificial animals and assistance for youngsters wanting to get married, had been transferred to a private bank account owned by al-Hilali, rather than the shared account the latter had with Muhammad Musa Nasr, which required the signatures of both men.[121]

Back in Jordan, Muhammad Musa Nasr and the other shaykhs apparently confronted al-Hilali with his alleged embezzlement, which he is said to have denied but eventually confessed to, including to donors in Kuwait. Supposedly not to cause a scene and embarrass the entire Imam al-Albani Centre, those involved wanted to keep the matter quiet if al-Hilali just agreed to return the money – which he is said to have partly done – and withdraw from the centre. Although he is claimed to have promised he would and a document is said to have been drawn up compelling him to cut ties with the Imam al-Albani Centre, he allegedly secretly left the meeting during which he was supposed to sign the document and fled. The other shaykhs are said to have gone looking for him afterwards, only to see him wandering around a hospital, from where they followed him to a restaurant where they "found him eating chicken and drinking a cocktail". The shaykhs appear to have tried to force him again to sign the document, but he refused.[122]

[121] *Seputar Korupsi Salim Hilali* (www.4shared.com/office/Ul2BWef8/SEPUTAR_KORUPSI_SALIM_HILALI.html, n.d. (accessed 2 April 2013)), 1–2. See also the "Al-Ṣundūq al-Aswad" files, published on the *Kull al-Salafiyyīn* website, which is run under the auspices of ʿAlī al-Ḥalabī. This document can be found at www.kulalsalafiyeen.com/vb/showthread.php?t=15620 and www.kulalsalafiyeen.com/vb/showthread.php?t=15620&page=3, 24 March 2010 (accessed 7 February 2013); Usāma al-ʿUtaybī, *Radd Usāma al-ʿUtaybī ʿalá ftirāʾāt Salīm al-Hilālī* (www.kulalsalafiyeen.com/vb/showthread.php?t=15620, 24 March 2010 (accessed 7 February 2013)).

[122] *Seputar*, 2–5 (the words cited can be found on 4); *Īlāf al-Salafiyyīn am "Ittilāf al-Salafiyyīn"?!!* (www.kulalsalafiyeen.com/vb/showthread.php?t=15620&page=2, 24 March 2010 (accessed 7 February 2014)); al-ʿUtaybī, *Radd.*

The embezzlement of funds from Kuwait was not the only charge levelled against al-Hilali. He was also accused of using 128,000 dollars for personal gain, even though that sum had been donated to the Imam al-Albani Centre by like-minded Muslims from Indonesia. This money, which was supposed to have been spent on laptops and setting up an undefined network called "The Future of Islam" (*mustaqbal al-Islām*), is said to have gone to al-Hilali's private bank account.[123] Much of this money is claimed to have been spent on buying land in Jordan by al-Hilali.[124] Moreover, he was also accused of selling the rights to one of his books to two different publishers.[125]

What to make of all of this? The accounts accusing al-Hilali are numerous and far more detailed than I have described here. Moreover, despite the divisions among quietist Salafis in Jordan, all those I interviewed about this agreed that al-Hilali had stolen the Imam al-Albani Centre's money, although al-Hilali's reputation as a serial plagiariser – deserved or not – may have influenced this image too. Furthermore, many of the writings about this matter also include scans of documents supposedly proving that al-Hilali had indeed received money from both Kuwait and Indonesia, had partly used it to enrich himself and buy land and had forged other shaykhs' signatures.[126]

The only one denying that al-Hilali was guilty of theft seems to be al-Hilali himself. He refuses to acknowledge any of the evidence against him, claims the accusations of theft are all lies and states that insofar money was taken that was not his, it has all been returned.[127] Instead, he says the reason he left the Imam al-Albani Centre was because some of its scholars were getting too close to the regime and its policies.[128] Although this claim seems plausible, given that the entire founding of the Imam al-Albani Centre was aimed at bringing quietist Salafism under state control, it does not deny the evidence against al-Hilali, of course. Moreover, this argument sounds odd coming from someone who was not only

[123] *Seputar*, 6.
[124] *Difāʿan ʿan Mashāyikh al-Urdunn* (www.kulalsalafiyeen.com/vb/showthread.php?t-15620, 24 March 2010 (accessed 7 February 2013)); *Seputar*, 7; al-ʿUtaybī, *Radd.*
[125] Al-ʿUtaybī, *Radd.*
[126] *Ilá Salīm al-Hilālī: Yarjá l-Takrīm bi-Tazwīdinā bi-Taqrīr* ... (www.kulalsalafiyeen.com/vb/showthread.php?t=15620&page=2, 24 March 2010 (accessed 7 February 2014)); *Min Awākhir Mā Tamma ktishāfuhu ʿan Salīm al-Hilālī 2010* (www.kulalsalafiyeen.com/vb/showthread.php?t=15620&page=3, 24 March 2010 (accessed 7 February 2013)); *Salīm al-Hilālī: Min Ayna La-ka* (www.kulalsalafiyeen.com/vb/showthread.php?t=15620&page=2, 24 March 2010 (accessed 7 February 2014)); *Seputar*, 12–20.
[127] Salīm b. ʿĪd al-Hilālī, *Al-Ajwiba al-Hilāliyya ʿalá baʿḍ al-Ittihāmāt al-ʿAṣriyya* (http://aloloom.net/vb/showthread.php?t=4842&p=19624&langid=5#post19624, 8 March 2010 (accessed 25 November 2013)).
[128] Interview with Salīm al-Hilālī, Amman, 28 January 2013.

heavily involved with the Imam al-Albani Centre but even its director and therefore presumably quite aware of why the centre had been founded.

In the end, the matter appears to have been hushed up and al-Hilali's dismissal from the Imam al-Albani Centre is said to have been presented as caused by a "difference in *manhaj*".[129] Meanwhile, relations between the culprit and the scholars now running the centre without him resemble those they have with Shaqra: al-Hilali lives on the margins of Jordanian quietist Salafism now and, ostracised by his fellow-scholars, is forced to publish his work in a Bahraini Salafi journal.[130] Al-Halabi also claims that al-Hilali has not repented for his alleged crimes, thereby blocking any reconciliation efforts between the scholars,[131] and the latter's claims of innocence have also been refuted by those close to the current leadership of the Imam al-Albani Centre.[132]

As with the claims of plagiarism mentioned earlier in this chapter, al-Hilali's alleged theft is ultimately a matter for detectives, not academics, to investigate, although it must be said that there is a fair amount of seemingly reliable evidence stacked against him. That this is a matter for a criminal investigation also applies to the wider accusation that al-Hilali was not alone in stealing funds from the Imam al-Albani Centre, but that scholars such as Mashhur b. Hasan and ʿAli al-Halabi were also involved in this. I have not seen any evidence of this, however, and some people who accused these scholars of theft even admitted that they did not have proof of their accusations. It must also be said that many of the charges I heard levelled against Mashhur b. Hasan and al-Halabi did not amount to more than questioning how poor Palestinian refugees such as they could afford the huge houses they live in now. Having visited many of these shaykhs at their homes, I can confirm that their houses are indeed quite big, but this is obviously no proof of any wrongdoing as such.

After the accusations of theft and corruption surfaced in the Jordanian media, the journalist Muhammad Abu Rumman wrote that quietist Salafism in the kingdom nowadays is loyal to the rulers, has a good relationship with the regime and is not a security issue, giving the

[129] Interview with a Jordanian Salafī who preferred to remain anonymous, Amman, January 2013.

[130] See, for instance, Salīm b. ʿĪd al-Hilālī, "Daʿwat Waḥdat al-Adyān fī l-Mīzān," *Al-Ṣaḥīfa al-Ṣādiqa*, no. 3 (1432 [2011]): 12–14; *id.*, "Al-Ikhtirāq al-Kabīr," *Al-Ṣaḥīfa al-Ṣādiqa*, no. 4 (1432 [2011]): 58–61.

[131] Interview with ʿAlī al-Ḥalabī, Amman, 27 June 2012.

[132] ʿAlī al-Ḥalabī, *Al-Ajwiba al-Ṣāʾiba ʿalá l-Daʿāwá l-Kādhiba ḥawla Markaz Imām al-Albānī* (www.alhalaby.com/play.php?catsmktba=1190, 22 December 2009 (accessed 1 April 2013)). This document can also be found at www.kulalsalafiyeen.com/vb/showthread.php?t=15620 and www.kulalsalafiyeen.com/vb/showthread.php?t=15620&page=2, 24 March 2010 (accessed 7 February 2013); al-ʿUtaybī, *Radd*.

movement "golden and powerful opportunities (*furaṣ qawiyya wa-dhahabiyya*) to work and be active in the country". Abu Rumman also touched on "the Salafi corruption" that had plagued the Imam al-Albani Centre in his article and stated that "it is not the first time there has been talk of corruption within this trend", reminding his readers of the "knowledge corruption and literary thefts" (i.e., plagiarism) that some scholars had been accused of earlier.[133] Although the quietist Salafi scholar Akram Ziyada responded to Abu Rumman's claims by pointing out that the theft at the Imam al-Albani Centre was "corruption of the Salafi" rather than "Salafi corruption", he did not deny the centre's closeness to the regime but, in fact, fully confirmed it.[134]

It appears that for some Salafis in Jordan, it is this dimension of "selling out" to the regime by squandering al-Albani's legacy of aloofist quietism in favour of a much more loyalist type, abetted by the enduring suspicions of plagiarism, ideological deviance and theft, that has come to dominate the kingdom's quietist Salafi trend. Although such perceptions may not be entirely justified, it cannot be denied that the "*fitna*" surrounding the death of al-Albani – the charges of plagiarism, the controversy about Shukri's book, the conflicts between al-Halabi, Abu Ruhayyim and Shaqra, the founding of the Imam al-Albani Centre and the accusations against al-Hilali – dealt a blow to the scholars' credibility and facilitated the further domestication of quietist Salafism in Jordan. Although the Imam al-Albani Centre successfully turned over a new leaf by restarting its activities after the problems abated in late 2011,[135] its Salafi utopia had definitely taken a turn towards loyalist quietism, which was deepened further in the years to come.

[133] Muḥammad Abū Rummān, "Ḥawla 'l-Fasād' al-Salafī," *Al-Ghad*, October 29, 2007 (http://alghad.com/index.php/article/451299.html, accessed 22 November 2013).
[134] Ziyāda, *"Fasād."*
[135] Interviews with ʿIṣām Hādī, Amman, 19 January 2013; ʿAlī al-Ḥalabī, 27 June 2012. See also the centre's website: http://alalbany.org/pageother.php?catsmktba=6753 (accessed 9 June 2015).

5 Quietist Salafism in Jordan after "9/11"

The official cover that the Imam al-Albani Centre gave quietist Salafis from accusations of being "extremists" came not a moment too soon: in the same year that the centre was founded, the "9/11" terrorist attacks in the United States occurred. From that moment on, the "war on terrorism" dominated American foreign policy during the period of the administration of the then President George W. Bush (2001–2009) through its invasions of Afghanistan in 2001 and Iraq in 2003 against the Taliban and the regime of Saddam Husayn, respectively. The American policy of fighting terrorism around the world also entailed supporting other countries dealing with terrorism. This would become quite relevant for Jordan – a longtime American ally in the region, particularly after it made peace with Israel in 1994[1] – when it experienced its own "9/11" in 2005.[2]

The American-led "war on terrorism" abetted the Jordanian state's domestication of quietist Salafis because it supported a growing trend within the regime to marginalise and fight radical Muslims and to promote the country as a beacon of "moderate" Islam in a turbulent Middle East. The quietist Salafi leadership, now officially organised through the Imam al-Albani Centre, also played a role in this development, often framing their utopia of the *salaf* in a way that squared neatly with the regime's official discourse. This chapter firstly focusses on how this domestication in the age of terrorism took place by looking at both the state's discourse and that of quietist Salafis themselves. It then, secondly, concentrates on the role of quietist Salafi scholars and their religious authority. Thirdly and finally, this chapter deals with the question of what it means to be a quietist Salafi in the kingdom today. These three topics show how the quietist Salafi utopia has ultimately become fully domesticated on an ideological, organisational and practical level.

[1] See, for example, Jack O'Connell (with Vernon Loeb), *King's Counsel: A Memoir of War, Espionage, and Diplomacy in the Middle East* (New York: W.W. Norton & Co., Inc., 2011).
[2] ICG, *Jordan's*; King Abdullah II, *Our*, 250–6.

Jordanian Salafis and the State in the Age of Terrorism

In his autobiographical work *Our Last Best Chance*, King ʿAbdallah II relates how, when he got back to Jordan from Great Britain after hearing about the terrorist attacks in the United States on 11 September 2001, he called his senior military officers together and let them know that he was "determined to help in the fight against these madmen. My officers", the king states, "were ready for Jordan to join in the fight; they had been battling militant extremists in Jordan for years, so they knew the harm they could do."[3] King ʿAbdallah II's willingness to assist the United States and step up counter-terrorism efforts in his own country were accompanied by much broader efforts to promote a "moderate Islam", as opposed to the "extremist Islam" allegedly represented by al-Qaʿida. This strategy brought the state and quietist Salafis together as allies and, as such, proved quite important in shaping relations between the regime and quietist Salafis after "9/11".

Jordan's Two-Pronged "War on Terrorism"

King ʿAbdallah II was, in fact, right when he said that his officers "had been battling militant extremists in Jordan for years". The kingdom had witnessed the rise of Jihadi-Salafism within its borders from the early 1990s, as we will see in Chapter 6. This helped lead to the formation of several loosely organised militant Islamist groups[4] that engaged in a number of bombings of cinemas and liquor stores, as well as attacks against Jordanian officials engaged in the peace process with Israel. Other (planned) attacks included those by the radical Jamaʿat al-Islah wa-l-Tahaddi (the Group of Reform and Challenge) against, among other targets, the American School in Amman, and the so-called Millennium Plot, which entailed blowing up several hotels in Jordan at the turn of the millennium.[5]

Although these attacks against various Jordanian targets prior to "9/11" were never the existential threat to the regime that the Nasserists in the 1950s or the Palestinian militant groups in the 1960s had posed, they were nevertheless serious security concerns. This was also the case with several events that took place after "9/11", like the assassination of Lawrence Foley, an American diplomat, in Amman in 2002[6] and the invasion of Iraq by an American-led coalition in 2003. The latter created a power vacuum in Jordan's neighbour in which militant groups could flourish, including the Jamaʿat al-Tawhid wa-l-Jihad (the Group of the Unity [of God] and Jihad), the organisation founded and led by the

[3] King Abdullah II, *Our*, 199. [4] Milton-Edwards, "Climate," 125–34.
[5] ICG, *Jordan's*, 10; Robbins and Rubin, "Rise," 68; Wiktorowicz, *Management*, 121–2.
[6] Ḥusayn, *Al-Zarqāwī*, 34–7.

Jordanian Jihadi-Salafi Abu Musʿab al-Zarqawi, who had been released from prison in 1999 and had subsequently gone to Iraq.[7]

While al-Zarqawi would later become especially known for his many attacks on Shiʿi civilians and American soldiers in Iraq, Jordanian authorities linked his name to the assassination of Foley as well. They did the same with the hotel bombings in Amman on 9 November 2005, in which 60 people were killed and 115 were injured and for which al-Zarqawi later claimed responsibility.[8] Given al-Zarqawi's attacks in Iraq, his and others' bombings in Jordan, the fact that ISIS – which occupied significant parts of Iraq and Syria in 2013 – had grown out of al-Zarqawi's organisation[9] and the kingdom's proximity to the violence in its neighbouring countries, Jordan was necessarily involved in this. It was therefore perhaps not surprising that the Jordanian regime increased its crackdown on terrorism and radical Islamist militancy after the early 2000s.[10] This was further increased after the so-called Arab Spring led to revolutions in various Arab countries, including Syria, which reportedly attracted several thousands of Jordanian jihad fighters, hundreds of whom are said to have been killed in Syria.[11]

The rise of ISIS (and later IS) caused Jordan to get even more involved in fighting Islamist militancy. In the late summer of 2014, an international coalition was formed to fight IS in both Iraq and Syria and Jordan became part of this, using air strikes against the group in Syria. The number of strikes was increased dramatically – though temporarily – after one Jordanian fighter pilot, Muʿadh al-Kasasiba, was captured by IS in December 2014 and – in retaliation for his bombing of the group's targets – was burned alive in a cage soon afterwards. Given the groundswell of sympathy among many Jordanians for al-Kasasiba's family and, in turn, for the military battle against IS,[12] the Jordanian regime has since been more involved in the fight against the Islamic State.[13]

7 Zelin, *War*, 1. 8 ICG, *Jordan's*, 1, 12. 9 Zelin, *War*, 1–4.

10 ICG, *Jordan's*, 12–4.

11 Mohammad Ghazal, "'At Least 250 Jordanian Jihadists Killed in Syria since 2011'," *The Jordan Times*, October 28, 2014 (http://jordantimes.com/at-least-250-jordanian-jihadists-killed-in-syria-since-2011, accessed 29 October 2014).

12 This issue – both expressions of solidarity with al-Kasāsiba's family and calls for revenge against IS – dominated the Jordanian press for days and was significantly present in the newspapers for weeks after it became known what had happened to the pilot. Moreover, after the pilot was killed, 95 percent of Jordanians considered IS a "terrorist movement" and 83 percent considered its actions "a threat to the security and stability in the region". See Taysīr al-Nuʿaymāt, "95% min al-Urdunniyyīn Yarawna an 'Dāʿish' Ḥaraka Irhābiyya," *Al-Ghad*, February 28, 2015 (http://alghad.com/articles/855571, accessed 2 March 2015).

13 Agence France-Presse (AFP), "Jordan Says It has Carried Out 56 Air Strikes Against ISIS," *The Guardian*, February 9, 2015 (www.theguardian.com/world/2015/feb/09/jordan-says-it-has-carried-out-56-air-strikes-against-isis, accessed 3 June 2015).

The Jordanian battle against various forms of Islamist militancy has not just been waged militarily, however, but was actually a two-pronged fight that also included a war of ideas that sought to counter the radical ideology underpinning many of the terrorists' actions and, simultaneously, promoted a different, "official" type of Islam as an alternative. Robbins and Rubin define "official Islam" as "the elements of religious authority that are under the direct or indirect control of the state" and "that support the political order or local political authority and its interests which are tied up with the interests of the state".[14] Although Jordan had long tried to include adherents to the subservient and decidedly apolitical Sufi trend in at least some of its official institutions in order to create a loyal group of government-employed scholars, these efforts were not always successful. Sufis in Jordan have virtually always, to be sure, been obedient and supportive of the authorities, but they sometimes resisted efforts to be included in "political" offices, partly out of fear of compromising the spiritual nature of their movement.[15] As such, unlike other countries in the region, which often coopted their religious institutions and authorities in order to shore up their own legitimacy soon after independence, Jordan was relatively late in doing so and only began to develop an "official Islam" after the Islamic Revolution in Iran in 1979.[16]

An important step towards the development of an "official Islam" was the founding of the Royal Academy for Islamic Civilisation Research in 1980, whose name was changed to the aforementioned Royal Aal al-Bayt Institute for Islamic Thought in 2000.[17] This institute organised conferences, invited Muslim scholars, published papers on Islamic issues and, through such activities, tried to promote a form of Islam that was a "moderate" antidote to the "extremist" ideology of militant Islamist groups. This development was further aided by more funding for mosques and the founding of the Advisory Council for Fatwas in 1984, measures that were partly meant to take the wind out of the sails of the increasingly politicised Muslim Brotherhood, which did very well in the parliamentary elections of 1989 and criticised the peace agreement with Israel in 1994.[18]

[14] Robbins and Rubin, "Rise," 61.

[15] Abū Haniyya, *Al-Ṭuruq*, 148–62. Interestingly, the "use" of Sufism by regimes to combat Jihādī-Salafism has also not been a resounding success in various countries. See Mark Sedgwick, "Sufis as 'Good Muslims': Sufism in the Battle against Jihadi Salafism," in *Sufis and Salafis in the Contemporary Age*, ed. Lloyd Ridgeon (London: Bloomsbury, 2015), 105–17.

[16] Robbins and Rubin, "Rise," 59–60.

[17] For more on the history and leadership of this institute, see http://aalalbayt.org/en/pastandpresent.html (accessed 4 June 2015).

[18] Robbins and Rubin, "Rise," 65–7.

From the second half of the 1990s, with the rise of radical Islam in the kingdom becoming more and more apparent, efforts to promote "official Islam" became increasingly clear, especially after 1999, when ʿAbdallah II became king. During his early years as monarch, he upgraded the importance of the Aal al-Bayt Institute by making his cousin, Prince Ghazi, its chairman of the Board of Trustees.[19] The latter was also involved in an important Jordanian effort to combat radical Islamist ideology, namely the Amman Message (Risalat ʿAmman) in 2004.[20] This was originally a sermon delivered in the presence of the king by the Jordanian Supreme Judge shaykh ʿIzz al-Din al-Tamimi in November 2004 that stressed that Islam is characterised by tolerance, moderation and freedom of religion.[21] It subsequently became a statement in favour of "moderate" Islam that was endorsed by Muslim scholars and politicians from all over the world.[22]

The specific conclusion of the Amman Message was threefold: (1) to conceive a wide definition of who is a Muslim (anyone subscribing to the recognised schools of Islamic law) so as to prevent the application of *takfīr* to other Muslims; (2) to emphasise a common core among all Muslims and that this is greater than what divides them; and (3) to ensure that giving fatwas should not be taken lightly and must only be undertaken by those who have the proper religious qualifications.[23] Building on these statements, conferences were organised to promote Sunni–Shiʿi understanding and to combat (the "extremist" use of) concepts like "jihad" and "*takfīr*"[24] and efforts were made to bolster the position of official religious institutions.[25] The regime also sought to support inter-religious relations, particularly between Christians and Muslims, through the 2005 Amman Interfaith Message,[26] the 2007 Muslim–Christian initiative known as "A Common Word"[27] and the Jordanian Interfaith Coexistence Research Centre.[28]

19 *Ibid.*, 68. 20 King Abdullah II, *Our*, 257.

21 ICG, *Jordan's*, 16; Robbins and Rubin, "Rise," 69.

22 For a list of the endorsements, see the Amman Message's website relevant section: http://ammanmessage.com/index.php?option=com_content&task=view&id=17&Itemid=31 (accessed 4 June 2015).

23 http://ammanmessage.com/index.php?option=com_content&task=view&id=91&Itemid=74 (accessed 4 June 2015); King Abdullah II, *Our*, 257–9.

24 Minzili, "Jordanian," 60–5. 25 Robbins and Rubin, "Rise," 69–70.

26 Royal Hashemite Court, *The Amman Interfaith Message* (n.p.: no publisher, 2005), 9–17, available at: http://ammanmessage.com/index.php?option=com_content&task=view&id=95&Itemid=54&limit=1&limitstart=0 (accessed 4 June 2015); King Abdullah II, *Our*, 259–60.

27 King Abdullah II, *Our*, 260; Robbins and Rubin, "Rise," 69.

28 See www.coexistencejordan.org/ (accessed 4 June 2015). I would like to thank Jillian Schwedler for bringing this website to my attention.

With the rise of ISIS/IS, known for its beheadings of civilians and other controversial forms of violence in the name of Islam, the perceived need for the Jordanian regime to promote a "moderate" image of the religion became even greater. The regime therefore doubled down on efforts to promote the "correct" image of Islam, associated mostly with "moderation" (*iʿtidāl*) and "tolerance" (*tasāmuḥ*).[29] Foreign Minister Nasir Juda stated that Jordan "rejects extremism and terrorism and is against everything that distorts the teachings of our kind religion".[30] Similarly, an official of the Ministry of Religious Endowments stated that "there is no moderate or immoderate Islam. There is one Islam[,] which is a faith of moderation, tolerance, forgiveness and acceptance of others, and there is extremism and terrorism, which are completely against Islam and Islamic teachings."[31] Both King ʿAbdallah II and his wife, Queen Raniya, therefore specifically called on Arabs and Muslims to spearhead the fight against radical Islam[32] and to speak out against it because "it's a fight that moderates have to win".[33] Given the past efforts by the state to promote an "official" and "moderate" Islam, it is not surprising that the king claimed that such efforts to combat radicals were actually attempts to "protect the Islamic religion"[34] and that the state's official Fatwa Department ruled that being a member of IS was

[29] "Al-Malik: Tawḥīd al-Juhūd li-l-Taṣaddī li-l-Fikr al-Mutaṭarrif," *Al-ʿArab al-Yawm*, January 27, 2015, 1; Muḥammad al-Daʿma, "Al-ʿĀhil al-Urdunnī: Al-Ḥarb ḍidda l-Irhāb Ḥarbunā wa-Yajibu an Nakūna fī Ṣufūf al-Ūlá li-l-Difāʿ ʿan Dīninā," *Al-Sharq al-Awsaṭ*, January 27, 2015 (http://aawsat.com/print/275271, accessed 27 January 2015); Mohammad Ghazal, "'Indonesia, Jordan to Promote True Image of Islam'," *The Jordan Times*, November 18, 2014 (http://jordantimes.com/indonesia-jordan-to-promote-true-image-of-islam, accessed 19 November 2014); Muʾayyad al-Ḥabāshina, "Mukāfaḥat Khaṭar al-Irhāb Shaʾn ʿArabī wa-Islāmī bi-l-Daraja al-Ūlá," *Al-Raʾy*, January 27, 2015, 1, 3.

[30] Petra News Agency, "Jūda: Al-Taṭarruf wa-l-Irhāb Yushawwihāni Taʿālīm Dīninā l-Samḥ," *Al-Dustūr*, January 28, 2015, 2.

[31] Mohammad Ghazal, "'More Engagement is Needed to Confront Terrorism'," *The Jordan Times*, January 26, 2015 (http://jordantimes.com/more-engagement-is-needed-to-confront-terrorism, accessed 27 January 2015).

[32] Samir Barhoum, "King Calls on Arabs, Muslims to Spearhead War on Terror, Radicalism," *The Jordan Times*, January 26, 2015 (http://jordantimes.com/king-calls-on-arabs-muslims-to-spearhead-war-on-terror-radicalism, accessed 26 January 2015).

[33] "Arab World Needs to Reclaim Its Narrative from Extremist Groups – Queen Rania," *The Jordan Times*, November 18, 2014 (http://jordantimes.com/arab-world-needs-to-reclaim-its-narrative-from-extremist-groups—queen-rania, accessed 19 November 2014).

[34] Petra News Agency, "Al-Malik: Al-Manṭiqa wa-Shuʿūbuhā Taqūdu Ḥarban ḍidda l-Tanẓīmāt al-Irhābiyya bi-Hadaf Ḥimāyat al-Dīn al-Islāmī al-Ḥanīf," *Al-Sabīl*, February 2, 2015, 9; Petra News Agency, "Al-Malik: Naḥmī l-Islām fī Ḥarbinā ʿalá l-Irhāb," *Al-Ghad*, February 9, 2015 (http://alghad.com/articles/852308, accessed 10 February 2015).

wrong and constituted disobedience to God and the Prophet Muhammad.[35] Groups such as IS, the king remarked earlier about radical Islamists in general, "have nothing to do with Islam and its message. Islam celebrates life; they seek to destroy it".[36]

Including Quietist Salafis in "Official Islam"

Considering Jordanian quietist Salafis' aversion against the terrorism of militant Islamist groups like al-Qaʿida and IS and their ideological commitment to subservience to the rulers, particularly after the death of al-Albani, they seem excellent allies in the state's two-pronged war on radical Islamism. Indeed, as we saw in the previous chapter, al-Halabi acknowledged that the Imam al-Albani Centre helped shield quietist Salafis from accusations of being "extremists". Its founding, which reinforced the loyalist tendencies within the movement (at the expense of its earlier aloofism) and officially brought the trend under the regime's bureaucratic control, should thus partly be seen in this context.

For its part, the regime seems quite aware that Salafis cannot simply be dismissed as "extremists" or "terrorists" altogether. Indeed, the king himself states that "the majority of Salafis do not condone terrorism or the killing of innocent civilians".[37] This belief is echoed by the Minister of Religious Endowments, Hayil ʿAbd al-Hafiz Dawud, in an interview from 2014 in which he states that the majority of imams "from among the Salafi trend are of the moderate trend (*al-tayyār al-muʿtadil*)".[38] In fact, when Lieutenant General Husayn al-Majali, then the head of General Security (and later the Interior Minister), was asked by a journalist about violent acts committed by "Salafis", he responded:

> We would like to distinguish between the peaceful Salafi trend (*al-tayyār al-Salafī al-musālim*) [and violent Salafis]. There are many [of the former], like shaykh al-Halabi. We have great respect for him and his group and their loyalty to the Hashimite leadership, to the ruler (*walī al-amr*) and to the homeland (*al-waṭan*).[39]

[35] Petra News Agency, " 'Al-Iftāʾ': Al-Intimāʾ li-'Dāʿish' Ḥarām wa-ʿIṣyān li-llāh wa-li-Rasūlihi," *Al-Būṣala*, April 13, 2015 (http://albosa.la/TVRFME9EQTErdQ==;, accessed 14 April 2015); Ḥamdān al-Ḥāj, "'Al-Iftāʾ' Tuḥarrimu l-Intimāʾ ilá l-Tanẓīmāt al-Irhābiyya wa-Takfīr al-Muslimīn," *Al-Dustūr*, April 14, 2015, 9.

[36] King Abdullah II, *Our*, 241. [37] *Ibid.*

[38] Khālid al-Khawājā, "Wazīr al-Awqāf: 'Khaṭar al-Taṭarruf' Mawjūd wa-Khuṭṭa Wāḍiḥa li-l-Taʿāmul maʿa Tadāʿiyātihi," *Al-Raʾy*, September 16, 2014, 8.

[39] "Al-Farīq Awwal al-Majālī: Lā Yajūzu l-Khalṭ bayna 'l-Rabīʿ al-ʿArabī' wa-Tajāwuz al-Qānūn," *Al-Ḥaqīqa al-Dawliyya*, June 27, 2012 (http://factjo.com/pages/print.aspx?id=20770, accessed 30 August 2012).

The fact that al-Halabi himself was the one who pointed out this article to me probably shows that quietist Salafis are not unaware of the regime's attitude towards them.[40]

Quietist Salafis thus seem to have become part of the regime's efforts to spread and promote a "moderate" type of Islam. This is confirmed by the aforementioned Amman Interfaith Message, which explicitly mentions "the legitimacy and common principles of all eight of the traditional schools of Islamic religious law (*madhhabs*) from the *Sunni, Shi'i* and *Ibadi* branches of Islam, and of *Sufi, Ash'ari* and moderate *Salafi* Islamic thought".[41] The quietist Salafi shaykh Akram Ziyada confirms this when he states that the regime has loosened control of the movement, particularly since 2003. He believes this has happened because "these *takfīrī*- or Jihadi-Salafis, especially the Jordanians among them, played a major role in [the aftermath of the war in] Iraq and the most important of them was Abu Mus'ab al-Zarqawi" and only quietist Salafis were deemed capable of rebutting their ideas.[42] Ziyada's analysis sounds plausible, particularly given the fact that after the hotel bombings in Amman in 2005, the regime asked al-Halabi to give a sermon in the presence of the king.[43] Seen in the context of the above, this should be interpreted as confirming that quietists in Jordan are now in the forefront of fighting radical Islamism alongside the state.

Yet despite their aversion to terrorism and their loyalty to the king, quietist Salafis are, in a sense, also unlikely candidates for the promotion of "moderate Islam". Their emphasis on doctrinal purity and outright rejection of other beliefs is clearly at odds with the tolerant and ecumenical approach to religion taken by the regime. Moreover, as Abu Rumman and Abu Haniyya have pointed out,[44] the regime remains sceptical of Salafis' long-term goal of the "Islamisation of society (*aslamat al-mujtama'*)" and is concerned about the shared doctrinal basis quietists have with political Salafis and Jihadi-Salafis, which sometimes leads those belonging to the former group to join the latter two.[45] This is reflected in the words of King 'Abdallah II himself, when he refers to Salafis as a "fundamentalist movement"[46] and

[40] Interview with 'Alī al-Ḥalabī, Amman, 27 June 2012.
[41] Royal Hashemite Court, *Amman*, 7–8. Italics are in the original.
[42] Interview with Akram Ziyāda, Amman, 28 June 2012.
[43] 'Alī b. Ḥasan b. 'Alī b. 'Abd al-Ḥamīd al-Ḥalabī al-Atharī, *Ḥadath Tafjīrāt 'Ammān: Naṣṣ Khuṭbat al-Jum'a allatī Ulqiyat bayna Yaday al-Malik 'Abdallāh al-Thānī, Malik al-Mamlaka al-Urdunniyya al-Hāshimiyya* (Amman: no publisher, 2005), 4.
[44] Abū Rummān and Abū Haniyya, *Al-Salafiyya al-Muḥāfaẓa*, 115.
[45] Although no research has been done on this, in a group interview I conducted with some 20 Jihādī-Salafis, about half turned out to have roots in quietist Salafism. Group interview with various Jihādī-Salafis, al-Ruṣayfa, 17 January 2009.
[46] King Abdullah II, *Our*, 241.

criticises their rejection of the learned, orthodox tradition of Islam in favour of a clean break with the *madhāhib*. "In the wrong hands", the king adds, "this can be very dangerous."[47]

Quietist Salafis' own discourse with regard to this issue reflects this tension of wavering between being ideal candidates to fight "extremism" alongside the state on the one hand and having religious beliefs that are quite different from the regime's on the other. They solve this by condemning terrorism and radical beliefs as the antithesis of Islam (and/or Salafism), just like the regime does, but – given their own less-than-tolerant views towards others – also make sure to emphasise that quietist Salafis are loyal to and fully supportive of the state in this respect. As such, their discourse on this topic clearly confirms the process of domestication they have gone through, moving from aloofist quietism to a much more loyalist strategy of explicit fealty to and cooperation with the state.

"Our Blessed Good Land": Quietist Salafis Join the State

In the years after "9/11", quietist Salafi *ʿulamāʾ* made quite clear that they did not support terrorist attacks. One Saudi scholar, writing in the Jordanian quietist Salafi journal *Al-Asala*, wonders about terrorists, asking his readers:

> Where is the manliness (*al-munūʾa*), the mercy (*al-raḥma*) and the humanity (*al-insāniyya*) with them?! What heart is this that disdains souls and possessions!? What mind is this that has the audacity to use violence against innocent people and to destroy the souls of the inviolable (*anfus al-maʿṣūmīn*)!? In fact, what soul is this that finds pleasure in shedding blood and scattering severed body parts?[48]

Quietist Jordanians similarly condemned the hotel bombings in Amman in 2005, with shaykh Muhammad Musa Nasr even dedicating an entire sermon to it,[49] and rejected the radicals by describing them as ignorant, rushing to judgement, violent and mistaken[50] and about whom scholars should not remain silent.[51] In a specially organised meeting at the Imam al-Albani Centre, quietist Salafi shaykhs also condemned IS and its killing of the Jordanian pilot Muʿadh al-Kasasiba, rejected the group's alleged

[47] *Ibid.*, 246–7.
[48] ʿAbd al-Raḥmān b. ʿAbd al-ʿAzīz al-Sudays, "Al-Irhāb Marfūḍ bi-Jamīʿ Ṣuwarihi wa-Ashkālihi," *Al-Aṣāla* 7, no. 40 (15 Dhū l-Ḥijja 1423 [17 February 2003]): 69.
[49] Muḥammad b. Mūsá Āl Naṣr, *Daʿāwá l-Jihād bayna al-Khanādiq . . . wa-l-Fanādiq* (www.almahajjah.net/Pages/3_ReportS_Pages/Arciv_Report_dawaJehad.htm, n.d. (accessed 2 April 2013)).
[50] ʿAlī b. Ḥasan b. ʿAlī b. ʿAbd al-Ḥamīd al-Ḥalabī al-Atharī, *Al-Fiʾa al-Ḍālla: Sabab Ḍalālihā! Wa-Abraz Simātihā!! Tajhīlan wa-Takfīran wa-Tafjīran* (n.p.: no publisher, 2004), 12–16.
[51] *Ibid.*, 23–55.

misuse of the writings of Ibn Taymiyya and explained the difference between jihad and IS's terrorism.[52]

Rather than simply condemning terrorism and violent acts committed in the name of Islam, quietist Salafis mostly engage in stressing that such attacks have nothing to do with their religion, thereby echoing the regime's central message. For example, al-Halabi, in his sermon for the king after the hotel bombings in Amman in 2005, states that the attack "that took place in our blessed good land (*baladinā l-ṭayyib al-mubārak*)" was done "in the name of religion", but that Islam has nothing to do with it.[53] In fact, he says, "every Muslim who believes in God and the last day is innocent (*barī'*) of this".[54] Other Jordanian quietist scholars echoed this, stating that terrorism "has no religion, no homeland, no identity. In fact, there are extremists and terrorists (*ghulāt wa-mutaṭarrifūn wa-irhābiyyūn*) in all religions and faiths (*kull milal wa-niḥal*)".[55]

Given the frequent associations of terrorism with Salafism, quietist scholars probably felt obliged to go further than simply dismissing the link between Islam and terrorist violence and to stress that Salafism had nothing to do with this either. An article in *Al-Asala* states that the person responsible for "9/11" "does not even have the slightest (*lā min qarīb wa-lā min ba'īd – lā fī qalīl wa-lā fī kathīr*) understanding of Salafism". In fact, "true Salafism – and Salafis who are true to their creed and their method (*al-Salafiyyun al-awfiyā' li-'aqīdatihim wa-manhajihim*) – are innocent of these acts (i.e., "9/11"), as innocent as the wolf was of the blood of the son of Ya'qub".[56] Another leader makes a similar point in response to the Amman bombings in 2005, stating that

> the true Salafi *da'wa* is the *da'wa* of mercy, wisdom, a middle position (*tawassuṭ*) and moderation.[57] It does not engage in these criminal acts – even in

52 Petra News Agency, "Jam'iyyat al-Imām al-Albānī: 'Iṣābat Dā'ish Jānabū l-Amāna fī Naql Kalām Ibn Taymiyya," *Al-Ghad*, March 1, 2015 (http://alghad.com/articles/855922).

53 Al-Ḥalabī, *Ḥadath*, 12. See also Muḥammad b. Mūsá Āl Naṣr, *Munīr 'Āmm 'alá Tafjīrāt 'Ammān al-Ijrāmiyya* (www.almahajjah.net/Pages/3_ReportS_Pages/Arciv_Report_TFgeratAMMAN.htm, n.d. (accessed 2 April 2013)); Abū 'Ubayda Mashhūr b. Ḥasan Āl Salmān, *Al-Salafiyya al-Naqiyya wa-Barā'atuhā min al-A'māl al-Radayya* (Amman: Al-Dār al-Athariyya, 2011), 14, who say almost literally the same, although the latter is not speaking of the Amman bombings in 2005.

54 Al-Ḥalabī, *Ḥadath*, 14.

55 "Al-Taqtīl al-A'má Fi'l Muḥarram Yabra'u l-Islām minhu!" *Al-Aṣāla* 10, no. 50 (15 Ramaḍān 1426 [18 October 2005]): 6.

56 "Wāqi'unā," 8. This is a reference to the Qur'ānic story of Yūsuf (Joseph), the son of Ya'qūb (Jacob), whose brothers had thrown him into a well and then later lied to his father that a wolf had killed him. See Q. 12: 7–18.

57 Similar words are also expressed in 'Alī al-Ḥalabī, *Taḥdhīrāt wa-Tanbīhāt ... Ḥawla Mā Jará – wa-Yajrī – min al-Taqtīl wa-l-Tafjīrāt* (www.alhalaby.com/play.php?catsmktba=2481, 2 January 2011 (accessed 2 April 2013)).

non-Muslim countries. In fact, it disapproves and is innocent of all sorts, forms and types of terrorism (*kull ṣuwar al-irhāb wa-ashkālihi wa-anwāʿihi*), beginning with intellectual terrorism (*irhāb al-fikr*) and ending with armed terrorism (*irhāb al-silāḥ*).[58]

Not surprisingly, when a group of Jihadi-Salafis in al-Zarqaʾ in April 2011 were involved in a clash with the police in which many of the latter got hurt, al-Halabi claimed that Salafis had nothing to do with this whatsoever, even though "most of the media" referred to the people involved in this incident as "Salafis".[59]

The problem for quietist Salafis is, of course, that "Salafism" is a contested term and that they are not the only ones appropriating it, as pointed out before. It is clear that this is frustrating to quietists, who claim that "this mixture of the names and realities has led to the defamation (*tashwīh*) of the image of the true Salafi *daʿwa*".[60] According to al-Halabi, incidents such as the hotel bombings in Amman in 2005 and the Jihadi-Salafi clash with the police in al-Zarqaʾ in 2011 as well as books written about Salafism only increase people's tendency to associate such violence with Salafism.[61] Mashhur b. Hasan blames "those who are not part of [Salafism, but who nevertheless] wear its clothes"[62] for this and calls on the media "to make the distinction between matters and to make known that we are innocent of these [terrorist] acts".[63] In this context, the aforementioned statement by the king in which he distinguishes between Salafis and radical Islamists is often referred to by al-Halabi. The latter praises the "trustworthy, wise word (*kalima ḥakīma amīna*)"[64] of "our ruler (*walī amrinā*)",[65] who "understood, through his wisdom (*ḥikmatihi*), his awareness (*waʿyihi*) and his inspired leadership (*qiyādatihi l-mulhama*), that there is a clear difference between the two trends [of Salafism and radical

58 "Al-Taqtīl," 5.

59 ʿAlī al-Ḥalabī, *Al-Salafiyya Barāʾ min Aḥdāth Madīnat al-Zarqāʾ* (www.alhalaby.com/play.php?catsmktba=2629, 15 April 2011 (accessed 2 April 2014)).

60 "Al-Salafiyya . . . wa-l-Irhāb!!" *Al-Aṣāla* 7, no. 39 (15 Jumādá l-Ākhira 1423 [24 August 2002]): 6.

61 ʿAlī b. Ḥasan b. ʿAlī b. ʿAbd al-Ḥamīd al-Ḥalabī al-Atharī, *Hādhihi Hiya l-Salafiyya: Daʿwat al-Īmān wa-l-Amn wa-l-Amān al-Manhajiyya al-ʿIlmiyya al-Tarbawiyya* (Medina: Dār al-Imām Muslim, 2011), 6, 8.

62 Āl Salmān, *Al-Salafiyya*, 34. 63 *Ibid.*, 36.

64 Al-Ḥalabī, *Hādhihi*, 4–5. The words quoted are on 5.

65 *Id.*, *Al-Daʿwa al-Salafiyya al-Hādiya wa-Mawqifuhā min al-Fitan al-ʿAṣriyya al-Jāriya wa-Bayān al-Asbāb al-Sharʿiyya al-Wāqiya* (n.p.: Mānshūrāt Muntadayāt Kull al-Salafiyyīn, 2011), 51; *id.*, *Al-Tafrīq al-Wāḍiḥ al-Mubīn li-Walī Amrinā "al-Malik ʿAbdallāh b. al-Ḥusayn" bayna "l-Takfīriyyīn" wa-"l-Salafiyyīn"* (www.alhalaby.com/catplay.php?catsmktba=4&page=10, 18 April 2011 (accessed 2 April 2013)).

Islamism]".[66] In fact, al-Halabi himself lists 26 differences between these two trends, ranging from views on jihad and revolts against the rulers to fasting and the extraction of evidence from scripture.[67]

These latter remarks by al-Halabi point to the second way quietists try to join the regime in its fight against terrorism and radical Islam: their emphasis on their loyalty to and support for the Jordanian state and its safety. Salafism, they imply, is a staunch ally in the kingdom's striving for safety and can be relied upon in this respect. This could already be discerned in al-Halabi's sermon after the hotel bombings in Amman in 2005, in which he briefly referred to "safety" (*al-amn*), "security" (*al-amān*) and "stability" (*al-istiqrār*).[68] A year later, Muhammad Musa Nasr stated that "Islam does not engage in shocking the safety of a safe country. This country is the little remaining remnant (*al-baqiyya al-qalīla al-bāqiya*) that is proud of its safety." He also stated that "we must preserve the safety of our country, oh servants of God, and know that safety is dependent on faith".[69]

The connection between faith and safety is developed further by Muhammad Musa Nasr in a booklet from 2006. He explains that "the believer believes that the safety of his country is a part of his creed, so he preserves the safety of his country because of creed, religion and worship, not because of politics, hypocrisy, trade or a job".[70] This safety is realised, he claims, through obedience to the ruler and advising him discreetly.[71] This emphasis on faith as a means to maintain safety echoes the piety Salafis promote as the best way to confront conflicts such as the Israeli–Palestinian dispute, as we saw in Chapter 2. Al-Halabi even states that the Salafi *da'wa* is "the *da'wa* of faith, safety and security"[72] that can realise "psychological and social safety" as well as "international and national security".[73] Because of this alleged connection between faith and the safety of a country, it is only natural for Salafis to support the rulers and, as Mashhur b. Hasan states citing another scholar, "to ask God – mighty and great is He – for success and luck for them".[74]

Al-Halabi takes this connection between Salafis and the safety of the Jordanian state a step further by pointing out that they are the most natural ally of the regime in its fight against radical Muslims. Firstly, he states that Sufis – who are equally apolitical and subservient to the rulers – have not really supported the king in his battle against the threat of

[66] *Al-Shaykh al-Ḥalabī fī Ḥiwār ma'a Batrā: Hunāka Khalṭ Kabīr bayna l-Tayyār al-Salafī wa-l-Takfīriyyīn* (www.alhalaby.com/play.php?catsmktba=2632, 18 April 2011 (accessed 1 April 2013)).
[67] Al-Ḥalabī, *Hādhihi*, 100–16. [68] *Id.*, 7, 9. [69] Āl Naṣr, *Munīr*.
[70] *Id.*, *Bayna l-Amn wa-l-Amān*, 8–9. The words quoted are on 9. [71] *Ibid.*, 27–8.
[72] Al-Ḥalabī, *Hādhihi*, 49. [73] *Ibid.*, 88. [74] Āl Salmān, *Al-Salafiyya*, 37.

terrorism, unlike quietist Salafis.[75] In fact, he even casts doubt on the safety of Sufism as a whole, linking it to Shiʿi Islam and pointing to the supposedly deviant beliefs that both these trends share.[76] At a time of fears of an Iranian-led Shiʿi "crescent" – a term coined by King ʿAbdallah II himself[77] – in the Arab world, such a connection between Sufism and Shiʿism can only be viewed as an attempt to vilify the former. This becomes even clearer when al-Halabi warns about the alleged attempts by Shiʿas to infiltrate Sunni countries through Sufism. The author adds, however, that "God – the exalted – has made the ruler of our country – may God preserve him and his rule – successful for a number of years in warning against the danger of the disgusting Shiʿas".[78]

Secondly, having discredited Sufis as disloyal to the regime in its battle against radical Islamists, al-Halabi underlines Salafis' own credentials in this respect by identifying Salafism with the Jordanian state. As we saw in Chapter 3, some of the kingdom's early religious scholars could plausibly be described as having some Salafi tendencies. Al-Halabi takes this a step further, however, by claiming that these tendencies were also present in the lives of the rulers of Jordan themselves. Particularly Husayn b. ʿAli and also King ʿAbdallah I and even King ʿAbdallah II are described as following the *salaf* and the Qurʾan and the Sunna.[79] By writing about the history of the kingdom's rulers like this, al-Halabi gives the impression that Salafism and the Hashimite dynasty have long been intertwined and, as such, are a natural combination. This support for the regime was emphasised when quietist scholars threw in their lot with the state by actively promoting the parliamentary elections of 2013. As mentioned before, quietist Salafis in Jordan are not supporters of democracy and elections, although they do believe that electing the least bad party or candidate is allowed. This reasoning provided them with the opening to support the parliamentary elections, which – given the regime's strong

[75] Al-Ḥalabī, *Mujmal*, 87–9.
[76] *Id.*, *Al-Daʿwa al-Salafiyya bayna l-Ṭuruq al-Ṣūfiyya wa-l-Daʿāwá al-Ṣaḥafiyya wa-l-Kashf al-Ṣila bayna l-Taṣawwuf wa-l-Afkār al-Shīʿiyya* (Amman: Al-Dār al-Athariyya, 2009), 35–76.
[77] Interview with King ʿAbdallāh II by Chris Matthews on Hardball, 12 September 2004. See www.nbcnews.com/id/6679774/ns/msnbc-hardball_with_chris_matthews/t/king-abdullah-ii-jordan/#.VXIUjlL4bal (accessed 5 June 2015). The phrase is used at 2: 18. This attitude by the king may seem surprising, given his ecumenical attitude. An explanation of this seeming contradiction may be that the regime promotes religious and sectarian tolerance, but is sceptical of Shiʿi political powers who may want to use sectarian identities to extend their own influence.
[78] Al-Ḥalabī, *Risāla*.
[79] *Id.*, *Mujmal Tārīkh*, 14–17, 29; *id.*, *Al-Daʿwa al-Salafiyya bayna l-Ṭuruq al-Ṣūfiyya*, 13–15.

emphasis on these in order to control the political opposition and channel discontent in a manageable way[80] – was a boon for the state.[81]

So how can the relationship between quietist Salafis and the Jordanian state be characterised with regard to the fight against terrorism and radical Islamism? Abu Rumman and Abu Haniyya refer to this relationship as "an unofficial 'deal'" between the two sides: the regime protects quietists and provides them with the means to spread their *daʿwa*, while quietists themselves preach a peaceful and subservient message.[82] This seems an accurate assessment, since it is clear what both sides get out of the relationship, but it is also obvious that quietists are not simply servants to the regime who are compelled to write the things they write. Given the entrenched apolitical ideology quietist Salafis adhere to and the increasingly loyalist tendencies found among them after al-Albani's death, quietists simply seem to share part of the regime's agenda.[83] Moreover, given this ideology and the strong emphasis on apoliticism and subservience that it entails, quietists could, in a sense, also be said to need the regime in order to define themselves as "moderates", different from the radicals they are agitating against. As such, this combination of factors has led to an increasing domestication of the quietist Salafi community and has more or less caused it to fill the shoes of the pre-1989 Muslim Brotherhood as a loyal Islamic supporter of the regime. The effect this has had on their scholars' religious authority is what we must turn to now.

Salafi Religious Authority in Jordan

The domestication of quietist Salafism in Jordan has been a multi-faceted process in which the regime did not so much subject the movement to its will, but in which quietist scholars themselves played an assertive role. This happened through quietists' apolitical ideology, their turn towards

[80] For more on such attempts to use democratisation as a means to ward off opposition and fundamental change, see Glenn E. Robinson, "Defensive Democratization in Jordan," *International Journal of Middle East Studies* 30, no. 3 (1998): 387–410.

[81] "Al-Ḥalabī: Al-Tayyār al-Salafī Sa-Yushārika fī l-Intikhābāt Taṣwītan," *Al-Sabīl*, November 9, 2012, 4; Taylor Luck, "Salafists to 'Get Out the Vote' for Upcoming Polls," *The Jordan Times*, November 8, 2012 (http://jordantimes.com/salafists-to-get-out-the-vote-for-upcoming-polls, accessed 9 November 2012); Petra News Agency, "Al-Shaykh al-Ḥalabī: Al-Urdunn Maḥdūd al-Mawārid Lakin Ghināhu l-Ḥaqīqī Yatamaththalu fī Amānihi l-Mashhūd la-hu wa-Shaʿbihi l-Ṣābir," *Al-Dustūr*, November 15, 2012, 8; *id.*, "Al-Shaykh al-Ḥalabī: Al-Urdunn Ghanī bi-Amnihi wa-Shaʿbihi l-Wafī l-Ṣābir," *Al-Raʾy*, November 15, 2012, 5.

[82] Abū Rummān and Abū Haniyya, *Al-Ḥall*, 220; *id.*, *Al-Salafiyya al-Muḥāfaẓa*, 10–11, 80–1, 113–15.

[83] Interviews with Abū l-Ḥajjāj Yūsuf b. Aḥmad al-ʿAlāwī, Māḥiṣ, 21 January 2014; Ibrāhīm al-ʿAsʿas, Amman, 14 January 2013; ʿIṣām Hādī, Amman, 19 January 2013; ʿĀyish Labābina, Irbid, 14 January 2014.

increasing loyalism over time, the results of their infighting and their conscious efforts to position themselves as "moderates" *vis-à-vis* radical Islamists. To some Salafis, ex-Salafis and non-Salafis I spoke to in Jordan, however, this is not how it appears. In their view, quietist Salafi scholars have entirely abandoned the independent attitude that al-Albani had always displayed towards the state and have basically sold their souls to the regime in return for money and influence. Although these accusations were mostly not substantiated by facts or a proper analysis of the situation, one does wonder how Jordanian quietist scholars maintain their religious authority in a movement that has changed significantly in its relationship with the state. This is particularly the case, of course, given the many accusations of plagiarism and fraud that have been levelled at some of quietist Salafism's most important scholars in Jordan.

Religious Authority

Following Weber, Krämer and Schmidtke define religious authority as the ability "to have one's rules and rulings followed, or obeyed, without recourse to coercive power".[84] In Sunni Islam, this is perhaps even more complicated than it is in, for example, Roman Catholicism. As Pierret points out: "From a historical point of view, the status of Sunni ʿalim has always been acquired through a process of reputation building rather than through institutional arrangements: since there is no Muslim equivalent of Christian ordination, [religious authority] depends on the informal assent of elder scholars and followers."[85] Simply put, "it is the willingness of *others* to credit any given person, group or institution with religious authority that ultimately renders it effective".[86] This means that, in the absence of a Muslim Vatican and a clerical hierarchy, religious authority in Sunni Islam is based on less tangible factors than a rank or position in an organisation. There are, of course, venerable centres of religious learning in the Muslim world – the Al-Azhar University in Cairo and the Islamic University of Medina come to mind – and high-ranking positions in, for example, one of Saudi Arabia's religious organisations do indicate one's seniority as a scholar. Yet the fact alone that there are several of such centres suggests that religious authority in Sunni Islam is less uniformly institutionalised than it is in Roman Catholicism.

[84] Gudrun Krämer and Sabine Schmidtke, "Introduction: Religious Authority and Religious Authorities in Muslim Societies. A Critical Overview," in *Speaking for Islam: Religious Authorities in Muslim Societies*, ed. Gudrun Krämer and Sabine Schmidtke (Leiden: Brill, 2000), 1.

[85] Pierret, *Religion*, 9–10. [86] Krämer and Schmidtke, "Introduction," 2.

The absence of a single centre of global religious authority in Islam has become even more obvious with the rise of the internet,[87] which has led not only to a greater availability of sources (particularly *ḥadīth*-collections and exegetical works (*tafāsīr*)) to a greater number of people, but has also led to what Mandaville refers to as "the pluralization of authority".[88] In a situation in which far more people (including lay persons) have access to and can have a say about a religious tradition like Islam (and much else besides), religious authority becomes even harder to define and more difficult to pinpoint, particularly when – on a global scale – there are so many competitors vying for people's attention.[89]

Still, the qualities or skills that a Sunni Muslim scholar or intellectual should have in order to be able to compete successfully with his or her challengers' religious authority, hard to quantify as they may be, do appear to be fairly clear. Various authors distinguish a recurrent set of characteristics that determine religious authority in the context described above. Some speak of "knowledge, conduct and charisma",[90] while others refer to scholars' "intellectual *formation*, their *vocation* and, crucially, their *orientation*"[91] or their knowledge, character and personality.[92] Although these three different sets of three qualities are not entirely synonymous, they are generally alike and overlap to a great extent.

The first characteristic – knowledge – refers first of all to the knowledge of the Islamic textual tradition, primarily the Qurʾan and the Sunna but also the scholarly writings based on those foundational texts. Knowledge does not stop there, however. Few would doubt, for instance, that the major *ʿulamāʾ* of Saudi Arabia are extremely knowledgeable of the scriptural sources of Islam. Yet their detractors – both Islamists and liberals – sometimes refer to them as *mashāyikh al-ḥayḍ* (the shaykhs of menstruation) because of the inordinate amount of time they spend ruling on aspects related to the female body at the expense of, for example, important societal or political issues.[93] Scholars seeking religious

[87] For a more general treatment of religious authority in relation to the internet, see Heidi Campbell, "Who's Got the Power? Religious Authority and the Internet," *Journal of Computer-Mediated Communication* 12, no. 3 (2007): 1043–62.

[88] Peter Mandaville, "Globalization and the Politics of Religious Knowledge: Pluralizing Authority in the Muslim World," *Theory, Culture & Society* 24, no. 2 (2007): 101–15.

[89] A dated but useful treatment of this phenomenon is Jon W. Anderson, "The Internet and Islam's New Interpreters," *New Media in the Muslim World: The Emerging Public Sphere*, ed. Dale F. Eickelman and Jon W. Anderson (Bloomington, IN: Indiana University Press, 1999), 41–56.

[90] Krämer and Schmidtke, "Introduction," 8. [91] Zaman, *Ulama*, 10.

[92] Quintan Wiktorowicz, *Radical Islam Rising: Muslim Extremism in the West* (Lanham, MD: Rowman & Littlefield Publishers, Inc., 2005), 137–8.

[93] Al-Rasheed, *Contesting*, 130–1.

authority should, therefore, ideally be knowledgeable in both religious and profane matters.[94] Moreover, they should also possess and express the knowledge that is doctrinally "right" or "sound". Credibility with regard to such knowledge – or, simply put, expertise – is quite important in persuading others, attracting followers and gaining authority. One's background, education and experiences can help establish such credibility.[95]

The second characteristic, labelled here as "character", is similarly important as an indicator of religious authority. This entails that one is not corrupt – both financially and morally – and that one does as one says. Such considerations with regard to sincerity are particularly important, of course, for movements like Salafism, whose adherents attach great value to a narrowly defined "truth" and to the following of a strict lifestyle. Other indicators of "character" revolve around relationships with benefactors or the state. If one compromises one's principles for financial or political gain, such discrepancies can be viewed as hypocritical, causing one's reputation to suffer. Similarly, an unwillingness to speak out on certain issues because it may result in unpleasant consequences can be seen as compromising one's character.[96]

Thirdly, personality – as well as the related "charisma" – is also important. If people can admire a scholar and are able to relate to and identify with him or her, this can lead to what Hass calls "source attractiveness". It enhances people's self-concepts and by imitating an "attractive" scholar or adopting his or her characteristics, people can positively affect their self-image and self-esteem.[97] Personality, however, also has to do with kindness to others, an openness to questions, the ability to relate to people's experiences, accessibility, not acting in a superior way, taking an interest in people's lives and remembering their names as well as being a good speaker who knows how to strike the right tone.[98]

[94] Wiktorowicz, *Radical*, 136–7.

[95] Robert D. Benford and David A. Snow, "Framing Processes and Social Movements: An Overview and Assessment," *Annual Review of Sociology* 26 (2000): 620–1; Marvin E. Goldberg and Jon Hartwick, "The Effects of Advertiser Reputation and Extremity of Advertising Claim on Advertising Effectiveness," *Journal of Consumer Research* 17 (1990): 172–3; R. Glen Hass, "Effects of Source Characteristics on Cognitive Responses and Persuasion," *Cognitive Responses in Persuasion*, ed. Richard E. Petty, Thomas M. Ostrom and Timothy C. Brock (Hillsdale, NJ: Lawrence Erlbaum Associates, 1981), 143–4; Carl I. Hovland and Walter Weiss, "The Influence of Source Credibility on Communication Effectiveness," *Public Opinion Quarterly* 15 (1951): 635–50.

[96] Wiktorowicz, *Radical*, 137–8, 144–7. On reputation, see also Goldberg and Hartwick, "Effects," 173–4.

[97] Hass, "Effects," 144–6.

[98] Wiktorowicz, *Radical*, 147–50.

Religious Authority Among Jordanian Quietists

Before we look at how the different aspects of religious authority as described above relate to quietist scholars in Jordan, we must first look at what may be considered the informal scholarly hierarchy of Jordanian quietists. This is indeed informal since no official jobs as president, leader or director of the community as a whole exist, yet positions of seniority can still be discerned. Based on criteria such as the number of publications, appearances in the media, their closeness to al-Albani and – perhaps most importantly – references to them by "ordinary" Salafis in conversations with me, it becomes clear that ʿAli al-Halabi is the most senior quietist Salafi scholar in Jordan today, followed closely by Mashhur b. Hasan. When asked who the most important quietist Salafi scholars in Jordan are, the names of these two men are mentioned very often, their lessons are well attended and the reverence students show for them exceeds that which they show to other shaykhs.[99]

A second group of senior quietist scholars include the other prominent students of al-Albani's, such as Muhammad Musa Nasr, Husayn al-ʿAwayisha, Akram Ziyada, Basim al-Jawabira and Ziyad al-ʿAbbadi. The first three are preachers or imams while the latter two work at the Faculty of Shariʿa of the University of Jordan. Except for Ziyada, all of these men have PhDs in Islamic subjects. Quietist Salafis in Jordan often refer to all of the above – who are in their forties, fifties or sixties – as "scholars" (*ʿulamāʾ*), while a third group of shaykhs is often "merely" labelled "knowledge seekers" (*ṭullāb ʿilm*) because their age, knowledge and experience is smaller than those of the "scholars". The latter include ʿUmar al-Butush, Hamza al-Majali, Firas Mashʿal, ʿAtiyya Hammad and Muhammad Khashshan. They are younger shaykhs who are in their thirties and whose relationship with al-Albani was mostly – if not entirely – an indirect one.

A fourth group of shaykhs consists, firstly, of people who may be scholars in their own right, but for whom living far from Amman means that they are less practically relevant on a national scale and more important in a local context. One of the most prominent of these is Jamal al-Shaykh, the imam of the al-Jasir Mosque in Irbid. Others include ʿImran Rabiʿ and Mansur al-Sharayiri. This group, secondly, also consists of people who are not so much prominent scholars but

[99] An example of the latter is the closing ceremony of the series of lectures at the Imām al-Albānī Centre on 19 June 2014, during which all of the shaykhs attending were given a certificate. The most senior scholars in attendance (Ḥusayn al-ʿAwāyisha, Mashhūr b. Ḥasan and Akram Ziyāda) were sitting behind a table and one of the younger shaykhs, ʿAṭiyya Ḥammād, decided to give his certificate specifically to shaykh Mashhūr, not to the others.

who have important positions in the Imam al-Albani Centre. These include primarily ʿAli Ahmad Khalid al-Kurdi, the current president of the Imam al-Albani Centre, and also his deputy and fellow leaders of the centre.[100]

Fifthly and finally, there is the marginalised group of shaykhs dealt with extensively in Chapter 4. This group consists of Muhammad Abu Ruhayyim, Muhammad Ibrahim Shaqra, Murad Shukri and Salim al-Hilali. The latter seems to have little if any following in Jordan anymore because of the accusations of fraud against him and the other three do not play much of a role in the wider quietist Salafi community anymore either. In the case of Abu Ruhayyim, this is not because of his lack of scholarly credentials but presumably because of his troublesome relationship with al-Halabi. Shaqra, for his part, is also a scholar, but is now in his eighties and does not seem to enjoy any following to speak of anymore. Shukri was never a scholar himself, but has focussed on writing poetry for years and does not play any meaningful role among quietist Salafis nowadays.[101]

The hierarchy mentioned above may be informal, but the position of scholars among quietists in Jordan is hugely important. This has a lot to do with the status of knowledge among Salafis. In fact, the movement I refer to as "quietist Salafism" is actually mostly labelled "knowledge Salafism" (*al-Salafiyya al-ʿilmiyya*) by adherents to the movement itself. Although this term is somewhat biased – after all, *all* Salafis (and not just quietists) claim to seek knowledge – it nevertheless indicates the value they attach to this concept. Several shaykhs whose lessons I attended emphasised the importance of knowledge of Islam or even focussed entirely on it, stressing that having the right knowledge is what separates Salafis from other branches of Islam.[102] It is therefore not surprising that *ʿulamāʾ* (literally: "the knowledgeable ones"), as the possessors of this knowledge, are of great importance and even indispensable to Salafis in Jordan, as several scholars make clear.[103] Scholars can, in fact, be seen as

[100] For a complete overview of the current administration of the Imām al-Albānī Centre, see http://alalbany.org/pageother.php?catsmktba=6753 (accessed 9 June 2015).

[101] It speaks for itself that these categories are not fixed. A good example of a shaykh who transcends the boundaries of these groups is ʿIṣām Hādī, al-Albānī's secretary. He grew up in the al-Hāshimī al-Shimālī neighbourhood of Amman (i.e., where Salafism in Jordan really got started), was very close to al-Albānī and has a good relationship with Shaqra and Shukrī, yet he was also invited to speak at the series of lectures organised by the Imām al-Albānī Centre in Amman in June 2014.

[102] Lessons by Bāsim al-Jawābira, Akram Ziyāda and Hamza al-Majali, Imām al-Albānī Centre, Amman, 11 June 2014; Manṣūr al-Sharāyirī, Imām al-Albānī Centre, Amman, 14 June 2014; Muḥammad Khashshān, Imām al-Albānī Centre, Amman, 18 June 2014; Firās Mashʿal, Imām al-Albānī Centre, 19 June 2014.

[103] Ḥusayn al-ʿAwāyisha, "Qabḍ al-ʿIlm ... wa-Atharuhu ...," *Al-Aṣāla* 1, no. 5 (15 Dhū l-Ḥijja 1413 [6 June 1993]): 31–3; Muḥammad b. Mūsá b. [sic!] Naṣr, "Al-ʿĀlim al-

the organisational backbone of the quietist Salafi movement in Jordan, particularly given its mostly informally organised structure in general.[104] This also has consequences in practice: when talking to "ordinary" Salafis during the initial stages of my field work, I was often referred to their shaykhs and quite a few even refused to be interviewed entirely until after I had spoken with their scholars. When asked why, they answered that the precise details of Salafism could best be explained by the scholars, thereby emphasising not only the importance of knowledge but also the central role of the *ʿulamāʾ* as the possessors of this knowledge.

The strong emphasis and reliance on scholars among Salafis does carry with it, of course, the danger that too much importance is attached to the shaykhs and that they are treated as meriting *taqlīd*, which is precisely what Salafis often reject when it comes to the schools of Islamic law. Interestingly, scholars seem to realise this danger. Students who attended the lessons at the Imam al-Albani Centre in 2014, for example, were given a number of books as a reward for completing the entire series of lectures. One of these was the book *Tahdhir al-Nasihin min al-Tahazzub li-l-ʿUlamaʾ wa-l-Murabbin* (The Warning of the Advisors Against Factionalism of the Scholars and the Educators), which deals precisely with this issue. Its author states that the most important thing for believers is to follow the revelation[105] and that scholars' fatwas are not binding and simply a reflection of what a particular shaykh believes to be right.[106] He also states that believers should only extend their *walāʾ* to God, Islam and Muslims collectively, not to a single scholar. Such a person should only be followed inasmuch as he adheres to the correct teachings of Islam. Dismissing the words of other shaykhs just to follow one scholar in particular, without evidence or knowledge, is actually a *bidʿa*, the author states.[107]

The actual religious authority of Jordan's quietist Salafi scholars nowadays has been affected by their move towards a more loyalist approach to the state and the many "scandals" that plagued the movement in the aftermath of al-Albani's death. With regard to knowledge, the scholars are still greatly respected among quietist Salafis. Although the accusation of being "neo-Murjiʾa" levelled against al-Halabi and others occasionally rears its head[108] and this certainly put some people

Rabbānī wa-Ḥājat al-Umma ilayhi," *Al-Aṣāla* 1, no. 3 (15 Shaʿbān 1413 [8 February 1993]): 41–3; *id.*, "Naṣāʾiḥ Muhimma ilá ʿUlamāʾ al-Umma," *Al-Aṣāla* 1, no. 6 (15 Ṣafar 1414 [4 August 1993]): 31–4.

104 Wiktorowicz, *Management*, 136–40. Though dated, Wiktorowicz's analysis is still largely correct.

105 Al-Mukhtār, *Taḥdhīr*, 79. 106 *Ibid.*, 82–3. 107 *Ibid.*, 87–95.

108 During one of his lessons, for example, Mashhūr b. Ḥasan was asked whether al-Ḥalabī was among the Murjiʾa, which Mashhūr denied. See www.youtube.com/watch?v=cNAWfdktErE (accessed 9 June 2015).

off,[109] even some of al-Halabi's critics admit that he really is a scholar. This also applies to quietists' use of the Arabic language. Unlike English, Arabic is divided into an elevated vernacular (*fuṣḥá*), used in the classical sources and – in a modernised form – in newspapers and books, and a commonly spoken, everyday variant (*ʿammiyya*). As Haykel has pointed out, an excellent command of the more literary *fuṣḥá* is seen as quite important to Salafis since this is the language in which the texts that they hold so dear were originally written down.[110] This tendency to try to speak good classical Arabic can be heard among many ordinary Salafis,[111] but particularly among scholars. During lessons I attended, I was often amazed at how fluently the shaykhs could speak in classical Arabic, which is a feat not achieved by many Arabs.

The question of character, secondly, is obviously more problematic for quietist Salafi scholars in Jordan, given all the accusations that were levelled against them in the years immediately prior to and after al-Albani's death. Even if only some of the things they are charged with by their opponents are true, the scholars – particularly al-Halabi and Mashhur b. Hasan – may come across as not living up to the standards they set for others. The many documents that have been written about the alleged plagiarism of some of the scholars as well as the accusations of theft by the same shaykhs expressed in several informal conversations I had with Salafis suggest that quite a number of people have become thoroughly disillusioned with them. This is also the case with the movement's increasingly loyalist tendencies. To some Salafis with whom I had informal conversations, particularly al-Halabi is an opportunist who will say and do whatever is needed to be looked upon favourably by the regime, which supposedly supports him with generous financial rewards.

Yet great numbers of quietist Salafis still flock to the lessons of these shaykhs and hold them in very high esteem indeed, despite the accusations and their loyalist ties with the regime. Several reasons can be given for this. Firstly, many young quietists may not be aware of these accusations because they were still children when the Salafi infighting took

[109] One person who was apparently put off by al-Ḥalabī's supposedly un-Salafī views on faith was the Saudi scholar al-Madkhalī, who used to be on very good terms with al-Ḥalabī. Al-Madkhalī apparently began criticising al-Ḥalabī, after which the latter wrote a large number of publications against his former friend. This subject is too big to deal with here, however.

[110] Haykel, "Nature," 35.

[111] I once visited a Salafī bookshop in downtown Amman, but found that the manager was still away for prayers. When I asked another Salafī how long it would take for the manager to be back, he answered: "*Khamsu daqāʾiq*." Such a formal way of saying something as simple as "five minutes" is typical of Jordanian Salafīs' attempts to speak *fuṣḥá*.

place. Similarly, a significant number of Salafis in Jordan are foreign, with many coming from sub-Saharan African countries or South-East Asia. They often live far outside Amman and may not have been aware of the "*fitna*" between the scholars either. Secondly, the increased domestication of Jordanian quietists may have represented a change with al-Albani's days, but in the broader Salafi movement, this is not at all exceptional. In Saudi Arabia, for example, strong ties between rulers and Salafi scholars are quite normal and, indeed, Islam has a long tradition of such relationships. Thirdly, many quietists may not believe the attacks on their scholars' character. As we saw in Chapter 4, there is indeed little evidence for some of the claims against the scholars, making this position of disbelief perhaps less naïve than it sounds. Fourthly, a final group of quietist Salafis may believe that the character of their scholars has been compromised, but still think they can learn a lot from them in terms of religious knowledge.[112]

The third aspect of religious authority distinguished above – personality – seems to work more unambiguously in the scholars' favour. The shaykhs whose lessons I attended or spoke with personally were not only kind and friendly people, but they were also very accessible to their students, often staying long after their lectures to answer questions. They were often engaging speakers and clearly involved their audience in what they were saying, asking them questions and making jokes. In one lesson taught by al-Halabi, for example, the pieces of paper that students use to write their questions on were continually brought to the shaykh by a little boy. The sight of this boy walking up and down the room to bring al-Halabi questions had a comedic effect, which was made even greater when the shaykh smiled at the boy and shook his hand, leading to laughter all around. This may not seem like much, but the fact that al-Halabi was willing to act more as a first among equals than as a high and mighty scholar made an impression on the students.[113]

Salafis in Jordan Today

The domestication of the quietist Salafi scholars and their movement in its various forms has thus had some effect on their religious authority, but not as much as one might have expected. So where does all of this leave Salafis in today's Jordan? The chapters of this book have so far dealt mostly with the *scholars* of the quietist

112 This discussion was heavily informed by an interview with a former Salafi who preferred to remain anonymous, Amman, January 2014.

113 Lesson by ʿAlī al-Ḥalabī, Imām al-Albānī Centre, Amman, 17 June 2014.

community. This can easily be justified by pointing to their crucial role as possessors of the knowledge that Salafis hold so dear, their acting as focal points of the Jordanian Salafi trend and their production of the ideology that quietists want to cleanse and teach. In other words, Salafi scholars deserve the attention they get. Yet what does it mean to be a quietist Salafi today and how does what we have seen before translate into everyday life as based on my many conversations with adherents to the trend and my attendance of many of their meetings?

Salafi Growth, Demographics and Activities

The actual number of (quietist) Salafis in Jordan is unknown. Although it is not clear what they base their estimates on, McCants mentions that there are some 7,000 Salafis in the kingdom,[114] which is similar to a number given by the Ministry of Interior in early 2015 (6,000–7,000, with some 1,500–2,000 sympathisers).[115] The latter number is given, however, in the context of estimates of radical Muslims in the country and may therefore refer more to Jihadi-Salafis than to Salafis in general. This is equally true with other numbers one finds in the Jordanian media.[116] The actual number of all Salafis together may therefore be quite a bit higher, but is unlikely to be in the many tens of thousands. Whatever the exact number is, however, it is clear that the movement has grown substantially since men like Muhammad Ibrahim Shaqra began preaching a Salafi message in the 1950s.

The reasons for this growth are less obvious in Jordan than in other countries. Pall shows, for example, how "recruitment" to the Salafi movement in Lebanon is part of a framing process that focusses heavily on socio-political issues that are highly relevant in the Lebanese context, such as Sunni–Shiʿi tensions, Sunni victimhood and the changes brought about by the revolts and revolutions collectively known as the "Arab Spring".[117] Although the idea that Islam is under attack does feature in quietist Salafi discourse in Jordan – as we saw in Chapter 2 – and the "Arab Spring" has not left the community untouched either – as Chapter 7 shows – Jordanian quietist discourse does not focus on these

[114] Will McCants, "A New Salafi Politics," *The New Salafi Politics* (Washington, DC: Project on Middle East Political Science, 2012), 6.

[115] Al-Sabīl, "Al-Dākhiliyya: 7 Ālāf Salafī fī l-Urdunn," *Al-Maqarr*, February 16, 2015 (www.maqar.com/?id=77192, accessed 3 March 2015).

[116] See, for example, Māhir Abū Ṭayr, "Tanẓīm Muwaḥḥad li-l-Salafiyya al-Jihādiyya fī l-Urdunn," *Al-Dustūr*, December 12, 2013, 16. This article refers specifically to Jihādī-Salafis, however.

[117] Pall, "Salafism," 266–79.

topics a lot, precisely because the movement is so apolitical.[118] This is also the case with Sunni–Shiʿi relations, although in a different way. To be sure, Chapter 2 has shown that quietist Salafis in Jordan are often virulently anti-Shiʿi. Yet as we saw above, this mostly relates to presumed conspiracies and plots going on *outside* Jordan, not in the kingdom itself. In that sense, the religiously quite homogeneous Jordan differs starkly from the multi-sectarian system in Lebanon and an anti-Shiʿi message is therefore far less likely to get people to join Salafism rather than any other movement.

Because quietist Salafism in Jordan is not an activist movement but an apolitical one focussed on religious doctrine, "conversion" may appear to be a better concept through which to analyse the growth of the trend than "recruitment". Snow and Machalek discuss the various ways of defining conversion, describing it as a "dramatic change" that can be sudden as well as gradual and can also take place as a series of multiple changes.[119] They also note that conversion concerns "a change in values, beliefs, and identities" and "the displacement of one universe of discourse by another or the ascendance of a formerly peripheral universe of discourse to the status of primary authority".[120]

Virtually all quietist Salafis that I talked to about this subject indicated that they had always been religious and even pious, but in different forms. Some had grown up in Salafi families, while most had a Sufi background or had been actively involved with the Muslim Brotherhood or the Jamaʿat al-Tabligh. They overwhelmingly described their development towards Salafism as "finally" ending up with "the truth". Although their embrace of Salafism undoubtedly led to a greater emphasis on the Qurʾan and the Sunna and a more specific view of how these should be read and interpreted, their change was very much a gradual one that remained within Sunni Islam. Indeed, given Salafis' reputation among some as being merely "pious Sunnis", it is not surprising that one often finds people attending Salafi sermons or lessons who do not look like Salafis at all.[121] This suggests that moving in and out of the Salafi community in Jordan is, in fact, a relatively fluid process, which is confirmed by my conversations with ex- Salafis , who sometimes maintain good ties with the community or keep up at least part of the

[118] Indeed, according to Usāma Shaḥāda, as cited by Abū Rummān and Abū Haniyya, many Salafis turn to quietism out of frustration about not being able to get anything done politically. Quietist Salafism, in that sense, constitutes a retreat from politics into learning and preaching, giving meaning to lives that would be wasted in politics. See Abū Rummān and Abū Haniyya, *Al-Salafiyya al-Muḥāfaẓa*, 109.

[119] David A. Snow and Richard Machalek, "The Sociology of Conversion," *Annual Review of Sociology* 10 (1984): 169.

[120] *Ibid.*, 170.

[121] I will deal with Salafī clothing and appearance later in this chapter.

lifestyle.[122] "Conversion" is thus an accurate but perhaps rather strong term to describe the process of joining the Salafi community in Jordan – perhaps "re-affiliation" is more precise in this context – although I have also met several people who converted to Salafism from a non-Islamic background, in which case the term seems more fully appropriate.

The quietist Salafi movement in Jordan has not just grown over the years, but its social and educational make-up has also changed. Salafis are still mostly from the poorer (and to a lesser extent middle) classes today and still mostly of Palestinian descent.[123] Yet their spread to more East Jordanian cities far removed from Amman, al-Zarqaʾ and al-Rusayfa, like Irbid and al-Ramtha in the north, al-Salt in the west and al-Tafila, al-ʿAqaba and al-Karak in the south,[124] suggests that more East Jordanians have joined the movement too.[125] Moreover, quietist Salafis' educational levels have gone up, with more and more getting a university education in *sharīʿa, ḥadīth* and other Islam-related subjects.[126]

The greater spread of quietist Salafism and the higher level of education among its adherents have perhaps helped in giving the quietist community in Jordan more visibility in society today. Its informally organised shaykh-centred structure is still in place, but the movement nowadays has more than just the Imam al-Albani Centre in Amman as an official outlet. Others include the Imam al-Albani Centre's Irbid branch, which organised a series of lessons in the al-Jasir Mosque in Irbid for the first time in 2014,[127] and Al-Dar al-Athariyya, a Salafi bookshop in downtown Amman founded by the Imam al-Albani Centre.[128] Others include the Jamʿiyyat al-Takaful al-Khayriyya (Solidarity Charity Association) in al-Ramtha, which mostly focusses on helping Syrian refugees fleeing the civil war in their home country.[129] The fact that an explicitly Salafi message can now be preached openly and on a large scale in centres and mosques throughout the country represents a clear difference with the situation during al-Albani's life, when this was still

[122] This contrasts with the situation in Lebanon, where people's choice for Salafism has much greater societal impact. See Pall, "Salafism," 131.
[123] Abū Rummān and Abū Haniyya, *Al-Salafiyya al-Muḥāfaẓa*, 106. [124] *Ibid.*, 105.
[125] This can also be seen in the make-up of (slightly) younger quietist scholars, several of whom – such as Ziyād al-ʿAbbādī and Muḥammad al-Majālī – are of East Jordanian descent.
[126] Interviews with Abū l-Ḥajjāj Yūsuf b. Aḥmad Āl ʿAllāwī, Amman, 21 January 2014; Shākir al-ʿĀrūrī, Amman, 23 January 2013.
[127] Signs promoting the Imām al-Albānī Centre's lessons in 2014 thanked Salafī organisations in Kuwait and Bahrain for their financial assistance. It appears that money from the Gulf continues to be a major source of financial aid for quietist Salafis in Jordan.
[128] Al-Ḥalabī, *Mujmal*, 116.
[129] For more on their activities, see their website at http://altkaful.net/ (accessed 10 June 2015).

limited and only partly allowed.[130] Quietist Salafi shaykhs even frequently travel abroad to take their *da'wa* to other countries such as the United States, Canada and various European countries.[131]

Another branch of Salafi activities that has developed over the last decade is the online sharing of information. A major player in this respect is the Kull al-Salafiyyin forum, which functions under the auspices of 'Ali al-Halabi. It contains a wealth of information on all kinds of topics, serves as a message board for lessons and lectures and allows quietists to discuss religious matters of mutual importance.[132] Other forms of social media are apparently not used very often by quietists in Jordan in general, but their scholars have popular and regularly updated Facebook accounts[133] (apart from their personal websites mentioned earlier), the Imam al-Albani Centre has its own YouTube channel[134] and al-Halabi, among others, is quite active on Twitter.[135]

Living Like the Prophet in Jordan

The increased institutionalisation of quietist Salafism – even if this is still on a relatively small scale – is a clear sign of the greater acceptance of (loyalist) quietist activities by the regime. This domestication is also apparent in the daily lifestyle of quietist Salafis in Jordan today. Although there has been a decade-long focus on *al-taṣfiya wa-l-tarbiya*, meaning that the everyday practice of doctrinal and ritual "purity" was always a major part of quietist Salafism, it seems to consist of little else nowadays. While controversial topics like foreign policy and *takfir* were discussed openly in al-Albani's days, they are now mostly just mentioned in the context of warning against "extremism", referred to in shaykhs' monologues or avoided entirely. Several shaykhs who were asked about politics during lessons I attended, for instance, politely said they did not want to talk about this.[136] A certain

130 Interviews with 'Alī al-Ḥalabī, Amman, 27 June 2012; Bāsim b. Fayṣal al-Jawābira, Amman, 26 June 2012; Akram Ziyāda, Amman, 28 June 2012.

131 Al-Ḥalabī, *Mujmal*, 116; interview with Akram Ziyāda, Amman, 28 June 2012.

132 See www.kulalsalafiyeen.com/vb/ (accessed 10 June 2015). For more on the reasons this forum was launched and how many subscribers it has, see 'Alī al-Ḥalabī, *Arba'a Ālāf "'Uḍw" fī "Muntadayāt Kull al-Salafiyyīn" Khilāl Sana wa-Niṣf – wa-l-Ḥamd li-llāh* (www.alhalaby.com/play.php?catsmktba=1852, 18 April 2010 (accessed 2 April 2013)); *id., Muntadá "Kull al-Salafiyyīn".. Limādhā?* (www.alhalaby.com/play.php?catsmktba=1049, 13 December 2009 (accessed 2 April 2013)).

133 Shaykhs having Facebook accounts include 'Alī al-Ḥalabī, Mashhūr b. Ḥasan and Bāsim b. Fayṣal al-Jawābira, among others.

134 See www.youtube.com/channel/UCKyqEtR7rNSugHWU2m2QanA (accessed 10 June 2015).

135 See https://twitter.com/alhalaby2010 (accessed 10 June 2015).

136 Lessons by Bāsim b. Fayṣal al-Jawābira, Imām al-Albānī Centre, Amman, 14 June 2014; 'Alī al-Ḥalabī, Imām al-Albānī Centre, Amman, 17 June 2014.

reluctance to discuss these issues is perhaps understandable given the number of Jordanians attracted to groups like IS in Syria and the earlier disputes on issues of *kufr* and *īmān*, but it does – in any case – show that the movement has become more careful and perhaps more focussed on uncontroversial matters of doctrine and everyday ritual.

In Salafis' daily lives, such a concentration on beliefs and practices that concern only people's personal religiosity is expressed in different ways. One of these is the spread of Salafi booklets – available at book markets organised outside mosques or at other Salafi activities – that usually state on the cover that they are "to be spread free of charge" and are thus ubiquitous and widely read among Salafis. They are often written by the Syrian Salafi scholar Muhammad b. Jamil Zaynu (1925–2010), who lived and worked in Saudi Arabia for much of his life but who also spent some time in Jordan, and deal with basic Islamic topics such as the five pillars of Islam,[137] the Prophet,[138] the first *sūra* of the Qurʾan,[139] the creed,[140] the idea that Salafis are *al-ṭāʾifa al-manṣūra,*[141] the centrality of *tawḥīd*[142] or the supposed dangers of Sufism.[143] Besides these doctrinal issues, however, some of them also deal with everyday questions such as the correct manners of Salafis,[144] the way the latter should raise their children[145] and the supposedly proper role and place of women.[146]

The reason Salafis in Jordan read such booklets goes back to the very core of their ideology, namely their claim to emulate the *salaf* – and particularly Muhammad – as closely and in as many spheres of life as possible. They are therefore, in a very literal sense, trying to live like the

137 Muḥammad b. Jamīl Zaynū, *Arkān al-Islām wa-l-Īmān min al-Kitāb wa-l-Sunna al-Ṣaḥīḥa* (Jeddah: Maṭbaʿat al-Amal, 1431 [2009/2010]).
138 *Id.*, *Min Badāʾiʿ al-Qaṣaṣ al-Nabawī al-Ṣaḥīḥ* (Riyadh: Majmūʿat al-Tuḥaf al-Nafāʾis al-Dawliyya, 1429 [2008]).
139 *Id.*, *Tafsīr wa-Bayān li-Aʿẓam Sūra fī l-Qurʾān* (Jeddah: Dār al-Khirāz, 1420 [1999/2000]).
140 Al-Lajna al-ʿIlmiyya fī Masjid al-Ṣādiq al-Amīn, *ʿAqīdatuka Ayyuhā l-Muslim* (Amman: Al-Dār al-Athariyya, 2014).
141 Majallat al-Bayān, *Risāla ilá Ṭalāʾiʿ al-Ṭāʾifa al-Manṣūra fī Bayt al-Maqdis wa-Aknāf Bayt al-Maqdis* (Riyadh: Al-Muntadá l-Islāmī, 2004).
142 Ṣāliḥ b. Fawzān al-Fawzān, *Kitāb al-Tawḥīd* (Cairo: Maṭābiʿ Ibn Taymiyya, n.d.).
143 Muḥammad b. Jamīl Zaynū, *Al-Ṣūfiyya fī Mīzān al-Kitāb wa-l-Sunna* (Jeddah: Dār al-Muḥammadī li-l-Nashr wa-l-Tawzīʿ, 1431 [2010]).
144 *Id.*, *Min Ādāb al-Islām li-Iṣlāḥ al-Fard wa-l-Mujtamaʿ* (Jeddah: Maṭbaʿat al-Amal, 1431 [2010]); *id.*, *Quṭūf min al-Shamāʾil al-Muḥammadiyya wa-l-Akhlāq al-Nabawiyya wa-l-Ādāb al-Islāmiyya* (Jeddah: Dār al-Khirāz, 1428 [2007]).
145 *Id.*, *Kayfa Nurabbī Awlādanā wa-Mā Huwa Wājib al-Ābāʾ wa-l-Abnāʾ* (Riyadh: Dār al-Ṣamīʿī, 1431 [2010]); *id.*, *Nidāʾ ilá l-Murabbīn wa-l-Murabbiyyāt li-Tawjīh al-Banīn wa-l-Banāt* (Riyadh: Dār al-Ṣamīʿī, 1429 [2008]).
146 *Id.*, *Takrīm al-Marʾa fī l-Islām* (Riyadh: Dār al-Qāsim li-l-Nashr, 1425 [2004/2005]).

Prophet in Jordan.[147] Their scholars are keen to advise them in these matters, offering pointers on how to prepare for and perform the *ḥajj*[148] and, particularly, prayer. Unlike the annual pilgrimage, prayer is obviously a ritual that recurs daily in Salafis' lives. Moreover, given its importance – it is one of the five pillars of Islam and must be performed, unlike the pilgrimage, which need only be embarked upon if one has the means to do so – it is imperative for Salafis to do it correctly. The essential Salafi guide to prayer in Jordan (and elsewhere) is al-Albani's book *Sifat Salat al-Nabi* (The Prophet's Way of Praying), which uses numerous *ḥadīth*s to describe every aspect of how Muhammad is said to have prayed.[149] Given the popularity of the book in Jordan, it is likely that the manner of prayer described in it has been widely adopted by quietist Salafis in the kingdom, probably because they want rituals – especially ones as important as prayer – to be done exactly right.[150]

Yet not all of al-Albani's rulings on this issue have been adopted. In another sign of his independence, he described in his book how the Prophet sometimes used to pray with his shoes on – unlike what is common practice among Muslims[151] – and therefore ruled that believers are allowed to do the same nowadays.[152] This is not, however, a practice I have observed among Jordanian Salafis, which may have something to do with the fact that to many inhabitants of the kingdom, Salafis are merely "pious Sunnis" and, as such, many non-Salafis visit their lessons and sermons as well. Taking off one's shoes before entering a mosque to pray may therefore simply be a way for Salafis in Jordan to avoid offending others and not seeking confrontation over such a relatively minor issue.[153]

[147] I am indebted to Ineke Roex for this subtitle, which I have adopted (and adapted) from the title she used for her dissertation: "Living like the Prophet in the Netherlands". See Roex, "Leven."

[148] ʿAlī b. Ḥasan [al-Ḥalabī], "Lā Ḥaraja.. Ayyuhā l-Ḥajīj!" *Al-Aṣāla* 1, no. 4 (15 Shawwāl 1413 [8 April 1993]): 76–7; Riyāḍ al-Ḥaqīl, "Zād al-Ḥāj," *Al-Aṣāla* 2, no. 11 (15 Dhū l-Ḥijja 1414 [26 May 1994]): 48–53; Salīm b. ʿĪd al-Hilālī, "Iḥdharū Ayyuhā l-Ḥajīj," *Al-Aṣāla* 1, no. 4 (15 Shawwāl 1413 [8 April 1993]): 78–9; Muḥammad b. Mūsá b. [sic!] Naṣr, "'Mā lā Budda minhu bayna Yaday al-Ḥajj'," *Al-Aṣāla* 1, no. 4 (15 Shawwāl 1413 [8 April 1993]): 72–5; Muḥammad Jamīl Zaynū, "Naṣāʾiḥ wa-Tawjīhāt ilá Ḥujjāj Bayt Allāh al-Ḥarām," *Al-Aṣāla* 2, no. 11 (15 Dhū l-Ḥijja 1414 [26 May 1994]): 45–7.

[149] Al-Albānī, *Ṣifat*, 49–150.

[150] This can also be seen in the many questions that are asked about prayer. See, for example, al-Albānī, *Al-Masāʾil*, 78–114; *id.*, "Masāʾil wa-Ajwibatuhā," *Al-Aṣāla* 2, no. 10: 42–3.

[151] For more on the issue of praying with one's shoes on and how this practice is rooted in *ḥadīth*s, see M.J. Kister, "'Do not Assimilate Yourselves ... ' *Lā Tashabbahū* ...," *Jerusalem Studies in Arabic and Islam* 12 (1989): 335–49.

[152] Al-Albānī, *Ṣifat*, 54–5.

[153] This is also what Gauvain describes in his study of Salafis in Egypt. See Gauvain, *Salafi*, 123–5.

The exact elements of the allegedly correct prayer are accompanied by a host of things that believers are supposed to say afterwards. In the al-Jasir Mosque in Irbid, huge signs hanging from the walls tell the believers that, in emulation of the Prophet, they have to utter several sentences mostly confirming the unity of God; say *subḥān Allāh* (God be praised), *al-ḥamd li-llāh* (praise be to God) and *Allāh akbar* (God is greatest) 33 times;[154] repeat several phrases confirming the unity of God again; and end with reciting several verses from the Qurʾan.[155] Such sayings are not limited to one mosque in Irbid, however, but are actually part of an elaborate system of *adhkār* (sayings of *ḥadīths* or Qurʾanic verses) that guide Salafis through the day and which have been collected in a small booklet, *Hisn al-Muslim* (The Fortress of the Muslim). Such utterings exist for when one awakens, gets dressed, leaves the house, enters or leaves a mosque, enters the house again, etcetera,[156] and are actually "performed" by Salafis throughout the day. Although I was told that refraining from uttering such *adhkār* was "merely" a minor sin, to Salafis they represent the constant emulation of the Prophet in daily life and, as such, embody much of what it means to be a Salafi in Jordan today.[157]

The fact that the example of the Prophet Muhammad is such an overbearing influence on Salafis' everyday lives may give the impression that living the life of a Salafi is extremely tiring. Although it might indeed have this effect on some and Salafis are perhaps unlikely to admit that having to live according to Muhammad's example is a burden to them, the quietists I talked to about this dismissed such fears, claiming that the practical emulation of the Prophet is something that comes naturally to them after a while.[158] When talking to quietist Salafis in Jordan, it is indeed striking how often they cite *ḥadīths* to back up the things they say. When having a drink on a hot day with some Salafis in a room with only one chair, for example, the quietists sipping their drinks would crouch on the floor, since they claim the Prophet preferred to drink while standing. Similarly, they – in emulation of Muhammad – would all hold their drinks in their

154 Typically, these phrases also need to be uttered exactly 33 times, not more or fewer times, since that is exactly what the Prophet is said to have done. Interview with Jamāl al-Shaykh, Irbid, 22 June 2014.

155 The exact words that should be uttered can be found in Saʿīd b. ʿAlī b. Wahf al-Qaḥṭānī, ed., *Ḥiṣn al-Muslim min Adhkār al-Kitāb wa-l-Sunna* (Cairo: Dār Ibn al-Haytham, 2010), 35–7.

156 Al-Qaḥṭānī, *Ḥiṣn*.

157 The importance of these *adhkār* is further emphasised by the fact that the booklet *Ḥiṣn al-Muslim* has also been commented on by shaykh Abū Muslim, a Salafī scholar from al-Zarqāʾ. See Abū Muslim Majdī b. ʿAbd al-Wahhāb al-Aḥmad, *Sharḥ Ḥiṣn al-Muslim min Adhkār al-Kitāb wa-l-Sunna* (Amman: Al-Dār al-Athariyya, 2012).

158 See also Gauvain, *Salafi*, 67, who found the same among Egyptian Salafis.

right hands. Salafis' attention to such details can lead to funny situations sometimes. A Salafi in Amman gave me a small bottle of orange juice once. When I shook it before opening it, he told me to stir it by twisting my wrist instead. My immediate response to him was: "Why? Is there a *ḥadīth* about this?" The fact that he started explaining to me that this had nothing to do with Islam and that it took him a few seconds to realise I was joking says less about his sense of humour, perhaps, than about the obvious nature of such a question in a Salafi context.

Such detailed attempts to live like the Prophet are also found in matters of hygiene,[159] eating[160] and language. This latter aspect expresses itself in the insistence on a correct pronunciation of the first *sūra* of the Qurʾan[161] and the use of special phrases that few people outside Salafi circles apply so consistently. Salafis' standard way of greeting other Muslims, for example, is *al-salām ʿalaykum wa-raḥmatullāh wa-barakātuhu* ("may peace, the mercy of God and his blessings be with you"), rather than more mundane greetings such as "hello" or "good morning". Similarly, instead of saying *shukran* ("thanks"), Salafis often use the phrase *jazāka llāh khayr* ("may God bless you for it") instead.[162] This desire to achieve "purity" of language – modelled on the Prophet and the Qurʾan – was also apparent in Salafis' desire to refer to me as a *Naṣrānī* (Christian), rather than a *Masīḥī*, a term preferred by many Arab Christians themselves. I was assured, however, that this was not out of any sense of hostility but simply because Christians are referred to in the Qurʾan as such.[163]

Salafi practices do not just entail following the example of the Prophet in remaining doctrinally pure, however, but also in keeping one's distance from customs considered evil. These can relate to issues such as smoking[164] or football. Shaykh Mashhur b. Hasan – while commending the exercise that football provides and relating this to the time of the Prophet[165] – warns against too close an attachment to any club[166] and states that any watching or playing of the sport should conform to the

[159] Al-Albānī, *Al-Masāʾil*, 59–77. See also Amghar, *Salafisme*, 154.
[160] Al-Ḥārith b. Zaydān al-Mazīdī, "Ādāb al-Ṭaʿām fī l-Sharīʿa al-Muṭṭahara," *Al-Aṣāla* 7, no. 38 (15 Rabīʿ al-Awwal 1423 [27 May 2002]): 68–75.
[161] Muḥammad b. Mūsá Āl Naṣr, *Al-Akhṭāʾ al-Wāqiʿa fī Qirāʾat Sūrat al-Fātiḥa min al-Muṣallīn wa-l-Aʾimma wa-l-Qāriʾīn* (Amman: Al-Dār al-Athariyya, 2008).
[162] See also Amghar, *Salafisme*, 148–9; Bonnefoy, *Salafism*, 49.
[163] See also Wiktorowicz, "Anatomy," 218–19.
[164] ʿAlī [b.] Ḥasan [b.] ʿAlī [b.] ʿAbd al-Ḥamīd [al-Ḥalabī], *Ḥukm al-Dīn fī l-Liḥya wa-l-Tadkhīn* (Beirut: Dār Ibn Ḥazm, 2002), 36–53.
[165] Abū ʿUbayda Mashhūr b. Ḥasan Āl Salmān, *Kurat al-Qadam bayna l-Maṣāliḥ wa-l-Mafāsid min Wujhat Naẓar Sharʿiyya* (Amman: Al-Dār al-Athariyya, 2009), 19–21.
[166] This is probably a reference to many Jordanian youngsters' extreme partisanship with regard to Spanish football clubs Barcelona and Real Madrid.

sharīʿa.[167] Given the huge popularity of football in Jordan,[168] refraining from watching it is no mean feat for Salafis. Even during the World Cup in 2014, however, quietists kept coming to lessons at the Imam al-Albani Centre in Amman, hardly looking up when people outside could be heard cheering because their favourite team had won.

Some issues may also be objectionable because they are associated with non-Muslims. The most apparent way in which this can be seen is Salafis' appearance, with which they strive to emulate Muhammad and look different from non-Muslims. Salafi women distinguish themselves from non-Muslims by wearing a headscarf (*ḥijāb*) and mostly also a veil and they sit separately from the men in mosques.[169] Salafi men often wear a white tunic known as a *thawb* or a *dishdasha*, mostly accompanied by a skullcap (*qulunsuwa*), which is sometimes covered by a piece of cloth known as a *shimāgh.*[170] Salafi beards, too, are distinctive for their length, which is not just a Qurʾanic and Prophetic command, they claim,[171] but also a means for Salafis to distinguish themselves from non-Muslims.[172] These outward signs of piety are, indeed, ubiquitous among Salafis in Jordan.[173]

More directly, this attitude is also expressed towards non-Muslims, including myself. Salafi relations with others are often justified by pointing to the need to do *daʿwa* and tell non-Muslims about the alleged beauty of Islam. Personally, I cannot count the number of times quietists tried to explain to me why Islam was superior and preferable to anything I might believe. Although this was annoying at times, it was never hostile or aggressive. In fact, one Salafi asked me once to explain the Christian concept of the Holy Trinity, a favourite subject among Salafis since it supposedly shows that Christianity is not really a monotheistic religion. I responded by saying that, to Christian theologians, this may be an issue they accept "without [asking] how" (*bi-lā kayfa*), invoking a concept we saw used by Hanbali theologians in Chapter 1. The Salafi I was talking with not only appreciated my use of a Hanbali concept to answer him, but it also satisfied his curiosity.

167 Āl Salmān, *Kurat*, 22–5.

168 I spent time in Jordan during one European Cup and one World Cup and even though Jordan itself did not participate, the matches were very popular indeed and sometimes whole streets were adorned with flags.

169 See also Amghar, *Salafisme*, 148.

170 Interview with Jamāl al-Shaykh, Irbid, 22 June 2014.

171 Al-Ḥalabī, *Ḥukm*, 21–3.

172 *Ibid.*, 24.

173 There are also some Salafis in Jordan who, based on what they claim is a Prophetic example, shave off their moustaches while maintaining their beards, but this is far less common.

Dealing with "unbelievers" such as myself can take quite different forms among Salafis in Jordan. When receiving a certificate indicating my completion of a series of lessons at the Imam al-Albani Centre in Amman in 2014, I noticed that it referred to me as a "brother". I remembered a fatwa on *al-walāʾ wa-l-barāʾ* by the Saudi shaykh Ibn Baz, however, which stated that Muslims are not allowed to refer to non-Muslims as "brothers"[174] and – strictly out of curiosity – asked how the centre reconciled labelling me as such with Ibn Baz's fatwa. The director of the centre did not respond verbally but looked slightly taken aback, perhaps knowing I had a point, the scholars looking on nodded in agreement with my citing of Ibn Baz and when I later told another Jordanian Salafi about this incident, he almost rolled over with laughter, with tears running down his face.

Thus, Salafi responses to everyday reality differ sometimes. Yet they are overwhelmingly guided by the principle of trying to live according to what they believe is the example of the Prophet. For Jordanian quietists nowadays, the Salafi utopia therefore finds expression in everyday rituals and customs, which is one sign of the movement's domestication. Another sign of this process is the trend's increased institutionalisation under the protection and even in the service of the regime and its two-pronged strategy of fighting "extremist" Islam. Opponents to this increasingly loyalist trend within quietist Salafism in Jordan have been marginalised and have therefore been unable to change or redirect this development. Outside of quietism, however, other streams of Salafism in Jordan have also been engaged in contesting the validity of the scholars' claims.

[174] ʿAbd al-ʿAzīz b. Bāz, *Lā Ikhwa bayna l-Muslimīn wa-l-Kāfirīn wa-Lā Dīn Ḥaqq Ghayr Dīn al-Islām* (www.binbaz.org.sa/node/8286, n.d. (accessed 16 June 2015)).

Part III

Contestation

6 Jihadi-Salafis Join the Fray

The two-pronged war on "extremist" Islam that the Jordanian regime has waged for several decades in varying degrees of intensity obviously targeted someone. Apart from global or transnational movements such as al-Qaʿida or the Islamic State, the regime was mostly concerned with fighting the phenomenon of Jihadi-Salafism within its own borders. As we saw in Chapter 1, Jihadi-Salafis apply *takfir* to the rulers of the Muslim world for the latter's alleged *ridda* (apostasy), as expressed in their failure to rule (entirely) according to Islamic law, and are willing to back up their beliefs with revolutionary jihad aimed at overthrowing these "apostate" regimes.

The states and their rulers in the Muslim world are not the only targets that Jihadi-Salafis in Jordan focus on, however. Their ideological wrath is also expressed towards the quietist Salafi community in the kingdom, showing that Jihadi-Salafis have a somewhat different view of reaching their desired utopia of an Islamic state and society and believe that the increasingly loyalist quietists are part of the problem, not the solution. This chapter therefore firstly focusses on the rise of and recent developments within Jihadi-Salafism in Jordan. It then moves on to the specific accusations that Jihadi-Salafis level at their quietist countrymen and how the former have started meddling in intra-quietist conflicts. Finally, I concentrate on the quietists' response to the attacks by Jihadi-Salafis. Their lashing out at their radical brethren again shows the increased domestication of the quietist Salafi scholars, so much so even that the regime at one point started adopting their discourse, rather than the other way round.

Jihadi-Salafism in Jordan

As we saw in Chapter 3, events in Saudi Arabia and Kuwait during the Gulf War in 1990 had a great impact on the quietist Salafi community in Jordan, resulting in the entrenchment of their apolitical ideology and leading to their becoming more loyalist in their approach towards the regime. This development was partly influenced by the influx of political

Salafis from Kuwait, yet the Salafis who had to leave this country after the Gulf War were not all politicos. Some of them were quietists while others – more importantly for this chapter – were Jihadi-Salafis. It is not clear how many of the latter entered Jordan from Kuwait in the early 1990s, but it is clear that one of them became the ideological godfather of the Jihadi-Salafi movement in Jordan and some would say even the entire world: Abu Muhammad al-Maqdisi. Unlike quietist Salafism in Jordan, the subjects of al-Maqdisi and Jihadi-Salafism in the kingdom have received a lot of scholarly attention (particularly from me) and it therefore suffices here to analyse the emergence and development of this trend and al-Maqdisi's role in it mostly on the basis of secondary literature.[1]

The Emergence of Jihadi-Salafism in Jordan

Abu Muhammad al-Maqdisi, whose real name is ʿIsam al-Barqawi, came to Jordan in 1992 as one of those many Palestinians whose roots lay in the West Bank when it was Jordanian territory. Born in Barqa (near Nablus) in 1959, he moved to Kuwait with his family when he was a small child and was raised there. Growing increasingly politicised through his contacts with members of the Muslim Brotherhood, he also tended towards the "purity" of Salafism and eventually found an ideological home in the nineteenth-century writings of Wahhabi scholars, which he discovered during his studies in Saudi Arabia in the early 1980s. After returning to Kuwait, he joined the many "Afghan Arabs" who went to Afghanistan/Pakistan to aid the jihad against the Soviet Union, although he did not actually engage in fighting there but concentrated on teaching in Peshawar, Pakistan. There, he met many of the people who would later go on to hold senior positions within the al-Qaʿida organisation, such as Ayman al-Zawahiri and Abu Musʿab al-Zarqawi. He subsequently returned to Kuwait, probably in the late 1980s, and eventually ended up in his new homeland in whose post-1967 territory he had never been before – Jordan.[2]

The situation al-Maqdisi encountered in the kingdom was one of tension and turbulence. The Palestinian intifada against Israeli occupation, although in its last throes, was still ongoing, which obviously affected Jordan – many of whose inhabitants are of Palestinian descent – a lot. Moreover, the falling oil prices after the Iran–Iraq war (1980–1988)

[1] The secondary literature on al-Maqdisī and Jihādī-Salafism is more extensive than what is mentioned in the footnotes to come. Since the relevant publications have already been mentioned in the introduction, however, I will not mention them all over again, but simply refer the most important and thorough work(s) on the specific sub-topics dealt with.

[2] Wagemakers, *Quietist*, 30–41.

meant that less financial aid from Gulf states and fewer remittances from Jordanians working in the oil industry were coming to the kingdom. This caused the regime to adopt far-reaching economic reforms, with the help of the International Monetary Fund (IMF), which led to taxes being raised and subsidies being cut. These measures led to protests, which the regime tried to deal with by announcing national parliamentary elections for the first time since 1967 in 1989.[3]

Because parliament was seen by the regime as a means to channel discontent, rather than as a reflection of the popular will, the democratic experiment ended in disappointment. This became painfully clear when the members of parliament (including those of the virulently anti-Israel Muslim Brotherhood) failed to stop Jordan from engaging in a peace process with the Jewish state in 1991. This not only resulted in an Israeli-Palestinian peace agreement in 1993 ("the Oslo Accords"), but also in the Wadi ʿAraba Agreement in 1994, which made peace between Israel and Jordan. Meanwhile, Jordanian "Afghans" who had left the kingdom to fight in Afghanistan were gradually returning to the country – including al-Zarqawi – believing they had participated in beating one superpower (the Soviet Union), only to find that another superpower (the United States) had just invaded neighbouring Iraq to drive its army out of Kuwait.[4]

It was in this eventful and turbulent period in Jordan's history that some Jordanians began to feel disillusioned about the Arab regimes, who had been unable to solve the conflict between Iraq and Kuwait themselves, and began to get a sense of losing control. Among such people, some turned to radical Islam and the loosely organised militant Islamist groups mentioned in Chapter 5. What these groups had in common was a general feeling of discontent towards the Jordanian regime, a rejection of the parliamentary way of expressing their contention and a tendency to commit violent acts. What they lacked, however, was an ideology that could unite them around a single cause. It was this that al-Maqdisi provided them with.[5]

While living in Kuwait, Saudi Arabia and Pakistan, al-Maqdisi had already written several books in which he clearly made use of the Salafi tradition, particularly as espoused by Wahhabi scholars, to justify jihad against Muslim regimes. Through his detailed use of the Salafi discussions on *īmān* and *kufr* that we saw in Chapter 1, he framed his opposition to Muslim regimes in a Salafi way, arguing that their alleged systematic unwillingness to apply the *sharīʿa* was a form of *kufr akbar*, meaning that no further verbal confirmation of their unbelief was necessary to justify

[3] *Ibid.*, 196–7. [4] *Ibid.*, 197–9. [5] *Ibid.*, 199–201.

applying *takfīr* to them.[6] This position is principally the same as that of major Saudi quietist Salafi scholars such as Muhammad b. Ibrahim Al al-Shaykh, Muhammad b. Salih al-ʿUthaymin and Salih b. Fawzan al-Fawzan.[7] He further used the very Salafi concept of *al-walāʾ wa-l-barāʾ* to argue that Muslim regimes were loyal to both "man-made laws" and non-Muslim countries rather than showing *walāʾ* to the *sharīʿa* and Islamic allies. Such supposedly misplaced loyalty equals *kufr*, al-Maqdisi holds, and should therefore be countered by *barāʾ* in its strongest form: jihad.[8] This way, al-Maqdisi justifies his opposition to Muslim regimes and his preferred solution in much more Salafi terms than other radical ideologues, such as Sayyid Qutb, had done before him.[9]

This thoroughly Salafi yet simultaneously anti-regime message provided unorganised radical Jordanians with the purpose and ideological coherence that they needed. This was underlined by the books and articles that al-Maqdisi wrote that applied his general beliefs to the situation in Jordan. These focus on the kingdom's "un-Islamic" constitution and laws, democracy and elections – which al-Maqdisi rejects for reasons largely similar to those we saw in Chapter 2 given by quietists – and practical advice for Jihadi-Salafis in Jordan.[10] At the same time, however, al-Maqdisi has long made clear that jihad is not always the right *manhaj* and that *daʿwa* is also important, if not more so, especially in situations in which a supposed ignorance of Islam exists or where there is no room for a jihad that has a chance to succeed and yield concrete results.[11] Al-Maqdisi has also expressed his opposition against what he labels "extremism in *takfīr*" (*al-ghulūw fī l-takfīr*) and the supposedly reckless use of jihad. Excommunication, he claims, must only be used after a thorough investigation of the person suspected of unbelief and cannot be applied to large groups of people, let alone to society as a whole. Jihad, similarly, should ideally be legitimate, effective and fruitful, so that it results in the founding of an Islamic emirate or state, rather than amounting to nothing more than mere fighting.[12]

Together with al-Zarqawi, who he met again back in Jordan, al-Maqdisi spread his message around the country by visiting people at home, photocopying his writings and even teaching unofficially in mosques. This was aided by certain people who would visit him and take his

[6] *Id.*, "Transformation," 95–101. [7] *Id., Quietist*, 65.
[8] *Id.*, "Enduring," 99–101; *id., Quietist*, 153–6, 165–74.
[9] For more on al-Maqdisī's ideology, see *id., Quietist*, esp. 51–93. [10] *Ibid.*, 223–5.
[11] *Ibid.*, 203–4, 228–30.
[12] *Id.*, "Protecting Jihad: The Sharia Council of the Minbar al-Tawhid wa-l-Jihad," *Middle East Policy* 18, no. 2 (2011): 149–52; *id., Quietist*, 227–9; *id.*, "Reclaiming," 525–9; *id.*, "Search," 404–13.

message back home, where they would preach it to a local audience, much like quietist Salafism was spread. One person who was particularly important in this respect was Raʾid Khuraysat, who was responsible for spreading al-Maqdisi's ideas in al-Salt but was later killed fighting in Iraq.[13] As such, al-Maqdisi gathered around him a group of mostly young Jihadi-Salafis who were attracted to his knowledge and ideology. This group, which was informally named Jamaʿat al-Muwahhidin (the Group of the Upholders of the Unity of God) or Jamaʿat al-Tawhid (the Group of the Unity of God), later became known as Bayʿat al-Imam (Fealty to the Imam), probably because of a mix-up with a name of another group. The reason it became known was that some of its members were planning an attack on an Israeli target in response to the killing of 29 Palestinians in Hebron by Israeli terrorist Baruch Goldstein in 1994. The plot was foiled by the security services, however, and the group ended up in gaol in the same year, where they stayed until 1999.[14]

While in prison, al-Maqdisi went on to spread his views and his writings were even smuggled out of his cell. At the same time, however, it became clear that in prison, the leadership of the group shifted more and more in the direction of al-Zarqawi. There seem to have been three reasons for this: firstly, al-Zarqawi was a tough and aggressive man of action, while al-Maqdisi had a much friendlier personality and wanted to focus on studying and writing; secondly, while al-Zarqawi wanted the group's efforts to focus on jihad abroad, al-Maqdisi felt that the time was right for *daʿwa* in Jordan itself; and thirdly, it became clear that al-Zarqawi, with his experience as a fighter in Afghanistan, had the type of jihadi authority that al-Maqdisi, who had never actually waged jihad, lacked. For these three reasons, al-Zarqawi appears to have been a more attractive leader for Jihadi-Salafi inmates than the bookish al-Maqdisi. The differences between the two men became even more explicit in 1999, when the entire group was released through a royal pardon on the occasion of King ʿAbdallah II's ascension to the throne; while al-Zarqawi left the country and became infamous for his role in many terrorist attacks in Iraq and elsewhere, al-Maqdisi remained in the kingdom and focussed on spreading his radical views there.[15]

Given al-Maqdisi's focus on *daʿwa* and his criticism of "extremism" in *takfir* and jihad, one can imagine that he was not too happy with al-Zarqawi's choice to go abroad and his behaviour in Iraq, which was often characterised by deadly attacks on civilians. His frustration over his former

[13] Interviews with Maḥmūd al-Kīlanī, al-Salṭ, 20 January 2014; a Jihādī-Salafī who preferred to remain anonymous, al-Salṭ, January 2014.

[14] Wagemakers, *Quietist*, 201, 202–5; *id.*, "Terrorist," 61–7.

[15] *Id.*, "Terrorist," 67–73.

pupil's actions reached such heights that he decided to write him a public letter in which he scolded al-Zarqawi for his behaviour – though in a brotherly fashion – and later repeated this criticism in several interviews. This, in turn, caused al-Zarqawi to respond and the relationship between the two men soured as a result.[16] Although al-Maqdisi appears to have been widely respected as a scholar among Jihadi-Salafis in Jordan, al-Zarqawi could be said to have been loved for his perceived bravery, action and willingness to wage jihad. This only increased when he was killed by the United States in Iraq in 2006. Al-Maqdisi's criticism of al-Zarqawi was not only uncalled for in the eyes of some admirers of the latter but also inappropriate given al-Zarqawi's stature as a jihad fighter who was later "martyred" for the cause. As a result, many of al-Zarqawi's staunch supporters in Jordan started criticising al-Maqdisi for his supposed weakness, his lack of jihadi credentials and the fact that he had the temerity to criticise their hero. To a certain extent, this criticism continues to this day.[17]

Jihadi-Salafism in Jordan Today and the Challenge of IS

Al-Maqdisi, though hugely important to the development of Jihadi-Salafism in Jordan, was not the only scholar this movement had. Another shaykh who had an impact on the community in Jordan and who would later go on to become one of the most prominent Jihadi-Salafi scholars in the world was Abu Basir al-Tartusi. Born as Mustafa Halima in Syria in 1959, he met al-Albani there before the latter went to Jordan and later moved to the kingdom himself, where he spent some time in the late 1980s.[18] During this time, he disputed al-Albani's ideas on *kufr* and published a book about this that can still be bought in Jordan today.[19] Although al-Tartusi's influence on the Jihadi-Salafi trend in Jordan is negligible because he later moved to Great Britain and eventually returned to Syria after the revolt against the regime there started in 2011, he did get to know the main quietist scholars during his time in the kingdom. As such, he would prove to be a valuable asset in the vilification of quietist Salafi scholars in Jordan, as we will see later on.[20]

16 Alshech, "Doctrinal," 422–33; Brooke, "Preacher," 52–66; Kazimi, "Virulent," 59–73.
17 Lahoud, "Search," 207–9; Wagemakers, "Reclaiming," 529–33.
18 Abū ʿAmr al-Battār, *Fatḥ al-Qadīr fī l-Taʿrīf bi-l-Shaykh Abī Baṣīr* (www.muslm.org/vb/showthread.php?368356, n.d. (accessed 27 August 2014)), 4, 6, 8–9. Since there are no page numbers in the document, I numbered the pages myself. I would like to thank Reuven Paz for providing me with this document.
19 Al-Ṭarṭūsī, *Al-Intiṣār*.
20 For more on Abū Baṣīr al-Ṭarṭūsī's life and ideology, see Joas Wagemakers, "Between Purity and Pragmatism? Abu Basir al-Tartusi's Nuanced Radicalism," in *Jihadi Thought and Ideology*, ed. Rüdiger Lohlker and Tamara Abu-Hamdeh (Berlin: Logos Verlag, 2013), 16–37.

A second scholar who was of some importance to the budding Jihadi-Salafi community in Jordan besides al-Maqdisi was ʿUmar b. Mahmud Abu ʿUmar, better known as Abu Qatada al-Filastini. Born near Bethlehem on the West Bank in 1960, Abu Qatada grew up in Amman in Jordan, where he went through several stages of religiosity, taking him from the Jamaʿat al-Tabligh to various forms of Salafism. Given the fact that he spent time teaching "Afghan Arabs" in Peshawar and had a formal religious education from universities in Jordan and Pakistan, he had the scholarly credentials to be of great influence to Jordanian Jihadi-Salafis. His travels to Malaysia, the United Arab Emirates and ultimately Great Britain in the early 1990s ensured that his influence was global, rather than local, however. He did try to set up a Salafi group in Jordan,[21] but given his absence from the kingdom after 1993, this petered out rather quickly.[22] In London, on the other hand, he became one of the central figures in the radical Islamist community and, as a result, was often in prison or under house arrest. Abu Qatada's importance to Jordan's Jihadi-Salafi community grew substantially, however, when he was deported to the kingdom from Great Britain in 2013.[23] Tried – but acquitted – on two separate terrorism charges,[24] Abu Qatada is now a free man and, together with al-Maqdisi, forms the scholarly backbone of the Jihadi-Salafi community in the kingdom today.

[21] Wagemakers, *Quietist*, 202.

[22] For more on Abū Qatāda's life and ideology, see Nesser, "Abū."

[23] Agence France-Presse (AFP), "Britain finally deports Abu Qatada to Jordan after decade long saga," *The Daily Telegraph*, July 7, 2013 (www.telegraph.co.uk/news/uknews/10164915/Britain-finally-deports-Abu-Qatada-to-Jordan-after-decade-long-saga.html, accessed 22 June 2015).

[24] "Al-Urdunn: Tabriʾat Abū Qatāda min Tuham al-Irhāb wa-Iṭlāq Sarāḥihi," *Al-Quds al-ʿArabī*, September 25, 2014, 1; "Al-Urdunn Yubriʾu l-Dāʿiya al-Islāmī Abū Qatāda," *Al-Sharq al-Awsaṭ*, September 24, 2014 (www.aawsat.com/home/article/187831, accessed 25 September 2014); Agence France-Presse (AFP), "Iṭlāq Sarāḥ 'Abū Qatāda' min Sijnihi fī Junūb al-Urdunn," *Al-Ḥayāt*, September 24, 2014 (http://alhayat.com/Articles/4743861, accessed 25 September 2014); Mohammad Ghazal, "Abu Qatada Cleared of Terrorism Charges," *The Jordan Times*, September 24, 2014 (http://jordantimes.com/abu-qatada-cleared-of-terrorism-charges, 24 September 2014); Ranya Kadri and Alan Cowell, "Militant Cleric Acquitted of Terrorism Charges," *The New York Times*, September 24, 2014 (http://nyti.ms/1mPYr6y, accessed 24 September 2014); Muwaffaq Kamāl, "'Amn al-Dawla' Tusdilu l-Sitār ʿalá Milaff 'Abū Qatāda' bi-l-Barāʾa min Tafjīrāt al-Alfiyya," *Al-Ghad*, September 25, 2014 (www.alghad.com/articles/827510, accessed 25 September 2014); Ghāzī al-Mirāyāt, "Al-Ifrāj ʿan Abī Qatāda baʿda Tabriʾatihi min Qaḍiyyat 'al-Tanẓīm al-Musallaḥ'," *Al-Raʾy*, September 25, 2014, 15; Ridād al-Qilāb, "Amn al-Dawla Tubriʾu Abā Qatāda," *Al-ʿArab al-Yawm*, September 25, 2014, 3; Rāʾid Rummān, "'Amn al-Dawla' Tufriju ʿan 'Abū Qatāda' li-ʿadam Kifāyat al-Adilla," *Al-Sabīl*, September 25, 2014, 5; Anas Ṣuwayliḥ, "Iṭlāq Sarāḥ Abī Qatāda baʿda Tabriʾatihi min Qaḍiyyat al-Alfiyya," *Al-Dustūr*, September 25, 2014, 7; Joas Wagemakers, *The Verdict of Abu Qatada al-Filastini* (www.jihadica.com/the-verdict-of-abu-qatada-al-filastini/, 26 June 2014 (accessed 22 June 2015)).

Although al-Maqdisi has been joined by Abu Qatada, meaning that the kingdom now hosts two of the most prominent – if not *the* most prominent – radical Islamic scholars alive, the movement also has a substantial second tier of shaykhs. These include spokesmen like Muhammad al-Shalabi – better known as Abu Sayyaf – in Maʿan, ʿAbd al-Fattah Shahada Hamid (Abu Muhammad al-Tahawi) from Irbid and Saʿd al-Hunayti from Amman, but also local leaders such as Jarrah al-Rahahila and Luqman al-Riyalat from al-Salt and Munif Samara from al-Zarqaʾ. Finally, the movement has some lower-rank scholars, namely ʿUmar Mahdi Al Zaydan from Irbid, Sami al-ʿUraydi (of unknown origins) and Abu ʿAbd al-Rahman Nur al-Din Bayram from al-Zarqaʾ.[25]

What these men used to have in common, apart from their Jihadi-Salafi ideas, was that they all supported al-Maqdisi in his disputes with al-Zarqawi's supporters, which focussed on jihadi authority and "purity" of doctrine in fighting a jihad.[26] This changed, however, with the advent of the so-called Arab Spring in late 2010, which drastically changed the status quo in parts of the Arab world. While Jihadi-Salafis had previously been united in their hostility to and support for jihad against the "apostate" regimes in Arab countries – even if they sometimes disagreed on the right strategy and tactics – they now witnessed rulers being toppled in Tunisia, Egypt, Libya, Yemen and possibly Syria. This meant that Jihadi-Salafis around the world suddenly had to start thinking about what to do next, rather than just focussing on what the current rulers were doing wrong, which led to new discussions and even intra-Jihadi-Salafi disputes on how to proceed in the aftermath of successful revolutions: should one accept peaceful means of contention or focus only on jihad? Must radical scholars and fighters take an inclusive approach to other anti-regime groups or stick to an exclusively Jihadi-Salafi banner?[27]

25 For more on each of these men, see Wagemakers, "Jihadi-Salafism." See also Sowell, "Jordanian." For more on Samāra, see Abū Rummān, *Anā*, 119–26. It should be noted that al-Ḥunayṭī, Āl Zaydān and al-ʿUraydī have left the country to join IS (in the case of the former two men) and Jabhat al-Nuṣra (in the case of the latter).

26 See, for instance, *Barāʾa min Fiʾat al-Ḍalāl Ghulāt al-Takfīr wa-Muʿtaqidātihim al-Zāʾigha* (www.tawhed.ws/r?i=t555vdqa, 15 November 2008 (accessed 12 November 2014)). Al-Maqdisī defends himself against a group of his Jordanian detractors in this document, which was signed by a number of these shaykhs, including al-Ṭaḥāwī, al-Raḥāḥila, Āl Zaydān, al-Riyālāt and Bayram. Others, such as Samāra and al-ʿUraydī, are known to be close to al-Maqdisī personally. Interview with Munīf Samāra, al-Zarqāʾ, 2 July 2014; group interview with various Jihādī-Salafis, al-Ruṣayfa, 17 January 2009.

27 Nelly Lahoud with Muhammad al-ʿUbaydi, *Jihadi-Discourse in the Wake of the Arab Spring* (www.ctc.usma.edu/posts/jihadi-discourse-in-the-wake-of-the-Arab-Spring, 2013 (accessed 24 April 2014)); Joas Wagemakers, "Al-Qāʿida's Post-Arab Spring Jihad: Confirmation or Re-Evaluation?" in *Violence in Islamic Thought: From European*

These divisions within Jihadi-Salafi circles became even greater – and more fiercely contested – with the rise of ISIS/IS, which claimed to be an Islamic state and even a caliphate. This led to a global Jihadi-Salafi debate on what an Islamic state should look like, with supporters of IS claiming that their group was the fulfilment of their long-held desire to have a caliphate, while opponents disagreed. This was especially the case in Jordan.[28] Given al-Maqdisi's preference for a legitimate, effective and fruitful jihad that leads to the founding of an Islamic state, one might expect him and his supporters to applaud the announcement of the caliphate by IS on 29 June 2014. This was not the case, however, since IS's beheadings of civilians, reintroduction of slavery and use of punishments for those who disagree with them represent precisely the type of behaviour that he has long criticised. Not everybody agrees with him on this point, however, and several of his former allies, like Al Zaydan and al-Hunayti, have since gone to Syria to join the Islamic State. Moreover, the divisions between pro-IS and anti-IS Jihadi-Salafi youngsters in Jordan are said to run through families and have even led to violence against some Jordanian opponents of IS.[29]

One person who has remained close to al-Maqdisi's point of view is his fellow-scholar Abu Qatada. Together with al-Maqdisi, he has become more and more critical of IS and has expressed this in increasingly harsh tones. While both scholars initially wanted to mediate between the al-Qaʿida-affiliated Jabhat al-Nusra and IS and expressed their criticism of the latter in rather veiled terms, they have become more and more explicit in their critique, often not mincing their words in describing IS's leaders.[30] This became even stronger after it became clear, in early 2015, that IS had burned Jordanian pilot Muʿadh al-Kasasiba alive. Although both scholars undoubtedly considered the pilot a combatant fighting on behalf of an "un-Islamic" regime, they strongly disagreed with the way he was killed. Al-Maqdisi negotiated with IS to get Sajida al-Rishawi – a failed suicide bomber involved in the hotel bombings in Amman in 2005 – released from a Jordanian prison in return for al-Kasasiba but failed because he claimed to have been betrayed by IS.[31] Al-Maqdisi went on to call IS

Imperialism to the Present Day, ed. Mustafa Baig and Robert Gleave (Edinburgh: Edinburgh University Press, forthcoming).

[28] Joas Wagemakers, "What Should an Islamic State Look Like? Jihādī-Salafī Debates on the War in Syria," *The Muslim World* (forthcoming).

[29] *Id.*, "Jihadi-Salafism." [30] *Id.*, "What."

[31] *Id.*, *Maqdisi in the Middle: An Inside Account of the Secret Negotiations to Free a Jordanian Pilot* (www.jihadica.com/maqdisi-in-the-middle-an-inside-account-of-the-secret-negotiations-to-free-a-jordanian-pilot/, 11 February 2015 (accessed 22 June 2015)). For al-Maqdisī's letter to IS, see "Naṣṣ Risālat al-Maqdisī li-l-Baghdādī ḥawla

"liars"[32] and Abu Qatada said they were "steeped in ignorance (*al-jahl*) and error (*al-ḍalāl*)".[33]

It is easy to see such intra-Jihadi-Salafi disputes between Jordanian supporters of IS and that group's opponents in the kingdom as simply a continuation of the earlier disagreements between the supporters of al-Maqdisi and those behind al-Zarqawi. While there are certainly similarities between the disputes, there are also differences. I have spoken to Jihadi-Salafis in Jordan, for instance, who were staunch supporters of al-Zarqawi or even fought alongside him in Iraq yet were also convinced that al-Zarqawi would have condemned IS's behaviour if he had still been alive today. Moreover, as we saw above, some of those supporting al-Maqdisi before the advent of the "Arab Spring" have now joined IS. The rise of the Islamic State has thus consolidated old fissures among Jihadi-Salafis in Jordan but has also created new ones, this time over whether IS's caliphate is really the desired utopia they have long called for or not. Whatever the case may be, IS has had a profound effect on the Jihadi-Salafi movement in Jordan because of the divisions it has created but also because of the steady erosion of al-Qaʿida's power structure it has led to, as al-Maqdisi and Abu Qatada – both al-Qaʿida-supporters – have openly admitted.[34] More important for this book, however, is that the Jihadi-Salafi movement in Jordan – including especially both scholars – have also turned their ire towards quietist Salafis.

Contesting Quietist Salafis

As we saw in Chapter 2, one of the issues dividing quietist Salafis in Jordan was the topic of faith, even if this was of less importance than the question of leadership that was analysed in Chapter 4. *Īmān* and *kufr* are not just important to quietist Salafis, however, but also to other Muslims – including Jihadi-Salafis. In the second half of the 1980s, when the Saudi scholar Safar al-Hawali wrote about quietist *ʿulamāʾ* being "modern-day Murjiʾa", al-Maqdisi also decided to write a book about this, thereby starting a trend of explicitly Jihadi-Salafi writings on

l-Kasāsiba," *Al-Ghad*, February 2, 2015 (http://alghad.com/articles/852017, accessed 9 February 2015).

32 "Al-Maqdisī: Fāwaḍtu Dāʿish bi-Shaʾn al-Kasāsiba wa-Wajadtuhum Kādhibūn," *Al-Ghad*, February 2, 2015 (http://alghad.com/articles/851761, accessed 6 February 2015).

33 "Abū Qatāda: 'Dāʿish ilá Zawāl," *Zād al-Urdunn al-Akhbārī*, February 2, 2015 (www.jordanzad.com/index.php?page=article&id=189046, accessed 6 February 2015).

34 Shiv Malik, Ali Younes, Spencer Ackerman and Mustafa Khalili, "How Isis Crippled al-Qaida," *The Guardian*, June 10, 2015 (www.theguardian.com/world/2015/jun/10/how-isis-crippled-al-qaida, accessed 10 June 2015).

this topic that relatively often concentrated on Jordanian quietists such as al-Albani, al-Halabi and, to a lesser extent, Shaqra. These accusations of Jordanian quietists being "modern-day Murji'a" echoed the intra-quietist discussions we saw earlier and even went so far that at one point in the late 2000s, the quietist and Jihadi-Salafi discussions became highly intertwined.

Accusing Quietists of Being Murji'a

"I originally wrote these papers in August/September 1987", writes al-Maqdisi in the introduction to his *Imta' al-Nazar fi Kashf Shubhat Murji'at al-'Asr* (The Delight of Looking into Uncovering the Spurious Arguments of the Modern-Day Murji'a), but he did not publish them straight away. It was not until he "saw the matter of the Murji'a get out of control in this country these days" that he decided to publish the book.[35] Al-Maqdisi distinguishes the different branches of the Murji'a and writes that, unlike the classical Murji'a, their alleged modern-day equivalents do not simply state that acts are not part of *īmān* but have a more sophisticated way of putting this. They claim, al-Maqdisi states, that sinful acts only cause the branches of faith (*shu'ab al-īmān*) to decrease, while leaving the core of faith untouched, unless there is a conscious admission of unbelief.[36] This means that a person's *īmān* cannot be taken away altogether by any single act, unless it is accompanied by *jaḥd, i'tiqād* or *istiḥlāl*. These "modern-day Murji'a" do this, al-Maqdisi claims, to turn the sins of the rulers of the Muslim world – who are supposedly not legislating according to God's will – into "sins and acts that do not decrease faith and do not destroy it".[37] Al-Maqdisi contends, however, that Muslim rulers really engage in systematic and structural *kufr akbar*, for which no extra verbal confession of unbelief is needed to justify *takfīr*. The unwillingness of the "modern-day Murji'a" to acknowledge this is not only doctrinally wrong, al-Maqdisi writes, but also lets "unbelieving" rulers off the hook.[38]

The discussion above is rather general. In a book published in 1996, however, al-Maqdisi becomes quite personal. Responding to al-Halabi's aforementioned controversial book *Al-Tahdhir min Fitnat al-Takfir*, published in 1996 on the basis of an earlier fatwa by al-Albani,[39]

[35] Abū Muḥammad al-Maqdisī, *Imtā' al-Naẓar fī Kashf Shubhāt Murji'at al-'Aṣr* (www.tawhed.ws/t, 1991/1992 (accessed July 2011)), 2.
[36] *Ibid.*, 6–7. [37] *Ibid.*, 28.
[38] *Ibid.*, 37–46. For a more detailed treatment of this book, see Ḥusnī, "Qirā'a," 167–73; Lav, *Radical*, 135–40.
[39] *Id.*, *Tabṣīr al-'Uqalā' bi-Talbisāt Ahl al-Tajahhum wa-l-Irjā'* (www.tawhed.ws/t, 1996 (accessed July 2011)), 8–9.

al-Maqdisi proceeds to refute the various arguments presented by al-Halabi. Among other things, he accuses al-Halabi of deviating from or even twisting the words of major classical scholars,[40] relying on and becoming part of the "scholars of the rulers" (*'ulamā' al-salāṭīn*),[41] mixing up the difference between *kufr akbar* and *kufr aṣghar*[42] and falsely acting as if the rulers of the Muslim world do apply (parts of) the *sharī'a*.[43] Al-Maqdisi subsequently also criticises the original fatwa by al-Albani, blaming the latter for interpreting references to *kufr* as referring only to minor unbelief and for accusing those who hold the "correct" position on this issue of extremism.[44] As a result, al-Maqdisi – although he explicitly does not apply *takfīr* to al-Halabi and al-Albani[45] – calls both scholars "modern-day Murji'a",[46] a label he also attaches to other Jordanian quietists, such as Murad Shukri and Salim al-Hilali.[47]

Although less extensively than al-Maqdisi, Abu Basir al-Tartusi also accuses Jordanian quietist scholars of being Murji'a. When asked for a fatwa on the question of al-Albani being a Murji', for instance, he answers that "shaykh al-Albani – may God have mercy on him – is considered a Murji' in questions of faith [. . .]".[48] The reason for this was found in al-Albani's supposedly deviant views on *īmān* and *kufr*,[49] an accusation he also levels at the shaykh's students in a separate treatise. Singling out Husayn al-'Awayisha, Muhammad Musa Nasr, Salim al-Hilali, 'Ali al-Halabi and Mashhur b. Hasan, he claims that these quietist scholars are guilty of *irjā'* in matters of faith since the difference between them and the classical Murji'a is "a superficial difference, not

40 *Ibid.*, 19–28, 52–4. 41 *Ibid.*, 29–33. 42 *Ibid.*, 41–51. 43 *Ibid.*, 64–74.

44 *Ibid.*, 100–61. See also Wagemakers, "Transformation," 99–101 for a more detailed discussion on this subject.

45 Al-Maqdisī, *Tabṣīr*, 171. 46 *Ibid.*, 170.

47 *Id.*, *Ruwaydan Ayyuhā l-Munhazimūna. Fa-A'dā'unā Yumayyizūna* (www.tawhed.ws/r?i=za33cn8f, 2002 (accessed 3 March 2014)), 1–4.

48 Abū Baṣīr al-Ṭarṭūsī, *Hal al-Albānī Murji'?* (www.tawhed.ws/pr?i=1104, n.d. (accessed 28 March 2013)). It is interesting that al-Ṭarṭūsī specifically mentions that al-Albānī is only among the Murji'a in certain issues, indicating that he cannot be seen as such in other respects. This is probably a reference to the idea that the "modern-day Murji'a" are also seen as loyal to the rulers of the Muslim world, which al-Albānī was not. A similar statement was made by al-Maqdisī, who wrote that while al-Albānī was among the Murji'a in matters of faith, he was never loyal to regimes, nor did he pledge allegiance to them, unlike many other scholars. This confirms his image as an aloofist quietist who was independent of regimes. E-mail message from Abū Muḥammad al-Maqdisī to the author, 21 September 2009.

49 See Abū Baṣīr al-Ṭarṭūsī, *Madhāhib al-Nās fī l-Shaykh Muḥammad Nāṣir al-Dīn al-Albānī* (www.tawhed.ws/r?i=s3usuben, 19 March 2001 (accessed 28 March 2013); *id.*, *Su'āl ḥawla Mawqif al-Albānī min Takfīr Tārik al-Ṣalāt* (www.tawhed.ws/pr?i=2356, n.d. (accessed 28 March 2013)).

an actual one".[50] The reason al-Tartusi says this is that the classical Murjiʾa did not include acts in faith and, as a result, stated that sinful acts did not affect the soundness of the religion, while the "modern-day Murjiʾa", he claims, do include acts in their definition of faith but nevertheless similarly believe that they are not a condition for the soundness of religion. "It is the same result", al-Tartusi states.[51] He also criticises Muhammad Ibrahim Shaqra – before he changed his mind and came out against al-Albani – for errors in this respect.[52]

Abu Qatada is slightly milder in his judgement of al-Albani. He praises the shaykh profusely as a great scholar of *ḥadīth*s, yet also admits he made mistakes.[53] These include, according to Abu Qatada, the fact that al-Albani "requires *istiḥlāl* in [applying] *takfīr* in [cases of] clear unbelief (*al-mukaffirāt al-ṣarīḥa*)".[54] He is nevertheless reluctant to refer to al-Albani as a Murjiʾ, preferring to call him "a man in whom there is *irjāʾ*", which he describes as someone who "does not build on this root [of the Murjiʾa] but perhaps falls into some of its requirements (*lawāzimihā*), its necessities (*muqtaḍayātihā*) or its branches (*furūʿihā*)".[55] He is much more critical of al-Albani's students, however, of whom he says that al-Albani himself "constantly warned against [their] mistakes, announcing repeatedly that he could teach [them], but that he could not raise [them as if they were his children]. Yet unfortunately, the shaykh became a prisoner of these students".[56] Abu Qatada singles out Shaqra for his close ties with the rulers of Jordan and scolds him for "loving King Husayn in God and also the rulers of the Gulf"[57] and "working as an advisor to the idol (*ṭāghūt*) crown prince in Jordan and not seeing any evil in loyalty to this ruler".[58] Such sentiments about quietist Salafis are echoed by other Jihadi-Salafis in Jordan as well.[59]

[50] Abū Baṣīr al-Ṭarṭūsī, *Mulāḥaẓāt wa-Rudūd ʿalá Risālat "Mujmal Masāʾil al-Īmān al-ʿIlmiyya fī Uṣūl al-ʿAqīda al-Salafiyya"* (www.tawhed.ws/a?a=0ybqpkdw, 25 April 2001 (accessed 24 February 2012)), 4.

[51] *Ibid.*, 5. See also 28–9.

[52] Al-Ṭarṭūsī, *Al-Intiṣār*, 14–15. See also footnote 1 in *ibid.*, 15.

[53] Abū Qatāda al-Filasṭīnī, *Naẓra Jadīda fī l-Jarḥ wa-l-Taʿdīl: Al-Albānī* (www.tawhed.ws/pr?i=1103, n.d. (accessed 28 March 2013)). This document was only available in html-format when I downloaded it. The information given here can be found on page 1 of the printout of this document.

[54] *Id.*, *Ḥawla Murjiʾat al-ʿAṣr* (www.tahwed.ws/r?i=57gqha8v, n.d. (accessed 9 June 2009)). This document was only available in html-format when I downloaded it. The information given here can be found on page 2 of the printout of this document.

[55] *Id.*, *Al-Farq bayna Rajul Murjiʾ wa-bayna Rajul fī-hi Irjāʾ* (www.tawhed.ws/pr?i=1220, n.d. (accessed 25 September 2009)). This document was only available in html-format when I downloaded it. The information given here can be found on page 1 of the printout of this document.

[56] *Ibid.*, 3. [57] *Ibid.*, 5. [58] *Ibid.*, 11.

[59] Interviews with various Jihādī-Salafis who preferred to remain anonymous, al-Salṭ, January 2014.

Meddling in Intra-Quietist Conflicts

The accusations expressed by Jihadi-Salafis that Jordanian quietist scholars are "modern-day Murjiʾa" are sometimes based on quietists' own writings, particularly al-Halabi's *Al-Tahdhir min Fitnat al-Takfir*. This is not surprising, since this book circulated widely among Salafis in Jordan, which must have irritated those who disagreed with it. In fact, al-Halabi himself, in his introduction to this book, explicitly refers to al-Tartusi, al-Maqdisi and Abu Qatada as "divergent deviants" (*al-munḥarifūn al-mukhālifūn*) and makes fun of their names:

> The first of them: this blind one who thinks of himself as "having insight (*baṣīran*)"[60] into what is correct (*bi-l-ṣawāb*)!
>
> The second of them: that perishable [man] (*al-hālik*) who reckons he is "immune (*ʿiṣām*)"[61] to the truth (*bi-l-ḥaqq*)!!
>
> The crowning touch on them (*wa-thālith athāfīhim*): this learned one (*al-mutaʿālim*) in whose ears Satan has urinated (*bāla l-shayṭān fī udhunayhi*), deceiving him (*mulabbasan ʿalayhi*), making it seem to him that he is "a thorn (*qatāda*)"[62] in the eyes of his opponents and an irritant in their throats (*shajan fī ḥulūqihim*)!!![63]

That this mockery of the Jihadi-Salafi shaykhs did not go unnoticed is clear from al-Maqdisi's writing, which explicitly mentions these words.[64] Jordanian Jihadi-Salafi criticism of the kingdom's "modern-day Murjiʾa" was thus always related to the intra-quietist ideological discussions we saw above and perhaps even a bit personal. Jihadi-Salafis did not start meddling in the conflict between al-Halabi and Shaqra, however, until the late 2000s.

As we saw in Chapter 4, Shaqra changed his mind about matters of faith and unbelief towards the late 1990s and, after al-Albani's death, even joined Muhammad Abu Ruhayyim in referring to al-Halabi and others as "neo-Murjiʾa". This did not go unnoticed to Jordan's Jihadi-Salafi scholars, who increasingly started taking Shaqra's side in his conflict with al-Halabi. Al-Maqdisi writes in one of his treatises, for example, that other quietist Salafis "left [Shaqra] and attacked him" when he confronted them with "the truth".[65] He even goes so far as to defend Shaqra in the introduction to a book by Muhammad Bu l-Nit,

[60] This is a reference to al-Ṭarṭūsī's *kunya* (the part of an Arabic name that means "father of…" or "mother of…") "Abū Baṣīr".
[61] This is a play on al-Maqdisī's given name, "ʿIṣām".
[62] This pun refers to "Abū Qatāda".
[63] Al-Ḥalabī, introduction to *Al-Taḥdhīr min Fitnat al-Ghuluw*, by al-Albānī, 48–9.
[64] Al-Maqdisī, *Tabṣīr*, 75–6.
[65] *Id.*, *Sarāb al-Tarājuʿāt wa-Asrāb al-Mutasāqiṭīn* (www.tawhed.ws/dl?i=31051001, 2010 (accessed 31 May 2010)), 3.

a Moroccan scholar.[66] In this publication, Bu l-Nit is sometimes critical of Shaqra,[67] but in a new edition of this book published by al-Maqdisi on his website, the latter writes in his introduction that Shaqra has changed since then and has retracted his earlier articles. In fact, al-Maqdisi states, "we have sat with him, visited him and got to know him from up close and we have found him a friend of the helpers of the religion (*muḥibban li-anṣār al-dīn*) and the jihad fighters".[68] That such visits between the two men actually took place became clear when a clip on YouTube surfaced of al-Maqdisi and Shaqra having a friendly chat together.[69]

Al-Tartusi, for his part, apparently even felt the need to apologise to Shaqra after the latter had a change of mind about issues related to *īmān* and *kufr*. He states that he criticised Shaqra in his works for belonging to "the people of *irjāʾ*", but now – after a telephone conversation with Shaqra – realises that he no longer deserves that label. Shaqra, however, apparently stated:

> There is no need for an apology, oh Abu Basir. You were right and correct. What you, Abu Muhammad al-Maqdisi and Abu Qatada wrote was correct and right. I say to people that you, Abu Muhammad al-Maqdisi and Abu Qatada were right and correct. There is no need for an apology. The possessor of the truth does not need to apologise for that about which he is right.[70]

These words were confirmed by Shaqra in my interview with him, in which he similarly stated that "I found Abu Muhammad al-Maqdisi to be honest and good (*fāḍil wa-ṭayyib*) and he has knowledge [...] and Abu Basir [al-Tartusi] too, like him, and Abu Qatada".[71]

It is statements such as these – as well as his change of mind about matters of faith and unbelief – that make it tempting to conclude that Shaqra has become a Jihadi-Salafi.[72] Yet given the fact that Shaqra still speaks rather proudly of his contacts with King Husayn,[73] it is unlikely that he can be classified as such. In fact, he is better described as

[66] For more on this book and its author, see Lav, *Radical*, 144–5.
[67] Muḥammad Bū l-Nīt, *Kashf al-Shubhāt (1) ʿAqīdat "al-Salafiyyīn" fī Mīzān Ahl al-Sunna wa-l-Jamāʿa* (Casablanca: Maṭābiʿ Afrīqiyā l-Sharq, 1998), 12–16.
[68] Abū Muḥammad al-Maqdisī, introduction to *ʿAqīdat Adʿiyāʾ al-Salafiyya fī Mīzān Ahl al-Sunna wa-l-Jamāʿa*, by Abū ʿAbdallāh Muḥammad Bū l-Nīt al-Marākishī (www.tawhed.ws/dl?i=0606091a, 2009 (accessed 30 September 2013)), 7.
[69] This video can be seen at www.youtube.com/watch?v=mttpgWh_vUs, 14 July 2010 (accessed 24 June 2015).
[70] Abū Baṣīr al-Ṭarṭūsī, *Li-l-Shaykh Muḥammad Ibrāhīm Shaqra ʿalayya Dayn!* (www.abubaseer.bizland.com/hadath/Read/hadath%2054.doc, 8 December 2008 (accessed 6 November 2012)). See also al-Battār, *Fatḥ*, 21–2; Lav, *Radical*, 160.
[71] Interview with Muḥammad Ibrāhīm Shaqra, Amman, 27 June 2012.
[72] This is, in fact, strongly suggested by Lav. See Lav, *Radical*, 163–4.
[73] Interview with Muḥammad Ibrāhīm Shaqra, Amman, 27 June 2012.

personally close to them, but not as an actual adherent to their ideas.[74] A more likely explanation for Shaqra's behaviour and statements is that he, after having felt rejected by his fellow quietists as their leader, sought a new audience that not only agreed with his views on faith and unbelief but also gave him the respect that he felt he was denied by quietist scholars. This was confirmed by al-Halabi when he quoted a fellow Salafi who had gone to the mosque Shaqra usually attended and "saw around him a group of [Jihadi-Salafis] who made him lead the way, who respected him and kissed his forehead".[75] It is probably this type of respect (along with his views on faith) that explains Shaqra's close personal ties with Jihadi-Salafis, rather than the suggestion that he has fully joined their side.

Despite implicitly getting involved in the intra-quietist leadership struggle and openly siding with Shaqra in this respect, Jordanian Jihadi-Salafi scholars make no mention of anything but the theological side of these conflicts. In other words, they interpret the disputes between al-Albani and al-Halabi on the one hand and Abu Ruhayyim and Shaqra on the other as solely dealing with faith and unbelief. That they missed the more important dimension of the leadership struggle is easily explained by the fact that they were outsiders – both as Jihadi-Salafis and as people residing outside Amman – who were not privy to the personal details of these conflicts. In fact, to a lot of Jordanian Salafis who – for ideological or geographical reasons or both – did not have an insider perspective on these disputes, the bone of contention was primarily theological.[76] This is even more the case for international Jihadi-Salafis who have commented on this issue. For them, as complete outsiders to these disputes, these conflicts were simply about the "correct" creed versus the "modern-day Murji'a".[77] The latter group, bruised by internal disputes and now also

[74] Interview with Marwān Shaḥāda, Amman, 9 June 2012.

[75] Interview with ʿAlī al-Ḥalabī, Amman, 27 June 2012.

[76] Interviews with Muʿādh al-ʿUtaybī, Irbid, 19 January 2014; Iḥsān al-ʿUtaybī, Irbid, 28 January 2014; Muḥammad al-Shalabī, Maʿān, 29 June 2014; Muṣṭafá al-Ṣurīfī, al-Salṭ, 30 June 2014.

[77] Ḥāmid b. ʿAbdallāh al-ʿAlī, *Bayān Ḥaqīqat al-Īmān wa-l-Radd ʿalá Murjiʾat al-ʿAṣr fī-Mā Khālafū fī-hi Maḥkam al-Qurʾān* (www.h-alali.net/b_open.php?id=a0dda88e-fb6b-1029-a701-0010dc91cf69, n.d. (accessed 31 August 2015)); Abū l-Faḍl ʿUmar al-Ḥuddūshī, *Ikhbār al-Awliyāʾ bi-Maṣnaʿ Ahl al-Tajahhum wa-l-Irjāʾ* (http://ia600809.us.archive.org/15/items/ekhbar-awlyaa/ekhbar-awlyaa.pdf, n.d. (accessed 31 August 2015)); Muḥammad al-Salafī al-Jazāʾirī, *Nathr al-Darr fī Tafnīd Shubhat Kufr dūna Kufr* (www.fichier-pdf.fr/2015/01/21/fichier-pdf-sans-nom-1/preview/page/1/, 2009 (accessed 31 August 2015)); Abū ʿUzayr ʿAbd al-Ilah Yūsuf al-Yūbī al-Ḥasanī al-Jazāʾirī, *Al-Kāshif fī Tarājuʿ ʿAlī al-Ḥalabī al-Jahmī al-Zāʾif* (www.tawhed.ws/dl?i=17051001, 2010 (accessed 4 October 2013)); Abū ʿUbayda ʿAbd al-Karīm al-Shādhilī, *Taʾsīs al-Naẓar fī Radd Shubah Mashāyikh Murjiʾat al-ʿAṣr* (www.tawhed.ws, 1420 [1999/2000] (accessed 3 September 2009); Abū ʿAbd al-Malik al-Tawḥīdī, *Kashf Mā Alqāhu Iblīs ʿalá Qalb ʿAbd*

suffering from Jihadi-Salafi charges of *irjāʾ*, did come up with a theologically suitable answer, however.

The Quietists Strike Back

Jordanian quietist Salafi scholars – and especially al-Halabi – have been the subject of quite a lot of theological abuse over the years coming from some of their fellow quietists in the kingdom itself as well as from Jihadi-Salafis from Jordan and elsewhere. Yet, as the quotation by al-Halabi on al-Tartusi, al-Maqdisi and Abu Qatada mentioned above suggests, quietists themselves can be rather polemical as well. This is also true in their ideological battle with Jordanian Jihadi-Salafis, which was by no means a one-sided affair in which only al-Halabi and like-minded scholars were taking all the blows. On the contrary, the charges of belonging to the "modern-day Murjiʾa" were deftly countered by quietists – and, again, especially al-Halabi – by accusing their opponents of belonging to the theological polar opposite of those supposedly "guilty" of *irjāʾ*: the Khawarij.

As I have pointed out elsewhere, terms such as "modern-day Murjiʾa"/ "neo-Murjiʾa" and "Khawarij" are part of a contest of theological mudslinging that is probably quite effective since such labels are partly correct, make use of complicated arguments that are difficult to disprove and avoid terms such as "unbelievers", which would clearly be inappropriate when levelled at pious Salafis.[78] For all three reasons, such labels are likely to stick. Moreover, just as applying "Murjiʾa" to quietists helps Jihadi-Salafis make the case that their opponents are lackeys to the regime, calling Jihadi-Salafis "Khawarij" serves the quietist agenda of portraying radicals as "extremists", thereby keeping the label of "Salafis" clean and aiding them in their attempt to distinguish themselves as "moderates". As such, this labelling by quietists – though perhaps meant less for public and regime consumption than for their own supporters – underlines their tendency towards loyalist quietism and serves their further domestication to the interests of the state.

al-ʿAzīz b. Rayyis al-Rayyis (www.tawhed.ws, 1430 [2009] (accessed 9 June 2009)); Abū Ṣakhr al-Yāfāwī, *Radd al-Iʿtidāʾāt Murjiʾat al-Khalaf ʿalá Manhaj al-Salaf* (www.tawhed.ws, n.d. (accessed 3 September 2009)); Abū Qatāda ʿAbd al-Khāliq al-Yamānī, *Murjiʾat al-ʿAṣr Murjifūn* (www.tawhed.ws/dl?i=16011008, n.d. (accessed 27 January 2010)); *id.*, *Al-Radd ʿalá Mā Qālahu l-Ḥalabī al-Daʿī fī Maqālat "Al-Salafiyya … al-Salafiyya al-Salafiyya" allatī Nushirat fī Jarīdat al-Ghad al-Urduniyya* (www.tawhed.ws/dl?i=22011003, n.d. (accessed 27 January 2010)).

[78] Wagemakers, "'Seceders'," 163.

Accusing Jihadi-Salafis of Being Khawarij

The direct reason quietists accuse Jihadi-Salafis of being like the Khawarij is twofold: firstly, quietists claim that, like the Khawarij rebelled against caliph ʿAli b. Abi Talib (r. 656–661), modern-day Jihadi-Salafis violently rebel against Muslim rulers or at least condone such behaviour; secondly, Jihadi-Salafis are accused of applying *takfīr* on the basis of "mere" major sins without verbal confirmation of sinful intention, thereby – in effect – excommunicating people on the basis of minor unbelief, just like the Khawarij did.[79] The accusation that Jordanian Jihadi-Salafis are like the Khawarij did not start with the conflicts after al-Albani's death, however. In fact, al-Albani himself has applied this term to Jihadi-Salafis.[80] From the late 1990s, this type of labelling by quietists did occur more frequently, however, which cannot be separated from either the disputes about faith and unbelief directly prior to and after al-Albani's death or the increasing tendencies by quietists to follow the regime's policy of denouncing "extremism".

With regard to the issue of "extremism" in *takfīr*, the legitimacy of this concept as such is not rejected by quietist Salafis,[81] but they do believe it can be dangerous in the hands of someone lacking the necessary knowledge or if the concept is applied too quickly.[82] The danger of the "*takfīrī*" ideology, quietists maintain, lies in the fact that it leads to excommunicating the rulers, starting revolutions against their regimes, insulting the scholars who have different views on this and committing murder of innocent Muslims (who, as alleged apostates, should supposedly be killed).[83] Interestingly, al-Halabi acknowledges that "*takfīrī* thought" dates from the beginning of Islam and he scolds those who doubt that such thinking is related to the religion or claim that it stems "from Zionist thought".[84] Nevertheless – and despite the allegedly deep Islamic roots of "*takfīr*ism" – al-Halabi states that its supposed adherents are wrong in claiming that they only excommunicate Muslims who have left the religion. They apply *takfīr*, he says, on the basis of sources about which the

[79] *Ibid.*, 154–6. [80] Abū Rummān and Abū Haniyya, *Al-Salafiyya al-Muḥāfaẓa*, 99.

[81] Al-Ḥalabī, *Al-Tabṣīr*, 20–1. [82] *Ibid.*, 35; *id.*, *Ḥadath*, 13–14.

[83] *Id.*, *Al-Fiʾa*, 8–10; *id.*, *Nadwa ʿan al-Fikr al-Takfīrī wa-Atharihi ʿalá l-Mujtamaʿ bi-Irbid* (www.alhalaby.com/play.php?catsmktba=2641, 25 April 2011 (accessed 1 April 2013)).

[84] *Id.*, "Min Mughālaṭāt Duʿāt 'al-Fikr al-Takfīrī'," *Al-Aṣāla* 10, no. 51 (15 Dhū l-Ḥijja 1426 [15 January 2006]): 21–2. The words quoted are on 22. Some scholars nevertheless trace such "*takfīrī*" ideas mainly to the Muslim Brotherhood and especially Sayyid Quṭb. See, for example, Saʿd al-Ḥaṣīn, "Fitnat al-Takfīr," *Al-Aṣāla* 6, no. 35 (15 Shaʿbān 1422 [2 November 2001]): 30–4.

scholars agree that they refer to minor unbelief only, not the major unbelief that is necessary to justify excommunication.[85]

Al-Halabi's mentioning of the long history of "*takfīrī*" thought, going all the way back to early Islam, is obviously a reference to the Khawarij, who are often described in Salafi discourse as exhibiting precisely the type of behaviour with regard to *takfīr* that quietists so object to. In Jordanian quietist publications, one will therefore often find references to the Khawarij. These are sometimes simply historical articles, indicating who the Khawarij were and why they were wrong in their views on faith,[86] seemingly partly meant to show that Salafis are not like that. Indeed, Jordanian quietists have written a number of articles in which they explicitly distance themselves from the Khawarij and show that Salafism differs greatly with the "*takfīrī*" practices of the former.[87] Instead, quietists maintain, Salafism is the genuine golden mean (*al-wasaṭiyya*) between the various extremes in Islamic theology, treading on the "straight path"[88] only.[89]

Still, it is clear that the definition of "Salafism" and the quietists' attempts to keep this label from being "tainted" by associations with the Khawarij is not the only reason they bring up this matter. Another, perhaps more important reason for this seems to lie in quietists' desire to provide those they deem "extremists" with a label that delegitimises them in a single word and puts their own accusations that quietists are "neo-Murji'a" in a new perspective. If, after all, "Khawarij" accuse quietists of being overly hesitant in their views on faith and unbelief, the latter must be doing something right since it is only natural that such "Khawarij" – precisely because they are "extremists" – would perceive of "the straight path" as being too moderate.

85 Al-Ḥalabī, "Min Mughālaṭāt," 22–3. For an extensive treatment of the issue of "extremism" in *takfīr* by a Jordanian quietist Salafī scholar, see Bāsim b. Fayṣal al-Jawābira's book *Extremism: The Causes, Effects and the Cure* (www.salafimanhaj.com, 2008 (accessed 8 October 2009)).

86 Abū ʿAbd al-Raḥmān Hishām al-ʿĀrif, "Fiqh al-Wuṣūl ilá 'l-Qimma!' ʿinda l-Khawārij," *Al-Aṣāla* 10, no. 48 (15 Rabīʿ al-Awwal 1426 [24 April 2005]): 32–3; Fatḥī ʿAbdallāh Sulṭān, "Manhaj Shaykh al-Islām fī Kashf Bidʿat al-Khawārij," *Al-Aṣāla* 5, no. 28 (15 Jumādá l-Ākhira 1420 [26 September 1999]): 18–31.

87 *Al-Shaykh al-Ḥalabī*; Abū ʿAbdallāh Fatḥī b. ʿAbdallāh al-Mawṣilī, "Mubādara Kashafat ʿan Uṣūl Ṣāḥibihā," *Al-Aṣāla* 9, no. 45 (15 Ṣafar 1425 [6 April 2014]): 26, 28.

88 This is a reference to Q. 1: 6, which states: "Guide us in the straight path (*al-ṣirāṭ al-mustaqīm*)".

89 Abū Anas Muḥammad b. Mūsá Āl Naṣr, "'Wa-ka-Dhālika Jaʿalnākum Umma Wasaṭan'," *Al-Aṣāla* 9, no. 46 (15 Rajab 1425 [31 August 2004]): 8–10; Amīn Muḥammad al-Buṭūsh, "Al-Wasaṭiyya fī l-Islām," *Al-Aṣāla* 6, no. 36 (15 Shawwāl 1422 [31 December 2001]): 24–9.

As such, Jordanian quietists regularly speak of "the Khawarij in every time and place"[90] or similar phrases, as if the Khawarij – or like-minded equivalents – still exist today, much like the charge of "neo-Murji'a" used by Jihadi-Salafis against quietists. Such "neo-Khawarij", as it were, are accused of twisting the texts of the Qur'an and the Sunna, acting without the *salaf*'s understanding of the sources, exhibiting extremism and conducting themselves with rudeness.[91] This results in *takfīr* on the basis of norms that are not Islamically legitimate, thereby creating *fitna* for the Muslim community,[92] bloodshed among Muslims and revolts against the rulers.[93] In applying the term "Khawarij" to any contemporary group, Jordanian quietists sometimes mention the Muslim Brotherhood[94] – seen by quietists as equally disruptive and responsible for civil strife – or specific people associated with that group.[95] More relevant for this study, however, is that quietists similarly use the label of "Khawarij" when referring to Jihadi-Salafis and their organisations, such as al-Qa'ida,[96] its leaders[97] and its branches.[98]

With regard to Jordan, quietists from that country make it quite clear that the kingdom's Jihadi-Salafis are equally worthy of the title of "Khawarij".[99] One scholar mentions several of the country's most prominent Jihadi-Salafis, such as Abu Qatada, Abu Sayyaf (Muhammad al-Shalabi), al-Zarqawi and al-Maqdisi, in this respect. The latter in particular is mentioned as having written books that are described as containing "the thought of the Khawarij".[100] Other scholars reach similar conclusions, singling out al-Maqdisi[101] as well as Abu Qatada and al-Tartusi.[102] The Jihadi-Salafis responsible for the clashes with the police in al-Zarqa' in April 2011 – from whom, as we saw above, quietists eagerly sought to distance themselves – are also described as "Khawarij".[103]

[90] Al-Buṭūsh, *Kashf*, 299.

[91] *Ibid.*, 299–300; al-Ḥalabī, *Al-Fi'a*, 12–3; Abū Usāma Salīm b. ʿĪd al-Hilālī, "Dalālat Aḥādīth al-Khawārij ʿalá Ḥajiyyat al-Manhaj al-Salafī?!" *Al-Aṣāla* 7, no. 40 (15 Dhū l-Ḥijja 1423 [17 February 2003]): 10–1.

[92] Al-Ḥalabī, *Al-Fi'a*, 11. [93] Al-Buṭūsh, *Kashf*, 300.

[94] ʿAlī al-Ḥalabī, *Hal "Laysa min al-Munīʿa wa-l-Rujūla Dhikr ʿUyūb 'al-Ikhwān' fī hādhā l-Awān" ka-Mā Naqalahu l-Baʿḍ ʿannī?* (www.alhalaby.com/play.php?catsmktba=3518, 25 August 2013 (accessed 26 August 2013)).

[95] Al-Hilālī, "Dalālat," 11. [96] Al-Buṭūsh, *Kashf*, 300–1.

[97] Al-Hilālī, "Dalālat," 11.

[98] "Mādhā Yanqimūna min Bilād al-Ḥaramayn?!" *Al-Aṣāla* 8, no. 43 (15 Jumādá l-Ākhira 1424 [14 August 2003]): 6–7.

[99] Interview with Muḥammad b. Mūsá Āl Naṣr, Amman, 20 June 2012.

[100] Al-Khaṭīb, *Ḥarakat*, 253–8. The words cited are on 256.

[101] Al-Ḥalabī, "Min Mughālaṭāt," 23. [102] Al-Hilālī, "Dalālat," 11.

[103] ʿAlī al-Ḥalabī, *Al-Khawārij wa-l-Khawārij al-Qaʿdiyya* (www.alhalaby.com/play.php?catsmktba=2813, 20 July 2011 (accessed 1 April 2013)).

The Regime Joins In

Quietist Salafi scholars in Jordan have fought the battle against Jihadi-Salafis through their discourse, labelling them "*takfīrī*s" and "Khawarij" in order to denounce and delegitimise them and to distance themselves from their practices. Their means to fight Jihadi-Salafis do not really go any further than this, however. Yet one scholar actively calls for fighting the "Khawarij". In a rather cunning way, after having established that modern-day groups like al-Qaʿida are Khawarij too, he cites classical scholar after scholar stating that the Khawarij – obviously in reference to the original group – must be fought.[104] This way, the full weight of classical Islamic scholarly authority can be employed to call for the crack-down on modern-day Jihadi-Salafi groups that did not even exist when these mediaeval *ʿulamāʾ* lived.

As we saw in Chapter 5, the Jordanian regime has fought radical Muslims for quite some time – both on the ideological and the military front – and has only increased its efforts in this respect since "9/11", with quietist Salafis seemingly following in its footsteps by portraying themselves as "moderate" and denouncing terrorism and "extremism". In the past few years, however, the regime – in an interesting turn of events – appears to be following quietist Salafis in their treatment of Jihadi-Salafis, at least when it comes to terminology. While the king has long referred to radical Muslims as "*takfīrī*s",[105] he appears to have adopted the practice of referring to Jihadi-Salafis as "Khawarij", particularly with the rise of IS since 2014.

In the context of the international coalition against the Islamic State, King ʿAbdallah II stated that "Khawarij groups must be fought".[106] In order to facilitate this fight, he later stated, "we must build a total method to defeat the Khawarij of our time (*Khawārij ʿaṣrinā*)" and "to wage war on the misguidance (*al-taḍlīl*) that these Khawarij practice".[107] The king similarly talked about "these terrorist gangs (*al-ʿiṣābāt al-irhābiyya*) among the Khawarij"[108] and how "today, we Muslims oppose a disgusting attack from the Khawarij who distort our religion to justify their detestable crimes (*jarāʾimihim al-faẓīʿa*)".[109] In fact, in an interview

[104] Al-Buṯīsh, *Kashf*, 309–18. [105] See, for example, King Abdullah II, *Our*, 241–2.

[106] Petra News Agency, "Al-Malik: Al-Ḥarb ʿalá l-Irhāb Ḥarb al-ʿArab wa-l-Muslimīn Awwalan," *Al-Dustūr*, March 10, 2015, 1.

[107] ʿUmar Muḥarama, "Al-Malik: Al-Ḥarb ʿalá l-Irhāb Nakhūḍuhā Naḥnu l-Muslimīn Difāʿan ʿan Dīninā wa-Qiyamihi l-Insāniyya al-Muthlá," *Al-Dustūr*, March 29, 2015, 5.

[108] Petra News Agency, "Al-Malik: ʿAlaynā an Nataḍāmana Dawman li-Nataṣaddá li-l-Irhāb Aynamā Kāna," *Al-Dustūr*, April 23, 2015, 2.

[109] Petra News Agency, "Al-Malik: Hazīmat al-Irhāb al-ʿĀlamī bi-Ḥājat li-Nahj Shumūlī," *Al-Dustūr*, June 12, 2015, 2.

with the American television channel Fox News, the king refers to IS as "Khawarij" several times, using a term whose meaning and significance few outside the Muslim world will immediately understand.[110]

These numerous references to "Khawarij" by King ʿAbdallah II to designate IS are not meant to say that the Jordanian regime has literally heard and adopted this term from quietists and is actually following the latter in its discourse on Jihadi-Salafis. In fact, the term "Khawarij" has been used by officials from other Muslim countries to denounce and delegitimise radicals for a long time, so Jordan is not unique in this respect.[111] It is striking, however, how wholeheartedly the Jordanian regime seems to have adopted this term, even more explicitly than quietist Salafis themselves. This does not suggest that the regime is trying to "out-Salafise" its own quietist scholars, but it does show to what extent the agendas and discourse of both actors converge, at least on this issue.

The active ideological resistance by quietists to Jihadi-Salafis as well as the regime's adoption of this "Khawarij" discourse are yet another indication of how the state and quietist Salafis in Jordan have grown increasingly close. To be sure, the discourse against "extremism" is rooted in beliefs that have been espoused by the regime and quietists for a much longer time, but its specific expressions do show how the growing domestication of a more and more loyalist quietist Salafi leadership has led to the use of a terminology by its scholars that is increasingly similar to that of the state. This has reached a point at which it almost seems as if the Jordanian state has become part of the quietist Salafi utopia sometimes. Although this may be an exaggeration, there is no doubt that the various aspects of domestication that we have seen throughout Chapters 2–6 meant that the quietist Salafi community in the kingdom was well prepared for a major political challenge that has swept through the Middle East in recent years and that has not left Jordan untouched either: the "Arab Spring".

110 "King Abdullah II: We're at war with 'outlaws of Islam'," *Fox News* (http://video.foxnews.com/v/4171242845001/king-abdullah-ii-were-at-war-with-outlaws-of-islam/?#sp=show-clips, 14 April 2015 (accessed 26 June 2015)). For a full (Arabic) transcript of the interview, see http://kingabdullah.jo/index.php/ar_JO/interviews/view/id/518/print/1.html, 14 April 2015 (accessed 22 June 2015).

111 See Kenney, *Muslim*, for how this term was employed to counter various types of Islamists in Egypt.

7 The Challenge of Political Salafism

On 17 December 2010, the Tunisian fruit vendor Muhammad al-Buʿazizi immolated himself in protest against the corruption and abuse of power that he was confronted with in his country. This incident, embedded in experiences about dictatorship, corruption and repression shared by many other Tunisians, sparked a series of demonstrations that culminated in a revolt that ultimately unseated the country's long-time president, Zayn al-ʿAbidin b. ʿAli. The events in Tunisia, in turn, inspired similar protests in other Arab countries, leading to the downfall of leaders in Egypt, Libya and Yemen too, although each state underwent this process in its own way and, at the time of writing (summer 2015), Syria is still embroiled in a civil war between its regime and various militant groups, the outcome of which cannot easily be predicted.

This series of revolts known as the "Arab Spring" sent shockwaves through the Middle East as regimes were seemingly being toppled everywhere. Although much of the "Arab Spring" ended in disappointment, it brought about substantial changes. One of these was the increased involvement of Salafis in politics. Both the general changes that the region underwent and the politicisation of certain Salafis had repercussions for Jordan.[1] This chapter therefore deals with political Salafism in the kingdom, emphasising developments after the "Arab Spring". It starts by analysing the rise of political Salafism in Jordan since its beginnings until the 2010s. I then give an in-depth account of one political Salafi

[1] For more on Jordan and the "Arab Spring", see *Jordan, Forever on the Brink* (Washington, DC: Project on Middle East Political Science, 2012); Shadi Hamid and Courtney Freer, *How Stable is Jordan? King Abdullah's Half-Hearted Reforms & the Challenge of the Arab Spring* (Doha: Brookings Doha Center, 2011); International Crisis Group (ICG), *Popular Protest in North Africa and the Middle East (IX): Dallying with Reform in a Divided Jordan*, Middle East/North Africa Report no. 118 (Amman/Brussels, 2012); Nur Köprülü, "Jordan since the Uprisings: Between Change and Stability," *Middle East Policy* 21, no. 2 (2014): 111–26; Sarah A. Tobin, "Jordan's Arab Spring: The Middle Class and Anti-Revolution," *Middle East Policy* 19, no. 1 (2012): 96–109; Sean L. Yom, "Tribal Politics in Contemporary Jordan: The Case of the Hirak Movement," *Middle East Journal* 68, no. 2 (2014): 229–47.

organisation's ideology in particular – the Jamʿiyyat al-Kitab wa-l-Sunna – including its views on the "Arab Spring". Finally, this chapter deals with how the Jordanian state and quietist Salafis have responded to the "threat" that political Salafism poses. Like the previous one, this chapter shows us a new side of Salafism in Jordan and one that was equally fervently fought by quietists, though with different arguments. It also shows us how years of domestication to the regime have created an image of the Salafi utopia among Jordan's main quietist scholars that is entirely loyalist.

The Rise of Political Salafism in Jordan

Despite the shift from al-Albani's aloofist quietism to al-Halabi's and others' loyalist version of the same type of Salafism, one thing remained the same for all quietists in Jordan: in practice, they limited the applicability of Islam to studying, cleansing the tradition, teaching and preaching. This focus on *al-taṣfiya wa-l-tarbiya*, which was discussed in Chapter 2, obviously came at the expense of paying attention to other aspects in life, including politics and society.[2] Given the fact that many Muslims believe they should get involved in these things too, it should come as no surprise that some Salafis in Jordan disagreed with the apolitical *manhaj* of al-Albani and his followers and, instead, wanted to broaden Salafism to include political action as well.[3]

The Rise of "Reformist" Salafism

As mentioned in Chapters 1 and 3, political Salafism in general as well as its adherents in Jordan in particular have been greatly influenced by the *ṣaḥwa* in Saudi Arabia and the writings of shaykh Abu ʿAbdallah ʿAbd al-Rahman b. ʿAbd al-Khaliq, who lives in Kuwait. Given the fact that many Jordanian Salafis are from Kuwait, it was especially Ibn ʿAbd al-Khaliq who had an impact on political or, as they call it, "reformist" Salafism in Jordan. In one of his writings, Ibn ʿAbd al-Khaliq states that while overthrowing Muslim rulers is not allowed, believers should, in their "method of changing wrong (*uslūb taghyīr al-munkar*)" in the rulers' policies, strive

[2] Again, by these words I do not mean that quietists do not talk about politics and society, but that they only discuss these through the prism of religion, as we saw in Chapter 2.

[3] My definition of "politics" used here is a fairly broad one that can be equated with "public affairs" (as opposed to private affairs). This is a fitting definition for the purpose of this book since it is precisely the "public" side of Islam that reformist Salafis in Jordan believe is ignored by quietists. For more on this, see Andrew Heywood, *Politics* (New York: Palgrave, 2002 [1997]), 7–9.

to forbid evil with their tongues and hearts.[4] Placing himself squarely between the violent revolts against regimes called for by Jihadi-Salafis[5] and the silent subservience of quietists, Ibn ʿAbd al-Khaliq states that in relations with the rulers, "dialogue and *daʿwa* with the tongue must be the only means for reform (*al-wasīla al-waḥīda li-l-iṣlāḥ*) in the midst of this *umma*".[6]

Another influential author to Jordanian "reformist" Salafis, the Sudanese Muhammad Abu Zayd Mustafa, builds on this idea of striving for Salafism-based political reform and allowing criticism of the ruler by actively calling for political participation. He mentions the various reservations Salafis have against this, including the idea that political participation would clash with the Salafi goal of *tarbiya*, would involve the "un-Islamic" concept of "democracy" and would mean running for public office.[7] The author counters this by pointing to the example of Yusuf (Joseph) in the Qurʾan,[8] who – according to Islamic tradition – accepted a high-ranking position in the Egyptian ruling hierarchy in pharaonic times when it became clear that he was the only person who could take care of "justice, reform and feeding the poor". This example is similar to the situation today, the author argues, in the sense that Muslims should get involved in calling for such reform if there is nobody else to do so.[9] Mindful of the Salafi application of *al-walāʾ wa-l-barāʾ*, the author states that Yusuf is proof of the fact that getting involved with unbelievers through politics does not mean one has to be loyal to them[10] and he also mentions other Islamic examples of legitimate Muslim cooperation with "unbelievers" to underline this point.[11]

Following a similar line of thinking, Ibn ʿAbd al-Khaliq states that "generally, the Islamic peoples want Islam and the Islamic *sharīʿa*", yet "they are ruled by governments that enforced or [still] enforce rules and laws that clash with Islam. There's no question that an effort should be made to amend these laws so that they become Islamically legitimate."[12] The fact that current laws are often "man-made" should not stop a Muslim from running for parliament, Ibn ʿAbd al-Khaliq says, since

> his entering parliament – while being a Muslim – does not compel him to participate, through his vote, in deciding on a law that clashes with the *sharīʿa*.

[4] ʿAbd al-Raḥmān b. ʿAbd al-Khāliq, *Al-Siyāsa al-Sharʿiyya fī l-Daʿwa ilá llāh* (Kuwait: Sharikat Bayt al-Maqdis li-l-Nashr wa-l-Tawzīʿ, 2006), 334.
[5] For more on this, see *ibid.*, 369–86. [6] *Ibid.*, 337.
[7] Muḥammad Abū Zayd Muṣṭafá, *Al-Mafhūm al-Salafī li-l-ʿAmal al-Siyāsī* (Riyadh: Maktabat Dār al-Salām, 1414 [1993/1994]), 16–19.
[8] See Q. 12. [9] Muṣṭafá, *Al-Mafhūm.*, 20. [10] *Ibid.*, 34. [11] *Ibid.*, 38–46.
[12] Muḥammad b. Maḥmūd al-Ṣāliḥ al-Sīlāwī, ed., *Ṣafaḥāt min Ḥayāt Dāʿiyat Faḍīlat al-Shaykh ʿAbd al-Raḥmān b. ʿAbd al-Khāliq* (n.p.: no publisher, 2007), 102–3.

It does not mean that he agrees with the man-made laws. In fact, he has entered [parliament] out of opposition to [such] laws and he wants their substitution and the substitution of the man-made constitution.[13]

Interestingly, Usama Shahada, a Palestinian-Jordanian baker from Amman and one of the most prominent "reformist" Salafis in Jordan not only supports such views but actually traces them back to al-Albani. Claiming that al-Albani was much more nuanced about political participation than the outright rejection that some of his students espouse now, he states that the shaykh's famous words "the good policy is to stay away from politics" actually constituted a political statement, not a religious one. According to Shahada, in other words, al-Albani simply meant that under the circumstances in which he lived at the time (a Syrian dictatorship), it was best to stay away from politics. This was not an absolute restriction, however, since al-Albani definitely believed in the validity of Islamic politics and even supported the election of Islamist parties if they were the least bad option available, Shahada states.[14] The author seems to say that if al-Albani had still been alive, he would have supported Shahada's point of view in this respect. This is obviously impossible to judge, but considering al-Albani's more nuanced views about participation in politics than what some of his more loyalist students preach today, it is clear that Shahada's attempt to appropriate the shaykh's legacy is not entirely far-fetched.

Ideas such as these entered Jordan through books and immigrants who had become acquainted with them through their experiences in (especially) Kuwait. It did not take long for them to be translated into action. The first and most prominent "reformist" organisation in Jordan doing so, the Jamʿiyyat al-Kitab wa-l-Sunna, was officially founded and registered with the Ministry of Culture in Amman in 1993.[15] Probably because it was registered with a ministry, it had to make extra sure that its activities would not raise the authorities' suspicion and, as a result, it focussed entirely on studying, teaching and preaching the Qurʾan and the Sunna in a way that seemingly did not differ much from what quietist Salafis had done for years.[16]

[13] *Ibid.*, 104.

[14] Shaḥāda, *Al-Daʿwa*, 69–70, 116–17, 138–9. For more on the author, see Abū Rummān, *Anā*, 172–80.

[15] "Liqāʾ 'al-Mirʾāt' maʿa Raʾīs Jamʿiyyat al-Kitāb wa-l-Sunna," *Al-Qibla* 1, no. 3 (2002): 36–7; Abū Rummān and Abū Haniyya, *Al-Ḥall*, 239; *id.*, *Al-Salafiyya al-Muḥāfaẓa*, 48; Dabbas, "Islamic," 239; Zāyid Ibrāhīm [Ḥammād], "Ḥawla Jamʿiyyat al-Kitāb wa-l-Sunna," *Al-Qibla* 4, nos. 10–11 (2005): 109; interview with Marwān Shaḥāda, Amman, 9 June 2012.

[16] Dabbas, "Islamic," 239–40; Wiktorowicz, *Management*, 129; *id.*, "Salafi," 227.

The difference between the Jamʿiyyat al-Kitab wa-l-Sunna and quietist Salafism was evident in several ways, one of which was its membership. As we saw in Chapter 5, quietist Salafis virtually always seem to have lived lives of piety and strong religiosity – albeit in "deviant" groups like the Muslim Brotherhood or the Jamaʿat al-Tabligh – before turning to Salafism. However, the early members of the Jamʿiyyat al-Kitab wa-l-Sunna were quite different. Hasan Abu Haniyya, for example, one of the group's founders and its first leader, was originally a man with leftist sympathies before becoming enamoured with Jihadi-Salafism. Similarly, one of Abu Haniyya's co-founders of the group, Marwan Shahada, was more motivated to join the group because of his pro-Palestinian militancy than by a long history of religiosity.[17]

Given the more diverse and also more overtly militant membership of the Jamʿiyyat al-Kitab wa-l-Sunna, it is perhaps not surprising that the group attracted quite a lot of unwanted attention from the authorities, especially given the rise of militant Islamist groups in the early 1990s that we saw before. State opposition to the Jamʿiyyat al-Kitab wa-l-Sunna was expressed in the long time it took the group to get a licence, threats against its members (including arrests and imprisonment for organising a supposedly dangerous political movement) and placing limits on its activities and ability to branch out to areas outside of East Amman.[18]

Because of the pressure applied to the Jamʿiyyat al-Kitab wa-l-Sunna, getting new members was difficult and even the existing leaders quit the group in the early 2000s.[19] Interestingly – and again showing the difference between the political Salafi mindset and that of quietists in Jordan – the members leaving the group generally did not remain loyal to their beliefs while fading into relative obscurity, like Murad Shukri, Muhammad Ibrahim Shaqra, Muhammad Abu Ruhayyim and Salim al-Hilali have done among quietists. Instead, they moved into entirely different directions. Some, like Abu Haniyya, Marwan Shahada and Ibrahim al-ʿAsʿas, became disillusioned with Salafism and pursued careers as researchers, using their personal experiences to inform others about Islamism. Others, like Waʾil al-Batiri and Bassam Nasir, made a name for themselves in journalism. Still others moved abroad or began working for the Jordanian government.[20] In fact, the man who briefly took over as temporary leader of the Jamʿiyyat al-Kitab wa-l-Sunna

[17] Interviews with Ḥasan Abū Haniyya, Amman, 9 August 2008, Amman, 9 June 2012; Marwān Shaḥāda, Amman, 9 June 2012. For more on Abū Haniyya, see Abū Rummān, *Anā*, 202–13.
[18] Wiktorowicz, *Management*, 129–31; *id.*, "Salafi," 227–8.
[19] Interview with Bassām Nāṣir, Amman, 16 June 2013.
[20] Interview with Marwān Shaḥāda, Amman, 11 January 2013.

after the group's implosion in the early 2000s, ʿAbd al-Fattah ʿUmar Abu l-Harith, emphasised his independence from any group since then.[21]

The Jamʿiyyat al-Kitab wa-l-Sunna has not been the only "reformist" Salafi organisation set up in Jordan, however. A few other organisations have also been founded that are said to have at least some "reformist" tendencies.[22] The most prominent of these is undoubtedly the Jamʿiyyat al-Irtiqaʾ al-Khayriyya (the Charitable Association of Progress),[23] which has its headquarters in Irbid. Founded in 2013 by Ihsan al-ʿUtaybi, another political Salafi from Kuwait strongly influenced by the writings of Ibn ʿAbd al-Khaliq, the Jamʿiyyat al-Irtiqaʾ al-Khayriyya became particularly active because of the Syrian civil war, which started in 2011 and brought a lot of refugees to Jordan.[24] Yet the organisation's current director, Ihsan al-ʿUtaybi's son Muʿadh, told me that the foundation of the group was *daʿwa*.[25] In fact, despite the group's name, its primary goals seem to be less related to charity than to studying and teaching the Qurʾan and the Sunna and spreading a message on the basis of these sources.[26]

Similarly influenced by Ibn ʿAbd al-Khaliq's writings and, more directly, by the political Salafism espoused by Ihsan al-ʿUtaybi is the Markaz Ibn Taymiyya al-Qurʾani (the Ibn Taymiyya Qurʾanic Centre), an institute of learning in the Palestinian refugee camp of al-Husn, near Irbid. Like the Jamʿiyyat al-Irtiqaʾ al-Khayriyya, it focusses on studying, teaching and *daʿwa* and it also dedicates some of its time and means to charity.[27] The latter also takes up a large part of the Jamʿiyyat al-Kitab wa-l-Sunna's time and money,[28] now under the guidance of Zayid Hammad,[29] who took over as leader from ʿAbd al-Fattah Abu l-Harith in the early 2000s. Much of this charity is directed towards the Syrian refugees in the north of Jordan, as the publications of the Jamʿiyyat al-Kitab wa-l-Sunna make clear.[30]

21 Interview with ʿAbd al-Fattāḥ ʿUmar Abū l-Ḥārith, Amman, 14 January 2013.
22 Interview with Marwān Shaḥāda, Amman, 9 June 2012.
23 Their website is located at www.alertiqaa.org/ (accessed 1 July 2015).
24 Interview with Iḥsān al-ʿUtaybī, Irbid, 28 January 2014.
25 Interview with Muʿādh al-ʿUtaybī, Irbid, 19 January 2014.
26 See *Jamʿiyyat al-Irtiqāʾ al-Khayriyya* (n.p.: no publisher, n.d.), 1–2. This is an information booklet given to me by Muʿādh al-ʿUtaybī.
27 Interview with Amīn al-Tubāsī, al-Ḥuṣn, 22 January 2014. Al-Tubāsī runs the Ibn Taymiyya Qurʾānic Centre.
28 Financially, the Jamʿiyyat al-Kitāb wa-l-Sunna is supported by Jordanians, but also by foreign donors from Kuwait, Qatar and Saudi Arabia. Interview with Aḥmad al-Dhuwayb, Amman, 15 January 2013. Al-Dhuwayb is the deputy director of Jamʿiyyat al-Kitāb wa-l-Sunna. See also www.youtube.com/watch?v=OjB6dm3E2Qs (from 13: 03, a list of donors is mentioned; accessed 1 July 2015).
29 For more on this man, see Abū Rummān, *Anā*, 159–71.
30 *ʿAṭāʾ bi-lā Ḥudūd* (n.p.: Jamʿiyyat al-Kitāb wa-l-Sunna, 2013); "Wafd min Jamʿiyyat al-Kitāb wa-l-Sunna Yushāriku fī Muʾtamar al-Āthār al-Nafsiyya wa-l-Ijtimāʿiyya

Considering the strong emphasis on Salafi *daʿwa* and charitable activities by political Salafi organisations, one could wonder what is so "reformist" about them and what distinguishes them from quietist Salafism. Indeed, partly for this reason, Muhammad Abu Rumman, a Jordanian journalist and expert on Islamist movements in the kingdom, has told me on several occasions that political Salafism does not really exist in Jordan.[31] Still, there are quite a number of Salafis who associate with this trend[32] and there is a clear difference between "reformist" Salafism in Jordan and the country's quietism. This difference lies in (a) the much broader range of topics that they deal with in their discourse, not limiting themselves to points of doctrinal purity at all, and (b) their willingness to engage with society through what they refer to as "*al-ʿamal*" (action). This attempt to make Salafism an ideology of public affairs is what makes it political, at least in their eyes.

As one "reformist" Salafi writer puts it, the rejection of public affairs by quietists "alienates the adherents to this [quietist Salafi] trend from the major and general issues of the *umma*, its concerns and its pains and separates the *daʿwa* from the reality and problems of the Muslims". This, in turn, "has disastrous consequences for the Salafi *daʿwa* itself", he writes. In such a scenario, "its fate will only be failure [...] and it will never constitute an effective movement for change (*ḥaraka taghyīriyya fāʿila*) [...] capable of returning the *umma* to its glories".[33] These words show precisely the basic difference between quietists and the Jamʿiyyat al-Kitab wa-l-Sunna, to whose specific ideology we must turn now.

The Ideology of the Jamʿiyyat al-Kitab wa-l-Sunna

Having started out as a rather heterogeneous group that also included Jihadi-Salafis, the Jamʿiyyat al-Kitab wa-l-Sunna was shut down in the early 2000s, but revived after members raised the matter in court and

li-l-Thawra al-Sūriyya," *Al-Qibla* 10, no. 23 (2012): 83–5; "Ahamm Injāzāt al-Jamʿiyya fī Ighāthat al-Lājiʾīn al-Sūriyyīn fī l-Urdunn," *Al-Qibla* 9, no. 22 (2012): 79–83; "Ahamm Injāzāt al-Jamʿiyya fī Ighāthat al-Lājiʾīn al-Sūriyyīn fī l-Urdunn," *Al-Qibla* 10, no. 23 (2012): 86–8. See also Sturla Godø Sæther, "Humanitarian Salafism: A Contradition in Terms? A Study of the Salafi Organisation 'The Book and the Sunna Society' and Their Efforts in Relief Work in Jordan" (MA thesis, University of Oslo, 2013).

31 Interviews with Muḥammab Abū Rummān, Amman, 11 August 2008, Amman, 19 June 2012.

32 One long-time political Salafī told me that the number of "reformists" may be as big as a third of the total number of Salafīs in the kingdom, which would amount to a few thousand persons.

33 Hishām ʿUlyān, "Al-Daʿwa al-Salafiyya ... Mulāḥaẓāt Naqdiyya," *Al-Qibla* 1, no. 3 (2002): 34–5.

were given permission to reopen the group's main branch in Amman.[34] Since then, under the direction of the activist Zayid Hammad, the group has become more narrowly "reformist" and more active as a charitable organisation.[35] Nowadays, the group's activities are spread over several branches across the country and – besides charitable action for Syrian refugees – include *daʿwa*, lessons, publishing a magazine (*Al-Qibla*) and organising summer camps for children.[36] Besides this engagement in public affairs, the ideology expressed by its members also remains explicitly political.

General Ideology

Although the Jamʿiyyat al-Kitab wa-l-Sunna does not have an ideological "programme" or a fixed set of ideas, the organisation does constitute a platform for "reformist" Salafis in Jordan who have a fairly homogeneous ideology. In many ways, "reformist" Salafi ideology is no different from the ideas espoused by the kingdom's quietist Salafis, however. This begins with the contested nature of the label "Salafism". According to Usama Shahada, it simply means "following the Book and the Sunna according to the way of the noble companions [of the Prophet Muhammad] in creed, jurisprudence, morals, method and [Islamically] legitimate politics".[37] The interpretation of these words (particularly the last few on politics) by "reformist" Salafis differ from the one adhered to by quietists, but the same words could, in principle, have been uttered by al-Halabi, for example.[38]

The division of Salafis into quietists, politicos and jihadis is something that "reformists" – like quietists – reject. They avoid the terms "traditional Salafism" and "knowledge Salafism",[39] which are mostly used to refer to quietists in Jordan. Waʾil al-Batiri, a former member of Jamʿiyyat al-Kitab wa-l-Sunna, even goes so far as to equate this trend with "the pledge of allegiance to the Arab rulers, listening to and obeying them for

[34] Interview with Marwān Shaḥāda, Amman, 11 January 2013.

[35] Interviews with ʿAbd al-Fattāḥ ʿUmar Abū l-Ḥārith, Amman, 14 January 2013; Zāyid Ḥammād, Amman, 19 January 2013.

[36] Ḥammād, "Ḥawla," 110; interviews with Zāyid Ḥammād, Amman, 19 January 2013; Marwān Shaḥāda, Amman, 11 January 2013.

[37] Shaḥāda, *Al-Daʿwa*, 16–17. See also *ibid.*, 28, where the author gives a slightly more detailed yet similar definition, and 76–9, where Shaḥāda explains what he means by the different elements of his definition.

[38] Other, similar definitions of Salafism by political Salafis in Jordan can be found in ʿAṣr b. Muḥammad al-Naṣr, "Al-Salafiyya al-Muʿāṣira: Ishkāliyyat al-Tārīkh wa-l-Khiṭāb," *Al-Qibla* 11, no. 24 (2013): 31–7; interview with ʿAbd al-Fattāh ʿUmar Abū l-Ḥārith, Amman, 14 January 2013.

[39] Shaḥāda, *Al-Daʿwa*, 16.

better or for worse (*fī l-munshiṭ wa-l-mukrah*) at a time when it calls [on people] to 'leave politics!' and [for] commitment to 'discrete advice' to the authorities". He also accuses quietist Salafis of being close to repressive leaders and concludes: "If this is knowledge [Salafism], welcome ignorance!! If it is correct to describe this 'Salafism' as 'knowledge', it is no more appropriate than describing the devil as the shaykh of Islam!!"[40]

"Reformist" Salafis are just as negative about Jihadi-Salafis. Like quietists, they deny that these are really Salafis.[41] They are blamed for applying *takfīr* to Muslims, waging jihad illegitimately and killing innocent people.[42] Shahada is particularly critical of Jordanian researchers Abu Rumman and Abu Haniyya for presenting Salafism as divided into three different branches, of which Jihadi-Salafism is one, which – in his view – is "not the result of a deep and wide study of the Salafi reality".[43] According to him, "Salafism has been a unified and unifying method (*manhaj mūḥad wa-mūḥid*) throughout history", it just differed slightly based on the context in which it found itself.[44] Shahada's alternative approach of Salafism is therefore to look at self-proclaimed Salafi organisations and see what kind of activities they engage in to know where they stand.[45]

As with quietists, political Salafis' rejection of both the term "Jihadi-Salafism" and the ideas of its adherents does not mean that they reject jihad. The latter concept, they say, is not beholden to Jihadi-Salafis. In fact, they roundly condemn the type of terrorist attacks usually associated with Jihadi-Salafism,[46] including the hotel bombings in Amman in 2005, to which several articles in a special issue of *Al-Qibla* were dedicated.[47] The concept of jihad itself, however, is described by

[40] Wāʾil ʿAlī al-Batīrī, "Al-Salafiyya 'al-Lā ʿIlmiyya'," *Al-Sabīl*, May 16, 2014, 6.

[41] Usāma Shaḥāda, *Laysa min al-Salafiyya fī l-Shayʾ* (http://osamash.maktoobblog.com/date/2009/11/, 20 November 2009 (website no longer available)).

[42] *Khabīr: Al-Khunūj min al-Ḥalqa al-Mufarragha bi-l-Urdunn Yaqtaḍī l-Iṣlāḥ* (http://main.islammessage.com/newspage.aspx?id=8380, 23 April 2011 (accessed 3 July 2015)); Shaḥādā, *Al-Daʿwa*, 16–17.

[43] Shaḥāda, *Al-Daʿwa*, 15–16. The words cited are on 15. [44] *Ibid.*, 24.

[45] *Ibid.*, 18–19.

[46] Abū Ḥamza Sayyid b. Muḥammad al-Minyāwī, *Talkhīṣ Fitnat al-Tafjīrāt wa-l-Ightiyālāt: Al-Asbāb – al-Āthār – al-ʿIlāj* (Amman: Jamʿiyyat al-Kitāb wa-l-Sunna – Lajnat al-Kalima al-Ṭayyiba, n.d.); Shaḥāda, *Al-Daʿwa*, 38–43, 47–58, 199–274.

[47] "Mutābaʿāt ... Mutābaʿāt ... Mutābaʿāt ... Mutābaʿāt ...," *Al-Qibla* 2, nos. 10–11 (2005): 98–108; Muḥammad al-ʿAbda, "Ḥayna Tataghallabu l-ʿĀṭifa," *Al-Qibla* 2, nos. 10–11 (2005): 94; Salmān b. Fahd al-ʿAwda, "Al-Qatl bi-Dam Bārid," *Al-Qibla* 2, nos. 10–11 (2005): 95–7; Lajnat al-Buḥūth wa-l-Dirāsāt, "Al-Nafs al-Maʿṣūma ... wa-l-Tatarrus: Aḥwāl ... wa-Aḥkām," *Al-Qibla* 2, nos. 10–11 (2005): 77–89; Shaḥāda, *Al-Daʿwa*, 44–6; ʿIṣām Zaydān, "Tafjīrāt ʿAmmān ... Tasāʾulāt ḥawla l-Hadaf wa-l-Mashrūʿ," *Al-Qibla* 2, nos. 10–11 (2005): 90–3.

"reformist" Salafis in Jordan as a legitimate military means to defend the *umma*[48] and as subject to certain rules that ensure that everything done conforms to the *sharīʿa*.[49]

Although political Salafis spend far more time talking about politics and society than quietists, they do focus on the things that all Salafis care about, such as the Qurʾan,[50] the study of *ḥadīth*s,[51] distancing themselves from early Islamic trends they disagree with,[52] *al-walāʾ wa-l-barāʾ*[53] and the question of faith.[54] With regard to the latter topic, the leader of the Jamʿiyyat al-Kitab wa-l-Sunna, Zayid Hammad, clearly distances himself from Jordanian quietists by stating that they only see acts as a condition of faith and thus of lesser value than belief in the heart and speech with the tongue, while "reformists" see acts as a full and integral part of faith.[55]

Other areas in which "reformist" Salafis strongly resemble their quietist brethren include their views on Shiʿas and women. Concerning the former, the publications by especially Usama Shahada, who has written a lot about Shiʿas, are just as negative about them as the writings by quietists, yet they focus more on the political role of Iran and alleged Shiʿi conspiracies working against supposed Sunni interests.[56] With regard to women, political Salafis seem to share quietists' conservatism, pointing out the need for and supposed benefits of headscarves,[57] the prohibition

48 Shaḥāda, *Al-Daʿwa*, 42–3.

49 Zāyid Ḥammād, "'Wa-Qātilū fī Sabīl Allāh . . . '," *Al-Qibla* 2, nos. 10–11 (2005): 10–13; Shaḥāda, *Al-Daʿwa*, 60–3.

50 Ṣalāḥ ʿAbd al-Fattāḥ al-Khālidī, "Ḥawla Nuzūl al-Qurʾān wa-Tanazzulātihi," *Al-Qibla* 11, no. 24 (2013): 11–14; Aḥmad Salīm, "Al-Iltifāt fī l-Qurʾān al-Karīm," *Al-Qibla* 11, no. 24 (2013): 15–19; Usāma Shaḥāda, "Maqāṣid al-Qurʾān," *Al-Qibla* 6, no. 16 (2008): 10–23.

51 ʿIdāb Maḥmūd al-Ḥamsh, "Al-Ḥadīth al-Jayyid ʿinda ʿUlamāʾ al-Rijāl ḥattá Nihāyat al-Qarn al-Rābiʿ," *Al-Qibla* 2, nos. 4–5 (2003): 88–103.

52 Usāma Shaḥāda, *Ḥālat al-Khawārij – Khaṭar al-Inḥirāf ʿan Manhaj al-Ṣaḥāba 1* (http://osamash.maktoobblog.com/date/2011/02/, 1 February 2011 (website no longer available)); *id.*, *Ḥālat al-Jabriyya wa-l-Qadariyya – Khaṭar al-Inḥirāf ʿan Manhaj al-Ṣaḥāba 2* (http://osamash.maktoobblog.com/date/2011/02/, 19 February 2011 (website no longer available)).

53 "Rukn al-Fatāwá," *Al-Qibla* 6, no. 16 (2008): 108.

54 Ibrāhīm Sarḥān, "Mawqif al-Ashāʿira min Ḥaqīqat al-Īmān," *Al-Qibla* 6, no. 16 (2008): 24–36.

55 "Liqāʾ 'al-Mirʾāt'," 38.

56 Zāyid Ḥammād, "Al-Shīʿa wa-Filasṭīn," *Al-Qibla* 6, no. 16 (2008): 78–95; Shaḥāda, *Al-Daʿwa*, 81–82; *id.*, "Limādhā Yufshilu l-Shīʿa Masīrat al-Waḥda al-Islāmiyya??" *Al-Qibla* 7, no. 18 (2009): 66–75; *id.*, *Min Tārīkh al-Ḥarakāt al-Islāmiyya maʿa l-Shīʿa wa-Īrān* (www.alrased.net, n.d.); *id.*, *Al-Mushkila al-Shīʿiyya* (www.alrased.net, 2008); *id.*, *Al-Sunna wa-l-Shīʿa: Ruʾya Wāqiʿiyya* (www.alrased.net, 2010); *id.*, "Al-Tashayyuʿ fī Khidmat al-Mashrūʿ al-Īrānī," *Al-Qibla* 6, no. 17 (2008): 78–80.

57 "Al-Ḥijāb," *Al-Qibla* 2, nos. 4–5 (2003): 200–3; Sāmī Najīb, "Ḥattá Lā Yakūna l-Ḥijāb Zayna," *Al-Qibla* 7, no. 18 (2009): 59–65.

of allowing women to be imams to men,[58] the idea that gender-mixing is not allowed,[59] the allegedly great number of rights that women have in Islam[60] and how Western initiatives to improve women's position in Muslim societies should be rejected as cultural invasions.[61]

Views on Politics

As similar as the general ideology of political Salafis connected with the Jamʿiyyat al-Kitab wa-l-Sunna may be to the basic ideas espoused by quietists, they are not the same. The differences between them become clearer when we look more closely at the "reformist" worldview and how their ideas on politics fit into this. As Usama Shahada told me: "States are founded on the principle that the people are a partner [in governing]. There is a left-wing partner, a secular one, a [Muslim] Brotherhood one, a nationalist one and a liberal one. Yet the Salafi one does not participate. Why [not]?"[62] This frustration over (Jordanian) quietists' unwillingness to get involved in politics is one indication of this difference, yet Shahada's complaint is not just related to direct involvement with the state, but is embedded in a more extensive and broader mindset that is specific to "reformist" Salafis.

The aforementioned former Salafi Ibrahim al-ʿAsʿas, who used to be a member of the Jamʿiyyat al-Kitab wa-l-Sunna, gives an indication of this political Salafi mindset by calling for "the revival of the culture of criticism (*thaqāfat al-naqd*) and the rejection of the culture of silence (*thaqāfat al-ṣamt*)".[63] Central in this "culture of criticism" is the concept of "change" (*taghyīr*). Citing Q. 13: 11 ("God changes not what is in a people (*inna llāh lā yughayyiru mā bi-qawm*), until they change what is in themselves (*ḥattá yughayyirū mā bi-anfusihim*)"), al-ʿAsʿas argues that

58 Aḥmad al-Dhuwayb, "Imāmat al-Marʾa," *Al-Qibla* 4, nos. 10–11 (2004): 14–18; Usāma Shaḥāda, *Taqwīḍ al-Islām min Dākhilihi … Imāmat al-Marʾa Numūdhajan* (http://osamash.maktoobblog.com/date/2010/06/, 27 June 2010 (website no longer available)).

59 Luṭf Allāh b. ʿAbd al-ʿAẓīm Khūja, "Kayfa Buniya Taḥrīm al-Ikhtilāṭ?" *Al-Qibla* 8, no. 20 (2010): 16–29.

60 Usāma Shaḥāda, *Iʿṭāʾ al-Nisāʾ Jamīʿ Ḥuqūqihinna l-Insāniyya wa-l-Dīniyya wa-l-Madaniyya* (http://osamash.maktoobblog.com/date/2007/09, 28 July 2007 (website no longer available)); *id., Mīrāth al-Marʾa Laysa Niṣf Mīrāth al-Rajul!!* (http://osamash.maktoobblog.com/date/2010/07/, 18 July 2010 (website no longer available)).

61 *Id., Ittifāqiyyat Sīdāw … bi-dūna Makyāj* (http://osamash.maktoobblog.com/date/2012/11/, 24 November 2012 (website no longer available)); *id., Marra Ukhrá … Limādhā Narfuḍu ttifāqiyyat Sīdāw* (http://osamash.maktoobblog.com/date/2013/01/, 18 January 2013 (website no longer available)).

62 Interview with Usāma Shaḥāda, Amman, 7 June 2012.

63 Ibrāhīm al-ʿAsʿas, *Raṣd al-Ẓawāhir – Hakadhā Naḥnu* … (n.p.: no publisher, 2011), 5.

people should have the will, the capacity and the "correct knowledge" to change.[64]

This may sound a bit vague, perhaps, and al-ʿAsʿas goes on to write things that members of the Jamʿiyyat al-Kitab wa-l-Sunna do not necessarily agree with, but one can nevertheless hear echoes of Shahada's lament about the lack of Salafi participation in this concept of a "culture of criticism". The idea that Salafis should actively participate in deciding about issues related to society and politics and view political developments (including the policies of the ruler) critically, rather than standing on the sidelines and simply accepting things as they are, is not only suggested by al-ʿAsʿas[65] but is also the basis of political Salafism in Jordan. Indeed, the concept of "reform" (*iṣlāḥ*) not only has a positive connotation for Muslims in general[66] but also forms one of the key terms used by "reformist" Salafis in Jordan today.

This attitude of wanting to engage in societal or political action to bring about change is typical of "reformist" Salafis in Jordan (including those of the Jamʿiyyat al-Kitab wa-l-Sunna), not because it is any less utopian than quietists' approach, but because it is more explicitly grounded in present-day reality. This also explains why political Salafis are more committed to social and political action: rather than investing only in people's eternal future in Paradise by cleansing and teaching various aspects of Islamic tradition that may one day result in a utopian Islamic state, as quietists do, "reformists" take a much greater interest in what goes on in the real world and are therefore far more willing to invest in the temporary aspects of life here on earth.

Political Salafis' greater interest in public affairs is evident from, for instance, their writings on the (growing) phenomenon of Western non-Muslim scholars studying Islam.[67] explanations of the economic crisis gripping much of the world in the late 2000s and early 2010s[68] and political analyses of foreign affairs.[69] An example of the latter is the Palestinian–Israeli conflict. While quietists nowadays, as we saw above,

64 *Ibid.*, 6–7. 65 *Ibid.*, 72.

66 Voll, "Renewal," 32–47. The word "*iṣlāḥ*" or linguistically related terms are often used positively in the Qurʾān. See, for example, Q. 2: 220; 4: 114; 11: 88.

67 "Ḥattá Tattabiʿu Millatahum," *Al-Qibla* 6, no. 16 (2008): 5–9; Ḥasan Abū Haniyya, "Al-Istishrāq wa-Tashkīl al-Ṣūra al-Namaṭiyya li-l-Islām," *Al-Qibla* 4, nos. 10–1 (2005): 27–36; Marwān Muḥammad Rushdī, "Al-Tarbiya al-Islāmiyya wa-l-Taḥaddiyāt al-ʿAqdiyya," *Al-Qibla* 7, no. 18 (2009): 45–8.

68 "Fa-dhanū bi-Ḥarb min Allāh wa-Rasūlihi – Azmat al-Rahn al-ʿAqārī," *Al-Qibla* 7, no. 18 (2009): 4–6; Tawfīq al-Jayyūsī, "Makhāṭir al-Ribā: Al-Ijtimāʿiyya wa-l-Iqtiṣādiyya," *Al-Qibla* 7, no. 18 (2009): 18–26; ʿAlāʾ al-Dīn Taysīr, "Al-Mushāraka al-Mutanāqiṣa," *Al-Qibla* 9, no. 21 (2011): 56–8.

69 Mūsá ʿAbd al-Raḥmān, "Al-Muslimūn fī l-Ṣīn," *Al-Qibla* 8, no. 20 (2010): 39–44; Muḥammad ʿĀdil ʿAql, "Turkiyā ... Qiṣṣat Najāḥ," *Al-Qibla* 10, no. 23 (2012): 70–2;

write about this dispute in terms of commitment to Islam, urging Palestinians to be pious, "reformist" Salafis deal with the conflict in different terms. Although they also write about, for example, the role of Jews or the Holy Land in the Qurʾan[70] or how the conflict could be a sign of end times,[71] "reformist" Salafis mostly focus on a much more narrowly political analysis of the dispute between Israelis and Palestinians. They write, for example, on alleged Israeli policies to undermine the al-Aqsa Mosque in Jerusalem and turn that city into an entirely Jewish one[72] or about supposed Israeli crimes against the Palestinians and what they see as the right of the latter to resist this through jihad.[73]

This is not to say that quietists never mention such things. (In fact, as we saw in Chapter 2, they do.) Yet analyses of international politics – even if only from a religious point of view – have become increasingly rare among Jordanian quietist scholars as the movement has turned more and more loyalist and has focussed much more narrowly on doctrinal and ritual "purity" in everyday life. "Reformists" therefore not only add a dimension that is lacking among today's leading quietist scholars but also seem to want to hold on to the much broader Salafi discourse from al-Albani's days, even if their method of applying this is different from the shaykh's.

In the discourse of "reformist" Salafis, a greater interest in public affairs is naturally accompanied by a wider application of "reform" than the one applied by quietists. While the latter strive to "reform" the scriptural tradition of Islam and, by extension, people's personal beliefs, political Salafis are willing to use Islam to tackle all kinds of problems. Usama Shahada, for example, points out that the reform he and other political Salafis in Jordan strive for goes back centuries and connects them with other reformers across the Middle East.[74] In fact, he even claims that

Zāyid Ibrāhīm Ḥammād, "Abʿād al-Tamarrud al-Ḥūthī fī l-Yaman," *Al-Qibla* 8, no. 20 (2010): 56–60.

70 "Filasṭīn fī l-Qurʾān al-Karīm . . . al-Arḍ al-Mubāraka," *Al-Qibla* 1, no. 2 (2002): 22–3; "Taʿriyat Banī Isrāʾīl Kamā Ṣawwarathā Āyāt al-Tanzīl," *Al-Qibla* 1, no. 2 (2002): 26–37; Bassām Nāṣir, "Ḥaqāʾiq al-Qurʾān Takshifu Khabāʾith al-Yahūd li-l-ʿIyān," *Al-Qibla* 1, no. 2 (2002): 17–21.

71 ʿAbd al-Fattāḥ ʿUmar [Abū l-Ḥārith], "Qitāl al-Muslimīn li-l-Yahūd . . . Hal Huwa Murtabaṭ bi-Ashrāṭ al-Sāʿa?!" *Al-Qibla* 1, no. 3 (2002): 61–5.

72 "Al-Quds Tuwājihu . . . 'al-Kharāb'," *Al-Qibla* 8, no. 20 (2010): 4–8; Muḥammad ʿĀyish, "Al-Masjid al-Aqṣá . . . Al-Nidāʾ Mā Qabla l-Akhīr . . . !" *Al-Qibla* 1, no. 2 (2002): 10–12; Jaʿfar Hādī Ḥasan, "Tahwīd al-Quds Yashmalu Bināʾ al-Haykal," *Al-Qibla* 1, no. 2 (2002): 24–5.

73 "Bayān min Jamʿiyyat al-Kitāb wa-l-Sunna bi-Khuṣūṣ Aḥdāth Ghazza," *Al-Qibla* 7, no. 18 (2009): 1; "Min Dayr Yāsīn ilá Janīn . . . al-Qātil Wāḥid," *Al-Qibla* 1, no. 2 (2002): 1.

74 Usāma Shaḥāda, *Min Tārīkh al-Iṣlāḥ al-Muʿāṣir* (http://osamash.maktoobblog.com/date/2011/04/, 13 April 2011 (website no longer available)).

reform was "the *manhaj* of the prophets".[75] As such, reform should not only be applied to the scriptural tradition of Islam, Shahada maintains, but also to one's own personality in order to become a better person.[76] to the entire Muslim community, legislation and the judiciary,[77] as well as to people's dialogue with secularism[78] and to tackling poverty.[79]

Particularly this last example suggests a hands-on approach – poverty is, after all, not alleviated by studying texts – and the Jamʿiyyat al-Kitab wa-l-Sunna provides exactly that through its charitable work among Syrian refugees. This approach of commitment to improving society is also apparent in the organisation's writings. One article in *Al-Qibla*, for instance, argues for a greater engagement with society by making sure that their discourse is understandable to both "the elite" (*al-khāṣṣa*) and the general population (*al-ʿāmma*).[80] To underline this desire to make sure that the Salafi *daʿwa* is not too complicated for people to understand, the Jamʿiyyat al-Kitab wa-l-Sunna has, for example, published a booklet containing brief and easy Qurʾanic exegesis.[81] Another article in *Al-Qibla* discusses the state of "Islamic action" in Jordan, reviewing the challenges of engaging with Jordanian society in an Islamic way, evaluating what has been achieved already and the positive and negative aspects of various Islamist movements.[82]

Such engagement with society and commitment to "Islamic action" suggest that the Jamʿiyyat al-Kitab wa-l-Sunna is more tolerant of other Islamic groups than quietist Salafis are and this does indeed seem to be the case with regard to the Jamaʿat al-Tabligh and the Muslim Brotherhood. Although "reformists" question the Jamaʿat al-Tabligh's commitment to scholarly knowledge – as do quietists – it is looked at favourably because of its activism, expressed in taking to the streets to share its message.[83] The Jamʿiyyat al-Kitab wa-l-Sunna seems to have an

[75] *Id., Al-Iṣlāḥ Manhaj al-Anbiyāʾ* (http://osamash.maktoobblog.com/date/2011/03/, 19 March 2011 (website no longer available)).

[76] *Id., Maʿālim al-Shakhṣiyya al-Iṣlāḥiyya* (http://osamash.maktoobblog.com/date/2011/04, 2 April 2011 (website no longer available)).

[77] *Id., Al-Iṣlāḥ al-Insānī al-Ijtimāʿī al-Siyāsī al-Waṭanī* (http://osamash.maktoobblog.com/date/2007/09, 28 September 2007 (website no longer available)).

[78] Bassām Nāṣir, "Al-Ijtihād wa-l-Tajdīd fī Ḥiwār ʿAlmānī Uṣūlī," *Al-Qibla* 4, nos. 10–11 (2005): 19–26.

[79] Sāmī Najīb Rashīd, "ʿIlāj Mushkilat al-Faqr," *Al-Qibla* 6, no. 17 (2008): 69–77.

[80] Muḥammad al-Duwaysh, "Al-Khiṭāb al-Daʿwī bayna l-ʿĀmma wa-l-Khāṣṣa," *Al-Qibla* 1, nos. 4–5 (2003): 7–8.

[81] Jamāl Yūsuf al-Humaylī, *Laṭāʾif al-Ishārāt fī Tafsīr Qiṣār Suwar al-Qurʾān* (Amman: Jamʿiyyat al-Kitāb wa-l-Sunna – Lajnat al-Kalima al-Ṭayyiba, 2012), 4–6.

[82] Muḥammad Sulaymān, "Ḥālat al-ʿAmal al-Islāmī fī l-Urdunn," *Al-Qibla* 2, nos. 4–5 (2003): 61–77.

[83] Bassām Nāṣir, "Jamāʿat al-Tablīgh wa-Hidāyat al-ʿIlm," *Al-Qibla* 2, nos. 4–5 (2003): 9–12.

even more nuanced attitude towards the Muslim Brotherhood. While "reformists" also suggest that the Brotherhood is not interested in knowledge and does not produce scholars,[84] they express far less hostility to them than quietists do. Deputy director of the Jamʿiyyat al-Kitab wa-l-Sunna Ahmad al-Dhuwayb told me that, despite ideological differences, his organisation cooperates with the Brotherhood whenever the situation – be it Syrian refugees or other charitable activities – demands this and that there is no clash between the two groups.[85] In fact, the more hawkish scholars associated with the Brotherhood sometimes even publish in *Al-Qibla*,[86] and Usama Shahada has even defended the group against negative regime-supported media attention.[87]

While there is clearly disagreement between Salafis in general and the Muslim Brotherhood over doctrinal issues, the latter's active engagement in parliamentary politics is certainly not held against them by "reformists", as quietists do. Particularly Usama Shahada has written about this issue. To him, politics and political participation are important parts of Islam and prominent Muslim leaders, from the Prophet himself to twentieth-century reformers, have shown that engaging in decision-making with regard to the ruling of a state – be it through relations with the rulers or opposition movements against colonial powers – is allowed.[88]

Interestingly, Shahada also describes what the desired outcome of such political participation – an Islamic state – should look like, based on the practices of the first caliphs. An Islamic state, Shahada claims, should be based on *ṭāʿa* and *bayʿa* to the leader,[89] but this should be done with the consent of the people, not by force, since the ruler is "an agent (*wakīl*) from the *umma* [working] in the administration of its affairs". The relationship between the ruler and the ruled should therefore not be one of oppressor and oppressed, but should be a contract between them in which the Muslims are a full partner who get a say in choosing their leader.[90]

[84] "Fī Ḥiwār," 98–9. [85] Interview with Aḥmad al-Dhuwayb, Amman, 15 January 2013.
[86] See, for instance, al-Khālidī, "Ḥawla"; *id.*, "Al-Tafsīr bi-l-Raʾy: Mafhūm wa-Ḍawābiṭ," *Al-Qibla* 10, no. 23 (2012): 12–15.
[87] Usāma Shaḥāda, *Munāṣara wa-Munāṣaḥa li-Jamāʿat al-Ikhwān al-Muslimīn* (http://osamash.maktoobblog.com/date/2012/12/, 8 December 2012 (website no longer available)).
[88] *Id.*, *Al-Daʿwa*, 64–9. [89] *Ibid.*, 93–4.
[90] *Id.*, *Khaṭar al-Inḥirāf ʿan Manhaj al-Ṣaḥāba 3 – Al-ʿAwda li-l-Thiyūqrāṭiyya* (http://osamash.maktoobblog.com/date/2011/02/, 19 February 2011 (website no longer available)); *id.*, *Al-Taṭawwur al-Siyāsī fī Dawlat al-Khulafāʾ al-Rāshidīn* (http://osamash.maktoobblog.com/date/2010/12/, 19 December 2010 (website no longer available)); *id.*, *Usus Dawlat al-Khulafāʾ al-Rāshidīn* (http://osamash.maktoobblog.com/date/2010/12, 19 December 2010 (website no longer available)). The words cited can be found in *ibid.*

It is the role Usama Shahada ascribes to the people that sets him and other members of the Jamʿiyyat al-Kitab wa-l-Sunna apart from their quietist brethren. While his mentioning of concepts like *ṭāʿa* and *bayʿa* suggests that he does not differ much from quietists, this is not the case. As Ahmad al-Dhuwayb states, Muslims should obey their leaders, but the latter should also obey God. If this is not the case, believers do not have to obey their leaders anymore either.[91] Thus, unlike quietists' support for rulers, which is rooted in ideology as well as a deep fear of chaos and anarchy, "reformists" obedience to leaders is conditional and hinges on their application of the *sharīʿa*, which some argue may be done gradually.[92]

As such, "reformists" get the people involved as a partner in political power in ways that quietists do not, which is one way of justifying the application of the *sharīʿa*: according to Shahada, Islam and the *sharīʿa* are "the basis of our country", as evidenced by state-sanctioned rituals such as Friday prayers, the fasting during Ramadan and Islamically inspired slogans. Thus, Islam and the *sharīʿa* are not imposed, but the choice of the people. Both Jordanian and Western secularists complaining about Salafi politics for being overtly Islamic, Usama Shahada writes, must therefore stop thinking that participation in politics is necessarily framed in secular terms and should, instead, get used to the idea that Muslims need not conform to their rules of the political game to be accepted.[93]

The above may suggest that "reformist" Salafis in Jordan accept democracy, but this is not the case. Although they seem to support the means of democracy (elections, term limits, etcetera), the idea of the people being ultimately in power clashes, they claim, with the idea that God is sovereign and the ultimate arbiter in the legal sphere. The *sharīʿa*, in other words, cannot be made subject to the will of the people. The latter therefore has to conform to the rules of Islam, not the other way around.[94] Usama Shahada, however, also doubts that democracy really

[91] Aḥmad al-Dhuwayb, "Ḥuqūq al-Ḥākim," *Al-Qibla* 9, no. 21 (2011): 59–63.

[92] Ḥasan Taysīr Shumūṭ, "Al-Tadarruj fī Taṭbīq al-Sharīʿa bayna l-Sharʿ wa-l-Wāqiʿ," *Al-Qibla* 10, no. 23 (2012): 16–19; Raʾfat Yaʿqūb, "Al-Tadarruj fī Taḥkīm al-Sharīʿa," *Al-Qibla* 10, no. 23 (2012): 20–30.

[93] Usāma Shaḥāda, *Al-Salafiyya wa-Asʾilat al-Mushāraka al-Siyāsiyya – 1* (http://osamash.maktoobblog.com/date/2012/10/, 13 October 2012 (website no longer available)); *id.*, *Al-Salafiyya wa-Asʾilat al-Mushāraka al-Siyāsiyya – 2* (http://osamash.maktoobblog.com/date/2012/10/, 19 October 2012 (website no longer available)). The words cited can be found in *ibid.*

[94] ʿIṣām Aḥmad, "Ḥaqīqat al-Dīmuqrāṭiyya," *Al-Qibla* 11, no. 24 (2013): 20–9; Usāma Shaḥāda, *Al-Salafiyya wa-Asʾilat al-Mushāraka al-Siyāsiyya – 3* (http://osamash.maktoobblog.com/date/2012/11/, 8 November 2012 (website no longer available)); ʿAbd al-Raḥīm b. Ṣamāyil al-Sulmī, "Siyādat al-Sharīʿa … 'al-Ḥadd al-Fāṣil bayna l-Islām wa-l-ʿAlmāniyya'," *Al-Qibla* 9, no. 22 (2012): 9–13.

constitutes "rule by the people", claiming that the large number of people who do not vote or may not vote (such as children or prisoners) as well as the influence of special interest groups and lobbies make a mockery of the idea of democracy as "rule by the people".[95] He also implicitly accuses secularists of not being true and consistent democrats, because if they were they would accept the people's democratic vote for Islamists.[96] It is precisely this scenario that became a concrete reality with the advent of the "Arab Spring".

Views on the "Arab Spring"

As mentioned, the revolutions in the Arab world brought about a wave of new political participation, with many people claiming their role in ruling their respective countries. Considering what "reformists" affiliated with the Jamʿiyyat al-Kitab wa-l-Sunna write on a "culture of criticism", "change", reform and political participation, it seems obvious that they would support such revolutions and this is indeed the case. *Al-Qibla*, for instance, published several articles that deal with the revolt against Syrian President Bashar al-Asad as a positive development and consider the various means and the legitimacy of overthrowing his regime.[97] Similarly, the Jamʿiyyat al-Kitab wa-l-Sunna's leader, Zayid Hammad, believes that the removal of dictatorships in the Arab world is a good thing and he sees it as the fulfilment of people's decades-old dreams,[98] a feeling shared by other "reformist" Salafis in Jordan.[99]

The belief that the "Arab Spring" is the culmination of long-term efforts by people in the Middle East to bring about change in their societies is particularly true with regard to Islamists, writes deputy director of the Jamʿiyyat al-Kitab wa-l-Sunna Ahmad al-Dhuwayb. These various types of Islamists, he claims, have a long history of striving for political reform. Through groups such as the Islamic Liberation Party, the Muslim Brotherhood and the Algerian Front Islamique du Salut as well as

95 Usāma Shaḥāda, *Al-Siyāda al-Shaʿbiyya … Al-Ukdhūba al-ʿAlmāniyya* (http://osamash.maktoobblog.com/date/2012/12/, 21 December 2012 (website no longer available)).
96 *Id., Hal al-ʿAlmāniyyūn Dīmuqrāṭiyyūn?* (http://osamash.maktoobblog.com/date/2011/07, 30 July 2011 (website no longer available)).
97 Ḥasan Abū Haniyya, "Bayna Masārāt al-Silmiyya wa-l-ʿAskariyya … Ayna Takmunu Maṣlaḥat al-Thawra al-Sūriyya?" *Al-Qibla* 9, no. 22 (2012): 39–43; Bassām Nāṣir, "Al-Thawra al-Sūriyya … Qirāʾa fī Khalfiyyāt wa-l-Dawāʿī wa-l-Asbāb," *Al-Qibla* 9, no. 22 (2012): 35–8; *id.*, "Thawrat Sūriyā wa-Aḥdāthuhā bi-Ruʾá wa-Naẓarāt Sharʿiyya," *Al-Qibla* 9, no. 22 (2012): 68–71.
98 Interview with Zāyid Ḥammād, Amman, 19 January 2013.
99 Interviews with Amīn al-Tubāsī, al-Ḥuṣn, 22 January 2014; Muʿādh al-ʿUtaybī, Irbid, 19 January 2014.

thinkers like Sayyid Qutb and the Pakistani ideologue Abu l-Aʿla Mawdudi (1903–1979), Islamists have long been in the forefront of political reform, al-Dhuwayb states.[100]

The primary means of political involvement during particularly the early stages of the "Arab Spring" was the demonstration. An article in *Al-Qibla* points out that Muslim scholars differ on this way of expressing discontent because demonstrations may clash with the belief that one should obey the ruler and could bring about more problems than they actually solve. If demonstrations are directed against rulers whose rule is not (entirely) Islamic, are organised as action for God (so not out of political or other motives), are legitimised by a fatwa from a scholar, will not lead to killing or the confiscation of property, will likely change things for the better and are not influenced by non-Muslims, one group of scholars allows them if no other means of contention is available.[101]

Naturally, given the above, "reformists" associated with the Jamʿiyyat al-Kitab wa-l-Sunna are quite supportive of Egyptian Islamists, claiming proudly that "in the revolutions of Egypt and Libya, religious youngsters were in the front line and the majority of victims were from among their ranks".[102] Usama Shahada echoes this sentiment, praising the fact that Egyptian Islamists, who used to be marginalised, arrested and imprisoned, have been elevated to positions of political power.[103] Although he criticises the Egyptian Muslim Brotherhood for, among other things, its alleged lack of a clear and precise ideology, Shahada – who supports the Egyptian Salafi Al-Nur Party – writes positively about Salafis' contributions to politics in Egypt, praises them for their strong method and knowledge and advises them not to rush into parliamentary life but to prepare carefully for this.[104]

Such sentiments with regard to Egyptian Salafis engaging in parliamentary politics show that "reformists" like Usama Shahada – unlike quietists in Jordan – look favourably upon founding political parties, including Salafi ones in the kingdom itself. Shahada points out in one of his articles that the "Arab Spring" has had several positive effects on Jordan's Salafis.

[100] Aḥmad al-Dhuwayb, "Tārīkh Mushārakat al-Islāmiyyīn fī l-Iṣlāḥ al-Siyāsī," *Al-Qibla* 10, no. 23 (2012): 47–59.

[101] Shākir al-ʿĀrūrī, "Muẓāharāt," *Al-Qibla* 9, no. 21 (2011): 14–22. See also Nāṣir, "Thawrat," 69.

[102] Zāyid Ḥammād, "Waddū Law Tudhinu fa-Yudhinūna," *Al-Qibla*ʿ 9, no. 21 (2011): 7.

[103] Suffice to say, these words were expressed before the removal from power of Muḥammad Mursī, the Muslim Brother who was the president of Egypt from 2012 to 2013.

[104] Usāma Shaḥāda, *Al-Islāmiyyūn wa-l-Marḥala al-Jadīda* (http://osamash.maktoobblog.com/date/2012/07/, 1 July 2012 (website no longer available)). For a more comprehensive assessment of Egyptian Salafism by Shaḥāda, see also *id.*, "Al-Madāris al-Salafiyya al-Muʿāṣira: Miṣr Numūdhijan," *Al-Qibla* 11, no. 24 (2013): 52–60.

One of these is that they are actually debating and taking positions on the revolutions in the Arab world. Others include a greater openness towards setting up Salafi organisations and engaging more in charitable activities. Shahada also mentions that efforts have been made to found a Salafi political party in Jordan, but that such efforts have failed until now because of the "immaturity" of Salafism in the kingdom as well as "official meddling that has thwarted some of these attempts".[105]

The benefits of such a Salafi party, Usama Shahada claims, are clear: Salafis will become an influential force in society, will have platforms from which to state their demands through official channels, will be able to make changes through parliament, will make other members of parliament stick to their promises, will show Salafism's true power in society and will translate their influence into the areas of culture, media and education.[106] Other (former) political Salafis affiliated with the Jamʿiyyat al-Kitab wa-l-Sunna in Jordan do not deny these benefits, but are sceptical of achieving them under the current circumstances. Like Shahada, they point to the supposed immaturity of the "reformist" Salafi movement in the kingdom and regime opposition to such a project,[107] but also to the lack of a strong Salafi infrastructure in Jordanian society on which they can build and the weakness of parliament, which would make founding such a Salafi party rather pointless.[108] Add to this that it is unclear what exactly such a party would stand for and how it would differ from the existing Islamist parties in Jordan[109] and it becomes apparent that no Salafi political party is likely to arise anytime soon. This has not stopped the state and quietist Salafis in Jordan from expressing their opposition to such efforts, however, to which we will now turn.

The State and Quietist Salafis "Fight" Political Salafism

Even though both the Jordanian state and al-Albani were quite favourably disposed towards the Muslim Brotherhood until the 1980s, the regime and quietists have become increasingly critical of that group, as we have seen above. For the state, it was the greater politicisation of the Brotherhood, the loss of its use as a loyal partner against dangerous

105 *Id.*, "Tafāʿulāt Salafiyyī al-Urdunn maʿa l-Rabīʿ al-ʿArabī wa-l-Āfāq al-Mustaqbaliyya," *Awrāq wa-Niqāshāt Muʾtamar "Al-Taḥawwulāt al-Salafiyya" – Al-Dalālāt, al-Tadāʿiyāt wa-l-Āfāq* (Amman: Friedrich Ebert Stiftung, 2013), 45–6.

106 *Id.*, *Al-Daʿwa*, 171–2.

107 Interviews with Aḥmad al-Dhuwayb, Amman, 15 January 2013; Zāyid Ḥammād, Amman, 19 January 2013; Marwān Shaḥāda, Amman, 9 June 2012.

108 Interview with Aḥmad al-Dhuwayb, Amman, 15 January 2013.

109 Interviews with Marwān Shaḥāda, Amman, 9 June 2012; Usāma Shaḥāda, Amman, 7 June 2012.

outside forces and its increasingly critical attitude towards the regime's policies that caused the relationship to deteriorate. To the increasingly loyalist quietist Salafi leadership in Jordan, the Muslim Brotherhood was both doctrinally unsound and far too politicised. Both the regime and quietist scholars have therefore had their own reasons to take a sceptical – if not outright hostile – attitude towards the Muslim Brotherhood. With the rise of political Salafism in the wake of the "Arab Spring", what might be described as a Salafi version of the Brotherhood increasingly started rearing its head, which was to the liking of neither the Jordanian regime nor the kingdom's leading quietist scholars.

The State: Bureaucratising Political Salafism

While quietist Salafis in Jordan have become increasingly loyalist in their relations with the regime, "reformist" Salafis seem to represent the non-violent mirror-image of this development: they claim to represent a type of Salafism that expresses al-Albani's broad and independent attitude to the state far better than leading quietist scholars do and, on top of that and unlike al-Albani, intend to actually engage in politics as well. The state, interestingly, has taken a similar approach to both trends: quietists have been domesticated in a long process involving several factors, including the founding of the Imam al-Albani Centre, through which the regime could control them; "reformists" have been dealt with likewise through their own organisations, including the Jamʿiyyat al-Kitab wa-l-Sunna.

As we saw earlier, "reformists" treat politics first and foremost as "public affairs", but – especially in the wake of the "Arab Spring" – also want to engage in the more narrow area of politics as "the art of government".[110] This has far more drastic consequences for the regime: while charitable activities are relatively uncontroversial and unable to harm the state's power and influence directly, "reformist" Salafis' focus on politics in the form of parliamentary participation and founding a Salafi party obviously represents a challenge to the Jordanian regime, not least because such action is taken partly out of opposition to current policies in the kingdom.

Because of the undesirability – from the regime's point of view – of yet another Islamist party, the Jordanian state has not allowed the development of political Salafism since the "Arab Spring" to go unchecked. As we saw earlier, several "reformist" Salafis spoke of regime pressure and meddling to stifle attempts at founding a Salafi party. It is not entirely clear how this pressure has been applied in practice, although there is

[110] For more on this, see Heywood, *Politics*, 5–7.

some anecdotal evidence to support the view that members of the intelligence services have actually visited individual "reformist" Salafis to convince them not to engage in parliamentary participation or founding a party.

More important, perhaps, than any pressure applied by the intelligence services on individual "reformists" are the regime's attempts to bureaucratise political Salafism in the kingdom. As mentioned above, the Jamʿiyyat al-Kitab wa-l-Sunna – the most likely organisation from which any political party would spring forth – is officially registered with the Ministry of Culture. This entails that it is a legal group, protected by law to pursue its charitable and social activities, yet it also means that the Jamʿiyyat al-Kitab wa-l-Sunna cannot embark on any explicitly political adventures – in the narrow, government-related sense – since that would be a matter for the Interior Ministry. Given that the latter is unlikely to allow a new political party – let alone a Salafi one, which is even less representative of the regime's ecumenical Islamic values than the Muslim Brotherhood – such a transfer from one ministry to the other would be quite pointless for the Jamʿiyyat al-Kitab wa-l-Sunna.[111]

However, the consequences of the Jamʿiyyat al-Kitab wa-l-Sunna's trying to found a political party would be greater than just wasting time and effort. Under the purview of the Ministry of Culture, the organisation has the freedom to engage in *daʿwa*, charitable work and other societal activities. Taking the leap into parliamentary politics by founding a party would possibly jeopardise all these since it could risk losing its position as a legally protected "cultural" organisation. The Jamʿiyyat al-Kitab wa-l-Sunna and other Salafi organisations in Jordan therefore have an interest in staying away from founding a political party, or at least until circumstances change or until they are willing to take the risk. It is for this reason that several former members of the Jamʿiyyat al-Kitab wa-l-Sunna have informally told me that the organisation has gradually grown closer to the regime. While this may be true, the group remains committed to political reform – at least in its discourse – and continues to express views about politics and the "Arab Spring" that are clearly at odds with the anti-revolutionary attitude espoused by the regime.[112]

[111] Interviews with Aḥmad al-Dhuwayb, Amman, 15 January 2013; Zāyid Ḥammād, Amman, 19 January 2013.

[112] Parts of this section are based on Joas Wagemakers, "The Dual Effect of the Arab Spring on Salafi Integration: Political Salafism in Jordan," in *Salafism after the Arab Awakening: Contending with People's Power*, ed. Francesco Cavatorta and Fabio Merone (London: Hurst & Co., 2016).

Quietists: Fighting *Fitna*

Unlike the Jordanian state, which apparently accepts "reformist" Salafism in the kingdom as long as it does not branch out into parliamentary politics, quietists are deeply concerned with the phenomenon as a whole, including its discourse on the "Arab Spring". Considering the leading quietist scholars' loyalty to their own Jordanian ruler, it is perhaps not surprising that they take a rather dim view of the revolts in the countries of the region.[113] This does not mean, however, that quietist scholars view the "Arab Spring" as one undifferentiated whole. In fact, they use the aforementioned distinction between obedience and a pledge of allegiance to distinguish between Egypt, Libya and Syria. In principle, quietist Salafi scholars in Jordan believe that leaders in all countries – Muslim or non-Muslim – deserve their *ṭāʿa*. In that sense, the fact that the Syrian President Bashar al-Asad is a member of the heterodox ʿAlawite branch of Islam does not make any difference to them. Yet when it comes to the much more active pledge of allegiance, they differentiate between countries that are ruled by Sunni rulers – like Jordan and, somewhat less explicitly, Egypt – on the one hand and countries ruled by leaders whose beliefs are doubted or simply not Sunni, like Libya and Syria.[114]

The situation is more complicated with regard to mere obedience, however, since this is where quietist scholars weigh the pros and cons of revolting against the regime. In principle, again, they are not in favour of any revolts since they generally believe that the result (chaos) will be worse than the problem (dictatorship). Yet in the cases of Libya and Syria, some – though certainly not all – quietist Salafi scholars expressed the view that the regimes in these countries are simply waging war against their own people, meaning that a revolt is allowed since the result of that is likely to be better than the problem.[115] This does not mean, however, that these scholars condone – let alone encourage – Muslim youngsters from all over the world to go to Syria to wage jihad there. This would clash with the policy of the Jordanian regime, yet quietist Salafis – though sceptical of any revolt – sometimes do see an uprising in Syria as the "least bad" option.[116] They therefore mostly express grief about the

113 Muwaffaq Kamāl, "Al-Ḥalabī: Lan Nushārika fī l-ʿAmal al-Siyāsī wa-Lā Māniʿ min Mumārasat Ḥaqq al-Intikhāb," *Al-Ghad*, May 29, 2012 (www.alwakeelnews.com/index.php?page=article&id=7628#.VZ4uo7X4bak, accessed 9 July 2015).

114 There is actually a difference of opinion between scholars about the former Libyan leader Muʿammar al-Qadhdhāfī, who was the *walī al-amr* according to Bāsim b. Fayṣal al-Jawābira but a Shiʿa unworthy of *bayʿa* to Ziyād al-ʿAbbādī. Interviews with Ziyād al-ʿAbbādī, Amman, 26 June 2012; Bāsim b. Fayṣal al-Jawābira, Amman, 26 June 2012.

115 Interviews with Muḥammad b. Mūsá Āl Naṣr, Amman, 20 June 2012; ʿAlī al-Ḥalabī, Amman, 27 June 2012.

116 *Liqāʾ Ṣaḥafī*; Kamāl, "Al-Ḥalabī."

situation in Syria,[117] point to the "non-Muslim" ʿAlawite background of its president[118] and state that only Syrians themselves are allowed to rise up against the regime in Damascus.[119]

The general attitude of Jordan's quietist Salafi leadership *vis-à-vis* the "Arab Spring" is thus one of scepticism and rejection. The central concept in all of this is "*fitna*", which quietists believe is the result of the different revolts. In the eyes of quietist scholars, a key instigator of such chaos can be found in the many demonstrations against the Arab regimes. According to quietist shaykh Husayn al-ʿAwayisha, who has written perhaps the most widely distributed Jordanian book on this matter, the *fitna* of the "Arab Spring" is caused by the lack of intra-Islamic cooperation, the absence of reformers, not practising "commanding right and forbidding wrong", sin, unbelief, the loss of the Prophet, the companions and knowledge as well as trickery and gambling with money and trade.[120] Demonstrations are not an answer to these problems, al-ʿAwayisha claims, since they are not part of Islam and do not constitute a form of "commanding right",[121] as some would have it.[122] In fact, demonstrations may begin peacefully but often lead to *fitna* and bloodshed, al-Halabi states,[123] and also often involve illegitimate gender-mixing.[124] As such, demonstrations against the regimes are rejected by quietists.[125]

In the eyes of Jordanian quietist scholars, a second cause of *fitna* during the aftermath of the "Arab Spring" was found in the emergence of political parties. Jordanian quietists' reasons to oppose political parties in general have already been dealt with in Chapter 2, but in the wake of

117 ʿAlī al-Ḥalabī, "*Sūriya*" ... *bayna l-Ālām* ... *wa-l-Āmāl – Kalimat Ḥaqq wa-Annat Ṣidq* (www.alhalaby.com/play.php?catsmktba=3016, 14 February 2012 (accessed 1 April 2013)).

118 *Id.*, *Kalimat Ḥaqq ʿIlmiyya fī Aḥdāth Sūriyya* (n.p.: Mānshūrāt Muntadayāt Kull al-Salafiyyīn, 2012), 38–50.

119 *Id.*, *Al-Mawqif al-Sharʿī min Fatwá "Muʾtamar al-Qāhira!" fī Ījāb al-Jihād fī "Sūriya" ʿalá ʿUmūm al-Muslimīn* (www.alhalaby.com/play.php?catsmktba=3495, 16 June 2013 (accessed 2 July 2013)); Kamāl, "Al-Ḥalabī."

120 Ḥusayn b. ʿAwda al-ʿAwāyisha, *Al-Fitan wa-Sabīl al-Najāt min-hā* (Amman: Al-Dār al-Athariyya, 2011), 12–24.

121 *Ibid.*, 96–9.

122 See, for example, Muḥammad Abū Fāris, "Ilá l-Mushārikīn fī Masīrat 'Inqādh al-Waṭan'," *Al-Sabīl*, October 4, 2012, 15. The author used to be one of the leading scholars of the Jordanian Muslim Brotherhood.

123 Al-Ḥalabī, *Al-Daʿwa al-Salafiyya al-Hādiya*, 10–11.

124 *Id.*, *Kalima ḥawla "Aḥdāth Miṣr" – 2* (www.alhalaby.com/play.php?catsmktba=2530, 30 January 2011 (accessed 1 April 2013)).

125 Many scholars also point to fatwas from major scholars about this subject. See, for example, al-ʿAwāyisha, *Al-Fitan*, 122–39; al-Ḥalabī, *Al-Daʿwa al-Salafiyya al-Hādiya*, 14–20; *id.*, *Taḥdhīrāt al-ʿUlamāʾ al-Thiqāt min al-Muẓāharāt bi-l-Adilla al-Bāhirāt wa-l-Naqḍ ʿalá l-Shubhāt al-Wāhiyāt* (Medina: Dār al-Imām Muslim, 2012).

the overthrow of especially President Husni Mubarak in Egypt, they were confronted with the sudden rise of numerous parties and presidential candidates, including Salafi ones. Although few quietist scholars have gone into great detail about this, al-Halabi has lamented this development,[126] particularly with regard to the Egyptian Salafi al-Nur Party, which was founded in the wake of the "Arab Spring".[127] He scolds Egyptian Salafis for welcoming the (originally Egyptian) political Salafi shaykh Ibn ʿAbd al-Khaliq from Kuwait as "the spiritual father of the Salafi *daʿwa*", while this title actually belongs to the quietist al-Albani, he writes.[128] He also tells them: "I do not understand why you have – quickly! – forgotten the advice of our shaykh, imam al-Albani [. . .] on the subject of 'politics' that 'the good policy is to stay away from politics'?!"[129]

Al-Halabi makes clear that he is not opposed to moral and religious reform but that this can best be done in a country not wrecked by revolts and demonstrations. He therefore praises Jordan as a "stable, safe country", which "in our conviction, is the greatest fortune of our country that is limited in its possibilities [yet] great in its safety and security. That is a fortune greater than all gold, silver, petrol and money."[130] The alternative to the "Arab Spring" that quietists offer, therefore, is more patience[131] and – especially – greater piety. Al-ʿAwayisha – bearing in mind what he saw as the causes of the "*fitna*" of the "Arab Spring" mentioned earlier – points to solutions such as letting God's word prevail,

[126] ʿAlī al-Ḥalabī, *"Ḥizb al-Nūr al-Salafī" wa-"l-Ikhwān al-Muslimūn" . . . Iʾtilāf am Ikhtilāf . . . am Mādhā?! Wa-Limādhā?* (www.alhalaby.com/play.php?catsmktba=2968, 18 December 2011 (accessed 1 April 2013)).

[127] *Id., Ilá "Ḥizb al-Nūr al-Salafī!!" Ammā Ān La-kum Taʿtabinī; fa-l-Ḥizbiyya Lā Tuntaju illā Ḥizbiyya* (www.alhalaby.com/play.php?catsmktba=3366, 28 December 2012 (accessed 1 April 2013)); *id., Ilá Salafiyyat "Ḥizb al-Nūr": Irjiʿū ilá "l-Thughūr" wa-Tarājaʿū ʿan "al-Juḥūr"* (www.alhalaby.com/play.php?catsmktba-3356, 13 December 2012 (accessed 1 April 2013)); *id., Ilá l-Salafiyyīn fī "Miṣr": Hādhā Tadhkīr "bi-Baʿḍ!" Naṣāʾiḥī "l-Sābiqa!" ilaykum: Maḥabba wa-Ḥirṣan . . . Laʿallakum* (www.alhalaby.com/play.php?catsmktba=3513, 18 August 2013 (accessed 19 August 2013)); *id., Ḥizbiyya wa-l-Salafiyya . . . Hal Yajtamiʿāni?! Maʿa l-Islāmī al-Ṣaḥafī "Usāma Shaḥāda" Numūdhajan* (www.alhalaby.com/play.php?catsmktba=3165, 24 June 2012 (accessed 1 April 2013)); *id., Tafṣīl wa-Taʾṣīl ḥawla Mā Yusammá bi-l-Aḥzāb al-Salafiyya* (www.alhalaby.com/play.php?catsmktba=3141, 13 May 2012 (accessed 1 April 2013)).

[128] *Id., Hal "Nazaʿat" = "Al-Miṣriyya!" Ikhwānanā l-Salafiyyīn fī "Miṣr" fī stiqbālihim "ʿAbd al-Raḥmān ʿAbd al-Khāliq?* (www.alhalaby.com/play.php?catsmktba=2999, 14 January 2012 (accessed 1 April 2013)).

[129] *Id., Naṣīḥa ilá l-Salafiyyīn fī "Miṣr" – bi-ʿĀmma – wa-ilayka – Ayyuhā l-Dāʿī l-Salafī – bi-Khāṣṣa* (www.alhalaby.com/play.php?catsmktba=2667, 24 May 2011 (accessed 2 April 2013)).

[130] Kamāl, "Al-Ḥalabī." [131] Interview with Aḥmad Muṣliḥ, Amman, 29 January 2013.

holding on to the Qur'an, the Sunna and the *manhaj* of the Prophet's companions, repenting for sins, mildness towards others and pleas to God.[132] The rulers should be obeyed and criticism against them should be expressed through discreet advice,[133] quietist Salafi shaykhs claim, and should be accompanied with *da'wa* to people in general.[134] Such *da'wa*, al-Halabi states – in reference to the square in central Cairo where Egyptian demonstrators demanded the removal of President Husni Mubarak – is "the real Liberation Square".[135]

Because Jordanian "reformist" Salafis never came close to leading anything resembling a revolution in the kingdom, did not demonstrate against the regime and only engaged in failed efforts to found a political party, quietist criticism of their discourse is less widespread than writings against the Salafi Al-Nur Party in Egypt, for example. Still, al-Halabi mentions that he has heard of Jordanians wanting to set up a Salafi party, but advises them to invest their efforts and their money in *da'wa* instead.[136] Some also express fear that any attempts to found a Salafi party in Jordan could jeopardise the quietist *da'wa* because the regime might associate such political activities with their own missionary project, just as quietists feared the association with Jihadi-Salafism, as we saw in Chapter 6.[137] Probably because of this fear – as well as the desire to "cleanse" Salafism of supposedly deviant beliefs – al-Halabi has criticised Usama Shahada for not only promoting Salafi political parties but also for the latter calling himself a Salafi. Unlike what the media call Shahada and like-minded others, al-Halabi states, their ideas about politics and founding parties are more influenced by Sufism and secularism than by Salafism.[138]

The "Arab Spring" thus shows that the loyalist quietist Salafi leadership in Jordan had become so domesticated by the time the first Arab revolts broke out that it did not need to reinvent itself, but could simply

[132] Al-'Awāyisha, *Al-Fitan*, 44–55.
[133] *Id.*, 142–7; al-Ḥalabī, *Al-Da'wa al-Salafiyya al-Hādiya*, 27–31; interview with Muḥammad Aḥmad Abū Laylá l-Atharī, al-Ruṣayfa, 26 January 2013.
[134] 'Alī al-Ḥalabī, *"Al-Da'wa al-Salafiyya" Ajallu min an Ta'ūla Ḥizban!* (www.alhalaby.com/play.php?catsmktba=2657, 13 May 2011 (accessed 2 April 2013)); *id., Ilá l-Salafiyyīn fī "Miṣr"*; interview with Akram Ziyāda, Amman, 28 June 2012.
[135] Al-Ḥalabī, *Al-Hudá*, 33; *id., Naṣīḥa.* [136] *Id., Tafṣīl.* See also *id., Al-Hudá*, 22.
[137] Interview with Fatḥī al-Mawṣilī, Amman, 23 January 2013.
[138] 'Alī al-Ḥalabī, "Al-Shaykh 'Alī al-Ḥalabī Yaruddu 'alá Usāma Shaḥāda: Tahdhīr al-Anām min al-Ḥizbiyya al-Mansūba li-l-Salafiyya wa-l-Islām," *Al-Ghad*, July 6, 2012 (www.alghad.com/index.php/article/562656.html (accessed 18 December 2013)). This article is also available in a slightly longer version at www.kulalsalafiyeen.com/vb/forumdisplay.php?f=3 (accessed 8 February 2013). See also al-Ḥalabī, *Al-Hudá*, 34–6, footnote 1.

apply its existing discourse – developed against earlier expressions of political Salafism as well as Jihadi-Salafis – to effectively ward off this challenge and nip it in the bud. Because the agendas of the state and quietist Salafis in the kingdom were so similar in this respect and because their discourse had become increasingly intertwined over the years, the quietist leadership acted as a sort of Salafi firewall against any attempts by "reformists" to copy the political efforts of their Egyptian counterparts. This way, the regime was secure in its support from quietists, while the latter could rest assured that whatever the outcome of their quest for a Salafi utopia would lead to, they – and not others – would be the ones to shape it.

Conclusion

As my Lebanese travel companion to Beirut mentioned in the Introduction stated: one can "talk about" Salafism in Jordan and, indeed, this book has dealt exactly with this topic, a growing movement among Sunni Muslims in the kingdom that includes several scholars and activists who are prominent not only on a national but also on an international level. These men adhere to the Salafi branch of Islam, whose adherents claim to emulate "the pious predecessors" (*al-salaf al-ṣāliḥ*, usually equated with the first three generations of Muslims) as closely and in as many spheres of life as possible. Although Jordan has long been a country where Islam is an important social and political factor – expressed in the prophetic lineage of the royal family, the country's official religious infrastructure and the bureaucratically controlled Islamist civil society organisations – non-radical Salafism in the country has received little academic attention so far. This book has addressed this gap in the literature by focussing on (1) the apolitical, quietist branch of Salafism in Jordan; (2) how this trend gradually transformed from being a subservient yet independent movement into one whose leaders are explicitly loyal to the regime; and (3) why this process I call "domestication" took place.

In Chapter 1, we saw that Salafism as a whole can be seen as a "grounded utopian movement", indicating its adherents' striving for the utopia represented by the *salaf* while simultaneously being grounded in the everyday practices by the actual members of the community in the here and now. This utopian "ideal place" is very old, in the sense that there have almost always been Muslims who strove to emulate the "pious predecessors" in some way. Although Salafism is seen by some as merely pious Sunni Islam, there are actually important legal and especially theological differences between Salafism and "orthodox" Sunni Islam. Salafism is also quite widespread. In the twentieth century, what we now know as Salafism was spread through Saudi "Wahhabi" propaganda, oil workers who went to the Gulf and adopted a Salafi lifestyle that they took home with them and the general search for an alternative to Arab socialism after the perceived defeat of this ideology in the June War against Israel in 1967.

The Salafi creed (*ʿaqīda*) places great emphasis on the central Islamic concept of *tawḥīd* (the unity of God) since it reinforces the monotheistic basis of the Muslim religion and distinguishes Salafism from popular rituals, like the worshipping of "saints", as well as other trends within Islam. The tendency to distinguish oneself as supposedly purer and more authentic than other Muslims can be found in many of Salafism's concepts, such as their living as "strangers" (*ghurabāʾ*) amidst allegedly misguided others and the idea that they belong to "the victorious group" (*al-ṭāʾifa al-manṣūra*) or "the sect saved [from hellfire]" (*al-firqa al-nājiya*). Salafis also avoid what they describe as "religious innovations" (*bidaʿ*, sing. *bidʿa*) and try to remain "pure" by displaying loyalty to God, Islam and fellow-Muslims while disavowing everything and everyone else (*al-walāʾ wa-l-barāʾ*). Other issues on which Salafis have outspoken views include the concepts of faith (*īmān*) and unbelief (*kufr*). Salafis generally believe that the former is embodied equally by belief in the heart, speech with the tongue and acts with the limbs, which distinguishes them from the early Islamic Murjiʾa, who excluded acts from faith. Salafis also hold that one may apply excommunication (*takfīr*) to someone who commits an act of unbelief, but often state the condition that the culprit needs to justify this act in his or her heart or speech. This distinguishes them from the early Islamic Khawarij, who are said to have generally applied *takfīr* even when this intention of unbelief was not apparent.

While the Salafi creed refers to beliefs, their method of applying this (*manhaj*) refers to practice. With regard to their method of reading the sources and worship, Salafis are very much alike, but they differ quite a lot in their method of dealing with politics and society. Three branches of Salafism can be distinguished: quietists, who avoid political action and focus on studying and the propagation of their message (*daʿwa*) instead; politicos, who do believe or actually engage in political action; and Jihadi-Salafis, who believe that jihad – a concept seen as legitimate by all Salafis – may not just be used against "unbelievers" (*kuffār*, sing. *kāfir*), but also within Muslim lands to overthrow regimes that are supposedly led by leaders guilty of apostasy (*ridda*) for not applying Islamic law (*sharīʿa*) entirely. Quietists, importantly, can further be divided into aloofists, who shun their regimes altogether and remain entirely independent, loyalists, who are loyal to their rulers and can be called upon to help or defend them, and propagandists, who actively propagate the supposed blessings of the regime and even attack those who doubt this.

Chapter 2 showed that Jordanian quietist Salafis, on which this book focusses in particular, share their basic ideology with Salafis worldwide.

Yet their one-time leader, Muhammad Nasir al-Din al-Albani, was known for his aloofism from political action and the rulers as well as his independent ideological attitude that focussed strongly on the sources and would not deviate from what he saw as the only correct ruling. Given the fact that al-Albani was the undisputed leader of the Salafi community in Jordan in the 1980s and 1990s, his aloofist quietism greatly influenced the movement in the kingdom and ensured that the quietist Salafi trend there had a strongly apolitical and independent streak.

One of the areas in which al-Albani was ideologically independent was his conviction that, unlike belief in the heart or speech with the tongue, acts – though part of faith – could not decrease *īmān* or take it away altogether, but could only increase it. This position was perceived as a clear deviation from the Salafi norm by several Jordanian quietists, including Muhammad Abu Ruhayyim and – in later years – Muhammad Ibrahim Shaqra. Both men went so far as to suggest (or even openly state) that al-Albani's views essentially amounted to excluding sinful acts from faith altogether and were therefore akin to the beliefs of the Murjiʾa. Although some of al-Albani's students defended him against this charge, particularly his prominent pupil ʿAli al-Halabi, they seemed to realise that their teacher held a position that, from a Salafi point of view, was hard to defend.

With regard to politics and society, quietist Salafis in Jordan advocate "the cleansing and teaching" (*al-taṣfiya wa-l-tarbiya*) of Islamic tradition from allegedly unlawful additions, dubious sources and religious innovations. Quietists see this as their way of "the jurisprudence of reality" (*fiqh al-wāqiʿ*), which shapes their assessment of and behaviour towards society. They use this concept, however, to better facilitate their *daʿwa*, not to engage in political action. The latter is not rejected by them in principle, but is delayed to an undetermined point in the future when society is ready for it. Contemporary politics, in the meantime, should be dealt with by displaying greater religious piety, in their view, while being obedient to the rulers. Quietists also reject democracy, elections, parties and Islamist movements such as the Muslim Brotherhood as means to express their contention, although they do allow voting for the least bad candidate in elections to ward off supposedly even worse choices in parliament.

In Chapter 3, we looked at the early history of quietist Salafism in Jordan, the impact al-Albani had on its development and the entrenchment of its apolitical ideology. Although there were some scholars in the early emirate and kingdom of (Trans)Jordan that could be described as having Salafi tendencies, Salafism did not become a real trend in the kingdom until Muhammad Ibrahim Shaqra and Ahmad al-Salik, who had both studied at the Al-Azhar University in Egypt, embraced Salafism and started preaching it in Amman. From there, their Salafi message was picked up by others and enjoyed a growing following. The trend really started growing, however, with the arrival of al-Albani.

Born in 1914 in Albania and raised in Syria, al-Albani was interested in Islamic reform from an early age and particularly applied this attitude to the study of the traditions of the Prophet Muhammad (*ḥadīth*s), which he submitted to a rigorous selection process, weeding out the "false" ones and adjusting doctrine on the basis of his findings. Partly because he had never enjoyed a formal religious education, but also because of his stubborn insistence on adhering to sources he deemed authentic, his findings were controversial among "orthodox" Sunni scholars, who preferred to base their rulings on the corpus of legal texts from their own school of Islamic law (*madhhab*), an attitude that al-Albani rejected. "The shaykh", as he is often referred to by his students, was also rather polemical and fiercely independent, both doctrinally and politically, and this made life more difficult for him under the already repressive regime in Syria. As a result, he decided to move to Jordan, where he settled in 1983 and quickly became the leading Salafi scholar.

Meanwhile, the 1980s and 1990s also witnessed the rise of political Salafism in the Gulf, particularly during and after the Iraqi invasion of Kuwait in 1990, when politicos were quite critical of Saudi Arabia's decision to allow 500,000 American troops into the country to defend it against a possible Iraqi attack. A regime crackdown on this criticism followed after the Gulf War was over, with quietist Salafis following suit by doubling down on their apolitical ideology against the politicised views of those critical of Saudi actions. This also applied to Jordanian quietists, who were far more informally organised than their brethren in the Gulf, but who nevertheless had strong ideological, personal and financial ties to them. This increased apoliticism by Jordanian quietists was expressed by, for example, becoming more critical of the Muslim Brotherhood, whose ideas had contributed to the development of political Salafism. As such, their already apolitical ideology became even more explicitly so during the 1990s, thereby further facilitating Jordanian quietist Salafism's eventual domestication by the regime.

Chapter 4 has dealt with the intra-Salafi conflicts among Jordanian quietists immediately prior to and after the death of al-Albani in 1999. These conflicts were strongly related to al-Albani's different views on faith, but this was not the main bone of contention, which can be said to have been religious authority and – ultimately – the leadership of the quietist Salafi community in Jordan. A contender for this position, ʿAli al-Halabi, was accused of plagiarism even before al-Albani's death. Although we can only be certain of this accusation with regard to one book, the impression of al-Halabi (and, to a lesser extent, other quietist Jordanian scholars) as a fraud was widespread. This was confirmed in the eyes of some when al-Halabi decided to add his name to the cover of a book on faith by a Jordanian quietist named Murad Shukri. Not only did this book express views on *īmān* that were seen as equally wrong as al-Albani's, but it later also turned out that al-Halabi had had no part in reading and verifying its text, as the cover claimed.

One quietist scholar whose view of al-Halabi as a deviant fraud was confirmed by Shukri's book was Muhammad Abu Ruhayyim, all the more so since al-Halabi had no formal education and a scholar like Abu Ruhayyim was unwilling to put up with such behaviour from a man he disdained for his supposed ignorance. This increased even more when al-Halabi edited one of al-Albani's fatwas on faith into a book, in which – according to Abu Ruhayyim – he expressed deviant views on *īmān* and twisted the words of major Salafi scholars. The controversy over this book eventually became an international affair, with Saudi scholars criticising al-Halabi too, but the latter's views on faith also became a target of critique from Shaqra, who differed with al-Halabi on the question of faith. This did not become a real problem, however, until after Shaqra was denied the leadership of the Jordanian quietist Salafi community after al-Albani's death in favour of al-Halabi, which frustrated Shaqra and caused him to double down on his position on faith. The leadership of the quietists in Jordan thus fell into the hands of al-Halabi, whose theological and political views towards the regime were more loyalist than those of either al-Albani or Shaqra.

Al-Halabi's position as the informal leader of the quietist community – and, thereby, the more loyalist direction he represented – was consolidated when the regime founded the Imam al-Albani Centre in Amman in 2001 and put the group of scholars around al-Halabi in charge of running it. This formally made the quietist Salafi leadership part of the bureaucratically controlled civil society in Jordan and thus more susceptible to the regime's wishes to domesticate the movement. As if the reputation of these scholars had not been damaged enough by accusations of plagiarism and ideological deviance, the director of the Imam al-Albani Centre, Salim al-Hilali, was also accused of stealing its funds and using them for his own personal benefit.

In Chapter 5, we read how the increased domestication of the quietist community aided the regime's efforts to fight terrorism, particularly after the attacks of 11 September 2001 in the United States. Although the regime fought Islamist militancy through military means, this also entailed promoting an official (i.e., regime-sponsored) "moderate" Islam of tolerance, peace and acceptance as an alternative to the radical ideology expressed by groups like al-Qaʿida. This trend was eagerly supported by quietist Salafis, who – through their rejection of terrorism, increasing loyalism and desire to be seen as distinct from "extremists" – shared part of the regime's discourse. They therefore explicitly denounced violence, rejected any link between terrorism and Islam/Salafism and expressed their loyalty to and support for the state and its safety as a religious duty.

Despite the many blows the quietist Salafi leadership has taken through accusations against them, their religious authority – summed up here as pertaining to having the right knowledge, character and personality – did not suffer as much as one might expect. Although there is no formal Salafi leadership structure in Jordan, it is clear that the scholars form the organisational backbone of the movement, that al-Halabi is the main scholar and that his ideological allies also enjoy great admiration from their followers. While the attacks on the scholars' character through accusations of plagiarism and being too close to the regime have damaged their religious authority among some, they are accepted as Salafi scholars because of their strong personalities and – especially – their great knowledge, particularly since Salafis see knowledge as extremely important.

The specific knowledge that quietist Salafis in Jordan focus on nowadays is much more narrowly geared towards achieving doctrinal and ritual "purity" than before. This was always important, but – given the scholars' ties with the state – it is also rather uncontroversial and unlikely to make them clash with the regime. The quietist Salafi community engaged in these efforts to live like the Prophet in Jordan is probably no greater than several tens of thousands of supporters. Many of them are from the poorer or middle classes, often of Palestinian but also of East Jordanian descent, increasingly educated and from all over the country. Interestingly, many quietists have been pious Muslims all their lives, even if they were members of the Jamaʿat al-Tabligh or the Muslim Brotherhood.

The rise and development of Jihadi-Salafism in Jordan was dealt with in Chapter 6. This trend came into existence when the kingdom was going through an economically and politically turbulent period, which caused some to become disillusioned with the regime and to turn to radical Islam, expressed in loosely organised militant groups without a clear ideology. This was provided for them by Abu Muhammad al-Maqdisi, one of the many Palestinians who had to leave Kuwait after the Gulf War, during which the Palestine Liberation Organisation (PLO) had sided with Iraq. Al-Maqdisi's ideology was not only fully Salafi and anti-regime, but simultaneously also criticised "extremism" in *takfīr* and jihad, particularly that of his former pupil Abu Musʿab al-Zarqawi, who would later go on to lead al-Qaʿida in Iraq. Because of the support al-Zarqawi enjoyed in Jordan among many Jihadi-Salafis, this led to a split within this Salafi subtrend between the scholarly led radicals who took a careful approach and the more action-oriented supporters of al-Zarqawi. Another split came about when the Islamic State (IS) rose to prominence in Iraq and Syria in 2013 and 2014, pitting those who recognised IS's policies and its claim to be a caliphate versus those who rejected the organisation and its actions.

An important part of Jordanian Jihadi-Salafi discourse dealt with attacking quietist Salafis in the kingdom, especially for their supposedly deviant views on faith. This suggests that quietists and Jihadi-Salafis are far apart and that the former may act as a "firewall" against the latter. This is, indeed, mostly the case, yet scholars such as al-Maqdisi have openly associated al-Albani and al-Halabi with the Murjiʾa, thereby echoing the earlier intra-quietist claims made by Abu Ruhayyim and Shaqra. This shows that there are links between the two subtrends that also suggest that quietism can act at least somewhat as a "conveyor belt" towards Jihadi-Salafism. While Jihadi-Salafis were unaware that the conflict between Shaqra and al-Halabi was more about leadership than theology, they implicitly sided with Shaqra in this conflict by re-evaluating their views on him after he was passed over for the leadership of quietists in Jordan and started criticising al-Halabi. Al-Maqdisi and others started praising him for coming round to the supposedly correct views on faith while Shaqra, frustrated over being sidelined by quietists, relished in this new-found respect for his position, even if it came from Jihadi-Salafis.

Quietists did not remain silent about such accusations from Jihadi-Salafis. They often referred to the latter as "Khawarij", the early Islamic polar opposite of the Murjiʾa. Since the Khawarij engaged in rebellion and were also quick to apply *takfīr*, the label was not only a theologically fitting reply to "Murjiʾa" but also effectively painted Jihadi-Salafis as "extremists". Moreover, it underlined the quietists' desire to disassociate radical Muslims from Salafism as a whole. Interestingly, the discourses of quietists and the state have become so intertwined on this point that the Jordanian regime is also regularly using the label of "Khawarij" to describe radical Muslims, particularly IS. Although the regime may not have adopted this term directly from quietists, its use by both of them does point to their similar agendas and, in turn, underlines quietists' increasingly domesticated position.

The topic of Chapter 7 was political Salafism in Jordan or, as its adherents call it, "reformist" Salafism. The latter developed in the 1990s against the backdrop of quietists' focus on *al-taṣfiya wa-l-tarbiya.* "Reformist" Salafis believed that Islam was about more than just doctrine and *da'wa* and, partly as a result of influence from like-minded scholars from especially Saudi Arabia and Kuwait, they set up the Jam'iyyat al-Kitab wa-l-Sunna (Book and Sunna Association) in 1993. Like other, later "reformist" organisations, this group was (and is) characterised by a broad Salafi discourse, which focusses far more on political and societal issues. Moreover, it also favours "Islamic action" by engaging in charitable activities.

With regard to its basic ideology, the Jam'iyyat al-Kitab wa-l-Sunna differs little from quietist Salafis. When it comes to politics and society, however, the organisation does not delay taking action until an undetermined point in the future, but wants to act now. Apart from their discourse and charitable activities, this expresses itself in a far more positive attitude towards Islamist groups, parliamentary participation and the series of revolutions in the Arab world after 2010 known collectively as the "Arab Spring". "Reformist" Salafis also applaud the founding of Salafi political parties in the wake of particularly the Egyptian revolution and some of them even have rudimentary plans to found a Salafi political party in Jordan, although these efforts have not yielded any results yet.

Considering the increasingly loyalist attitude of quietists towards the state and the latter's attempts to control civil society so as not to allow it to develop into political or security "threats", neither the quietist Salafi leadership in Jordan nor the country's regime look favourably upon the rise of political Salafism. The state has therefore tried to control "reformist" Salafism and particularly the Jam'iyyat al-Kitab wa-l-Sunna by providing them with space to engage in "cultural" activities while simultaneously blocking any avenues towards political participation. Quietists, in the meantime, have generally denounced the "Arab Spring" and its expressions (demonstrations, revolts and new (Salafi) political parties). As an alternative, they have suggested patience, *da'wa*, personal piety and obedience and discreet advice to the rulers, thereby showing once again how the independent quietist Salafi movement once led by al-Albani has been fully domesticated.

Salafism in Jordan: A Tale of Two Bookshops

If one goes to downtown Amman and drives to 'Abdali, a busy area in the capital, one will find a square often used for markets. Opposite this square is a street that, on one side, is filled with numerous shops, including many bookshops. Two of these are run by quietist Salafis, yet they are quite different. One of them, Al-Dar al-Athariyya, is owned by the Imam al-Albani Centre, stacked with only Salafi books on doctrine and ritual "purity" and run by a very friendly and hospitable manager called Ishaq. Some ten metres away, the second Salafi bookshop, Al-Dar al-ʿUthmaniyya, is located. Independently owned and run by a slightly older yet equally friendly and hospitable quietist named Salih, it sells Salafi books of a much wider variety, as well as publications on a host of other, unrelated topics such as computer programming or courses in English.

These two bookshops, being located very close to each other yet selling quite a different selection of books and being run in two divergent ways, exemplify quietist Salafism in Jordan today. While one trend has become highly loyalist to the regime, is officially organised through the Imam al-Albani Centre and focusses almost exclusively on doctrine and rituals, another has tried to retain its aloofism from the state, is independent and sees Salafism as less narrow. Although the first trend is the most visible, the most influential and the most powerful among Jordanian quietist Salafis, the second one still exists, despite not having any prominent leaders or scholars. In the meantime, the distance between them is significant, but relatively small, just like that between the bookshops.

The first branch of quietist Salafism in Jordan has not become loyalist because the regime simply submitted it to its will or bought its subservience, as critics of quietist Salafism in general and those in Jordan in particular sometimes claim. This transformation from aloofist quietism to a loyalist (and sometimes perhaps even propagandist) version of the same branch is actually more complex. Firstly, quietist Salafism in Jordan, by its very nature, was always apolitical and obedient to the rulers through its ideology, which was not just a tool for mobilisation but also a set of deeply held beliefs. Secondly, the movement's adherents themselves reinforced this apoliticism in their confrontation with political Salafism in the 1990s. Thirdly, the internal conflicts among quietists right before and after the death of al-Albani were entirely of the movement's own making. Although quietists had always lived in an environment ultimately controlled by the regime, it was not until 2001 that the latter really stepped in to organise quietist Salafism and even then the shaykhs had a say in it themselves. Since then, there have been clear incentives from the regime towards quietists to stay loyal to the state and various phenomena – the rise of terrorism, Jihadi-Salafism and political Salafism – have reinforced this trend.

The regime has thus certainly played a role in domesticating the quietist Salafi community in Jordan through the explicit inclusion of its leaders in the state's sphere of influence, but to deny the movement's leaders their agency in this "moderation" would be a misrepresentation of what has clearly been a much more nuanced and dynamic process. The reasons for the movement's domestication therefore lie in its ideology, its response to others, its internal dynamics, the influence of the state and – for reasons having to do with ideology as well as interests – quietists' conscious embrace of the regime's role. Through this increasingly loyalist attitude, Jordanian quietist Salafi shaykhs and their community have come to resemble somewhat the Salafi religious establishment in Saudi Arabia, which has long been loyally tied to that country's regime. This also partly explains the lack of substantial opposition to the domestication process of quietists' leaders: compared to the situation of Saudi quietist Salafi scholars – who dominate much of the trend's discourse worldwide – the present Jordanian context is not at all out of the ordinary. For many quietists in Jordan, there may even be little difference between the kingdom's dominant loyalist quietists and those who have tried to remain aloofist and independent, just like the two bookshops in ʿAbdali may seem alike. Beneath the surface, however, there are fissures that are unlikely to disappear anytime soon. Yet both trends and their respective bookshops do have in common that each will keep claiming al-Albani's legacy, cleansing and teaching their way to the Salafi utopia.

Glossary

Note: several of the terms mentioned here have multiple meanings. I have chosen to focus only on those meanings used in this study. Terms used only once are not listed here, but explained where they occur in the text.

ahl al-ḥadīth – an early Islamic trend and precursor to Salafism (q.v.) that relied heavily on *ḥadīths* (q.v.) in establishing its rulings, at the expense of relying on considered opinion (*raʾy*, q.v.). They were opposed by the *ahl al-raʾy* (q.v.). There are also modern-day movements bearing this name or similar ones.

ahl al-raʾy – an early Islamic trend that relied heavily on considered opinion (*raʾy*, q.v.) in establishing its rulings, at the expense of relying on *ḥadīths* (q.v.). They were opposed by the *ahl al-ḥadīth* (q.v.).

ahl al-Sunna wa-l-jamāʿa – the branch of Islam that claims to follow the example of the Prophet (Sunna) and belong to the group (*jamāʿa*) that, according to a *ḥadīth* (q.v.), will be saved from hellfire. The term is applied by Salafis (q.v.) to themselves but is also used by Sunni Muslims in general. See also *al-ṭāʾifa al-manṣūra*, *al-firqa al-nājiya*.

ʿaqīda – creed. This is a highly important term for Salafis (q.v.) since they attach great value to following the right path and therefore often pay much attention to its details.

barāʾ – see *al-walāʾ wa-l-barāʾ*.

bayʿa – an oath of allegiance. Some quietist Salafis (q.v.) in Jordan have expressed the willingness to pledge allegiance to King ʿAbdallah II of Jordan.

bidʿa (pl. *bidaʿ*) – innovation. Salafis (q.v.) regard *bidaʿ* as undesirable and wrong since they are considered illegitimate additions to Islam that compromise the religion's supposed purity. See also *tajdīd*.

daʿwa – the call to Islam. This is the preferred method (*manhaj*, q.v.) of engaging with society for quietist Salafis (q.v.) in general.

fiqh – Islamic jurisprudence. This term plays a minor role in Salafism (q.v.), whose adherents concentrate far more on creed (*ʿaqīda*, q.v.).

fiqh al-wāqiʿ – the jurisprudence of reality. A term used by Jordanian Salafis (q.v.) to indicate their willingness to inform themselves about society in order to facilitate their *daʿwa* (q.v.).

al-firqa al-nājiya – the saved sect, the group that, according to a *ḥadīth* (q.v.), will be saved from hellfire. Salafis (q.v.) believe that they are part of this group. See also *ahl al-Sunna wa-l-jamāʿa*, *al-ṭāʾifa al-manṣūra*.

fitna (pl. *fitan*) – chaos, strife. Quietist Salafis (q.v.) often describe Jihadi-Salafis as causing *fitna* through their jihad and excommunication (*takfīr*, q.v.) of Muslim rulers. They also often see the partisanship (*ḥizbiyya*, q.v.), demonstrations and political involvement of political Salafis as causing *fitna*.

ghurabāʾ (sing. *gharīb*) – strangers. According to a *ḥadīth* (q.v.), Muslims are called upon to be strangers among the people around them. Salafis (q.v.) apply this term to themselves to explain and justify their being different from others.

ḥadīth (pl. *aḥādīth* but given as *ḥadīth*s in this study) – a story consisting of a chain of transmitters (*isnād*) and some content (*matn*) containing information about or from the first generations of Muslims, particularly the Prophet Muhammad. *Ḥadīth*s have played a major role in the formation of Islamic law (*sharīʿa*, q.v.) and in the doctrines and publications of Salafis (q.v.).

ḥajj – Islamic pilgrimage to Mecca. This is one of the five pillars of Islam.

hijra – emigration. Most often used in Islamic history to refer to the emigration of the Prophet Muhammad from Mecca to Medina in 622 AD, but also applied to modern-day religiously motivated emigration, such as the perceived duty to move from non-Muslim countries to Muslim countries. See also *al-walāʾ wa-l-barāʾ*.

ḥizbiyya – partisanship. Quietist Salafis (q.v.) accuse the Muslim Brotherhood and political Salafis of being in favour of partisanship, thereby directing their loyalty to a party rather than to God, Islam and Muslims and dividing the *umma* (q.v.).

ijtihād – independent reasoning on the basis of the scriptural sources of Islam without necessarily remaining within the limits of one Islamic legal school of thought (*madhhab*, q.v.). *Ijtihād* is the opposite of blind emulation (*taqlīd*, q.v.).

īmān – faith. The opposite of unbelief (*kufr*, q.v.). According to Salafis (q.v.), faith consists of belief in the heart (*al-iʿtiqād bi-l-qalb*), speech with the tongue (*al-qawl bi-l-lisān*) and acts with the limbs (*al-aʿmāl bi-l-jawāriḥ*), although some Salafis ascribe different value to the latter.

irjāʾ – postponement. The term is linked to the Murjiʾa (q.v.), an early

Islamic trend advocating the postponement of judgement over a person's sins and leaving it to God.

iṣlāḥ – reform. This term is favourably looked upon by all Salafis (q.v.), but especially by political Salafis in Jordan, who apply the term to various areas of life.

al-istiʿāna bi-l-kuffār – the act of asking non-Muslims for help, especially against other Muslims in times of war. It is seen by most modern Salafi (q.v.) scholars as part of loyalty and disavowal (*al-walāʾ wa-l-barāʾ*, q. v.). According to many Salafi scholars, *al-istiʿāna bi-l-kuffār* is strictly forbidden.

istiḥlāl – making or considering something that is forbidden (*ḥarām*) permissible (*ḥalāl*). With regard to the question of unbelief (*kufr*, q. v.), having the belief that something wrong is actually right is one of the conditions that turn minor unbelief (*kufr aṣghar*, q.v.) into major unbelief (*kufr akbar*, q.v.), thereby expelling its culprit from Islam. See also *iʿtiqād, jaḥd.*

iʿtiqād – conviction. With regard to the question of unbelief (*kufr*, q.v.), the conviction that one is committing a sin without refraining from it is one of the conditions that turn minor unbelief (*kufr aṣghar*, q.v.) into major unbelief (*kufr akbar*, q.v.), thereby expelling its culprit from Islam. See also *istiḥlāl, jaḥd.*

jaḥd – negation. With regard to the question of unbelief (*kufr*, q.v.), the negation of the supposed truth of Islam and its rulings is one of the conditions that turn minor unbelief (*kufr aṣghar*, q.v.) into major unbelief (*kufr akbar*, q.v.), thereby expelling its culprit from Islam. See also *iʿtiqād, istiḥlāl.*

juḥūd – see *jaḥd.*

kabīra (*kabāʾir*) – a major sin. It can be equated with minor unbelief (*kufr aṣghar*, q.v.) and should not be confused with major unbelief (*kufr akbar*, q.v.).

kāfir (pl. *kuffār*/*kāfirūn*) – unbeliever, non-Muslim.

kamāl al-dīn – the perfection of the religion. This is a level of faith (*īmān*, q.v.) on which sins do not harm faith as a whole, Salafis (q.v.) believe, but on which good beliefs, speech and action can increase it. See also *ṣiḥḥat al-dīn, wājib al-dīn.*

Khawarij (sing. Khariji) – seceders. The term refers to an early Islamic group that is said to have seceded from the majority of Muslims and supposedly applied excommunication (*takfīr*, q.v.) of other Muslims for acts of minor unbelief (*kufr aṣghar*, q.v.). The label is often used by quietist Salafis (q.v.) to de-legitimise Jihadi-Salafis. In that sense, the term "Khawarij" is the opposite of "Murjiʾa" (q.v.). See also *irjāʾ*.

kufr – unbelief. The opposite of *īmān* (q.v.). Salafis (q.v.) divide *kufr* into major unbelief (*kufr akbar*, q.v.), which expels its culprit from Islam, and minor unbelief (*kufr aṣghar*, q.v.), which does not, unless it is accompanied by *iʿtiqād* (q.v.), *istiḥlāl* (q.v.) or *jaḥd* (q.v.). See also *shirk*.

kufr akbar – major unbelief. According to Salafis (q.v.), this level of unbelief (*kufr*, q.v.) expels the culprit from Islam. See also *īmān*, *kufr aṣghar*, *shirk*.

kufr aṣghar – minor unbelief. According to Salafis (q.v.), this level of unbelief (*kufr*, q.v.) is a serious violation of Islam, but does not expel the culprit from Islam. See also *īmān*, *kufr akbar*, *shirk*.

kufr dūna kufr – unbelief less than unbelief. This phrase is used by quietist Salafis (q.v.) to indicate that certain types of unbelief (*kufr*, q.v.) are not major unbelief (*kufr akbar*, q.v.) but minor unbelief (*kufr aṣghar*, q.v.), which means that applying excommunication (*takfīr*, q.v.) to the culprit is not allowed. The phrase is derived from words ascribed to ʿAbdallah b. ʿAbbas (c.619–687). See also *īmān*.

madhhab (pl. *madhāhib*) – Islamic legal school. In Sunni Islam, there are four schools of law: the Hanafi, Hanbali, Maliki and Shafiʿi legal schools. Each is usually treated as legitimate in the eyes of the others, but Salafis (q.v.) in Jordan reject the blind emulation (*taqlīd*, q.v.) of any one school of law and instead advocate independent reasoning on the basis of the scriptural sources of Islam (*ijtihād*, q.v.).

manhaj – method. The term refers to the method of applying the creed (*ʿaqīda*, q.v.) that Salafis (q.v.) follow in their treatment of the sources, worship and dealing with society. It is a very important concept since the *manhaj* is partly responsible for setting Salafis apart from each other and from other Sunni Muslims.

mujaddid (pl. *mujaddidūn*) – renewer. According to tradition, every hundred years will see a new and important renewer in Islam. See also *tajdīd*.

Murjiʾa – an early Islamic trend advocating the postponement (*irjāʾ*, q.v.) of judgement over a person's sins and leaving it to God. Quietist Salafis (q.v.) unwilling to apply excommunication (*takfīr*, q.v.) to rulers of Muslim countries are often accused by Jihadi-Salafis of being like the Murjiʾa. See also Khawarij.

raʾy – considered opinion. A means for Muslim scholars (*ʿulamāʾ*, q.v.) to create new rulings on the basis of existing texts using one's own or others' opinions. Salafis (q.v.) reject this but distinguish it from independent reasoning (*ijtihād*, q.v.), which they see as a legitimate form of deriving rulings from the text. See also *ahl al-raʾy*.

ṣaḥwa – revival. In this book, the term refers to the Saudi movement that was inspired by Salafism (q.v.) and the ideas of the Muslim Brotherhood and grew in importance from the 1960s onwards.

It played a major role in the opposition to the Saudi regime in the 1990s.

salaf – see *al-salaf al-ṣāliḥ*.

al-salaf al-ṣāliḥ – the pious predecessors. Usually refers to the first three generations of Muslims who, according to a *ḥadīth* (q.v.), are the best in Islamic history. Salafis (q.v.) claim to try to emulate these generations as much and in as many spheres of life as possible.

Salafis – see Salafism.

Salafism – the trend in Islam whose adherents claim to try to emulate the first three generations of Muslims (*al-salaf al-ṣāliḥ*, q.v.) as much and in as many spheres of life as possible.

sharīʿa – Islamic law. The term refers to the path Muslims should follow, which is supposedly embodied by the numerous writings on Islamic legal issues. Because Salafis (q.v.) believe that religious innovations (*bidaʿ*, sing. *bidʿa*, q.v.) have crept into this system of laws throughout the centuries, they reject the *sharīʿa* as it is understood by many other Muslims (i.e., the systems of the different legal schools (*madhāhib*, sing. *madhhab*, q.v.) developed by *ʿulamāʾ* (q.v.) throughout the course of Islamic history). Salafis' own alternative remains rather vague, however.

shaykh – patriarch, leader, title for a religious scholar or for someone respected for other reasons. See also *ʿulamāʾ*.

shirk – polytheism. Salafis (q.v.) see Muslims guilty of *shirk* as unbelievers (*kuffār*, sing. *kāfir*, q.v.). See also *kufr*.

shūrá – consultation. Islamists who want to incorporate democracy into their ideas sometimes use this term as a supposedly Islamic form of democracy. Salafis generally reject this.

ṣiḥḥat al-dīn – the soundness of the religion. This is a level of faith (*īmān*, q.v.) on which the occurrence of sins is so serious that they expel the culprit from Islam, Salafis (q.v.) believe. See also *kamāl al-dīn*, *wājib al-dīn*.

ṭāʿa – obedience. Quietist Salafis (q.v.) are strongly in favour of obedience to the rulers of the Muslim world because they believe it is their religious duty and because they do not want to create strife (*fitna*, q.v.).

tabdīl – exchange. It refers to the complete exchange of Islamic law (*sharīʿa*, q.v.) with another system of laws or a non-Islamic constitution. According to some Salafis (q.v.), this act of exchange is such a clear example of unbelief (*kufr*, q.v.) that no further proof of someone's true intentions is necessary. It thereby expels the culprit from Islam.

al-ṭāʾifa al-manṣūra – the victorious group. This term refers to the Muslims who are, on the basis of *ḥadīth* (q.v.), believed to be the only victorious group on Judgement Day. Salafis (q.v.) believe they are part of this group. See also *ahl al-Sunna wa-l-jamāʿa, al-firqa al-nājiya.*

tajdīd – renewal. See also *mujaddid.*

takfīr – excommunication of other Muslims, declaring other Muslims to be unbelievers (*kuffār*, sing. *kāfir*, q.v.). While Jihadi-Salafis (q.v.) advocate this when dealing with the rulers of Muslim countries, quietist Salafis acknowledge the legitimacy of the concept as such but see its application to Muslim rulers in general as a sign of extremism.

takfīrī – excommunicator. This is a derogatory term used by quietist Salafis (q.v.) to suggest that Jihadi-Salafis' ideology revolves around (illegitimately) excommunicating the rulers of Muslim countries. See also Khawarij.

ṭālib ʿilm (pl. *ṭullāb ʿilm*) – a student of (religious) knowledge, a knowledge seeker. A term that many Salafis (q.v.) apply to themselves, thereby indicating that they see themselves as seekers of the correct knowledge of Islam. See also shaykh, *ʿulamāʾ*.

taqlīd – blind emulation of a particular school of law (*madhhab*, q.v.). Jordanian quietist Salafis (q.v.) reject this. See also *ijtihād.*

tarbiya – see *al-taṣfiya wa-l-tarbiya.*

taṣfiya – see *al-taṣfiya wa-l-tarbiya.*

al-taṣfiya wa-l-tarbiya – cleansing and teaching. Quietist Salafis (q.v.) in Jordan use this term to indicate their *manhaj* (q.v.) for dealing with society. It refers to their efforts to "cleanse" Islamic traditions from supposedly inauthentic *ḥadīths* (q.v.) and *bidaʿ* (sing. *bidʿa*, q.v.) so as to attain an entirely "purified" Islam, which must subsequently be taught to others.

tawḥīd – the unity of God. This is a strong focal point in Salafism (q.v.) and in Islam as a whole. Salafis (q.v.) divide *tawḥīd* into three different types: *tawḥīd al-rubūbiyya* (the unity of lordship), *tawḥīd al-asmāʾ wa-l-ṣifāt* (the unity of names and attributes) and *tawḥīd al-ulūhiyya* (the unity of divinity). The first refers to basic ideas of monotheism such as that there is only one God and Creator; the second refers to God's unique nature and incomparability; and the third form refers to the idea that only God may be worshipped.

ʿulamāʾ (sing. *ʿālim*) – scholars, particularly religious scholars. Among Jordanian Salafis (q.v.), *ʿulamāʾ* form the organisational backbone of the movement. They are held in great esteem as the possessors of old and the producers of new knowledge. Informally, they are seen as more knowledgeable than *ṭullāb ʿilm* (sing. *ṭālib ʿilm*, q.v.). See also shaykh.

umma – the worldwide community of Muslims.

wājib al-dīn – the compulsory of the religion. This is a level of faith (*īmān*, q.v.) on which sins harm faith, Salafis (q.v.) believe, but do not expel the culprit from Islam. See also *kamāl al-dīn*, *ṣiḥḥat al-dīn*.

walāʾ – see *al-walāʾ wa-l-barāʾ*.

al-walāʾ wa-l-barāʾ – loyalty and disavowal. *Walāʾ* refers to the friendship, loyalty and dedication Muslims should show to God, Islam and their co-religionists, while *barāʾ* denotes the distance, disavowal, hatred and enmity Muslims should show towards everything else. While many scholars interpret this concept solely in a social and apolitical way, others treat it as a concept relevant to situations of military conflict, during which Muslims should always side with their fellow believers against non-Muslims. See also *al-istiʿāna bi-l-kuffār*.

walī al-amr (pl. *wulāt al-amr*) – the ruler. Quietist Salafis (q.v.) believe the ruler should be obeyed and, in case of criticism, should be given advice (*naṣīḥa*). Political Salafis, however, believe protests and/or political participation are allowed, and Jihadi-Salafis believe the *walī al-amr* may be fought if he is an apostate (*murtadd*).

Bibliography

Below is a non-exhaustive list of sources. For reasons of space, the references to newspapers, YouTube videos and *ḥadīth* collections have been omitted.

Interviews

During my fieldwork in Jordan, I have benefited greatly from many informal conversations I had with Salafis and others, as well as from actual interviews with some who wished to remain anonymous. These have been omitted from the following list, which shows only those semi-structured interviews with the people who allowed me to use their names.

Ziyād al-ʿAbbādī, Amman, 26 June 2012

Ḥasan Abū Haniyya, Amman, 9 August 2008, 13 January 2009, 9 June 2012

ʿAbd al-Fattāḥ ʿUmar Abū l-Ḥārith, Amman, 14 January 2013

Yāsir Abū Hilāla, Amman, 7 August 2008

Muḥammad Abū Ruḥayyim, Amman, 16 January 2013

Ḥusayn Abū Rummān, Amman, 11 August 2008

Muḥammad Abū Rummān, Amman, 11 August 2008, 19 June 2012

Abū Muslim Majdī b. ʿAbd al-Wahhāb al-Aḥmad, al-Zarqāʾ, 18 June 2013

Abū l-Ḥajjāj Yūsuf b. Aḥmad al-ʿAlawī, Māḥiṣ, 21 January 2014

Muḥammad b. Mūsá Āl Naṣr, Amman, 20 June 2012

Mashhūr b. Ḥasan Āl Salmān, Amman, 27 June 2012

Ḥāzim al-Amīn, Beirut, 14 August 2008

Shākir al-ʿĀrūrī, Amman, 23 January 2013

Ibrāhīm al-ʿAsʿas, Amman, 14 January 2013

Muḥammad Aḥmad Abū Laylá l-Atharī, al-Ruṣayfa, 26 January 2013

Ḥusayn al-ʿAwāyisha, Amman, 28 June 2012

Wāʾil al-Batīrī, Amman, 11 January 2014

Fāris Brayzāt, Amman, 6 August 2008

Aḥmad al-Dhuwayb, Amman, 15 January 2013

ʿIkrima Gharāyiba, Amman, 15 January 2009

Ashraf Gharbiyya, al-Ruṣayfa, 3 July 2014

ʿIṣām Hādī, Amman, 19 January 2013

ʿAlī al-Ḥalabī, Amman, 19 January 2009, 27 June 2012; via e-mail, 17 June 2013
Zāyid Ḥammād, Amman, 19 January 2013
Shadi Hamid, Amman, 11 August 2008
Salīm al-Hilālī, Amman, 28 January 2013
Fuʾād Ḥusayn, Amman, 5 August 2008
Isḥāq b. Yaḥyá, Amman, 11 June 2012
Bāsim b. Fayṣal al-Jawābira, Amman, 26 June 2012
Maḥmūd al-Kīlānī, al-Salṭ, 20 January 2014
Samīḥ Khurays, Amman, 14 January 2009
ʿĀyish Labābina, Irbid, 14 January 2014
Ṣāliḥ al-Laḥḥām, Amman, 21 January 2013
Abū Muḥammad al-Maqdisī, Amman, 13 January 2009; al-Ruṣayfa, 17 January 2009
Fatḥī al-Mawṣilī, Amman, 23 January 2013
ʿAbd al-Malik Besfort Maxhuni, al-Zarqāʾ, 18 January 2014
Aḥmad Muṣliḥ, Amman, 29 January 2013
Bassām Nāṣir, Amman, 16 June 2013
Fādī Qarāqara, Amman, 16 June 2012
Yūsuf Rabāba, Amman, 12 January 2009
ʿUrayb al-Rantāwī, Amman, 12 August 2008
Munīf Samāra, al-Zarqāʾ, 2 July 2014
Marwān Shaḥāda, Amman, 13 January 2009, 9 June 2012, 11 January 2013
Usāma Shaḥāda, Amman, 12 January 2009, 7 June 2012, 10 January 2013
Muḥammad al-Shalabī, Maʿān, 29 June 2014
Muḥammad Ibrāhīm Shaqra, Amman, 27 June 2012
Jamāl al-Shaykh, Irbid, 22 June 2014
Murād Shukrī, Amman, 17 January 2013
Muṣṭafá l-Ṣurīfī, al-Salṭ, 30 June 2014
Walīd ʿUthmān Tāsh, al-Zarqāʾ, 26 January 2014
Amīn al-Tubāsī, al-Ḥuṣn, 22 January 2014
Iḥsān al-ʿUtaybī, Irbid, 28 January 2014
Muʿādh al-ʿUtaybī, Irbid, 19 January 2014
Akram Ziyāda, Amman, 28 June 2012

Websites and Forums

Please note that some of these websites may no longer be accessible.

http://aalalbayt.org/en/news.html
http://alathary.net
http://alawaysheh.com
http://alhalaby.net/main/Default.aspx
http://almahajjah.net/Pages/2_Dr_Pages/2_1_DR.htm
http://aloloom.net

http://altkaful.net/
http://ammanmessage.com
http://ifpo.hypotheses.org
http://kingabdullah.jo
http://madkhalis.com
http://main.islammessage.com
http://osamash.maktoobblog.com
http://turntoislam.com
https://sunnahtube.files.wordpress.com
www.4salaf.com
www.addyaiya.com
www.alalbany.net
www.alertiqaa.org
www.alhalaby.com
www.alifta.net
www.almahajjah.net
www.al-sunna.net
www.binbaz.org.sa
www.coexistencejordan.org
www.gallup.com
www.hudson.org
www.ict.org.il
www.kulalsalafiyeen.com
www.majles.alwkah.net
www.mashhoor.net
www.mediafire.com
www.muslm.org
www.oriold.uzh.ch/static/hegira.html
www.saaid.net
www.salafimanhaj.com
www.salafipublications.com
www.tawhed.ws
www.themadkhalis.com/md
www.ui.se/eng
www.washingtoninstitute.org

Media

Agence France-Presse
Al-ʿArab al-Yawm
Al-Būṣala
Al-Dustūr
Al-Ghad
Al-Ḥaqīqa al-Dawliyya
Al-Ḥayāt
Al-Jazīra
Al-Maqarr

Al-Quds al-ʿArabī
Al-Raʾy
Al-Ribāṭ News
Al-Sabīl
Al-Sharq al-Awsaṭ
ʿAmmūn
The Daily Telegraph
The Economist
Fox News
The Guardian
The Jordan Times
NBC News
The New York Times
Petra
Ṣawt al-Shaʿb
Shīḥān News
Zād al-Urdunn al-Akhbārī

Articles, Books, Fatwas, Reports and Unpublished Manuscripts

Primary Sources (Arabic, English and French)

"Ahamm Injāzāt al-Jamʿiyya fī Ighāthat al-Lājiʾīn al-Sūriyyīn fī l-Urdunn." *Al-Qibla* 9, no. 22 (2012): 79–83.
"Ahamm Injāzāt al-Jamʿiyya fī Ighāthat al-Lājiʾīn al-Sūriyyīn fī l-Urdunn." *Al-Qibla* 10, no. 23 (2012): 86–8.
"Aḥwāl al-ʿĀlam al-Islāmī." *Al-Aṣāla* 1, no. 1 (15 Rabīʿ al-Thānī 1413 [13 October 1992]): 75–6.
"Aḥwāl al-ʿĀlam al-Islāmī." *Al-Aṣāla* 1, no. 2 (15 Jumādá l-Ākhira 1413 [11 December 1992]): 77–9.
"Aḥwāl al-ʿĀlam al-Islāmī." *Al-Aṣāla* 1, no. 5 (15 Dhū l-Ḥijja 1413 [6 June 1993]): 78–80.
"Aḥwāl al-ʿĀlam al-Islāmī." *Al-Aṣāla* 3, nos. 15–16 (15 Dhū l-Qaʿda 1415 [15 April 1995]): 133–4.
"Ajwibat al-ʿAllāma al-Albānī ʿalá Asʾilat Jabhat al-Inqādh – al-Jazāʾir." *Al-Aṣāla* 1, no. 4 (15 Shawwāl 1413 [8 April 1993]): 15–22.
"Al-Ḥijāb." *Al-Qibla* 2, nos. 4–5 (2003): 200–3.
"Al-Ḥubb fī llāh wa-l-walāʾ." *Al-Aṣāla* 1, no. 2 (15 Jumādá l-Ākhira 1413 [11 December 1992]): 81–2.
"Al-Quds Tuwājihu … 'al-Kharāb'." *Al-Qibla* 8, no. 20 (2010): 4–8.
"Al-Rawāfiḍ al-Shīʿa wa-Mawāqifuhum al-Shanīʿa min Ahl al-Sunna wa-l-Sharīʿa!!" *Al-Aṣāla* 11, no. 54 (15 Dhū l-Ḥijja 1427 [6 December 2006]): 5–6.
"Al-Salafiyya Ẓāhira – bi-Idhn Allāh." *Al-Aṣāla* 7, no. 38 (15 Rabīʿ al-Awwal 1423 [27 May 2002]): 5–8.

"Al-Salafiyya. Wāḥida." *Al-Aṣāla* 6, no. 31 (15 Muḥarram 1422 [9 April 2001]): 5–6.
"Al-Salafiyya . . . wa-l-Irhāb!!" *Al-Aṣāla* 7, no. 39 (15 Jumādá l-Ākhira 1423 [24 August 2002]): 5–8.
"Al-Taqtīl al-Aʿmá Fiʾl Muḥarram Yabraʾu l-Islām minhu!" *Al-Aṣāla* 10, no. 50 (15 Ramaḍān 1426 [18 October 2005]): 5–6.
"Bayān min Hayʾat Kibār al-ʿUlamāʾ ḥawla Masʾalat al-Takfīr." *Al-Aṣāla* 5, no. 28 (15 Jumādá l-Ākhira 1420 [26 September 1999]): 90–3.
"Bayān min Jamʿiyyat al-Kitāb wa-l-Sunna bi-Khuṣūṣ Aḥdāth Ghazza." *Al-Qibla* 7, no. 18 (2009): 1.
"Bayna Lughat al-ʿArab wa-Fahm al-Salaf." *Al-Aṣāla* 5, nos. 25–6 (15 Muḥarram 1421 [20 April 2000] – 15 Rabīʿ al-Awwal 1421 [18 June 2000]): 17–24.
"Fa-dhanū bi-Ḥarb min Allāh wa-Rasūlihi – Azmat al-Rahn al-ʿAqārī." *Al-Qibla* 7, no. 18 (2009): 4–6.
"Fatāwá l-Lajna al-Dāʾima fī Masʾalat al-Ḥukm bi-Ghayr Mā Anzala llāh." *Al-Aṣāla* 5, no. 29 (15 Shaʿbān 1421 [13 November 2000]): 77–8.
"Fī Ḥiwār Maftūḥ maʿa l-Murāqib al-ʿĀmm li-Jamāʿat al-Ikhwān al-Muslimīn fī l-Urdunn." *Al-Qibla* 1, no. 3 (Summer 2002): 94–114.
"Filasṭīn fī l-Qurʾān al-Karīm . . . al-Arḍ al-Mubāraka." *Al-Qibla* 1, no. 2 (2002): 22–3.
"Hal al-ʿAmal Sharṭ Ṣiḥḥa fī l-Īmān am Sharṭ Kamāl?" *Al-Aṣāla* 5, nos. 25–6 (15 Muḥarram 1421 [20 April 2000] – 15 Rabīʿ al-Awwal 1421 [18 June 2000]): 133–9.
"Ḥaqīqat al-ʿUdwān." *Al-Aṣāla* 7, no. 40 (Dhū l-Ḥijja 1423 [17 February 2003]): 4–6.
"Ḥattá Tattabiʿu Millatahum." *Al-Qibla* 6, no. 16 (2008): 5–9.
"Ḥiwār maʿa Faḍīlat al-Shaykh Faqīh al-Zamān Muḥammad b. Ṣāliḥ al-ʿUthaymīn Ḥafaẓahu llāh." *Al-Aṣāla* 5, no. 28 (15 Jumādá l-Ākhira 1420 [26 September 1999]): 71–8.
"Iṭfāʾ al-Fitna." *Al-Aṣāla* 9, no. 45 (15 Ṣafar 1425 [6 April 2004]): 5–6.
"Lā Salām illā bi-l-Islām." *Al-Aṣāla* 2, no. 8 (15 Jumādá l-Ākhira 1414 [30 November 1993]): 5–7.
"Liqāʾ 'al-Mirʾāt' maʿa Raʾīs Jamʿiyyat al-Kitāb wa-l-Sunna." *Al-Qibla* 1, no. 3 (2002): 36–9.
"Mādhā Yanqimūna min Bilād al-Ḥaramayn?!" *Al-Aṣāla* 8, no. 43 (15 Jumādá l-Ākhira 1424 [14 August 2003]): 5–7.
"Masʾalat al-Irjāʾ." *Al-Aṣāla* 5, nos. 25–6 (15 Muḥarram 1421 [20 April 2000] – 15 Rabīʿ al-Awwal 1421 [18 June 2000]): 115–32.
"Min Dayr Yāsīn ilá Janīn . . . al-Qātil Wāḥid." *Al-Qibla* 1, no. 2 (2002): 1.
"Mutābaʿāt . . . Mutābaʿāt . . . Mutābaʿāt . . . Mutābaʿāt . . ." *Al-Qibla* 2, nos. 10–11 (2005): 98–108.
"Rukn al-Fatāwá." *Al-Qibla* 6, no. 16 (2008): 105–13.
"Ṣirāʿunā maʿa l-Yahūd Ṣirāʿ Wujūd Lā Ṣirāʿ Ḥudūd." *Al-Aṣāla* 5, no. 30 (15 Shawwāl 1421 [11 January 2001]): 5–6.
"Taḥrīr Qawl Ibn ʿAbbās – Raḍiya llāh ʿanhu: 'Kufr Dūna Kufr'." *Al-Aṣāla* 5, nos. 25–6 (15 Muḥarram 1421 [20 April 2000] – 15 Rabīʿ al-Awwal 1421 [18 June 2000]): 79–114.

"Takfīr Tārik al-Ṣalāt." *Al-Aṣāla* 5, nos. 25–6 (15 Muḥarram 1421 [20 April 2000] – 15 Rabīʿ al-Awwal 1421 [18 June 2000]): 25–77.
"Taʿriyat Banī Isrāʾīl Kamā Ṣawwarathā Āyāt al-Tanzīl." *Al-Qibla* 1, no. 2 (2002): 26–37.
"Tarjamat Faḍīlat al-Shaykh al-Muḥaddith ʿAbd al-Qādir al-Arnāʾūṭ (Raḥimahu llāh)." *Al-Qibla* 4, nos. 10–11 (November 2005): 37–54.
"Wafd min Jamʿiyyat al-Kitāb wa-l-Sunna Yushāriku fī Muʾtamar al-Āthār al-Nafsiyya wa-l-Ijtimāʿiyya li-l-Thawra al-Sūriyya." *Al-Qibla* 10, no. 23 (2012): 83–5.
"Wāqiʿunā l-Alīm wa-Mustaqbalunā l-Wāʿid." *Al-Aṣāla* 6, no. 35 (15. Shaʿbān 1422 [2 November 2001]): 5–11.
ʿAbd al-Raḥmān, Mūsá. "Al-Muslimūn fī l-Ṣīn." *Al-Qibla* 8, no. 20 (2010): 39–44.
ʿAbda, Muḥammad al-. "Ḥayna Tataghallabu l-ʿĀṭifa." *Al-Qibla* 2, nos. 10–11 (2005): 94.
Abū Fāris, Muḥammad ʿAbd al-Qādir. *Al-Mushāraka fī l-Wizāra fī l-Anẓima al-Jāhiliyya*. N.p.: No publisher, 1991.
Abū Haniyya, ʿAlī b. Muḥammad. *Tuḥfat al-Ṭālib al-Abī bi-Tarjamat al-Shaykh al-Muḥaddith ʿAlī b. Ḥasan al-Ḥalabī*. N.p.: Manshūrāt Muntadayāt Kull al-Salafiyyīn, 2011.
Abū Haniyya, Ḥasan. "Al-Istishrāq wa-Tashkīl al-Ṣūra al-Namaṭiyya li-l-Islām." *Al-Qibla* 4, nos. 10–11 (2005): 27–36.
"Bayna Masārāt al-Silmiyya wa-l-ʿAskariyya ... Ayna Takmunu Maṣlaḥat al-Thawra al-Sūriyya?" *Al-Qibla* 9, no. 22 (2012): 39–43.
Abū l-ʿAynayn, Aḥmad b. Ibrāhīm. *Al-Intiṣār li-l-Ḥaqq wa-Ahl al-ʿIlm al-Kibār wa-l-Radd ʿalá Man Ramá l-Shaykh Muḥammad Nāṣir al-Dīn al-Albānī Raḥimahu llāh bi-l-Tasāhul*. Kuwait: Maktabat al-Imam al-Zuhbī, 2004.
Abū l-Ḥārith, ʿAbd al-Fattāḥ ʿUmar. "Qitāl al-Muslimīn li-l-Yahūd ... Hal Huwa Murtabaṭ bi-Ashrāṭ al-Sāʿa?!" *Al-Qibla* 1, no. 3 (2002): 61–5.
Abū Lūz, Abū Anas ʿAlī b. Ḥusayn. *Fitnat al-Takfīr*. Riyadh: Dār al-Waṭan, 1417 [1996–1997].
Fitnat al-Takfīr. Riyadh: Dār Ibn Khuzayma, 1997.
Abū Lūz, ʿAlī b. Ḥasan. "Ẓāhirat al-Iʿtiṣāmāt wa-l-Muẓāharāt wa-l-Thawrāt al-Shaʿbiyya wa-l-Iḍrāb fī Fatāwá l-Aʾimma wa-l-ʿUlamāʾ." *Al-Aṣāla* 5, no. 30 (15 Shawwāl 1421 [11 January 2001]): 59–65.
Abū Ruḥayyim, Muḥammad. *Ḥaqīqat al-Khilāf bayna l-Salafiyya al-Sharʿiyya wa-Adʿiyāʾihā*. www.tawhed.ws/dl?i=ynh8cqba, 1998.
Ḥaqīqat al-Īmān ʿinda l-Shaykh al-Albānī. www.tawhed.ws/dl?i=d7pgztyu, 2001.
Introduction to *Masʾalat al-Īmān fī Kaffatay al-Mīzān*, edited by Abū ʿUzayr ʿAbd al-Ilāh Yūsuf al-Yūbī al-Ḥasanī al-Jazāʾirī, 5–18. Amman: Dār al-Maʾmūn, 2006.
Aḥmad, Abū Muslim Majdī b. ʿAbd al-Wahhāb al-. *Sharḥ Ḥiṣn al-Muslim min Adhkār al-Kitāb wa-l-Sunna*. Amman: Al-Dār al-Athariyya, 2012.
Aḥmad, ʿIṣām. "Ḥaqīqat al-Dīmuqrāṭiyya." *Al-Qibla* 11, no. 24 (2013): 20–9.
Āl ʿAbd al-ʿAzīz, Mūsá b. ʿAbdallāh, ed. *Al-Maqālāt al-Manhajiyya fī "Ḥizb al-Taḥrīr" wa-l-Jamāʿāt al-Takfīriyya min "Al-Majalla al-Salafiyya" li-l-Imāmayn Ibn Bāz wa-l-Albānī*. Riyadh: Dār al-Buḥūth wa-l-Dirāsāt al-Muʿāṣira wa-l-Tarājum, 2006.

Āl ʿAbd al-Raḥmān, Abū Ṭalḥa ʿUmar b. Ibrāhīm. *Ḥukm al-Sharīʿa fī l-Zawāj min al-Shīʿa*. Cairo: Dār al-Minhāj, 2004.

Āl ʿAlāwī, Yūsuf b. Aḥmad. *Al-Ṣaḥāba Jīl al-Qudwa*. N.p.: No publisher, 2013.

Al-Bayān, Majallat. *Risāla ilá Ṭalāʾiʿ al-Ṭāʾifa al-Manṣūra fī Bayt al-Maqdis wa-Aknāf Bayt al-Maqdis*. Riyadh: Al-Muntadá l-Islāmī, 2004.

Āl Ḥumayyid, Saʿd b. ʿAbdallāh b. ʿAbd al-ʿAzīz. Introduction to *Rafʿ al-Lāʾima ʿan Fatwá l-Lajna al-Dāʾima*, edited by Muḥammad b. Sālim al-Dawsarī, 11–14. www.tawhed.ws/dl?i=ev70m465, n.d.

Āl Naṣr, Abū Anas Muḥammad b. Mūsá. "Al-ʿĀlim al-Rabbānī wa-Ḥājat al-Umma ilayhi." *Al-Aṣāla* 1, no. 3 (15 Shaʿbān 1413 [8 February 1993]): 41–3.

Al-Akhṭāʾ al-Wāqiʿa fī Qirāʾat Sūrat al-Fātiḥa min al-Muṣallīn wa-l-Aʾimma wa-l-Qāriʾīn. Amman: Al-Dār al-Athariyya, 2008.

Al-Rāfiḍa wa-Dawruhum fī l-Manṭiqa. www.almahajjah.net/Pages/3_ReportS_Pages/Arciv_Report_Rafedah.htm, n.d.

"ʿĀqibat Ahl al-Bidaʿ." *Al-Aṣāla* 5, no. 27 (15 Rabīʿ al-Ākhir 1421 [18 July 2000]): 17–18.

Awluwiyyāt al-Daʿwa ilá llāh. www.almahajjah.net/Pages/3_ReportS_Pages/Arciv_Report_aulauiat.htm, n.d.

Daʿāwá l-Jihād bayna al-Khanādiq ... wa-l-Fanādiq. www.almahajjah.net/Pages/3_ReportS_Pages/Arciv_Report_dawaJehad.htm, n.d.

Ḥarb Ṣalībiyya Jadīda Yaʿuddu la-hā Bābā l-Fātīkān. www.almahajjah.net/Pages/3_ReportS_Pages/Arciv_Report_HrbFtekan.htm, n.d.

Iʿmāl al-Naẓar fī l-Radd ʿalá Man Ankara l-Jamʿ fī l-Ḥaḍar bi-ʿUdhr al-Maṭar. Amman: Al-Dār al-Athariyya, 2003.

Jarīmat al-Ghishsh: Aḥkāmuhā wa-Ṣuwarihā wa-Āthārihā l-Mudammira. Dubai: Maktabat al-Furqān, 2008.

La-Kum Allāh Yā Ahlunā fī Ghazza al-Abiyya. www.almahajjah.net/Pages/7_Others_Files/GAZA_File.htm, n.d.

"'Mā lā Budda minhu bayna Yaday al-Ḥajj'." *Al-Aṣāla* 1, no. 4 (15 Shawwāl 1413 [8 April 1993]): 72–5.

"Makhāṭir Taghrīb al-Mujtamaʿāt al-Muslima." *Al-Aṣāla* 10, no. 49 (15 Jumādá l-Ākhira 1426 [22 July 2005]): 29–33.

Munīr ʿĀmm ʿalá Tafjīrāt ʿAmmān al-Ijrāmiyya. www.almahajjah.net/Pages/3_ReportS_Pages/Arciv_Report_TFgeratAMMAN.htm, n.d.

"Nakbat al-ʿAṣr bi-Mawt Imām al-ʿAṣr." *Al-Aṣāla* 4, no. 23 (15 Shaʿbān 1420 [24 November 1999]): 21–7.

"Naṣāʾiḥ Muhimma ilá ʿUlamāʾ al-Umma." *Al-Aṣāla* 1, no. 6 (15 Ṣafar 1414 [4 August 1993]): 31–4.

"Taḥdhīr al-Birriyya min ʿIbādat al-Aṣnām al-Bashariyya." *Al-Aṣāla* 1, no. 2 (15 Jumādá l-Ākhira 1413 [11 December 1992]): 25–9.

"'Wa-ka-Dhālika Jaʿalnākum Umma Wasaṭan'." *Al-Aṣāla* 9, no. 46 (15 Rajab 1425 [31 August 2004]): 8–10.

"Wa-Man Yushriku bi-llāh fa-kaʾannamā Kharra min al-Samāʾ." *Al-Aṣāla* 1, no. 1 (15 Rabīʿ al-Thānī 1413 [13 October 1992]): 5–8.

"Wujūb Taʿāwun al-Muslimīn ʿalá l-Birr wa-l-Taqwá." *Al-Aṣāla* 1, no. 2 (15 Jumādá l-Ākhira 1413 [11 December 1992]): 7–11.

Wujūb Ta'āwun al-Muslimīn [sic!] *'alá l-Birr wa-l-Taqwá*. http://almahajjah.net/print.php?action=printf&&id=155, 16 May 2010.

Āl Salmān, Abū 'Ubayda Mashhūr b. Ḥasan. "Al-'Amaliyyāt al-Fidā'iyya: A-Hiya Intiḥāriyya?! Am Istishhādiyya?! Al-Ḥalqa al-Rābi'a." *Al-Aṣāla* 7, no. 39 (15 Jumādá l-Ākhira 1423 [24 August 2002]): 28–41.

"Al-'Amaliyyāt al-Fidā'iyya: A-Hiya Intiḥāriyya?! Am Istishhādiyya?! Al-Ḥalqa al-Thālitha." *Al-Aṣāla* 7, no. 38 (15 Rabī' al-Awwal 1423 [27 May 2002]): 44–57.

"Al-'Amaliyyāt al-Fidā'iyya: A-Hiya Intiḥāriyya?! Am Istishhādiyya?! Al-Ḥalqa al-Thāniya." *Al-Aṣāla* 7, no. 37 (15 Ṣafar 1423 [28 April 2002]): 41–7.

"Al-'Amaliyyāt al-Fidā'iyya: A-Hiya Intiḥāriyya?! Am Istishhādiyya?! Al-Ḥalqa al-Ūlá." *Al-Aṣāla* 6, no. 36 (15 Shawwāl 1422 [31 December 2001]): 35–45.

"Al-Farq bayna l-Ṣaghīra wa-l-Kabīra." *Al-Aṣāla* 7, no. 40 (15 Dhū l-Ḥijja 1423 [17 February 2003]): 19–26.

"Al-Farq bayna l-Ṣaghīra wa-l-Kabīra – 2." *Al-Aṣāla* 8, no. 41 (15 Ṣafar 1424 [18 April 2003]): 54–60.

"Al-Farq bayna l-Ṣaghīra wa-l-Kabīra – 3." *Al-Aṣāla* 8, no. 42 (15 Rabī' al-Thānī 1424 [16 June 2003]): 43–53.

"Al-Farq bayna l-Ṣaghīra wa-l-Kabīra – 4." *Al-Aṣāla* 8, no. 43 (15 Jumādá l-Ākhira 1424 [14 August 2003]: 51–8.

"Al-Farq bayna l-Ṣaghīra wa-l-Kabīra – 5." *Al-Aṣāla* 8, no. 44 (15 Shawwāl 1424 [10 December 2003]): 45–9.

"Al-Fitan wa-'Awāmil al-Taghyīr." *Al-Aṣāla* 2, no. 8 (15 Jumādá l-Ākhira 1414 [30 November 2013]): 11–13.

Al-Imām al-Albānī wa-Jamā'at al-Tablīgh: 'Awāṣim wa-Qawāṣim, Sawābiq wa-Bawā'iq. Amman: Al-Dār al-Athariyya, 2010.

Al-Salafiyya al-Naqiyya wa-Barā'atuhā min al-A'māl al-Radayya. Amman: Al-Dār al-Athariyya, 2011.

Al-Salafiyyūn wa-Qaḍiyyat Filasṭīn fī Wāqi'inā l-Mu'āṣir. Nicosia: Markaz Bayt al-Maqdis li-l-Dirāsāt al-Tawthīqiyya, 2006 [2002].

Al-Siyāsa allatī Yurīduhā l-Salafiyyūn. Amman: Al-Dār al-Athariyya, 2005.

Introduction to *Juhūd al-Imām al-Albānī Nāṣir al-Sunna wa-l-Dīn fī Bayān 'Aqīdat al-Salaf al-Ṣāliḥīn fī l-Īmān bi-llāh Rabb al-'Ālamīn*, edited by Aḥmad Ṣāliḥ Ḥusayn al-Jabbūrī, 5–34. Amman: Al-Dār al-Athariyya, 2008.

Kurat al-Qadam bayna l-Maṣāliḥ wa-l-Mafāsid min Wujhat Naẓar Shar'iyya. Amman: Al-Dār al-Athariyya, 2009.

"Ma'ālim fī Fiqh al-Shaykh al-Albānī." *Al-Aṣāla* 4, no. 23 (15 Sha'bān 1420 [24 November 1999]): 33–6.

Āl 'Ubaykān, 'Abd al-Muḥsin b. Nāṣir. "Ḥukm Muwālāt wa-Muẓāharat al-Kuffār?" *Al-Aṣāla* 8, no. 44 (15 Shawwāl 1424 [10 December 2003]): 13–17.

Albānī, Muḥammad Nāṣir al-Dīn al-. *Al-'Aqīda al-Ṭaḥāwiyya: Sharḥ wa-Ta'līq*. Beirut: Al-Maktab al-Islāmī, 1993.

"Al-Da'wa al-Salafiyya: Uṣūluhā ... Maqāṣiduhā ... Asbāb al-Nuhūf [sic!] bi-hā." *Al-Aṣāla* 5, no. 27 (15 Rabī' al-Ākhir 1421 [18 July 2000]): 74–8.

"Al-Fatāwá." *Al-Aṣāla* 4, no. 19 (15 Dhū l-Qa'da 1419 [3 March 1999]): 73–7.

Al-Fatāwá Kuwaytiyya wa-l-Fatāwá al-Ustrāliyya. Cairo: Dār al-Ḍiyā', 2007.

Al-Masāʾil al-ʿIlmiyya wa-l-Fatāwá al-Sharʿiyya: Fatāwá l-Shaykh al-ʿAllāma Muḥammad Nāṣir al-Dīn al-Albānī fī l-Madīna wa-l-Imārāt. Edited by ʿAmr ʿAbd al-Munʿim Salīm. Ṭanṭā: Dār al-Ḍiyāʾ, 2006.
Al-Salafiyya: Haqīqatuhā, Uṣūluhā, Mawqifuhā min al-Madhāhib, Shubha ḥawlahā li-Faḍīlat al-Shaykh al-Mujaddid Muḥammad Nāṣir al-Dīn al-Albānī. Edited by ʿAmr ʿAbd al-Munʿim Salīm. N.p.: Dār al-Ḍiyāʾ, 2006.
Al-Taṣfiya wa-l-Tarbiya wa-Ḥājat al-Muslimīn ilayhimā. Amman: Al-Maktaba al-Islāmiyya, 1421 [2000/2001].
Al-Tawassul: Anwāʿuhu wa-Aḥkāmuhu. Beirut and Damascus: No publisher, 1397 [1395; 1977 [1975]].
Al-Tawḥīd Awwalan Yā Duʿāt al-Islām!! N.p.: Dār al-Hudá al-Nabawī, 1999.
Fitnat al-Takfīr. www.saaid.net/book/open.php?cat=1&book=174, n.d.
Ḥukm Tārik al-Ṣalāt. Riyadh: Dār al-Jalālayn, 1992.
Jilbāb al-Marʾa al-Muslima fī l-Kitāb wa-l-Sunna. Hebron and Amman: Maktabat Dandīs, 2002.
Kashf al-Niqāb ʿammā fī Kalimāt Abī Ghurra min al-Abāṭīl wa-l-Iftirāʾāt. N.p.: No publisher, 1978 [1975].
"Kull Bidʿa Ḍalāla." *Al-Aṣāla* 4, no. 21 (15 Rabīʿ al-Ākhir 1420 [29 July 1999]): 73–7.
"Masāʾil wa-Ajwibatuhā." *Al-Aṣāla* 2, no. 10 (15 Shawwāl 1414 [28 March 1994]): 38–43.
"Masāʾil wa-Ajwibatuhā." *Al-Aṣāla* 4, no. 18 (15 Muḥarram 1418 [23 May 1997]): 69–74.
"Masāʾil wa-Ajwibatuhā: Al-Masāʾil al-Lubnāniyya (2)." *Al-Aṣāla* 2, no. 9 (15 Shaʿbān 1414 [28 January 1994]): 86–90.
"Masāʾil . . . wa-Ajwibatuhā." *Al-Aṣāla* 3, no. 17 (15 Dhū l-Ḥijja 1416 [4 April 1996]): 70–1.
Manzalat al-Sunna fī l-Islām wa-Bayān annahu Lā Yustaghná ʿanhā bi-l-Qurʾān. Al-Ṣafāt: Al-Dār al-Salafiyya, 1984.
Ṣalāt al-ʿĪdayn fī l-Muṣallá Hiya l-Sunna. Beirut and Damascus: Al-Maktab al-Islāmī, 1986.
Ṣifat Ṣalāt al-Nabī – Ṣallá llāh ʿalayhi wa-l-Sallam – min al-Takbīr ilá l-Taslīm ka-annaka Tarāhā. Beirut and Damascus: Al-Maktab al-Islāmī, 1987.
Suʾāl wa-Jawāb ḥawla Fiqh al-Wāqiʿ. Amman: Al-Maktaba al-Islāmiyya, 1422 [2000/2001].
Taḥdhīr al-Sājid min Ittikhādh al-Qubūr Masājid. Beirut and Damascus: Al-Maktab al-Islāmī, 1398 [1377; 1978 [1957/1958]].
Albānī, Muḥammad Nāṣir al-Dīn al- et al. "Masāʾil ʿAṣriyya fī l-Siyāsa al-Sharʿiyya." *Al-Aṣāla* 1, no. 2 (15 Jumādá l-Ākhira 1413 [11 December 1992]): 16–24.
ʿAlī, Ḥāmid b. ʿAbdallāh al-. *Bayān Ḥaqīqat al-Īmān wa-l-Radd ʿalá Murjiʾat al-ʿAṣr fī-Mā Khālafū fī-hi Maḥkam al-Qurʾān*. www.h-alali.net/b_open.php?id=a0dda88e-fb6b-1029-a701-0010dc91cf69, n.d.
Al-Shaykh al-Ḥalabī fī Ḥiwār maʿa Batrā: Hunāka Khalṭ Kabīr bayna l-Tayyār al-Salafī wa-l-Takfīriyyīn. www.alhalaby.com/play.php?catsmktba=2632, 18 April 2011.

ʿAnbarī, Khālid b. ʿAlī b. Muḥammad al-. *Al-Ḥukm bi-Ghayr Mā Anzala llāh wa-Uṣūl al-Takfīr*. Cairo: Dār al-Minhāj, 2003.
"Al-Ṭarīq ilá l-Ḥukm bi-Mā Anzala llāh." *Al-Aṣāla* 2, no. 10 (15 Shawwāl 1414 [28 March 1994]): 17–23.
"Faṣl al-Khiṭāb fī Man Lam Yaḥkum bi-l-Sunna wa-l-Kitāb." *Al-Aṣāla* 1, no. 6 (15 Ṣafar 1414 [4 August 1993]): 12–16.
ʿAnzī, Saʿūd b. Mulūḥ b. Sulṭān al-. "Al-Bayʿa bayna l-Ḍawābiṭ al-Sharʿiyya wa-l-Tanẓīmāt al-Ḥizbiyya." *Al-Aṣāla* 8, no. 41 (15 Ṣafar 1424 [18 April 2003]): 33–42.
ʿAql, Muḥammad ʿĀdil. "Turkiyā … Qiṣṣat Najāḥ." *Al-Qibla* 10, no. 23 (2012): 70–2.
ʿĀrif, Abū ʿAbd al-Raḥmān Hishām al-. "Fiqh al-Wuṣūl ilá 'l-Qimma!' ʿinda l-Khawārij." *Al-Aṣāla* 10, no. 48 (15 Rabīʿ al-Awwal 1426 [24 April 2005]): 32–3.
ʿĀrūrī, Shākir b. Tawfīq al-. "Aʿẓam al-Dhunūb: al-Shirk." *Al-Aṣāla* 2, no. 7 (15 Rabīʿ al-Thānī 1414 [2 October 1993]): 12–15.
Al-Ashʿariyya fī Mīzān al-Ashāʿira – Al-Juzʾ al-Awwal. N.p.: No publisher, 2011.
Daʿwat Nabī llāh ʿĪsá – ʿalayhi l-Salām – ilá l-Tawḥīd Wafqa l-Tawrāt wa-l-Injīl. N.p.: No publisher, 2009.
"Muẓāharāt." *Al-Qibla* 9, no. 21 (2011): 14–22.
ʿAsʿas, Ibrāhīm al-. *Al-Salaf wa-l-Salafiyyūn: Ruʾya min al-Dākhil*. Beirut: Dār al-Bayāriq, 1994.
Raṣd al-Ẓawāhir – Hakadhā Naḥnu …. N.p.: No publisher, 2011.
ʿAṭāʾ bi-lā Ḥudūd. N.p.: Jamʿiyyat al-Kitāb wa-l-Sunna, 2013.
Atharī, Abū ʿAbdallāh ʿAbd al-Raḥīm b. al-ʿArabī al-. *Difāʿan ʿan Mashāyikh al-Urdunn*. www.kulalsalafiyeen.com/vb/showthread.php?t=15620, 24 March 2010 [originally published Shawwāl 1428 [October–November 2007]].
Atharī, Abū Muḥammad al-. "Nashāṭ al-Rāfiḍa fī Turkiyā." *Al-Aṣāla* 2, no. 9 (15 Shaʿbān 1414 [28 January 1994]): 64–70.
Atharī, Ibn Ḥamd al-. *Mudhakkira fī l-Rudūd ʿalá Jahālāt al-Ḥalabī wa-Sariqāt al-ʿIlmiyya*. http://alathary.net/vb2/attachment.p… ntid=695&stc=1, n.d.
ʿAwāyisha, Ḥusayn b. ʿAwda al-. *Al-Fitan wa-Sabīl al-Najāt min-hā*. Amman: Al-Dār al-Athariyya, 2011.
Kalima fī l-Daʿwa wa-l-Taḥdhīr min al-Bidʿa. http://alawaysheh.com/print.php?id=445, 4 October 2012.
Limādhā l-Islām wa-l-Tawḥīd? http://alawaysheh.com/print.php?id=248, 16 February 2011.
"Manhaj al-Shaykh al-Albānī fī l-Tazkiya." *Al-Aṣāla* 4, no. 23 (15 Shaʿbān 1420 [24 November 1999]): 44–5.
Masʾalat al-Muwālāt. http://alawaysheh.com/print.php?id=504, 16 February 2013.
"Qabḍ al-ʿIlm … wa-Atharuhu …" *Al-Aṣāla* 1, no. 5 (15 Dhū l-Ḥijja 1413 [6 June 1993]): 31–3.
ʿAwāyisha, Ḥusayn b. ʿAwda al-, Muḥammad b. Mūsá Āl Naṣr, Salīm b. ʿĪd al-Hilālī, ʿAlī b. Ḥasan al-Ḥalabī al-Atharī and Mashhūr b. Ḥasan Āl Salmān.

Mujmal Masāʾil al-Īmān al-ʿIlmiyya fī Uṣūl al-ʿAqīda al-Salafiyya. www.mediafire.com/view/?ehqmw6g0mr599bn, 29 August 2000.
ʿAwda, Salmān b. Fahd al-. "Al-Qatl bi-Dam Bārid." *Al-Qibla* 2, nos. 10–11 (2005): 95–7.
ʿĀyish, Muḥammad. "Al-Masjid al-Aqṣá . . . Al-Nidāʾ Mā Qabla l-Akhīr . . . !" *Al-Qibla* 1, no. 2 (2002): 10–12.
Barāʾa min Fiʾat al-Ḍalāl Ghulāt al-Takfīr wa-Muʿtaqidātihim al-Zāʾigha. www.tawhed.ws/r?i=t555vdqa, 15 November 2008.
Batīrī, Wāʾil al-. *ʿIṣābat al-Surrāq al-Muttaḥida!* www.tawhed.ws/r?i=1502094c, n.d.
Luṣūṣ al-Nuṣūṣ. www.tawhed.ws/r?i=0504091k, n.d.
Sariqa ʿIlmiyya. www.tawhed.ws/r?i=0606091d, n.d.
Battār, Abū ʿAmr al-. *Fatḥ al-Qadīr fī l-Taʿrīf bi-l-Shaykh Abī Baṣīr*. www.muslm.org/vb/showthread.php?368356, n.d.
Bū l-Nīt, Muḥammad. *Kashf al-Shubhāt (1) ʿAqīdat "al-Salafiyyīn" fī Mīzān Ahl al-Sunna wa-l-Jamāʿa*. Casablanca: Maṭābiʿ Afrīqiyā l-Sharq, 1998.
Būṭī, Muḥammad Saʿīd Ramaḍān al-. *Al-Salafiyya Marḥala Zamaniyya Mubāraka Lā Madhhab Islāmī*. Beirut/Damascus: Dār al-Fikr al-Muʿāṣir/Dār al-Fikr, 2010 [1988].
Buṭūsh, Abū ʿAbdallāh and ʿUmar b. ʿAbd al-Ḥamīd al-. *Kashf al-Astār ʿammā fī Tanẓīm al-Qāʿida min Afkār wa-Akhṭār*. Amman: Al-Dār al-Athariyya, 2009.
Buṭūsh, Amīn Muḥammad al-. "Al-Wasaṭiyya fī l-Islām." *Al-Aṣāla* 6, no. 36 (15 Shawwāl 1422 [31 December 2001]): 24–9.
Dawsarī, Muḥammad b. Sālim al-. *Rafʿ al-Lāʾima ʿan Fatwá l-Lajna al-Dāʾima*. www.tawhed.ws/dl?i=ev70m465, n.d.
Daydāt, Aḥmad. *Mādhā Taqūlu l-Tawrāt wa-l-Injīl ʿan Muḥammad – Ṣallá llāh ʿalayhi wa-Sallam?* Al-Dammām: Dār Ibn al-Jawzī, 1990.
Dhuwayb, Aḥmad al-. "Ḥuqūq al-Ḥākim." *Al-Qibla* 9, no. 21 (2011): 59–63.
"Imāmat al-Marʾa." *Al-Qibla* 4, nos. 10–11 (2004): 14–18.
"Tārīkh Mushārakat al-Islāmiyyīn fī l-Iṣlāḥ al-Siyāsī." *Al-Qibla* 10, no. 23 (2012): 47–59.
Difāʿan ʿan Mashāyikh al-Urdunn. www.kulalsalafiyeen.com/vb/showthread.php?t-15620, 24 March 2010.
Duwaysh, Muḥammad al-. "Al-Khiṭāb al-Daʿwī bayna l-ʿĀmma wa-l-Khāṣṣa." *Al-Qibla* 1, nos. 4–5 (2003): 7–8.
Fātiḥ, Umm Muḥammad al-. "Ilá Mawākib al-Ṣādiqīn 1." *Al-Aṣāla* 2, no. 7 (15 Rabīʿ al-Thānī 1414 [2 October 1993]): 40–8.
"Ilá Mawākib al-Ṣādiqīn 2." *Al-Aṣāla* 2, no. 8 (15 Jumādá l-Ākhira 1414 [30 November 1993]): 63–9.
Fawzān, Ṣāliḥ b. Fawzān al-. *Kitāb al-Tawḥīd*. Cairo: Maṭābiʿ Ibn Taymiyya, n.d.
Why Manhaj? http://turntoislam.com/community/threads/why-manhaj-methodology-by-shaykh-saalih-bin-fawzaan-al-fawzaan.25431/, n.d.
Filasṭīnī, Abū Qatāda al-. *Al-Farq bayna Rajul Murjiʾ wa-bayna Rajul fī-hi Irjāʾ*. www.tawhed.ws/pr?i=1220, n.d.
Ḥawla Murjiʾat al-ʿAṣr. www.tahwed.ws/r?i=57gqha8v, n.d.
Naẓra Jadīda fī l-Jarḥ wa-l-Taʿdīl: Al-Albānī. www.tawhed.ws/pr?i=1103, n.d.

Hādī, ʿIṣām Mūsá. "Ḥayāt Aḥmad al-Sālik." Unpublished manuscript in possession of the author, n.d.

Muḥaddith al-ʿAṣr al-Imām Muḥammad Nāṣir al-Dīn al-Albānī kamā ʿAraftuhu. Al-Jubayl: Dār al-Ṣadīq, 2003.

"Ṣafaḥāt min Ḥayāt al-ʿAllāma Muḥammad Nasīb al-Rifāʿī." Unpublished manuscript in possession of the author, n.d.

Ḥāj, Khālid Muḥammad ʿAlī al-. "Al-Islām wa-l-Tarbiya." *Al-Aṣāla* 3, nos. 15–16 (15 Dhū l-Qaʿda 1415 [15 April 1995]): 45–55.

Ḥalabī al-Atharī, Abū l-Ḥārith ʿAlī b. Ḥasan b. ʿAlī b. ʿAbd al-Ḥamīd al-. "'. . . Lā Tattakhidhū ʿAduwwī wa-ʿAduwwakum Awliyāʾ." *Al-Aṣāla* 1, no. 6 (15 Ṣafar 1414 [4 August 1993]): 8–9.

Al-Ajwiba al-Mutalāʾima ʿalá Fatwá l-Lajna al-Dāʾima ḥawla Kitābay l-Taḥdhīr *wa*-l-Ṣayḥat al-Nadhīr *fī l-Radd ʿalá Duʿāt al-Takfīr.* www.4salaf.com/vb/showthread.php?t=5986, n.d.

Al-Ajwiba al-Ṣāʾiba ʿalá l-Daʿāwá l-Kādhiba ḥawla Markaz Imām al-Albānī. www.alhalaby.com/play.php?catsmktba=1190, 22 December 2009.

"Al-ʿAllāma al-Albānī wa-Juhūduhu fī l-ʿAqīda." *Al-Aṣāla* 4, no. 23 (15 Shaʿbān 1420 [24 November 1999]): 37–9.

Al-Bayʿa bayna l-Sunna wa-l-Bidʿa ʿinda l-Jamāʿāt al-Islāmiyya. Amman: Al-Maktaba al-Islāmiyya, 1985.

"Al-Daʿwa al-Salafiyya" Ajallu min an Taʾūla Ḥizban! www.alhalaby.com/play.php?catsmktba=2657, 13 May 2011.

Al-Daʿwa al-Salafiyya al-Hādiya wa-Mawqifuhā min al-Fitan al-ʿAṣriyya al-Jāriya wa-Bayān al-Asbāb al-Sharʿiyya al-Wāqiya. N.p.: Mānshūrāt Muntadayāt Kull al-Salafiyyīn, 2011.

Al-Daʿwa al-Salafiyya bayna l-Ṭuruq al-Ṣūfiyya wa-l-Daʿāwá al-Ṣaḥafiyya wa-l-Kashf al-Ṣila bayna l-Taṣawwuf wa-l-Afkār al-Shīʿiyya. Amman: Al-Dār al-Athariyya, 2009.

Al-Fiʾa al-Ḍālla: Sabab Ḍalālihā! Wa-Abraz Simātihā!! Tajhīlan wa-Takfīran wa-Tafjīran. N.p.: No publisher, 2004.

Al-Hudá wa-l-Nūr fī Hatk Suttūr al-Ḥizbiyya Dhāt al-Shurūr wa-Bayān annahā min Ḍalālāt al-Bidaʿ wa-Muḥaddathāt al-Umūr. N.p.: Mānshūrāt Muntadayāt Kull al-Salafiyyīn, 2012.

Al-Iʿlān bi-Barāʾat Ahl al-Sunna wa-l-Īmān min Daʿwá "Waḥdat al-Adyān." www.alhalaby.com/play.php?catsmktba=2242, 2 August 2010.

Al-Khawārij wa-l-Khawārij al-Qaʿdiyya. www.alhalaby.com/play.php?catsmktba=2813, 20 July 2011.

Al-Mawqif al-Sharʿī min Fatwá "Muʾtamar al-Qāhira!" fī Ījāb al-Jihād fī "Sūriya" ʿalá ʿUmūm al-Muslimīn. www.alhalaby.com/play.php?catsmktba=3495, 16 June 2013.

Al-Qawl al-Maʾmūn fī Takhrīj Mā Warada ʿan Ibn ʿAbbās fī Tafsīr wa-Man Lam Yaḥkum bi-mā Anzala llāh fa-Ulāʾika Hum al-Kāfirūn. Al-Dammām: Dār al-Hijra, 1989.

Al-Radd al-Burhānī fī l-Intiṣār li-l-ʿAllāma al-Muḥaddith al-Imām al-Shaykh Muḥammad Nāṣir al-Dīn al-Albānī. ʿAjman: Maktabat al-Furqān, 2002.

Al-Salafiyya Barāʾ min Aḥdāth Madīnat al-Zarqāʾ. www.alhalaby.com/play.php?catsmktba=2629, 15 April 2011.

"Al-Salafiyya ... wa- ... l-Ḥizbiyya ... " *Al-Aṣāla* 1, no. 2 (15 Jumādá l-Ākhira 1413 [11 December 1992]): 51–3.

Al-Shaykh Muḥammad Ibrāhīm Shaqra. Shukran Jazīlan la-ka. www.alhalaby.com/play.php?catsmktba=3169, 28 June 2012.

Al-Shīʿa Fitnat al-ʿAṣr Yā Saʿādat Muftī Miṣr! www.alhalaby.com/play.php?catsmktba=969, 12 December 2009.

Al-Shīʿa Taghzū "Miṣr"! bi-Amwālihā wa Shubhātihā wa-Shahwātihā; fa-ntabihū wa-Tayqaẓū wa-ḥdhanī! www.alhalaby.com/play.php?catsmktba=3438, 7 April 2013.

"Al-Shirk ... bayna l-Qubūr ... wa-l-Quṣūr!!" *Al-Aṣāla* 1, no. 3 (15 Shaʿbān 1413 [8 February 1993]): 18–20.

Al-Tabṣīr bi-Qawāʿid al-Takfīr. Cairo: Dār al-Minhāj, 2004.

Al-Tafrīq al-Wāḍiḥ al-Mubīn li-Walī Amrinā "al-Malik ʿAbdallāh b. al-Ḥusayn" bayna "l-Takfīriyyīn" wa-"l-Salafiyyīn." www.alhalaby.com/catplay.php?catsmktba=4&page=10, 18 April 2011.

ed. *Al-Taḥdhīr min Fitnat al-Takfīr.* N.p.: No publisher, 1996.

Al-Tanbīhāt al-Mutawāʾima fī Nuṣrat Ḥaqq al-Ajwiba al-Mutalāʾima ʿalá Fatwá l-Lajna al-Dāʾima wa-l-Naqḍ ʿalá Aghālīṭ wa-Mughālaṭāt Rafʿ al-Lāʾima!!! United Arab Emirates: Maktabat Dār al-Ḥadīth, 2003.

Al-Taʿrīf wa-l-Tanbiʾa bi-Taʾṣīlāt al-ʿAllāma al-Shaykh al-Imām Asad al-Sunna al-Humām Muḥammad Nāṣir al-Dīn al-Albānī – Raḥimahu llāh – fī Masāʾil al-Īmān wa-l-Radd ʿalá l-Murjiʾa. www.alhalaby.com/play.php?catsmktba=3430, 2009.

Al-Taṣfiya wa-l-Tarbiya: Muḥāḍara li-l-Shaykh al-Ḥalabī. www.alhalaby.com/play.php?catsmktba=1078, 14 December 2009.

Al-ʿUdwān al-Ghāshim ʿalá Ghazzat Hāshim. Amman: Al-Dār al-Athariyya, 2009.

"Al-Walāʾ wa-l-Barāʾ wa-l-Balāʾ!" *Al-Aṣāla* 11, no. 54 (15 Dhū l-Ḥijja 1427 [6 December 2006]): 18–20.

"Aqsām al-Tawḥīd." *Al-Aṣāla* 1, no. 4 (15 Shawwāl 1413 [8 April 1993]): 23–6.

Arbaʿa Ālāf "ʿUḍw" fī "Muntadayāt Kull al-Salafiyyīn" Khilāl Sana wa-Niṣf – wa-l-Ḥamd li-llāh. www.alhalaby.com/play.php?catsmktba=1852, 18 April 2010.

ed. *Ḍawābiṭ al-Amr bi-l-Maʿrūf wa-l-Nahy ʿan al-Munkar ʿinda Shaykh al-Islām Ibn Taymiyya.* N.p.: Al-Aṣāla, 1994.

Fiqh al-Wāqiʿ bayna l-Naẓariyya wa-l-Taṭbīq. Ramallah: Sharakat al-Nūr, 1420 [1999/2000] [1412 [1991/1992]].

Gleaming Pearls in Destroying the False Claim that Imaam al-Albanee Agrees with the Murjiʾah! https://sunnahtube.files.wordpress.com/2013/05/salafimanhaj_gleamingpearls.pdf, 2006–2008.

Ḥadath Tafjīrāt ʿAmmān: Naṣṣ Khuṭbat al-Jumʿa allatī Ulqiyat bayna Yaday al-Malik ʿAbdallāh al-Thānī, Malik al-Mamlaka al-Urdunniyya al-Hāshimiyya. Amman: No publisher, 2005.

Hādhihi Hiya l-Salafiyya: Daʿwat al-Īmān wa-l-Amn wa-l-Amān al-Manhajiyya al-ʿIlmiyya al-Tarbawiyya. Medina: Dār al-Imām Muslim, 2011.

"Hadhihi l-Daʿwa. Man la-hā?!" *Al-Aṣāla* 2, no. 11 (15 Dhū l-Ḥijja 1414 [26 May 1994]): 32–4.

Hal Aqarra? Am Nafá? ʿAlī al-Ḥalabī bi-annahu Tilmīdh al-Albānī. www.alhalaby.com/play.php?catsmktba=1193, 22 December 2009.

Hal "Laysa min al-Munīʿa wa-l-Rujūla Dhikr ʿUyūb 'al-Ikhwān' fī hādhā l-Awān" ka-Mā Naqalahu l-Baʿḍ ʿannī? www.alhalaby.com/play.php?catsmktba=3518, 25 August 2013.

Hal "Nazaʿat" = "Al-Miṣriyya!" Ikhwānanā l-Salafiyyīn fī "Miṣr" fī stiqbālihim "ʿAbd al-Raḥmān ʿAbd al-Khāliq? www.alhalaby.com/play.php?catsmktba=2999, 14 January 2012.

"Ḥizb al-Nūr al-Salafī" wa-"l-Ikhwān al-Muslimūn" ... Iʾtilāf am Ikhtilāf ... am Mādhā?! Wa-Limādhā? www.alhalaby.com/play.php?catsmktba=2968, 18 December 2011.

Ḥizbiyya wa-l-Salafiyya ... Hal Yajtamiʿāni?! Maʿa l-Islāmī al-Ṣaḥafī "Usāma Shaḥāda" Numūdhajan. www.alhalaby.com/play.php?catsmktba=3165, 24 June 2012.

Ḥukm al-Dīn fī l-Liḥya wa-l-Tadkhīn. Beirut: Dār Ibn Ḥazm, 2002.

Ijābat al-Sāʾil ʿan Ḥukm Asliḥat al-Dammār al-Shāmil. Amman: Al-Dār al-Athariyya, 2009.

Ilá "Ḥizb al-Nūr al-Salafī!!" Ammā Ān La-kum Taʿtabinū; fa-l-Ḥizbiyya Lā Tuntaju illā Ḥizbiyya. www.alhalaby.com/play.php?catsmktba=3366, 28 December 2012.

Ilá l-Salafiyyīn fī "Miṣr": Hādhā Tadhkīr "bi-Baʿḍ!" Naṣāʾiḥī "l-Sābiqa!" ilay-kum: Maḥabba wa-Ḥirṣan ... Laʿallakum. www.alhalaby.com/play.php?catsmktba=3513, 18 August 2013.

Ilá Salafiyyat "Ḥizb al-Nūr": Irjiʿū ilá "l-Thughūr" wa-Tarājaʿū ʿan "al-Juḥūr." www.alhalaby.com/play.php?catsmktba-3356, 13 December 2012.

ʿIlm Uṣūl al-Bidaʿ: Dirāsa Takmīliyya Muhimma fī ʿIlm Uṣūl al-Fiqh. Riyadh and Jeddah: Dār al-Rāya li-l-Nashr wa-l-Tawzīʿ, 1992.

Introduction to *Al-Taḥdhīr min Fitnat al-Ghulūw fī l-Takfīr* by Muḥammad Nāṣir al-Dīn al-Albānī, 5–66. Bīr Nabālā: Sharikat Nūr, 2002 [1996].

Kalāmī fī Takfīr al-Qawl bi-"Waḥdat al-Adyān" – wa-Mā ilayhā – qabla Iḥdá wa-ʿIshrīn Sana. www.alhalaby.com/play.php?catsmktba=2331, 26 August 2010.

Kalima ḥawla "Aḥdāth Miṣr" – 2. www.alhalaby.com/play.php?catsmktba=2530, 30 January 2011.

Kalimat Ḥaqq ʿIlmiyya fī Aḥdāth Sūriyya. N.p.: Mānshūrāt Muntadayāt Kull al-Salafiyyīn, 2012.

Kalimatī fī Majlis al-Ṣulḥ maʿa Faḍīlat al-Shaykh Muḥammad Shaqra – Wafaqahu llāh. www.alhalaby.com/play.php?catsmktba=3461, 25 April 2013.

Kayfa Naruddu ʿalá Man Yatamassaku bi-Kalām al-Shaykh: Annaka Lasta min Talāmīdhihi? www.alhalaby.com/play.php?catsmktba=229, 14 November 2009.

"Lā Ḥaraja. Ayyuhā l-Ḥajīj!" *Al-Aṣāla* 1, no. 4 (15 Shawwāl 1413 [8 April 1993]): 76–7.

Liqāʾ al-Shaykh ʿAlī al-Ḥalabī fī Ṣaḥīfat al-Sūsina. www.alhalaby.com/play.php?catsmktba=3172, 3 July 2012.

Liqāʾ Ṣaḥafī maʿa Mawqiʿ (… Awar Jū …) maʿa Shaykhinā ʿAlī b. Ḥasan al-Ḥalabī – Ḥafiẓahu llāh. www.alhalaby.com/play.php?catsmktba=3181, 5 July 2012.

"Madārik al-Naẓar fī l-Siyāsa bayna l-Taṭbīqāt al-Sharʿiyya wa-l-Infiʿālāt al-Ḥamāsiyya." *Al-Aṣāla* 5, no. 28 (15 Jumādá l-Ākhira 1420 [26 September 1999]): 48–50.

Masāʾil ʿIlmiyya fī l-Daʿwa wa-l-Siyāsa al-Sharʿiyya. Amman: Al-Dār al-Athariyya, 2010.

"Min Mughālaṭāt Duʿāt ʻal-Fikr al-Takfīrī'." *Al-Aṣāla* 10, no. 51 (15 Dhū l-Ḥijja 1426 [15 January 2006]): 21–4.

Mujmal Tārīkh al-Daʿwa al-Salafiyya fī l-Diyār al-Urdunniyya. Amman: Al-Dār al-Athariyya, 2009.

Muntadá "Kull al-Salafiyyīn." Limādhā? www.alhalaby.com/play.php?catsmkt ba=1049, 13 December 2009.

Nadwa ʿan al-Fikr al-Takfīrī wa-Atharihi ʿalá l-Mujtamaʿ bi-Irbid. www.alhalaby .com/play.php?catsmktba=2641, 25 April 2011.

"Naṣāʾiḥ wa-Tawjīhāt Faḍīlat al-Shaykh ʿAlī b. Ḥasan ʿAlī al-Ḥalabī." In *Naṣāʾiḥ wa-Tawjīhāt al-Mufakkirīn wa-ʿUlamāʾ al-Islām li-l-Jamāʿāt wa-l-Aḥzāb al-Islāmiyya*, edited by Niẓām Salāma Sakkijhā, 305–15. Amman: Al-Maktaba al-Islāmiyya, 1999.

Naṣīḥa ilá l-Salafiyyīn fī "Miṣr" – bi-ʿĀmma – wa-ilayka – Ayyuhā l-Dāʿī l-Salafī – bi-Khāṣṣa. www.alhalaby.com/play.php?catsmktba=2667, 24 May 2011.

"Qāhī lā Ḍayr … ": "Wa-l-Ṣulḥ Khayr … " Awrāq … fī Kāʾinat "al-Ṣulḥ wa-l-Ittifāq" maʿa l-Shaykh Muḥammad Shaqra … Faqra Faqra! Amman: Al-Dār al-Athariyya, 2004.

Radd Qawl Man Qāla bi-Taḥrīm al-Jamʿiyyāt Muṭlaqan. www.alhalaby.com/pl ay.php?catsmktba=3179, 4 July 2012.

Risāla ilá Kull Man Wallāhu llāh Umūr al-Muslimīn fī l-Muḥādharat min Tasallul al-Shīʿa ʿibra l-Mutaṣawwifīn. www.alhalaby.com/play.php?catsmktb a=3470, 5 May 2013.

Ṣayḥat Nadhīr bi-Khaṭar al-Takfīr. www.alhalaby.com/play.php?catsmktb a=2925, 1997.

"Sūriya" … bayna l-Ālām … wa-l-Āmāl – Kalimat Ḥaqq wa-Annat Ṣidq. www .alhalaby.com/play.php?catsmktba=3016, 14 February 2012.

Tafṣīl wa-Taʾṣīl ḥawla Mā Yusammá bi-l-Aḥzāb al-Salafiyya. www.alhalaby .com/play.php?catsmktba=3141, 13 May 2012.

Taḥdhīrāt al-ʿUlamāʾ al-Thiqāt min al-Muẓāharāt bi-l-Adilla al-Bāhirāt wa-l-Naqḍ ʿalá l-Shubhāt al-Wāhiyāt. Medina: Dār al-Imām Muslim, 2012.

Taḥdhīrāt wa-Tanbīhāt … Ḥawla Mā Jará – wa-Yajrī – min al-Taqtīl wa-l-Tafjīrāt. www.alhalaby.com/play.php?catsmktba=2481, 2 January 2011.

Taʾyīd, lā Taqlīd maʿa Kalimat Faḍīlat al-Shaykh al-Muftī fī Sayyid Quṭb. www .alhalaby.com/play.php?catsmktba=1133, 16 December 2009.

Wafāt Faḍīlat al-Shaykh Yūsuf al-Barqāwī – ʿAlam min Aʿlām Madīnat al-Zarqāʾ. www.kulalsalafiyeen.com/vb/printthread.php?t=11556, 21 October 2009.

Ḥammād, Zāyid Ibrāhīm. "Abʿād al-Tamarrud al-Ḥūthī fī l-Yaman." *Al-Qibla* 8, no. 20 (2010): 56–60.

"Al-Shīʿa wa-Filasṭīn." *Al-Qibla* 6, no. 16 (2008): 78–95.

"Ḥawla Jamʿiyyat al-Kitāb wa-l-Sunna." *Al-Qibla* 4, nos. 10–11 (2005): 109–11.

"Waddū Law Tudhinu fa-Yudhinūna." *Al-Qibla* 9, no. 21 (2011): 7–13.

"'Wa-Qātilū fī Sabīl Allāh . . . '." *Al-Qibla* 2, nos. 10–11 (2005): 10–13.

Ḥamsh, ʿIdāb Maḥmūd al-. "Al-Ḥadīth al-Jayyid ʿinda ʿUlamāʾ al-Rijāl ḥattá Nihāyat al-Qarn al-Rābiʿ." *Al-Qibla* 2, nos. 4–5 (2003): 88–103.

Ḥaqīl, Riyāḍ al-. "Zād al-Ḥāj." *Al-Aṣāla* 2, no. 11 (15 Dhū l-Ḥijja 1414 [26 May 1994]): 48–53.

Ḥasan, Jaʿfar Hādī. "Tahwīd al-Quds Yashmalu Bināʾ al-Haykal." *Al-Qibla* 1, no. 2 (2002): 24–5.

Ḥaṣīn, Saʿd al-. "Al-Taqrīb bayna Ahl al-Firaq wa-l-Adyān am Radduhum Jamīʿan ilá l-Waḥyayn?" *Al-Aṣāla* 9, no. 47 (15 Dhū l-Qaʿda 1425 [27 December 2004]): 50–4.

"Fī l-Walāʾ wa-l-Barāʾ al-Sharʿī wa-l-Ḥarakī." *Al-Aṣāla* 4, no. 20 (15 Muḥarram 1420 [1 May 1999]): 22–5.

"Fitnat al-Takfīr." *Al-Aṣāla* 6, no. 35 (15 Shaʿbān 1422 [2 November 2001]): 30–4.

Ḥawālī, Ṣafar b. ʿAbd al-Raḥmān al-. *Ẓāhirat al-Irjāʾ fī l-Fikr al-Islāmī*, vol. II. www.tawhed.ws/dl?i=xc88bqeg, 1985/6.

Ḥāyik, Abū Ṣuhayb Khālid al-. *Fa-ltaqamahu l-Ḥūt*. www.tawhed.ws/r?i=1502092n, 11 Jumādá l-Ūlá 1429 [17 May 2008].

Hakadhā Badaʾa "Musalsil al-Sariqāt" ʿinda Man Yantasibūna li-l-Salaf Zūran! www.tawhed.ws/r?i=0504096s, 18 Jumādá l-Ūlá [25 May 2008].

Liqāʾ maʿa l-Shaykh Rāʾid Ṣabrī ḥawla Sariqāt Mashhūr Ḥasan Āl Salmān li-Kutubihi wa-Kitābihi "Kashf al-Mastūr ʿan Sariqāt Mashhūr." www.addyaiya.com/uin/arb/Viewdataitems.aspx?ProductId=309, 27 Muḥarram 1430 [24 January 2009].

Hilālī, Abū Usāma Salīm b. ʿĪd al-. *Al-Ajwiba al-Hilāliyya ʿalá baʿḍ al-Ittihāmāt al-ʿAṣriyya*. http://aloloom.net/vb/showthread.php?t=4842&p=19624&langid=5#post19624, 8 March 2010.

"Al-Daʿwa wa-l-Nūr . . . " *Al-Aṣāla* 1, no. 1 (15 Rabīʿ al-Thānī 1413 [13 October 1992]): 37–40.

"Al-Ikhtirāq al-Kabīr." *Al-Ṣaḥīfa al-Ṣādiqa*, no. 4 (1432 [2011]): 58–61.

Al-Jamāʿāt al-Islāmiyya fī Ḍawʾ al-Kitāb wa-l-Sunna bi-Fahm Salaf al-Umma. Amman: Al-Dār al-Athariyya, 2004.

"Al-Mujtamaʿ al-Islāmī al-Muʿāṣir wa-l-Taḥaddī al-Ḥaḍārī 1." *Al-Aṣāla* 9, no. 45 (15 Ṣafar 1425 [6 April 2004]): 30–3.

Al-Mustaqbal li-l-Islām bi-Manhaj al-Salaf al-Kirām. Cairo: Dār al-Imām Aḥmad, 2007.

"Al-Salafiyyūn wa-l-Siyāsa." *Al-Aṣāla* 4, no. 18 (15 Muḥarram 1419 [23 May 1997]): 29–33.

"Dalālat Aḥādīth al-Khawārij ʿalá Ḥajiyyat al-Manhaj al-Salafī?!" *Al-Aṣāla* 7, no. 40 (15 Dhū l-Ḥijja 1423 [17 February 2003]): 10–13.

"Daʿwat Waḥdat al-Adyān fī l-Mīzān." *Al-Ṣaḥīfa al-Ṣādiqa*, no. 3 (1432 [2011]): 12–14.

"Iḥdharū Ayyuhā l-Ḥajīj." *Al-Aṣāla* 1, no. 4 (15 Shawwāl 1413 [8 April 1993]): 78–9.

Limādhā Ikhtartu l-Manhaj al-Salafī? Cairo: Dār al-Imām Aḥmad, 2008.

"Limādha l-Manhaj al-Salafī." *Al-Aṣāla* 1, no. 1 (15 Rabīʿ al-Thānī 1413 [13 October 1992]): 17–25.

"Man Hiya l-Ṭāʾifa al-Manṣūra?" *Al-Aṣāla* 1, no. 2 (15 Jumādá l-Ākhira 1413 [11 December 1992]): 30–9.

Manzalat al-ʿIlm wa-l-ʿUlamāʾ ʿinda l-Ḥarakāt al-Islāmiyya al-Muʿāṣira. Cairo: Dār al-Imām Aḥmad, 2008.

"Marāḥil Tadwīn al-ʿAqīda." *Al-Aṣāla* 1, no. 1 (15 Rabīʿ al-Thānī 1413 [13 October 1992]): 11–14.

Maṭlaʿ al-Fajr fī Fiqh al-Zajr bi-l-Hajr wa-maʿahu Bayān Manhaj al-Salaf al-Ṣāliḥ fī Muʿāmalat Ahl al-Bidaʿ wa-l-Ahwāʾ. Cairo: Dār al-Imām Aḥmad, 2005.

"Min Bidaʿ al-Ṣiyām wa-l-Qiyām fī Ramaḍān." *Al-Aṣāla* 1, no. 3 (15 Shaʿbān 1413 [8 February 1993]): 73–6.

"Shaykhunā l-Albānī. Muḥaddithan." *Al-Aṣāla* 4, no. 23 (15 Shaʿbān 1420 [24 November 1999]): 28–32.

Hirās, Muḥammad Khalīl. "Jihād al-Rasūl – Ṣallá llāh ʿalayhi wa-Sallam – fī Sabīl al-Tawḥīd." *Al-Aṣāla* 10, no. 50 (15 Ramaḍān 1426 [18 October 2005]): 15–18.

Ḥuddūshī, Abū l-Faḍl ʿUmar al-. *Ikhbār al-Awliyāʾ bi-Maṣnaʿ Ahl al-Tajahhum wa-l-Irjāʾ*. http://ia600809.us.archive.org/15/items/ekhbar-awlyaa/ekhbar-awlyaa.pdf, n.d.

Humaylī, Jamāl Yūsuf al-. *Laṭāʾif al-Ishārāt fī Tafsīr Qiṣār Suwar al-Qurʾān*. Amman: Jamʿiyyat al-Kitāb wa-l-Sunna – Lajnat al-Kalima al-Ṭayyiba, 2012.

Ibn ʿAbd al-Khāliq, ʿAbd al-Raḥmān. *Al-Siyāsa al-Sharʿiyya fī l-Daʿwa ilá llāh*. Kuwait: Sharikat Bayt al-Maqdis li-l-Nashr wa-l-Tawzīʿ, 2006.

Ibn ʿAbd al-Laṭīf, Saʿd b. Muḥammad. "Qirāʾa fī l-Muʾtamar al-Khāmis li-l-Taqrīb bayna Ahl al-Sunna wa-l-Shīʿa!!" *Al-Aṣāla* 1, no. 5 (15 Dhū l-Ḥijja 1413 [6 June 1993]): 41–5.

Ibn Badawī, ʿAbd al-ʿAẓīm. "Al-Taḥdhīr min al-Shirk wa-l-Ḥathth ʿalá l-Tawḥīd." *Al-Aṣāla* 2, no. 11 (15 Dhū l-Ḥijja 1414 [26 May 1994]): 17–24.

"Maẓāhir Shirkiyya 1." *Al-Aṣāla* 2, no. 8 (15 Jumādá l-Ākhira 1414 [30 November 1993]): 14–17.

"Maẓāhir Shirkiyya 2." *Al-Aṣāla* 2, no. 9 (15 Shaʿbān 1414 [28 January 1994]): 14–16.

Ibn Bāz, ʿAbd al-ʿAzīz. "Asbāb Ḍaʿf al-Muslimīn Amām ʿAduwwihim wa-Wasāʾil al-ʿIlāj li-Dhālika 1." *Al-Aṣāla* 8, no. 42 (15 Rabīʿ al-Thānī 1424 [16 June 2003]): 54–60.

"Asbāb Ḍaʿf al-Muslimīn Amām ʿAduwwihim wa-Wasāʾil al-ʿIlāj li-Dhālika 2." *Al-Aṣāla* 8, no. 43 (15 Jumādá l-Ākhira 1424 [14 August 2003]): 34–7.

"Asbāb Ḍaʿf al-Muslimīn Amām ʿAduwwihim wa-Wasāʾil al-ʿIlāj li-Dhālika 3." *Al-Aṣāla* 9, no. 45 (15 Ṣafar 1425 [6 April 2004]): 40–4.

Lā Ikhwa bayna l-Muslimīn wa-l-Kāfirīn wa-Lā Dīn Ḥaqq Ghayr Dīn al-Islām. www.binbaz.org.sa/node/8286, n.d.

"Min Fatāwá l-Shaykh ʿAbd al-ʿAzīz b. Bāz." *Al-Aṣāla* 4, no. 21 (15 Rabīʿ al-Ākhir 1420 [29 July 1999]): 78–9.
Ilá Salīm al-Hilālī: Yarjá l-Takrīm bi-Tazwīdinā bi-Taqrīr... www.kulalsalafiyeen.com/vb/showthread.php?t=15620&page=2, 24 March 2010.
Īlāf al-Salafiyyīn am "Ittilāf al-Salafiyyīn"?!! www.kulalsalafiyeen.com/vb/showthread.php?t=15620&page=2, 24 March 2010.
Jabbūrī, Aḥmad Ṣāliḥ Ḥusayn al-. *Juhūd al-Imām al-Albānī Nāṣir al-Sunna wa-l-Dīn fī Bayān ʿAqīdat al-Salaf al-Ṣāliḥīn fī l-Īmān bi-llāh Rabb al-ʿĀlamīn.* Amman: Al-Dār al-Athariyya, 2008.
Jamʿiyyat al-Irtiqāʾ al-Khayriyya. N.p.: No publisher, n.d.
Jarbūʿ, ʿAbdallāh al-. "Al-Īmān al-Sharʿī wa-l-Dalālat al-Nuṣūṣ ʿalayhi." *Al-Aṣāla* 6, no. 36 (15 Shawwāl 1422 [31 December 2001]): 30–4.
Jawābira, Bāsim b. Fayṣal al-. *Extremism: The Causes, Effects and the Cure*. www.salafimanhaj.com, 2008.
Jawnam, ʿAbdallāh b. Muḥammad al-. "Shurūṭ Lā Ilāha illā llāh." *Al-Aṣāla* 4, no. 24 (15 Shawwāl 1420 [22 January 2000]): 21–5.
Jayyūsī, Tawfīq al-. "Makhāṭir al-Ribā: Al-Ijtimāʿiyya wa-l-Iqtiṣādiyya." *Al-Qibla* 7, no. 18 (2009): 18–26.
Jazāʾirī, Abū ʿUzayr ʿAbd al-Ilah Yūsuf al-Yūbī al-Ḥasanī al-. *Al-Kāshif fī Tarājuʿ ʿAlī al-Ḥalabī al-Jahmī al-Zāʾif*. www.tawhed.ws/dl?i=17051001, 2010.
Masʾalat al-Īmān fī Kaffatay al-Mīzān. Amman: Dār al-Maʾmūn, 2006.
Jazāʾirī, Muḥammad al-Salafī al-. *Nathr al-Darr fī Tafnīd Shubhat Kufr dūna Kufr*. www.fichier-pdf.fr/2015/01/21/fichier-pdf-sans-nom-1/preview/page/1/, 2009.
Kātib, ʿAbd al-Ṣamad b. Muḥammad al-. "... ilayka Ayyatuhā l-Marʾa al-Muslima." *Al-Aṣāla* 2, no. 9 (15 Shaʿbān 1414 [28 January 1994]): 59–61.
Khabīr: Al-Khurūj min al-Ḥalqa al-Mufarragha bi-l-Urdunn Yaqtaḍī l-Iṣlāḥ. http://main.islammessage.com/newspage.aspx?id=8380, 23 April 2011.
Khālidī, Ṣalāḥ ʿAbd al-Fattāḥ al-. "Al-Tafsīr bi-l-Raʾy: Mafhūm wa-Ḍawābiṭ." *Al-Qibla* 10, no. 23 (2012): 12–15.
"Ḥawla Nuzūl al-Qurʾān wa-Tanazzulātihi." *Al-Qibla* 11, no. 24 (2013): 11–14.
Khamīs, Muḥammad b. ʿAbd al-Raḥmān al-. "Al-Tawḥīd ʿinda Ahl al-Sunna wa-Aqsāmuhu." *Al-Aṣāla* 6, no. 31 (15 Muḥarram 1422 [9 April 2001]): 25–31.
Khatib, Ahmad Mouaz al-. "Al-Tamaddun al-Islami: Passé et présent d'une association réformiste Damascène." *Maghreb-Machrek*, no. 198 (2008–2009): 79–89.
Khaṭīb, Muḥammad Māhir ʿAbd al-Karīm al-. *Ḥarakat al-Ikhwān al-Muslimīn: ʿAraḍ wa-Naqd*. Amman: Al-Bayrūnī, 2012.
Khūja, Luṭf Allāh b. ʿAbd al-ʿAẓīm. "Kayfa Buniya Taḥrīm al-Ikhtilāṭ?" *Al-Qibla* 8, no. 20 (2010): 16–29.
Khumayyis, Muḥammad ʿAbd al-Raḥmān al-. "Mafāhīm Khāṭiʾa ḥawla l-Awliyāʾ." *Al-Aṣāla* 2, no. 9 (15 Shaʿbān 1414 [28 January 1994]): 71–5.
Kuwaytī, Aḥmad al-. *Al-Kashf al-Mathālī ʿan Sariqāt Salīm al-Hilālī*. http://alhalaby.net/main/articles.aspx?article_no=412, n.d.
Lajna al-Dāʾima li-l-Buḥūth wa-l-Iftāʾ, Al-. "Fatwa no. 20212." www.alifta.net/Search/ResultDetails.aspx?languagename=ar&lang=ar&view=result&fat

waNum=&FatwaNumID=&ID=10899&searchScope=3&SearchScopeLevels1=&SearchScopeLevels2=&highLight=1&SearchType=exact&SearchMoesar=false&bookID=&LeftVal=0&RightVal=0&simple=&SearchCriteria=allwords&PagePath=&siteSection=1&searchkeyword=217133216177216167216175032216180217131216177217138#firstKeyWordFound, n.d.

"Fatwa no. 21517." www.alifta.net/Search/ResultDetails.aspx?languagename=ar%26lang=ar&view=result&fatwaNum=&FatwaNumID=&ID=10901&searchScope=3&SearchScopeLevels1=&SearchScopeLevels2=&highLight=1&SearchType=exact&SearchMoesar=false&bookID=&LeftVal=0&RightVal=0&simple=&SearchCriteria=allwords&PagePath=&siteSection=1&searchkeyword=216185217132217138032216173216179217134032216167217132216173217132216168217138#firstKeyWordFound, n.d.

"Waḥdat al-Adyān aw al-Taqrīb baynahā." *Al-Aṣāla* 4, no. 18 (15 Muḥarram 1418 [23 May 1997]): 22–8.

Lajna al-ʿIlmiyya fī Masjid al-Ṣādiq al-Amīn, Al-. *ʿAqīdatuka Ayyuhā l-Muslim.* Amman: Al-Dār al-Athariyya, 2014.

Lajnat al-Fatwa fi Markaz al-Imam al-Albani. "Rukn al-Fatāwá." *Al-Aṣāla* 10, no. 50 (15 Ramaḍān 1426 [18 October 2005]): 70–6.

Liqāʾ Shabakat Anā l-Muslim maʿa l-Shaykh al-Duktūr Muḥammad Abū Ruḥayyim. www.saaid.net/leqa/1.htm, n.d.

Madanī, Aḥmad b. Muḥammad al-Dahlawī al-. *Tārīkh Ahl al-Ḥadīth: Taʿyīn al-Firqa al-Nājiya wa-annahā Ṭāʾifat Ahl al-Ḥadīth.* Medina: Maktabat al-Ghurabāʾ al-Athariyya, 1417 AH [1996/1997].

Mahdī, Muḥammad b. Muḥammad b. Aḥmad al-. "Ḥuqūq al-Ṭifl al-Tarbawiyya fī l-Islām." *Al-Aṣāla* 2, no. 10 (15 Shawwāl 1414 [28 March 1994]): 44–8.

Manfikhī, Muḥammad Farīz. "Waqfāt maʿa Kitāb Al-Salafiyya Marḥala Zamaniyya Mubāraka Lā Madhhab Islāmī (li-Muḥammad Saʿīd al-Būṭī) (Al-Ḥalqa al-Ūlá)." *Al-Aṣāla* 3, nos. 13–14 (15 Rajab 1415 [18 December 1994]): 73–86.

"Waqfāt maʿa Kitāb Al-Salafiyya Marḥala Zamaniyya Mubāraka Lā Madhhab Islāmī li-Muḥammad Saʿīd al-Būṭī, Al-Ḥalqa al-Thāniya." *Al-Aṣāla* 3, nos. 15–16 (15 Dhu l-Qaʿda 1415 [15 April 1995]): 62–74.

Mansī, Muḥammad Badr. "Ahammiyyat al-Tawḥīd fī Wāqiʿ al-Muslimīn Jamāʿāt wa-Afrādan 1." *Al-Aṣāla* 1, no. 5 (15 Dhū l-Ḥijja 1413 [6 June 1993]): 13–17.

"Ahammiyyat al-Tawḥīd fī Wāqiʿ al-Muslimīn Jamāʿāt wa-Afrādan 2." *Al-Aṣāla* 1, no. 6 (15 Ṣafar 1414 [6 June 1993]): 17–20.

Maqdisī, Abū ʿAbd al-Raḥmān Hishām al-ʿĀrif al-. "Madá Khaṭūrat Ahl al-Ahwāʾ wa-l-Bidaʿ." *Al-Aṣāla* 7, no. 37 (15 Ṣafar 1423 [28 April 2002]): 19–26.

Maqdisī, Abū Muḥammad al-. *Imtāʿ al-Naẓar fī Kashf Shubhāt Murjiʾat al-ʿAṣr.* www.tawhed.ws/t, 1991/1992.

Introduction to *ʿAqīdat Adʿiyāʾ al-Salafiyya fī Mīzān Ahl al-Sunna wa-l-Jamāʿa*, by Abū ʿAbdallāh Muḥammad Bū l-Nīt al-Marākishī, 4–8. www.tawhed.ws/dl?i=0606091a, 2009.

Ruwaydan Ayyuhā l-Munhazimūna. Fa-Aʿdāʾunā Yumayyizūna. www.tawhed.ws/r?i=za33cn8f, 2002.

Sarāb al-Tarāju'āt wa-Asrāb al-Mutasāqiṭīn. www.tawhed.ws/dl?i=31051001, 2010.

Tabṣīr al-'Uqalā' bi-Talbisāt Ahl al-Tajahhum wa-l-Irjā'. www.tawhed.ws/t, 1996.

Maqdisī, Hishām al-'Ārif al-. "Al-Yahūd wa-l-Naṣārá fī Ḍaw' al-Qur'ān wa-l-Sunna." *Al-Aṣāla* 6, no. 31 (15 Muḥarram 1422 [9 April 2001]): 7–12.

Ma'rībī, Abū l-Ḥasan al-. "Raf' al-Ḥijāb 'an al-Farq bayna Da'wat Ahl al-Sunna wa-Da'wat Ahl al-Bida' wa-l-Aḥzāb." *Al-Aṣāla* 5, no. 27 (15 Rabī' al-Ākhir 1421 [18 July 2000]): 55–9.

Mawṣilī, Abū 'Abdallāh Fatḥī b. 'Abdallāh al-. "Mubādara Kashafat 'an Uṣūl Ṣāḥibihā." *Al-Aṣāla* 9, no. 45 (15 Ṣafar 1425 [6 April 2014]): 25–9.

Mazīdī, Al-Ḥārith b. Zaydān al-. "Ādāb al-Ṭa'ām fī l-Sharī'a al-Muṭṭahara." *Al-Aṣāla* 7, no. 38 (15 Rabī' al-Awwal 1423 [27 May 2002]): 68–75.

Min Awākhir Mā Tamma ktishāfuhu 'an Salīm al-Hilālī 2010. www.kulalsalafiyeen.com/vb/showthread.php?t=15620&page=3, 24 March 2010.

Minyāwī, Abū Ḥamza Sayyid b. Muḥammad al-. *Talkhīṣ Fitnat al-Tafjīrāt wa-l-Ightiyālāt: Al-Asbāb – al-Āthār – al-'Ilāj*. Amman: Jam'iyyat al-Kitāb wa-l-Sunna – Lajnat al-Kalima al-Ṭayyiba, n.d.

Miṣrī, Muḥammad 'Abd al-Hādī al-. *Ma'ālim Manhaj Ahl al-Sunna wa-l-Jamā'a*. Amman: Jam'iyyat al-Kitāb wa-l-Sunna – Lajnat al-Kalima al-Ṭayyiba, 2011.

Mukhtār, Abū l-'Abbās 'Imād Ṭāriq b. 'Abd al-'Azīz al-. *Taḥdhīr al-Nāṣiḥīn min al-Taḥazzub li-l-'Ulamā' wa-l-Murabbīn*. Amman: Al-Dār al-Athariyya, 2008.

Munāẓarat Muḥammad Abū Ruḥayyim li-'Alī al-Ḥalabī. www.tawhed.ws/c?i=296, n.d.

Muṣṭafá, Muḥammad Abū Zayd. *Al-Mafhūm al-Salafī li-l-'Amal al-Siyāsī*. Riyadh: Maktabat Dār al-Salām, 1414 [1993/1994].

Najīb, Sāmī. "Ḥattá Lā Yakūna l-Ḥijāb Zayna." *Al-Qibla* 7, no. 18 (2009): 59–65.

Nāṣir, Bassām. "Al-Ijtihād wa-l-Tajdīd fī Ḥiwār 'Almānī Uṣūlī." *Al-Qibla* 4, nos. 10–11 (2005): 19–26.

"Al-Thawra al-Sūriyya ... Qirā'a fī Khalfiyyāt wa-l-Dawā'ī wa-l-Asbāb." *Al-Qibla* 9, no. 22 (2012): 35–8.

"Ḥaqā'iq al-Qur'ān Takshifu Khabā'ith al-Yahūd li-l-'Iyān." *Al-Qibla* 1, no. 2 (2002): 17–21.

"Jamā'at al-Tablīgh wa-Hidāyat al-'Ilm." *Al-Qibla* 2, nos. 4–5 (2003): 9–12.

"Thawrat Sūriyā wa-Aḥdāthuhā bi-Ru'á wa-Naẓarāt Shar'iyya." *Al-Qibla* 9, no. 22 (2012): 68–71.

Naṣr, 'Aṣr b. Muḥammad al-. "Al-Salafiyya al-Mu'āṣira: Ishkāliyyat al-Tārīkh wa-l-Khiṭāb." *Al-Qibla* 11, no. 24 (2013): 31–7.

Nu'mān, 'Abd al-Mu'man Muḥammad al-. "Maqām al-Tawḥīd ...." *Al-Aṣāla* 2, no. 12 (15 Ṣafar 1415 [24 July 1994]): 13–14.

Qaḥṭānī, Sa'īd b. 'Alī b. Wahf al-, ed. *Ḥiṣn al-Muslim min Adhkār al-Kitāb wa-l-Sunna*. Cairo: Dār Ibn al-Haytham, 2010.

Qāsimī, Muḥammad Jamāl al-Dīn al-. *Iṣlāḥ al-Masājid min al-Bida' wa-l-'Awābid*. Beirut and Damascus: Al-Maktab al-Islāmī, 1983.

Qaysī, Marwān al-. "Al-Thaqāfa ... wa-l-Ghazw al-Thaqāfī 1." *Al-Aṣāla* 2, no. 7 (15 Rabīʿ al-Thānī 1414 [2 October 1993]): 63–6.

"Al-Thaqāfa ... wa-l-Ghazw al-Thaqāfī 2." *Al-Aṣāla* 2, no. 8 (15 Jumādá l-Ākhira 1414 [30 November 1993]): 57–62.

"Al-Usra wa-Qawāʿid al-Sulūk al-ʿĀʾilī 1." *Al-Aṣāla* 1, no. 2 (15 Jumādá l-Ākhira 1413 [11 December 1992]): 67–70.

"Al-Usra wa-Qawāʿid al-Sulūk al-ʿĀʾilī 2." *Al-Aṣāla* 1, no. 3 (15 Shaʿbān 1413 [8 February 1993]): 44–6.

Rājiḥī, ʿAbd al-ʿAzīz b. Fayṣal al-. *Al-Fāriq bayna l-Muḥaqqiq wa-l-Sāriq*. www.saaid.net/Doat/rajhi/1.htm, published at various dates in 2000 and 2002.

Rashīd, Sāmī Najīb. "ʿIlāj Mushkilat al-Faqr." *Al-Qibla* 6, no. 17 (2008): 69–77.

Riḍā, Muḥammad Rashīd. *Ḥuqūq al-Nisāʾ fī l-Islām*. Beirut and Damascus: Al-Maktab al-Islāmī, 1984.

Royal Hashemite Court. *The Amman Interfaith Message*. N.p.: No publisher, 2005.

Rushdī, Marwān Muḥammad. "Al-Tarbiya al-Islāmiyya wa-l-Taḥaddiyāt al-ʿAqdiyya." *Al-Qibla* 7, no. 18 (2009): 40–8.

Sadḥān, ʿAbd al-ʿAzīz b. Muḥammad b. ʿAbdallāh al-. *Al-Imām al-Albānī Durūs wa-Mawāqif wa-ʿIbar*. Riyadh: Dār al-Tawḥīd, 2008.

Sadlān, Ṣāliḥ b. Ghānim al-. "Wāqiʿ al-Umma al-Islāmiyya al-Dāʾ wa-l-Dawāʾ." *Al-Aṣāla* 1, no. 4 (15 Shawwāl 1413 [8 April 1993]): 40–8.

Salām, Aḥmad. "Hal Naḥnu Qawm Salafiyyūn (1)?" *Al-Aṣāla* 3, nos. 13–14 (15 Rajab 1415 [18 December 1994]): 117–21.

Ṣāliḥ, Umm ʿAbdallāh Najlāʾ al-. "ʿAwāmil Bināʾ Shakhṣiyyat al-Marʾa al-Muslima." *Al-Aṣāla* 8, no. 44 (15 Shawwāl 1424 [10 December 2003]): 77–82.

"Dawr al-Marʾa al-Muslima fī Tamkīn al-Waḥda al-Islāmiyya." *Al-Aṣāla* 10, no. 48 (15 Rabīʿ al-Awwal 1426 [24 April 2005]): 73–82.

"Ukhtāhu Kūnī Khayr Mutāʿ." *Al-Aṣāla* 11, no. 53 (15 Rajab 1427 [10 August 2006]): 77–81.

Salīm, Aḥmad. "Al-Iltifāt fī l-Qurʾān al-Karīm." *Al-Qibla* 11, no. 24 (2013): 15–19.

Salīm, ʿAmr ʿAbd al-Munʿim. *Barāʾat al-Dhimma bi-Nuṣrat al-Sunna: Al-Difāʿ al-Sunnī ʿan al-Albānī wa-l-Jawāb ʿan Shubah Ṣāḥib "Al-Taʿrīf."* Ṭanṭā: Dār al-Ḍiyāʾ, n.d.

Salīm al-Hilālī: Min Ayna La-ka. www.kulalsalafiyeen.com/vb/showthread.php?t=15620&page=2, 24 March 2010.

Sarḥān, Ibrāhīm. "Mawqif al-Ashāʿira min Ḥaqīqat al-Īmān." *Al-Qibla* 6, no. 16 (2008): 24–36.

Seputar Korupsi Salim Hilali. www.4shared.com/office/Ul2BWef8/SEPUTAR_KORUPSI_SALIM_HILALI.html, n.d.

Shaʿbān, Abū ʿAbd al-Raḥmān Muḥammad b. Surūr. *Al-Shaykh al-Albānī wa-Manhajahu fī Taqrīr Masāʾil al-Iʿtiqād*. Riyadh: Dār al-Kiyān, 2007.

Shādhilī, Abū ʿUbayda ʿAbd al-Karīm al-. *Taʾsīs al-Naẓar fī Radd Shubah Mashāyikh Murjiʾat al-ʿAṣr*. www.tawhed.ws, 1420 [1999/2000].

Shaḥāda, Usāma. *Al-Daʿwa al-Salafiyya: Maqālāt fī Mafhūmihā, Tārīkhihā wa-Tabāyunihā ʿan Jamāʿāt al-ʿUnf wa-l-Taṭarruf*. N.p.: No publisher, n.d.

Al-Iṣlāḥ al-Insānī al-Ijtimāʿī al-Siyāsī al-Waṭanī. http://osamash.maktoobblog.com/date/2007/09, 28 September 2007.
Al-Iṣlāḥ Manhaj al-Anbiyāʾ. http://osamash.maktoobblog.com/date/2011/03/, 19 March 2011.
Al-Islāmiyyūn wa-l-Marḥala al-Jadīda. http://osamash.maktoobblog.com/date/2012/07/, 1 July 2012.
"Al-Madāris al-Salafiyya al-Muʿāṣira: Miṣr Numūdhijan." *Al-Qibla* 11, no. 24 (2013): 52–60.
Al-Mushkila al-Shīʿiyya. www.alrased.net, 2008.
Al-Salafiyya wa-Asʾilat al-Mushāraka al-Siyāsiyya – 1. http://osamash.maktoobblog.com/date/2012/10/, 13 October 2012.
Al-Salafiyya wa-Asʾilat al-Mushāraka al-Siyāsiyya – 2. http://osamash.maktoobblog.com/date/2012/10/, 19 October 2012.
Al-Salafiyya wa-Asʾilat al-Mushāraka al-Siyāsiyya – 3. http://osamash.maktoobblog.com/date/2012/11/, 8 November 2012.
Al-Siyāda al-Shaʿbiyya ... Al-Ukdhūba al-ʿAlmāniyya. http://osamash.maktoobblog.com/date/2012/12/, 21 December 2012.
Al-Sunna wa-l-Shīʿa: Ruʾya Wāqiʿiyya. www.alrased.net, 2010.
"Al-Tashayyuʿ fī Khidmat al-Mashrūʿ al-Īrānī." *Al-Qibla* 6, no. 17 (2008): 78–80.
Al-Taṭawwur al-Siyāsī fī Dawlat al-Khulafāʾ al-Rāshidūn. http://osamash.maktoobblog.com/date/2010/12/, 19 December 2010.
Hal al-ʿAlmāniyyūn Dīmuqrāṭiyyūn? http://osamash.maktoobblog.com/date/2011/07, 30 July 2011.
Ḥālat al-Jabriyya wa-l-Qadariyya – Khaṭar al-Inḥirāf ʿan Manhaj al-Ṣaḥāba 2. http://osamash.maktoobblog.com/date/2011/02/, 19 February 2011.
Ḥālat al-Khawārij – Khaṭar al-Inḥirāf ʿan Manhaj al-Ṣaḥāba 1. http://osamash.maktoobblog.com/date/2011/02/, 1 February 2011.
Iʿṭāʾ al-Nisāʾ Jamīʿ Ḥuqūqihinna l-Insāniyya wa-l-Dīniyya wa-l-Madaniyya. http://osamash.maktoobblog.com/date/2007/09, 28 July 2007.
Ittifāqiyyat Sīdāw ... bi-dūna Makyāj. http://osamash.maktoobblog.com/date/2012/11/, 24 November 2012.
Khaṭar al-Inḥirāf ʿan Manhaj al-Ṣaḥāba 3 – Al-ʿAwda li-l-Thiyūqrāṭiyya. http://osamash.maktoobblog.com/date/2011/02/, 19 February 2011.
Laysa min al-Salafiyya fī l-Shayʾ. http://osamash.maktoobblog.com/date/2009/11/, 20 November 2009.
"Limādhā Yufshilu l-Shīʿa Masīrat al-Waḥda al-Islāmiyya??" *Al-Qibla* 7, no. 18 (2009): 66–75.
Maʿālim al-Shakhṣiyya al-Iṣlāḥiyya. http://osamash.maktoobblog.com/date/2011/04, 2 April 2011.
"Maqāṣid al-Qurʾān." *Al-Qibla* 6, no. 16 (2008): 10–23.
Marra Ukhrá ... Limādhā Narfuḍu ttifāqiyyat Sīdāw. http://osamash.maktoobblog.com/date/2013/01/, 18 January 2013.
Min Tārīkh al-Ḥarakāt al-Islāmiyya maʿa l-Shīʿa wa-Īrān. www.alrased.net, n.d.
Min Tārīkh al-Iṣlāḥ al-Muʿāṣir. http://osamash.maktoobblog.com/date/2011/04/, 13 April 2011.

Mīrāth al-Mar'a Laysa Niṣf Mīrāth al-Rajul!! http://osamash.maktoobblog.com/date/2010/07/, 18 July 2010.
Munāṣara wa-Munāṣaḥa li-Jamā'at al-Ikhwān al-Muslimīn. http://osamash.maktoobblog.com/date/2012/12/, 8 December 2012.
"Tafā'ulāt Salafiyyī al-Urdunn ma'a l-Rabī' al-'Arabī wa-l-Āfāq al-Mustaqbaliyya." *Awrāq wa-Niqāshāt Mu'tamar "Al-Taḥawwulāt al-Salafiyya" – Al-Dalālāt, al-Taḍā'iyāt wa-l-Āfāq*, 44–7. Amman: Friedrich Ebert Stiftung, 2013.
Taqwīḍ al-Islām min Dākhilihi… Imāmat al-Mar'a Numūdhajan. http://osamash.maktoobblog.com/date/2010/06/, 27 June 2010.
Usus Dawlat al-Khulafā' al-Rāshidūn. http://osamash.maktoobblog.com/date/2010/12, 19 December 2010.
Shāmī, Abū 'Abdallāh al-. "Al-Duktūr al-Būṭī min Khilāl Kutubihi!!!" *Al-Aṣāla* 2, no. 11 (15 Dhū l-Ḥijja 1414 [26 May 1994]): 59–66.
"Al-Duktūr al-Būṭī min Khilāl Kutubihi!! (2)." *Al-Aṣāla* 2, no. 12 (15 Ṣafar 1415 [24 July 1994]): 64–70.
Shāmī, Iyād Muḥammad al-. *Ārā' al-Imām al-Albānī al-Tarbawiyya.* Amman: Al-Dār al-Athariyya, 2009.
Shamrānī, 'Abdallāh b. Muḥammad al-. *Mazāliq fī l-Taḥqīq.* www.tawhed.ws/r?i=72ffkf2o, n.d.
Shaqra, 'Āṣim Muḥammad Ibrāhīm. *Al-Rudūd al-'Ilmiyya al-Sunniyya Yaruddu fī-hi l-Kitāb 'alá Mā Jā'a min Hujūm 'alá l-Shaykh Muḥammad Ibrāhīm Shaqra fī 'adaday al-Aṣāla 25 wa-26.* N.p.: No publisher, 2000.
Shaqra, Muḥammad Ibrāhīm. "Al-Dīmuqrāṭiyya wa-l-Ta'addudiyya al-Ḥizbiyya." *Al-Aṣāla* 1, no. 1 (15 Rabī' al-Thānī 1413 [13 October 1992]): 26–30.
Al-Dufū'āt al-Ghawānī wa-l-Istinbāṭāt al-Rawānī li-Iẓhār Wajh al-Ḥaqq fī Mas'alat 'Iṣmat Azwāj al-Nabī – Ṣallá llah 'alayhi wa-Sallam – allatī Ikhtalafa 'alayhā Nasīb al-Rifā'ī wa-Nāṣir al-Dīn al-Albānī. N.p.: No publisher, 2003.
"Al-Shaykh Muḥammad Nasīb al-Rifā'ī: Ṣafḥa Da'wiyya Ṭuwiyat?!" *Al-Aṣāla* 1, no. 3 (15 Sha'bān 1413 [8 February 1993]): 21–9.
"Al-Taṭarruf al-Dīnī … Ma'ná!!" *Al-Aṣāla* 1, no. 2 (15 Jumādá l-Ākhira 1413 [11 December 1992]): 46–50.
Ayna Taqa'u "Lā ilāha illā llāh" fī Dīn al-Murji'a al-Judud? www.saaid.net/book/open.php?cat=88&book=1312, n.d.
"Ḍawābiṭ al-Amr bi-l-Ma'rūf wa-l-Nahy 'an al-Munkar Tadhkīran li-l-Khāṣṣa wa-Bayānan li-l-'Āmma." *Al-Aṣāla* 3, nos. 15–16 (15 Dhū l-Qa'da 1415 [15 April 1995]): 36–44.
Hiya l-Salafiyya Nisbatan wa-'Aqīdatan wa-Manhajan. www.saaid.net/book/open.php?cat=1&Book=44, 2000 [1992].
Introduction to *Al-Kāshif fī Tarāju' 'Alī al-Ḥalabī al-Jahmī al-Zā'if*, by Abū 'Uzayr 'Abd al-Ilah Yūsuf al-Yūbī al-Ḥasanī al-Jazā'irī, 5–12. www.tawhed.ws/dl?i=17051001, 2010.
Introduction to *Ḥaqīqat al-Īmān 'inda l-Shaykh al-Albānī*, by Muḥammad Abū Ruḥayyim, 5–8. www.tawhed.ws/dl?i=d7pgztyu, 2001.
"Jaffat al-Ṣuḥuf wa-Rufi'at al-Aqlām." *Al-Aṣāla* 4, no. 23 (15 Sha'bān 1420 [24 November 1999]): 15–20.

"Kalimat Ḥaqq fī Futyā l-ʿAllāma Muḥammad Nāṣir al-Dīn al-Albānī ḥawla Hijrat al-Muḍṭahadīn min al-Muslimīn." *Al-Aṣāla* 2, no. 7 (15 Rabīʿ al-Th ānī 1414 [2 October 1993]): 49–62.

Mādhā Yanqimūna min al-Shaykh?! N.p.: No publisher, n.d.

Tanwīr al-Afhām ilá baʿḍ Mafāhīm al-Islām. www.saaid.net/book/open.php?ca t=1&book=43, 2000 [1985].

Sharḥ al-ʿAqīda al-Ṭaḥāwiyya li-l-ʿAllāma Ibn Abī l-ʿIzz al-Ḥanafī. Beirut/Cairo: Al-Maktab al-Islāmī/Dār al-Salām, 2011.

Shaybānī, Muḥammad b. Ibrāhīm al-. *Mukhtaṣar Kitāb al-Albānī: Jihāduhu wa-Ḥayātuhu l-ʿIlmiyya*. Kuwait: Markaz al-Makhṭūṭāt wa-l-Turāth wa-l-Wathāʾiq, 1998.

Shukrī, Murād. "Al-Shaykh Muḥammad Nasīb al-Rifāʿī – Raḥimahu llāh." *Al-Aṣāla* 1, no. 3 (15 Shaʿbān 1413 [8 February 1993]): 30.

Iḥkām al-Taqrīr li-Aḥkām Masʾalat al-Takfīr. Riyadh: Dār al-Ṣamīʿī, 1994.

"Thalāthūn ʿĀmman min Tārīkh al-Daʿwa al-Salafiyya fī l-Mamlaka al-Urdunniyya (1980–2010)." Unpublished manuscript in possession of the author, n.d.

Shumūṭ, Ḥasan Taysīr. "Al-Tadarruj fī Taṭbīq al-Sharīʿa bayna l-Sharʿ wa-l-Wāqiʿ." *Al-Qibla* 10, no. 23 (2012): 16–19.

Sīlāwī, Muḥammad b. Maḥmūd al-Ṣāliḥ al-, ed. *Ṣafaḥāt min Ḥayāt Dāʿiyat Faḍīlat al-Shaykh ʿAbd al-Raḥmān b. ʿAbd al-Khāliq*. N.p.: No publisher, 2007.

Sudays, ʿAbd al-Raḥmān b. ʿAbd al-ʿAzīz al-. "Al-Irhāb Marfūḍ bi-Jamīʿ Ṣuwarihi wa-Ashkālihi." *Al-Aṣāla* 7, no. 40 (15 Dhū l-Ḥijja 1423 [17 February 2003]): 65–70.

Sulaymān, Muḥammad. "Ḥālat al-ʿAmal al-Islāmī fī l-Urdunn." *Al-Qibla* 2, nos. 4–5 (2003): 61–77.

Sulaymān, Yūsuf. "Kalima ḥawla l-Jihād." *Al-Aṣāla* 3, no. 17 (15 Dhū l-Ḥijja 1416 [4 April 1996]): 96–8.

Sulmī, ʿAbd al-Raḥīm b. Ṣamāyil al-. "Maṣādir al-Talaqqī ʿinda Ahl al-Bidaʿ." *Al-Aṣāla* 2, no. 7 (15 Rabīʿ al-Thānī 1414 [2 October 1993]): 28–35.

"Siyādat al-Sharīʿa … 'al-Ḥadd al-Fāṣil bayna l-Islām wa-l-ʿAlmāniyya'." *Al-Qibla* 9, no. 22 (2012): 9–13.

Sulṭān, Fatḥī ʿAbdallāh. "Ḍawābiṭ al-Kalām fī Anwāʿ al-Kufr wa-Taqsīmātihā." *Al-Aṣāla* 5, no. 29 (15 Shaʿbān 1421 [13 November 2000]): 66–76.

"Manhaj Shaykh al-Islām fī Kashf Bidʿat al-Khawārij." *Al-Aṣāla* 5, no. 28 (15 Jumādá l-Ākhira 1420 [26 September 1999]): 18–31.

Ṣūmālī, ʿUthmān b. Muʿallim al-. "Al-Farq bayna l-Jihād fī Sabīl Allāh wa-l-Khurūj ʿalá l-Ḥukkām." *Al-Aṣāla* 4, no. 21 (15 Rabīʿ al-Ākhir 1420 [29 July 1999]): 43–50.

"Baʿḍ al-Ḍawābiṭ fī Fiqh al-Amr bi-l-Maʿrūf wa-l-Nahy ʿan al-Munkar." *Al-Aṣāla* 4, no. 22 (15 Jumādá l-Ākhira 1420 [26 September 1999]): 60–6.

"Shurūṭ al-Jihād fī Sabīl Allāh." *Al-Aṣāla* 6, no. 31 (15 Muḥarram 1422 [9 April 2001]): 62–8.

Ṭālib, Nūr al-Dīn, ed. *Maqālāt al-Albānī*. Riyadh: Dār al-Aṭlas, 2000.

Ṭarṭūsī, ʿAbd al-Munʿim Muṣṭafá Ḥalīma Abū Baṣīr al-. *Al-Intiṣār li-Ahl al-Tawḥīd wa-l-Radd ʿalá Man Jādala ʿan al-Ṭawāghīt: Mulāḥaẓāt wa-Rudūd*

ʿalá Sharīṭ "Al-Kufr Kufrān" li-l-Shaykh Muḥammad Nāṣir al-Dīn al-Albānī. Beirut: Dār al-Bayāriq, 1996.

Hal al-Albānī Murjiʾ? www.tawhed.ws/pr?i=1104, n.d.

Li-l-Shaykh Muḥammad Ibrāhīm Shaqra ʿalayya Dayn! www.abubaseer.bizland.com/hadath/Read/hadath%2054.doc, 8 December 2008.

Madhāhib al-Nās fī l-Shaykh Muḥammad Nāṣir al-Dīn al-Albānī. www.tawhed.ws/r?i=s3usuben, 19 March 2001.

Mulāḥaẓāt wa-Rudūd ʿalá Risāla "Mujmal Masāʾil al-Īmān al-ʿIlmiyya fī Uṣūl al-ʿAqīda al-Salafiyya." www.tawhed.ws/a?a=0ybqpkdw, 25 April 2001.

Suʾāl ḥawla Mawqif al-Albānī min Takfīr Tārik al-Ṣalāt. www.tawhed.ws/pr?i=2356, n.d.

Tawḥīdī, Abū ʿAbd al-Malik al-. *Kashf Mā Alqāhu Iblīs ʿalá Qalb ʿAbd al-ʿAzīz b. Rayyis al-Rayyis.* www.tawhed.ws, 1430 [2009].

Taysīr, ʿAlāʾ al-Dīn. "Al-Mushāraka al-Mutanāqiṣa." *Al-Qibla* 9, no. 21 (2011): 56–8.

ʿUbaydī, ʿAwnī Jaddūʿ al-. *Sukkān al-Urdunn wa-Filasṭīn: Al-Manābit wa-l-Uṣūl.* Amman: No publisher, 2014.

ʿUbaylān, ʿAbdallāh b. Ṣāliḥ al-. "Durūs fī Manhaj al-Salaf." *Al-Aṣāla* 4, no. 22 (15 Jumādá l-Ākhira 1420 [26 September 1999]): 33–9.

ʿUlyān, Hishām. "Al-Daʿwa al-Salafiyya . . . Mulāḥaẓāt Naqdiyya." *Al-Qibla* 1, no. 3 (2002): 34–5.

ʿUmarī, Salmān. *Ḥiwār Jarīdat* Al-Jazīra *maʿa l-Shaykh Yūsuf al-Barqāwī.* www.al-sunna.net/articles/file.php?id=3213, 23 Dhū l-Ḥijja [10 April 1999].

ʿUtaybī, Usāma al-. *Radd Usāma al-ʿUtaybī ʿalá ftirāʾāt Salīm al-Hilālī.* www.kulalsalafiyeen.com/vb/showthread.php?t=15620, 24 March 2010.

ʿUthaymīn, Muḥammad b. Ṣāliḥ al-. "Kalimat al-Tawḥīd: Faḍluhā wa-Maʿnāhā." *Al-Aṣāla* 3, nos. 15–16 (15 Dhū l-Qaʿda 1415 [15 April 1995]): 13–16.

Wānilī, Khayr al-Dīn al-. "Al-Aḥkām allatī Tamyīz bi-hā l-Marʾa ʿan al-Rajul 2." *Al-Aṣāla* 6, no. 35 (15 Shaʿbān 1422 [2 November 2001]): 62–70.

"Al-Aḥkām allatī Tamyīz bi-hā l-Marʾa ʿan al-Rajul 3." *Al-Aṣāla* 6, no. 36 (15 Shawwāl 1422 [31 December 2001]): 64–6.

"Al-Aḥkām allatī Tamyīz bi-hā l-Marʾa ʿan al-Rajul 4." *Al-Aṣāla* 7, no. 37 (15 Ṣafar 1423 [28 April 2002]): 55–60.

"Ibn Taymiyyat al-Qarn al-ʿIshrīn." *Al-Aṣāla* 4, no. 23 (15 Shaʿbān 1420 [24 November 1999]): 63–4.

Yāfāwī, Abū Ṣakhr al-. *Radd al-Iʿtidāʾāt Murjiʾat al-Khalaf ʿalá Manhaj al-Salaf.* www.tawhed.ws, n.d.

Yamanī, Abū Qatāda. *Al-Radd ʿalá Mā Qālahu l-Ḥalabī al-Daʿī fī Maqālat "Al-Salafiyya . . . al-Salafiyya al-Salafiyya" allatī Nushirat fī Jarīdat al-Ghad al-Urdunnī.* www.tawhed.ws/dl?i=22011003, n.d.

Yamānī, Abū Qatāda ʿAbd al-Khāliq al-. *Murjiʾat al-ʿAṣr Murjifūn.* www.tawhed.ws/dl?i=16011008, n.d.

Yaʿqūb, Raʾfat. "Al-Tadarruj fī Taḥkīm al-Sharīʿa." *Al-Qibla* 10, no. 23 (2012): 20–30.

Zaʿtarī, Saʿd b. Fatḥī b. Saʿīd al-. *Tanbīh al-Faṭīn li-Tafāhut Taʾṣīlāt "ʿAlī al-Ḥalabī" l-Miskīn wa-llatī Khālafa bi-hā Nahj al-Salaf al-Awwalīn.* Cairo/Fez: Dār ʿIlm al-Salaf/Dār al-Tawḥīd, 2009.

Zaydān, ʿIṣām. "Tafjīrāt ʿAmmān . . . Tasāʾulāt ḥawla l-Hadaf wa-l-Mashrūʿ." *Al-Qibla* 2, nos. 10–11 (2005): 90–3.
Zaynū, Muḥammad b. Jamīl. *Al-Ṣūfiyya fī Mīzān al-Kitāb wa-l-Sunna*. Jeddah: Dār al-Muḥammadī li-l-Nashr wa-l-Tawzīʿ, 1431 [2010].
Arkān al-Islām wa-l-Īmān min al-Kitāb wa-l-Sunna al-Ṣaḥīḥa. Jeddah: Maṭbaʿat al-Amal, 1431 [2009/2010].
Kayfa Nurabbī Awlādanā wa-Mā Huwa Wājib al-Ābāʾ wa-l-Abnāʾ. Riyadh: Dār al-Ṣamīʿī, 1431 [2010].
Min Ādāb al-Islām li-Iṣlāḥ al-Fard wa-l-Mujtamaʿ. Jeddah: Maṭbaʿat al-Amal, 1431 [2010].
Min Badāʾiʿ al-Qaṣaṣ al-Nabawī al-Ṣaḥīḥ. Riyadh: Majmūʿat al-Tuḥaf al-Naf āʾis al-Dawliyya, 1429 [2008].
"Naṣāʾiḥ wa-Tawjīhāt ilá Ḥujjāj Bayt Allāh al-Ḥarām." *Al-Aṣāla* 2, no. 11 (15 Dhū l-Ḥijja 1414 [26 May 1994]): 45–7.
Nidāʾ ilá l-Murabbīn wa-l-Murabbiyyāt li-Tawjīh al-Banīn wa-l-Banāt. Riyadh: Dār al-Ṣamīʿī, 1429 [2008].
Quṭūf min al-Shamāʾil al-Muḥammadiyya wa-l-Akhlāq al-Nabawiyya wa-l-Ādāb al-Islāmiyya. Jeddah: Dār al-Khirāz, 1428 [2007].
Tafsīr wa-Bayān li-Aʿẓam Sūra fī l-Qurʾān. Jeddah: Dār al-Khirāz, 1420 [1999/2000].
Takrīm al-Marʾa fī l-Islām. Riyadh: Dār al-Qāsim li-l-Nashr, 1425 [2004/2005].
Ziyāda, Akram b. Muḥammad b. *"Fasād" al-Salafī, Lā "al-Fasād" al-Salafī*. www.majles.alwkah.net/t9059/, 30 October 2007.
"Ṭūbá li-Man Lam Yanqaṭiʿ ʿAmalahu ʿanhu." *Al-Aṣāla* 4, no. 23 (15 Shaʿbān 1420 [24 November 1999]): 50–2.
Zuhayrī, Samīr b. Amīn al-. *Muḥaddith al-ʿAṣr Muḥammad Nāṣir al-Dīn al-Albānī*. Riyadh: Dār al-Mughnī. 1421 [2000[1999]].

Secondary Sources (Arabic, Dutch, English, French, German)

Abdul Kazem, Ali. "The Muslim Brotherhood: The Historic Background and the Ideological Origins." In *Islamic Movements in Jordan* (translation George A. Musleh), edited by Jillian Schwedler, 13–43. Amman: Al-Urdun al-Jadid Research Center/Sindbad Publishing House, 1997.
Abir, Mordechai. *Saudi Arabia: Government, Society and the Gulf Crisis*. London and New York: Routledge, 1993.
Abou Zahab, Mariam. "Salafism in Pakistan: The Ahl-e Hadith Movement." In *Global Salafism: Islam's New Religious Movement*, edited by Roel Meijer, 126–42. London: Hurst & Co., 2009.
Abū Haniyya, Ḥasan. *Al-Marʾa wa-l-Siyāsa min Manẓūr al-Ḥarakāt al-Islāmiyya fī l-Urdunn*. Amman: Friedrich Ebert Stiftung, 2008.
Al-Ṭuruq al-Ṣūfiyya: Durūb Allāh al-Rūḥiyya; Al-Takayyuf wa-l-Tajdīd fī Siyāq al-Taḥdīth. Amman: Friedrich Ebert Stiftung, 2011.
Abu-Odeh, Adnan. *Jordanians, Palestinians & the Hashemite Kingdom in the Middle East Peace Process*. Washington, DC: United States Institute of Peace, 1999.
Abū Rummān, Muḥammad. "Al-Māḍī fī l-Ḥāḍir . . . al-Taṣfiya wa-l-Tarbiya ʿinda l-Albānī." *Rimāḥ al-Ṣaḥāʾif: Al-Salafiyya al-Albāniyya wa-Khuṣūmuhā*. Dubai: Markaz al-Misbār li-l-Dirāsāt wa-l-Buḥūth, 2010), 65–88.

Anā Salafī: Baḥth fī l-Huwiyya al-Wāqiʿiyya wa-l-Mutakhayyala ladá l-Salafiyyīn. Amman: Friedrich Ebert Stiftung, 2014.

Abū Rummān, Muḥammad and Ḥasan Abū Haniyya. *Al-Ḥall al-Islāmī: Al-Islāmiyyūn wa-l-Dawla wa-Rihānāt al-Dīmuqrāṭiyya wa-l-Amn*. Amman: Friedrich Ebert Stiftung, 2012.

Al-Salafiyya al-Jihādiyya fī l-Urdunn baʿda Maqtal al-Zarqāwī: Muqārabat al-Huwiyya, Azmat al-Qiyāda wa-Ḍabābiyyat al-Ruʾya. Amman: Friedrich Ebert Stiftung, 2009.

Al-Salafiyya al-Muḥāfaẓa: Istrātījiyyat "Aslamat al-Mujtamaʿ" wa-Suʾāl al-ʿAlāqa "al-Muntasiba" maʿa l-Dawla. Amman: Friedrich Ebert Stiftung, 2010.

Adraoui, Mohamed-Ali. *Du Golfe aux banlieues: Le salafisme mondialisé*. Paris: Presses Universitaires de France, 2013.

"Être salafiste en France." In *Qu'est-ce que le salafisme?*, edited by Bernard Rougier, 231–41. Paris: Presses Universitaires de France, 2008.

"Salafism in France: Ideology, Practices and Contradictions." In *Global Salafism: Islam's New Religious Movement*, edited by Roel Meijer, 364–83. London: Hurst & Co., 2009.

Ahady, Anwar ul-Haq. "Saudi Arabia, Iran and the Conflict in Afghanistan." In *Fundamentalism Reborn? Afghanistan and the Taliban*, edited by William Malley, 117–34. New York: New York University Press.

Allen, Charles. *God's Terrorists: The Wahhabi Cult and the Hidden Roots of Modern Jihad*. Cambridge, MA: Da Capo Press, 2006.

Alon, Yoav. *The Making of Jordan: Tribes, Colonialism and the Modern State*. London and New York: I.B. Tauris, 2009 [2007].

Alshech, Eli. "The Doctrinal Crisis within the Salafi-Jihadi Ranks and the Emergence of Neo-Takfirism." *Islamic Law and Society* 21, no. 4 (2014): 419–52.

Amawi, Abla M. "The 1993 Elections in Jordan." *Arab Studies Quarterly* 16, no. 3 (1994): 15–27.

Amghar, Samir. *Le salafisme d'aujourd'hui: Mouvements sectaries en Occident*. Paris: Michalon Éditions, 2011.

"Quietisten, Politiker und Revolutionäre: Die Entstehung und Entwicklung des salafistischen Universums in Europa." In *Salafismus: Auf der Suche nach dem wahren Islam*, edited by Behnam T. Said and Hazim Fouad, 381–410. Freiburg: Herder, 2014.

Amīn, Ḥazim al-. *Al-Salafī al-Yatīm: Al-Wajh al-Filasṭīnī li-"l-Jihād al-ʿĀlamī" wa-"l-Qāʿida."* Beirut and London: Dār al-Sāqī, 2011.

Amin, Kamaruddin. "Nasiruddin al-Albani on Muslim's Sahih: A Critical Study of his Method." *Islamic Law and Society* 11, no. 2 (2004): 149–76.

Anderson, Jon W. "The Internet and Islam's New Interpreters." In *New Media in the Muslim World: The Emerging Public Sphere*, edited by Dale F. Eickelman and Jon W. Anderson, 41–56. Bloomington, IN: Indiana University Press, 1999.

Antonius, George. *The Arab Awakening*. New York: Capricorn Books, 1965 [1946].

Arberry, A.J. *The Koran Interpreted*. New York: Touchstone, 1955.

Aruri, Naseer H. *Jordan: A Study in Political Development (1921–1965)*. The Hague: Martinus Nijhoff, 1972.

Ashton, Nigel. *King Hussein of Jordan: A Political Life*. New Haven and London: Yale University Press, 2008.

Atawneh, Muhammad Al. *Wahhābī Islam Facing the Challenges of Modernity: Dār al-Iftā in the Modern Saudi State*. Leiden: Brill, 2010.

Ayoob, Mohammed and Hasan Kosebalaban, ed. *Religion and Politics in Saudi Arabia: Wahhabism and the State*. Boulder, CO: Lynne Rienner Publishers, 2009.

Baehr, Dirk. *Kontinuität und Wandel in der Ideologie des Jihadi-Salafismus*. Bonn: Bouvier Verlag, 2009.

Becker, Carmen. "Following the Salafi Manhaj in Computer-Mediated Environments: Linking Everyday Life to the Qur'ān and the Sunna." In *The Transmission and Dynamics of the Textual Sources of Islam: Essays in Honour of Harald Motzki*, edited by Nicolet Boekhoff-van der Voort, Kees Versteegh and Joas Wagemakers, 421–41. Leiden: Brill, 2011.

"Learning to be Authentic: Religious Practices of German and Dutch Muslims Following the Salafiyya in Forums and Chat Rooms." PhD diss., Radboud University, Nijmegen, 2013.

"Muslims on the Path of the Salaf al-Salih: Ritual Dynamics in Chat Rooms and Discussion Forums." *Information, Communication & Society* 14, no. 8 (2011): 1181–203.

Benford, Robert D. and David A. Snow. "Framing Processes and Social Movements: An Overview and Assessment." *Annual Review of Sociology* 26 (2000): 611–39.

Bizri, Nader el-. "God: Essence and Attributes." In *The Cambridge Companion to Classical Islamic Theology*, edited by Tim Winter, 121–40. Cambridge: Cambridge University Press, 2008.

Blankinship, Khalid. "The Early Creed." In *The Cambridge Companion to Classical Islamic Theology*, edited by Tim Winter, 33–54. Cambridge: Cambridge University Press, 2008.

Bonnefoy, Laurent. "How Transnational is Salafism in Yemen?" In *Global Salafism: Islam's New Religious Movement*, edited by Roel Meijer, 321–41. London: Hurst & Co., 2009.

"L'illusion apolitique: Adaptations, évolutions et instrumentalisations du salafisme Yéménite." In *Qu'est-ce que le salafisme?*, edited by Bernard Rougier, 137–59. Paris: Presses Universitaires de France, 2008.

"Salafism in Yemen: A 'Saudisation'?" In *Kingdom without Borders: Saudi Arabia's Political, Religious and Media Frontiers*, edited by Madawi Al-Rasheed, 245–62. London: Hurst & Co., 2008.

Salafism in Yemen: Transnationalism and Religious Identity. London: Hurst & Co., 2011.

"Violence in Contemporary Yemen: State, Society and Salafis." *The Muslim World* 101 (2011): 324–46.

Bonner, Michael. *Jihad in Islamic History*. Princeton and Oxford: Princeton University Press, 2006.

Bonney, Richard. *Jihād: From Qur'ān to bin Laden*. New York: Palgrave, 2004.

Boukhars, Anouar. "The Challenge of Terrorism and Religious Extremism in Jordan." *Strategic Insights* 5, no. 4 (2006).

Boulby, Marion. *The Muslim Brotherhood and the Kings of Jordan, 1945–1993*. Atlanta, GA: Scholars Press, 1999.

Brachman, Jarret M. *Global Jihad: Theory and Practice*. London and New York: Routledge, 2009.

Brandon, James. "Jordan's Jihad Scholar al-Maqdisi is Freed from Prison." *Terrorism Monitor* 6, no. 7 (2008): 3–6.

Brisard, Jean-Charles (with Damien Martinez). *Zarqawi: The New Face of Al-Qaeda*. New York: Other Press, 2005.

Brooke, Steven. "The Preacher and the Jihadi." In *Current Trends in Islamist Ideology*, vol. III, edited by Hillel Fradkin, Husain Haqqani and Eric Brown, 52–66. Washington, DC: Hudson Institute, 2006.

Brown, Jonathan A.C. "Is Islam Easy to Understand or Not? Salafis, the Democratization of Interpretation and the Need for the Ulema." *Journal of Islamic Studies* 26, no. 2 (2015): 117–44.

The Canonization of al-Bukhārī and Muslim: The Formation and Function of the Sunnī Ḥadīth Canon. Leiden: Brill, 2007.

Burgat, François and Muhammad Sbitli. "Les salafis au Yémen ou ... la modernisation malgré tout." *Chroniques yéménites*, 10 (2002).

Burke, Jason. *Al-Qaeda: The True Story of Radical Islam*. London and New York: I.B. Tauris, 2004 [2003].

Caillet, Romain. *Le proces d'Abū Muḥammad al-Maqdisī et le delit d'opinion dans un état autoritaire*. Les carnets de l'Ifpo: http://ifpo.hypotheses.org/2556, 2011.

"Note sur l'espace public salafi en Jordanie." In *Villes, pratiques urbaines et construction nationale en Jordanie*, edited by Myriam Ababsa and Rami Daher, 307–27. Beirut: Presses de l'ifpo, 2011.

"Trajectoires de salafis français en Égypte." In *Qu'est-ce que le salafisme?*, edited by Bernard Rougier, 257–71. Paris: Presses Universitaires de France, 2008.

Campbell, Heidi. "Who's Got the Power? Religious Authority and the Internet." *Journal of Computer-Mediated Communication* 12, no. 3 (2007): 1043–62.

Caryl, Christian. "The Salafi Moment." In *The New Salafi Politics*, 8–10. Washington, DC: Project on Middle East Political Science, 2012.

Charillon, Frédéric and Alain Mouftard. "Jordanie: Les elections du 8 novembre 1993 et le processus de paix." *Monde Arabe Maghreb Machrek*, no. 144 (1994): 40–54.

Chittick, William C. "Ṣūfī Thought and Practice." In *The Oxford Encyclopedia of the Islamic World*, vol. V, edited by John L. Esposito, 207–16. Oxford: Oxford University Press, 2009.

Clark, Janine A. *Islam, Charity, and Activism: Middle-Class Networks and Social Welfare in Egypt, Jordan, and Yemen*. Bloomington and Indianapolis, IN: Indiana University Press, 2004.

Cleveland, William L. and Martin Bunton. *A History of the Modern Middle East*. Boulder, CO: Westview Press, 2013 [1994].

Commins, David. *Islamic Reform: Politics and Social Change in Late Ottoman Syria*. New York and Oxford: Oxford University Press, 1990.

"Le salafisme en Arabie Saoudite." In *Qu'est-ce que le salafisme?*, edited by Bernard Rougier, 25–44. Paris: Presses Universitaires de France, 2008.

The Wahhabi Mission and Saudi Arabia. London and New York: I.B. Tauris, 2006.

Cook, David. *Understanding Jihad*. Berkeley and Los Angeles: University of California Press, 2005.

Cook, Michael. *Commanding Right and Forbidding Wrong*. Cambridge: Cambridge University Press, 2001.

"On the Origins of Wahhabism." *Journal of the Royal Asiatic Society* 2, no. 2 (1992): 191–202.

Coulson, N.J. *A History of Islamic Law*. Edinburgh: Edinburgh University Press, 1999 [1964].

Dabbas, Hamed. "Islamic Centers, Associations, Societies, Organizations, and Committees in Jordan." In *Islamic Movements in Jordan* (translation George A. Musleh), edited by Jillian Schwedler, 193–259. Amman: Al-Urdun al-Jadid Research Center/Sindbad Publishing House, 1997.

Dalacoura, Katerina. *Islamist Terrorism and Democracy in the Middle East*. Cambridge: Cambridge University Press, 2011.

Dann, Uriel. *King Hussein and the Challenge of Arab Radicalism: Jordan, 1955–1967*. New York and Oxford: Oxford University Press, 1989.

Dantschke, Claudia. "'Da habe ich etwas gesehen, was mir einen Sinn gibt.' – Was macht Salafismus attraktiv und wie kann man diesem entgegenwirken?" In *Salafismus: Auf der Suche nach dem wahren Islam*, edited by Behnam T. Said and Hazim Fouad, 474–502. Freiburg: Herder, 2014.

Daynī, Yūsuf al-. "Rimāḥ al-Ṣaḥā'if: Al-Iḥtirāb 'alá Tamthīl al-Salafiyya bayna l-Albāniyya wa-Khuṣūmihā." In *Rimāḥ al-Ṣaḥā'if: Al-Salafiyya al-Albāniyya wa-Khuṣūmuhā*, 7–36. Dubai: Markaz al-Misbār li-l-Dirāsāt wa-l-Buḥūth, 2010.

Della Porta, Donatella and Mario Diani. *Social Movements: An Introduction*. Malden, MA: Blackwell Publishing, 2006 [1999].

DeLong-Bas, Natana J. *Wahhabi Islam: From Revival and Reform to Global Jihad*. Oxford: Oxford University Press, 2004.

Duderija, Adis. "Neo-Traditional Salafi Qur'an-Sunna Hermeneutics and its Interpretational Implications." *Religion Compass* 5, no. 7 (2011): 314–25.

Dziri, Bacem. "'Das Gebet des Propheten, als ob Du es sehen würdest': Der Salafismus als 'Rechtsschule' des Propheten?" In *Salafismus: Auf der Suche nach dem wahren Islam*, edited by Behnam T. Said and Hazim Fouad, 132–59. Freiburg: Herder, 2014.

Elmaz, Orhan. "Jihadi-Salafist Creed: Abu Muhammad al-Maqdisi's Imperatives of Faith." In *New Approaches to the Analysis of Jihadism: Online and Offline*, edited by Rüdiger Lohlker, 15–36. Göttingen: Vienna University Press, 2012.

Escobar Stemmann, Juan José. "Islamic Activism in Jordan." *Athena Intelligence Journal* 3, no. 3 (2008): 7–18.

Ess, Josef van. *Theologie und Gesellschaft im 2. und 3. Jahrhundert Hidschra, vol. II*. Berlin and New York: Walter de Gruyter, 1992.

Fadel, Mohammed. "The Social Logic of Taqlīd and the Rise of the Mukhtaṣar." *Islamic Law and Society* 3, no. 2 (1996): 193–233.

Fahad, Abdulaziz H. al-. "From Exclusivism to Accommodation: Doctrinal and Legal Evolution of Wahhabism." *New York University Law Review* 79, no. 2 (2004): 485–519.

Fandy, Mamoun. "CyberResistance: Saudi Opposition Between Globalization and Localization." *Comparative Studies in Society and History* 41, no. 1 (1999): 124–47.

"Egypt's Islamic Group: Regional Revenge." *Middle East Journal* 48, no. 4 (1994): 607–25.

Saudi Arabia and the Politics of Dissent. New York: Palgrave, 1999.

Fattah, Hala. "'Wahhabi' Influences, Salafi Responses: Shaikh Mahmud Shukri and the Iraqi Salafi Movement, 1745–1930." *Journal of Islamic Studies* 14, no. 2 (2003): 127–48.

Figueira, Daurius. *Salafi Jihadi Discourse of Sunni Islam in the 21st Century: The Discourse of Abu Muhammad al-Maqdisi and Anwar al-Awlaki.* Bloomington, IN: iUniverse, Inc., 2011.

Filiu, Jean-Pierre. "The Local and Global Jihad of al-Qaʿida in the Islamic Maghrib." *Middle East Journal* 63, no. 2 (2009): 213–26.

Firestone, Reuven. *Jihad: The Origin of Holy War in Islam.* Oxford: Oxford University Press, 1999.

Fouad, Hazim. "Postrevolutionärer Pluralismus: Das salafistische Spektrum in Ägypten." In *Salafismus: Auf der Suche nach dem wahren Islam*, edited by Behnam T. Said and Hazim Fouad, 229–64. Freiburg: Herder, 2014.

Gaborieau, Marc. "The Transformation of Tablīghī Jamāʿat into a Transnational Movement." In *Travellers in Faith: Studies of the Tablīghī Jamāʿat as a Transnational Islamic Movement for Faith Renewal*, edited by Muhammad Khalid Masud, 121–38. Leiden: Brill, 2000.

Gallup. *Poll of the Islamic World: Perceptions of Western Culture.* www.gallup.com/poll/5458/poll-islamic-world-perceptions-western-culture.aspx, 12 March 2002.

Gardet, L. "Īmān." In *Encyclopaedia of Islam New Edition*, vol. III, edited by B. Lewis, V.L. Ménage, Ch. Pellat and J. Schacht, 1170–4. Leiden: Brill, 1986.

Gauvain, Richard. *Salafi Ritual Purity: In the Presence of God.* London and New York: Routledge, 2013.

Gerges, Fawaz A. *The Far Enemy: Why Jihad Went Global.* Cambridge: Cambridge University Press, 2005.

Ghabra, Shafeeq. "Palestinians in Kuwait: The Family and the Politics of Survival." *Journal of Palestine Studies* 17, no. 2 (1988): 62–83.

Gharaibeh, Mohammad. "Zur Glaubenslehre des Salafismus." In *Salafismus: Auf der Suche nach dem wahren Islam*, edited by Behnam T. Said and Hazim Fouad, 106–31. Freiburg: Herder, 2014.

Gharāyiba, Ibrāhīm. *Jamāʿat al-Ikhwān al-Muslimīn fī l-Urdunn, 1946–1996.* Amman: Markaz al-Urdunn al-Jadīd/Dār Sindbād li-l-Nashr, 1997.

Gold, Dore. *Hatred's Kingdom: How Saudi Arabia Supports the New Global Terrorism.* Washington, DC: Regnery Publishing, Inc., 2003.

Goldberg, Marvin E. and Jon Hartwick. "The Effects of Advertiser Reputation and Extremity of Advertising Claim on Advertising Effectiveness." *Journal of Consumer Research* 17 (1990): 172–9.

Görke, Andreas. "Prospects and Limits in the Study of the Historical Muḥammad." In *The Transmission and Dynamics of the Textual Sources of Islam: Essays in Honour of Harald Motzki*, edited by Nicolet Boekhoff-van der Voort, Kees Versteegh and Joas Wagemakers, 137–51. Leiden: Brill, 2011.

Griffel, Frank. "What Do We Mean By 'Salafi'? Connecting Muḥammad ʿAbduh with Egypt's Nūr Party in Islam's Contemporary Intellectual History." *Die Welt des Islams* 55, no. 2 (2015): 186–220.

Gūl, Muḥammad and Zāhid Kāmil. "Al-Khiṭāb al-Siyāsī li-l-Salafiyya al-Albāniyya." In *Rimāḥ al-Ṣaḥāʾif: Al-Salafiyya al-Albāniyya wa-Khuṣūmuhā*, 91–113. Dubai: Markaz al-Misbār li-l-Dirāsāt wa-l-Buḥūth, 2010.

Habib, Randa. *Hussein and Abdullah: Inside the Jordanian Royal Family* (translation Miranda Tell) London: Saqi, 2010.

Haddad, Simon. "Fath al-Islam in Lebanon: Anatomy of a Terrorist Organization." *Studies in Conflict & Terrorism* 33, no. 6 (2010): 548–69.

Hafez, Mohammed M. *Suicide Bombers in Iraq: The Strategy and Ideology of Martyrdom*. Washington, DC: United States Institute of Peace, 2007.

Why Muslims Rebel: Repression and Resistance in the Islamic World. Boulder, CO: Lynne Rienner, 2003.

Hallaq, Wael B. "On the Origins of the Controversy about the Existence of Mujtahids and the Gate of Ijtihād." *Studia Islamica* 63 (1986): 129–41.

Sharīʿa: Theory, Practice, Transformations. Cambridge: Cambridge University Press, 2009.

"Was the Gate of Ijtihad Closed?" *International Journal of Middle East Studies* 16, no. 1 (1984): 3–41.

Hamdeh, Emad. "The Emergence of an Iconoclast: Muḥammad Nāṣir al-Dīn al-Albānī and His Critics." PhD diss., University of Exeter, 2014.

Hamid, Sadek. "The Attraction of 'Authentic' Islam: Salafism and British Muslim Youth." In *Global Salafism: Islam's New Religious Movement*, edited by Roel Meijer, 384–403. London: Hurst & Co., 2009.

Hamid, Shadi *Temptations of Power: Islamists and Illiberal Democracy in a New Middle East*. Oxford: Oxford University Press, 2014.

Hamid, Shadi and Courtney Freer. *How Stable is Jordan? King Abdullah's Half-Hearted Reforms & the Challenge of the Arab Spring*. Doha: Brookings Doha Center, 2011.

Hamidullah, Muhammad. *The Muslim Conduct of State*. Lahore: Sh. Muhammad Ashraf, 1996.

Harmsen, Egbert. *Islam, Civil Society and Social Work: Muslim Voluntary Welfare Associations in Jordan Between Patronage and Empowerment*. Amsterdam: Amsterdam University Press, 2008.

Hasan, Noorhaidi. "Ambivalent Doctrines and Conflicts in the Salafi Movement in Indonesia." In *Global Salafism: Islam's New Religious Movement*, edited by Roel Meijer, 169–88. London: Hurst & Co., 2009.

"Saudi Expansion, the Salafi Campaign and Arabised Islam in Indonesia." In *Kingdom without Borders: Saudi Arabia's Political, Religious and Media*

Frontiers, edited by Madawi Al-Rasheed, 263–81. London: Hurst & Co., 2008.

Laskar Jihad: Islam, Militancy, and the Quest for Identity in Post-New Order Indonesia. Ithaca, NY: Cornell Southeast Asia Program Publications, 2006.

Hass, R. Glen. "Effects of Source Characteristics on Cognitive Responses and Persuasion." In *Cognitive Responses in Persuasion*, edited by Richard E. Petty, Thomas M. Ostrom and Timothy C. Brock, 141–72. Hillsdale, NJ: Lawrence Erlbaum Associates, 1981.

Haykel, Bernard. "Jihadis and the Shiʿa." In *Self-Inflicted Wounds: Debates and Divisions within al-Qaʿida and its Periphery*, edited by Assaf Moghadam and Brian Fishman, 202–23. West Point, NY: Combating Terrorism Center, 2010.

"On the Nature of Salafi Thought and Action." In *Global Salafism: Islam's New Religious Movement*, edited by Roel Meijer, 33–57. London: Hurst & Co., 2009.

Revival and Reform in Islam: The Legacy of Muhammad al-Shawkani. Cambridge: Cambridge University Press, 2003.

"The Salafis in Yemen at a Crossroads: An Obituary of Shaykh Muqbil al-Wadiʿi of Dammaj (d. 1422/2001)." *Jemen Report* 2 (2002): 28–37.

Hegghammer, Thomas. *Jihad in Saudi Arabia: Violence and Pan-Islamism since 1979*. Cambridge: Cambridge University Press, 2010.

"Jihadi-Salafis or Revolutionaries? On Religion and Politics in the Study of Militant Islamism." In *Global Salafism: Islam's New Religious Movement*, edited by Roel Meijer, 244–66. London: Hurst & Co., 2009.

Hellmich, Christina. "Creating the Ideology of Al Qaeda: From Hypocrites to Salafi-Jihadists." *Studies in Conflict & Terrorism* 31 (2008): 111–24.

Heywood, Andrew. *Politics*. New York: Palgrave, 2002 [1997].

Høigilt, Jacob and Frida Nome. "Egyptian Salafism in Revolution." *Journal of Islamic Studies* 25, no. 1 (2014): 33–54.

Holden, David and Richard Johns. *The House of Saud: The Rise and Rule of the Most Powerful Dynasty in the Arab World*. New York: Holt, Rinehart and Winston, 1981.

Hourani, Albert. *Arabic Thought in the Liberal Age, 1798–1939*. Cambridge: Cambridge University Press, 1983 [1962].

Hovland, Carl I. and Walter Weiss. "The Influence of Source Credibility on Communication Effectiveness." *Public Opinion Quarterly* 15 (1951): 635–50.

Hroub, Khaled. "Salafi Formations in Palestine: The Limits of a De-Palestinised Milieu." In *Global Salafism: Islam's New Religious Movement*, edited by Roel Meijer, 221–43. London: Hurst & Co., 2009.

Ḥusayn, Fuʾād. *Al-Zarqāwī: Al-Jīl al-Thānī li-l-Qāʿida*. Beirut: Dār al-Khayyāl, 2005.

Ḥusnī, Aḥmad. "Qirāʾa fī Kitāb Imtāʿ al-Naẓar fī Kashf Shubhāt Murjiʾat al-ʿAṣr." *Al-Misbār*, no. 5 (2007): 167–73.

International Crisis Group (ICG). *Jordan's 9/11: Dealing with Jihadi Islamism*. ICG Middle East Report no. 47. Amman and Brussels, 2005.

International Crisis Group (ICG). *Popular Protest in North Africa and the Middle East (IX): Dallying with Reform in a Divided Jordan*. ICG Middle East/North Africa Report no. 118. Amman/Brussels, 2012.

International Crisis Group (ICG). *Tentative Jihad: Syria's Fundamentalist Opposition*. ICG Middle East Report no. 131. Damascus and Brussels, 2012.

International Institute for Counter-Terrorism. *The Jihadi Forums: An Open Forum with Abu Muhammad al-Maqdisi*. www.ict.org.il/Article.aspx?ID=155, 2010.

Izutsu, Toshihiko. *Ethico-Religious Concepts in the Qur'ān*. Montreal: McGill University Press, 2002.

Jackson, Sherman. "Taqlīd, Legal Scaffolding and the Scope of Legal Injunctions in Post-Formative Theory." *Islamic Law and Society* 3, no. 2 (1996): 165–92.

Jansen, Johannes J.G. *The Neglected Duty: The Creed of Sadat's Assassins and Islamic Resurgence in the Middle East*. New York: MacMillan, 1986.

Johnsen, Gregory D. *The Last Refuge: Yemen, al-Qaeda, and America's War in Arabia*. New York and London: W.W. Norton & Co., 2013.

Jolen, Judith. "The Quest for Legitimacy: The Role of Islam in the State's Political Discourse in Egypt and Jordan (1979–1996)." PhD diss., Catholic University Nijmegen, 2003.

Jordan, Forever on the Brink. Washington, DC: Project on Middle East Political Science, 2012.

Katulis, Brian, Hardin Lang and Mokhtar Awad. *Jordan in the Eye of the Storm: Continued U.S. Support Necessary as Regional Turmoil Continues*. Washington, DC: Center for American Progress, 2014.

Katz, Kimberly. *Jordanian Jerusalem: Holy Place and National Spaces*. Gainesville, FL: University Press of Florida, 2005.

Kazimi, Nibras. "A Virulent Ideology in Mutation: Zarqawi Upstages Maqdisi." In *Current Trends in Islamist Ideology*, vol. II, edited by Hillel Fradkin, Husain Haqqani and Eric Brown, 59–73. Washington, DC: Hudson Institute, 2005.

"Zarqawi's Anti-Shi'a Legacy: Original or Borrowed?" In *Current Trends in Islamist Ideology*, vol. IV, edited by Hillel Fradkin, Hussain Haqqani and Eric Brown, 53–72. Washington, DC: Hudson Institute, 2006.

Kenney, Jeffrey T. *Muslim Rebels: Kharijites and the Politics of Extremism in Egypt*. Oxford: Oxford University Press, 2006.

Kepel, Gilles. *Jihad: The Trail of Political Islam* (translation Anthony F. Roberts). Cambridge, MA, and London: Belknap/Harvard University Press, 2002.

Muslim Extremism in Egypt: The Prophet and the Pharaoh (translation Jon Rothschild). Berkeley and Los Angeles: University of California Press, 2003 [1986].

The War for Muslim Minds: Islam and the West (translation Pascale Ghazaleh). Cambridge, MA, and London: Belknap/Harvard University Press, 2004.

Khadduri, Majid. *The Islamic Law of Nations: Shaybānī's Siyar*. Baltimore: The Johns Hopkins Press, 1966.

War and Peace in the Law of Islam. Baltimore: The Johns Hopkins Press, 1955.

King Abdullah II of Jordan. *Our Last Best Chance: The Pursuit of Peace in a Time of Peril*. New York: Viking, 2011.

Kister, M.J. "'Do not Assimilate Yourselves ... ' Lā Tashabbahū ...." *Jerusalem Studies in Arabic and Islam* 12 (1989): 321–71.

"Notes on an Account of the Shura Appointed by 'Umar b. al-Khattab." *Journal of Semitic Studies* 9 (1964): 320–6.

Koning, Martijn de. "Changing Worldviews and Friendship: An Exploration of the Life Stories of Two Female Salafis in the Netherlands." In *Global Salafism: Islam's New Religious Movement*, edited by Roel Meijer, 404–23. London: Hurst & Co., 2009.

"'Moge Hij onze ogen openen': De radicale utopie van het 'salafisme'." *Tijdschrift voor Religie, Recht en Beleid* 2, no. 2 (2011): 47–61.

Zoeken naar een "zuivere" islam: Geloofsbeleving en identiteitsvorming van jonge Marokkaans-Nederlandse moslims. Amsterdam: Bert Bakker, 2008.

Koning, Martijn de, Joas Wagemakers and Carmen Becker. *Salafisme: Utopische idealen in een weerbarstige praktijk*. Almere: Parthenon, 2014.

Köpfer, Benno. "*Ghuraba'* – das Konzept der Fremden in salafistischen Strömungen: Von Namen eines Terrorcamps zum subkulturellen Lifestyle." In *Salafismus: Auf der Suche nach dem wahren Islam*, edited by Behnam T. Said and Hazim Fouad, 442–73. Freiburg: Herder, 2014.

Köprülü, Nur. "Jordan since the Uprisings: Between Change and Stability." *Middle East Policy* 21, no. 2 (2014): 111–26.

Krämer, Gudrun. "Good Counsel to the King: The Islamist Opposition in Saudi Arabia, Jordan, and Morocco." In *Middle East Monarchies: The Challenge of Modernity*, edited by Joseph Kostiner, 257–87. Boulder, CO: Lynne Rienner Publishers, 2000.

Krämer, Gudrun and Sabine Schmidtke. "Introduction: Religious Authority and Religious Authorities in Muslim Societies. A Critical Overview." In *Speaking for Islam: Religious Authorities in Muslim Societies*, edited by Gudrun Krämer and Sabine Schmidtke, 1–14. Leiden: Brill, 2000.

Lacroix, Stéphane. "Between Revolution and Apoliticism: Nasir al-Din al-Albani and his Impact on the Shaping of Contemporary Salafism." In *Global Salafism: Islam's New Religious Movement*, edited by Roel Meijer, 58–80. London: Hurst & Co., 2009.

"L'apport de Muhammad Nasir al-Din al-Albani au salafisme contemporain." In *Qu'est-ce que le salafisme?*, edited by Bernard Rougier, 45–64. Paris: Presses Universitaires de France, 2008.

Les islamistes saoudiens: Une insurrection manquée. Paris: Presses Universitaires de France, 2010.

Sheikhs and Politicians: Inside the New Egyptian Salafism. Doha: Brookings Institution, 2012.

Lahoud, Nelly with Muhammad al-ʿUbaydi. *Jihadi-Discourse in the Wake of the Arab Spring*. www.ctc.usma.edu/posts/jihadi-discourse-in-the-wake-of-the-Arab-Spring, 2013.

Lahoud, Nelly. "In Search of Philosopher-Jihadis: Abu Muhammad al-Maqdisi's Jihadi Philosophy." *Totalitarian Movements and Political Religions* 10, no. 2 (2009): 205–20.

The Jihadis' Path to Self-Destruction. New York: Columbia University Press, 2010.

Lahoud-Tatar, Carine. *Islam et politique au Koweït*. Paris: Presses Universitaire de France, 2011.

"Koweït: Salafismes et rapports au pouvoir." In *Qu'est-ce que le salafisme?*, edited by Bernard Rougier, 123–35. Paris: Presses Universitaires de France, 2008.

Lajnat al-Buhuth wa-l-Dirasat. "Al-Nafs al-Maʿṣūma ... wa-l-Tatarrus: Aḥwāl ... wa-Aḥkām." *Al-Qibla* 2, nos. 10–11 (2005): 77–89.

Landau-Tasseron, Ella. "The 'Cyclical Reform': A Study of the Mujaddid Tradition." *Studia Islamica* 70 (1989): 79–117.

Lauzière, Henri. "The Construction of Salafiyya: Reconsidering Salafism from the Perspective of Conceptual History." *International Journal of Middle East Studies* 42, no. 3 (2010): 369–89.

Lav, Daniel. *Radical Islam and the Revival of Medieval Theology*. Cambridge: Cambridge University Press, 2012.

Lenfant, Arnaud. "L'évolution du salafisme en Syrië au XXe siècle." In *Qu'est-ce que le salafisme?*, edited by Bernard Rougier, 161–78. Paris: Presses Universitaires de France, 2008.

Lesch, Ann M. "Palestinians in Kuwait." *Journal of Palestine Studies* 20, no. 4 (1991): 42–54.

Loidolt, Bryce. "Managing the Global and Local: The Dual Agendas of Al Qaeda in the Arabian Peninsula." *Studies in Conflict & Terrorism* 34, no. 2 (2011): 102–23.

Lund, Aron. *Syria's Salafi Insurgents: The Rise of the Syrian Islamic Front*. UI Occasional Papers no. 17. www.ui.se/eng/upl/files/86861.pdf, March 2013.

Lynch, Marc. "Islam Divided Between Salafi-jihad and the Ikhwan." *Studies in Conflict & Terrorism* 33, no. 6 (2010): 467–87.

State Interests and Public Spheres: The International Politics of Jordan's Identity. New York: Columbia University Press, 1999.

Madelung, Wilferd. "Early Sunni Doctrine Concerning Faith as Reflected in the Kitāb al-Īmān of Abū ʿUbayd al-Qāsim b. Sallām (d. 224/839)." *Studia Islamica* 32 (1970): 233–54.

Der Imam al-Qasim ibn Ibrahim und die Glaubenslehre der Zaiditen. Berlin: Walter de Gruyter & Co., 1965.

Religious Trends in Early Islamic Iran. New York: State University of New York Press, 1988.

"The Early Murjiʾa in Khurāsān and Transoxania and the Spread of Ḥanafism." *Islam* 59 (1982): 32–9.

Mandaville, Peter. *Global Political Islam*. London and New York: Routledge, 2007.

"Globalization and the Politics of Religious Knowledge: Pluralizing Authority in the Muslim World." *Theory, Culture & Society* 24, no. 2 (2007): 101–15.

Transnational Muslim Politics: Reimagining the Umma. London and New York: Routledge, 2004 [2001].

Masbah, Mohammed. "In Richtung politischer Partizipation: Die Mäβigung der marokkanischen Salafisten seit Beginn des 'Arabische Frühlungs'." In *Salafismus: Auf der Suche nach dem wahren Islam*, edited by Behnam T. Said and Hazim Fouad, 297–319. Freiburg: Herder, 2014.

Masud, Muhammad Khalid. "The Growth and Development of the Tablīghī Jamāʿat in India." In *Travellers in Faith: Studies of the Tablīghī Jamāʿat as a Transnational Islamic Movement for Faith Renewal*, edited by Muhammad Khalid Masud, 3–43. Leiden: Brill, 2000.

Matthee, Rudi. "Egyptian Oppostion on the Iranian Revolution." In *Shi'ism and Social Protest*, edited by Juan R.I. Cole and Nikki R. Keddie, 47–74. New Haven and London: Yale University Press, 1986.

McAdam, Doug. *Political Process and the Development of Black Insurgency, 1930–1970*. Chicago: University of Chicago Press, 1999 [1982].

McCants, Will. "A New Salafi Politics." In *The New Salafi Politics*, 6–8. Washington, DC: Project on Middle East Political Science, 2012.

Mdaires, Falah Abdullah al-. *Islamic Extremism in Kuwait: From the Muslim Brotherhood to al-Qaeda and other Islamist Political Groups*. London and New York: Routledge, 2010.

Meijer, Roel. "Introduction." In *Global Salafism: Islam's New Religious Movement*, edited by Roel Meijer, 1–32. London: Hurst & Co., 2009.

"Politicising *al-Jarḥ wa-l-Taʿdīl*: Rabīʿ b. Hādī al-Madkhalī and the Transnational Battle for Religious Authority." In *The Transmission and Dynamics of the Textual Sources of Islam: Essays in Honour of Harald Motzki*, edited by Nicolet Boekhoff-van der Voort, Kees Versteegh and Joas Wagemakers, 375–99. Leiden: Brill, 2011.

ed. *Global Salafism: Islam's New Religious Movement*. London: Hurst & Co., 2009.

Metcalf, Barbara Daly. *Islamic Revival in British India: Deoband, 1860–1900*. Oxford: Oxford University Press, 2002 [1982].

Milton-Edwards, Beverley. "Climate of Change in Jordan's Islamist Movement." In *Islamic Fundamentalism*, edited by Abdel Salam Sidahmed and Anoushiravan Ehteshami, 123–42. Boulder, CO: Westview Press, 1996.

Milton-Edwards, Beverley and Peter Hinchcliffe. *Jordan: A Hashemite Legacy*. London & New York: Routledge, 2009.

Minzili, Yair. "The Jordanian Regime Fights the War of Ideas." In *Current Trends in Islamist Ideology*, vol. V, edited by Hillel Fradkin, Hussain Haqqani and Eric Brown, 55–69. Washington, DC: Hudson Institute, 2007.

Morabia, Alfred. *Le Gihad dans l'Islam medieval: Le "combat sacré" des origins au XIIe siècle*. Paris: Albin Michel, 1993.

Mouline, Nabile. *Les clercs de l'islam: Autorité religieuse et pouvoir politique en Arabie Saoudite, XVIIIe-XXIe siècle*. Paris: Presses Universitaires de France, 2011.

Napoleoni, Loretta. *Insurgent Iraq: Al Zarqawi and the New Generation*. New York: Seven Stories Press, 2005.

Nedza, Justyna. "'Salafismus': Überlegungen zur Schärfung einer Analysekategorie." In *Salafismus: Auf der Suche nach dem wahren Islam*, edited by Behnam T. Said and Hazim Fouad, 80–105. Freiburg: Herder, 2014.

Nesser, Petter. "Abū Qatāda and Palestine." *Die Welt des Islams* 53, nos. 3–4 (2013): 416–48.

O'Connell, Jack (with Vernon Loeb). *King's Counsel: A Memoir of War, Espionage, and Diplomacy in the Middle East*. New York: W.W. Norton & Co., Inc., 2011.

Olidort, Jacob. *The Politics of "Quietist" Salafism*. Washington, DC: The Brookings Institution, 2015.

Page, Michael, Lara Challita and Alistair Harris. "Al Qaeda in the Arabian Peninsula: Framing Narratives and Prescriptions." *Terrorism and Political Violence* 23, no. 2 (2011): 150–72.

Pall, Zoltan. *Kuwaiti Salafism and Its Growing Influence in the Levant*. Washington, DC: Carnegie Endowment for International Peace, 2014.

Lebanese Salafis between the Gulf and Europe: Development, Fractionalization and Transnational Networks of Salafism in Lebanon. Amsterdam: Amsterdam University Press, 2013.

"Salafism in Lebanon: Local and Transnational Resources." PhD diss., Utrecht University, 2014.

Pampus, K.H. *Über die Rolle der Ḫāriǧīya im frühen Islam*. Wiesbaden: Verlag Otto Harrassowitz, 1980.

Pessagno, J. Meric. "The Murjiʾa, Īmān and Abū ʿUbayd." *Journal of the American Oriental Society* 95, no. 3 (1975): 382–94.

Peters, Rudolph. "Idjtihād and Taqlīd in 18th and 19th Century Islam." *Die Welt des Islams* 20, nos. 3–4 (1980): 131–45.

Jihad in Classical and Modern Islam. Princeton: Markus Wiener Publishers, 1996.

Pierret, Thomas. *Religion and State in Syria: The Sunni Ulama from Coup to Revolution*. Cambridge: Cambridge University Press, 2013.

Podeh, Elie. "The Bayʿa: Modern Political Uses of Islamic Ritual in the Arab World." *Die Welt des Islams* 50, no. 1 (2010): 117–52.

Price, Charles, Donald Nonini and Erich Fox Tree. "Grounded Utopian Movements: Subjects of Neglect." *Anthrological Quarterly* 81, no. 1 (2008): 127–59.

Rabil, Robert G. *Salafism in Lebanon: From Apoliticism to Transnational Jihadism*. Washington, DC: Georgetown University Press, 2014.

Radi, Lamia. "Les Palestiniens du Koweit en Jordanie." *Monde arabe Maghreb Machrek*, 144 (1994): 55–65.

Rasheed, Madawi Al-. *A History of Saudi Arabia*. Cambridge: Cambridge University Press, 2002.

Contesting the Saudi State: Islamic Voices from a New Generation. Cambridge: Cambridge University Press, 2007.

"The Local and the Global in Saudi Salafi Discourse." In *Global Salafism: Islam's New Religious Movement*, edited by Roel Meijer, 301–20. London: Hurst & Co., 2009.

"The Minaret and the Palace: Obedience at Home and Rebellion Abroad." In *Kingdom without Borders: Saudi Arabia's Political, Religious and Media Frontiers*, edited by Madawi Al-Rasheed, 199–219. London: Hurst & Co., 2008.

Redissi, Hamadi. "The Refutation of Wahhabism in Arabic Sources." In *Kingdom without Borders: Saudi Arabia's Political, Religious and Media Frontiers*, edited by Madawi Al-Rasheed, 157–81. London: Hurst & Co., 2008.

Rentz, George S. *The Birth of the Islamic Reform Movement in Saudi Arabia: Muḥammad b. ʿAbd al-Wahhāb (1703/4–1792) and the Beginnings of Unitarian Empire in Arabia*. London: Arabian Publishing Ltd., 2004.

Rimāḥ al-Ṣaḥāʾif: Al-Salafiyya al-Albāniyya wa-Khuṣūmuhā. Dubai: Markaz al-Misbār li-l-Dirāsāt wa-l-Buḥūth, 2010.

Rizvi, Sayyid Muhammad. "Muhibb al-Din al-Khatib: A Portrait of a Salafi-Arabist (1886–1969)." MA thesis, Simon Fraser University, 1991.

Robbins, Michael and Lawrence Rubin. "The Rise of Official Islam in Jordan." *Politics, Religion & Ideology* 14, no. 1 (2013): 59–74.

Robins, Philip. *A History of Jordan*. Cambridge: Cambridge University Press, 2004.

Robinson, Glenn E. "Defensive Democratization in Jordan." *International Journal of Middle East Studies* 30, no. 3 (1998): 387–410.

Roex, Ineke. "Leven als de profeet in Nederland: Over de salafi-beweging en democratie." PhD diss., University of Amsterdam, 2013.

Rogan, Eugene L. "Bringing the State Back: The Limits of Ottoman Rule in Jordan, 1840–1910." In *Village, Steppe and State: The Social Origins of Modern Jordan*, edited by Eugene L. Rogan and Tariq Tell, 32–57. London and New York: British Academic Press, 1994.

Frontiers of the State in the Late Ottoman Empire. Cambridge: Cambridge University Press, 1999.

Rougier, Bernard. "Fatah al-Islam: Un réseau jihadiste au coeur des contradictions libanaises." In *Qu'est-ce que le salafisme?*, edited by Bernard Rougier, 179–210. Paris: Presses Universitaires de France, 2008.

"Introduction." In *Qu'est-ce que le salafisme?*, edited by Bernard Rougier, 1–21. Paris: Presses Universitaires de France, 2008.

"Le jihad en Afghanistan et l'emergence du salafisme-jihadisme." In *Qu'est-ce que le salafisme?*, edited by Bernard Rougier, 65–86. Paris: Presses Universitaires de France, 2008.

ed. *Qu'est-ce que le salafisme?* Paris: Presses Universitaires de France, 2008.

Everyday Jihad: The Rise of Militant Islamism among Palestinians in Lebanon (translation Pascale Ghazaleh). Cambridge, MA, and London: Harvard University Press, 2007 [2004].

Rubin, Barnett. "Arab Islamists in Afghanistan." In *Political Islam: Revolution, Radicalism, or Reform?*, edited by John L. Esposito, 179–206. Boulder, CO, and London: Lynne Rienner, 1997.

Ryad, Umar. *Islamic Reformism and Christianity: A Critical Reading of the Works of Muḥammad Rashīd Riḍā and His Associates (1898–1935)*. Leiden: Brill, 2009.

Ryan, Curtis R. *Jordan in Transition: From Hussein to Abdullah*. Boulder, CO: Lynne Rienner Publishers, 2002.

Saab, Bilal Y. and Magnus Ranstorp. "Securing Lebanon from the Threat of Salafist Jihadism." *Studies in Conflict & Terrorism* 30, no. 10 (2007): 825–55.

Sæther, Sturla Godø. "Humanitarian Salafism: A Contradition in Terms? A Study of the Salafi Organisation 'The Book and the Sunna Society' and Their Efforts in Relief Work in Jordan." MA thesis, University of Oslo, 2013.

Said, Behnam T. "Salafismus und politische Gewalt under deutscher Perspektive." In *Salafismus: Auf der Suche nach dem wahren Islam*, edited by Behnam T. Said and Hazim Fouad, 193–226. Freiburg: Herder, 2014.

Said, Behnam T. and Hazim Fouad, eds. *Salafismus: Auf der Suche nach dem wahren Islam*. Freiburg: Herder, 2014.

Salem, Elie Adib. *Political Theory and Institutions of the Khawarij*. Baltimore: Johns Hopkins University Press, 1956.

Salem, Isam Kamel. *Islam und Völkerrecht: Das Völkerrecht in der islamischen Weltanschauung*. Berlin: EXpress Edition, 1984.

Salibi, Kamal. *The Modern History of Jordan*. London and New York: I.B. Tauris, 2006 [1993].

Salomon, Noah. "The Salafi Critique of Islamism: Doctrine, Difference and the Problem of Islamic Political Action in Contemporary Sudan." In *Global Salafism: Islam's New Religious Movement*, edited by Roel Meijer, 143–68. London: Hurst & Co., 2009.

Sarhan, Saud al-. "The Creeds of Aḥmad Ibn Ḥanbal." In *Books and Bibliophiles: Studies in Honour of Paul Auchterlonie on the Bio-Bibliography of the Muslim World*, edited by Robert Gleave, 29–44. N.p.: Gibb Memorial Trust, 2014.

Schacht, Joseph "An Early Murciʾite Treatise." *Oriens* 17 (1964): 96–117.

An Introduction to Islamic Law. Oxford: Oxford University Press, 1982 [1964].

Schulze, Reinhard. *Islamischer Internationalismus im 20. Jahrhundert: Untersuchungen zur Geschichte der islamischen Weltliga*. Leiden: Brill, 1990.

Schwartz, Stephen. *The Two Faces of Islam: Saudi Fundamentalism and its Role in Terrorism*. New York: Anchor Books, 2003.

Schwedler, Jillian. "A Paradox of Democracy? Islamist Participation in Elections." *Middle East Report*, no. 209 (1998): 25–9.

Faith in Moderation: Islamist Parties in Jordan and Yemen. Cambridge: Cambridge University Press, 2006.

Sedgwick, Mark. "Sufis as 'Good Muslims': Sufism in the Battle against Jihadi Salafism." In *Sufis and Salafis in the Contemporary Age*, edited by Lloyd Ridgeon, 105–17. London: Bloomsbury, 2015.

Shaḥāda, Marwān b. Aḥmad. "Al-Salafiyya al-Albāniyya: Qirāʾa Naqdiyya." In *Rimāḥ al-Ṣaḥāʾif: Al-Salafiyya al-Albāniyya wa-Khuṣūmuhā*, 115–31. Dubai: Markaz al-Misbār li-l-Dirāsāt wa-l-Buḥūth, 2010.

Sharqāwī, Ṭāhir al-. "Abū Muḥammad al-Maqdisī . . . Thunāʾiyyat al-Muqaddas wa-l-ʿUnf." *Al-Misbār*, no. 5 (2007): 131–43.

Shavit, Uriya. "Can Muslims Befriend Non-Muslims? Debating al-walāʾ wa-l-barāʾ (Loyalty and Disavowal) in Theory and Practice." *Islam and Christian-Muslim Relations* 25, no. 1 (2014): 67–88.

"Is Shura a Muslim Form of Democracy? Roots and Systemization of a Polemic." *Middle Eastern Studies* 46 (2010): 349–74.

"The Wasaṭī and Salafī Approaches to the Religious Law of Muslim Minorities." *Islamic Law and Society* 19 (2012): 416–57.

Shehabi, Saeed. "The Role of Religious Ideology in the Expansionist Policies of Saudi Arabia." In *Kingdom without Borders: Saudi Arabia's Political, Religious and Media Frontiers*, edited by Madawi Al-Rasheed, 183–97. London: Hurst & Co., 2008.

Shishani, Murad Batal al-. "Jihad Ideologue Abu Muhammad al-Maqdisi Challenges Jordan's Neo-Zarqawists." *Terrorism Monitor* 7, no. 20 (2009): 3–4.

"Jordan's New Generation of Salafi-Jihadists Take to the Streets to Demand Rule by Shariʿa." *Terrorism Monitor* 9, no. 18 (2011): 7–9.

"The Dangerous Ideas of the Neo-Zarqawist Movement." *CTC Sentinel* 2, no. 9 (2009): 18–20.

"The Neo-Zarqawists: Divisions Emerge between Jordan's Salafist Militants." *Terrorism Focus* 5, no. 39 (2008).

Shlaim, Avi. *Lion of Jordan: The Life of King Hussein in War and Peace*. New York: Albert A. Knopf, 2008.

The Politics of Partition: King Abdullah, the Zionists, and Palestine 1921–1951. Oxford: Oxford University Press, 1998 [1988].

Shryock, Andrew. *Nationalism and the Genealogical Imagination: Oral History and Textual Authority in Tribal Jordan*. Berkeley, Los Angeles and London: University of California Press, 1997.

Sirriyeh, Elizabeth. "Wahhabis, Unbelievers and the Problems of Exclusivism." *BRISMES Bulletin* 16, no. 2 (1989): 123–32.

Sirry, Mun'im. "Jamāl al-Dīn al-Qāsimī and the Salafi Approach to Sufism." *Die Welt des Islams* 51, no. 1 (2011): 75–108.

Snow, David A. and Richard Machalek. "The Sociology of Conversion." *Annual Review of Sociology* 10 (1984): 167–90.

Sowell, Kirk. *Jordanian Salafism and the Jihad in Syria*. www.hudson.org/research/11131-jordanian-salafism-and-the-jihad-in-syria, 2015.

Springer, Devin R., James L. Regens and David N. Edger. *Islamic Radicalism and Global Jihad*. Washington, DC: Georgetown University Press, 2009.

Steinberg, Guido. "Jihadi-Salafism and the Shi'is: Remarks about the Intellectual Roots of anti-Shi'ism." In *Global Salafism: Islam's New Religious Movement*, edited by Roel Meijer, 107–25. London: Hurst & Co., 2009.

Religion und Staat in Saudi-Arabien: Die wahhabitische Gelehrten, 1902–1953. Würzburg: Ergon Verlag, 2002.

"Saudi-Arabien: Der Salafismus in seinem Mutterland." In *Salafismus: Auf der Suche nach dem wahren Islam*, edited by Behnam T. Said and Hazim Fouad, 265–96. Freiburg: Herder, 2014.

"The Wahhabi Ulama and the Saudi State: 1745 to the Present." In *Saudi Arabia in the Balance: Political Economy, Society, Foreign Affairs*, edited by Paul Aarts and Gerd Nonneman, 11–34. London: Hurst & Co., 2005.

Sulaymān, Ḥasan. "Mawqif al-Salafiyya al-Albāniyya min al-Jamā'āt al-Islāmiyya." In *Rimāḥ al-Ṣaḥā'if: Al-Salafiyya al-Albāniyya wa-Khuṣūmuhā*, 133–55. Dubai: Markaz al-Misbār li-l-Dirāsāt wa-l-Buḥūth, 2010.

Susser, Asher. "The Jordanian Monarchy: The Hashemite Success Story." In *Middle East Monarchies: The Challenge of Modernity*, edited by Joseph Kostiner, 87–115. Boulder, CO: Lynne Rienner Publishers, 2000.

Swidler, Ann. "Culture in Action: Symbols and Strategies." *American Sociological Review* 51 (1986): 273–86.

Taji-Farouki, Suha. *Fundamental Quest: Hizb al-Tahrir and the Search for the Islamic Caliphate*. London: Grey Seal Books, 1996.

Tamimi, Aymenn Jawad al-. "The Dawn of the Islamic State of Iraq and ash-Sham." In *Current Trends in Islamist Ideology*, vol. XVI, edited by Hillel Fradkin, Hussain Haqqani, Eric Brown and Hassan Mneimeh, 5–15. Washington, DC: Hudson Institute, 2014.

"The Islamic State of Iraq and al-Sham." *Middle East Review of International Affairs* 17, no. 3 (2013): 19–44.

Tarrow, Sidney. *Power in Movement: Social Movements, Collective Action and Politics*. Cambridge: Cambridge University Press, 2011 [1994].

Teitelbaum, Joshua. "Duelling for Daʿwa: State vs. Society on the Saudi Internet." *Middle East Journal* 56, no. 2 (2002): 222–39.

Holier Than Thou: Saudi Arabia's Islamic Opposition. Washington, DC: Washington Institute for Near East Policy, 2000.

The New Salafi Politics. Washington, DC: Project on Middle East Political Science, 2012.

Thomas, Dominique. "Le role d'Internet dans la diffusion de la doctrine salafiste." In *Qu'est-ce que le salafisme?*, edited by Bernard Rougier, 87–102. Paris: Presses Universitaires de France, 2008.

Timani, Hussam S. *Modern Intellectual Readings of the Kharijites*. New York: Peter Lang Publishing, 2008.

Tobin, Sarah A. "Jordan's Arab Spring: The Middle Class and Anti-Revolution." *Middle East Policy* 19, no. 1 (2012): 96–109.

Traboulsi, Samer. "An Early Refutation of Muḥammad ibn ʿAbd al-Wahhāb's Reformist Views." *Die Welt des Islams* 42, no. 3 (2002): 373–415.

Troquer, Yann le and Rozenn Hommery al-Oudat. "From Kuwait to Jordan: The Palestinians' Third Exodus." *Journal of Palestine Studies* 28, no. 3 (1999): 37–51.

Vassiliev, Alexei. *The History of Saudi Arabia*. London: Saqi Books, 2000 [1998].

Verskin, Alan. *Oppressed in the Land? Fatwās on Muslims Living under Non-Muslim Rule from the Middle Ages to the Present*. Princeton: Markus Wiener Publishers, 2013.

Vloten, G. van. "Irdjā." *Zeitschrift der Deutschen Morgenländischen Gesellschaft* 45, no. 2 (1891): 161–71.

Voll, John O. "Renewal and Reform in Islamic History: *Tajdid* and *Islah*." In *Voices of Resurgent Islam*, edited by John L. Esposito, 32–47. Oxford: Oxford University Press, 1983.

Wagemakers, Joas. "A Purist Jihadi-Salafi: The Ideology of Abu Muhammad al-Maqdisi." *British Journal of Middle Eastern Studies* 36, no. 2 (2009): 281–97.

A Quietist Jihadi: The Ideology and Influence of Abu Muhammad al-Maqdisi. Cambridge: Cambridge University Press, 2012.

"A Terrorist Organization that Never Was: The Jordanian 'Bayʿat al-Imam' Group." *Middle East Journal* 68, no. 1 (2014): 59–75.

"Abu Muhammad al-Maqdisi: A Counter-Terrorism Asset?" *CTC Sentinel* 1, no. 6 (2008): 7–9.

"Al-Qāʿida's Post-Arab Spring Jihad: Confirmation or Re-Evaluation?" In *Violence in Islamic Thought: From European Imperialism to the Present Day*, edited by Mustafa Baig and Robert Gleave. Edinburgh: Edinburgh University Press, forthcoming.

"An Inquiry into Ignorance: A Jihādī-Salafī Debate on *Jahl* as an Obstacle to *Takfīr*." In *The Transmission and Dynamics of the Textual Sources of Islam:*

Essays in Honour of Harald Motzki, edited by Nicolet Boekhoff-van der Voort, Kees Versteegh and Joas Wagemakers, 301–27. Leiden: Brill, 2011.

"Between Purity and Pragmatism? Abu Basir al-Tartusi's Nuanced Radicalism." In *Jihadi Thought and Ideology*, edited by Rüdiger Lohlker and Tamara Abu-Hamdeh, 16–37. Berlin: Logos Verlag, 2013.

"Contesting Religious Authority in Jordanian Salafi Networks." In *Perseverance of Terrorism: Focus on Leaders*, edited by Marko Milosevic and Kacper Rekawek, 111–25. Amsterdam: IOS Press, 2014.

"De 'godfather' van de jihad: Abu Mohammed al-Maqdisi." *ZemZem: Tijdschrift over het Midden-Oosten, Noord-Afrika en islam* 3, no. 3 (2007): 79–85.

"Defining the Enemy: Abū Muḥammad al-Maqdisī's Radical Reading of Sūrat al-Mumtaḥana." *Die Welt des Islams* 48, nos. 3–4 (2008): 348–71.

"Framing the 'Threat to Islam': Al-Wala' wa-l-Bara' in Salafi Discourse." *Arab Studies Quarterly* 30, no. 4 (2008): 1–22.

"In Search of 'Lions and Hawks': Abū Muḥammad al-Maqdisī's Palestinian Identity." *Die Welt des Islams* 53, nos. 3–4 (2013): 388–415.

"Invoking Zarqawi: Abu Muhammad al-Maqdisi's Jihad Deficit." *CTC Sentinel* 2, no. 6 (2009): 14–7.

"Jihadi-Salafism in Jordan and the Syrian Conflict." In *Religious Extremism in Insurgency & Counterinsurgency in Syria: A New Launching Pad for Global Terrorism*, edited by Nico Prucha. London and New York: Routledge, forthcoming.

Maqdisi in the Middle: An Inside Account of the Secret Negotiations to Free a Jordanian Pilot. www.jihadica.com/maqdisi-in-the-middle-an-inside-account-of-the-secret-negotiations-to-free-a-jordanian-pilot/, 11 February 2015.

"Protecting Jihad: The Sharia Council of the Minbar al-Tawhid wa-l-Jihad." *Middle East Policy* 18, no. 2 (2011): 148–62.

"Reclaiming Scholarly Authority: Abu Muhammad al-Maqdisi's Critique of Jihadi Practices." *Studies in Conflict & Terrorism* 34, no. 7 (2011): 523–39.

"Revisiting Wiktorowicz: Categorising and Defining the Branches of Salafism." In *Salafism After the Arab Awakening: Contending with People's Power*, edited by Francesco Cavatorta and Fabio Merone. London: Hurst & Co., 2016.

"Salafistische Strömungen und ihre Sicht auf *al-wala' wa-l-bara'* (Loyalität und Lossagung)." In *Salafismus: Auf der Suche nach dem wahren Islam*, edited by Behnam T. Said and Hazim Fouad, 55–79. Freiburg: Herder, 2014.

"'Seceders' and 'Postponers'? An Analysis of the 'Khawarij' and 'Murji'a' Labels in Polemical Debates between Quietist and Jihadi-Salafis." In *Contextualising Jihadi Thought*, edited by Jeevan Deol and Zaheer Kazmi, 145–64. London: Hurst & Co., 2012.

"Soennitische islamisten en de erfenis van de Islamitische Revolutie." *ZemZem: Tijdschrift over het Midden-Oosten, Noord-Afrika en islam* 4, no. 4 (2008): 55–59.

"The Dual Effect of the Arab Spring on Salafi Integration: Political Salafism in Jordan." In *Salafism after the Arab Awakening: Contending with People's Power*,

edited by Francesco Cavatorta and Fabio Merone. London: Hurst & Co., 2016.
"The Enduring Legacy of the Second Saudi State: Quietist and Radical Wahhabi Contestations of al-Walāʾ wa-l-Barāʾ." *International Journal of Middle East Studies* 44, no. 1 (2012): 93–110.
"The Transformation of a Radical Concept: *Al-Walaʾ wa-l-Baraʾ* in the Ideology of Abu Muhammad al-Maqdisi." In *Global Salafism: Islam's New Religious Movement*, edited by Roel Meijer, 81–106. London: Hurst & Co., 2009.
The Verdict of Abu Qatada al-Filastini. www.jihadica.com/the-verdict-of-abu-qatada-al-filastini/, 26 June 2014.
"What Should an Islamic State Look Like? Jihādī-Salafī Debates on the War in Syria." *The Muslim World* (forthcoming).
Wahid, Din. "Nurturing the Salafi *Manhaj*: A Study of Salafi *Pesantren*s in Contemporary Indonesia." PhD diss., Utrecht University, 2014.
Watt, William Montgomery. *Islamic Philosophy and Theology*. Edinburgh: Edinburgh University Press, 1962.
The Formative Period of Islamic Thought. Oxford: One World, 1998 [1973].
Weismann, Itzchak. "Between Ṣūfī Reformism and Modernist Rationalism: A Reappraisal of the Origins of the Salafiyya from the Damascene Angle." *Die Welt des Islams* 41, no. 2 (2001): 206–37.
"Genealogies of Fundamentalism: Salafi Discourse in Nineteenth-Century Baghdad." *British Journal of Middle Eastern Studies* 36, no. 2 (2009): 267–80.
Taste of Modernity: Sufism, Salafiyya, and Arabism in Late Ottoman Damascus. Leiden: Brill, 2001.
Wensinck, A.J. *The Muslim Creed: Its Genesis and Historical Development*. London: Frank Cass & Co. Ltd., 1965.
White, Jeffrey, Andrew J. Stabler and Aaron Y. Zelin. *Syria's Military Opposition: How Effective, United or Extremist?* WINEP Policy Focus 128. www.washingtoninstitute.org/policy-analysis/view/syrias-military-opposition-how-effective-united-or-extremist, September 2013.
Wiedl, Nina. "Geschichte des Salafismus in Deutschland." In *Salafismus: Auf der Suche nach dem wahren Islam*, edited by Behnam T. Said and Hazim Fouad, 411–41. Freiburg: Herder, 2014.
Wiktorowicz, Quintan. "Anatomy of the Salafi Movement." *Studies in Conflict & Terrorism* 29, no. 3 (2006): 207–39.
"Civil Society as Social Control: State Power in Jordan." *Comparative Politics* 33, no. 1 (October 2000): 43–61.
Radical Islam Rising: Muslim Extremism in the West. Lanham, MD: Rowman & Littlefield Publishers, Inc., 2005.
The Management of Islamic Activism: Salafis, the Muslim Brotherhood, and State Power in Jordan. Albany, NY: State University of New York Press, 2001.
"The Salafi Movement in Jordan." *International Journal of Middle East Studies* 32, no. 2 (2000): 219–40.
"The Salafi Movement: Violence and Fragmentation of a Community." In *Muslim Networks from Hajj to Hiphop*, edited by Miriam Cooke and

Bruce B. Lawrence, 208–34. Chapel Hill and London: University of North Carolina Press, 2005.

ed. *Islamic Activism: A Social Movement Theory Approach*. Bloomington and Indianapolis, IN: Indiana University Press, 2005.

Wiktorowicz, Quintan and Suha Taji-Farouki. "Islamic NGOs and Muslim Politics: A Case from Jordan." *Third World Quarterly* 21, no. 4 (2000): 685–99.

Wilson, Mary C. *King Abdullah, Britain and the Making of Jordan*. Cambridge: Cambridge University Press, 1987.

Wood, Simon A. *Christian Cricitisms, Islamic Proofs: Rashīd Riḍā's Modernist Defense of Islam*. Oxford: Oneworld, 2008.

Yilmaz, Samet. "Der Salafismus in der Türkei." In *Salafismus: Auf der Suche nach dem wahren Islam*, edited by Behnam T. Said and Hazim Fouad, 350–78. Freiburg: Herder, 2014.

Yom, Sean L. "Tribal Politics in Contemporary Jordan: The Case of the Hirak Movement." *Middle East Journal* 68, no. 2 (2014): 229–47.

Zaman, Muhammad Qasim. *The Ulama in Contemporary Islam: Custodians of Change*. Princeton and Oxford: Princeton University Press, 2002.

Zelin, Aaron Y. *The War between ISIS and al-Qaeda for Supremacy of the Global Jihadist Movement*. WINEP Research Notes no. 20. www.washingtoninstitute.org/policy-analysis/view/the-war-between-isis-and-al-qaeda-for-supremacy-of-the-global-jihadist, June 2014.

Index

ʿAbbadi, Ziyad al-, 161
ʿAbd al-Nasir, Gamal, 5, 37, 38, 111
ʿAbdallah. *See* King ʿAbdallah
ʿAbdallah II. *See* King ʿAbdallah II
ʿAbduh, Muhammad, 35
abode of Islam. *See dār al-Islām*
Abu Ghudda, ʿAbd al-Fattah, 102, 103
Abu Hanifa al-Nuʿman b. Thabit, 46
Abu Haniyya, Hasan, 6, 18, 151, 157, 205, 209
Abu Jaʿfar Ahmad b. Muhammad al-Tahawi. *See* Tahawi, Abu Jaʿfar Ahmad b. Muhammad al-
Abu Layla l-Athari, Muhammad Ahmad, 115
Abu l-Harith, ʿAbd al-Fattah ʿUmar, 206
Abu l-Hasan al-Ashʿari. *See* Ashʿari, Abu l-Hasan al-
Abu Muhammad al-Maqdisi. *See* Maqdisi, Abu Muhammad al-
Abu Qatada al-Filastini. *See* Filastini, Abu Qatada al-
Abu Qura, ʿAbd al-Latif, 10
Abu Ruhayyim, Muhammad, 76, 80, 81, 124–37, 143, 162, 192, 194, 205, 229, 231, 233
Abu Rumman, Muhammad, 6, 18, 142, 143, 151, 157, 207, 209
Abu Sayyaf. *See* Shalabi, Muhammad al-
Abu ʿUmar, ʿUmar b. Mahmud. *See* Filastini, Abu Qatada al-
acts with the limbs. *See īmān, aʿmāl bi-l-jawāriḥ, al-*
advice. *See naṣīḥa* (pl. *naṣāʾiḥ*)
Advisory Council for Fatwas, 147
Afghani, Jamal al-Din al-, 35
Afghanistan, 58, 180
  Afghan Arabs fighting in, 58, 180, 181, 183, 185
  American invasion of (2001), 144
ahl al-ḥadīth, 30, 31, 33, 237, *See also ahl al-raʾy*
ahl al-raʾy, 30, 31, 237, 240, *See also ahl al-ḥadīth*
ahl al-Sunna wa-l-jamāʿa, 29, 237, 238, 242, *See also* Islam, Sunni Islam
ahl-e ḥadīth, 33, 34
Al al-Shaykh ʿAbd al-ʿAziz b. ʿAbdallah, 112
Al al-Shaykh, Muhammad b. Ibrahim, 52, 104, 130, 182
Al Nasr, Muhammad b. Musa, 61, 67, 68, 79, 107, 115, 116, 118, 137, 139, 140, 152, 155, 161, 190
Al Zaydan, ʿUmar Mahdi, 186, 187
Albani, Muhammad Nasir al-Din al-, 2, 17, 18, 43, 52, 55, 61, 64, 65, 72, 87, 99, 109, 110, 111, 114, 115, 116, 119, 120, 121, 124, 126, 127, 128, 131, 132, 133, 134, 135, 136, 137, 138, 139, 150, 161, 165, 168, 169, 171, 190, 202, 213, 224, 231
  banned from Jordan, 108
  childhood of, 100–1, 230
  criticism of, 103–4
  death of, 24, 59, 95, 117, 118–19, 127, 132, 134, 138, 143, 157, 163, 164, 192, 196, 230, 231, 235
  in Jordan, 95, 105–9, 132, 184, 230
  in Saudi Arabia, 17, 104–5
  in Syria, 100–4, 105, 138, 184
  independent attitude of, 24, 54, 70–1, 74, 107, 137, 139, 143, 158, 202, 220, 229, 230, 234
  influence on Salafism in Jordan, 23, 55, 95, 96, 100–9, 229, 230, 236
  on *fiqh al-wāqiʿ*, 84
  on *ḥadīth* criticism, 17, 118
  on *īmān* and *kufr*, 75–8, 79, 80, 81, 189, 190, 191, 192–5, 196, 229, 230, 231, 233
  on politics, 83–4, 88, 89, 91, 204, 220, 224
  on *takfīr*, 75–8

Albani (cont.)
on *taṣfiya wa-l-tarbiya, al-*, 82–4
on *walāʾ wa-l-barāʾ, al-*, 68
on *tark al-ṣalāt*, 80
onties with Muslim Brotherhood in Jordan, 106, 219
onties with Muslim Brotherhood in Syria, 102–3
Albani, Nuh Najati l-, 100, 101
Albania, 100, 102, 230
Shkodër, 100
Algeria, 38, 88, 217
ʿAli b. Abi Talib, 72, 196
Alon, Yoav, 3
Alusi, Mahmud Shukri al-, 35
America. *See* United States of America
Amman Interfaith Message, 148, 151
Amman Message, 148
amr bi-l-maʿrūf wa-l-nahy ʿan al-munkar, al-, 62, 203, 223
Ansar al-Sunna al-Muhammadiyya, 55
anthropomorphism, 41
apostasy. *See ridda*
apostate. *See murtadd* (pl. *murtaddūn*)
ʿaqīda, 34, 39–50, 51, 60, 66, 67, 71, 82, 91, 97, 111, 118, 125, 131, 153, 155, 170, 194, 208, 228, 237, 240
ʿaql, 35, 41, 42, 51
Aqsa Mosque, Al-, 4, 213
Arab nationalism, 4, 10
Arab Revolt (1916), 4
Arab Spring, 18, 24, 57, 146, 166, 186, 188, 200, 201, 202, 217–19, 220, 221, 222–6, 234
Arabian Peninsula, 3, 33, *See also* Saudi Arabia
Arab-Israeli conflict, 5–6, 10, 18, 53, 69, 155, 212, 213, *See also* Israel; Palestinians
Black September, 5, 11
intifada (1987), 180
Oslo Accords (1993), 6, 181
peace negotiations, 6, 181
Wadi ʿAraba Agreement (1994), 6, 144, 147, 181
war in 1948, 5
war in 1967, 5, 37, 38, 228
war in 1973, 106
Zionism, 4, 10
Arnaʾut, ʿAbd al-Qadir al-, 102
Asad, Bashar al-, 16, 217, 222
Asala, Al-, 22, 62, 81, 115, 118, 134, 135, 137, 138, 152, 153
ʿAsʿas, Ibrahim al-, 65, 66, 205, 211, 212
Ashʿari, Abu l-Hasan al-, 47, 48
Ashʿariyya, 41, 42, 47, 102, 151, *See also kalām*; Maturidiyya; theology
asking non-Muslims for help. *See walāʾ wa-l-barāʾ, al-, istiʿāna bi-l-kuffār, al-*
Atatürk, Mustafa Kemal, 100
ʿAttar, ʿIsam al-, 102
ʿAwayisha, Husayn al-, 79, 107, 116, 118, 137, 139, 161, 190, 223, 224
ʿAwda, Salman al-, 55, 109, 110, 111
Azhar University, Al-, 98, 99, 132, 158, 230

Bahrain, 142
Banna, Hasan al-, 10, 106, 112
barāʾ. *See walāʾ wa-l-barāʾ, al-*
Barqawi, ʿIsam al-. *See* Maqdisi, Abu Muhammad al-
Barqawi, Yusuf al-, 99, 100
Batiri, Waʾil al-, 122, 123, 205, 208
bayʿa, 87, 91, 215, 216, 222, 237
Bayʿat al-Imam, 183
Bayram, Abu ʿAbd al-Rahman Nur al-Din, 186
belief in the heart. *See īmān, iʿtiqād bi-l-qalb, al-*
Ben Ali, Zine El Abidine. *See* Ibn ʿAli, Zayn al-ʿAbidin
bidʿa (pl. *bidaʿ*), 43, 51, 66, 67, 89, 91, 99, 101, 105, 163, 228, 229, 237, 241, 242
Bin Laden, Osama, 2, 58
Bitar, Muhammad Bahjat al-, 101
blind emulation. *See taqlīd*
Bosnia, 64, 86
Bu l-Nit, Muhammad, 192, 193
Buʿazizi, Muhammad al-, 201
Bunton, Martin, 1
Bush, George W., 144
Buti, Muhammad Saʿid Ramadan al-, 65, 103
Butush, ʿUmar al-, 161

call to Islam. *See daʿwa*
Canada, 169
chaos. *See fitna* (pl. *fitan*)
Christianity, 3, 39, 50, 71, 86, 96, 148, 158, 173, 174
Bible, 71
Greek Orthodoxy, 3
Roman Catholicism, 158
Vatican, 158
Christians. *See* Christianity
cleansing and teaching. *See taṣfiya wa-l-tarbiya, al-*
Cleveland, William L., 1
Cold War, 58
colonialism, 4

commanding right and forbidding wrong. *See amr bi-l-ma'rūf wa-l-nahy 'an al-munkar, al-*
Common Word, A, 148
compulsion. *See ikrāh*
compulsory of the religion. *See īmān, wājib al-dīn*
confession of faith. *See shahāda*
consensus. *See ijmā'*
considered opinion. *See ra'y*
conspiracies, 68–9, 72, 73, 167, 211
consultation. *See shūrá*
conviction. *See i'tiqād*
creed. *See 'aqīda*
Crusaders, 69

Dar al-Athariyya, Al-, 168, 235
dār al-Islām, 53, 57
Dar al-'Uthmaniyya, Al-, 235
da'wa, 52, 53, 63, 82, 84, 85, 86, 90, 100, 105, 107, 120, 133, 135, 138, 139, 140, 153, 154, 155, 157, 169, 174, 182, 183, 203, 206, 207, 208, 214, 221, 224, 225, 228, 229, 234
Dawsari, Muhammad b. Salim al-, 130, 131
Dawud, Hayil 'Abd al-Hafiz, 150
democracy, 88, 89, 90, 156, 181, 182, 203, 216, 217, 229, 241, *See also* elections; *shūrá*
demonstrations, 55, 56, 85, 201, 218, 223, 224, 225, 234, 238
Dhunaybat, 'Abd al-Majid al-, 90, 91
Dhuwayb, Ahmad al-, 215, 216, 217, 218
disavowal. *See barā'*
disobedience. *See ma'ṣiya*
Dubai, 18

education. *See taṣfiya wa-l-tarbiya, al-*
Egypt, 1, 37, 38, 39, 95, 98, 106, 109, 111, 186, 201, 203, 218, 222, 224, 225, 226, 230, 234
  Cairo, 38, 98, 158, 225
elections, 11, 52, 55, 88, 147, 156, 181, 182, 204, 216, 229, *See also* democracy; *shūrá*
emigration. *See hijra*
exchange. *See tabdīl*
excommunication. *See takfīr*
excommunicator. *See takfīrī*

Facebook, 169
Fairouz, 1
faith. *See īmān*
Fandy, Mamoun, 37
fāsiq, 49, *See also kabīra* (pl. *kabā'ir*); *kāfir* (pl. *kuffār*); *kufr*; *ma'ṣiya*; *murtadd* (pl. *murtaddūn*); *ridda*; *shirk*; *takfīr*; *takfīrī*
fatwas, 7, 21, 22, 54, 70, 104, 112, 114, 124, 126, 128, 129, 130, 131, 135, 138, 148, 149, 163, 175, 189, 190, 218, 231
Fawzan, Salih b. Fawzan al-, 51, 52, 182
Fi Zilal al-Qur'an, 111
Filastini, Abu Qatada al-, 2, 16, 185, 186, 187, 188, 191, 192, 193, 195, 198
fiqh, 34, 74, 83, 101, 104, 118, 208
  fiqh al-wāqi', 84, 85, 229, 238
firqa al-nājiya, al-, 40, 42, 66, 228, 237, 238, 242, *See also ṭā'ifa al-manṣūra, al-*
First World War, 4
fitna (pl. *fitan*), 74, 87, 119, 143, 165, 198, 223, 224, 238, 241
Fitnat al-Takfir, 127, 128
Foley, Lawrence, 145, 146
following the sources. *See ittibā'*
Fox Tree, Erich, 28
Front Islamique du Salut (FIS), 88, 217

Gauvain, Richard, 19
gender-mixing. *See ikhtilāṭ*
Gerges, Fawaz, 57
Gharaibeh, Mohammed, 41
Ghost Dance movement, 28
ghurabā' (sing. *gharīb*), 42, 43, 228
Goldstein, Baruch, 183
Great Britain, 4, 145, 184, 185
  London, 58, 185
Greater Syria. *See* Sham, Al-
grounded utopian movements, 28
Guatemala, 28
Gulf War, 55, 56, 69, 70, 109, 111, 113, 140, 179, 180, 181, 230, 232

Hadi, 'Isam, 70, 84, 121
*ḥadīth*s, 2, 17, 19, 28, 29, 30, 31, 32, 36, 39, 40, 42, 43, 61, 64, 65, 67, 70, 74, 83, 101, 102, 103, 104, 107, 118, 159, 168, 171, 172, 173, 191, 210, 230, 237, 238, 241, 242, *See also* Prophet Muhammad; Sunna
Haj Hasan Mosque, 23
ḥajj, 96, 171
Halabi, 'Ali al-, 76, 77, 79, 80, 81, 84, 85, 86, 96, 97, 107, 110, 111, 112, 115, 116, 118, 119–37, 138, 139, 142, 143, 150, 151, 153, 154, 155, 156, 161, 162, 163, 164, 165, 169, 189, 190, 192–5, 196, 197, 202, 208, 223, 224, 225, 229, 231, 232, 233

Halima, Mustafa. *See* Tartusi, Abu Basir al-
Hamdeh, Emad, 70
Hamid, Shadi, 20
Hammad, ʿAtiyya, 161
Hammad, Zayid, 206, 208, 210, 217
Haqiqat al-Khilaf bayna l-Salafiyya al-Sharʿiyya wa-Adʿiyaʾiha fi Masaʾil al-Iman, 124
Hashimite dynasty, 4, 6, 7, 10, 150, 156
Hawali, Safar al-, 55, 75, 109, 110, 111, 112, 188
Hawwa, Saʿid, 102
Haykel, Bernard, 35, 164
helping non-Muslims. *See walāʾ wa-l-barāʾ, al-*, *iʿānat al-kuffār*
hijra, 45, 70
Hilali, Salim al-, 79, 118, 119, 122, 123, 137, 139–43, 162, 190, 205, 231
Hisn al-Muslim, 172
History of the Modern Middle East, A, 1
Hizb al-Nur, 218, 224, 225
Hizb al-Tahrir al-Islami, 9, 10, 18, 90, 217
ḥizbiyya, 53, 89, 91, 103, 238
Hizbullah, 72
Hunayti, Saʿd al-, 186, 187
Husayn. *See* King Husayn
Husayn b. ʿAli, 4, 97, 156
Husayn, Saddam, 71, 144
Husayni Mosque in Amman, Al-, 98

ʿibāda, 51, 155, 228
Ibn ʿAbbas, ʿAbdallah, 78, 80, 134, 240
Ibn ʿAbd al-Khaliq, Abu ʿAbdallah ʿAbd al-Rahman, 56, 109, 113, 120, 121, 122, 123, 202, 203, 206, 224
Ibn ʿAbd al-Wahhab, Muhammad, 33, 64, 98
Ibn ʿAli, Zayn al-ʿAbidin, 201
Ibn al-ʿUthaymin. *See* ʿUthaymin, Muhammad b. Salih al-
Ibn al-Wazir, Muhammad b. Ibrahim, 32
Ibn ʿAtiq, Hamd, 34
Ibn ʿAtiq, Saʿd, 34
Ibn Baz, ʿAbd al-ʿAziz, 52, 54, 70, 80, 99, 104, 175
Ibn Hajar al-ʿAsqalani, 124
Ibn Hanbal, Ahmad, 29, 31, 32, 91
Ibn Hasan, Mashhur, 79, 106, 107, 115, 118, 119, 122, 123, 137, 139, 142, 154, 155, 161, 164, 173, 190
Ibn Qayyim al-Jawziyya, Shams al-Din, 32, 77
Ibn Saʿud, Muhammad, 33
Ibn Taymiyya, Taqi al-Din Ahmad, 32, 33, 44, 118, 130, 153
ideology, 19, 20, 21, 27, 42, 55, 58, 59, 60–91, 95, 109, 110, 111, 112, 113, 116, 119, 126, 127, 134, 144, 147, 148, 157, 166, 170, 179, 180, 181, 182, 183, 192, 194, 195, 196, 199, 200, 202, 207–19, 228, 229, 230, 231, 232, 233, 234, 235, 236
ignorance. *See jahl*
Ihkam al-Taqrir li-Ahkam Masʾalat al-Takfir, 123
ijmāʿ, 30
ijtihād, 32, 34, 104, 124, 238, 240, 242, *See also ittibāʿ*; *taqlīd*
ikhtilāṭ, 73, 223
ikrāh. *See kufr*, excuses for
ʿilm, 62, 105, 107, 115, 131, 133, 139, 159–60, 162, 163, 165, 166, 183, 196, 209, 214, 215, 218, 223, 232
Ilyas, Mawlana Muhammad, 8
Imam al-Albani Centre, 23, 119, 137, 144, 150, 152, 162, 163, 168, 169, 174, 175, 220, 231, 235
īmān, 23, 46–50, 51, 60, 74–81, 123, 124, 125, 126, 127, 128, 129, 131, 132, 134, 135, 155, 170, 181, 188–91, 192, 193, 194, 196, 197, 210, 228, 229, 230, 231, 233, 238, 239, 240, 241, 242, *See also kufr*
  aʿmāl bi-l-jawāriḥ, al-, 46, 47, 48, 50, 75, 76, 77, 79, 80, 123, 124, 134, 136, 189, 191, 210, 228, 229, 238
  increase and decrease of, 48, 75, 76, 79, 124, 189, 229
  iʿtiqād bi-l-qalb, al-, 46, 47, 48, 75, 76, 77, 79, 80, 124, 129, 210, 228, 229, 238
  kamāl al-dīn, 49, 76, 79, 124, 136, 241, *See also īmān*, *ṣiḥḥat al-dīn*; *wājib al-dīn*
  qawl bi-l-lisān, al-, 46, 47, 48, 75, 76, 77, 79, 80, 210, 228, 229, 238
  ṣiḥḥat al-dīn, 48, 49, 76, 191, 239, 241, *See also īmān*, *kamāl al-dīn*; *wājib al-dīn*
  wājib al-dīn, 48, 49, 76, 79, 239, 241, 243, *See also īmān*, *kamāl al-dīn*; *ṣiḥḥat al-dīn*
Imtaʿ al-Nazar fi Kashf Shubhat Murjiʾat al-ʿAsr, 189
inclusion-moderation thesis, 20, 21, 236
independent reasoning. *See ijtihād*
India, 8, 9, 33, 34
Indian subcontinent, 32, 33
Indonesia, 141
innovation. *See bidʿa* (pl. *bidaʿ*)
interest. *See maṣlaḥa* (pl. *maṣāliḥ*)

International Monetary Fund (IMF), 181
Iran, 7, 38, 72, 108, 156, 180
Islamic Revolution in (1979), 38, 108, 147
Teheran, 38
Iraq, 1, 15, 35, 55, 56, 71, 108, 113, 146, 151, 180, 181, 183, 184, 188, 230, 233
American invasion of (2003), 18, 70, 144, 145
Baghdad, 72
irjāʾ, 47, 134, 190, 191, 193, 195, 238, 239, 240, *See also* Murjiʾa
iṣlāḥ, 56, 101, 113, 203, 212, 213, 214, 217, 218, 221, 224
Islam
ʿAlawites, 222, 223
Ibadi Islam, 151
Shiʿa Islam, 38, 72, 108–9, 146, 148, 151, 156, 166, 167
Sufism, 8, 72, 96, 97, 98, 99, 101, 102, 103, 105, 151, 155, 156, 167, 170, 225
Sunni Islam, 3, 7, 11, 27, 29, 30, 31, 36, 37, 39, 41, 42, 43, 65, 66, 72, 87, 96, 108, 148, 151, 156, 158, 159, 166, 167, 171, 210, 222, 227, 230, 237, 240, 274, *See also ahl al-Sunna wa-l-jamāʿa*
Islamic Action Front (IAF), 11
Islamic jurisprudence. *See fiqh*
Islamic law. *See sharīʿa*
Islamic Liberation Party. *See* Hizb al-Tahrir al-Islami
Islamic State (IS), 2, 9, 59, 146, 149, 150, 152, 153, 170, 179, 187, 188, 199, 200, 233
Islamic State of Iraq and al-Sham (ISIS). *See* Islamic State (IS)
Islamic University of Medina, 99, 104, 110, 158
Islamism, 2, 6, 16, 18, 20, 51, 58, 88, 91, 105, 122, 145, 146, 147, 148, 150, 151, 154, 155, 156, 157, 158, 159, 181, 185, 205, 207, 217, 218, 219, 220, 229, 232, 234, 241
Israel, 4, 5, 37, 38, 70, 86, 106, 144, 145, 180, 181, 183, 213, *See also* Arab-Israeli conflict; Palestinians
istiḥlāl, 49, 50, 78, 79, 81, 124, 189, 191, 239, 240, *See also iʿtiqād; jaḥd*
iʿtiqād, 49, 50, 78, 81, 124, 189, 239, 240, *See also istiḥlāl; jaḥd*
ittibāʿ, 32
iẓhār al-dīn, 44, 45, *See also walāʾ wa-l-barāʾ, al-*
jaḥd, 49, 50, 78, 81, 124, 189, 239, 240, *See also istiḥlāl; iʿtiqād*
jahl. *See kufr*, excuses for
jamāʿa, 39, 62, 84, 237
Jamaʿat al-Islah wa-l-Tahaddi, 145
Jamaʿat al-Muwahhidin, 183
Jamaʿat al-Tawhid, 183
Jamaʿat al-Tawhid wa-l-Jihad, 145
Jamaica, 28
Jami, Muhammad b. Aman al-, 54, *See also* Jamis
Jamis, 54, *See also* Jami, Muhammad b. Aman al-
Jamʿiyyat al-Irtiqaʾ al-Khayriyya, 206
Jamʿiyyat al-Kitab wa-l-Sunna, 56, 202, 204–6, 207–19, 220, 221, 234
Jamʿiyyat al-Takaful al-Khayriyya, 168
Jamʿiyyat Ihyaʾ al-Turath al-Islami, 55, 56, 109, 113, 140
Jamʿiyyat Waqf al-Turath al-Islami, 55
Jasir Mosque, Al-, 23, 161, 168, 172
Jawabira, Basim b. Faysal al-, 61, 106, 116, 137, 161
Jerusalem, 4, 213
Jews. *See* Judaism
jihad, 53–4, 57, 58, 70, 146, 148, 153, 155, 180, 182, 183, 184, 186, 187, 193, 209, 213, 222, 228, 233, 238
classical jihad, 57, 58
global jihad, 57
revolutionary jihad, 46, 57, 179, 181, 182
Jolen, Judith, 7
Jordan, 1, 2, 37, 53, 55, 59
"East Jordanians", 5, 116, 168
"Palestinian Jordanians", 5, 70, 115, 168, 180, 204
ʿAbdali neighbourhood in Amman, 234, 236
Amman, 1, 10, 22, 23, 66, 98, 113, 115, 116, 134, 137, 145, 165, 168, 173, 174, 175, 185, 186, 194, 204, 205, 208, 230, 231, 234
ʿAqaba, Al-, 168
army of, 6
attempted coup in 1957, 5, 10
attempted coup in 1970, 5
civil society in, 7–8
conservative secularism in, 6
government of, 6
Hashimi al-Shimali neighbourhood in Amman, Al-, 98, 100, 105, 115
history of, 2–6, 156
Husn, Al-, 206
Irbid, 23, 113, 116, 161, 168, 172, 186, 206

Jordan (cont.)
  Islam in, 6–11
  Jamaʿat al-Tabligh in, 8–9, 10, 18, 90, 116, 167, 185, 205, 214, 232
  Karak, Al-, 116, 168
  Maʿan, 116, 186
  Marj al-Hammam, 23
  official Islamic institutes in, 7, 147–50, 227
  Palestinian refugees in, 5, 206
  parliament of, 6, 9
  promotion of "moderate" Islam in, 144, 145, 147–57, 232
  Ramtha, Al-, 168
  regime of, 4, 6, 7, 109, 116, 119, 137, 138, 139, 141, 142, 143, 145–50, 151, 152, 157, 158, 164, 169, 175, 179, 181, 196, 199–200, 219–21, 222, 226, 231, 232, 233, 234, 235, 236
  Royal Court of, 6
  Rusayfa, Al-, 115, 168
  Salt, Al-, 105, 168, 183, 186
  security services of, 6
  Sufism in, 8, 147, 155, 156, 167
  Tafila, Al-, 168
  Tayba, Al-, 61
  tribalism in, 3, 4, 6
  West Bank as part of, 5
  Zarqaʾ, Al-, 76, 99, 105, 115, 119, 154, 168, 186, 198
Jordanian Interfaith Coexistence Research Centre, 148
Joseph. *See* Yusuf
Juda, Nasir, 149
Judaism, 10, 39, 50, 69, 71, 72, 78, 80, 86, 213
juḥūd. *See jaḥd*
jurisprudence of reality. *See fiqh, fiqh al-wāqiʿ*

kabīra (pl. *kabāʾir*), 48, 49, 50, 196, *See also fāsiq*; *kāfir* (pl. *kuffār*); *kufr*; *maʿṣiya*; *murtadd* (pl. *murtaddūn*); *ridda*; *shirk*; *takfīr*; *takfīrī*
kāfir (pl. *kuffār*), 45, 49, 76, 78, 79, 80, 124, 195, 203, 228, 239, 241, 242, *See also fāsiq*; *kabīra* (pl. *kabāʾir*); *kufr*; *maʿṣiya*; *murtadd* (pl. *murtaddūn*); *ridda*; *shirk*; *takfīr*; *takfīrī*
kalām, 42, 43, 51, *See also* theology
Kalimat ila l-Ukht al-Muslima, 120
Kasasiba, Muʿadh al-, 146, 152, 187
Khalayila Mosque, 23
Khalifa, Muhammad ʿAbd al-Rahman, 10
khalwa, 73
Khashshan, Muhammad, 161
khaṭaʾ. *See kufr*, excuses for
Khatib, Muhibb al-Din al-, 96
Khawarij (sing. Khariji), 47, 48, 50, 91, 195–200, 228, 233, 239, 240, 242, 283
Khomeini, Ruhollah, 108
King ʿAbdallah, 4, 6, 97, 156
  assassination of, 4
  ties with Muslim Brotherhood, 10
  ties with Zionists, 4
King ʿAbdallah II, 6, 7, 11, 87, 145, 148, 149, 150, 151, 153, 154, 156, 183, 199, 200, 237
  ascent to the throne of, 6
  ties with Muslim Brotherhood, 11
King Husayn, 6, 7, 108, 109, 114, 133, 191, 193
  ascent to the throne of, 5
  death of, 6
  ties with Muslim Brotherhood, 10–11
King Talal, 4, 5
Kingdom of Jordan. *See* Jordan
knowledge. *See ʿilm*
knowledge seeker. *See ṭālib ʿilm* (pl. *ṭullāb ʿilm*)
Koran. *See* Qurʾan
Krämer, Gudrun, 158
kufr, 46–50, 51, 60, 74–81, 123, 124, 126, 128, 129, 170, 181, 182, 184, 188–91, 192, 193, 194, 196, 197, 223, 228, 238, 239, 240, 241, *See also fāsiq*; *kabīra* (pl. *kabāʾir*); *kāfir* (pl. *kuffār*); *maʿṣiya*; *murtadd* (pl. *murtaddūn*); *ridda*; *shirk*; *takfīr*; *takfīrī*
  excuses for, 49, 188, 209
  kufr akbar, 49, 50, 77, 81, 181, 189, 190, 197, 239, 240
  kufr ʿamalī, 77, 78, 79, 80
  kufr aṣghar, 49, 50, 77, 80, 190, 196, 239, 240
  kufr dūna kufr, 78, 80, 134
  kufr iʿtiqādī, 77, 78
Kull al-Salafiyyin internet forum, 99, 169
Kurdi, ʿAli Ahmad Khalid al-, 162
Kuwait, 23, 55, 95, 109, 111, 113–14, 116, 120, 140, 141, 179, 180, 181, 202, 204, 206, 224, 230, 232, 234

Lauzière, Henri, 35
Lav, Daniel, 119, 126, 127
leaving prayer. *See tark al-ṣalāt*
Lebanon, 1, 72, 95, 100, 108, 166, 167, 227
  Beirut, 1, 227
Libya, 38, 186, 201, 218, 222
loyalty and disavowal. *See walāʾ wa-l-barāʾ, al-*

Machalek, Richard, 167
madhhab (pl. *madhāhib*), 30, 31, 32, 33, 37, 39, 64, 65, 99, 101, 102, 103, 104, 124, 148, 151, 152, 163, 230, 238, 240, 241, 242
  Hanafi *madhhab*, 7, 46, 48, 75, 100, 101
  Hanbali *madhhab*, 32, 34, 41, 42, 47, 48, 65, 74, 99, 102, 104, 105, 174
  Shafiʿi *madhhab*, 7
Madkhali, Rabiʿ b. Hadi al-, 52, 54, 110, 112, *See also* Madkhalis
Madkhalis, 54, *See also* Madkhali, Rabiʿ b. Hadi al-
Majali, Hamza al-, 161
Majali, Husayn al-, 150
major sin. *See kabīra* (pl. *kabāʾir*)
major unbelief. *See kufr, kufr akbar*
Malaysia, 185
Manar, Al-, 101
Mandaville, Peter, 52, 53, 159
manhaj (pl. *manāhij*), 51–9, 60, 62, 82, 83, 85, 111, 112, 142, 153, 182, 202, 208, 209, 214, 225, 228, 237, 242
Maqdisi, Abu Muhammad al-, 2, 15, 16, 21, 46, 180, 181–4, 185, 186, 187, 188, 189–90, 192–5, 198, 232, 233
Markaz Ibn Taymiyya al-Qurʾani, 206
Mashʿal, Firas, 161
maʿṣiya, 48, 150, *See also fāsiq*; *kabīra* (pl. *kabāʾir*); *kāfir* (pl. *kuffār*); *kufr*; *murtadd* (pl. *murtaddūn*); *ridda*; *shirk*; *takfīr*; *takfīrī*
maṣlaḥa (pl. *maṣāliḥ*), 88
Maturidiyya, 41, 42, *See also* Ashʿariyya; *kalām*; theology
Mawdudi, Abu l-Aʿla, 218
Maya movement, 28
McCants, William, 166
Mecca, 4, 96, 97, 238
Medina, 104, 238
Meijer, Roel, 52, 53, 112
metaphorical interpretation. *See taʾwīl*
method. *See manhaj* (pl. *manāhij*)
Middle East, 1, 4, 200, 201, 213, 217
minor unbelief. *See kufr, kufr aṣghar*
Misbar, Al-, 18
mistake. *See khaṭaʾ*
Mongols, 72
monotheism. *See tawḥīd*
Mubarak, Husni, 224, 225
Muhammad. *See* Prophet Muhammad
mujaddid (pl. *mujaddidūn*), 43, 240, 242
Muqbil b. Hadi al-Wadiʿi. *See* Wadiʿi, Muqbil b. Hadi al-
Murjiʾa, 46, 47, 48, 50, 75, 76, 81, 110, 124, 126, 128, 129, 131, 135, 136, 163, 188–91, 192, 194, 195, 197, 198, 228, 229, 233, 238, 239, 240, 266, *See also irjāʾ*
murtadd (pl. *murtaddūn*), xi, 57, 106, 179, 186, 196, *See also fāsiq*; *kabīra* (pl. *kabāʾir*); *kāfir* (pl. *kuffār*); *kufr*; *maʿṣiya*; *ridda*; *shirk*; *takfīr*; *takfīrī*
Muslim Brotherhood, 18, 53, 90, 108, 110, 111, 114, 180, 198, 211, 217, 229, 238
  in Egypt, 10, 38, 55, 57, 218
  in Jordan, 10–11, 90–1, 99, 106, 108, 116, 147, 157, 167, 181, 205, 214–15, 219, 220, 221, 230, 232
  in Syria, 38, 55, 103
Muslim community. *See umma*
Muslim World League, 38
Mustafa, Muhammad Abu Zayd, 203
Muʿtazila, 41, 42, 47, 48

Nabatean kingdom of Petra, 2
Nabhani, Taqi al-Din al-, 9
Najd. *See* Saudi Arabia, Najd
naṣīḥa (pl. *naṣāʾiḥ*), 52, 87, 155, 209, 225, 234, 243
Nasir, Bassam, 205
Nasr, Muhammad Musa. *See* Al Nasr, Muhammad b. Musa
Nasser, Gamal Abdul. *See* ʿAbd al-Nasir, Gamal
Nasserism, 5, 10, 37, 145
negation. *See jaḥd*
Nonini, Donald, 28
Nur Party, Al-. *See* Hizb al-Nur

oath of allegiance. *See bayʿa*
obedience. *See ṭāʿa*
oil, 37, 181, 227
Olidort, Jacob, 53
orthodoxy, 8, 41, 42, 65, 98, 99, 103, 152, 227, 230
Ottoman Empire, 3, 4
Our Last Best Chance, 7, 145

Pakistan, 33, 58, 180, 181, 185
  Peshawar, 180, 185
Palestinians, 4, 5, 10, 70, 86, 113, 114, 118, 145, 180, 183, 213, 232, *See also* Arab-Israeli conflict; Israel
  Gaza Strip, 86
  Palestine, 4, 10
  Palestine Liberation Organisation (PLO), 113, 233
  Palestinian nationalism, 4

Palestinians (cont.)
refugees, 5, 59, 113, 119, 133, 142
West Bank, 5, 113, 180, 185
Pall, Zoltan, 27, 166
partisanship. *See ḥizbiyya*
people of considered opinion. *See ahl al-ra'y*
people of the Prophetic tradition. *See ahl al-ḥadīth*
perfection of the religion. *See īmān, kamāl al-dīn*
Permanent Council for Knowledge Studies and Fatwas, 124, 126, 129, 130, 131, 135
Petra. *See* Nabatean Kingdom of Petra
Pierret, Thomas, 65, 158
piety, 8, 9, 53, 73, 90, 116, 155, 167, 171, 174, 195, 205, 224, 227, 229, 232, 234
pilgrimage. *See ḥajj*
pious predecessors. *See* Salafism, *salaf al-ṣāliḥ, al-*
polytheism. *See shirk*
postponement. *See irjā'*
Price, Charles, 28
Prince Ghazi, 148
Prophet Muhammad, 2, 4, 6, 28, 30, 31, 39, 40, 43, 44, 61, 62, 64, 71, 72, 77, 82, 83, 104, 150, 169, 170, 171, 172, 173, 174, 175, 208, 215, 223, 225, 230, 232, 237, 238, 277, *See also ḥadīth*s; Sunna
protests. *See* demonstrations

Qa'ida, al-, 16, 54, 58, 59, 64, 145, 150, 179, 180, 187, 188, 198, 199, 232, 233
Jabhat al-Nusra, 59, 187
Qa'ida in Iraq, al-, 2, 15, 58
Qa'ida in the Islamic Maghrib (North Africa), al-, 58
Qa'ida on the Arabian Peninsula (Saudi Arabia and Yemen), al-, 58
Qalqili, 'Abdallah al-, 97
Qasimi, Jamal al-Din al-, 35, 101
Qattan, Ibrahim al-, 97
Qaysi, Marwan al-, 69
Qibla, Al-, 22, 208, 209, 214, 215, 217, 218
Queen Raniya, 149
Qur'an, 7, 8, 9, 19, 30, 31, 32, 33, 34, 35, 36, 41, 42, 50, 51, 79, 83, 85, 86, 88, 89, 91, 103, 156, 159, 167, 170, 172, 173, 174, 198, 203, 204, 206, 208, 210, 213, 214, 225
Qur'anic exegesis. *See tafsīr*
Qutb, Muhammad, 110
Qutb, Sayyid, 57, 106, 110, 111–12, 123, 182, 218

Rabi', 'Imran, 161
radicalisation, 20, 21, 39
Ra'fat, Muhammad al-, 106
Rahahila, Jarrah al-, 186
Rahma Mosque, Al-, 23
Rastafari movement, 28
rationalism, 47, *See 'aql*
ra'y, 30, 31, 43, 237, 240
reform. *See iṣlāḥ*
renewal. *See tajdīd*
renewer. *See mujaddid* (pl. *mujaddidūn*)
revelation. *See waḥy*
revival. *See ṣaḥwa*
Rida, Muhammad Rashid, 96, 101
ridda, 179, 228, *See also fāsiq; kabīra* (pl. *kabā'ir*); *kāfir* (pl. *kuffār*); *kufr; ma'ṣiya; murtadd* (pl. *murtaddūn*); *shirk; takfīr; takfīrī*
Rifa'i, Muhammad Nasib al-, 99, 100
Rishawi, Sajida al-, 187
ritual purity, 169, 170–5, 235
rituals, 45, 170–5, 235
Riyalat, Luqman al-, 186
Robbins, Michael, 147
Rogan, Eugene L., 3
Royal Aal al-Bayt Institute for Islamic Thought, 65, 147, 148
Royal Academy for Islamic Civilisation Research, 147
Rubin, Lawrence, 147
ruler. *See walī al-amr* (pl. *wulāt al-amr*)

Sadat, Anwar al-, 38, 39
ṣaḥwa, 55, 56, 109, 110, 111, 113, 114, 202
Sahyat Nadhir bi-Khatar al-Takfir, 129
Sa'id, 'Abd al-Rahim, 99
Sa'id, Hammam, 99
salaf. See Salafism, *salaf al-ṣāliḥ, al-*
Salafis. *See* Salafism
Salafism
accusations of plagiarism among Salafis in Jordan, 119–26, 127, 141, 142, 143, 158, 164, 231, 232
accusations of theft among Salafis in Jordan, 119, 139–43, 158, 162, 164, 231
as a contested term, 29–30
as a contested term in Jordan, 61–2, 154, 225
as related to modernist Salafis, 35–6
as related to orthodox Sunni Islam, 31–2, 42

as related to Wahhabism, 33–4, 37–8
categorisation of, 51–9, 228
categorisation of Salafism in Jordan, 62–3, 208–9
clothing of, 43
clothing of Salafis in Jordan, 174
condemnation of terrorism among Salafis in Jordan, 150–7
conflicts among Salafis in Jordan, 117, 118–43, 158, 164, 230–1, 235
contestation of Jihadi-Salafism in Jordan, 196–8, 233
contestation of political Salafism in Jordan, 222–6
definition of, 241, 2, 28–30, 53, 55, 57, 227
definition of Salafism in Jordan, 208
domestication of Salafism in Jordan, 19, 55, 59, 60, 91, 95, 109, 117, 119, 137, 139, 143, 144, 152, 157, 165, 169, 175, 179, 195, 200, 202, 220, 225, 227, 230, 231, 233, 234, 236
economic background of Salafis in Jordan, 116, 168, 232
educational background of Salafis in Jordan, 116, 168, 232
female adherents to Salafism in Jordan, 22, 74
gender relations among Salafis in Jordan, 73–4, 170, 210, 211
history of Salafism in Jordan, 95–117, 118–43, 144–75, 229–32
īmān and *kufr* among Salafis in Jordan, 74–81
importance of Arabic language to Salafis in Jordan, 164
in academic literature, 11–18, 19
in Egypt, 12, 55, 57, 218, 224, 225, 226
in Europe, 13
in France, 14
in Germany, 13
in Great Britain, 13
in Gulf countries, 11
in Indonesia, 13
in Kuwait, 11, 55, 56, 57, 109, 113, 114, 140
in Lebanon, 12, 55, 56, 59
in Morocco, 57
in Pakistan, 12
in Saudi Arabia, 12, 109
in Sudan, 13
in Syria, 13
in the Netherlands, 14
in the Palestinian territories, 13
in Turkey, 13
in Yemen, 12
influence Kuwait on Salafism in Jordan, 95, 113–14, 116
influence Saudi Arabia on Salafism in Jordan, 95, 97, 109–13, 116
Jihadi-Salafism, 21, 46, 47, 53, 57–9, 60, 64, 90, 151, 194, 203, 209, 226, 228, 238, 239, 240, 242, 243, 276
Jihadi-Salafism in Jordan, 14, 15, 16, 59, 145, 146, 154, 166, 179–200, 205, 207, 208, 225, 232–3, 235
language use of Salafis in Jordan, 173
leadership ambitions within Salafism in Jordan, 119, 126–37, 230, 231, 233
minority rights among Salafis in Jordan, 71–2
number of adherents to Salafism in Jordan, 166
on the internet, 14
opposition to Salafism in Jordan, 65–6
organisational structure of Salafism in Jordan, 55, 114–16, 137, 144, 163, 168–9, 230, 232
Palestinian descent of many adherents to Salafism in Jordan, 15, 115, 116, 168
political Salafism, 55–7, 59, 60, 69, 70, 75, 109, 110, 113, 114, 151, 180, 228, 230, 235, 238, 239, 243
political Salafism in Jordan, 56, 59, 201–26, 234, 235
politics in relation to, 243, 52–3, 55
politics in relation to Salafism in Jordan, 82–91, 202, 229
precursors to, 30–3, 36, 39, 237
quietist Salafism, 19, 21, 23, 24, 52–5, 59, 60, 228, 237, 239, 240, 241, 242, 243
reception of Sayyid Qutb among Salafis in Jordan, 111–12
reformist Salafism in Jordan. *See* Salafism, political Salafism in Jordan
religious authority among Salafis in Jordan, 127, 131, 132, 133, 135, 136, 144, 157, 158–65, 230, 232
religious background of Salafis in Jordan, 116, 167–8
salaf al-ṣāliḥ, al-, 2, 19, 28, 29, 30, 32, 33, 34, 35, 36, 37, 39, 40, 43, 60, 61, 62, 63, 64, 85, 95, 100, 101, 109, 119, 144, 156, 170, 198, 227, 241
social background of Salafis in Jordan, 166–7, 168, 232
spread of, 36–9
theological views of, 39–50
views on jihad, 53–4

Salafism (cont.)
  views on jihad among Salafis in Jordan, 63–4
  views on Shi'as, 45
  views on Shi'as among Salafis in Jordan, 108–9, 156, 167, 210
  views on Sufism, 45, 170, 225
  views on Sufism among Salafis in Jordan, 72, 155–6
Salik Mosque in Amman, Al-, 98, 100
Salik, Ahmad al-, 98, 99, 100, 105, 230
Salik, Muhammad al-, 98
Samara, Munif, 186
San'ani, Muhammad b. Isma'il al-, 32
Saudi Arabia, 7, 23, 34, 37–9, 45, 52, 54, 55, 56, 69, 70, 74, 75, 95, 99, 102, 104, 107, 109–13, 114, 116, 120, 124, 125, 129, 130, 135, 152, 158, 159, 165, 170, 175, 179, 180, 181, 182, 188, 202, 227, 230, 231, 234, 236
  Muslim Brotherhood exiles in, 38, 55, 56, 111, 240
  Najd, 33
  Riyadh, 39
saved sect. *See firqa al-nājiya, al-*
Schmidtke, Sabine, 158
scholars. *See 'ulamā'* (sing. *'ālim*)
schools of Islamic law. *See madhhab* (pl. *madhāhib*)
Schwedler, Jillian, 20
seclusion. *See khalwa*
Second World War, 37
Shafi'i, Muhammad b. Idris al-, 31
Shah Wali Allah, 33
shahāda, 40, 77
Shahada Hamid, 'Abd al-Fattah. *See* Tahawi, Abu Muhammad al-
Shahada, Marwan, 205
Shahada, Usama, 113, 204, 208, 209, 210, 211, 212, 213, 214, 215, 216, 218, 219, 225
Shalabi, Muhammad al-, 186, 198
Sham, Al-, 3
Shaqra, 'Asim Muhammad Ibrahim, 135,
Shaqra, Muhammad Ibrahim, 80, 81, 98, 99, 100, 105, 108, 109, 110, 118, 119, 126, 127, 128, 129, 131–7, 138, 139, 142, 143, 162, 166, 189, 191, 192–5, 205, 229, 230, 231, 233
Sharayiri, Mansur al-, 161
sharī'a, 6, 7, 10, 30, 31, 43, 45, 50, 57, 64, 78, 81, 85, 88, 148, 168, 174, 179, 181, 182, 190, 203, 210, 216, 228, 230, 238, 241
Shawish, Zuhayr al-, 102, 103
Shawkani, Muhammad b. 'Ali al-, 32
shaykh (pl. *shuyūkh*), 8, 9, 17, 23, 34, 43, 52, 54, 62, 69, 76, 77, 84, 96, 97, 99, 103, 104, 105, 107, 108, 109, 112, 115, 116, 118, 120, 122, 130, 132, 133, 135, 136, 138, 140, 141, 142, 148, 150, 151, 152, 159, 161, 162, 163, 164, 165, 168, 169, 173, 175, 184, 186, 190, 191, 192, 202, 204, 209, 213, 223, 224, 225, 230, 235, 236, 241, 242, 254
Shaykh, Jamal al-, 161
Shinqiti, Muhammad al-Khadir al-, 97
shirk, 40, 47, 67, 72, 86, 91, 240, 241, *See also fāsiq*; *kabīra* (pl. *kabā'ir*); *kāfir* (pl. *kuffār*); *kufr*; *ma'ṣiya*; *murtadd* (pl. *murtaddūn*); *ridda*; *takfīr*; *takfīrī*
showing the religion. *See iẓhār al-dīn*
Shukri, Murad, 119, 123–6, 127, 128, 129, 137, 143, 162, 190, 205, 231
shūrá, 88, 89, *See also* democracy; elections
Siba'i, Mustafa al-, 102
Sifat Salat al-Nabi, 171
sinner. *See fāsiq*
Snow, David A., 167
social media, 169
Social Movement Theory (SMT), 20
soundness of the religion. *See īmān, ṣiḥḥat al-dīn*
South Asia, 65
South-East Asia, 165
Soviet Union, 58
  invasion of Afghanistan, 58, 180, 181
speculative theology. *See kalām*
speech with the tongue. *See īmān, qawl bi-l-lisān, al-*
strangers. *See ghurabā'* (sing. *gharīb*)
strife. *See fitna* (pl. *fitan*)
sub-Saharan Africa, 165
Sudan, 203
Sunna, 30, 31, 32, 33, 34, 35, 36, 51, 83, 85, 86, 88, 89, 91, 103, 156, 159, 167, 198, 204, 206, 208, 225, 237, *See also ḥadīth*s; Prophet Muhammad
Surur, Muhammad, 111
Syria, 1, 35, 38, 59, 65, 72, 95, 96, 99, 100, 102, 103, 104, 105, 106, 107, 108, 109, 111, 114, 146, 168, 170, 184, 186, 187, 204, 206, 208, 214, 215, 222, 223, 230, 233
  Aleppo, 99, 102
  civil war in, 16, 18, 53, 168, 184, 201, 206, 217, 223
  Damascus, 100, 102, 103, 105, 223

ṭāʿa, 86, 87, 208, 215, 216, 222, 225, 229, 234, 235, 241
tabdīl, 50, 78, 81, 241
tafsīr, 83, 111, 159, 214
Tahawi, Abu Jaʿfar Ahmad b. Muhammad al-, 46, 75
Tahawi, Abu Muhammad al-, 186
Tahdhir al-Nasihin min al-Tahazzub li-l-ʿUlamaʾ wa-l-Murabbin, 163
Tahdhir al-Umma min Taʿliqat al-Halabi ʿala Aqwal al-Aʾimma, 129
Tahdhir min Fitnat al-Takfir, Al-, 127, 128, 189, 192
ṭāʾifa al-manṣūra, al-, 40, 42, 66, 170, 228, 237, 238, 241, *See also firqa al-nājiya, al-*
tajdīd, 43, 237, 240, 242
takfīr, 49, 50, 60, 74, 75, 81, 87, 91, 106, 111, 123, 128, 129, 130, 136, 148, 169, 179, 182, 183, 189, 190, 191, 196, 197, 198, 209, 228, 233, 239, 240, 242, *See also fāsiq*; *kabīra* (pl. *kabāʾir*); *kāfir* (pl. *kuffār*); *kufr*; *maʿṣiya*; *murtadd* (pl. *murtaddūn*); *ridda*; *shirk*; *takfīrī*
takfīrī, 151, 196, 197, 199, *See also fāsiq*; *kabīra* (pl. *kabāʾir*); *kāfir* (pl. *kuffār*); *kufr*; *maʿṣiya*; *murtadd* (pl. *murtaddūn*); *ridda*; *shirk*
Takruri Mosque in Amman, Al-, 98, 100
Talal. *See* King Talal
Taliʿat al-Baʿth al-Islami, 106
ṭālib ʿilm (pl. *ṭullāb ʿilm*), 123, 161, 242
Taliban, 144
Tamaddun al-Islami, Al-, 101
Tamimi, ʿIzz al-Din al-, 148
taqlīd, 32, 34, 35, 101, 163, 238, 240, 242, *See also ijtihād*; *ittibāʿ*
tarbiya. *See taṣfiya wa-l-tarbiya, al-*
tark al-ṣalāt, 77, 80, 124, 134
Tartusi, Abu Basir al-, 184, 190, 191, 192, 193, 195, 198
taṣfiya. *See taṣfiya wa-l-tarbiya, al-*
taṣfiya wa-l-tarbiya, al-, 82, 83, 84, 85, 86, 87, 91, 113, 116, 169, 202, 203, 212, 225, 229, 234, 236, 242
tawḥīd, 40–2, 46, 51, 62, 66, 71, 86, 99, 101, 170, 172, 228, 242
  tawḥīd al-asmāʾ wa-l-ṣifāt, 40, 41, 42, 97, 242
  tawḥīd al-ʿibāda. *See tawḥīd, tawḥīd al-ulūhiyya*
  tawḥīd al-rubūbiyya, 40, 242
  tawḥīd al-ulūhiyya, 40, 41, 50, 242
taʾwīl, 41
terrorism, 16, 27, 54, 63, 144, 145–57, 183, 199, 209, 231, 232, 235
  attacks in Jordan of 9 November 2005, 144, 146, 151, 152, 153, 154, 155, 187, 209
  attacks in London of 7 July 2005, 58
  attacks in US of 11 September 2001, 16, 58, 144, 145, 152, 153, 199, 231
theology, 39, 41, 42, 45, 46, 47, 65, 91, 97, 119, 125, 127, 134, 136, 194, 195, 197, 227, 231, 233
traditionists. *See ahl al-ḥadīth*
Transjordan. *See* Jordan
tribalism. *See* Jordan, tribalism in
Tunisia, 186, 201
Turkey, 1, 98, 100
Twitter, 169

ʿulamāʾ (sing. *ʿālim*), xi, 2, 19, 20, 21, 23, 24, 29, 30, 32, 33, 34, 35, 36, 39, 40, 41, 44, 46, 48, 50, 51, 52, 54, 55, 56, 61, 62, 63, 65, 70, 72, 75, 79, 80, 81, 85, 88, 89, 97, 99, 100, 102, 103, 104, 106, 107, 108, 109, 110, 111, 112, 115, 116, 118, 119, 120, 122, 123, 124, 126, 127, 128, 129, 130, 131, 132, 133, 136, 137, 141, 142, 143, 144, 147, 148, 152, 153, 156, 157–65, 166, 169, 171, 175, 179, 180, 181, 182, 184, 186, 187, 188, 190, 191, 192, 193, 194, 195, 196, 198, 199, 200, 202, 213, 215, 218, 220, 222, 223, 224, 227, 229, 230, 231, 232, 233, 234, 235, 236, 239, 240, 241, 242, 243
Umm al-Qura University, 125
umma, 31, 33, 39, 40, 61, 83, 85, 86, 88, 203, 207, 210, 215, 238
unbelief. *See kufr*
unbelief less than unbelief. *See kufr, kufr dūna kufr*
unbeliever. *See kāfir* (pl. *kuffār*)
United Arab Emirates, 108, 185
United States of America, 28, 57, 69, 70, 71, 112, 144, 145, 146, 169, 181, 184, 200, 230, 231
unity of divinity. *See tawḥīd, tawḥīd al-ulūhiyya*
unity of God. *See tawḥīd*
unity of lordship. *See tawḥīd, tawḥīd al-rubūbiyya*
unity of names and attributes. *See tawḥīd, tawḥīd al-asmāʾ wa-l-ṣifāt*
unity of worship. *See tawḥīd, tawḥīd al-ʿibāda*
University of Jordan, 22, 125, 161

ʿUraydi, Sami al-, 128, 186
ʿUtaybi, Ihsan al-, 113, 206
ʿUtaybi, Muʿadh al-, 206
ʿUthaymin, Muhammad b. Salih al-, 52, 54
utopia, 28, 30, 33, 35, 36, 39, 40, 43, 60, 74, 91, 95, 100, 109, 116, 119, 143, 144, 175, 179, 188, 200, 202, 212, 226, 227, 236

victorious group. *See ṭāʾifa al-manṣūra, al-*

Wadiʿi, Muqbil b. Hadi al-, 52
Wahhabism, 33, 34, 36, 37–9, 43, 55, 70, 74, 99, 102, 103, 104, 110, 180, 181, 227, *See also* Salafism
waḥy, 42
walāʾ. *See walāʾ wa-l-barāʾ, al-*
walāʾ wa-l-barāʾ, al-, 44–6, 51, 68, 70, 71, 74, 163, 175, 182, 203, 210, 228, 237, 239
  iʿānat al-kuffār, 45
  istiʿāna bi-l-kuffār, al-, 45, 70, 239, 243
  legislative interpretation of, 45–6
  muwālāt, 69
  personal interpretation of, 44–5, 68–9
  political interpretation of, 45, 69, 70
  tawallī, 69
walī al-amr (pl. *wulāt al-amr*), 52, 53, 54, 63, 86, 87, 150, 154, 243
Weber, Max, 158
Wiktorowicz, Quintan, 16, 17, 51, 52, 95, 110
worship. *See ʿibāda*

Yemen, 186, 201
YouTube, 169, 193
Yusuf, 203

Zahirat al-Irjaʾ fi l-Fikr al-Islami, 75, 110
Zarqawi, Abu Musʿab al-, 2, 15, 16, 146, 151, 180, 181, 182, 183–4, 186, 188, 198, 233
Zawahiri, Ayman al-, 58, 180
Zaynu, Muhammad b. Jamil, 170
Ziyada, Akram, 115, 118, 137, 143, 151, 161
Zogu, Ahmet, 100

CPSIA information can be obtained
at www.ICGtesting.com
Printed in the USA
LVOW12*0331170517
534737LV00009B/165/P

9 781107 163669